Alaska
a travel survival kit

Jim DuFresne

Alaska – a travel survival kit
   3rd edition

Published by
   Lonely Planet Publications
   Head Office: PO Box 617, Hawthorn, Vic 3122, Australia
   US Office: PO Box 2001A, Berkeley, CA 94702, USA

Printed by
   Colorcraft Ltd, Hong Kong

Photographs by
   Alaska Division of Tourism (ADT), Al Giddings (AG), Anchorage Visitors Bureau (AVB),
   Camp Alaska Tours (CAT), Camp Denali (CD), Deanna Swaney (DS), Ellen DuFresne (ED),
   Jim DuFresne (JD), John Svenson (JS), National Park Service (NPS), St Elias Alpine Guides (SEAG),
   US Fish & Wildlife Service (USFW), US Forest Service (USFS)
   Front cover: Humpback Whale Tail (AG), The Image Bank
   Back cover: Caribou (DS) & Fishing near Lake Clark (ADT)

Illustrations by
   John Svenson on page Nos 18, 19, 21, 37, 45, 51, 172, 252, 271, 311 & 338

First published
   June 1983

This edition
   January 1991

Although the authors and publisher have tried to make the information as
accurate as possible, they accept no responsibility for any loss, injury or
inconvenience sustained by any person using this book.

National Library of Australia Cataloguing in Publication Data

DuFresne, Jim
   Alaska, a travel survival kit.

   3rd ed.
   Includes index.
   ISBN 0 86442 101 X.

   1. Alaska – Description and travel – 1981 – Guide-books. I. Title.

   917.98045

   text © Jim DuFresne 1990
   maps © Lonely Planet 1990
   photos © photographers as indicated 1990
   illustrations © John Svenson & Lonely Planet 1990

Jim DuFresne

Jim (pictured) is a former sports and out-doors editor of the *Juneau Empire* and the first Alaskan sportswriter to win a national award from Associated Press. He is presently a freelance writer, specialising in outdoor and travel writing. His previous books include *Tramping in New Zealand* (Lonely Planet) and wilderness guides to Isle Royale, Voyageurs and Glacier Bay national parks.

John Svenson

Artist mountaineer John Svenson has lived in Alaska for the past 2 decades and his woodcuts, water colours and illustrations have appeared in national outdoor maga-zines as well as art galleries throughout the Northwest. During the summer, he works as a climbing guide, and though his trade has taken him to the summits of four continents, Alaska has always remained his inspirational mecca.

From the Author

My deepest appreciation goes to my old Juneau housemates Jeff and Sue Sloss and a legion of Lonely Planet travellers who went to Alaska with this book in hand and then took the time to drop me a line. They include Hans Gullestrup (a professor in Denmark), Jacqui Kerslake of British Columbia, Jeff Williams of Australia, Christine Gruttke, John Rowland and especially Ken Zimmer-men of Montana for his seven-page letter written in the heart of downtown Talkeetna.

I received considerable assistance from Nandita Lai of the Fairbanks Visitor Bureau, Pamela Hjorteset of the Ketchikan Visitor Bureau, Connie Taylor of the Cordova Chamber of Commerce, Suzi Bock of the Matanuska-Susitna Visitor Bureau, Cathy Clark of the Seward Chamber of Commerce, Liz Arend from the Municipality of Anchor-age and especially Jeffery Osborn of the Anchorage Visitor Bureau.

Also lending me a hand were Linda Levernock of Camp Denali, Bob Jacobs of St Elias Alpine Guides, Tim Adams of CampAlaska, Larry Edwards of Baidarka Boats in Sitka and Ike Waits of Wild Rose

Guidebooks. Assisting me from the US Forest Service were Neil Hagadorn, Mark Madrid, Esther Bingham, James Cochrane, Scott Russell and Wayne Nicholls. Connie Hill did the same for the US Fish & Wildlife Service.

At the other end of the world in Australia, Tony Wheeler and Jim Hart of Lonely Planet gave me the encouragement to enlarge this travel guide while their down-under staff cleaned it up and put it together.

But in the end this book is written for three women who have always inspired me to travel and experience Alaska: to my wife, Peggy; to Bonnie in Gustavus; and most of all to my sister, Ellen (1949-1978), who lost her life in the land she loved. May Alaska always cherish her soul.

From the Publisher

This edition of Alaska was edited at the Lonely Planet office in Australia by Alan Tiller, and Trudi Canavan was responsible for design, illustrations, cover design and maps.

Thanks must also go to Deanna Swaney, Dianne Clark and Tom Smallman for provid-ing extra information; Susan Mitra for all her help with proofing and editorial guidance;

Anne Jeffree and Tamsin Wilson for additional illustrations; and Sharon Wertheim for indexing.

This Book

We greatly appreciate the contributions of travellers who took the time and energy to write to us. Writers (apologies if we've misspelt your name) to whom thanks must go include:

Martin Aunsborg (Dk), Jenne Boyd (UK), Luigi Cerri (It), Demaree (USA), Laura Gibbons (USA), Karen Johanne Gravesen (Dk), Christine Gruttke (USA), Randy Herr (USA), Gregory Johns (USA), Jacqui Kerslake (C), Todd Mazur (Aus), R Miller (USA), Julie Nock (UK), Peter Roberts (USA), Rosalind Rude (USA), Sandy Schroth (USA), K Shannon (NZ), Frank Waaamer (USA), S Ward (USA), James O Whittaker (USA), Jeff Williams (Aus)

Aus – Australia, C – Canada, Dk – Denmark, It – Italy, NZ – New Zealand, USA – United States of America.

Warning & Request

Things change: prices go up, schedules change, good places go bad and bad places go bankrupt – nothing stays the same. So if you find things better or worse, recently opened or long since closed, please write and tell us and help make the next edition better!

Your letters will be used to help update future editions and, where possible, important changes will also be included as a Stop Press section in reprints.

All information is greatly appreciated and the best letters will receive a free copy of the next edition, or any other Lonely Planet book of your choice.

Contents

Introduction

THE AURA OF ALASKA

It isn't the mountains, sparkling lakes or glaciers that draw travellers to Alaska every year but the magic in the land; an irresistible force that tugs on those who dream about the north country.

No area in the United States of America possesses the mystical pull that this land has. It ignites the imagination of people who live in the city but long to wander in the woods. Its mythical title of the 'Final Frontier' is as true today as it was in the past when Alaska's promise of adventure and the lure of quick wealth brought the first invasion of miners to the state in 1898 for the Klondike gold rush. Today, they have been replaced by travellers and backpackers but the spirit of adventure is still the same.

Travellers, drawn to Alaska by its colour-ful reputation, are stunned by the grandeur of what they see and often go home penni-less. There are mountains, glaciers and rivers in other parts of North America but few are on the same scale or as overpowering as those in Alaska. To see a brown bear ram-bling up one side of a mountain valley or to sit in a kayak and watch a 5 mile (8 km) wide glacier continually calve ice off its face are experiences of natural beauty that perma-nently change your way of thinking.

If nature's handiwork doesn't effect you, then the state's overwhelming size will. Everything in Alaska is big, that is every-thing except its population. The total population is 523,000 and almost half of them live in one city, Anchorage. Yet the state is huge at 591,004 sq miles (1,536,610 sq km) which makes it a fifth of the size of the

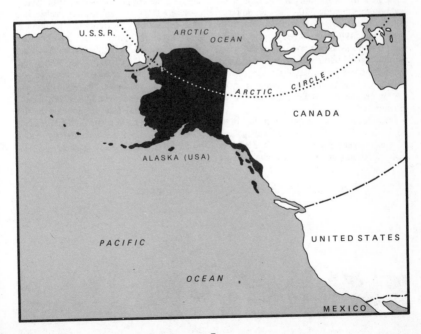

United States; as big as England, France, Italy and Spain put together; bigger than the next three largest states in the USA combined; or 120 times larger than the US state of Rhode Island. There is more than 1 sq mile (2.6 sq km) for every Alaska resident; if Manhattan Island in New York City was populated to the same density there would be 16 people living on the island.

In Alaska, you have the third longest river in North America, 17 of the country's 20 highest peaks and 5000 glaciers, with one larger than Switzerland. You also have arctic winters that are one long night and arctic summers that are one long day. You can find king crabs that measure 3 feet (1 metre) from claw to claw, brown bears that stand over 12 feet (4 metres) tall and farmers who grow 70 lb (31 kg) cabbages and 30 lb (13 kg) turnips after a summer of 20 hour days.

Two things that have reached legendary proportions in Alaska are the state's mosquitoes and its prices. There are always tales among travellers about a plate of eggs, toast and potatoes costing $20 or insects so large that campers have to beat them back with sticks, but myths are spread by those who went home bug bitten and broke. For most people, a good bottle of bug dope will keep the mosquitoes away, while the aim of this book is to show you how to avoid many of the high prices and still see the wonders of the north country.

Despite Alaska's reputation for high prices, it's still possible for backpackers and overseas travellers to experience the land on a so-called budget trip because the greatest things the state has to offer – prime wilderness, abundant wildlife, clear water, miles of hiking trails, in general the great outdoors – are either free or cost little to experience.

If you are low on funds but are willing to camp, hike or sit on a mountain peak to soak up the sunshine and scenery, then you can afford a trip to Alaska. If, on the other hand, you insist on staying in hotels, eating in restaurants and dancing in nightclubs, then the legendary Alaskan prices will quickly become a reality.

Within the state, ranging 1400 miles (2240 km) from north to south and 2400 miles (3840 km) from east to west, are several regions which make up Alaska's character, each as distinctive as the countries in Europe. You can begin your travels in the rainy, lush Southeast and end them at the Arctic tundra – a vast, treeless plain where the sun never sets during the summer.

The weather and scenery change dramatically from one region to the next. In the summer, the temperatures can range from a cool 50°F (10°C) in Glacier Bay to a sizzling 95°F (35°C) on a hot August afternoon in Fairbanks. In some years, rainfall can measure less than 2 inches (51 mm) in areas above the Arctic Circle, or more than 300 inches (7600 mm) at the little town of Port Walter in the Southeast.

For the purpose of budget travel, Alaska has been divided into six regions in this book, with the main focus on the five areas which can be easily reached either by road or by the State Marine Ferry system.

Dall Sheep

Facts about Alaska

HISTORY

Alaska's history is a strange series of spurts and sputters. Although today it is viewed as a wilderness paradise, it has often in the past been regarded as a frozen wasteland, suitable only for Eskimos and polar bears. When some resource was uncovered, however, a short period of prosperity and exploitation followed; first of sea-otter skins, then gold, salmon, oil and most recently, untouched wilderness. After each was exhausted the land slipped back into oblivion.

The First Alaskans

The first Alaskans migrated from Asia to North America 30,000 to 40,000 years ago during an ice age that lowered the sea level and gave rise to a 900 mile (1450 km) land bridge spanning Siberia and Alaska. The nomadic groups were not bent on exploring the new world but on following the animal herds that provided them with food and clothing. Although many tribes wandered deep into North and South America, four ethnic groups – the Athabascans, Aleuts, Eskimos and the coastal tribes of Tlingits and Haidas – remained in Alaska and made the harsh wilderness their homeland.

The First Europeans

The first written record of the state was made by Virtus Bering, a Danish navigator sailing for the Czar of Russia. Bering's trip in 1728 proved that America and Asia were two separate continents, and 13 years later, on a second voyage, he went ashore near Cordova to become the first European to set foot in Alaska.

Bering and many of his crew were killed in a shipwreck during that journey, but the survivors brought back fur pelts and tales of fabulous seal and otter colonies – Alaska's first boom was under way. The Russians wasted little time in overrunning the Aleutian Islands and quickly established a settlement on Kodiak Island. Chaos followed as bands of Russian hunters robbed and murdered each other for furs while the peaceful Aleutian Indians, living near the hunting grounds, were almost annihilated.

By the 1790s, Russia had organised the Russian-American Company to regulate the fur trade and ease the violent competition. However, tales of the enormous wealth in the Alaskan wildlife trade brought several other countries to the frigid waters. Spain claimed the entire North American west coast, including Alaska, and sent several explorers to the Southeast region. These early visitors took boat loads of furs but left neither settlers or forts, only a few Spanish names.

The British arrived when Captain James Cook began searching the area for the mythical Northwest Passage between the Pacific and Atlantic oceans. The French sent Jean de La Perouse, who in 1786 made it as far as Lituya Bay on the southern coast of Alaska. By the 1790s, Cook's shipmate, George Vancouver, had returned on his own and charted the complicated waters of the Southeast's Inside Passage.

After depleting the fur colonies in the Aleutians, the Russians moved their territorial capital from Kodiak to Sitka in the Southeast and built a second fort near the mouth of Stikine River in 1834 to prevent the British from moving into the area. That fort, which was named St Dionysius at the time, eventually evolved into the small lumbering and fishing town of Wrangell.

When a small trickle of American adventurers began to arrive, four nations had a foot in the Panhandle of Alaska. Spain and France were squeezed out of the area by the early 1800s while the British were reduced to leasing selected areas from the Russians.

The Sale of Alaska

By the 1860s, the Russians found themselves badly overextended. Their involvement in Napoleon's European wars, a declining fur industry and the long lines of shipping

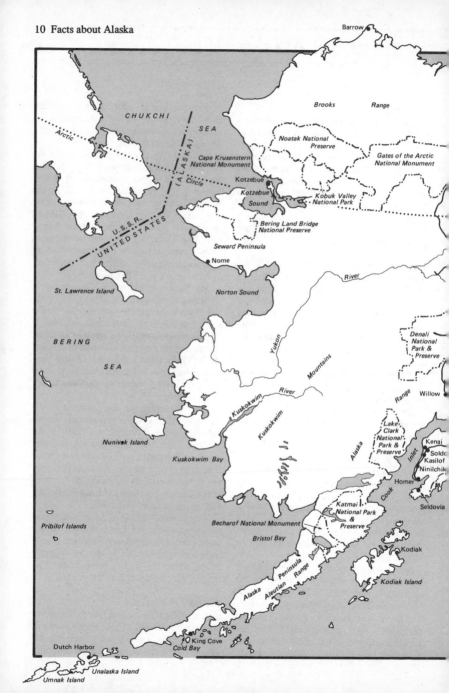

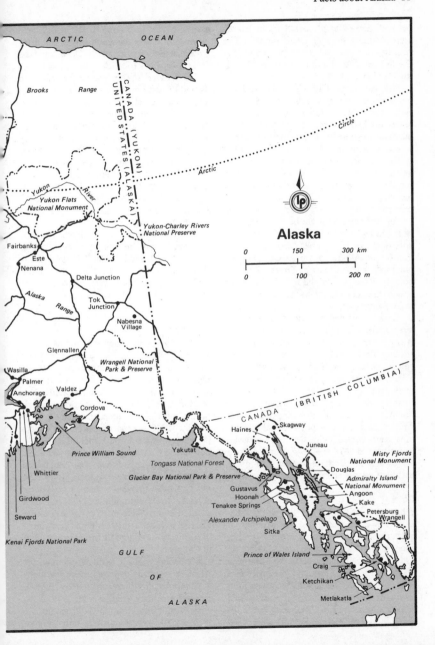

between Sitka and the heartland of Russia were draining their national treasury. The country made several overtures to the USA for the sale of Alaska and fishers from Washington State pushed for it.

The American Civil War delayed the negotiations and it wasn't until 1867 that Secretary of State William H Seward, with extremely keen foresight, signed a treaty to purchase the state for $7.2 million – less than 2 cents an acre (0.4 hectare). By then the US public was in an uproar over the 'Frozen Wasteland'. Newspapers called it 'Seward's Ice Box' or 'Walrussia', while one senator heatedly compared Alaska to a 'sucked orange' as little was left of the rich fur trade.

On the Senate floor, the battle to ratify the treaty lasted 6 months before the sale was approved. On 18 October 1867, the formal transfer of Alaska to the Americans took place in Sitka, while nearby Wrangell, a town both the Russians and the British controlled at one time, changed flags for the third time in its short existence.

Alaska remained a lawless, unorganised territory for the next 20 years, with the US Army in charge at one point and the Navy at another. This great land, remote and inaccessible to all but a few hardy settlers, remained a dark, frozen mystery to most people. Eventually its riches were uncovered one by one. First it was whales, taken mostly in the Southeast and later in the Bering Sea and the Arctic Ocean. Next the phenomenal salmon-runs were tapped, with the first canneries being built in 1878 at Klawock on Prince of Wales Island. Both industries brought a trickle of people and prosperity to Alaska.

Gold

What brought Alaska into the world limelight, however, was gold. The promise of quick riches and the adventure of the frontier became the most effective lure Alaska ever had. Gold was discovered in the Gastineau Channel in the 1880s and the towns of Juneau and Douglas sprang up overnight, living off the very productive Treadwell and Alaska-Juneau mines. Circle City in the Interior suddenly emerged in 1893 when gold

was discovered in nearby Birch Creek. Three years later, one of the world's most colourful gold rushes took place in the Klondike of the Yukon Territory (Canada).

Often called 'the last grand adventure', the Klondike gold rush took place when the country and much of the world was suffering through a severe recession. Thousands of people quit their jobs and sold their homes to finance a trip through Southeast Alaska to the newly created boom town of Skagway. From this tent city, almost 30,000 prospectors tackled the steep Chilkoot Trail to Lake Bennett, where they built crude rafts to float the rest of the way to the goldfields; an equal number returned home along the route, broke and disillusioned.

The number of miners who made a fortune was small, but the tales and legends that emerged were endless. The Klondike stampede, though it only lasted from 1896 to the early 1900s, was Alaska's most colourful era and earned it the reputation of the country's last frontier.

Statehood

By the 1900s, the attention of the miners shifted from the Klondike to Nome and then Fairbanks, a boom town that was born when Felix Pedro discovered gold 12 miles (19.2 km) north of the area in 1902. The gold mines and the large Kennecott Copper Mines north of Cordova also stimulated the state's growth and the 1900 census estimated the state's population to be 60,000, including 30,000 non-natives. Alaskans, who moved their capital from Sitka to Juneau that year, began to clamour for more say in their future. The US Congress first gave them a nonvoting delegate to Washington in 1906 and then assisted in setting up a territorial legislature that met at Juneau in 1913. Three years later, the territory submitted its first statehood bill to Congress.

Statehood was set aside when many of Alaska's residents departed south for high-paying jobs that were created by WW I. Ironically, it took another war, WW II, to push Alaska firmly into the 20th century.

The USA experienced its only foreign

invasion on home soil when the Japanese attacked the Attu Islands and bombed Dutch Harbor in the Aleutian Islands during WW II. Congress and military leaders panicked and rushed to develop and protect the rest of Alaska. Large army and air-force bases were built and thousands of military personnel were sent to run them. But it was the famous Alcan (also known as the Alaska Highway) that was the single most important project of the military build-up. The 1520 mile (2540 km) road was a major engineering feat and became the only overland link between Alaska and the rest of the USA.

The road was built by the military but it was the residents that benefited as it stimulated the development of Alaska's natural resources. The growth lead to a new drive for statehood to fix what many felt was Alaska's status of '2nd class citizenship' in Washington, DC. Early in 1958, Congress approved a statehood act which Alaskans quickly accepted, and on 3 January 1959, President Dwight Eisenhower proclaimed the land the 49th State of the Union.

The Modern State

Alaska entered the 1960s full of promise and then disaster struck: the most powerful earthquake ever recorded in North America (8.6 on the Richter scale) hit Southcentral Alaska on Good Friday morning in 1964. Over 100 lives were lost and the damage was estimated at $500 million. In Anchorage, office buildings sank below the ground while a tidal wave wiped out the entire community of Valdez. In Kodiak and Seward, 32 feet (9.8 metres) of the coastline slipped into the Gulf of Alaska, while Cordova lost its entire harbour as the sea rose 16 feet (4.9 metres).

If the natural catastrophe left the newborn state in a shambles, then it was a gift from nature that rushed it to recovery and beyond. Alaska's next boom took place in 1968 when massive oil deposits were discovered underneath Prudhoe Bay in the Arctic Ocean. The value of the oil doubled after the worldwide Arab oil embargo of 1973 but it couldn't be touched until there was a pipeline to transport it to the warm-water port of Valdez. The

pipeline, in turn, couldn't be built until the US Congress, which still administered most of the land, settled the intense controversy between industry, environmentalists and indigenous Indians with historical claims.

The Alaska Native Claims Settlement Act of 1971 was an unprecedented piece of legislation that opened the way for a group of oil companies to undertake the construction of the 789 mile (1270 km) pipeline. The oil began to flow in 1977, but during the brief years of pipeline construction Anchorage developed into a fully fledged modern city and Fairbanks burst at the seams as the transport centre for much of the project. Along with four-digit weekly salaries, there was an astronomical rise in prices for basic items such as housing and food in Fairbanks, which some residents feel never came down with the wages.

In the end, however, oil has given Alaska an economic base that is the envy of many other states; its residents enjoy the highest per-capita income in the country. The state's budget is in the billions and legislators in Juneau have transformed Anchorage into a stunning city with sports arenas, libraries and performing-arts centres, while virtually every Bush town has a million-dollar school. During the late 1970s and 80s, it was difficult for Alaska's residents to see beyond the gleam of the oil dollar.

Their rude awakening came on 11 March 1989 with the biggest oil spill in US history. The accident occurred when the *Exxon Valdez*, an Exxon Oil supertanker, rammed a reef and spilled almost 11 million gallons (41.7 million litres) of north-slope crude into the bountiful waters of Prince William Sound. Alaskans and the rest of the country watched in horror as the spill quickly became far too large for booms to contain the oil. Within months, more than 700 miles (1120 km) of coastline was tainted as Gulf of Alaska currents dispersed streamers of oil and tar balls.

State residents were shocked as oil began to appear from the glacier-carved cliffs of Kenai Fjords to the bird rookeries of Katmai National Park, and from lonely Cook Islet beaches to the salmon streams on Kodiak Island. In the first 3 months, workers picked up the oil-soaked bodies of 26,000 sea birds, 787 sea otters and 57 bald eagles, and Valdez experienced another boom as the centre of the clean-up effort that employed 9000 workers, 800 boats and 45 oil skimmers. But the best this highly paid army could do was scrape 364 miles (582 km) of shoreline before the on-coming winter weather shut down the effort in September.

In the end, many Alaskans felt betrayed by Big Oil, the very companies that had fed them so well in the past. The unfortunate event may be just the latest round in Alaska's greatest debate – exploitation of the wilderness. The issue moved to centre stage when industry, conservationists and the government came head to head over a single paragraph in the Native Claims Settlement Act, known simply as *d-2*, that called for the preservation of 80 million acres (32 million hectares) of Alaskan wilderness. Most residents used it to cover the entire issue of federal interference with the state's resources and future.

The resulting battle was a tug of war about how much land the US Congress would preserve, to what extent industries such as mining and logging would be allowed to develop, and what permanent residents would be allowed to purchase. The fury over wilderness reached a climax when on the eve of his departure from office in 1980, President Jimmy Carter signed the Alaska Lands Bill into law, setting aside over 100 million acres (40 million hectares) for national parks and preserves with a single stroke of the pen.

The problems of how to manage America's remaining true wilderness are far from over. Oil-company officials, already preparing for the day the Prudhoe Bay fields run dry, have been eyeing other wilderness areas such as the Arctic National Wildlife Refuge and Bristol Bay, home of Alaska's greatest salmon runs.

All this alarms environmentalists who say pipelines, oil drills and the activity associated in removing the oil will forever disrupt one of the last true wilderness areas on earth

– not just a park or a bay but a complete ecosystem. Others doubt that environmentalists can win this battle, not in a state where 85% of its revenue comes from the oil industry.

Also at the core of the issue are both 'locking up the land' and federal interference in the lives of Alaskans. Largely as the result of their remoteness, Alaskans have always been extremely independent, resenting anyone who travelled north with a book of rules and regulations. To most Alaskans, Washington, DC, is a foreign capital.

Today's Alaskans tend to be young and spirited in work and play. They are individualistic in their lifestyles, following few outside trends and adhering only to what their environment dictates. They are lovers of the outdoors, though they don't always seem to take care of it, and generally extend a warm welcome to travellers. Occasionally you might run into one who is boastfully loud as he spins and weaves tales of unbelievable feats while slapping you on the back. In this land of frontier fable, that's not being obnoxious – that's being colourful.

GEOGRAPHY
Southeast
Also known as the Panhandle, Southeast Alaska is a 500 mile (800 km) coastal strip that extends from Dixon Entrance, north of Prince Rupert, to the Gulf of Alaska. In between are the hundreds of islands (including Prince of Wales Island, the third largest island in the USA) of the Alexander Archipelago and a narrow strip of coast separated from Canada's mainland by the glacier-filled Coastal Mountains.

Winding through the middle of the region is the Inside Passage waterway, the lifeline for the isolated communities as the rugged terrain prohibits road building. High annual rainfall and mild temperatures have turned the Southeast into rainforest which is broken up by majestic mountain ranges, glaciers and fjords that surpass those in Norway.

The area has many small fishing and lumbering towns as well as the larger

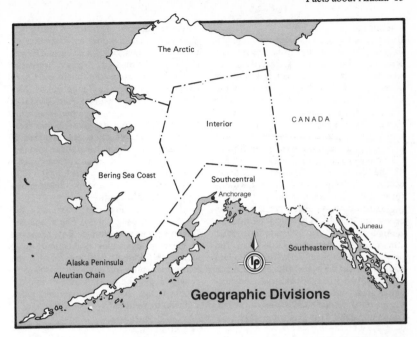

Geographic Divisions

communities of Ketchikan, Sitka and Juneau, which is the state capital and considered by many to be the most scenic city in Alaska. Other highlights of the region include the wilderness areas of Glacier Bay, Admiralty Island, Misty Fjord and Tracy Arm, and the White Pass Railroad, built in the days of the Klondike gold rush. Because the State Marine Ferry connects the Southeast to Seattle (USA) and Prince Rupert (Canada), it is the cheapest and often the first area visited by travellers.

Southcentral

This region curves 650 miles (1040 km) from the Gulf of Alaska, past Prince William Sound to Kodiak Island. Like the Southeast, it is a mixture of rugged mountains, glaciers, steep fjords and virgin forests, and includes the Kenai Peninsula, a superb recreational area for backpacking, fishing and boating. To the south-west is Kodiak Island, home to

much of Alaska's crab industry and the Kodiak bear, the largest species of brown bear in the state. To the east of the Kenai Peninsula is Prince William Sound, a bay that used to be famous for the Columbia Glacier and as a mecca for kayakers and adventurers – now infamous as the sight of the Exxon oil spill.

The weather along the coastline can often be rainy and stormy but the summers are usually mild and have their share of sunshine. The peninsula is served by road from Anchorage and by the State Marine Ferry which crosses Prince William Sound and runs to Kodiak.

Highlights of the region are the historical and charming towns of Homer, Seward, Cordova and Hope, while backpackers will find many opportunities for outdoor adventure in the wilderness areas of the Chugach National Forest, Kenai National Wildlife Refuge and the outlying areas around Kodiak, Cordova and Valdez.

Anchorage

Because of the city's size and central location, Anchorage has to be viewed as a separate region; one that is passed through whether you want to deal with an urban area or not. At first glance, Anchorage appears to be like any other city – billboards, traffic jams, fast-food restaurants and what seems like hordes of people. Among this uncontrolled urban sprawl, however, is a city that in recent years has blossomed on the flow of oil money. While older cities in the Lower 48 (the continental USA) often worry about decaying city centres, Anchorage has transformed its city centre with such capital projects as a sports arena, performing-arts centre and 70 miles (110 km) of bike paths.

Anchorage also has a feature most other cities don't – wilderness at its doorstep. The nearby Chugach State Park, Turnagain and Knik arms, and the Matanuska Valley (home of the softball-size radishes) make Anchorage an area worth spending a little time in, if for no other reason than having to arrive, depart or pass through it at some stage.

The Interior

This area includes three major roads – the George Parks, Glenn and Richardson highways – that cut across the centre of the state and pass a number of forests, state parks and recreational areas, including Denali National Park & Preserve, Alaska's number one attraction. The heartland of Alaska offers warm temperatures in the summer and ample opportunities for outdoor activities in some of the state's most scenic and accessible areas. With the Alaska Range to the north, the Wrangell and Chugach mountains to the south and the Talkeetna Mountains cutting through the middle, the Interior has a rugged appearance matching that of either Southeast or Southcentral Alaska but without much of the rain and cloudy weather.

Fairbanks

The boom town of both the gold-rush days and later the pipeline construction to Prudhoe Bay has settled down a little, but it still retains much of its colourful and hardcore Alaskan character. A quick trip through Fairbanks is often a disappointment to most travellers, as Alaska's second largest city is very spread-out. Located in the flat valley floor formed by the Tanana and Chena rivers, with the Alaska Range and Mt Mc-Kinley far off in the distance, Fairbanks lacks the dramatic setting many other areas offer. However, the true delights of this free-wheeling frontier town are revealed if sufficient time is spent here. In the summer, Fairbanks can be an unusually warm place with temperatures often reaching 80°F to 90°F (27°C to 32°C), and the midnight sun only sets for a few hours.

The surrounding area, especially the White Mountains, Circle, Eagle and the Dalton Highway to Prudhoe Bay, has some of the most interesting backcountry areas accessible by road. Fairbanks is also the transport centre for anybody wishing to venture above the Arctic Circle or into the Brooks Range, site of many national parks and wildlife refuges.

The Bush

This region covers a vast area that includes the Brooks Range, Arctic Alaska, Western Alaska on the Bering Sea, and the Alaska Peninsula and Aleutian Islands which make up the out-reaching western arm of the state. The Bush is larger than the other five regions put together and is separated from them by great mountains and mighty rivers.

Occasionally, there are ways of beating the high cost of getting to the far reaches of the state, but for the most part travelling to the Bush involves small chartered aircraft, or 'bush planes'. These aeroplanes are a common method of travel through much of the state but, unfortunately, are prohibitively expensive for many budget travellers.

Except for the larger communities of Nome, Kotzebue and Barrow, independent travel in Bush villages is difficult unless you have a contact. If you have just stepped off a chartered aeroplane, the small, isolated villages may appear closed, unfriendly and have very limited facilities.

For those who do make an effort to leave

the roads, Bush Alaska offers a lifestyle that is rare in other areas of the USA, and, for the most part, is unaffected by the state's booming summer tourist industry. Climate in the summer can range from a chilly 40°F (4°C) in the treeless and nightless Arctic tundra to the wet and fog of the Bering Sea coast, where the terrain is a flat land of lakes and slow-moving rivers.

CLIMATE & THE 24 HOUR DAY

It makes sense that a place as large and diverse as Alaska would have a climate to match. The effects of oceans surrounding 75% of the state, the mountainous terrain and the low angle of the sun give Alaska an extremely variable climate and daily weather that is famous for being unpredictable.

The Interior can top 90°F (32°C) during the summer, yet 6 months later in the same region the temperature can drop to -60°F (-51°C). Fort Yukon holds the state record for maximum temperature at 100°F (37.7°C) in June 1915, yet it once recorded a temperature of -78°F (-60°C).

For the most part, Southeast and Southcentral Alaska have high rainfall with temperatures that only vary 40°F (22°C) during the year. Anchorage, shielded by the Kenai Mountains, has an annual rainfall of 15 inches (380 mm) and averages 60°F to 70°F (15°C to 21°C) from June to August. Juneau averages 57 inches (1450 mm) of rain or snow annually, while Ketchikan gets 154 inches (3900 mm) a year, most of which is rain, as the temperatures are extremely mild even in the winter.

Residents will tell you, however, that averages don't mean a thing. There have been summers when it has rained just about every day, and there have been Aprils when every day has been sunny and dry. A good week in Southcentral and Southeast Alaska during the summer will include three sunny days, two overcast ones and two when you will have to pull your rain gear out or duck for cover.

In the Interior and up around Fairbanks, precipitation is light but temperatures can fluctuate by more than 100°F (37.4°C)

during the year. In the summer, the average daytime temperature can range from 55°F to 75°F (12°C to 23°C) with a brief period in late July to early August where it will top 80°F (27°C) or even 90°F (32°C). At night, temperatures can drop sharply to 45°F (7°C) or even lower, and freak snowfalls can occur in the valleys during July or August, with the white stuff lasting a day or two.

The climate in the Bush varies. The region north of the Arctic Circle is cool most of the summer with temperatures around 45°F (7°C), and annual rainfall is less than 4 inches (100 mm). Other areas such as Nome in Western Alaska or Dillingham in Southwest Alaska aren't much warmer and tend to be foggy and rainy much of the summer.

In most of Alaska, summers are a beautiful mixture of long days and short nights, making the great outdoors even more appealing. At Point Barrow, Alaska's northernmost point, the sun never sets for 2½ months from May to August. The longest day is on 21 June (equinox), when the sun sets for only 2 hours in Fairbanks, 4 hours in Anchorage and 5 to 6 hours in the Southeast.

Even after the sun sets in late June and July, it is replaced not by night, but by a dusk that still allows good visibility. The midnight sun allows residents and visitors to undertake activities at hours undreamed of in most other places – 6 mile hikes after dinner, bike rides at 10 pm or softball games at midnight. It also causes most people, even those with the best window shades, to wake up at 4 or 5 am.

No matter where you intend to travel or what you plan to do, bring protection against Alaska's climate. This should include warm clothing, rain gear and a covering if you are camping out. Alaska's weather is unpredictable and often changes when least expected – don't be left out in the cold.

FLORA & FAUNA

From the road, most visitors see more wildlife in Alaska than they do in a lifetime elsewhere. From the trail, such encounters are often the highlight of the entire trip; you can spot an animal, watch it quietly and marvel at the experience when it moves on leisurely.

Moose are widespread throughout the state but are frequently sighted along the Alcan, in the Interior and on the Kenai Peninsula. Some of these animals can weigh up to 1600 lb (720 kg) and have been known to invade the city limits of Anchorage during severe winters. Caribou, of which there are an estimated 600,000 living in Alaska's 13 herds, are more difficult to view as they range from the Interior north to the Arctic Sea. The best place to see caribou is Denali National Park, where they are occasionally seen from the park road.

Other mammals encountered during alpine treks include Dall sheep and mountain goats in alpine regions of Southeast and Southcentral Alaska. In the lowlands, hikers have a chance to view red fox, beaver, pine marten, snowshoe hare, red squirrel and on rare occasions wolves or even a wolverines.

Marine mammals most commonly spotted include harbour seals, sea otters, sea lions, harbour porpoises and killer whales, or Orcas, whose high black and white dorsal fin makes them easy to identify from a distance. The two most common whales seen in coastal waters are the humpback, with its hump-like dorsal fin and long flippers, and the smaller minke whale.

The salmon runs are one of Alaska's most amazing sights and are common throughout much of the state. From late July to mid-September, many coastal streams are choked with salmon swimming upstream to spawn. You won't see just one here and there, but thousands – so many that they have to wait their turn to swim through narrow gaps of shallow water. The salmon are famous for their struggle

against the current, their magnificent leaps over waterfalls, and for covering stream banks with carcasses afterwards. There are five kinds of salmon in Alaska; sockeye (also referred to as red salmon), king (chinook), pink (humpie), coho (silver) and chum.

Equally impressive in Alaska's wilderness is the bald eagle, the majestic and powerful bird that is the symbol of a nation. While elsewhere the bird is almost extinct, in Alaska it

thrives in strong numbers. The eagle can be sighted almost daily in most of the Southeast and is common in Prince William Sound. It also migrates once a year in a spectacle that exceeds even the salmon runs. As many as 1500 bald eagles gather along the Chilkat River north of Haines from late October to December. They come to feed on the late chum-salmon run and create an amazing scene during the bleakness of early winter. Bare trees, without a leaf remaining, support 80 or more white-headed eagles, four or five to a branch.

The flora of Alaska, like everything in the state, is diverse, changing dramatically from one region to the next. There are 33 native species of trees, the fewest of any state in the USA, and only 12 of these are classified as large trees more than 70 feet (20 metres) in height. Not surprising, nine of these species are found in the coastal regions of Southeast and Southcentral Alaska.

In these areas, mild temperatures in winter and summer and frequent rains produce lush coniferous forests of Sitka spruce (the state tree) and western hemlock. Any opening in the forest is often a bog or filled with alder or spiny devil's club, a mildly poisonous plant that often results in a rash on contact. The tree line is often between 2000 and 3000 feet (600 to 900 metres) where thick alder takes over until finally giving way to alpine meadows.

In the Interior, the large area of plains and hills between the Alaska Range and the Brooks Range is dominated by boreal forest of white spruce, cottonwood and paper birch, while on north-facing slopes and in moist lowlands you'll find a stunted forest of scrawny black spruce. Continue travelling north and you'll enter a zone known as Taiga, characterised by muskeg, willow thickets and more stunted spruce, before entering the tundra of the Arctic coastal region.

The Arctic tundra is a bizarre world, a treeless area except for a few small stands on gravel flood plains of rivers. Plant life hugs the ground; even willow trees that only grow 6 inches (15 cm) in height still produce pussy willows. Other plants, including grasses, mosses and a variety of tiny flowers, provide a carpet of life for a short period in July and August despite little precipitation and a harsh climate.

Perhaps the flora that interests hikers and visitors the most are Alaska's wild berries. Blueberries are found throughout much of the state while in the Southeast you'll encounter huge patches of huckleberries and salmonberries. Other species include blackberries, raspberries, highbush cranberries and straw-berries. If you plan to feast on berries, take time to learn which ones are inedible. The most common poisonous one is the bane-berry, found in the Southeast and the Interior, which often appears as a white berry.

GOVERNMENT

The government sector in Alaska is very strong, especially in Juneau, the capital city of Alaska. Statewide, one in every three people are paid for government work, while in Juneau it's estimated that two-thirds of the residents work for either the federal, state or city government. The result is a lopsided pay scale with workers in the private sector rarely having a salary comparable with government workers.

All this government is most obvious when the state legislature and its army of aids and advisors convene in Juneau for the annual session. From across Alaska, 40 state representatives and 20 state senators arrive and take up temporary residence in the city until April to draw up a budget, spend the oil money and pass bills. Legislation is then passed onto the governor, who either signs them into law or vetoes the measures. The best way to understand Alaska state politics and its colourful history is to join one of the free tours offered at the Alaska State Capitol in Juneau.

Alaska, like three other states in the USA, has only one US state representative and two US Senators because of its small population. Local government consists of 1st, 2nd and 3rd class boroughs and cities along with hundreds of unincorporated villages, the category that most Bush communities fall into.

ECONOMY

Alaska's economy is fuelled by oil. Oil and gas revenues annually account for almost 90% of the gross state product. Because of Prudhoe Bay, the largest oil field in the USA, Alaska is the richest state in the Union. The average annual income of an Alaskan is close to $20,000 as compared to $12,000 nationally. Commercial fishing is the second largest industry in the state as the Alaskan fleet contributes almost 25% of the country's annual catch, including nearly all canned salmon produced in the USA. Tourism is the state's third largest industry while mining, logging and, to a very small degree, farming also contribute to the economy.

POPULATION

Alaska, the largest state in the USA, has the smallest population. Permanent residents, not including the large influx of seasonal workers in the fishing and tourist industries, number 523,000, with over half of them living in the Anchorage Bowl area. It is estimated that only 30% of the state's population were born in Alaska while 25% have moved there in the last 5 years. This means that the average resident is young (26 to 28), mobile and mostly from the US west coast. Eskimos and other indigenous groups make up only 14% of the total population while ethnic groups of Japanese, Filipinos and Blacks represent less than 5%.

The five largest cities in Alaska are Anchorage (pop 218,979) Fairbanks (pop 72,000), Juneau (pop 29,370), Kodiak (pop 14,203) and Ketchikan (pop 12,982).

PEOPLE & CULTURE

Long before Bering's journeys to Alaska, other groups of people had made their way there and established a culture and lifestyle in one of the world's harshest environments. The first major invasion, which came across the land bridge from Asia, was by the Tlingits and the Haidas (who settled throughout the Southeast and British Columbia), and the Athabascans (a nomadic tribe that lived in the Interior). The other two major groups were the Aleuts of the Aleutian Islands and the Eskimos, or Inuit, who settled on the coast of the Bering Sea and the Arctic Ocean; both groups are believed to have migrated only 3000 years ago but were well established by the time the Europeans arrived.

The Tlingit and Haida cultures were advanced, as the tribes had permanent settlements including large clan houses. They were noted for their excellent woodcarving, most notably poles, called *totems*, that can still be seen today in most Southeast communities. The Tlingits were spread throughout the Southeast in large numbers and occasionally went as far south as Seattle in their large dugout canoes. Both groups had few problems gathering food as fish and game were plentiful in the Southeast.

Not so for the Aleuts and the Eskimos. With much colder winters and cooler summers, both groups had to develop a highly effective sea-hunting culture to sustain life in the harsh regions of Alaska.

Aleutian Islands. The Eskimos were unsurpassed carvers of ivory, jade and soapstone; many support themselves today by continuing the art.

The indigenous people, despite their harsh environment, were numerous until the white people brought guns, alcohol and disease that destroyed the Indians' delicate relationship with nature and wiped out entire villages. At one time, there were an estimated

This was especially true for the Eskimos who could not have survived the winters without their skilled ice-hunting techniques. In the spring, armed with only jade-tipped harpoons, the Eskimos stalked and killed 60 ton (54,420 kg) bowhead whales in skin-covered kayaks called *bidarkas* and *umikaks*.

The Aleuts were known for some of the finest basket weaving in North America, using the highly prized Attu grass of the

20,000 Aleuts living on almost every island of the Aleutian chain. It took the Russians only 50 years to reduce the population (mainly through forced labour) to less than 2000. The whalers who arrived at Eskimo villages in the mid-1800s were similarly destructive.

Today, there are almost 70,000 indigenous people living in Alaska of which half are Eskimos, or Inuit. They are no longer nomadic but live in permanent villages which have replaced the tribe and range in size from less than 30 people to 3100 in Barrow, the largest centre of indigenous people in Alaska.

Most indigenous people in the Bush still depend on some level of subsistence, but today their houses are constructed of modern materials and often heated by electricity or oil. Visitors are occasionally shocked when they fly hundreds of miles into a remote area only to see TV antennas sticking out of cabins, community satellite dishes, people drinking Coca-Cola or children listening to Michael Jackson tapes on their boom box.

All indigenous people received a boost in 1971 when Congress passed the Native Claims Settlement Act in an effort to allow oil companies to build a pipeline across their traditional lands. The act created the Alaska Native Fund and formed 12 regional corporations, controlled and administered by the local tribes, that invested and developed the $900 million and 44 million acres (17.6 million hectares) received for their historical lands.

Today, all indigenous people hold stock in their village corporations and receive dividends when it turns a profit. Although a few have floundered and lost money, one of them, Sealaska of Juneau, has done so well managing its lands and investing its funds that the corporation is ranked among the 500 largest companies in America.

To give indigenous Alaskans time to understand capitalism and private ownership, a concept that was completely foreign to their ancestors, the Settlement Act stated that stock couldn't be sold until 1991. In that year, after 2 decades of waiting, the indigenous population can do what they want with their corporation's stock – corporations that still control millions of acres in Alaska, including mineral rights and timber. Many indigenous Alaskans fear that their culture will die at the hands of monetary greed. 'Young people look at land in the white sense, as real estate', said one native leader. 'They will be offered a good price, they'll sell and then it will be gone.'

In a campaign against stock sales, some corporations are promoting 'spirit movements', a return to traditional values and heritage. Smaller villages isolated in the Bush have even gone a step further by

demanding 'tribal sovereignty', the right to bypass state and federal laws to control their taxation, education, fish and game regulations, law enforcement and other traditional government functions. By 1989, state attorneys were in court contesting half a dozen cases involving tribal sovereignty and more were expected.

HOLIDAYS & FESTIVALS

Alaskans do their fair share of celebrating, much of it during the summer. One of the biggest celebrations in the state is the Summer Solstice on 21 June, the longest day of the year. Fairbanks holds the best community festival, with a variety of events including midnight baseball games (played without the use of artificial light) and hikes to local hills to view the midnight sun. Nome stages a week-long Midnight Sun Festival while Barrow stages a 'Sun will not set for 83 days' Festival and many towns have unofficial celebrations.

Independence Day (4 July) is a popular holiday around the state when the larger communities of Ketchikan, Juneau, Anchorage and Fairbanks sponsor well-planned events. Perhaps even more enjoyable during this time of year is a visit to a small settlement such as Gustavus, Seldovia or Talkeetna, where you cannot help but be swept along with the local residents in an afternoon of old-fashion celebrating that usually ends with a square dance in the evening.

Salmon and halibut derbies that end with cash prizes for the heaviest fish caught are regular events around the coastal regions of Alaska, with Juneau and Seward having the largest. Although most travellers are ill prepared to compete in such fishing contests, watching the boats returning to the marina with their catch makes for an interesting afternoon.

State fairs, though small compared to those in the Lower 48, are worth attending if for no other reason than to see what a 70 lb (32 kg) cabbage looks like. They all take place in August and include the Alaska State Fair at Palmer, the Tanana Valley Fair at

Fairbanks, the Southeast State Fair at Haines and smaller ones at Kodiak, Delta Junction and Ninilchik.

Regional Festivals & Celebrations
The regional festivals and celebrations in Alaska include:

April
  Spring Arts Festival, Homer
  Alyeska Spring Carnival, Girdwood
  Alaska Folk Festival, Juneau
  Copper Day Celebrations, Cordova
  State Drama Festival, Haines
  Piuraagiaqta Spring Festival, Barrow
May
  Little Norway Festival, Petersburg
  Miner's Day Celebration, Talkeetna
  Crab Festival, Kodiak
  Polar Bear Swim, Nome
  Buffalo Wallow Jamboree, Delta Junction
June
  Summer Music Festival, Sitka
  Nenana River Daze, Nenana
  Renaissance Festival, Anchorage
  Nuchalowayaa Festival, Tanana
  Summer Solstice, Fairbanks
  Midnight Sun Festival, Nome
  All Alaska Logging Championships, Sitka
  Whaling Festival, Barrow
  White-water Weekend, Valdez
  Basically Bach Festival, Anchorage
  Iditarod Extravaganza, Palmer
  Colony Days Summerfest, Palmer
July
  Moose Dropping Festival, Talkeetna
  Summer Arts Festival, Fairbanks
  Golden Days, Fairbanks
  Soapy Smith's Wake, Skagway
  Forest Fair, Girdwood
  Gold Rush Days, Valdez
  Bear Paw Festival, Chugiak-Eagle River
  Bluegrass Festival, Palmer
  Progress Days, Soldotna
  Water Festival, Wasilla
August
  Blueberry Festival, Ketchikan
  Tanana Valley Fair, Fairbanks
  Southeast Alaska State Fair, Haines
  State Fair and Rodeo, Kodiak
  Deltana Fair, Delta Junction
  AgriFair, Ninilchik
  Alaska State Fair, Palmer
  Scottish Highland Games, Anchorage
  St Herman's Pilgrimage, Kodiak

September
  Oktoberfest, Anchorage
  Fall Fest, Dillingham
  Taste of Homer, Homer
October
  Alaska Day Celebration, Sitka
  October Arts Festival, Petersburg
  Oktoberfest, Fairbanks

Tourist offices can provide exact dates and further information on various events.

State Holidays
The state holidays for Alaska include:

1 January
  New Year's Day
16 January
  Martin Luther King Day
16 February
  President's Day
30 March
  Seward's Day
April
  Easter
25 May
  Memorial Day
4 July
  Independence Day
7 September
  Labor Day
12 October
  Columbus Day
18 October
  Alaska Day
11 November
  Veteran's Day
26 November
  Thanksgiving
25 December
  Christmas

ALASKAN ENGLISH
English is spoken all across Alaska but it is tinted with Alaskan words and phrases that make it almost a tongue of its own. Most of these words are of native Alaskan origin or a colourful combination coined by some local character. The following list should be of some assistance when you get confused but is by no means a complete text of Alaskan English.

Alcan (or Alaska Highway) – The only overland link between the state and the rest of the country. Although the highway is almost completely paved now, completing a journey across this legendary road is still a special accomplishment that earns you a slash mark on the side of your pick-up truck.

aurora borealis (or northern lights) – A spectacular show on clear nights, possible almost any time of the year. The mystical snakes of light that weave across the sky from the northern horizon are the result of gas particles colliding with solar electrons. Best viewed from the Interior, away from city lights, late summer to winter.

bidarka – A skin-covered sea kayak used by the Aleuts.

blanket toss – An activity originating with the Eskimos in which a hunter was tossed into the air with a skin so he could search for whales offshore.

blue cloud – What Southeasterners call a break in the clouds.

break-up – A phrase applied to rivers when the ice suddenly begins to disintegrate and flows downstream. Many residents also use it to describe spring in Alaska when the rains come, the snows melt and everything turns to mud and slush.

bunny boots – Large, oversized and usually white plastic boots used extensively in subzero weather to prevent feet from freezing.

The Bush – Any area in the state either not connected by road to Anchorage or which does not have a State Marine Ferry dock in town.

cache – A small hut or storage room built high off the ground to keep supplies and spare food away from roaming bears and wolves. The term, however, has found its way onto the neon signs of everything from liquor stores to pizza parlours in the cities.

cabin fever – A winter condition in which cross-eyed Alaskans go stir-crazy in their one-room cabins because of too little sunlight and too much time spent indoors.

capital move – The political issue that raged

in the early 1980s which concerned moving the state capital from Juneau closer to Anchorage. The issue was buried somewhat in a 1982 state election when residents rejected the funding for the move north.

cheechako – Tenderfoot, greenhorn or somebody trying to survive their first year in Alaska.

chum – Not your mate or good buddy but a nickname for the dog salmon.

clearcut – A hated sight for environmentalists, this is an area where loggers have cut every tree, large and small, leaving nothing standing. A traveller's first view of one, often from a state ferry, is a shocking sight.

d-2 – A phrase that covers the lands issue of the late 1970s, pitting environmentalists against developers over the federal government's preservation of 100 million acres (40 million hectares) of Alaska wilderness as wildlife reserves, forests and national parks.

developers – Those residents of Alaska who favour development of the state's natural resources and land through such endeavours as logging and mining, as opposed to preserving it in national parks.

Eskimo ice cream – A traditional food made of whipped berries, seal oil and snow.

fish wheel – A wooden trap that scoops salmon or other large fish out of a river into a holding tank by utilising the current as power.

greenies – A nickname for environmentalists and others who celebrated the passage of the Alaska Lands Bill.

humpie – A nickname for the humpback, or pink salmon, the mainstay of the fishing industry in the Southeast.

ice worm – A small, thin black worm that thrives in glacial ice; made famous by a Robert Service poem.

Lower 48 – The way Alaskans describe the continental United States.

mukluks – Lightweight boots of seal skin trimmed with fur, made by the Eskimos.

moose nuggets – Hard, smooth little objects dropped by moose after a good meal. Some enterprising resident in Homer has capitalised on them by baking, varnishing and trimming them with evergreen leaves to sell during Christmas as Moostletoe.

muskeg – The bogs in Alaska where layers of matted plant life float on top of stagnant water. A bad place to hike or pitch a tent.

no-see-um – Nickname for the tiny gnats found throughout much of the Alaska wilderness, especially the Interior and areas in the Brooks Range.

outside – To residents, any place that isn't Alaska.

permafrost – Permanently frozen subsoil that covers two-thirds of the state.

petroglyphs – Ancient rock carvings.

potlatch – A traditional gathering of indigenous people held to commemorate any memorable occasion.

qiviut – The wool of the musk ox that is often woven into garments.

scat – Any animal droppings but usually used to describe that of a bear. If it is dark brown or bluish and somewhat square in shape, a bear has passed through. If it is steaming, it's eating blueberries around the next bend.

sourdough – Any old-timer in the state, who some say is 'sour on the country but without enough dough to get out'. More recently arrived residents believe anybody who has survived an Alaskan winter qualifies as a sourdough. The term also applies to a yeasty mixture used to make bread or pancakes rise.

stinkhead – an Eskimo 'treat' made by burying a salmon head in the sand. Leave the head to ferment for up to 10 days, then dig it up, wash off the sand and enjoy!

Southeast sneakers – Also known as Ketchikan tennis shoes, Sitka slippers, Petersburg pumps and a variety of other names. These are the tall, reddish-brown rubber boots Southeast residents wear when it rains and often when it doesn't.

taku wind – Juneau's sudden gusts of wind that may exceed 100 miles (160 km) per hour in the spring and fall. Often the winds cause another strange phenomenon – horizontal rain which, as the name indicates, comes straight at you instead of falling down on you. In Anchorage and throughout the Interior, these sudden rushes of air over or through mountain gaps are called 'williwaws'.

tundra – Often used to refer to the vast, treeless Arctic plains.

ulu – A fan-shaped knife that indigenous people use to chop and scrape meat. Now the gift shops use them to lure tourists.

Lynx

Facts for the Visitor

VISAS

If you are travelling to Alaska from overseas there are one or two things you need depending on your nationality: a passport (except for USA and Canadian citizens who only need a driver's license or voter registration card) and at least one visa, possibly two. Obviously a US visa is needed, but if you're taking either the Alcan (also called the Alaska Highway) or the State Marine Ferry from Prince Rupert in British Columbia then you will also need a Canadian visa. The Alcan begins in Canada, requiring travellers to pass from the USA into Canada and back into the USA again.

Travellers from western Europe and most Commonwealth nations do not need a Canadian visa and can get a 6 month travel visa to the USA without too much paperwork or waiting. All visitors must have an onward or return ticket to enter the USA and sufficient funds to pass into Canada. Those arriving at the Canadian border with less than US$250 will most likely be turned back.

Vaccinations are not required for either country and only people who have been on a farm during the past 30 days will be detained by immigration officials. Travellers are allowed to bring all personal goods (including camping gear or hiking equipment) into the USA and Canada free of duty, along with food for 2 days and up to 50 cigars, 200 cigarettes and 40 oz (1.2 litres) of liquor or wine.

There are no forms to fill out if you are a foreign visitor bringing any vehicle into Alaska whether it is a bicycle, motorcycle or a car; nor are there forms for hunting rifles or fishing gear. Hunting rifles (handguns and automatic weapons are prohibited) must be registered in your own country and you should bring proof of this. There is no limit to the amount of money you can bring into Alaska but anything over US$5000 must be registered with customs officials.

A word of warning: overseas travellers should be aware of the procedures to re-enter the USA. Occasionally visitors get stuck in Canada without the necessary papers to enter Alaska after passing through the Lower 48. Canadian immigration officers often caution people who they feel might have difficulty returning to the USA.

EMPLOYMENT

Tales of astronomical wages for jobs on the Alaska Pipeline and other high paying employment are, unfortunately, either exaggerated or nonexistent today. Except for brief hiring booms, like the Exxon oil spill clean-up, the cold reality is that Alaska has one of the highest unemployment rates in the country, averaging 11% annually and often reaching 20% during the winter.

Many summer travellers arrive thinking they will get work on a fishing boat after hearing of someone earning $10,000 in 6 weeks by getting a percentage of the catch on a good boat. After discovering they lack the deck-hand experience necessary for any kind of position on a fishing vessel, they end up cleaning salmon in a cannery for minimum wages ($3.85 per hour).

Summer employment in Alaska is possible but be realistic about what you will be paid and look in the right places. Search out tourist-related business such as hotels, restaurants, bars and resorts who need additional short-term help to handle the influx of customers. Other places such as the US Forest Service and national parks also hire a large number of temporary workers during the summer. But be aware that these agencies, like many canneries, recruit their workers during the winter and have little if anything to offer someone passing through in June or July.

Those people whose sole interest is working for a summer in Alaska rather than travelling should begin looking the winter before. Start by contacting regional offices of the US Forest Service, national parks or

the chambers of commerce in fishing communities such as Petersburg, Juneau, Kodiak or Sitka. You can also get some information from the Alaska State Employment Service (Box 3-7000, Juneau, Alaska 99802) though they tend to do everything they can to discourage outsiders from seeking jobs in Alaska.

MONEY & COSTS

Alaskans use the same currency as the rest of the USA, American dollars (US$) – only they use a lot more of it. The state is traditionally known for having the highest cost of living in the country, though places like southern California, San Francisco and New York City have caught up if not surpassed it in some costs like housing. There are two reasons for the high prices in Alaska: the long distances needed to transport everything and the high cost of labour.

To buy a dozen eggs in Fairbanks will cost your more than in other parts of the USA, around $1.30 to $1.60, but to walk into a cafe and have two of them cooked and served is where the high prices slap you in the face like a July snowfall. In the restaurants, not only are the transport costs added to the price, but so are the high salaries of the chef, waitress and busboy who put them sunny-side up on your table.

The trick to budget travel, or beating the high prices, is to avoid the labour cost. Buy your own food in a market and cook it at the youth hostel or campsite. Use public transport or better still hitchhike; sleep in campgrounds and enjoy your favourite brew

around a campfire at night. It is the restaurants, bars, hotels and taxi companies, with their inflated peak-season prices, that will quickly drain your money pouch.

A rule of thumb for Alaskan prices is that they are lowest in Ketchikan and increase gradually as you go north. Overall, the Southeast has the best bargains because of inexpensive barge transport from Seattle (the supply centre for the area). Barges arrive weekly in Southeast Alaska, bringing all the necessities of life. The trip takes several days and fresh food such as bread and milk is frozen before shipping. If you walk into a store and find all the milk half frozen, don't be alarmed – the barge just arrived.

Anchorage and to some extent Fairbanks are the exceptions to the rule as they have competitive prices due to their large populations and business communities. When travelling in the Bush, on the other hand, be prepared for anything. The cost of fresh food, gasoline or lodging can be two or three times what it is anywhere else in the state. It is here that the tales of $25 breakfasts were conjured up, and in some isolated Bush villages these stories might not be too mythical.

On the average, a loaf of day-old bread will cost $1.50 to $1.80, while locally baked bread will cost from $2 to $2.50. Half a gallon (2 litres) of milk costs from $1.90 to $2.70, apples cost from 79 cents to $1.20 per lb ($1.80 to $2.60 per kg) and hamburger is anywhere from $2 per lb ($4.40 per kg) in the large cities to over $3.50 per lb ($7.70 per kg) in a small town. When buying fresh fruit and vegetables take the time to look over them closely, especially in small town markets. It is not too uncommon to buy a stalk of celery and later discover the middle of it is spoiled.

A US gallon (3.7 litres) of gasoline can cost anywhere from $1.50 in large commercial areas to $2.50 or more at some deserted station off the road. A single room in the cheapest motels or hotels costs from $35 to $40 per night while many state and federal campgrounds charge $5 per tent site and privately owned campgrounds cost anywhere from $7 to $15 a night.

The National Bank of Alaska (NBA) is the largest bank in the state with offices in almost every village and town on the heavily travelled routes. The NBA, open Monday to Friday from 10 am to 3 pm, can meet the needs of most visitors. Many branches of the NBA and other banks are open evenings on Wednesday and Friday or have drive-up windows that stay open late. The popular brands of travellers' cheques are widely used around the state and many merchants also accept Canadian money, though they usually burn you on the exchange rate.

Note All prices quoted in this book are in US dollars unless otherwise stated.

A$1 = $0.82
UK£1 = $1.98
C$1 = $0.91
NZ$1 = $0.63
DM 1 = $0.67

Tipping
Tipping in Alaska, like the rest of the USA, is expected; the going rate for restaurants, hotels and taxi drivers is about 15%.

TOURIST INFORMATION
The first place to write to while planning your adventure is the Alaska Division of Tourism (PO Box E-301, Juneau, Alaska 99811; tel (907) 465-2010, fax (907) 586-8399) where you can request a copy of the *Alaska State Vacation Planner*, a 120 page annually updated magazine.

Travel information is easy to obtain once you are on the road as almost every city, town and village has a tourist contact centre whether it be a visitors bureau, chamber of commerce or a hut near the ferry dock. They are good sources for free maps, information on local accommodation and directions to the nearest campground or hiking trail.

GENERAL INFORMATION
Post
Planning to write home or to friends? Send it 1st class by sticking a 25 cent stamp on the envelope or by using a 39 cent airgram for overseas destinations. Surface mail, slow anywhere in the USA, can take up to a month moving to or from Alaska.

To receive mail while travelling in Alaska, have it sent c/o General Delivery to a post office along your route. Although everybody passes through Anchorage (zip code (post code) 99510), it's probably better to choose smaller towns like Juneau (99801), Ketchikan (99901), Seward (99664), Tok (99780) or Delta Junction (99737). Post offices are supposed to keep letters for 10 days before returning them, although smaller ones may keep letters longer, especially if your letters have 'Please Hold' on the front written in big red crayon. If you are planning to stay at youth hostels, those are the best addresses to leave with letter writers.

Telegrams and mailgrams can be sent anywhere from Alaska by calling (800) 478-9500 and money orders can be received at banks in most communities, certainly the ones budget travellers pass through.

Telephones
Telephone area codes are simple in Alaska; the entire state shares 907 expect Hyder which uses 604.

Electricity
Voltage in Alaska is 110/120 volts – the same as everywhere else in the USA.

Time
In 1983, Alaska reduced its time zones from four to two in an effort to help commerce and

communications between its cities. With the exception of four Aleutian Island communities and Hyder, a small community on the Alaska/British Columbia border, the entire state shares the same time zone, Alaska Time, which is 1 hour earlier than Pacific Standard Time, in which Seattle falls.

When it is noon in Anchorage, it is 9 pm in London, 4 pm in New York and 7 am in Melbourne the following day.

Business Hours

Banks and post offices in Alaska are generally open from 9 am to 5 pm Monday to Friday. Other business hours are variable but many shops are open until 10 pm during the week, from 10 am to 6 pm Saturday and from noon to 5 pm Sundays.

Weights & Measures

Alaska uses the imperial system of measurement. Weight is measured in ounces (oz) and pounds (lb), volume is measured in pints and gallons, and length in inches, feet and yards.

A conversion table is provided at the back of this book for people more comfortable with metric measurement.

MEDIA

There are 33 daily, weekly and trade newspapers in Alaska, though most are eight pages of local news, softball scores and advertising. The largest daily in the state is the *Anchorage Daily News*, a 1st class newspaper that captured the Pulitzer Prize in the 1970s with its stories on the Alaska Pipeline. The next biggest daily is its competitor, the *Anchorage Times*, while the *Fairbanks Daily News Miner* is one of the state's finest papers. The *Seattle Post-Intelligencer* is flown into the Southeast daily and the usual news magazines, *Time* and *Newsweek*, are available, though they are a week old by the time they reach the newsstand.

HEALTH

Pre-Departure Preparations

Health Insurance The cost of health care in the USA is extremely high and Alaska is no exception. A travel insurance policy to cover theft, loss and medical proble... a wise idea. There are a wide va... policies and your travel agent will have re... ommendations. The international student travel policies handled by the Student Travel Association (STA) or other student travel organisations are usually good value. Some policies offer lower and higher medical expenses options but the higher one is chiefly for countries like the USA which have extremely high medical costs. Check the small print:

1 Some policies specifically exclude 'dangerous activities' such as motorcycling and even trekking. If such activities are on your agenda, you don't want that sort of policy.
2 You may prefer a policy which pays doctors or hospitals direct rather than you having to pay on the spot and claim later. If you do have to claim later, make sure you keep all documentation. Some policies ask you to call back (reverse charges) to a centre in your home country where an immediate assessment of your problem is made.
3 Check if the policy covers ambulances or an emergency flight home. If you have to stretch out you will need two seats and somebody has to pay for them!

Medical Kit A small, straightforward medical kit is a wise thing to carry, especially if you plan to venture away from populated areas. A possible kit list includes:

• Paracetamol (called acetominophen in North America) – for pain or fever.
• Antihistamine (such as Benadryl) – useful as a decongestant for colds, for allergies, to ease itching from insect bites or stings, or to help prevent motion sickness.
• Antibiotics – useful if you're travelling in the wilderness, but they must be prescribed and you should carry the prescription with you.
• Kaokin and pectin preparation (Pepto-Bismol), and Imodium or Lomotil – for bouts of giardia or stomach upsets.

... treatment of
...ticularly import-
...dren.

...hrome and antibiotic
...ry' spray – for cuts and

...n – to ease irritation from
bi...

• Ban... and Band-aids – for minor injur-
ies.
• Scissors, tweezers and a thermometer –
mercury thermometers are prohibited by airlines.
• Insect repellent, sunscreen, suntan lotion,
chap stick and water purification tablets.
• Space Blanket – to be used for warmth or
as an emergency signal.

Water Purification

Tap water in Alaska is safe to drink but it is
wise to purify surface water that is to be used
for cooking and drinking. The simplest way
of purifying water is to boil it thoroughly.
Technically this means boiling it for 10
minutes, something which happens very
rarely! Remember that at high altitude water
boils at a lower temperature, so germs are
less likely to be killed.

Simple filtering will not remove all
dangerous organisms, so if you cannot boil
water it should be treated chemically. Chlo-
rine tablets (Puritabs, Steritabs or other
brand names) will kill many but not all
pathogens. Iodine is very effective in purifying water and is available in tablet form (such
as Potable Aqua), but follow the directions
carefully and remember that too much iodine
can be harmful.

If you can't find tablets, tincture of iodine
(2%) or iodine crystals can be used. Two
drops of tincture of iodine per quart (or litre)
of clear water is the recommended dosage;
the treated water should be left to stand for
30 minutes before drinking. Iodine crystals
can also be used to purify water but this is a
more complicated process, as you have to
first prepare a saturated iodine solution.
Iodine loses its effectiveness if exposed to air
or damp so keep it in a tightly sealed con-
tainer. Flavoured powder will disguise the

taste of treated water and is a good idea if you
are travelling with children.

Water from glacial rivers may appear
murky but it can be drunk, if necessary, in
small quantities. The murk is actually fine
particles of silt scoured from the rock by the
glacier and drinking too much of it has been
known to clog up internal plumbing

Giardia

Giardia, sometimes called 'beaver fever', is
an intestinal parasite present in contaminated
water. The symptoms are stomach cramps,
nausea, a bloated stomach, watery, foul-
smelling diarrhoea and frequent gas. Giardia
can appear several weeks after you have been
exposed to the parasite. The symptoms may
disappear for a few days and then return; this
can go on for several weeks. Metronidazole,
known as Flagyl, is the recommended drug,
but it should only be taken under medical
supervision. Antibiotics are of no use.

Sunburn & Windburn

Sunburn and windburn should be primary
concerns for anyone planning to spend time
bushwalking or travelling over snow and ice.
The sun will burn you even if you feel cold
and the wind will cause dehydration and skin
chafing. Use a good sunblock and a moisture
cream on exposed skin, even on cloudy days.
A hat provides added protection and zinc
oxide or some other barrier cream for your
nose and lips is recommended for those
spending anytime on the ice or snow.

Reflection and glare off the ice and snow
can cause snow blindness, so high-protection
sunglasses should be considered essential for
any sort of glacier visit.

Hypothermia

Perhaps the most dangerous health threat in
the arctic regions is hypothermia. Hypothermia occurs when the body loses heat faster
than it can produce it and the core temperature of the body falls. It is surprisingly easy
to progress from very cold to dangerously
cold due to a combination of wind, wet clothing, fatigue and hunger, even if the air
temperature is above freezing.

It is best to dress in layers; silk, wool and some of the new artificial fibres are all good insulating materials. A hat is important, as a lot of heat is lost through the head. A strong, waterproof outer layer is essential, as keeping dry is vital. Carry basic supplies, including food containing simple sugars to generate heat quickly and lots of fluid to drink.

Symptoms of hypothermia are exhaustion, numb skin (particularly toes and fingers), shivering, slurred speech, irrational or violent behaviour, lethargy, stumbling, dizzy spells, muscle cramps and violent bursts of energy. Irrationality may take the form of sufferers claiming they are warm and trying to take off their clothes.

To treat hypothermia, first get the patient out of the wind and/or rain, remove their clothing if its wet and replace it with dry, warm clothing. Give them hot liquids – not alcohol – and some high-calorie, easily digestible food. This should be enough for the early stages of hypothermia, but if it has gone further it may be necessary to place victims in warm sleeping bags and get in with them. Do not rub patients, place them near a fire or remove their wet clothes in the wind. If possible, place a sufferer in a warm (not hot) bath.

Motion Sickness

Since a great deal of travel in Alaska is done by boat and much of the overland travel is over rough, unsurfaced roads, motion sickness can be a real problem for those prone to it.

Eating lightly before and during a trip will reduce the chances of motion sickness. If you are prone to motion sickness, try to find a place that minimises disturbance – near the wing on aircrafts, close to midships on boats and near the centre of buses. Fresh air usually helps; reading or cigarette smoke doesn't. Commercial antimotion-sickness preparations, which can cause drowsiness, have to be taken before the trip commences; when you're feeling sick it's too late. Ginger is a natural preventative and is available in capsule form.

Rabies

Rabies is found in Alaska, especially among small rodents such as squirrels and chipmunks in wilderness areas; it is caused by a bite or scratch from an infected animal. Any bite, scratch or even lick from a mammal should be cleaned immediately and thoroughly. Scrub with soap and running water, and then clean with an alcohol solution. If there is any possibility that the animal is infected, medical help should be sought immediately. Even if the animal is not rabid, all bites should be treated seriously as they can become infected or can result in tetanus. A rabies vaccination is now available and should be considered if you are in a high-risk category – for instance, handling or working with animals.

WOMEN TRAVELLERS

Perfumes or scented cosmetics, including deodorants, should not be worn in areas where you are likely to encounter bears as the smell will attract them. Women who are menstruating should also be cautious. Women should also be alert to the dangers of hitchhiking, especially when they are travelling alone – use common sense and don't be afraid to say no to lifts.

DANGERS & ANNOYANCES

There are many dangers and annoyances associated with the Alaskan wilderness; these range from problems with bears and insects to the dangers of blue-water paddling – for more information on these topics see the Wilderness chapter.

FILM & PHOTOGRAPHY

The most cherished items you can take home from your trip are pictures and slides of Alaska's powerful scenery. Much of the state is a photographer's dream and your shutter finger will be tempted by mountain and glacier panoramas, bustling waterfronts and diverse wildlife encountered during paddling and hiking trips. Even if you have never toted a camera before, seriously consider taking one to Alaska.

A small, fixed-lens, so-called 'no-mind'

(just point and shoot!) 35 mm camera is OK for a summer of backpacking in the north country. If, however, you want to get a little more serious about photography you need a full 35 mm camera with a couple of lenses.

To photograph wildlife in its natural state, a 135 mm or larger telephoto lens is needed to make the animal the main object in the picture. A two-times converter is also handy in this respect, while a wide-angle lens of 28 to 35 mm adds considerable dimension to scenic views. Keep in mind the rainy weather that will be encountered during your trip; a waterproof camera bag is an excellent investment, especially if a great deal of your time will be spent in the woods.

Most photographers find that Kodachrome (ASA 64 or ASA 100) is the best all-around film, especially when photographing glaciers or snowfields where the reflection off the ice and snow is strong. A few rolls of high-speed film (ASA 200 or 400) are handy for nature photography as the majority of wildlife will be encountered at dusk and dawn, periods of low light. Bring all your own film if possible; in the large cities and towns it will be expensive, up to $12 for a roll of Kodachrome (36 exposures), while in smaller communities you may have a hard time finding the type of film you want.

ACCOMMODATION
Camping
Bring a tent – then you will never be without inexpensive accommodation in Alaska. There are no cheap bed & breakfast places as found in Europe and the number of youth hostels is limited, but there are state, federal and private campgrounds from Ketchikan to Fairbanks. Nightly fees range from nothing to $14 per tent in some of the more deluxe private campgrounds.

It is also a widely accepted practice among backpackers to just wander into the woods and find a spot to pitch a tent. With the exception of Anchorage, Fairbanks and one or two other cities, you can walk a mile (1.6 km) or so from most towns and find yourself in an isolated wooded area. It may not be an 'officially designated campsite', but if back-

packers are clean and orderly, locals are more than happy to overlook this fact.

Your tent should be light (under 5 lb/2 kg) and complete with a good rain fly; if it has been on more than its fair share of trips, consider waterproofing the rain fly and tent floor before you leave. The new free-standing dome tents work best, as in many areas of the state the ground is rocky and difficult to sink a peg into. Along with the tent, bring a thin foam sleeping pad (not a bulky air mattress); it will soften the hard ground and help you keep warm by putting a layer of insulation between your sleeping bag and the moisture that will seep through the tent floor.

Youth Hostels
The once-struggling Alaska Council of American Youth Hostels has grown considerably in the last few years and now has almost 12 hostels scattered around the state. Although the number varies from summer to summer, the mainstays of the system are the hostels in Anchorage, Juneau, Ketchikan, Sitka, Haines, Delta Junction and Tok. The first hostel you check into is the best source of information on which youth hostels are open and which have been closed down.

The hostels range from a Quonset hut in Fairbanks to a huge house in Juneau, four blocks from the capitol building, that has a common room with a fireplace, cooking facilities and showers. In between is everything from church basements and rustic cabins with wood heating to the Mentasta Mountain Wilderness Lodge that can only be reached after a 6 mile (9.8 km) hike from the road. Perhaps the most important hostel for many budget travellers is the Anchorage International Hostel, which recently moved closer to the city centre and the bus terminal.

The hostel fees range from $5 to $10 for a 1 night stay, more if you are a nonmember. Some hostels accept reservations and others don't; each hostel's particulars will be discussed later in this guide. Be aware that hostelling means separate male and female dormitories, house parents, chores assigned for each day you stay and curfews. Also, the hostels are closed during the day – even

Top: Harbour seals on icebergs in Glacier Bay (JD)
Left: Bald eagle in Southeast Alaska (ADT)
Right: Sitka deer on Admiralty Island (USFS)

Top: Floatplane at sunset (USFW)
Bottom: Ski plane over Glacier (AVB)

when it rains. They are strict about these and other rules such as no smoking, drinking and illegal drugs. Still, youth hostels are the best bargains for accommodation in Alaska and the best place to meet other budget travellers and backpackers.

For more information on Alaska's youth hostels before you depart on your trip, write to or call the Alaska Council of American Youth Hostels (tel (907) 276-7772), 700 H St, Anchorage, Alaska 99501.

Bed & Breakfasts

It is now possible to stay in a B&B from Ketchikan to Anchorage, Cordova, Fairbanks, and all the way to Nome and Bettles. What was once a handful of private homes catering to travellers in the early 1980s is now a network of hundreds. For travellers who want nothing to do with a sleeping bag or tent, B&Bs can be an acceptable compromise between sleeping on the ground and high-priced motels and lodges. Some B&Bs are bargains and most have rates below that of major hotels. Still, they are not cheap and you should plan on spending anywhere from $30 to $75 per night for a room.

Some B&Bs are in small, out-of-the-way communities such as Angoon, Gustavus, McCarthy or Talkeetna where staying in a private home can be a unique and interesting experience. All recommend reservations in advance but it is often possible, in cities like Anchorage, Juneau and Fairbanks where there are many B&Bs, to obtain a bed the day you arrive by calling around. Details about B&Bs will be covered in the regional chapters. For more information before your trip or to make reservations contact the following B&B associations in Alaska:

Southeast Alaska
    Alaska Bed & Breakfast Association, PO Box 21890, Juneau 99802 (tel (907) 586-2959)
Southcentral Alaska
    Alaska Private Lodging, PO Box 200047, Anchorage 99520 (tel (907) 258-1717)
Anchorage
    Stay with a Friend, 3605 Arctic Boulevard, Suite 173, Anchorage 99503 (tel (907) 344-4006)

Fairbanks
    Fairbanks Bed & Breakfast, PO Box 74573, Fairbanks 99707 (tel (907) 452-4967)
Kodiak
    Kodiak Bed & Breakfast Service, 308 Cope St, Kodiak 99615 (tel (907) 486-5367)

Roadhouses

Roadhouses, found along the highways, are another option. The authentic roadhouses that combine cabins with a large lodge/dining room are slowly being replaced by modern motels, but some can still be found that offer rustic cabins and sleep two to four people for $40 to $70 per night. A few of the roadhouses, those with a roaring blaze in the stone fireplace and an owner who acts as chef, bartender and late-night storyteller, are charming.

Hotels & Motels

Hotels and motels are the most expensive lodging you can book. Although there are a few bargain bunkhouses, the average single room in an 'inexpensive' hotel costs from $30 to $35 and a double costs from $40 to $50; these are the places down by the waterfront with shared bathrooms. Better hotels in each town will be even more costly, with Anchorage's best places charging close to $150 per night.

The other problem with hotel & motels is that they tend to be full during much of the summer. Without being part of a tour or having advanced reservations, you may have to search for an available bed in some cities. In small villages, you could be out of luck as they may only have one or two places to choose from.

Wilderness Lodges

These are off the beaten path and usually require a bush plane or boat to reach them. The vast majority need advance booking and offer rustic cabins with saunas and ample opportunities to explore the nearby area by foot, canoe or kayak (they provide the boats). The lodges are designed for people who want to 'escape into the wilderness' without having to endure the 'hardship' of a tent, freeze-dried dinners or a small camp stove. The prices range from $150 to $250 per person per day and include all meals.

FOOD

The local supermarket will provide the cheapest food whether you want to live on a diet of fruit and nuts or cook full meals at the youth hostel. The larger cities will have several markets which offer competitive prices and a good selection of fruit and vegetables during the summer.

While strolling down the aisles also keep an eye out for fresh Alaskan seafood, especially in Southeast markets. Local seafood is not cheap but it is renown throughout the country for its superb taste. The most common catches are king salmon steaks at $5 to $6 per lb ($11 to $13 per kg), whole Dungeness crab at $3 to $5 per lb ($6.50 to $11 per kg) and prawns, which are large shrimp, at $8 to $9 per lb ($17.50 to $20 per kg). The larger markets will also have halibut, smoked salmon and cooked king crab.

Alaska is no longer so remote that America's fast-food (and cheapest) restaurants have not reached it. Back in the late 1970s only Anchorage and Fairbanks had a *McDonald's*. Now you can order a Big Mac in Ketchikan, Juneau and Kodiak, while other chains such as *Pizza Hut, Burger King, Wendy's* and *Taco Bell* are just as widespread. There is even a *Dairy Queen* in Kotzebue and a *Baskin Robbins Ice Cream Shop* on the island of Attu at the end of the Aleutian Island chain.

Although these fast-food outlets are cheap, if for no other reason than you don't have to leave a tip, their prices still reflect the high cost of living in Alaska as a Big Mac will cost you between $2 and $2.50 and a small french fries will cost 80 cents.

Much of the state, however, is safe from the fast-food invasion and the smaller towns you pass through will offer only a local coffee shop or cafe. Breakfast, which many places serve all day, is the best bargain; a plate of eggs, toast and hash browns will cost

Brewed and Bottled in Juneau, Alaska

$4 to $6 while a cup of coffee will cost 75 cents to $1.

One popular eating event during the summer in most of the state, but especially the Southeast, is the salmon bake; a dinner costs from $14 to $18 but it is worth trying at least once. The salmon is caught locally, grilled, smothered with somebody's homemade barbecue sauce and often served in an all-you-can-eat fashion. One of the best bakes is in Juneau, next to the Last Chance Mining Museum, where the cost of the meal includes your first beer, live entertainment and beautiful mountain scenery. There is another excellent salmon bake in Fairbanks.

DRINKS
Alcohol

The legal drinking age in Alaska is 21 and only the churches outnumber the bars. Except for 70 native towns like Bethel or Angoon, where alcohol is prohibited, it is never very difficult to find an open bar or liquor store. That and the long, dark winters explains why Alaska has the highest alcoholism rate per capita in the USA, especially among the indigenous people. Bar hours vary but there are always a few places that open their doors at 9 am and don't close until 5 am.

Bars in the larger cities vary in their decor and many offer live entertainment, music and dancing. The bars in smaller towns are good places to have a brew and mingle with people from the fishing industry, loggers or other locals passing through. All serve the usual American beer found in the north-west (Miller, Rainier, Olympia) and usually one or two of that fine Canadian brew, charging around $3 for a 12 oz (360 ml) bottle. During the summer, don't be alarmed if you walk into a bar for a couple of beers with the sun still up and walk out while it's rising again, missing the night entirely.

DRUGS

A few words to clear up the myths that surround Alaska's drug laws. Technically, marijuana is legal when used in the privacy of your home and you are in possession of less than 1 oz (28 g). Although it is not a law, the State Supreme Court has ruled that the use of the drug is the right of an individual. Alaska is the only state in the country where marijuana is actually legal but don't expect a drug paradise when you arrive.

Marijuana, which comes to Alaska mostly from Hawaii and California, is extremely hard to find and usually quite costly, often three times what it might sell for elsewhere in the USA. Many residents who are regular smokers grow their own or purchase it from somebody who does. Home-grown is considerably cheaper but of low quality because of the short growing season in the summer.

It is against the law to smoke marijuana in public places such as parks, bars or the State Marine Ferry, and there are severe penalties for those arrested while doing so. It is also foolhardy to carry it when hitchhiking or driving along the Alcan as you have to pass through the close inspection of immigration officers at two borders.

In recent years, the state legislators have tried to make marijuana illegal but have failed each time. The use of other drugs is against the law and results in severe penalties, especially for cocaine which is heavily abused in Alaska.

BOOKS

The following publications will aid travellers heading north to Alaska. A few of the more popular ones can be found in any good bookstore but most are available only in Alaska or by writing to the publisher. A good alternative, however, is to write to Wild Rose Guidebooks, an Anchorage-based distributor of more than 50 Alaskan guides and maps for travel, fishing, camping and natural history as well as recreational books for hikers, backpackers and kayakers. Send for their catalogue by writing to Wild Rose Guidebooks, PO Box 240047, Anchorage, Alaska 99524. A list of hiking and wilderness guidebooks can be found in the Books section of the Wilderness chapter.

Travel Guides

The Milepost (Alaska Northwest Books, 22026 20th Ave SE, Bothell, Washington 98021; 586 pp, $14.95), unquestionably the most popular travel guide, is put out every year. While it has good information, history and maps of Alaska and western Canada, its drawbacks include its large size – at 8 by 11 inches (21 by 28 cm) it is impossible to slip into the side pocket of a backpack – and that it is written for travellers who are driving. Listings of restaurants, hotels and other businesses are also limited to advertisers.

The Alaska Wilderness Milepost (Alaska Northwest Books, 22026 20th Ave Southeast, Bothell, Washington 98021; 400pp, $14.95) used to be a slim section in Milepost but it has now been split into a guidebook of its own by the publisher. Perhaps the most comprehensive guide to Bush Alaska, the parts of Alaska that can't be reached by road, as it covers more than 250 remote towns and villages. It's smaller format, 6 by 9 inches (15 by 23 cm), also makes it easier to store in a pack.

Adventuring in Alaska by Peggy Wayburn (Sierra Club Books, 530 Bush St, San Francisco, California 94108; 375 pp, $10.95) is a good general guidebook to the many new national parks, wildlife preserves and other remote regions of Alaska. It also contains excellent 'how-to' information on undertaking wilderness expeditions in the state, whether the mode of travel is canoeing, kayaking or hiking.

Alaska's Southeast: Touring the Inside Passage by Sarah Eppenbach (Pacific Search Press, 222 Dexter Ave North, Seattle, Washington 98109; 304 pp, $11.95) offers some of the most comprehensive accounts of the Southeast's history and culture, although it lacks detailed travel information. It does a superb job giving you a feeling for each town and area of the Panhandle.

The Inside Passage Traveler by Ellen Searby (Windham Press, Box 1332, Juneau, Alaska 99802; 216 pp, $10.95) is another travel guide devoted to the Southeast as written by a former State Marine Ferry crew member. It is mediocre overall but there is good information on the smaller communities that can be reached by the State Marine Ferry.

Alaska's Parklands, The Complete Guide by Nancy Simmerman (The Mountaineers, 306 2nd Ave West, Seattle, Washington 98119; 336 pp, $15.95) is the encyclopedia of Alaska wilderness, covering over 110 state and national parks and wilderness areas. It lacks detailed travel information and guides to individual canoe and hiking routes but does a thorough job of covering the scenery, location, wildlife and activities available in each preserve.

Alaska Vacation Planner (Alaska State Division of Tourism, Box E-301, Juneau, Alaska 99801; 120 pp, $2 for postage and handling) is updated annually by the Alaska State Division of Tourism and is an index of bus companies, air charters, hotels, wilderness lodges and camping facilities; it also lists statewide attractions, festivals and guide companies. Prices are included with some business descriptions but not all – a handy publication to have while planning your trip.

General

Alaska by James A Michener (Fawcett Books, New York, NY); whether you love or hate him as an author, just about everybody agrees that James Michener leaves no stone unturned in writing about a place. He usually

begins with the creation of the mountains and rivers, and 1000 pages later brings you to the present; his novel of Alaska is no different. Michener actually spent three summers in Sitka researching the book and the result is an overview of the state's history that few books can provide. A bit wordy for my literary taste but many others rave about the book.

Coming into the Country by celebrated author John McPhee (Bantam Books, New York, NY) takes a mid-1970s look at Alaska in a book that is 600 pages shorter and considerably lighter than Michener's effort. McPhee's experiences included a kayak trip down the Kobuk River in the Brooks Range, living in the town of Eagle for a while and spending time in Juneau during the height of the capital move issue. All of the stories provide an excellent insight into the state and the kind of people who live there.

City Visitor Guides

Various large and small newspapers around the state put out special visitors' guides at the beginning of the summer. All are filled with local history, information, things to do and trails to hike in the area where the newspaper circulates. The guides are free and are usually found at numerous locations (restaurants, bars, hotel lobbies) around town. If you write to them, most newspapers will send you a copy of the publication before you depart, though they may charge you a small handling and shipping fee. The various cities in Alaska that have newspaper guides are:

Anchorage
> *The Anchorage Times Visitors' Guide*, The Anchorage Times, PO Box 40, Anchorage 99510

Fairbanks
> *Interior & Arctic Alaska Visitors' Guide*, Fairbanks Daily News Miner, Box 710, Fairbanks 99707

Haines
> *Haines Sentinel*, Chilkat Valley News, PO Box 630, Haines 99827

Homer
> *Homer Tourist Guide*, The Homer News, 3482 Landing St, Homer 99603

Juneau
    Juneau Guide, Juneau Empire, 235 2nd St, Juneau 99801
Ketchikan
    Ketchikan Visitors' Guide, Ketchikan Daily News, PO Box 7900, Ketchikan 99901
Petersburg
    Viking Visitor Guide, Petersburg Pilot, PO Box 930, Petersburg 99833
Skagway
    Skagway Alaskan, The Skagway News, PO Box 1898, Skagway 99840
Sitka
    All About Sitka, Sitka Daily Sentinel, PO Box 799, Sitka 99835
Valdez
    Valdez/Cordova Visitors' Guide, Valdez Vanguard, PO Box 157, Valdez 99686
Wrangell
    The Wrangell Guide, Wrangell Publishing Inc, PO Box 798, Wrangell 99929

ACTIVITIES
Alaska on a Shoestring

For all the expense and energy involved in getting to Alaska, it should not be a 7 day/6 night fling through five cities. To truly appreciate several regions of the state, or even one, visitors need to take the time to meet the people, hike the trails and view some of nature's most impressive features. You can drive or hitchhike from Anchorage to Fairbanks in 1 day, but in your hurry you will miss small and interesting towns like Talkeetna or outdoor opportunities like the canoe routes in the Nancy Lake State Recreational Area.

This is where backpacking has a distinct advantage over a package tour – with much time and few obligations, you can slowly make your way through the state, stopping when it pleases you and moving on when it doesn't. Often a quaint little village or sea port will be especially inviting and you can pitch your tent along the beach for a few days or even a few weeks.

Although the State Division of Tourism also promotes visiting Alaska in the winter, summer is when the vast majority of travellers choose to come. The tourist high season is from late June to August, through you can visit the state anytime from mid-April to late September and expect reasonably mild weather with only an occasional freak snowfall or cold spell.

Many travellers who have less than 3 weeks to spare spend it entirely in the Southeast, taking the State Marine Ferry from Bellingham in the US state of Washington. Those who want to see the Southeast and then move further north to Fairbanks, Denali National Park and Anchorage need at least a month and should possibly plan on returning from Anchorage by air. Any less time would be a rush job through a land where one simply cannot afford to hurry.

It's wise to start your trip at the beginning of the summer in case you want to extend your stay another month or even longer. One of the most common stories among residents is how somebody came to visit Alaska for 6 weeks and ended up staying 6 years. Once there, Alaska is a hard land to leave.

The Best of Alaska

There is much to do and see in Alaska. The following are my favourite 10 attractions, but there are many others. Twenty-two outstanding wilderness trips are listed in the Trekking and Paddling sections of the Wilderness chapter.

...uttle bus along the Denali & Preserve road to view the ...rior chapter).

...passage on one of the three special Su... ...rine Ferry runs from Kodiak to Dutch .Harbor on the Alaskan Peninsula (Bush chapter).

3 Flying into a US Forest Service cabin for a few days (Wilderness chapter).

4 Viewing the northern lights from the University of Alaska campus in Fairbanks (Fairbanks chapter).

5 Travelling to Tenakee Springs aboard the State Marine Ferry and soaking in the village's hot springs (Southeast chapter).

6 Taking a glacier cruise on Prince William Sound, either to Kenai Fjords, College Fjord or the State Marine Ferry past Columbia Glacier (Southcentral chapter).

7 Hiking into Mentasa Mountains Hostel and spending a night (Interior chapter).

8 Riding the White Pass & Yukon Railroad from Skagway (Southeast chapter).

9 Viewing the Midnight Sun on or near 21 June (summer solstice) from Eagle Summit off the Steese Highway (Fairbanks chapter).

10 Travelling to and spending a night in McCarthy (Southcentral Chapter).

WHAT TO BRING
Clothes

With nights that freeze and days that fry, layering is the only way to dress for Alaskan summers without having to take a pair of shipping trunks. It's an accepted fact in the north country that several light layers of clothing are warmer than a single heavy one. With layers you trap warm air near the body to act as an insulation against the cold. Layers are also easy to strip off when the midday sun begins to heat up.

Instead of a heavy coat, pack a long-sleeve jersey, or woollen sweater, and a windbreaker/parka; they are easier to pack and more versatile for Alaska's many changes of weather. A woollen hat and mittens are necessary items to fend away the cold night air, freak snowfalls or the chilly rain of the Southeast. Leave the umbrellas at home and instead take a waterproof nylon jacket with

a hood for rain protection, and a pair of rain pants if your plans include day hikes or wilderness expeditions.

The number of luxury restaurants, hotels and entertainment spots is growing in the large Alaskan cities; even in Juneau there is now a bar with a dress code, amusing the residents when it opened in 1984. Along with the proper dress, these places have high prices to match. For the most part, Alaska is still a land of jeans, hiking boots (or brown rubber boots in Southeast) and woollen shirts which is the acceptable attire for the vast majority of restaurants, bars and hotels throughout this state. If you are going to backpack around the north on a budget, there is no reason to take anything that isn't comfortable, functional in the harsh environment and easy to pack and wash.

There is no need to buy a pair of the brown rubber boots that you'll see throughout the Southeast, but you should wax or 'grease' your boots to protect your feet from rain and the wet brush on the trail. The new ultralight boots on the market today are fine for most of the hikes described in this book but not all. If your plans include glacier walking and serious ascents into the mountains, traditional all-leather boots (that feel like cement blocks on your feet) are still required footwear.

It is best to avoid anything with goosedown fillings such as jackets or sleeping bags, as wet feathers tend to clump and lose

most of their insulating power. Polyester fibre is the most common filling used by Alaskans.

Camping & Expedition Equipment

If you plan on extended trips into the wilderness, you will need to have suitable equipment such as a tent, a sleeping bag, a camp stove, maps and a compass. For more specific information about what equipment to take, see the What to Bring section in the Wilderness chapter.

Wolverine

Getting There

Many travellers from the Lower 48 mistakingly think that a trip to Alaska is like visiting another state of the USA. It isn't; getting to the north country is as costly and complicated as travelling to a foreign country. Plan ahead and check around for the best possible deal on airline flights or bus tickets.

If you are coming from the US mainland, there are three ways of getting to Alaska: the Alcan (also known as the Alaska Highway), the Inside Passage waterway, or flying in from a number of cities. If you are coming from Asia or Europe, it is also possible to fly direct to Anchorage, the Alaskan crossroad for any airline that flies the polar route. Tokyo and New York are just 7 hours away from Anchorage and London is 9 hours away.

AIR

The quickest and easiest (but unfortunately the most expensive) way to reach Alaska is to fly there. A number of major US domestic carriers offer regular services from the Lower 48 to Alaska, and 10 international airlines stop over in Anchorage. They all have special fares and travel promotions, and it is well worth the effort to check out all possibilities before purchasing a ticket.

Tickets generally fall into two basic types: regular fares, which no budget traveller would ever be caught purchasing; and Advance Purchase Excursion (Apex) or 'Supersavers' that require round-trip tickets to be booked 14 to 30 days in advance and have a maximum number of days you can stay. The US domestic airlines also offer a special price to passengers travelling on Tuesdays and Wednesdays – off-peak days for the airline industry. While Alaska Airlines have off-season rates for those who travel between December and May.

From the USA
Seattle and Portland are the traditional depar-

ture points within the USA for air travel to Alaska, but now you can book a nonstop flight to Anchorage from a number of cities including San Francisco, St Louis, Minneapolis and Honolulu. Direct flights to Anchorage or flights via Seattle are also offered from cities such as Boston, Washington DC, San Diego, Los Angeles, New Orleans, Houston, Dallas and Chicago.

Alaska Airlines is by far the largest carrier of travellers to Alaska and offers an Apex return fare from Seattle to Anchorage for $438. The only requirement is that you book it 14 days in advance and return within a year. Similar return fares between Seattle and Juneau are $340 and between Seattle and Fairbanks $502.

United Airlines offer a $589 Apex return fare from Chicago to Anchorage, and Delta Airlines flies from Salt Lake City to Anchorage for a round-trip fare of $540. The US domestic airlines can be contacted on the following toll-free numbers for information on fares and schedules: Alaska Airlines (800) 426-0333; United Airlines (800) 874-0412; Northwest Airlines (800) 225-2525; and Delta Airlines (800) 221-1212.

In short, air travel is the best way to go if you plan to spend 3 weeks or less touring Alaska, as most tickets allow you one or two stopovers on each leg of the flight. However, if you are planning to spend a month or the entire summer venturing through the state, it is cheaper to use the State Marine Ferry or jump on a bus.

From Asia & Europe
The international carriers that make stops in Anchorage are Korean Air, Japan Airlines, Air France, British Airways, KLM Royal Dutch Airlines, Lufthansa German Airlines, Sabena Belgian World Airlines, Swissair, China Airlines and SAS Scandinavian Airlines. Most of them offer Apex fares. From Europe, Sabena Belgian traditionally offers the lowest rates to Anchorage.

A random sample of international Apex return fares are Amsterdam to Anchorage $1245, London to Anchorage $995, Frankfurt to Anchorage $434, Brussels to Anchorage $1037, and Tokyo to Anchorage $785. Again it pays to check them out. At times, it may be cheaper to take an Apex flight to Seattle or Los Angeles and then purchase a second ticket from there to Alaska with one of the domestic carriers.

From Australia & New Zealand

Most travellers from this region fly to the US west coast (Los Angeles, San Francisco or Seattle) first, and then either fly with a US domestic airline, drive or take the State Marine Ferry to Alaska. Discount fares from Australia & New Zealand to the US west coast range from A$1200 to A$1600 return depending on the time of travel. Carriers on this route include Qantas, Continental Airlines, Air New Zealand and United Airlines.

Japan Airlines (JAL) have a flight from Sydney to Anchorage via Tokyo for around A$2600 one way.

OVERLAND – THE ALCAN

What began in April 1942 as an unprecedented construction project during the heat of WW II ended 8 months later as the first overland link between the Lower 48 and Alaska, known formally as the Alaska-Canada Military Highway and affectionately as the Alcan. Today, the Alcan (also known as the Alaska Highway) is a road through the vast wilderness of north-west Canada and Alaska; a spectacular drive enjoyed by thousands of travellers each summer who take their time to soak up the scenery, wildlife and clear, cold streams along the way.

For those with the time, the Alaska Highway is a unique way to travel north. The trip is an adventure in itself; the 1520 mile (2450 km) road is a legend among highways

and to complete the journey is a feather in any traveller's cap. *Mile 0* of the Alcan is at Dawson Creek in British Columbia, while the other end is at Fairbanks (although residents of Delta Junction will debate that).

The Alcan is now entirely asphalt-paved, and although sections of jarring potholes, frost heaves (the rippling effect of the pavement caused by freezing and thawing) and loose gravel still prevail, they are nothing like the rough conditions it was famous for 10 or 15 years ago. The era of lashing spare fuel cans to the side of the car and gasoline stations every 250 miles (400 km) are also gone. Food, petrol and lodging can be found every 20 to 50 miles (32 to 80 km) along the highway, with 100 miles (160 km) being the longest stretch between fuel stops.

There are several ways to get to the Alcan: you can begin in the US states of Washington, Idaho or Montana and pass through Edmonton or Jasper in Alberta or Prince George in British Columbia, Canada. There are also several ways of travelling the highway: bus, car, a combination of marine ferry and bus or the cheapest of all – hitch-hiking.

Bussing the Alcan

A combination of buses will take you from Seattle via the Alcan to Anchorage, Fairbanks, Skagway or Haines for a moderate cost. There are no direct bus services from the Lower 48 to Alaska; travellers have to be patient as services are more limited than those in the rest of the country. But by doing so, the cost of reaching Alaska is cheap compared to flying or taking the State Marine Ferry.

Greyhound You can purchase a one-way ticket to Whitehorse in British Columbia for $149 from the Greyhound station in the centre of Seattle on the corner of 8th Ave and

Stewart St. The bus departs at least three times a week on Monday, Wednesday and Friday; more often if the demand is high during the summer. Call the station (tel (206) 628-5530) to double-check exact departure days and times. You switch to a Greyhound Lines of Canada bus at the Vancouver station, 150 Dunsmuir St, and continue your journey north changing buses again at Prince George and Dawson Creek in British Columbia. The continuous trip with no overnight stopovers takes 52 hours.

Beginning from Vancouver, it's C$191 for a one-way ticket to Whitehorse, the Yukon capital. When planning your trip, keep in mind that most Greyhound special offers, such as Ameripass (unlimited travel for 7 days), do not apply to Yukon or Alaska destinations. Greyhound maintains a toll-free US telephone number (tel (800) 237-8211), and it tends to change its schedule and rates almost monthly.

Alaskon Express Once you've reached Whitehorse, you change to an Alaskon Express bus (the former White Pass & Yukon Line) for the next leg of the journey. Operated by Gray Line of Alaska from May to September, you can pick up the buses either at Westmark Klondike Inn, 2288 2nd Ave, or in the Greyhound Bus Terminal at the north end of 2nd Ave.

Buses depart the Yukon capital on Friday and Tuesday at noon, stay overnight at Beaver Creek in the Yukon and then continue to Anchorage the next day, reaching the city at 6.16 pm. You can also depart the bus earlier at Tok, Glennallen or Palmer. On Sunday and Wednesday, buses depart Whitehorse at noon for Haines, reaching the Southeast Alaska town and ferry terminal port at 6.30 pm.

As a testimony to the popularity of the Chilkoot Trail, an Alaskon Express bus departs daily from Whitehorse for Skagway, stopping along the way to pick up backpackers coming off the popular trek. On Sunday, Wednesday, Tuesday and Friday it leaves Whitehorse at 4.30 pm, arriving at Skagway

2 hours later; on Saturday, Monday and Thursday it departs at 2.30 pm.

You can also go overland to Fairbanks, something that was hard to do in the past. Catch the Tuesday Alaskon Express bus from Whitehorse to Beaver Creek, and then on Wednesday transfer to the 8 am bus that arrives in Fairbanks at 3.30 pm. A nice thing about these buses is that you can flag them down along the road or in a small town, which is good if you have been sitting around for most of the morning trying to thumb a ride out of a town like Haines Junction. Can you imagine doing that to a Greyhound bus in the Lower 48? The driver would still be laughing.

The one-way fare from Whitehorse to Anchorage is $140, to Fairbanks $129, Haines $71 and to Skagway $51; keep in mind that these fares do not include lodging at Beaver Creek. In Whitehorse, call (403) 667-2223 for current bus information. If you are still in the planning stages of your trip, call the toll-free US number for Gray Line of Alaska, (800) 544-2206; by January they can provide schedules, departure times and rates for the following summer.

Norline Coaches This was the Canadian bus company that used to provide the final link between Whitehorse and Alaska but now it runs between Whitehorse and Dawson City to the north. From June to September, buses depart from the Whitehorse Bus Terminal on Monday, Wednesday and Friday at 9 am and arrive in Dawson City the same day; the one-way fare is C$66.

While many feel this is the more scenic and adventurous route into Alaska, there is no bus transport beyond Dawson City and the hitch across the border through Chicken and down to Tok can be a long wait at times. For current rates and schedules call Norline on (403) 668-3355.

Bus Tours Other companies with bus services to Alaska sell the trip as 'tours' and include overnight lodging in the fare. This sends the price beyond the reach of most budget travellers. The one exception is

Green Tortoise Alternative Travel, the company with recycled buses whose seats have been replaced with foam-covered platforms, sofas and dinettes.

When not sleeping on the bus during night drives, Green Tortoise groups use state and federal campgrounds for accommodation and make an effort to include hiking, rafting and other outdoor activities on their itinerary. Food is not included in the fare but the bus travellers pool their funds to purchase goods in bulk and then prepare it in group cook-outs.

On Green Tortoise tours, group interaction is a large part of the experience. Everybody pitches in during meal time and spontaneous volleyball matches or Frisbee games are frequent activities during rest breaks. Beer and wine are allowed on the bus and people are encouraged to bring musical instruments. Although passengers could be any age, the vast majority of people are in their 20s to early 30s.

The company runs a 4 week tour through Alaska in July and August which includes cruising through Southeast Alaska on the State Marine Ferry as well as stops in the Yukon Territory, Fairbanks, Denali National Park, Kenai Peninsula and then returning home along the Alcan. The bus can be picked up in San Francisco (California), Eugene and Portland (Oregon) or Seattle (Washington). The fare, $1300, covers everything except food and side trips. Food is another $140 if you participate in the group kitchen, and almost everybody does.

For more information write to Green Tortoise, Box 24459, San Francisco, California 94124; or you can call a variety of offices around the USA, including San Francisco (415) 821-0803, Seattle (206) 324-7433 or New York (212) 431-3348.

Driving the Alcan

Without a doubt, driving your own car to Alaska allows you the most freedom. You can leave when you want, stop where you feel like it and pretty much make up your itinerary as you travel along. It's not exactly cheap driving to Alaska, and that's not even

considering the wear and tear and thousands of miles you'll clock up on your vehicle. The final bill will depend on where you're coming from, where you stay at night (campground, cabins or a lodge) and what you eat (food prepared by yourself or from cafes along the way).

Recently, two travellers wrote that they spent $341 for gasoline on the 4618 mile (7388 km), 17 day trip from the US state of Michigan to Fairbanks as well as $56 in camping fees and $100 for food (keep in mind they left home with a case of peanut butter). In the end, they wrote, driving the Alcan cost them $35 a day and a baseball-size crack in their windshield. But the adventure was worth it and they were able to hang their home-town sign at Watson Lake with the hundreds of others left by those who have conquered the highway.

If you're contemplating this car trip, remember that the condition of your tyres is very important. The Alcan may be paved but it's constantly under repair and stretches of frost heaves and pot holes are common, especially on the Canadian side; worn tyres don't last long here. Even your spare, and you *must* have one, should be fairly new.

The windscreen wipers are another important item. Replace them before you depart and carry an extra set along with a gallon of solvent for the windscreen-washer reservoir. Dust, dirt and mud make good visibility a constant battle while driving. Also bring a jack, wrenches and other assorted tools, spare hoses and fan belts, and hope you never have to use them.

Some travellers use an insect screen, others put plastic headlight covers or a wire-mesh screen over the headlights, and others place a rubber mat or piece of carpet between the gas tank and securing straps. All this is to protect the vehicle from the worse danger on the road – flying rocks that are kicked up by truck-and-trail rigs passing you.

By far the worst problem on the Alcan and many other roads in Alaska and the Yukon is dust; that's why even on the hottest days, you see most cars with their windows up. To control dust in a campervan or trailer, reverse the roof vent on your rig so it faces forward. Then keep it open a few inches while driving, creating air pressure inside to combat the incoming dust.

It's always good to·have Canadian currency on hand to purchase gasoline and not depend on the small stations along the way to cash your travellers' cheques for you. One or two of the major gasoline credit cards come in handy, especially if you have a major breakdown. The other thing to keep in mind is that Tourism Yukon operates a number of visitor reception centres that provide a wealth of information and maps for drivers. The ones along the Alcan are:

Watson Lake
  The Alaska Highway Interpretive Center is at the junction of the Alcan and Campbell St (tel (403) 536-7469)
Whitehorse
  The Visitor Center, 302 Steele St, is at 3rd Ave in the T C Richards Building (tel (403) 667-2915)
Haines Junction
  The Visitor Center, Kluane National Park Headquarters (tel (403) 634-2345)
Beaver Creek
  The Visitor Center is at *Mile 1202* (1923 km) of the Alcan (tel (403) 862-7321)

Books If you are planning to drive to and around Alaska, here are two specialised guidebooks that were written to be read as you bump and rattle your way through the north country. Both books can be obtained through Wild Rose Guidebooks (tel (907) 274-0471), PO Box 240047, Anchorage, Alaska 99525.

Roadside Geology of Alaska by Cathy Connor & Daniel O'Haire (Mountain Press Publishing, Missoula, Montana; 1988, 250 pp, $12.95) does an excellent job of covering the geology of Alaska you see from the road and how it shaped the state's history and development. Every road and sea route is covered, even dead-end roads in the Southeast, and along the way you learn what happened during the Good Friday Earthquake and why miners turned up gold on the beaches of Nome – not dull reading by any means.

The Highway Angler is by Gunnar

Pedersen (Wild Rose Guidebooks; 1989, 258 pp, $19.95). The author describes almost 200 streams, rivers, lakes and saltwater fishing spots in Southcentral Alaska that can be reached by a car and fished from the water's edge. Local maps and road mileages are also provided as well as information on inexpensive fishing adventures in the Kenai Peninsula, around Anchorage, in the Matanuska Valley and up the Glenn and Parks highways.

Hitching the Alcan

If you are properly prepared and havé sufficient time, thumbing the Alcan can be an easy way to see the country, meet people and save money. Many travellers thumb from Los Angeles to Anchorage, Fairbanks or Juneau in 7 to 10 days for under $100. I once did it in 4 days, and that included a half-day wait at Haines Junction. There are, however, many 'do's', 'don'ts' and 'ifs' to hitching the highway.

The Alcan seems to inspire the pioneer spirit in travellers who drive it. Drivers are good about picking up hitchhikers, much better than those across the Lower 48 – the only problem is that there aren't as many of them. In some places along the route you may have to wait 30 minutes or longer before a car passes by. During the summer, the number of vehicles increases significantly, but if you're attempting the trip in early spring or late fall, be prepared to wait hours or even overnight at one of a handful of junctions along the way.

All hitchhikers should be self-sufficient with a tent, some food, water, warm clothing and a good book or two. While in many parts of the country a long wait can make you go stir-crazy, along the Alcan it isn't so bad. In fact, if the weather is good, it is enjoyable to sit out in the wide open land, surrounded by mountains and clean air. Hitchhikers must be patient and not overanxious to reach their destination. Moving through the USA and southern Canada, you will get the usual short and long rides from one city to the next. Once you make it to Dawson Creek, it will probably only take you one or two longer rides to reach your destination.

Any part of the Alcan can be slow, but some sections are notorious. The worst can be Haines Junction, the crossroads in the Yukon where southbound hitchhikers occasionally have to stay overnight before catching a ride to Haines in Southeast Alaska. Longer waits may also occur if you are heading home in late summer or early fall and thumbing out of Glennallen, Tok or Delta Junction back into Canada and the Lower 48. The same holds true for those trying to hitchhike north from Dawson Creek in spring and early summer. A sign with your destination on it helps, as does displaying your backpack, which tells drivers you're a summer traveller.

The hardest part of the trip for many is crossing the US-Canadian border. Canadian officials usually pull cars over if the passengers are not of the same nationality as the driver, and they will ask to see proof of sufficient funds. Anybody without prearranged transport is required to have $80 per day to travel through Canada or a total of $200 to $250.

The Canadians are not hassling hitchhikers when they do this, they're just making sure that visitors don't get stuck somewhere for a week because they ran out of money. On the way to Alaska, most travellers will have these funds; on the way back, however, it may be difficult if you are at the end of your trip and without money.

Possible solutions are to catch a ride with someone driving the entire way or with a Canadian willing to tell officials you are a friend visiting. Three places to make contacts for a ride back to the Lower 48 are the Anchorage Youth Hostel; the Wood Center in the middle of University of Alaska campus in Fairbanks, which has a noticeboard for students offering or needing rides; and the Chamber of Commerce hospitality centre in Tok, where the free coffee pulls in many drivers before they continue into Canada. If you are heading north, the noticeboard outside the tourist office in Dawson Creek is worth checking as it often contains messages from people looking for somebody to help with fuel costs.

With luck, it can take you less than a week to hitchhike from Seattle to Fairbanks or Anchorage, but to be on the safe side, plan on the trip taking 7 to 8 days. The route from Seattle to Alaska is good as it is the most direct and has the most traffic to Dawson

Creek. This combines hitching along the Interstate 5 in Washington to the Canadian border, the Trans-Canada Highway 1 to Cache Creek, and Highway 97 north to Dawson Creek and the Alcan.

An alternative to hitching the entire Alaska Highway is to take the State Marine Ferry from Bellingham in Washington to Haines and start hitching from there, cutting the journey in half but still travelling along the highway's most spectacular parts. Haines, however, is a town of about 1100 people and traffic is light on the road to the Alcan at Haines Junction. It is best to hustle off the ferry and begin thumbing as vehicles unload, so that you can try to catch a driver heading north. Or seek out a lift while you are still on the boat by taping a notice outside the ship's cafeteria or showers.

A couple more 'do's' and 'don'ts' for those attempting this great adventure in hitchhiking. Taking drugs across the border is risky if you are driving and downright foolish when hitchhiking, as both Canadian and American customs officials make it a habit to search hitchhikers. With only a backpack, it's tough to hide drugs in a place where they won't look.

It is also good to have your Canadian money before leaving southern Canada; once hitching, it is hard to stop at a bank. Most businesses along the Alcan take American money, but they either give less than the normal 25% to 30% difference on the exchange rate or give none at all.

Discuss your travel plans with the driver and make sure that they don't let you off at some deserted corner. This isn't a major problem if you're self-sufficient, but it's still nice to be near a town when waiting for a ride. No matter when you attempt the highway, make sure you have warm clothing, mittens, boots and a woollen hat; don't underestimate the weather and its ability to turn freezing cold at any time.

Keep in mind that there is a youth hostel at Tok (no phone) with 10 beds and tent space; call the Tok Visitor Center (tel (907) 883-5667) for information. There is also a youth hostel (tel (907) 895-5074) further along the Alcan near Delta Junction, just off the highway.

Finally, keep a journal – the Alaska Highway legend will live on long after it has been conquered because the road and the people you meet are one-of-a-kind.

SEA
The Inside Passage
Leaving Bellingham As an alternative to the Alcan or to avoid doubling back on the highway, you can travel the Southeast's Inside Passage, a waterway made up of thousands of islands, fjords and mountainous coastlines. To many, the Southeast is the most beautiful area in the state and the Alaskan Marine Ferries are the country's best public transport bargain.

The large 'blue canoes' of the State Marine Highway are equipped with observation decks, food services, bars, lounges and solariums with deck chairs. You can rent a stateroom for overnight trips but most backpackers head straight for the solarium and sleep in one of the deck chairs or on the floor with a sleeping pad. On long-distance hauls from Bellingham, travellers sometimes even pitch their dome tents.

With its leisurely pace, travel on the marine ferries is a delightful experience. The midnight sun is warm and apart from the scenery, the possibility of sighting whales, bald eagles or sea lions keeps most travellers at the side of the ship. This is also an excellent way to meet other backpackers heading for a summer in the north country.

A big change in the state ferry system occurred in 1990 when Bellingham replaced Seattle as the new southern terminus of the Alaska Marine Highway. The new terminus includes an information centre, ticket office, luggage lockers and an outdoor seating area with a nice view of Bellingham Bay and the surrounding hills. It's 10 minutes north of the Bellingham International Airport in the historic Fairhaven shopping district, 87 miles (139 km) north of Seattle. From the Interstate 5 Highway, you depart west on Fairhaven Parkway (exit 250) for 1.1 miles (1.7 km) and then turn right onto 12th St where signs will direct you to the terminus at the end of Harris Ave.

The ferries are extremely popular during the peak season from June to August. Reservations are needed for cabin or vehicle space and for walk-on passengers on departures from Bellingham. Space for summer sailings from Bellingham is often filled by April, forcing walk-on passengers to wait stand-by for an available spot.

If you plan to depart Bellingham in June or July, it is best to make reservations. The state ferry's reservation office will take written requests anytime and telephone requests from the first working day of January for summer sailings. As telephone lines are jammed most of the time after the first day of the year, it is wise to send in a written request as soon as you can figure out your itinerary.

The summer sailing schedule comes out in December and you can obtain one by contacting the Alaska Marine Highway (tel (907) 465-3941), PO Box R, Juneau, Alaska 99811. There is now a toll-free telephone number (tel (800) 642-0066 from the Lower 48) to handle schedule requests and reservations.

The ferries to Alaska stop first at Prince Rupert in British Columbia, and then continue onto Ketchikan in Alaska. Most ferries then depart for Wrangell, Petersburg, Sitka, Juneau, Haines and Skagway before heading back south. A trip from Bellingham to Juneau takes 2½ to 4 days depending on the route. Most ferry terminals are a few miles out of town and the short in-port time doesn't allow passengers to view the area without making it a stopover. However, walk-on passengers can make as many stopovers as they wish without additional cost.

For example, if you purchase a ticket from Bellingham to Haines, you can spend a few days at the fishing village of Petersburg and then catch the next ferry north without having to purchase another ticket or make a reservation. Just make sure that you stop at the purser's office and get a stopover coupon before leaving the boat.

If you intend to use the ferries to view the Southeast, obtain a current schedule and keep it handy at all times. State ferries stop almost every day at larger centres like Juneau, but the smaller villages may only have one ferry every 3 or 4 days and many places won't have a service at all.

There are six ships working Southeast Alaska; four of them are larger vessels that sail the entire route from Bellingham to Skagway. The *Columbia*, *Malaspina*, *Matanuska* and *Taku* all have cabins, lounges, eating facilities and public showers for both walk-on passengers and cabin renters.

The other two ships are smaller, do not have cabins, and serve out-of-the-way villages from Juneau or Ketchikan. In the summer, the *Aurora* sails between Ketchikan, Kake, Hollis, Petersburg and Prince Rupert. The *Le Conte* stops at Juneau, Hoonah, Angoon, Sitka, Kake, Tenakee Springs, Skagway, Haines and Petersburg, and makes a special run to Pelican once a month. The *Chilkat*, the original ship of the fleet, is no longer in service during the summer and only operates in the winter when another vessel is in dry dock.

If you plan to just pass through the Southeast on your way north, purchase a ticket from Bellingham to Haines and make a few stopovers at places that take your fancy. If you plan to spend a good deal of time or the entire summer in the region, purchase a ticket to Juneau and then use that as your base, taking shorter trips to other towns on the *Le Conte*. The fare for walk-on passengers from Bellingham to Haines is $214, while the ticket from Bellingham to Juneau is $200.

One way to save money is to take a bus or hitchhike to Prince Rupert in British Columbia where the dramatic mountain scenery begins, and hop on the ferry from there. The fare from Prince Rupert to Haines is $104 and to Juneau $90. Fares for travel within the Southeast include: Ketchikan to Juneau $66; Petersburg to Juneau $38; Juneau to Haines $18; Haines to Skagway $12; and Juneau to Angoon $20.

The State Department of Transportation

puts out a brochure entitled the *Alaska Marine Highway*, but here are a few tips they don't tell you. When boarding in Bellingham, it is best to scramble to the solarium and either stake out a lounge chair or at least an area on the floor. The solarium and observation deck are the best places to sleep as the air is clean and the night-time peace is unbroken. The other place to crash out is the indoor lounges, which can be smoky, noisy or both.

At last reports, backpackers were still allowed to pitch free-standing tents near the solarium, but there's always discussion among ferry officials to ban this practice. The tents tend to take up more space than two people really need in an already popular and crowded section of the ship.

Food on board is inexpensive compared to what you will pay on shore, but it is cheaper to bring your own grub and eat it in the solarium or the cafeteria. Some backpackers bring their own tea bags, coffee or Cup-a-Soup and then just purchase the cup of hot water. The pursers, however, do not allow any camp stoves to be used on board and are very strict about enforcing this. Bringing your own liquor is also prohibited as there is a bar aboard the larger ships, but I have yet to see a cruise where a happy traveller isn't handing out beers from an ice-chest in the solarium.

There is now a tariff for carrying on bicycles or kayaks, but compared to the cost of bringing a car or motorcycle it is nothing. The cost is only $32 to take what ferry officials call an 'alternative means of conveyance' from Bellingham to Haines. A bicycle can be a handy way to see at least part of a town without disembarking for a few days, while a summer (or even a lifetime) can be spent using the ferry system to hop from one wilderness kayak trip to another.

Above all else, when using the Alaska Marine Ferry system, check and double-check the departures of ferries once you have arrived in the Southeast. It is worth a phone call to the terminus to find out the actual arrival and departure times; the state ferries are notorious for being late or breaking down and having their departures cancelled. It's something that happens every summer without fail.

Leaving Prince Rupert If the Alaska State Ferries are full in Bellingham, one alternative is to begin your cruise in Seattle onboard British Columbia Ferries, switching to the Alaska line in Prince Rupert.

From Pier 48 in the centre of Seattle at 101 Alaskan Way South, catch a British Columbia (BC) Stena Line ferry to Victoria on Vancouver Island. During the summer, boats depart twice daily with the *Princess Marguerite*, designed for foot passengers only, departing at 8 am and the *Vancouver Island Princess*, which is capable of carrying vehicles, leaving at 10 am. It's a 4½ hour trip, and a one-way fare for walk-on passengers is $29. For pretrip planning call (800) 962-5984 for an update on rates and schedules and in Seattle dial (206) 441-5560 for ferry information.

Once you land on Vancouver Island, head north to Port Hardy and catch the BC Ferry to Prince Rupert. From this Canadian city, there is a much better chance to board the Alaska Marine Ferry because there are five vessels that connect Prince Rupert to Southeast Alaska. Port Hardy can be reached by bus from Victoria on Pacific Coast Lines (tel (604) 385-4411), which leaves once a day for a one-way fare of C$51. The bus depot is at 710 Douglas St, behind the Empress Hotel in the centre of Victoria.

At Port Hardy, the BC Ferry *Queen of the North* sails to Prince Rupert one day and returns to Vancouver Island the next, maintaining this every-other-day schedule from 1 June to the end of September. The trip is scenic and the daylight voyage takes 15 hours; the one-way fare for walk-on passengers is C$68. The same ship also makes a stop once a week at the isolated town of Bella Bella in British Columbia.

More information and complete schedules for the BC Ferries can be obtained by calling or writing to BC Ferries (tel (604) 386-3431), 1112 Fort St, Victoria, British Columbia, Canada V8V 4V2. In Vancouver call (604) 669-1211 and in Seattle call (206)

441-6865 for ferry information and reservations.

Leaving Hyder, Alaska Finally, if for some strange reason you can't catch an Alaska State Ferry at Prince Rupert, there's one last alternative to waiting. Make your way east along the Yellowhead Highway from Prince Rupert and then head north along the Cassiar Highway. Hitching is about the only way to travel this route if you don't have a vehicle as there is no bus service. You need to travel 99 miles (158 km) along the scenic Cassiar Highway and then turn off at Meziadin Lake for Stewart. Right across the border from the British Columbia town is Hyder, a Southeast Alaska hamlet of about 50 people with a few cafes, bars and gift shops.

During the summer, the Alaska State Ferry *Aurora* usually departs from here every Friday at 2.15 pm for Ketchikan, where you can continue north on one of several other boats. The one-way fare from Hyder to Ketchikan is $30.

Note It is important to double check the departure time for the Hyder ferry as it may leave on Pacific Time as opposed to Alaska Time.

Mink

Getting Around

Touring Alaska on limited funds means not departing from the roads and not travelling in areas without a State Marine Ferry dock. However, budget travellers shouldn't worry because although the roads and the marine highway (the cheapest forms of travel) cover only a quarter of the state, this quarter comprises the most popular regions of Alaska and includes the major attractions, parks and cities.

Even if there is a road to your destination, travel around Alaska is unlike travel in any other state of the USA. The overwhelming distances between regions and the fledgeling public transport system makes getting around almost as hard as getting there. Any long visit to Alaska usually combines transport by car, bus, marine ferry, train and often a bush plane for access into the wilderness.

AIR
Surviving the Bush Plane Ride
I met the classic bush pilot in Yakutat, Alaska. I arrived at the airport on board a sleek Alaska Airlines Boeing 737 and was immediately hustled over to a small hangar where there was this sputtering machine that appeared to be dripping something and was held together by baling wire. Next to it was 'Sourdough' dressed in faded jeans, cowboy boots and a TWA cap, spitting out long streams of tobacco juice. I would have known him anywhere, even without his plane – the famous Alaskan bush pilot, a lovable north-country character who is in many ways the last great adventurer in a frontier that is quickly becoming a regulated piece of real estate.

My group was headed for 10 days of wilderness kayaking in Russell Fjord and he was the only pilot available with a beach-lander. After he proceeded to pack the plane to its roof with gear, somebody asked him how he knew what his plane could safely carry. 'See that wheel in the back,' he said, 'as long as it

gets off the runway'. We all squeezed in and took off.

When you want to see more than the roadside attractions, you go to a dirt runway or small airfield outside of town and climb into a bush plane. With 75% of the state not accessible by road, these small, single-engine planes are the backbone of intrastate transport. They carry residents and supplies to desolate areas of the Bush, take anglers to some of the best fishing spots in the country and drop off backpackers in the middle of prime, untouched wilderness.

The person at the controls is a bush pilot, someone who might be fresh out of the Air Force or somebody who arrived in Alaska 'way bee-for statehood' and learned to fly by trial and error. A ride with him is not only transport to isolated areas and a scenic overview of the state but it sometimes includes an earful of flying tales – some believable, some not.

Don't be alarmed when you hear that Alaska has the highest number of aeroplane crashes per capita in the country – it also has the greatest percentage of pilots. One in every 45 residents has a licence, and one resident in 65 owns a plane. That's eight times more pilots and 14 times more planes per capita than any other state in the USA. Bush pilots are safe flyers who know their territory and its weather patterns; they don't want to go down any more than you do.

A ride in a bush plane is essential if you want to go beyond the common sights and see some of Alaska's most memorable scenery. In the larger cities of Anchorage, Fairbanks, Juneau and Ketchikan it pays to check around before chartering. In most small towns and villages, however, you will be lucky if there is a choice. In the following regional chapters, air-taxi services are listed under the town or area from which they operate.

Bush aircraft include float planes that land and take off on water and beach-landers with

oversized tyres that can use rough gravel shorelines as air strips. Others are equipped with skis to land on glaciers, sophisticated radar instruments for stormy areas like the Aleutian Islands, or boat racks to carry canoes or hard-shell kayaks.

The fares differ with the type of plane, its size, the number of passengers and the amount of flying time. On the average, a Cessna 185 that can carry three passengers and a limited amount of gear will cost up to $250 to charter for an hour of flying time. A Cessna 206, a slightly larger plane that will hold four passengers, costs around $400. Keep in mind that when chartering a plane to drop you off at an isolated Forest Service cabin or for a wilderness trek, you must pay for both the air time to your drop-off point and for the return to the departure point.

As a general rule, if one of the domestic carriers, Alaska Airlines or the intrastate carrier MarkAir, has a flight to your destination, it will be the cheapest way of flying there. Alaska Airlines provides the most extensive service for travel within Alaska. A sample of their one-way fares for intrastate flights are: Anchorage to Fairbanks $116; Juneau to Cordova $141; Juneau to Anchorage $192; Anchorage to Nome $231; and Anchorage to Kodiak $138.

Before chartering your own plane, check out all the possibilities first. Most air-taxi companies have regularly scheduled flights to small towns and villages in six to nine-seater aircraft with single-seat fares that are a fraction of the cost of chartering an entire plane. Others offer a 'mail flight' to small villages which are run on a regular basis with one or two seats available to travellers.

Even when your destination is a Forest Service cabin or some wilderness spot, check with the local air-taxi companies; it is a common practice to match up a party departing from the cabin with another that's arriving, so that the air-charter costs can be split by filling the plane on both runs.

Air travel in small bush planes is expensive, but the more passengers, the cheaper the charter; two people chartering an entire plane, no matter what the distance, is a costly exercise.

Booking a plane is easy and can often be done the day before or at the last minute if need be. Double-check all pick-up times and places when flying to a wilderness area. Bush pilots fly over the pick-up point and if you are not there, they usually return, call the Forest Service and still charge you for the flight.

When flying in and out of bays, fjords or coastal waterways, check the tides before determining your pick-up time. It is best to schedule pick-ups and drop-offs at high tide or else you may end up tramping 0.5 mile (0.8 km) through mud flats.

If a pilot doesn't want to fly, don't push

the subject, just reschedule your charter. The pilot is the best judge of weather patterns and can see, or sometimes feel, bad flying conditions when others can't. Always schedule extra days around a charter flight. It's not uncommon to be 'socked in' by weather for a day or two until a plane can fly in. Don't panic, they know you are there. Think of the high school basketball team in the mid-1960s which flew to King Cove in the Aleutians for a weekend game. They were 'socked in' for a month before they could fly out again.

When travelling to small Bush towns, a scheduled flight or mail run is the cheapest way to go. Don't hesitate, however, to charter a flight to some desolate wilderness spot on your own; the best that Alaska has to offer is usually just a short flight away.

BUS

Regular bus services within Alaska are limited, but they are available between the larger towns and cities for independent travellers (as opposed to package tours) at reasonable rates. The only problem is that as one bus company goes under another appears, so the phone numbers, schedules, rates and pick-up points change drastically from one summer to the next. It pays to call ahead after arriving in Alaska to make sure that buses are still running to where you want to go.

Alaska-Yukon

This bus company is an arm of Alaska Sightseeing which mainly sells package tours, not seats for independent travellers; their high fares reflect this. Still, you can travel by Alaska-Yukon between Anchorage and Fairbanks ($120), Anchorage and Denali ($95) or Valdez and Fairbanks, although in almost every case somebody else is running the same route for a lot less.

Schedules and departure points are given in the regional chapters. Reservations are not required but are recommended by the company; they will also ship bicycles for an additional fee. For information call or write to Alaska Sightseeing (tel (800) 637-3334 –

toll-free number), 349 Wrangell Ave, Anchorage, Alaska 99501.

Alaskon Express

These buses are the Gray Line motorcoaches which mainly serve travellers needing transport along the last leg of the Alcan from Whitehorse into Haines, Skagway, Anchorage or Fairbanks (see the Alcan section in the Getting There chapter). You can also use the bus line to travel from Anchorage to Glennallen ($48), from Fairbanks to Tok ($40) or from Delta Junction to Fairbanks ($20).

From Haines, you can book a passage on Alaskon Express for the 2 day run to Anchorage which leaves every Friday and Tuesday for $173; this fare does not include overnight lodging at Beaver Creek. Local passenger boarding points, departure times and phone numbers are given in later chapters. For information or reservations while planning your trip, contact Gray Line of Alaska (tel (800) 544-2206 – toll-free number), 300 Elliott Ave West, Seattle, Washington 98119.

Seward Bus Lines

This company provides services between Anchorage and Seward, and an interconnecting bus with Alaska Intercity Line from Seward to Homer. A bus leaves Seward daily at 9 am, reaches Anchorage at noon and then departs for the return run at 5.30 pm; the one-way fare is $25. Along the way you can get off at Summit Lake and hop on an Alaska Intercity bus to Homer for $35. Pick up these buses at 550 Railway Ave in Seward and at Alaska Samovar Inn, 720 Gambell St in Anchorage. Call (907) 224-3608 for current schedules and rates.

Alaska Intercity Lines

Alaska Intercity began services in 1989 and provides an important link from Anchorage to towns on the west side of the Kenai Peninsula. This stretch is never hard to hitchhike in the summer but for those who don't like standing on the side of the road Intercity Lines now provides an alternative. The bus leaves daily from Sunday to Friday at 7 am and makes pick ups at a number of Anchorage hotels, including Westmark at 720 5th Ave, the Sheraton at 401 East 6th Ave, Days Inn at 321 5th Ave and the Clarion Hotel at 4800 Spenard Rd. It then heads south reaching Soldotna at noon, Kenai at 12.30 pm and Homer at 3.30 pm where it turns around and heads back to Anchorage.

Fares from Anchorage are $27.50 to Soldotna and Kenai and $37.50 to Homer. Let's hope this company stays in business, but call (907) 279-3221 just to make sure it has.

Alaska-Denali Transit
This is a budget bus company which runs a 2 day trip once a week from Anchorage to Haines via Denali National Park, Fairbanks and Tok. Being a small outfit, the schedules change from summer to summer so check with them before you travel. The one-way fare from Anchorage to Denali is $35, to Fairbanks $55, and to Haines $115.

The van leaves from Anchorage every Saturday at 8.00 pm, departs Denali at 2.00 pm Saturday and Fairbanks at 5.30 pm Saturday, and arrives in Haines at 8.00 pm Sunday. On the return journey, the van leaves Haines at 8.00 am Tuesdays, departs Fairbanks at 1.30 pm Wednesday and Denali at 4.00 pm Wednesday, and arrives in Anchorage at 9.30 pm Wednesdays. Pick-up points include the Anchorage Youth Hostel, the Denali Park Hotel, the Fairbanks Hostel (Tanana Fairgrounds), the Fairbanks Visitor Center and the Haines Visitor Center.

Tickets and information can be obtained from Alaska-Denali Transit, PO Box 4557, Anchorage, Alaska 99510; tel (907) 273-3331.

TRAIN
In a state the size of Alaska, the logistics of building a railroad line were overwhelming at the turn of the century; many private companies tried but failed, leading to federal government intervention in 1912. Three years later, construction began on a route from the tent city of Anchorage to the boom town of Fairbanks. The line cut its way over what was thought to be impenetrable mountains, across raging rivers and through a wilderness as challenging as any construction crew had faced in the history of American railroading.

No wonder it took them 8 years to build the Alaska Railroad. Today, it stretches 470 miles (766 km) from Seward to Fairbanks, and despite the state's heavy dependence on air travel, the railroad remains a vital artery in moving people and goods across Alaska's interior. It is so important to Alaskans, that the state purchased the line from the federal government in 1985 for $23.3 million, making it the only state-owned commercial line in the country.

The Alaska Railroad provides a good and inexpensive means of transport for travellers, and the scenery on each route is spectacular. Hitching along the George Parks Highway is cheaper, sure, but few travellers, even those counting their dimes, regret booking a seat on the line and viewing one of the world's most pristine wilderness areas from the train's comfortable and, if you're willing to pay a little extra, gracious carriages.

Anchorage to Fairbanks
The Alaska Railroad operates a year-round service between Fairbanks and Anchorage, and summer services from late May to mid-September between Anchorage and Whittier on Prince William Sound, and from Anchorage to Seward. Although the 114 mile (184 km) trip down to Seward is a spectacular ride, unquestionably the most popular run is the 336 mile (541 km) trip from Anchorage to Fairbanks with a stop at Denali National Park. Heading north, the train passes within 46 miles (74 km) of Mt McKinley at *Mile 279* (447 km), a stunning sight from the train's viewing domes on a clear day, and then slows down to cross the 918 foot (275 metre) bridge over Hurricane Gulch, one of the most spectacular views of the trip.

North of the Denali National Park, the train hugs the side of the Nenana River Canyon, passes numerous views of the

Alaska Range and, 60 miles (97 km) south of Fairbanks, crosses the 700 foot (210 metre) Mears Memorial Bridge over the Tanana River, one of the longest single-span bridges in the world. Before the bridge was completed, this was the end of the line in both directions as people and goods were then ferried across the river to waiting cars on the other bank.

From late May to mid-September, two express trains run daily between Anchorage and Fairbanks with stops at Wasilla, Talkeetna, Denali National Park and Nenana. The express trains are geared for out-of-state travellers as they offer vista-dome cars for all passengers to share, reclining seats and a full dining and beverage service. You can also take your own food and drink on board, which isn't a bad idea as dinner on the train can cost between $15 and $20.

The northbound train departs Anchorage daily at 8.30 am, reaches Denali National Park at 3.50 pm and Fairbanks at 8 pm. The southbound train departs Fairbanks at 8 am, reaches Denali National Park at 12.30 pm and Anchorage at 8 pm. The one-way fare from Anchorage to Denali National Park is $62, and $88 to Fairbanks; from Fairbanks to Denali it is $33. From late September to mid-May the schedule changes to one train per week, which departs Anchorage at 8.30 am on Saturday and then leaves Fairbanks at 8 am on Sunday for the return trip.

For those who want to experience the railroad's golden era and travel in luxury, both Tour Alaska and Gray Line operate two-deck superdome cars which are hooked onto the end of the train. The cars were built in the 1950s, in the twilight of elegant rail service, by the Pullman-Standard Company at $320,000 a piece, which would be something like $2.5 million today. The tour companies obtained 14 of them and renovated the cars' delicately etched mirrors, oak tables, thick carpeting and plushy upholstered seats. Gray Line operates the McKinley Explorer cars and charges $130 one-way from Anchorage to Fairbanks; meals are extra, of course. Tour Alaska (tel

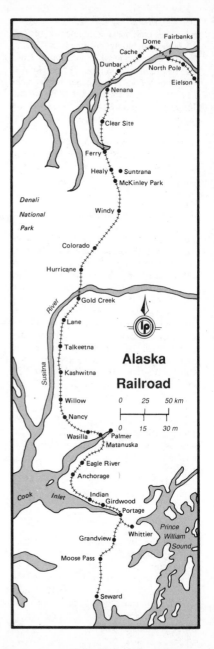

(800) 835-8907 – toll free) operates Midnight Sun cars at similar prices.

The Alaska Railroad still makes a 'milk run' in which a train stops at every town and can even be flagged down by backpackers, anglers and mountain climbers emerging from their treks at the railroad tracks. The run used to extend all the way to Fairbanks but now stops at Hurricane Gulch, where it turns around and heads back to Anchorage the same day. Still, the trip takes you pass Mt McKinley and into some remote areas of the state and allows you to mingle with more local residents than you would on the express train.

During the May to mid-September summer season, this diesel train departs Anchorage at 6.30 am and returns by 4.30 pm on Wednesday and Saturday. On Sunday, it departs at noon and returns by 10.30 pm. The rest of the year it only makes the trip on the first Thursday of the month, departing Anchorage at 8.30 am; a round-trip ticket is $88.

There are a few things to keep in mind when travelling by train from Anchorage to Fairbanks. Arrive at the depot at least 15 minutes before departure as the express trains leave on time. Sit on the east side of the train if you want to see the mileposts, and for the best scenery sit on the west side for the stretch from Anchorage to Denali and then on the east side north of there.

The windows in all carriages are big but taking pictures through them is less than satisfactory due to their distorting curves and the dust on them. To avoid this, step outside to the platform between cars to shoot photos. Railroad and historic buffs might be interested in obtaining a copy of the *Ride Guide to the Historic Alaska Railroad* by Laura Zahn & Anita Williams which provides insights along the way and can be purchased at the depot bookstores or through Wild Rose Guidebooks (PO Box 240047, Anchorage, Alaska 99524).

Finally, it pays to book early on this popular train; in Anchorage call (907) 265-2494. Before your trip call the toll free number, (800) 544-0552; or write to Alaska Railroad, PO Box 107500, Anchorage, Alaska 99510.

Anchorage to Whittier

The rail service from Anchorage to Portage and Whittier during the summer is timed to meet the arrivals and departures of the Alaska Marine Ferry, MV *Bartlett*, which crosses the Prince William Sound to Valdez on a scenic cruise that passes the Columbia Glacier.

The first leg from Anchorage to Portage is made by bus which leaves the Anchorage depot at 11.45 am daily and then transfers its passengers to a waiting train. You arrive in Whittier at 2 pm and the ferry departs at 3 pm. The train then departs Whittier at 3.30 pm, and later transfers passengers to a bus which arrives in Anchorage at 5.30 pm.

Even if you don't plan to take the marine ferry across Prince William Sound, the trip to Whittier can be a fun day trip as it is a scenic and interesting town. The train ride, although only 40 minutes long, includes two tunnels, one of which is 13,090 feet (3990 metres) long. The train shuttle makes several round trips daily; the one-way fare from Anchorage to Whittier is $18, while the Portage to Whittier trip is $7.50.

Tickets for the Whittier shuttle can be purchased from conductors at Portage. No reservations are taken for the rail service between Anchorage and Whittier, but passengers with confirmed ferry tickets have priority on boarding the 1.30 pm train from Portage.

Anchorage to Seward

Some say the ride between Anchorage and Seward is one of the most spectacular train trips in the world, rivalling those in the Swiss Alps or the New Zealand train that climbs over Arthur's Pass in the Southern Alps. From Anchorage, the 114 mile (184 km) trip begins by skirting the 60 mile (97 km) long Turnagain Arm on Cook Inlet where travellers can study the bore tides. After leaving Portage, the train swings south and climbs over mountain passes, across deep river gorges and comes within 0.5 mile (0.8 km) of three glaciers; Spencer, Bartlett and Trail. The trip ends in Seward, a quaint town that is surrounded by mountains on one side and Resurrection Bay on the other.

The service only operates from late May to early September on Thursday to Monday with a special run on 4 July. The train departs Anchorage at 7 am and reaches Seward at 11 am. It departs Seward the same day at 6 pm and reaches Anchorage at 10 pm; the one-way fare is $35, round-trip $60.

White Pass & Yukon Railroad

The White Pass & Yukon Railroad, a historical narrow-gauge railroad, was built during the height of the Klondike gold rush in 1898 and connected Skagway to Whitehorse. It was the first railroad to be built in Alaska and at that time the most northern line in North America.

The railroad was carved out of the rugged mountains by workers who, in places, had to be suspended by ropes from vertical cliffs in order to chip and blast the granite away. It followed the 40 mile (65 km) White Pass Trail from Skagway to Lake Bennett where the miners would build rafts to float the rest of the way to Dawson City on the Yukon River. The line reached Whitehorse in 1900 and by then had made the Chilkoot Trail obsolete.

The railroad also played an important role in building the Alcan during WW II and was then used for transporting ore by mining companies in the Yukon Territory. In 1982, after world metal prices fell and the Canadian mines closed, operation of the White Pass & Yukon Railroad was suspended. But it has always been a popular tourist attraction, especially with big cruise ships, and in 1988, under the name of White Pass & Yukon Route, the railroad resumed limited service.

Today, it's still the incredible ride it must have been for the Klondike miners. The White Pass & Yukon Railroad has one of the steepest grades in North America as it climbs from sea level in Skagway to 2885 feet (865 metres) at White Pass in only 20 miles (32.6 km). The mountain scenery is fantastic, the old narrow gauge cars intriguing, and the trip is a must for anyone passing through Southeast Alaska.

The train runs from late May to September and offers a 1 day summit excursion, a Chilkoot Trail service (see the Trekking section in the Wilderness chapter for details) and a scheduled through-service for travellers who actually want to use it as a means of transport to Whitehorse and the Alcan. Northbound trains depart Skagway daily at 1 pm and arrive in Fraser at 2.30 pm, where passengers transfer to buses which arrive in Whitehorse at 6.30 pm (Pacific Time). Southbound buses depart Whitehorse at 8.30 am (Pacific Time), and the train leaves Fraser at 10.20 am arriving in Skagway at noon. The one-way fare from Skagway to Whitehorse is $89.

Knowing the history of this train, reservations wouldn't be a bad idea and can be made before your trip by calling the toll-free number (800) 343-7373, or writing to the White Pass & Yukon Route (tel (907) 983-2217), PO Box 435, Skagway, Alaska 99840.

BOAT

State Marine Ferry

In the Southeast, the State Marine Ferry replaces bus services and operates from Juneau or Ketchikan to Skagway, Haines, Hoonah, Tenakee Springs, Angoon, Sitka, Kake, Petersburg, Hyder and Hollis, with an occasional special run to the tiny fishing village of Pelican (see the Inside Passage section in the Getting There chapter for more details).

There are also marine ferry services in Southcentral and Southwest Alaska, where the MV *Bartlett* and the MV *Tustumena* connect towns along Prince William Sound and the Gulf of Alaska. The Southwest marine ferry does not connect with the Southeast line, but travellers can get around that by picking up an Alaska Airlines flight from Juneau to Cordova for $141 to continue their ferry trip around the Alaskan coast.

The *MV Bartlett* sails from Cordova and Valdez to Whittier across Prince William Sound, passing the Columbia Glacier along the way. The MV *Tustumena* provides a service between Seward, Homer and Seldovia on the Kenai Peninsula; Port Lions and Kodiak on Kodiak Island; and Valdez and Cordova on the eastern shore of Prince William Sound.

Four times during the summer – in mid-May, June, July and September – the MV *Tustumena* also makes a special run to Sand Point, King Cove, Cold Bay and Dutch Harbor at the end of the Alaska Peninsula. The cruise takes 5 days from Kodiak and is the cheapest way to see part of Alaska's stormy arm (see the Southwest section in the Bush chapter).

Sample fares for marine ferry travel along the Southwest routes for walk-on passengers are:

Valdez to Cordova	$26
Valdez to Whittier	$54
Valdez to Seward	$54
Seward to Kodiak	$48
Homer to Kodiak	$42
Kodiak to Dutch Harbor	$176
Homer to Seldovia	$14

DRIVING
Car Rental
Having your own car in Alaska, as in any other place, provides freedom and flexibility that cannot be obtained from public transport. Car rental, however, is a costly way to travel for one or two people. In Alaska, it isn't the charge per day for the rental but the mileage rate and the distances covered that make it so expensive; drivers will find petrol only slightly more expensive than in the rest of the USA.

The Alaska tourist boom of the 1980s has produced a network of cheap car rental companies that offer rates almost 50% lower than those of national firms such as Avis, Hertz and National Car Rental. The largest of these is All Star Car Rental, which has offices in 11 Alaskan towns including Anchorage, Fairbanks, Kenai, Ketchikan, Petersburg, Wrangell and Sitka. Their rates begin at $29.95 per day, and in many towns you'll receive 100 free miles but after that it's 25 cents per mile.

Other companies include Payless Rent-A-Car and Rent-A-Wreck. The cars, though functional, are not pretty and are occasionally stubborn about starting up right away. If there are three or four people splitting the cost, car rental can often be as cheap or cheaper than taking a bus, with all the freedom of a car. In Fairbanks, it is a great way to see the region north of the city where there is no public transport apart from bush planes.

All the used-car rental companies will be listed in the regional chapters under the towns where they maintain offices. All Star, however, maintains a toll-free number (800) 426-5243 for those who want to reserve a car in advance of their trip.

Motorhome Rental
You can also rent a motorhome in Alaska. More than a dozen companies, almost all of them based in Anchorage, will rent you a motorhome, ranging from 20 to 35 feet (6 to 11 metres) in length, that accommodates up to six people. The price can vary from $100 to $150 per day but again you have to consider all the extra charges. Many offer a 100 free miles per day and 25 cents per mile for any additional mileage.

You also have to pay for insurance and possibly even a 'housekeeping kit' – the pots, pans and sheets you'll need to survive. It's best to anticipate a daily fee of between $150 to $200 but when divided between four to six people it comes out to around $35 a day per person for both transport and a soft bed at night. Not such a bad deal if you can round up several other people who want to share the same itinerary. Other costs include gasoline, food and camping sites.

It's best to reserve a motorhome in advance if possible. A few of the larger Anchorage rental companies include Alaska Panorama Fleet (tel (907) 562-1401); Clippership Motorhome Rentals (tel (907) 276-6491); and Great Alaska Holidays (tel (800) 642-6462 – toll-free).

BICYCLE
For those who want to bike it, Alaska offers a variety of cycling adventures on paved

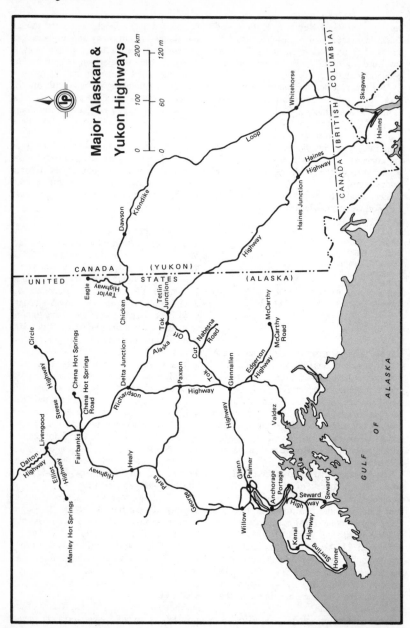

Major Alaskan &
Yukon Highways

roads during long days with comfortably cool temperatures. Most cyclists hop on the State Marine Ferry, where they can carry their bike on for a small charge. The individual Southeast communities are good places to gear up for the longer rides up north.

From Haines, you can catch an Alaskon Express bus, there is no charge for the bike, to Tok or Anchorage in the heart of Alaska. You can also take your bike on Alaska Airlines for a $30 excess baggage fee each way; it doesn't have to be crated but is merely handed over to the ticket officials at the counter.

Summer cyclists have to take some extra precautions in Alaska. There are few towns with comprehensively equipped bike shops so it is wise to carry not only metric tools but also a tube-patch repair kit, brake cables, spokes, brake pads and any other parts that might be needed during the trip.

Due to the high rainfall, especially in the Southeast, waterproof saddle bags are useful, as are tyre fenders. Rain gear is a must, and storing gear in zip-lock plastic bags within your side saddles is not being over-cautious. Warm clothing, mittens and a woollen hat should be carried, along with a tent and rain tarpaulin.

Some roads do not have much of a shoulder – the Seward Highway between Anchorage and Girdwood being the classic example – so cyclists should utilise the long hours of sunlight to pedal when the traffic is light in such areas. It is not necessary to carry a lot of food, as you can easily restock every couple of days on all major roads.

Most cyclists avoid gravel, but biking the Alcan, an increasingly popular trip, does involve some short gravel breaks in the paved asphalt. When riding along gravel roads, figure on making 50% to 70% of your normal distance and take spare inner tubes – flat tyres will be a daily occurrence.

The following cities and towns in Alaska have bike shops that offer a good selection of spare parts and information on riding in the local area. However, by the end of the summer many are low on, or completely out of, certain spare parts.

Anchorage
    The Bicycle Shop, 1035 West Northern Lights Blvd (tel (907) 272-5219)
    Gary King Sporting Goods, 202 East Northern Lights Blvd (tel (907) 279-7454)
    REI Co-op, 1200 West Northern Lights Blvd (tel (907) 272-4565)
Fairbanks
    Beaver Sports, 2400 College Rd (tel (907) 479-2494)
    Campbell Sports, 609 3rd St (tel (907) 452-2757)
Juneau
    Adventure Sports, 9105 Mendenhall Mall Rd (tel (907) 789-5696)
Sitka
    Southeast Diving & Sport Shop, 203 Lincoln St (tel (907) 747-8279)

The following are the more common long-distance trips undertaken by cyclists during the summer in Alaska.

Anchorage to Fairbanks

This ride can be done comfortably in 5 to 6 days along the George Parks Highway, and is 360 miles (580 km) along a flat road with scattered sections of rolling hills. Highlights are the impressive views of Mt McKinley and an interesting side trip into Denali National Park where cyclists can extend their trip with a ride along the gravel park road. Many cyclists take the Alaska Railroad part of the way and then bike the rest; there is an excess baggage charge for carrying your bicycle on the train.

Anchorage to the Kenai Peninsula

There is an endless number of possible bike trips or combinations of biking and hiking adventures in the Kenai Peninsula. You can also utilise the Southwest runs of the Alaska State Marine Ferry. A common trip is to cycle from Anchorage to Homer, take the ferry to Kodiak, then return via Seward and pedal back to Anchorage.

This is a 7 to 12 day trip depending on how much time you spend in Homer and Kodiak; the distance by bike is 350 miles (560 km) with an additional 400 miles (640 km) by ferry. Bikes can also be used to hop from one hiking trail to another in some of Alaska's most pleasant backcountry. Or, you can cycle to Portage, combine the rail and ferry transport across Prince William Sound to Valdez and then head north.

Fairbanks to Valdez

This is perhaps one of the most scenic routes cyclists can undertake and also one of the hardest. The 6 to 7 day trip follows the Richardson Highway from Delta Junction to Glennallen and then goes onto Valdez; a total of 375 miles (600 km). It includes several hilly sections and tough climbs over Isabel Pass before Paxson, and Thompson Pass at 2771 feet (845 metres), 25 miles (40 km) east of Valdez.

New brake pads are a must, along with rain gear and warm clothing, as the long ride downhill from Thompson Pass is often a cold and wet one. From Valdez, you can take a ferry across Prince William Sound and head back to Anchorage, or backtrack to the Glenn Highway and eventually to Anchorage.

North Star Bicycle Route

This 3400 mile (5440 km) ride is a summer-long adventure that begins in Missoula (Montana) and ends in Anchorage. Along the way you cross the Canadian Rockies, pick up the Alcan in British Columbia, pedal through the Yukon Territory and follow Alaskan highways from Tok to Anchorage.

Although the Alcan is now paved, miles of rough surface still exist due to construc-

tion work, making this a trip only for experienced cyclists looking for a grand adventure. The trip can be reduced significantly by either bussing part of the route in Canada (see the Bussing the Alcan section in the Getting There chapter) or by utilising the State Marine Ferry from Bellingham. It is 446 miles (714 km) from Haines to Tok, and 328 miles (525 km) from Tok to Anchorage, a ride that can be done comfortably in 5 days.

Those interested in this route would do well to read *The North Star Bicycle Route* while planning the trip. You can obtain copies of this 24 page booklet by sending $6.95 to the Bicycle Travel Association (tel (406) 721-1776), PO Box 8308, Missoula, Montana 59807. This nonprofit bicycle travel association also sells several other guides including *The Canadian Rockies Bicycling Guide* ($9.95) that would come in handy for anybody contemplating this once-in-a-lifetime ride.

You might also consider the *Alaska Bicycle Touring Guide* ($16.95, 328 pp, 1989), which is the first guide put together for touring Alaska on two wheels. It's been called the 'bicycling equivalent of the Milepost' for its thorough description of routes throughout the state, including two that go above the Arctic Circle. Look for it in Alaskan bookstores or order it before your trip through Wild Rose Guidebooks, PO Box 240047, Anchorage, Alaska 99524.

Black Bear

The Wilderness

Alaska is many things, but first and foremost it is the great outdoors; you go there for the mountains, the trails, the wildlife and the camping. If retrieving the morning newspaper is all the fresh air you can handle, Alaska can be a dull place. But if you're a camper, hiker, backpacker or someone who likes to spend a lot of time at scenic lookouts, the north country has two things for you – extensive wilderness areas and long days to enjoy them in.

Compared to the cost of getting there, the cost of enjoying most of the backcountry is relatively low. Hiking is free and even the most expensive camping fee is cheap compared to what motels will charge. Camping areas vary across Alaska from places with cosy lounges and heated bathrooms to out-of-town clearings.

The different adventures available in Alaska vary as much; you can take a 3 hour hike on a well-maintained trail that begins from the centre of Juneau or a 1 week trek in Denali National Park where there are no trails at all.

The best way to enter the state's wilderness is to begin with a day hike the minute you step off the State Marine Ferry or depart from the Alcan. Once having experienced a taste of the woods, many travellers forgo the cities and spend the rest of their trip taking long-term adventures into the backcountry. Make the most of Alaska's immense surroundings.

THE WILDERNESS EXPERIENCE

Alaska, which covers over 550,000 sq miles (1.4 million sq km), is serviced by only 5000 miles (8000 km) of public highway. Most of the recent tourist boom is centred around these roads and visitors tend to cling to them. Ironically, this causes the state, with all its space, to have its share of over-crowded parks and campgrounds.

Residents of Alaska know this and tend to stay away from heavily touristed places like Denali National Park during the middle of summer. They also know how to escape into the backcountry – those wearing Sierra Club T-shirts call it a 'wilderness experience'. Others throw a backpack together and say they're 'going out the road for a spell'. It's all the same – a journey into the woods, away from the city, neighbours, TV and other signs of human existence. That is the greatest enjoyment Alaska can offer anyone; a week of nothing but nature in all its splendour.

You have to be careful on such adventures. In a true wilderness experience, you are completely on your own. However, don't let the lack of communication with the civilised world prevent you from venturing into the wilderness; that's the best part. On an ideal trip, you won't meet another person outside your party, see a boat or hear the hum of a bush plane.

In this perfect tranquillity, all worries and pressures of day-to-day living are cast aside and you begin to discover yourself in the natural setting. More enjoyment and satisfaction can be derived from a few days in the wilderness than from a 3 week bus tour. Some people, once they enter, never get it out of their blood.

Local hiking trails and camping areas are covered in the regional chapters. The 22 trips described in this chapter are popular wilderness excursions that backpackers can do on their own if they are properly equipped and have sufficient outdoor experience. They are either maintained trails or natural paddling routes enjoyed by backpackers every year. Some trips cannot provide a true 'wilderness experience', as they are too popular during the summer, but many are isolated and offer a glimpse of pristine backcountry.

Those who didn't come to Alaska with the right gear or who lack camping knowledge can still escape into the woods and return safely. There are two ways of doing this. The first way is to join a guided expedition where equipment, group organisation and knowledge of the area are supplied. Guided expeditions, which cover the state, range from half a day to 3 weeks and cost between $125 and $150 per person per day (a list of guide companies is given at the end of this chapter). The other way to sample the wilderness, without enduring a 20 mile (32 km) hike or hiring the services of a tour guide, is to rent a Forest Service cabin.

GENERAL INFORMATION
Who Controls What
With almost three-quarters of the state locked up, it's good to know what federal or state agency administers the land you want to hike on. Almost all of the recreational areas, parks and forests, including the campgrounds and trails in them, are controlled by one of five agencies.

US Forest Service This federal bureau handles the Tongass and Chugach national forests which cover practically all of the Southeast and Eastern Kenai Peninsula, including Prince William Sound. The US Forest Service (USFS) can provide information on the 190 public-use cabins it maintains, along with hiking, kayaking, canoeing and other recreational opportunities in its domain. Most USFS campgrounds charge from $5 to $8 per day, depending on the facilities, and have a 14 day limit. The addresses for the main USFS offices are given in the Accommodation section of this chapter but there are also smaller offices in Craig, Wrangell, Hoonah and Yakutat.

In the Southeast, each USFS office has a copy of the *Southeast Alaska Community Opportunity Guide*, which is put together by the Forest Service and contains information about camping, trails, fishing areas and cabins throughout Tongass National Forest. If you plan to spend any time in a Southeast town, it is well worth your while to venture to the USFS office and thumb through this reference guide.

National Park Service The National Park Service administers Denali, Glacier Bay and Katmai national parks and preserves, all of which have maintained campgrounds and are accessible by either an Alaska Airlines flight or by road. The seven campgrounds in Denali National Park are scattered across the park; Morino Campground at the entrance to the park is a free, no-frills area for backpackers.

Two other national parks, Kenai Fjords and Wrangell-St Elias, also have roads leading into them but their facilities are not nearly as well developed for visitors as the first three national parks mentioned – of course many consider that a plus. Without the visitor centres, campervan hook-ups, hot showers and expensive lodges, these national parks escape the mid-summer crush of tourists that the other parks suffer.

There are three other national parks (Gates of the Arctic, Kobuk Valley and Lake Clark) and three national preserves (Aniachak, Noatak and Yukon-Charley Rivers) that are administered by the National Park Service. All of them are only accessible by bush plane or boat and offer no facilities within the park. Most visitors reach them through guide companies who venture into the wilderness areas by raft, kayak or foot.

The National Park Service also maintains numerous national monuments and national historical parks. For addresses and more information on the individual parks, check the regional chapters. For general information on all parks, contact the main National Park Service offices: Alaska Public Lands Information Center (tel (907) 271-2737), 605 West 4th Ave, Suite 105, Anchorage, Alaska 99501-2231; and the National Park Service (tel (907) 586-7137), 709 West 9th St, Juneau, Alaska 99801

Bureau of Land Management The Bureau of Land Management (BLM) is the federal agency that maintains much of the wilderness around and north of Fairbanks. It has developed 25 camping areas and five public-use cabins in the Interior as well as two popular trails (Pinnell Mountain and White Mountain) both located off the highways north of Fairbanks. Camping, free in BLM campgrounds, is handled on a first-come first-serve basis. The cabins, $15 a night, are all within 100 miles (160 km) of Fairbanks.

The BLM offices have good publications on the Taylor Highway, a secondary road that is an adventure in itself, and national wild rivers such as the Gulkana, Fortymile and Delta. For more information contact the BLM District Office (tel (907) 474-2343), 1150 University Ave, Fairbanks, Alaska 99709 or the BLM District Office (tel (907) 822-3217), PO Box 147, Glennallen, Alaska 99588.

US Fish & Wildlife Service This arm of the Department of the Interior administers 16 wildlife refuges in Alaska that total more than 77 million acres (31 million hectares). The largest, Yukon Delta that surrounds Bethel in Western Alaska, is almost 20 million acres (8 million hectares).

The purpose of wildlife refuges is to protect habitats; visitor use and developed recreational activities are strictly an after thought. Most of the refuges are in remote areas of the Bush, with few, if any, developed facilities – guide companies are the only means by which most travellers visit them. The one exception is Kenai National Wildlife Refuge, which can be reached by road from Anchorage. This preserve has 15 campgrounds, of which the Kenai-Russian River Campground is by far the most popular, and over 200 miles (320 km) of hiking trails and water routes, including the popular Swanson River Canoe Route.

The Kodiak National Wildlife Refuge, although considerably more remote and more expensive to reach than Kenai, does offer nine wilderness cabins similar to USFS cabins for $15 per night. For more information about individual areas, see the regional chapters. For general information contact the Regional Office (tel (907) 786-3487), US Fish & Wildlife Service, 1011 East Tudor Rd, Anchorage, Alaska 99503.

Alaska Division of Parks The Alaska Division of Parks and Outdoor Recreation controls more than 100 areas in the Alaska State Park system, ranging from the 1.5

million acre (600,000 hectare) Wood-Tikchik State Park, north of Dillingham on Bristol Bay, to small wayside parks along the highway. The areas also include state trails, campgrounds, wilderness parks and historical sites, all maintained by the state.

Among the more popular parks which offer a variety of recreational opportunities are Chugach, Denali State Park south of Mt McKinley, Nancy Lake Recreational Area just south of Willow, Captain Cook State Recreation Area on the Kenai Peninsula and Chilkat State Park south of Haines. Most campgrounds cost $5 a night with a couple of the more popular ones charging $10 a night.

For travellers planning to spend a summer camping in Alaska, a state park camping pass, allowing unlimited camping for a year, is a wise investment at $50. The state parks division also rents out recreational cabins in the Southeast, Southcentral and the Interior regions for $20 to $25 a night. To obtain an annual Alaska Camping Pass in advance, send a cheque or money order to one of the following offices: Alaska Division of Parks (tel (907) 276-2653), PO Box 107001, Anchorage, Alaska 99510, or the Alaska Division of Parks, 400 Willoughby Center, Juneau, Alaska 99801.

Backpacking

Camping, hiking and backpacking in Alaska are more dangerous than in most other places. The weather is more unpredictable, the climate harsher, and encounters with wildlife a daily occurrence. Unpredictable situations like getting lost, snow storms in the middle of the summer or being 'socked in' by low clouds and fog for days while waiting for a bush plane happen annually to hundreds of backpackers in Alaska.

If you're planning to wander beyond road-side parks, don't take your adventure lightly. You must be totally independent in the wilderness – a new experience for most city dwellers. You need the knowledge and equipment to sit out bad weather, endure an overturned boat or assist an injured member of your party.

The information and suggestions in this chapter are only a guide to backpacking in Alaska, not a complete lesson on surviving the outdoors. For that you should consult a survival manual such as *Walking Softly in the Wilderness* by John Hart (Sierra Club Books); be prepared before you enter the woods.

Backcountry Conduct

It is wise to check in with the US Forest Service (USFS) office or National Park headquarters before entering the backcountry. By letting them know your intentions, you'll get peace of mind knowing that someone knows you're out there. If there is no ranger office in the area, the best place to advise of your travel plans is the air charter service responsible for picking-up your party.

Do not harass wildlife while travelling in the backcountry. Avoid startling an animal, as it will most likely flee, leaving you with a short and forgettable encounter. If you flush a bird from its nest, leave the area quickly, as an unattended nest leaves the eggs vulnerable to predators. Never attempt to feed wildlife; it is not healthy for you or the animal.

Finally, be thoughtful when in the wilderness as it is a delicate environment. Carry in

your supplies and carry out your trash, never littering or leaving garbage to smoulder in a fire pit. Always put out your fire and cover it with natural materials or better still don't light a fire in heavily travelled areas. Use biodegradeable soap and do all washing away from water sources. In short, practice low-impact no-trace camping and leave no evidence of your stay. Only then can an area remain a true wilderness.

DANGERS & ANNOYANCES
Drinking Water

Alaska's water is affected by *giardia lamblia*, or 'beaver fever' as it is known among backpackers. The parasite is found in surface water, particularly beaver ponds, and is transmitted between humans and animals. For information on water purification and how to treat giardia, see the Health section in the Facts for the Visitor chapter.

Water from glacial rivers may appear murky but it can be drunk, if necessary, in small quantities, athough drinking too much of it tends to clog up the internal plumbing. The murk is actually fine particles of silt scoured from the rock by the glacier.

Insects

Alaska is notorious for its biting insects. In the cities and towns you have few problems, but out in the woods you'll have to contend with a variety of insects, including mosquitoes, black flies, white-socks, no-see-ums and deer flies. Coastal areas, with their cool summers, have smaller numbers of insects than the Interior. Generally, camping on a beach where there is some breeze is better than pitching a tent in the woods. In the end, just accept the fact that you will be bitten.

Mosquitoes can often be the most bothersome pest. They emerge from hibernation before the snow has entirely melted away, peak in late June and are around until the first frost. It's the female of the species who is after your blood, and they're most active early in the morning and at dusk. Luckily, even a slight wind grounds them. You can combat mosquitoes by wearing light colours,

Top: St Elias National Park (SEAG)
Left: Backpackers, Glacier Bay (JD)
Right: Hikers on White Thunder Ridge in Glacier Bay (JS)

Top: Ski Plane dropping off mountain climbers (AVB)
Bottom: Alyeska Ski Resort (ADT)

a snug-fitting parka and by tucking your pant's legs into your socks or boots.

The best protection by far is a high potent insect repellent; the best contain a high percentage of DEET (diethyltoluamide), the active ingredient. A little bottle of Musk Oil or Cutters can cost $5 or $6 (they contain 100% DEET) but it's one of the best investments you will make.

Unfortunately, repellents are less effective, and some people say useless, against black flies and no-see-ums. Their season runs from June to August and their bite is far more annoying. The tiny no-see-um bite is a prolonged prick after which the surrounding skin becomes inflamed and itches intermittently for up to a week or more. Unlike the mosquito, these insects will crawl into your hair and under loose clothing in search of bare skin.

Thus, the best protection and a fact of life in Alaska's backcountry are long-sleeved shirts, socks that will allow you to tuck your pants into them and a snug cap or woollen hat. One other item that comes in handy is an after-bite medication. Most of them rub on and contain ammonia; while it might drive away your tent partner, it does soothe the craving to scratch the assortment of bites on your arms and neck.

Bears

You could spend the entire summer in Alaska without ever seeing a bear, or you could be on an early-morning stroll in Juneau and see one scrambling towards the woods a block away from the Governor's Mansion. The fact is, as one ranger put it, 'no matter where you travel in Alaska, you'll never be far from a bear'.

Too often, travellers decide to skip a wilderness trip because they hear a local tell a few bear stories. Your own equipment and outdoor experience should determine whether you take a trek into the woods, not the possibility of meeting a bear on the trail. You have a much better chance of being mugged in Los Angeles than getting mauled by a bear in Alaska.

The best way to avoid bears is to follow a few common-sense rules. Bears do not roam the backcountry looking for hikers to maul; they only charge when they feel trapped, when a hiker comes between a sow and her cubs or when they are enticed by food. It is a good practice to sing or clap when travelling through thick bush so you don't bump into one. That has happened, and usually the bear feels threatened and has no choice but to defend itself. Don't camp near bear food sources or in the middle of an obvious bear path. Stay away from thick berry patches, streams choking with salmon or beaches littered with bear scat.

Other people attach 'bear bells' all over their backpack, boots and clothing. Bells will alert any bear in the immediate area, but unfortunately will also scare all other wildlife, even the species you want to see. The constant ringing not only eliminates the chances to view animals but blocks out the natural sounds of the woods that ease the mind and fill the soul with wonder.

Leave the pet at home; a frightened dog only runs back to its owner and most dogs are no match for a bear. Set up your 'kitchen' – the spot where you will cook and eat – 30 to 50 yards/metres away from your tent. In coastal areas, many backpackers eat in the tidal zone, knowing that when the high tide comes in all evidence of food will be washed away.

At night try, to place your food sacks 10 feet (3 metres) or more off the ground by hanging them in a tree, placing them on top of a tall boulder or putting them on the edge of a rock cliff. In a treeless, flat area, cover up the food sacks with rocks. A bear is not going to see the food bags, it's going to smell them; by packaging all food items in zip-lock plastic bags, you greatly reduce the animal's chances of getting a whiff of your next meal.

And please, don't take food into the tent at night. Don't even take toothpaste, hand lotion, suntan oils or anything with a smell. If a bear smells a human, it will leave; anything else might encourage it to investigate.

If you do meet a bear on the trail, *do not* turn and run. Stop, make no sudden moves and begin talking calmly to it. Bears have

Brown Bears

extremely poor eyesight and speaking helps it understand that you are there. If it doesn't take off right away, back up slowly before turning around and departing the area. A bear standing on its hind legs is not on the verge of charging, only trying to see you better. When a bear turns sideways or begins a series of woofs, it is only challenging you for space – just back away slowly and leave.

Most bear charges are bluffs, with the animal veering off at the last minute. Experienced backpackers handle a charge in different ways. Some throw their packs 3 feet (1 metre) in front of them, as this will often distract the bear long enough for them to back away. Others fire a hand-held signal flare over the bear's head (but never at it) in an attempt to use the noise and sudden light to scare it away. If an encounter is imminent, drop into a fetal position and place your hands behind your neck.

Some people carry a gun to fend off bear charges. This is a skilled operation if you are a good shot, a foolish one if you are not. With a gun, you must drop a charging bear with one or two shots; it will be extremely dangerous if only wounded.

Be extremely careful in bear country, but don't let their reputation keep you out of the woods.

ACCOMMODATION
Camping
Choosing a spot to pitch a tent in a campground is easy, but in the wilderness the choice is more complicated and should be made carefully to avoid problems in the middle of the night. Through much of Alaska, especially the Interior, river bars are the best place to pitch a tent. Strips of sand or small gravel patches along rivers provide good drainage and a smoother surface on which to pitch a tent than tussock grass.

Take time to check out the area before unpacking your gear. Avoid animal trails (whether the tracks be moose or bear), areas with bear scat, and berry patches with ripe fruit. In late summer, it is best to stay away from streams choked with salmon runs.

In the Southeast and other coastal areas of Alaska, search out beaches and ridges with southern exposures; they provide the driest conditions in these rainy zones. Old glacier and stream outwashes (sand or gravel deposits) make ideal campsites as long as you stay well above the high-tide line. Look for the last ridge of seaweed and debris on the shore and then pitch your tent another 20 to 30 yards/metres above that to avoid waking up with salt water flooding your tent. Tidal fluctuations along Alaska's coast are among the largest in the world; up to 30 feet (9 metres) in some places.

Forest Service Cabins

Built and maintained by the US Forest Service (USFS), the cabins are scattered throughout the Tongass National Forest (practically the entire Southeast), the Chugach National Forest on the Kenai Peninsula, and different islands and bays in Prince William Sound. For the most part, the cabins are rustic log cabins or A-frames with wood-burning stoves, plywood bunks, pit toilets and often a rowboat if the cabins are on a lake. They are usually located near remote lakes or streams, along coastal beaches or above the timberline.

A few cabins can be reached by hiking, but for most a bush plane or chartered boat has to drop you off and then return for you. The cabins are an ideal way to sneak into the woods and separate yourself from the world without having to undertake rigorous backcountry travel.

Although there are a few free shelters, the vast majority of cabins cost $20 per night to rent but can comfortably hold parties of six or more. You can reserve them 180 days in advance by sending the total payment and the dates you want the cabins to the various Forest Service offices which administer them.

During the summer, the cabins are heavily used by both locals and travellers, and have a limit of 7 consecutive nights per party. In the Chugach National Forest, there is a 3 day limit on hike-in cabins from May to August. Some are so popular that the Forest Service holds a lottery among all the reservation requests sent 179 days in advance, in order to determine who will be allowed to occupy them during peak periods of the summer.

The cabins provide excellent shelter from bad weather but you have to bring your own bedding (sleeping bag and ground pad), food and cooking gear, including a small backpacker's stove for when the wood pile is wet. Other items that come in handy are insect repellent, matches, candles and a topographical map of the surrounding area. The

USFS also recommends that any water obtained from nearby lakes should be purified (see the Health section in the Facts for the Visitor chapter for information on water purification and Giardia).

Of the 190 USFS public-use cabins, almost 150 of them are in the Southeast and are accessible from Ketchikan, Petersburg, Juneau or Sitka. If you don't make reservations but have a flexible schedule, it is still possible to rent one. During the summer, USFS offices in the Southeast maintain lists of the cabins and dates still available. There are always a few cabins available for a couple of days in the middle of the week, although they are most likely the remote ones requiring more flying time (and thus money) to reach. The most accessible ones are usually booked solid by the time June rolls around.

In the regional chapters, a description of selected cabins is given under the names of towns they are most accessible from. These cabins are special because they can either be reached in 30 minutes or less by bush plane or have some intriguing feature nearby, such as natural hot springs or a glacier.

For a complete list of cabins in the Southeast, write to the following USFS offices in Alaska, which will forward a booklet describing each cabin in its district along with details about the surrounding terrain and the best way to travel to it.

Chatham Area Supervisor
204 Siginaka Way, Sitka 99835 (tel (907) 747-6671)
Forest Service Information Centre
Box 1628, Juneau 99802 (tel (907) 586-8751)
Ketchikan Area Supervisor
Federal Building, Ketchikan 99901 (tel (907) 225-3101)
Stikine Area Supervisor
PO Box 309, Petersburg 99833 (tel (907) 772-3871)

The Chugach National Forest in Southcentral has 39 cabins, including seven along the Resurrection Trail and two on the Russian Lakes Trail. There are also a couple of cabins in the Cordova area that can be reached by foot, but the rest are accessible only by air or boat. For a complete list of cabins and bookings in the Chugach National Forest, write to the following USFS district offices in Alaska.

Anchorage Ranger District
   201 East 9th Ave, Suite 206, Anchorage 99501 (tel (907) 271-2599)
Cordova Ranger District
   PO Box 280, Cordova 99574 (tel (907) 424-7661)
Seward Ranger District
   PO Box 390, Seward 99664 (tel (907) 224-3374)

BOOKS

A great deal of reference material is available to assist backpackers in finding their way along the trail or to give them a better understanding of the natural world around them. The following books can be found in good Alaskan bookstores or can be obtained directly from Wild Rose Guidebooks, PO Box 240047, Anchorage, Alaska 99524.

Hiking Guides

55 Ways to the Wilderness in Southcentral Alaska by Nancy Simmerman & Helen Nienhueser (Mountaineer-Books, 306 2nd Ave West, Seattle, Washington 98119; 1985, 176 pp, $10.95) is a hiking guide with the most up-to-date information covering popular trails around the Kenai Peninsula, the Anchorage area and from Palmer to Valdez. The text includes maps, distances and estimated trekking times.

15 Hikes in Denali by Don Croner (Trans-Alaska Publishing Company, 200 West 34th Ave, Anchorage, Alaska; 1989, 42 pp, $7.95) is a large format guide which outlines 15 hikes in Denali National Park, ranging from short day hikes to 40 mile (64 km) treks. This second edition also contains additional information and drawings covering plants, birds and geology of the park. It's a good purchase if you plan an extended trip to the park.

Alaska Wilderness; Exploring the Central Brooks Range by Robert Marshall (Wild Rose Guidebooks, PO Box 240047, Anchorage, Alaska, 99524; 1989, 175 pp, $12.95) was written and published in the 1930s and

then republished in 1989 for the simple reason that the mountains, rivers, passes and terrain of the central Brooks Range have not changed. What Marshall saw and many of the routes he explored are still the popular ones today.

Juneau Trails by the US Forest Service (1983, 60 pp, $2), a little green book, is a bible for Juneau hikers as it describes 26 trails around the capital city – perhaps the best area for hiking in Alaska. The guidebook includes maps, distances, rating of the trails and location of trailheads along with brief descriptions of the route. The book can be obtained at the USFS information centre in the Centennial Building on Egan Drive in Juneau, but you have to ask for it.

Sitka Trails by the US Forest Service (72 pp, $2) is similar to *Juneau Trails* and covers 30 hiking trails around Sitka and its nearby coastline. Each trail has a one paragraph description, rough map and information on access and special features. Either write ahead of time or stop at Sitka Ranger District, 204 Siginaka Way, Alaska 99835.

Discover Southeast Alaska with Pack and Paddle by Margaret Piggott (Mountaineer Books), a long-time guidebook to the water routes and hiking trails of the Southeast, should soon reappear as an updated new edition after being out of print for several years. Text and maps cover hiking and paddling routes from Ketchikan to Skagway.

Paddling Guides

The Coastal Kayaker by Randel Washburne (Globe Pequot Press, Old Chester Rd, PO Box Q, Chester, Connecticut 06412; 1983, 224 pp, $11.95) deals mostly with the art of blue-water kayaking and how to survive in the coastal wilderness of British Columbia and Southeast Alaska. It contains paddling notes and basic maps for seven different areas, including four in the Southeast.

A Guide to Alaska's Kenai Fjords by David Miller (Wilderness Images, Anchor Cove, PO Box 1367, Seward, Alaska 99664; 1987, 116 pp, $8.95). A coastal paddling guide to the Kenai Fjords National Park with route descriptions and maps. The author provides an overview of the area plus specific information about protected coves, hikes, fishing tips and protected areas for kayakers to arrange drop-offs and pick-ups.

Glacier Bay National Park: A Backcountry Guide to the Glaciers and Beyond by Jim DuFresne (Mountaineer-Books; 1988, 144 pp, $8.95) is a complete guide to Glacier Bay's backcountry. Along with introductory material on the park, the book contains information on kayak rentals, transport up the bay and detailed descriptions of water and land routes in this trail-less park; maps are included.

Alaska Paddling Guide by Jack Mosby & David Dapkus (J&R Publishers, PO Box 140264, Anchorage, Alaska 99514; 1986, 113 pp, $7.95) is a statewide guide which covers 110 possible water trips, many have road access. Descriptions of the journeys are brief but practical information such as access points, trip length and a rough map are provided.

General

Guide to the Birds of Alaska is by Robert Armstrong (Alaska Northwest Books, 130 2nd Ave South, Edmonds, Washington 98020; 1990, 332 pp, $19.95). To ornithologists, Alaska is the ultimate destination. More than 400 species of birds have been spotted in the state and this guide has information on identification, distribution and habitat on 335 of them. Along with text, the books contains colour photographs of the species, drawings and a bird check list.

A Guide to Alaskan Seabirds by the Alaska Natural History Association, 2525 Gambell St, Anchorage, Alaska 99503 (1982, 40 pp, $4.95) is a thin guide to the birds that thrive along coastal Alaska. It has excellent drawings for easy identification.

Wild, Edible & Poisonous Plants of Alaska by Dr Christine Heller (Alaska Natural History Association; 88 pp, $2.50), a handy little guide, is an excellent companion on any hike, as it contains both drawings and colour photos of Alaskan flora, including edible plants, berries and wildflowers.

A Guide to Wildlife Viewing in Alaska

(Wild Rose Guidebooks; 1983, 170 pp, $12.95) is an Alaska Department of Fish & Game sponsored guide which covers the best opportunities to view wildlife by regions and seasons. The first chapter explains how to find wildlife and the following chapters cover Alaska's 14 different types of wildlife habitats.

ACTIVITIES
Blue-water Paddling

Blue-water in Alaska refers to the coastal areas of the state that are characterised by extreme tidal fluctuations, cold water temperatures and the possibility of high winds and waves. Throughout Southeast and Southcentral Alaska, the open canoe gives way to the kayak, and blue-water paddling is the means of escape into the coastal wilderness.

Don't confuse white-water kayaking with ocean touring. River running in light, streamlined kayaks with helmets, wet suits and Eskimo rolls has nothing to do with paddling coastal Alaska in ocean-touring kayaks. Every year, hundreds of backpackers with canoeing experience arrive in the north country and undertake their first blue-water kayak trip in such protected areas as Muir Inlet in Glacier Bay National Park or Tracy Arm Fjord, south of Juneau.

Tidal fluctuations are the main concern in blue-water areas. Paddlers should always pull their boats above the high-tide mark and secure it by tying a line to a rock or tree. A tide book for the area should be in the same pouch as the topographical map – paddlers schedule days around the changing tides, travelling with the tidal current or during slack tide for easy paddling. Check with local rangers for the narrow inlets or straits where rip tides or whirlpools might form, and always plan to paddle these areas during slack tides.

Cold coastal water, rarely above 45°F (7°C) in the summer, makes capsizing more than unpleasant. Even with a life jacket, survival time in the water is less than 2 hours; without one it is considerably less. Plan your trip to run parallel with the shoreline and

Blue-water Paddling

arrange your schedule so you can sit out rough weather without missing your pick-up date. If you do flip, stay with the boat and attempt to right it and crawl back in. Trying to swim to shore in arctic water is risky at best.

Give a wide berth to marine mammals such as sea lions, seals and especially any whales that are seen during a paddle. Glacial ice should also be treated with respect. It is unwise to approach a glacier face closer than 0.5 mile (0.8 km) as icebergs can calve suddenly and create a series of unmanageable waves and swells. Never try to climb onto a floating iceberg as they are extremely unstable and can roll without warning.

Framed backpacks are almost useless in kayaks; gear is better stowed in duffle bags or small day packs. Carry a large supply of assorted plastic bags, including several garbage bags. All gear, especially sleeping bags and clothing, should be stowed in

plastic bags, as water tends to seep in even when you seal yourself in with a cockpit skirt. Other equipment taken along on any blue-water paddle should include an extra paddle, a large sponge for bailing the boat, sunglasses and sunscreen, extra lines and a repair kit of duct tape and a tube of silicon sealant for fibreglass cracks.

Wilderness Fishing

Many people have a fish-per-cast vision of angling in Alaska. They expect every river, stream and lake, no matter how close to the road, to be bountiful and often go home disappointed when their fishing efforts produce little to brag about. Serious anglers visiting Alaska carefully research the areas to be fished and are equipped with the right gear and tackle. They often pay for guides or book a room at remote camps or lodges where rivers are not 'fished out' by every passing motorist.

If, however, you plan to undertake a few wilderness trips, by all means pack along a rod, reel and some tackle. It's now possible to purchase a backpacking rod that breaks down into five sections and has a light reel; it takes up less room than your soap, shaving cream and wash rag. In the Southeast and Southcentral regions, backpackers can catch cutthroat trout, rainbow trout and Dolly Vardens, a fish similar to the other two. Further north, especially around Fairbanks, you'll get grayling, with its sail-like dorsal fin, and arctic char; during August, salmon seem to be everywhere.

If angling is just a second thought, attach a light line for simplicity, something in the 4 to 6 lb (2 to 3 kg) range, and take along a small selection of spinners and spoons. After you arrive, you can always purchase the lures used locally, but in most wilderness streams I've rarely had a problem catching fish on Mepps spinners, sizes Nos 1 to 3. Other lures that work well are Pixies, Dare Devils and Krocodiles.

For fly fishing a No 6 rod with a matching No 6 floating line or sinking tip is well suited for Dolly Vardens, cutthroat trout and pink salmon. For other species of salmon a No 7 or No 8 rod and line are better choices. For ease of travel, rods should break down and be in a case.

A nonresident's fishing license is $36 a year (as compared to only $10 for residents) or you can purchase a 3 day license for $10 or a 14 day license for $20; every bait shop in the state sells them. The Alaska Department of Fish & Game puts out a variety of material including the *Recreational Fishing Guide*. You can obtain the 72 page guide ($4) by writing to the Department of Fish & Game (tel (906) 465-4112), PO Box 3-2000, Juneau, Alaska 99811.

Perhaps the most comprehensive guide to fishing Alaska is the recently released, *Fishing Alaska on $20 a Day* by Christopher & Adela Batin, available from Alaska Angler Publications (tel (800) 446-2286 – toll free), PO Box 83550, Fairbanks, Alaska 99708 for $23.95. It is based on Forest Service cabin accommodation that can be rented for $20 a day. The 338 page guide describes each cabin, fishing in the immediate area and gateway city, and provides good introductory material. The authors suggest that some of Alaska's best sport fishing lies on the doorsteps of the state's 200 recreational cabins.

WHAT TO BRING
Day-Hike Equipment
Too often, visitors undertake a day hike with little or no equipment and then, 3 hours from the trailhead, get caught in bad weather wearing only a flimsy cotton jacket. Worse still, they suffer a major mishap such as losing the trail and have to spend a long night in the woods without food, matches or warm clothing.

Along with your large, framed backpack, take a soft day pack or rucksack with you to Alaska. These small knapsacks are ideal for day hikes and should contain waterproof clothing, woollen mittens and hat, a knife, high-energy food (chocolate), matches, map and compass, metal drinking cup and insect repellent.

Expedition Equipment
For longer treks and adventures into the wilderness, backpackers should double-check their equipment before they leave home, as opposed to scurrying around some small Alaska town trying to locate a camp stove or a pair of glacier goggles. Most towns in Alaska will have at least one store with a wall full of camping supplies, but prices will be high and by mid to late summer certain items will be out of stock.

You don't need to arrive with a complete line of the latest Gortex, but then again, that $4.95 plastic rain suit probably won't last more than a few days in the woods. Bring functional and sturdy equipment to Alaska and you will go home after a summer of wilderness adventures with much of it intact.

Clothing Alaska has traditionally been wool country. Wool insulates not only against snow and cold but also against the constant drizzle, which is usually one of the main causes of hypothermia. Even when wet, wool will keep you warm, and it dries much faster than cotton.

However, wool is gradually giving way to the new synthetic pile or spun artificial fibres which possess the same qualities; they may even outperform wool under severe wet and cold conditions. The drawback is that the jersey of acrylic piling costs twice as much as a good old woollen jacket. Take your pick but avoid cotton items (jacket, socks and blue jeans) and outerwear that contains goose down, as they are useless when wet.

On any trip longer than 2 days you should have two to three pairs of woollen socks, along with woollen mittens and a knitted hat; woollen pants and shirts are not going too far as the weather can change suddenly. Dress in layers – or like an artichoke, as residents say – for maximum containment of body heat. Always carry a heavy jersey or jacket for the evenings, and waterproof clothing should be on the top of everybody's pack.

Boots The traditional footwear is the heavy leather hiking boot that has been smeared on the outside with half a can of bees wax. More and more backpackers, however, are opting for the new lightweight nylon boots made by sporting-shoe companies like Nike or Hi-Tech. These are lighter to pack and easier on the feet than leather boots, while providing all the foot protection and ankle support needed on most trails and wilderness trips other than technical mountaineering. Normal tennis shoes are not enough for the trails but are handy to have as a change of footwear at night or for fording rivers and streams.

Tent Coming to Alaska without a lightweight tent is like going to Hawaii without a beach towel. It's the biggest cost-saver you can bring. The tent doesn't have to be fancy, but it should have a rain fly which can double as a shade during long summer days when the sun is out long after you've gone to bed. Make sure the netting around the doors and windows is bug proof and will prevent you from turning into a nightly smorgasbord for any mosquito that passes by.

If the tent is more than 4 years old, waterproof the floor and rain fly before departing on your trip.

Sleeping Bag This is a good item to bring whether you plan on camping or not, as it is also very useful in youth hostels, on board the State Marine Ferry and in seedy hotels when you're not sure what's crawling in the mattress.

There has been many an all-night discussion among backpackers on the qualities of down versus synthetic fibres. What can't be argued though is down's quality of clumping when wet. In rainy Southeast and South-central Alaska, this means trouble during most wilderness trips. Along with a sleeping bag, bring an insulated foam pad to sleep on – it will reduce much of the ground chill. In the Interior, you will often be sleeping just inches away from permafrost, or permanently frozen ground.

Camp Stove Cooking dinner over a crackling campfire may be a romantic notion while you're planning your trip, but it is an inconvenience and often a major headache when you're actually on the trail. Bring a reliable backpacker's stove and make life simple in the woods. Rain, strong winds and a lack of available wood will hamper your efforts to build a fire, while some preserves like Denali National Park won't even allow campfires in the backcountry.

Remember, you cannot carry white gas or other camp-stove fuels on an airline flight but just about every small town or park visitor centre will stock it.

Map & Compass Backpackers should not only carry a compass into the wilderness but should have some basic knowledge of how to use it correctly. You should also have the correct US Geological Survey (USGS) map for the area in which you are planning to travel.

USGS topographical maps come in a variety of scales but hikers and kayakers prefer the smallest scale of 1:63,360, where each inch equals a mile. The free maps of Tongass and Chugach national forests sent by the US Forest Service will not do for any wilderness adventure, as they cover too much and lack the detail that backpackers rely on.

USGS maps cost $2.50 a section and can generally be purchased at bookstores, sports shops or camping stores in the last Alaskan town from which you enter the backcountry. However, it is not uncommon for the stores to be out of the maps covering popular areas. If possible, order your maps ahead of time from the main office, USGS Western Distribution Branch, Denver Federal Centre, PO Box 25286 Denver, Colorado 80225; first write and ask for a free index of maps for Alaska.

Sun Protection Alaska has long hours of sunlight during the summer and the sun's rays are even more intense when they are reflected off snow or water. All backpackers should bring a cap with a visor on it and a small tube of sun screen to save at least one layer of skin on their nose. If you plan to do any kayaking, canoeing or alpine hiking around snowfields, you should also plan on bringing a pair of dark sunglasses, known by many locals as 'glacier goggles'.

Food You can buy food in almost any town or village at the start of most trips. If travelling to Glacier Bay, Denali or Katmai national parks, don't plan on purchasing your main supply of food at the park headquarters; stock up at the last major town you pass through.

Trekking

The following trips are along routes that are popular and well developed. Backpackers still need the proper gear and knowledge but can undertake these adventures on their own without the services of a guide. Always check with the offices or park headquarters listed for current trail conditions. A few of the trails have US Forest Service (USFS) cabins along the way, but these must be reserved well in advance. Bring a tent on any wilderness trek.

CHILKOOT TRAIL
Denali National Park may be the most popular park in Alaska, but the Chilkoot is unquestionably the most famous trail and often the most used during the summer; more than 2000 hikers follow it annually. It is the same route used by the Klondike gold miners in the 1898 to 1900 gold rush and is not so much a wilderness adventure as a history lesson.

The well-developed and well-marked trail is littered from one end to the other with artefacts of the era – everything from entire ghost towns and huge mining dredges to a lone boot lying next to the trail. The trip is 33 to 35 miles (53 to 56 km) long (depending on where you exit) and includes the Chilkoot Pass – a steep climb up loose rocks to 3550 feet (1082 metres), where most hikers use all fours to scramble over the loose rocks. The trail can be attempted by anyone in good physical condition with the right equipment

and enough time. The hike normally takes 4 to 5 days, though it can be done in 2 to 3 days by experienced trekkers.

Before 1982, one of the more popular highlights of the hike was riding the White Pass & Yukon Railroad back to Skagway. In 1981, the last summer the train ran before it ceased operations, 2500 hikers tackled the Chilkoot. The historic railroad has since been reorganised and recently resumed service; it remains to be seen if the trail again draws such a large number of hikers – most likely it will.

Experiencing the Chilkoot and returning on the White Pass & Yukon Railroad is probably the ultimate Alaska trek, combining great scenery, a first-hand view of history and an incredible sense of adventure. Best of all, it's affordable even for budget travellers.

Getting Started
The Chilkoot Trail can be hiked from either direction (starting at Skagway or Lake Bennett) but it is actually easier from Lake Bennett. However, there is something about following the footsteps of the Klondike miners that makes this such a special adventure. As gold miners did at the turn of the century, most hikers also arrive at Skagway, the historical gold-rush town, by ferry and spend a day or so walking the wooden sidewalks and purchasing supplies from stores with false fronts. They then continue north along the Chilkoot Trail.

From Skagway, make your way to Dyea, 8 miles (13 km) to the north-west and the site of the trailhead. *Mile 0* of the Chilkoot is just before the Taiya River crossing. Near the trailhead is the Dyea Camping Area (22 sites, no fee) and a National Park Service ranger station. You can reach Dyea by either hitch-hiking or contacting a number of taxi services in town. Pioneer Taxi (tel (907) 983-2623) charges $10 per person for a ride out to the trailhead, which seems to be the going rate.

Getting Back
At the northern end of the trail, hikers can catch the White Pass & Yukon Railroad from

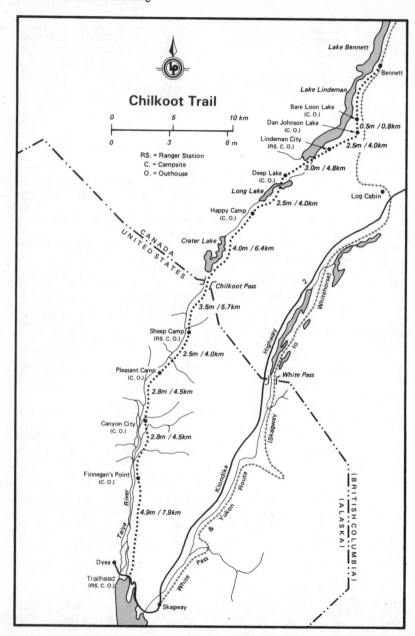

Chilkoot Trail

0		5		10 km
0	3			6 m

RS. = Ranger Station
C. = Campsite
O. = Outhouse

Lake Bennett

Bennett

Lake Lindeman

Bare Loon Lake
(C. O.)

Dan Johnson Lake
(C. O.)

0.5m / 0.8km

Lindeman City
(RS. C. O.)

2.5m / 4.0km

3.0m / 4.8km

Deep Lake
(C. O.)

Long Lake

Log Cabin

2.5m / 4.0km

Happy Camp
(C. O.)

Crater Lake

4.0m / 6.4km

CANADA
UNITED STATES

Chilkoot Pass

3.5m / 5.7km

Highway 2 to Whitehorse

Sheep Camp
(RS. C. O.)

2.5m / 4.0km

Pleasant Camp
(C. O.)

White Pass

2.8m / 4.5km

Canyon City
(C. O.)

2.8m / 4.5km

(Skagway)

Finnegan's Point
(C. O.)

Klondike

Yukon Route

4.9m / 7.9km

Taiya River

&

Dyea

White

Pass

Trailhead
(RS. C. O.)

Skagway

(BRITISH COLUMBIA)
(ALASKA)

mid-June to mid-September, but the trip begins with a track motorcar service from Bennett to Fraser. At Fraser you transfer to the narrow gauge train for the scenic ride to Skagway. The motorcar departs Bennett daily at 8.30 pm and 1.15 pm and the fare from Bennett to Skagway is $67. You can also catch the track car at Lindeman, a new stop at *Mile 37.7* (60.3 km) where the trail first joins the track. From Skagway, the train departs at 7.45 am and 1 pm for those who want to begin at the northern trailhead.

There are also two other ways to leave the trail at the northern end: you can hike 6 miles (10 km) south from Bare Loon Lake Campground to the Log Cabin on Klondike Highway or take the track car from the Lindeman station to the Log Cabin. An Alaskon Express bus stops daily at the Log Cabin on its way south to Skagway. On Saturday, Monday and Thursday the bus departs at 4.30 pm; the rest of the week it departs at 6.30 pm.

A north travelling bus reaches the warming hut at 10.45 am on Saturday, Monday and Thursday on its way to Whitehorse and 9.15 am the rest of the week. The one-way fare from Log Cabin to Skagway is $16 and from Log Cabin to Whitehorse is $51. The bus company can be contacted in Skagway during the summer at (907) 983-2241; all departures from Log Cabin are given in Yukon Time.

The alternative is Chilkoot Boat Tours, the ferry service which sprang up after the White Pass & Yukon Railroad ceased operations. The ferry carries hikers from the trail's end across Lake Bennett to Carcross, where you can catch an Alaskon Express bus north or south. Arrangements are made at site No 20 of the Lake Bennett Campground or by calling (403) 668-7766 in Whitehorse. The vast majority of hikers walk out to the Klondike Highway.

More Information

Stop at the National Park Service visitor centre in the refurbished railroad depot on the corner of 2nd Ave and Broadway, Skagway, for current weather and trail conditions, exhibits and films on the area's history, and hiking maps. It's hard to get lost on the Chilkoot Trail as there seems to be an orange marker every 50 yards/metres. For more information contact the National Park Service (tel (907) 983-2921) at PO Box 517, Skagway, Alaska 99840.

Section	miles	km
Dyea to Canyon City	7.7	12.4
Canyon City to Sheep Camp	5.3	8.5
Sheep Camp to Chilkoot Pass	3.5	5.6
Chilkoot Pass to Happy Camp	4.0	6.4
Happy Camp to Deep Lake	2.5	4.0
Deep Lake to Lindeman City	3.0	4.8
Lindeman to Bare Loon Lake	3.0	4.8
Bare Loon Lake to Log Cabin	6.0	9.6
Bare Loon to Lake Bennett	4.0	6.4

RESURRECTION PASS TRAIL

Located in the Chugach National Forest, this 39 mile (62 km) trail was carved by prospectors in the late 1800s and today is the most popular hiking route on the Kenai Peninsula. The trip can be done in 3 days by a keen hiker but most people prefer to do it in 5 to 7 days to make the most of the immense beauty of the region and the excellent fishing in Trout, Juneau and Swan lakes.

There is a series of eight US Forest Service (USFS) cabins along the route for $20 per night. They have to be reserved in advance at the USFS office in Anchorage and, being quite popular, are fully-booked for most of the summer which makes last-minute reservations almost impossible. Most hikers take a tent and a camp stove, as fallen wood can sometimes be scarce during the busy summer.

Getting Started

The northern trailhead is 20 miles (32 km) from the Seward Highway and 4 miles (6.4 km) south of Hope on Resurrection Creek Rd. Hope, an historical mining community founded in 1896 by gold seekers, is a charming, out-of-the-way place to visit, but Hope Highway is not an easy road to hitchhike. Patience is the key as eventually someone will give you a lift.

From Hope Highway you turn south at the

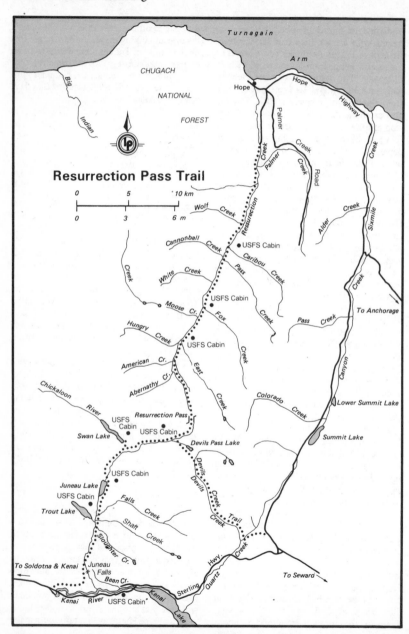

posted Resurrection Pass Trail signs onto Resurrection Creek Rd, passing the fork to Palmer Creek Rd. The southern trailhead is on the Sterling Highway, near Cooper Landing or 53 miles (85 km) east of Soldotna and 106 miles (171 km) south of Anchorage. Hitchhiking is easy on the Sterling and Seward highways in either direction, or you can hop on an Intercity bus out of Anchorage (see the Bus section in the Getting Around chapter). A quarter of a mile (0.4 km) east of the southern trailhead along the Sterling Highway is the Russian River USFS Campground (84 campsites, $6 per night for tents) and the trailhead for the Russian Lakes Trail.

An alternative route that avoids travelling to the remote northern trailhead is the Devils Pass Trail, which is posted at *Mile 39* (62.4 km) of the Seward Highway, 88 miles (142 km) south of Anchorage. The 10 mile (16 km) path leaves the highway and climbs to Devil's Pass at 2400 feet (720 metres), where it joins the Resurrection Pass Trail. By using the Devils Pass Trail and the lower portion of Resurrection Pass Trail, you can hike from the Seward Highway to the Sterling Highway in 2 days.

More Information

For more information on the trail or reserving cabins along it, contact the USFS office for the Anchorage District: Chugach National Forest (tel (907) 261-2500), 201 East 9th St, Suite 206, Anchorage, Alaska 99501.

Bull Moose

Section	miles	km
Resurrection Creek Rd to Caribou Creek Cabin	6.9	11.1
Caribou Creek to Fox Creek Campsite	4.7	7.6
Fox Creek to East Creek Cabin	2.8	4.5
East Creek to Resurrection Pass	4.9	7.9
Resurrection Pass to Devil's Pass Cabin	2.1	3.4
Devil's Pass to Swan Lake Cabin	4.4	7.1
Swan Lake to Juneau Lake Cabin	3.3	5.3
Juneau Lake to Trout Lake Cabin	2.7	4.3
Trout Lake to Juneau Creek Falls	2.3	3.7
Juneau Creek Falls to Sterling Highway	4.4	7.1

RUSSIAN LAKES TRAIL

This 21 mile (34 km), 2 day hike is an ideal alternative for those who do not want to over-extend themselves in the Chugach National Forest. The trail is well travelled, well maintained and well marked during the summer and not too demanding on the legs. Most of the hike is a pleasant forest walk broken up by patches of wildflowers, ripe berries, lakes and streams.

The walk's highlights include the possibility of viewing moose or bears, the impressive glaciated mountains across from Upper Russian Lake or, for those carrying a fishing pole, the chance to catch your own dinner. The trek offers good fishing for Dolly Varden, rainbow trout and salmon in the upper portions of the Russian River, rainbow

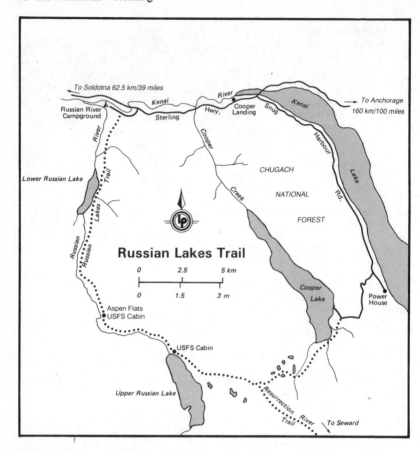

trout in Lower Russian Lake, Aspen Flats and Upper Russian Lake, and Dolly Varden in Cooper Lake near the eastern trailhead.

If you plan ahead, there are two USFS cabins on the trail for $20 per night but you need to reserve them in advance. One is on Upper Russian Lake, 9 miles (14.4 km) from the Cooper Lake trailhead. The second is at Aspen Flats, another 3 miles (4.8 km) northwest along the trail or 12 miles (19 km) from the western trailhead.

Getting Started

It is easier to start from the Cooper Lake trailhead, the higher end of the trail. To reach the trailhead, turn off at *Mile 47.8* (76.5 km) of Sterling Highway onto Snug Harbour Rd. The road leads 12 miles (19.3 km) to Cooper Lake and ends at a marked parking lot and the trailhead.

The western trailhead is on a side road marked Russian River USFS Campground at *Mile 52.7* (84.3 km) of the Sterling Highway. Hike 0.9 mile (1.4 km) to the end of the campground road to reach a parking lot at the beginning of the trail. If you're planning to camp at Russian River the night before starting the trek, keep in mind that the camp-

ground is extremely popular during the salmon-running season and fills up with anglers by early afternoon.

More Information

For more information on the trail or to reserve cabins, contact the Anchorage District USFS Office (tel (907) 261-2500), 201 East 9th St, Suite 206, Anchorage, Alaska 99501.

Section	miles	km
Cooper Lake trailhead to		
junction of Resurrection River Trail	5	8.0
trail junction to		
Upper Russian Lake Cabin	4	6.4
Upper Russian Lake to		
Aspen Flats Cabin	3	4.8
Aspen Flats to		
Lower Russian Lake	6	9.6
Lower Russian Lake to		
Russian River Campground	3	4.8

JOHNSON PASS TRAIL

In the same area as the Resurrection Pass and Russian Lakes trails, and nearly as popular, is the Johnson Pass Trail, a 2 day and 23 mile (37 km) hike over an alpine pass 1500 feet (450 metres) in elevation. The trail was originally part of the Old Iditarod Trail blazed by prospectors from Seward to the golden beaches of Nome, and later was used as part of the old Seward mail route.

Most of the trail is fairly level, which makes for easy hiking, while anglers will find arctic grayling in Bench Lake and rainbow trout in Johnson Lake. Plan to camp at either Johnson Lake or Johnson Pass, but keep in mind that these places are above the

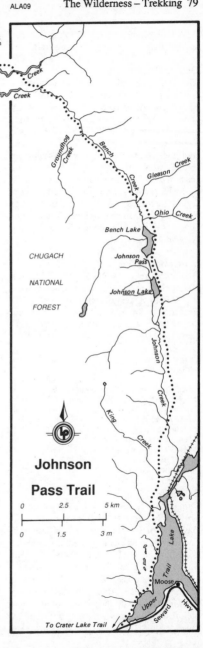

Johnson
Pass Trail

tree line, making it necessary to carry a small stove. There are no cabins on this trail.

Getting Started

The trail can be hiked from either direction. The northern trailhead is at *Mile 64* (103 km) of the Seward Highway or 96 miles (154 km) south of Anchorage; there is a gravel road marked Forest Service Trail No 10 that leads a short way to a parking lot and the trail. The trail goes south over Johnson Pass and then to the shore of Upper Trail Lake before reaching the Seward Highway again at *Mile 32.5* (52.3 km). Hitchhiking to or from either end of the trail is easy during the summer, or arrangements can be made with Seward Bus Lines (see the Bus section in the Getting Around chapter).

More Information

Because the trail lies in the Chugach National Forest, contact the Anchorage District USFS Office (tel (907) 261-2500), 201 East 9th St, Suite 206, Anchorage, Alaska, 99501 for more information and trail conditions.

Section	miles	km
northern trailhead to		
Bench Creek Bridge	3.8	6.1
Bench Creek Bridge to Bench Lake	5.5	8.8
Bench Lake to Johnson Pass	0.7	1.1
Johnson Pass to Johnson Lake	0.6	1.0
Johnson Lake to		
Johnson Creek Bridge	5.1	8.2
Johnson Creek Bridge to		
Upper Trail Lake	3.7	5.9
Upper Trail Lake to		
Seward Highway	3.6	5.8

COASTAL TRAIL

Caines Head State Recreation Area is a 6000 acre (2400 hectares) park on Resurrection Bay south of Seward. This area has long been favoured by boat and kayak enthusiasts who go ashore to explore the remains of Fort McGilvray and the South Beach Garrison, old WW II outposts that were built as a result of the Japanese attack on the Aleutian Islands. Along with the remains of an Army pier, firing platforms and the 'garrison ghost town' at South Beach, the park also has much

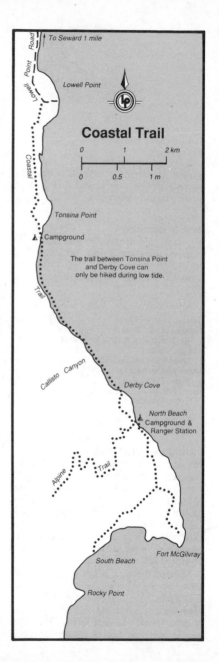

natural beauty including a massive headland that raises 650 feet (195 metres) above the water and provides sweeping views of Resurrection Bay.

The Coastal Trail is a 4.5 mile (7.3 km) one-way hike from Lowell Point to North Beach, where you can continue along old army roads to Fort McGilvray and South Beach. Along the way you pass a walk-in campground, vault toilets and a picnic shelter at Tonsina Point, and a campground, picnic shelter and ranger station at North Beach. This makes an excellent overnight trip, combining history with great scenery and a opportunity to climb a spur trail into alpine areas; it's also affordable as the trailhead is an easy walk from Seward.

Getting Started
The trailhead is at the end of Lowell Point Rd, a mile (1.6 km) south of Seward's ferry terminal. Before leaving town, purchase a tide book; the 3 mile (4.8 km) stretch between Tonsina Point and North Beach can only be hiked during low tide. Plan to leave Seward 2 hours before low tide to avoid becoming stranded along the way. Due to steep cliffs along the shoreline, it's not possible to follow the beach from the trailhead to Tonsina Point. The trek to North Beach is a 2 to 3 hour walk at which point you have to stay until the next low tide (12 hours later) before returning.

More Information
For a brochure on the park, stop at the Caines Head State Recreation Area office (tel 224-3434) on the 2nd floor of the City/State Building at the corner of 5th Ave and Adams St in Seward.

Section	miles	km
northern trailhead to Tonsina Point	1.5	2.4
Tonsina Point to North Beach	3.0	4.9
North Beach to Fort McGilvray	2.0	3.2
North Beach to South Beach	2.5	4.1

PINNELL MOUNTAIN TRAIL
The midnight sun is the outstanding sight on the Pinnell Mountain Trail, a 24 mile (39 km) trek, 85 miles (137 km) north-east of Fairbanks on the Steese Highway. From 18 to 25 June, the sun never sets on the trail, giving hikers 24 hour days. The polar phenomenon of the sun sitting above the horizon at midnight can be viewed and photographed at several high points on the trail, including the Eagle Summit trailhead.

The route is mostly tundra ridgetops that lie above 3500 feet (1050 metres) and can be steep and rugged at times. The other highlight of the trip are the wildflowers (unmatched in much of the state) which carpet the arctic-alpine tundra slopes, beginning in late May and peaking in mid-June. Hikers may spot small bands of caribou along with grizzly bears, rock rabbits and an occasional wolf or lynx. The views from the ridge tops are spectacular, with the Alaska Range visible to the south and the Yukon Flats to the north.

Getting Started
The trail is a 3 day adventure, if you hike it at 8 miles (13 km) a day. Most hikers begin at the Eagle Summit trailhead on *Mile 107.3* (172.6 km) of the Steese Highway, the higher end of the trail. The western end lies at Twelvemile Summit, closer to Fairbanks at *Mile 85* (137 km) of the Steese Highway. There are two three-sided shelters built by the Youth Conservation Corps (YCC) which are open to anyone without reservations or fees. It is still necessary to bring a tent with good bug netting; use the shelters as your kitchen.

Snow cover can be expected in May (with patches remaining to June) and mid-September. These are good sources of water which is scarce on this trail. Bring at least 2 quarts (2 litres) of water per person and then refill your supply at either snow patches, springs or tundra pools at every opportunity. Boil or filter all standing water from pools and slow-running springs.

The winds can be brutal in this barren region, as there are no trees to slow the gusts that can come howling over the ridges. Bring

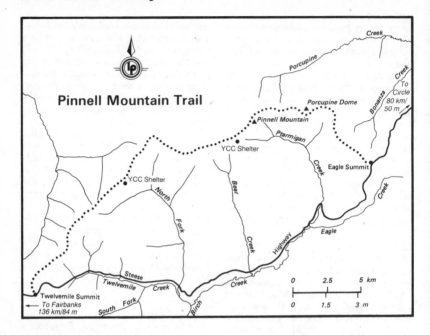

Pinnell Mountain Trail

a wind screen for your camp stove, otherwise cooking dinner can become a long ordeal.

Traffic on the Steese Highway is light this far out of Fairbanks, but there is a trickle. A Bureau of Land Management (BLM) traffic survey reported that an average of 800 vehicles per day use the road and most hikers end up hitching back to the trailhead where they began.

If there are two or more of you, an alternative is to rent a car through All Star Car Rental in Fairbanks (tel (907) 479-4229), $32.95 per day plus mileage, and combine the trip with a drive to Circle Hot Springs or the wilderness town of Circle on the Yukon River. Also check into Spell of the Yukon Tours (tel (907) 455-6128), a small company with package tours that include a night at the hot springs – you may be able to arrange transport to the trailheads and back. There is a gasoline station and restaurant at *Mile 101* (162 km) of the Steese Highway, but stock up in Fairbanks.

More Information

For trail conditions or a free trail map, contact the Bureau of Land Management office in Fairbanks by writing to BLM District Office (tel (907) 474-2200), 1150 University Ave, Fairbanks, Alaska 99709-3844.

Section	miles	km
Eagle Summit trailhead to		
Porcupine Dome	5.0	8.0
Porcupine Dome to 1st YCC shelter	4.0	6.4
1st shelter to 2nd YCC shelter	7.0	11.2
2nd shelter to Twelvemile Summit	7.0	11.2

WHITE MOUNTAIN TRAIL

The Bureau of Land Management (BLM), which maintains the Pinnell Mountain Trail, also administers the White Mountain Trail. This 21 mile (34 km) return route winds through dense spruce forest, traverses scenic alpine ridgetops and arctic tundra, and ends at Beaver Creek in the foothills of the majestic White Mountains.

White Mountain Trails
Beaver Creek Canoe Route

White Mountain Trail & Beaver Creek Canoe Route

On the banks of the creek is the Borealis-Le Fevre Cabin which can be reserved for $15 a night. Reservations aren't really necessary as the last 2.5 miles (4 km) of this trail drops off the ridgeline and descends into a muskeg area where hikers must ford up to four streams. The cabin receives little use during the summer as most parties end the day camping above the tree line as opposed to dealing with the low-lying swamp.

Even stopping short of the cabin, the hike is a steady 2 day walk from the trailhead at *Mile 28* (45 km) of the Elliott Highway, 31 miles (50 km) north of Fairbanks. As on the Pinnell Mountain Trail, you need to bring water which is scarce in the alpine sections. Highlights of the trek are the views on top of Wickersham Dome, which include Mt Mc-Kinley, the White Mountains and the Alaskan Range.

Getting Started

Don't confuse the White Mountain Summer Trail (also called Summit Trail), which was made for hikers, with the Winter Trail (Wickersham Trail), 4.5 miles (7.2 km) closer to Fairbanks on the Elliott Highway. The Winter Trail was cut for snow machines,

Borealis Le-Fevre Cabin

cross-country skiing and people using snow shoes, and leads through swampy, muskeg lowlands. The two trails meet up 2 miles (3.2 km) south of the Borealis-Le Fevre Cabin.

Stock up with provisions in Fairbanks; the last place to purchase food and gasoline is at Fox on the junction of the Steese and Elliott highways. There is usually more traffic on the Elliott Highway than on the back portions of the Steese, but it is still slow for hitchhiking.

More Information
The BLM District Office in Fairbanks (tel (907) 474-2200), 1150 University Ave, Fairbanks, Alaska 99709-3844, can supply a free map that lacks topographical detail but contains plenty of information on the trail. The office will also have current information on trail conditions and the availability of water, and is the place to reserve the Borealis-Le Fevre Cabin.

Section	miles	km
Summer trailhead to		
Wickersham Creek	2.0	3.2
Wickersham Creek to		
Wickersham Dome	2.0	3.2
Wickersham Dome to		
Winter Trail junction	13.0	21.0
trail junction to		
Borealis-Le Fevre Cabin	2.0	3.2

MT EIELSON CIRCUIT – DENALI NATIONAL PARK
Denali National Park & Preserve is a paradise for backpackers – especially backpackers on a budget. You could spend days or even weeks at the park and only pay for the food you eat and the $3 entry fee.

The reserve is divided into 43 backcountry zones and only a regulated number of overnight hikers, usually from two to 12, are allowed into each area. In the height of the summer, it may be difficult to get a permit into the section of your choice and other sections will be closed off entirely when the impact of visitors is too great for wildlife. The number of visitors tapers off dramatically in late August. Many people consider the end of August to mid-September as the prime time to see the park as the crowds and bugs are gone and the autumn colours are setting in.

There are many treks in the park. If time allows, begin by taking a ride on the shuttle bus and doing a day hike to get acquainted with a trail-less park, fording streams and rivers, and reading your topographical map accurately; then plan an overnight excursion. The Mt Eielson Circuit, 14 miles (22.5 km) long, is a leisurely 2 day walk, or a 3 day trek if a day is spent scrambling up any of the nearby peaks.

The hike offers an excellent opportunity to view Mt McKinley, Muldrow Glacier or an abundance of wildlife. The route begins and ends at the Eielson Visitor Center and involves climbing 1300 feet (390 metres) through the pass between Mt Eielson and Castle Peak. The most difficult part of the walk, however, is crossing Thorofare River, which should be done in tennis shoes with an ice axe or sturdy pole in hand.

From Eielson Visitor Center, *Mile 66* (106 km) of the park road, you begin the route by dropping down the steep hill to Gorge Creek, crossing it and continuing south to the Thorofare River. Follow the tundra shelf along the east side of the river until you cross Sunrise Creek, which flows into the Thorofare.

The Thorofare River must then be forded

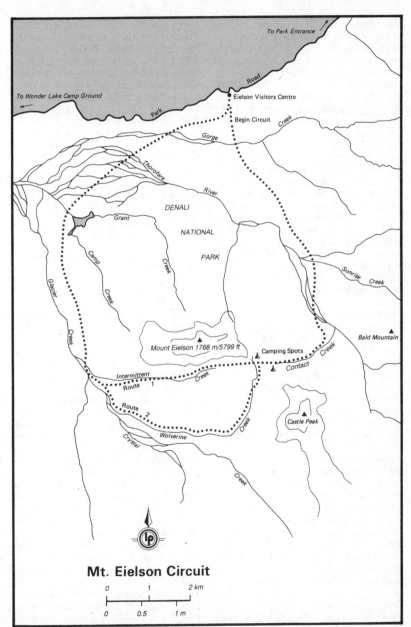

Mt. Eielson Circuit

with extreme caution. Once on the west bank of the river, continue hiking south until you reach the junction of Contact Creek and the Thorofare River. The creek is due west of Bald Mountain Summit and leads up to the pass between Mt Eielson and Castle Peak. The pass, at an elevation of 4700 feet (1400 metres), is a good place to spend the night, as views of Mt McKinley are possible in clear weather.

From the pass, hike west towards Intermittent Creek, where rock cairns point the way. The creek leads to the gravel bars of Granite Creek on the south-west side of Mt Eielson. This section of the river makes for easy hiking or a good campsite for those who want to tackle Mt Eielson from the west side, its most manageable approach. Head north along Glacier Creek until you reach the flood plain with the many braids of Camp Creek and the Thorofare River woven across it. Cross the channels and proceed north-east towards the Eielson Visitor Center.

Getting Started

There is information about the park in the Denali National Park section in the Interior chapter. There are several ways of getting to the park from either Fairbanks or Anchorage, including a handful of bus companies and the Alaska Railroad (see the Bus and Train sections in the Getting Around chapter).

Once at the park, most backpackers stay at the free Morino Campground and then obtain their backcountry permit from the Riley Creek Visitor Center. Permits are handed out on a first-come, first-serve basis but the zones around the Eielson Visitor Center are extremely popular and if you arrive in July or early August it might be a 2 or 3 day wait before you obtain one. Both visitor centres sell topographical maps; the Mt Eielson Circuit is contained on one section – Mt McKinley B-1. There is a small store within the park headquarters that sells food and camp-stove fuel, but it is best to stock up in Anchorage or Fairbanks.

More Information

For a shoe-box full of free information about the park, contact the Denali National Park & Preserve (tel (907) 683-2686 – recorded message), PO Box 9, Denali Park, Alaska 99755. If you are in Anchorage, contact the National Park Service centre for information about Denali or any national park in Alaska at the Alaska Public Lands Information Center (tel (907) 271-2737), 605 West 4th Ave, Anchorage, Alaska 99501.

Section*	miles	km
Eielson Visitor Center to		
Gorge Creek	1.0	1.6
Gorge Creek to		
Sunrise-Thorofare junction	2.0	3.2
junction to Contact Creek	1.0	1.6
Contact Creek to Pass Summit	1.2	1.9
Pass Summit to Glacier Creek	3.3	5.3
Glacier Creek to flood plains	2.5	4.0
flood plains to Eielson Visitor Center	3.0	4.8

* This is a route not a trail, so all distances are rough estimates only.

DEER MOUNTAIN TRAIL

Located in Ketchikan, the Deer Mountain Trail is often the first hike visitors do in the north country, and rarely does it disappoint them. The trail is a steady but manageable climb to the sharp peak above the city, with incredible views of the Tongass Narrows and the surrounding area.

What many backpackers don't realise is that the Deer Mountain Trail is only part of a challenging, overnight alpine trail system. This 11 mile (17.7 km) trip, which includes spending the night in a free USFS cabin, begins with the 3 mile (4.8 km) Deer Mountain Trail which leads into the Blue Lake Trail. This path is a natural route along an alpine ridge extending 4 miles (6.4 km) north to John Mountain. Here, hikers can return to the Ketchikan road system by taking the John Mountain Trail for 2 miles (3.2 km) to Upper Silvis Lake and then following an old access road from the hydroplant on Lower Silvis Lake to the parking lot off Beaver Falls Highway.

Deer Mountain is a well-maintained and heavily used trail during the summer. Even though it is a steady climb, the hike to the

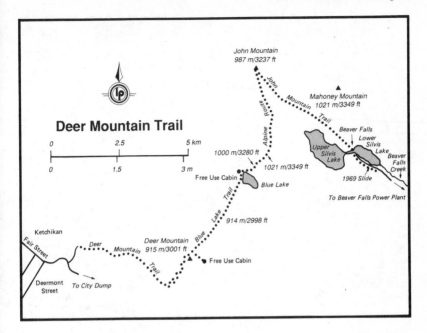

Deer Mountain Trail

John Mountain
987 m/3237 ft

Mahoney Mountain
1021 m/3349 ft

John Mountain Trail

Alpine Route

Beaver Falls

Lower
Silvis
Lake

Upper
Silvis
Lake

Beaver
Falls
Creek

1000 m/3280 ft

1021 m/3349 ft

Free Use Cabin

Blue Lake

1969 Slide

To Beaver Falls Power Plant

Blue Lake Trail

914 m/2998 ft

Ketchikan

Fair Street

Deer Mountain Trail

Deer Mountain
915 m/3001 ft

Free Use Cabin

Deermont
Street

To City Dump

0   2.5   5 km

0   1.5   3 m

summit is not overly difficult. A quarter of a mile (0.4 km) before the summit you pass the junction to Blue Lake and the posted trail to the Deer Mountain USFS Cabin. The cabin, located above the tree line, sleeps eight and is filled on a first-come, first-serve basis. The Blue Lake Trail crosses alpine country with natural but good footing, although in rainy weather it may be difficult to follow. The scenery from the trail is spectacular.

Within 2 miles (3.2 km) from the junction of the Deer Mountain Trail, you arrive at a second free-use USFS cabin on the shore of Blue Lake. This cabin also sleeps eight and, at 2700 feet (810 metres), is above the tree line in a scenic setting.

The John Mountain Trail has 20% grades on the first mile from Upper Silvis Lake and then goes through alpine country; the trail is marked by a series of steel posts. It is a fairly difficult track to follow and presents hikers with a challenge in reading their topographical maps and choosing the right route.

Getting Started

The trailhead for the Deer Mountain Trail can be reached by following the gravel road from the corner of Fair and Deermount streets in Ketchikan, past a subdivision towards the city dump. Just before reaching the dump, a trail sign points left to a side road which leads to the trailhead and small parking lot.

To get to the start of the John Mountain Trail, hitchhike 12.9 miles (20.8 km) east of Ketchikan along the South Tongass Highway (also known as the Beaver Falls Highway) to its end at the power plant. There is a 2 mile (3.2 km) hike along an old access road from the power plant at the tidewater to the hydroplant on Lower Silvis Lake.

As the road to Upper Silvis Lake was destroyed by a landslide, some scrambling up the steep hillside is necessary. There are a couple of ways to reach the upper lake; one begins on the roof of the lower lake power-house, following an old outlet stream course.

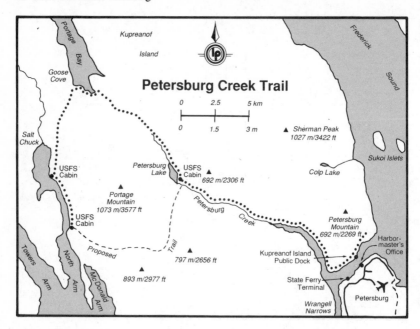

The John Mountain Trail begins at the old outlet at the western end of the upper lake.

More Information

The cabins and trails are maintained by the US Forest Service (USFS), which have their main headquarters and visitor centre in the Federal Building on Stedman St in Ketchikan. You can contact them for trail conditions or more information at USFS Office (tel (907) 225-3101), Federal Building, Ketchikan, Alaska 99901.

Section	miles	km
Deer Mountain trailhead to		
Deer Mountain Summit	3.1	5.0
Summit to Blue Lake Cabin	2.2	3.5
Blue Lake Cabin to John Mountain	2.0	3.2
John Mountain to Upper Silvis Lake	2.0	3.2
Upper Silvis Lake to		
South Tongass Highway	2.0	3.2

PETERSBURG CREEK TRAIL

A short hop across the Wrangell Narrows

from the fishing community of Petersburg is Petersburg Creek and the first of four trails that can be combined into a circular hike connecting two US Forest Service (USFS) cabins. The Petersburg Creek Trail has been brushed and re-marked and now provides backpackers with a wilderness opportunity and access to USFS cabins that don't require expensive bush-plane travel. Both cabins need to be reserved and cost $20 per night.

Petersburg Creek Trail is entirely planked, but those planning to go onto Portage Bay or Salt Chuck should consider carrying along a pair of rubber boots or 'Southeast sneakers', as you will encounter wet muskeg areas or stretches flooded out by beaver dams. Also bring a fishing pole, as there are good spots in the creek for Dolly Varden and cutthroat trout. In August and early September, there are large coho-salmon runs throughout the area that attract anglers and bears.

The trek begins across Wrangell Narrows from Petersburg at the Kupreanof Island public dock. From the dock a partial board-walk leads south for 2 miles (3.2 km) past a handful of cabins and then turns north-west up the tidewater arm of the creek, located almost directly across Wrangell Narrows from the ferry terminal.

A well-planked trail goes from the saltwater arm and continues along the northern side of the freshwater creek to the Petersburg Lake USFS Cabin on the eastern end of the lake. From the cabin, a second trail continues north to Portage Bay, and though some sections might be hard to follow, it is marked with a series of blue diamond-shaped blazes on the trees.

Leading west from the trail to Portage Bay is the trail to Salt Chuck; you definitely need rubber boots to make it through the wet sections on this path. It's the most challenging of the three trails but Salt Chuck East USFS Cabin, an A-Frame with a extended side, is in a beautiful spot that is surrounded by mountains. The cabin is equipped with a row boat and there's good trout fishing nearby. The cabin is often reserved well in advance during the August salmon runs, but it is easy to obtain from mid-June to late July.

Someday the USFS plans to turn this into a circular route by building a trail around the south side of Portage Mountain from Salt Chuck back to the Petersburg Lake USFS Cabin. But that project is continually being postponed due to lack of funds. Most backpackers can handle the trek into Petersburg Lake but to go beyond is a trip for those with experience in wilderness travel.

Getting Started

The only hitch to this trip is getting across Wrangell Narrows to the public dock on Kupreanof Island. The USFS office above the post office in Petersburg provides a list of charter-boat operators and places to rent a skiff. This can be expensive as a boat can cost as much as $150. The cheapest and probably the easiest way to get across Wrangell Narrows is to hitch a ride with one of the boats that cross the narrows every day.

Go to the skiff float in the North Harbor (Old Harbor) near the Harbormaster's office

on the waterfront and ask around for boats crossing. A small population lives on the other side of the narrows so boats are constantly crossing, though at times you might have to wait a bit. Also try to inquire at the Harbormaster's office, though at times they tend to discourage this practice.

Those who arrive at Petersburg with their own kayak can paddle to the creek during high tide to avoid much of the hike along the tidewater arm. This is one trip that you'll want good waterproof clothing and rubber boots. Bring a tent or plan on reserving the cabins at least 2 months in advance; even earlier if you want to tackle the route in August during the coho-salmon runs.

More Information

The Petersburg District USFS office is on the 2nd floor of the post office along Main St. Make sure you contact the office before embarking to double-check on trail conditions and the status of the new trail from Salt Chuck to Petersburg Lake. Contact them at Petersburg Ranger District (tel (907) 772-3871), PO Box 1328, Petersburg, Alaska 99833.

Section	miles	km
Kupreanof Island dock to tidewater arm	2.0	3.2
tidewater arm to Petersburg Creek	3.0	4.8
trail by creek to USFS cabin	6.5	10.4
USFS cabin to Portage Bay	5.5	8.8
Portage Bay to Salt Chuck East Cabin	6.0	9.6

DAN MOLLER TRAIL

Across the Gastineau Channel from the centre of Juneau is the Dan Moller Trail. It was originally built during the 1930s for downhill skiers and at one time had three warming huts and two toll ropes along it. Today, the skiers continue along the North Douglas Highway to the Eaglecrest Ski Area, while the Dan Moller Trail has become a popular access to the alpine meadows in the middle of Douglas Island.

The trail is 3.3 miles (5.3 km) and leads to a beautiful alpine bowl where the US Forest Service (USFS) has restored the remaining ski cabin. As with all USFS cabins, you have

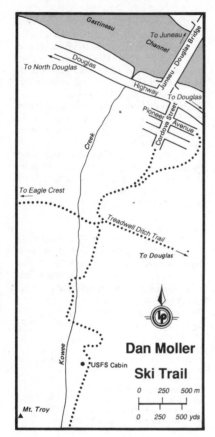

Juneau Youth Hostel. You can easily walk to it or catch the minibus to Douglas and get off at Cordova St, which leads to a growth of apartments and condominiums known as West Juneau. From Cordova St, turn left (south-east) onto Pioneer Ave and follow it to the end of the pavement.

The trail begins past the fifth house on the right where there is a trailhead and a small parking area. An old jeep track serves as the first part of the trail before it emerges into open muskeg. Most of it is planked but waterproof boots are a must. The hike is a steady climb to the alpine bowl but is not overly tiring; plan on 6 hours for the round trip.

More Information
Contact the USFS office in Juneau for trail conditions and reserving the Dan Moller USFS Cabin: Juneau District Office (tel (907) 586-8751), Juneau Centennial Hall, 101 Egan Drive, Juneau, Alaska 99801.

Section	miles	km
Youth Hostel to Dan Moller trailhead	1.5	2.4
Dan Moller trailhead to		
junction with Treadwell Ditch Trail	0.8	1.3
trail junction to upper cabin	2.5	4.0

WOLF POINT – GLACIER BAY NATIONAL PARK
Nestled in the northern part of Alaska's Southeast is the state's frozen gem – the Glacier Bay National Park & Preserve. The preserve has spectacular mountain scenery, impressive fjord-like bays and inlets, and abundant wildlife including harbour seals, whales and porpoises. However, its major draw card for visitors and outdoor enthusiasts is its tidewater glaciers – those magnificent frozen rivers that roar, rumble and thunder into the upper reaches of the bay, filling the water with sculptured ice.

Glacier Bay is not just another trail-less park in Alaska's wilderness; it should be viewed as a marine park, with the kayak being the most practical way of travelling the backcountry. Every summer, uninformed visitors are disappointed that there are no

to reserve it in advance ($20 per night) but from 10 am to 5 pm it's shared by everybody as a warming hut.

Even if you can't secure the cabin, don't pass up this trail. Camping in the alpine bowl is superb and an afternoon or an extra day can be spent scrambling up and along the ridge that surrounds the bowl and forms the backbone of Douglas Island. From the ridge, there are scenic views of Douglas Island, Admiralty Island and Stephens Passage.

Getting Started
The trailhead is 1.5 miles (2.4 km) from the

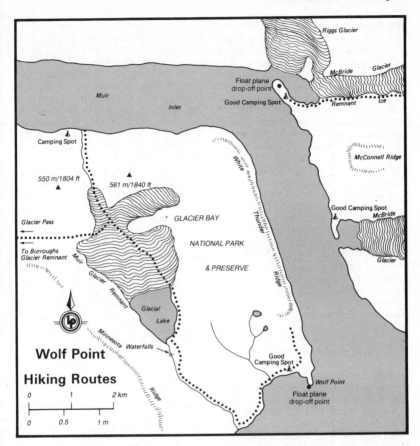

glaciers near Bartlett Cove (park headquarters), and it is impossible to hike to the nearest one, some 40 miles (64 km) up the bay. The most common way to explore the park is to rent a kayak, board a tour boat and spend a few days paddling the well-protected inlets up Glacier Bay.

Backpackers who want nothing to do with small boats, double-bladed paddles and spray skirts still have an opportunity to explore the park and view glaciers. Wolf Point, located in Muir Inlet, is one of the few areas where hikers can spend several days exploring the park on foot and view a number

of glaciers. Unfortunately, the only way to reach it is by float plane as Muir Inlet was recently designated a wilderness area and ruled off limits to all motorised boat traffic, including the tour boat that used to drop off kayakers and hikers.

The cove formed by Wolf Point is a river delta that offers good camping. From here it is an easy 1.2 mile (1.9 km) climb to White Thunder Ridge at 700 feet (213 metres), where there are good views of McBride and Riggs glaciers. The most popular overnight trip from Wolf Point is to hike north across the Muir Glacier Remnant, reaching Muir

Inlet again where the ice pack is thick and mother seals and their pups rest on icebergs.

To reach Muir Glacier Remnant, hike 0.5 mile (0.8 km) along the shoreline south of Wolf Point to the second river that flows into Muir Inlet; this is the larger river of the two and is much too wide and deep to ford. Follow the river bank for 0.6 mile (1 km) and you will approach a large waterfall. At this point you will be forced to hike up a steep bank and into the thick alder around the falls for a quarter of a mile (0.4 km), but you will emerge to the stunning sight of Muir Glacier Remnant and the glacial lake in front of it.

After hiking around the lake, climb onto the ice and head towards the distinct 800 foot (244 metre) rock knob that extends from White Thunder Ridge into the ice field. On the topographic maps it is shown as surrounded by ice, but that is no longer true. Directly west of this is Glacier Pass, while to the north the ice continues towards a pass between a pair of 1800 feet (549 metre) knobs. Once beyond these knobs you follow a stream down to the shoreline of Muir Inlet. This far up Muir Inlet the terrain is bare and very rocky, forcing you to search a little for a flat spot on which to pitch your tent.

Getting Started

Turn to the Glacier Bay section in the Southeast chapter for general information about Glacier Bay National Park & Preserve. Once at Bartlett Cove, backpackers can stay in the free campground while preparing for their excursion up the bay. Call at the visitor centre on the foot of the dock to obtain a backcountry permit and to purchase the proper topographic maps (for Wolf Point you will need two: Skagway A-4 and Mt Fairweather D-1). Then arrange transport to the area through Glacier Bay Air from its desk in the Glacier Bay Lodge.

You must pack waterproof clothing, pants, parka and a camp stove. Stock up on supplies in Juneau to avoid having to purchase anything in Gustavus, the small settlement just outside Bartlett Cove. Stagnant glacial remnants are composed of ice with a rough surface, filled with minerals and rocks that

offer good footing. Crampons are not needed, though some hikers carry an ice axe or stout pole with them to check cracks before stepping over them.

For the most part, Muir Remnant is a gently sloping, unbroken section of glacier except for areas around the fringes and a few crevasses here and there. It is best to stay away from such areas when hiking over the ice, and you should always travel in pairs.

The overnight trip from Wolf Point to the other side of Muir Inlet is a 6.5 mile (10.4 km) walk, and is a challenge for experienced hikers only. If you have the equipment and the time, this adventure will provide more intimate experiences of the park's backcountry than a day spent on a crowded tour boat.

More Information

In Juneau, the US Forest Service office in the Centennial Hall supplies information on Glacier Bay along with maps and hand-outs. For information before you depart, contact the National Park Service (tel (907) 697-2230), Glacier Bay National Park, Gustavus, Alaska 99826.

Section*	miles	km
Wolf Point to Glacial River	0.5	0.8
mouth of river inland to Glacial Lake	0.9	1.5
around Glacial Lake to		
Muir Remnant	1.2	1.9
across Muir Remnant to		
800 foot (244 metre) knob	1.1	1.8
from the knob, north to Muir Inlet	2.7	4.3

* This is a route not a trail, so all distances are rough estimates only.

VALLEY OF 10,000 SMOKES – KATMAI NATIONAL PARK

Katmai National Park & Preserve, an expensive side trip, is an intriguing place for a long-term wilderness adventure. A series of volcanic eruptions in 1912 left the area with unique land formations, including the popular Valley of 10,000 Smokes with its eerie, barren landscape. Wildlife is plentiful, with brown bear the most prominent animal. Moose live in most parts of the park and the

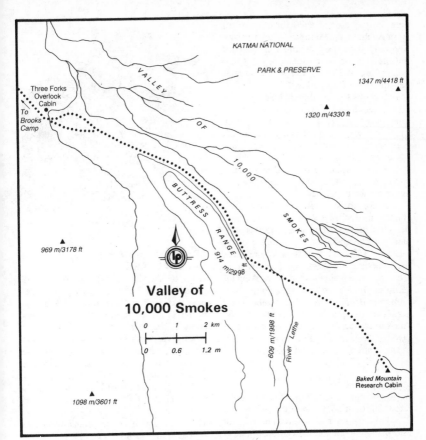

KATMAI NATIONAL

PARK & PRESERVE

1347 m/4418 ft

VALLEY

Three Forks
Overlook
Cabin

To
Brooks
Camp

OF

1320 m/4330 ft

10,000

BUTTRESS

RANGE

SMOKES

914 m/2998 ft

969 m/3178 ft

**Valley of
10,000 Smokes**

0   1   2 km

0   0.6   1.2 m

609 m/1998 ft

River Lethe

Baked Mountain
Research Cabin

1098 m/3601 ft

fishing is often said to be among the best in Alaska, as Katmai is an important spawning area for salmon.

The Valley of 10,000 Smokes is the most popular route for backpacking in Katmai, even though few of the famed '10,000 smokes' are active today. It begins with a short trail from Three Forks Overlook at the end of the park road to Windy Creek on the floor of the valley. A well-defined route then leads 12 miles (19.9 km) south-east across the valley to a research cabin on the side of Baked Mountain.

The hike is considered fairly difficult and

includes some steep trekking along the foot-hills of the Buttress Range, followed by a drop down to the River Lethe, a major fording. From the river, you head for the divide between Broken Mountain, 3785 feet (1154 metres), and Baked Mountain, 3695 feet (1126 metres). You then head south-east to climb the short but steep slope of Baked Mountain to the cabin.

Getting Started

Turn to the Katmai National Park section in the Bush chapter for travel information to and from Katmai National Park, but be prepared to pay around $400 for a return trip from Anchorage, 290 miles (466 km) away. The only developed facilities in the park, outside of a couple of expensive wilderness lodges, are at Brooks Camp, the summer headquarters of the park.

At Brooks Camp, there is lodging, a restaurant and a park store which sells limited quantities of freeze-dried food, topographic maps and white gas for camp stoves. The park store also rents tents, canoes, camp stoves and fishing poles among other things. It is best to stock up on food and fishing tackle in Anchorage to avoid emptying your entire money pouch here.

Like Denali National Park, Katmai has a shuttle bus that travels the park road almost daily but, unlike Denali's free bus, it is operated by a concessionaire. A return trip on the bus costs $50 and a spot should be reserved the night before. Hikers who have a week in the park can skip the bus fare by walking the 23 miles (36.8 km) out to Three Forks Overlook from Brooks Camp. The weather in the area can be consistently poor even by Alaskan standards; the skies are clear only 20% of the summer and from September onwards strong winds are frequent.

More Information

In Anchorage, contact the Alaska Public Land Information Center (tel (907) 271-2737) at the corner of 4th Ave and F St for information about Katmai National Park. If you're planning to visit the park, it is best to write ahead for information to Katmai National Park (tel (907) 246-3305), PO Box 7, King Salmon, Alaska 99613.

Section	miles	km
Brooks Camp to Three Forks via		
Park Rd	23.0	36.8
Three Forks to Windy Creek*	1.0	1.6
Windy Creek to River Lethe via		
the Buttress Range*	7.0	11.2
River Lethe to		
Baked Mountain Cabin*	4.0	6.4

* Marked distances are rough estimates only.

Dall Sheep

DIXIE PASS – WRANGELL-ST ELIAS NATIONAL PARK

Even by Alaskan standards, Wrangell-St Elias National Park is a large tract of wilderness. At 13.2 million acres (5.3 million hectares) it's the largest US National Park, contains the most peaks over 14,500 feet (4350 m) in North America and has the greatest concentration of glaciers in the continent. The park is a mountainous wilderness as three mountain chains (Wrangell, St Elias and Chugach) converge here. Wildlife in the park includes Dall sheep, three herds of caribou, moose and, of course, lots of bears. The rivers are full of grayling, while trout thrives in the lakes.

The most common trek is to spend 1 or 2 days hiking up to the Kennecott Mines and then Root Glacier (see the Wrangell-St Elias National Park section in the Southcentral chapter). Dixie Pass offers a longer, more rugged and truer wilderness adventure into the interior of this park. The trek up to Dixie Pass and back is 20 miles (32 km), but plan to camp there at least 1 or 2 extra days to take in the alpine beauty and explore the nearby ridges. This itinerary requires 3 to 4 days and is of moderate difficulty.

The trip begins from McCarthy Rd by hiking 2.5 miles (4 km) up the Nugget Creek/Kotsina Rd and then another 1.3 miles

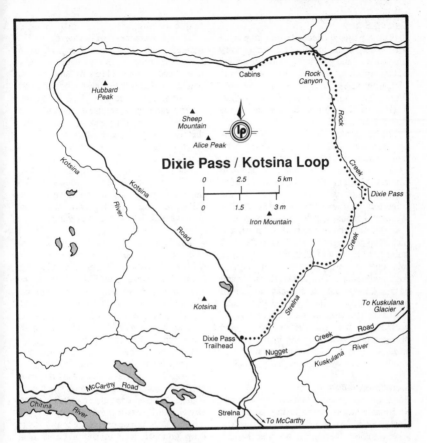

Dixie Pass / Kotsina Loop

(2 km) along Kotsina Rd after Nugget Rd splits off to the north-east. The Dixie Pass trailhead is posted on the right-hand side of Kotsina Rd and begins as a planked path down to Strelna Creek and then continues along the west side of the creek for 3 miles (5 km) to the first major confluence.

After fording the creek, continue to follow the trail for another 4 miles (6.5 km) to the final ascent to the pass. It's a 10 mile (16 km) hike from the trailhead to Dixie Pass which offers superb scenery, good camping and opportunities to spend an extra day or two hiking the ridges.

Either backtrack or, for the more adventurous, return along the Kotsina Trail Loop. This trail begins by descending the pass and following Rock Creek north 5.5 miles (9 km) to the Upper Kotsina River drainage area. The route involves hiking the west side of the creek and then fording it at Pass Creek to avoid a canyon area. Where Rock Creek merges into Kotsina River, you can pick up Kotsina Rd for the final 25 miles (41 km) back to the Dixie Pass trailhead. In all, the Kotsina Trail Loop is a 45 mile (73 km) hike that requires 5 to 7 days and experience in wilderness travel.

Getting Started

Pick up supplies at Glennallen and stop at the park headquarters to fill out a backcountry trip itinerary and obtain your US Geological Survey quadrangle maps (Valdez C-1 and McCarthy C-8). Then arrange travel with Wrangell Mt Bus Adventures (tel (907) 822-5519 in McCarthy) from the junction of the Richardson and Glenn highways.

The bus departs Glennallen for McCarthy on Monday, Wednesday and Friday; the return fare costs $80. Alternatively, you can save a few dollars by hitching down to Chitina, which is OK along the Richardson Highway but the last 33 miles on the Edgerton Highway can be difficult. The Wrangell Mt bus will also pick you up here.

Make arrangements to be dropped off and picked up at Nugget Creek/Kotsina Rd, 13.5 miles (22 km) east of Chitina and then continue onto McCarthy to see more of this great park's wilderness. This trip is affordable and easy to arrange but you still have to be well prepared; it could take several days to reach you if you have a mishap. Bears may be present anywhere and stream fording must be attempted with extreme caution. Pack extra food, good waterproof clothing and woollens as the weather can change quickly.

More Information

For more information, contact the Wrangell-St Elias National Park headquarters (tel (907) 822-5235), PO Box 29, Glennallen, Alaska 99588. During the summer there is also a ranger station (tel (907) 823-2205) at Chitina.

Section	miles	km
McCarthy Rd to trailhead	3.8	6.2
trailhead to Strelna Creek	2.5	4.0
Strelna Creek to Dixie Pass	7.5	12.2
Dixie Pass to Upper Kotsina River	5.5	9.0
Kotsina River to trailhead via road	25.0	40.7

Paddling

MISTY FJORDS

The Misty Fjords National Monument, which encompasses 2.3 million acres (928,491 hectares) of wilderness, lies between two impressive fjords – Behm Canal, 117 miles (188 km) long, and Portland Canal, 72 miles (116 km) long. The two natural canals give the preserve its trademark of extraordinarily deep and long fjords with sheer granite walls that rise thousands of feet out of the water. Misty Fjords is named after the rainy weather that seems to hover over it much of the year; the annual rainfall is 14 feet (4.2 metres)!

But don't let the rain put you off, Misty Fjords is an incredible place to spend a few days paddling. Lush forests, dramatic waterfalls plunging out of granite walls and diverse wildlife make the monument a kayaker's delight.

The destination for many kayakers are the smaller but equally impressive fjords of Walker Cove and Punchbowl Cove in Rudyerd Bay, off Behm Canal. The vegetation in this monument is dense spruce-hemlock rainforest, while the abundant wildlife includes sea lions, harbour seals, killer whales, brown and black bears, mountain goats, moose and bald eagles.

Ketchikan is the departure point for most trips into Misty Fjord. Several tour boats run day trips into the area and there are the usual expensive sightseeing flights on small bush planes. Kayakers can either paddle out of the city (a 7 to 12 day trip for experienced paddlers only) or utilise one of the tour boats to drop you off deep in Behm Canal near Rudyerd Bay and protected water.

Those contemplating paddling all the way from Ketchikan have to keep in mind that the currents around Point Alava and Alava Bay are strong and tricky, often flowing in unusual patterns. Rounding the point into Behm Canal should be done at slack tide, which means leaving the city at high tide. The 3 to 4 mile (4.8 to 6.4 km) crossing of Behm Canal should also be done with caution, as northerly winds can create choppy conditions.

The Misty Fjords National Monument, which is administered by the US Forest Service (USFS), has 15 cabins (reservations

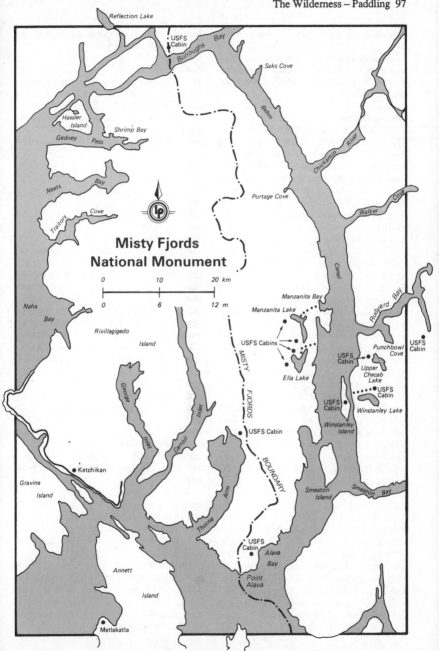

Reflection Lake

USFS Cabin

Burroughs Bay

Saks Cove

Bahm

Chickamin River

Hassler Island

Shrimp Bay

Gedney Pass

Neets Bay

Traitors Cove

Portage Cove

Walker Cove

Misty Fjords National Monument

| 0 | 10 | 20 km |
| 0 | 6 | 12 m |

Manzanita Bay

Manzanita Lake

Rudyerd Bay

USFS Cabin

USFS Cabins

Punchbowl Cove

USFS Cabin

Upper Checab Lake

Naha Bay

Rivillagigedo Island

Ella Lake

USFS Cabin

USFS Cabin

MISTY

FJORDS

Winstanley Lake

Winstanley Island

George Inlet

Carroll Inlet

USFS Cabin

BOUNDARY

Smeaton Island

Smeaton Bay

Ketchikan

Gravina Island

Thorne Arm

USFS Cabin

Alava Bay

Annett Island

Point Alava

Metlakatla

needed, $20 rental fee) and 15 miles (24 km) of trails. Two of the cabins, at Alava Bay and Winstanley Island, are right on Behm Canal and allow kayakers to end a day of paddling at the doorstep of a cabin. Many of the others are a short hike inland.

Getting Started

Outdoor Alaska, a Ketchikan tour company, offers many services for kayakers to Misty Fjords, including a variety of boat and plane trips into the monument. The company will drop you off and pick you up anywhere in the preserve for $150; a boat leaves on Wednesday, Friday, Saturday and Sunday. This allows inexperienced paddlers to avoid much of the open water of Behm Canal and to experience only the protected and spectacular areas of Rudyerd Bay or Walker Cove.

For the same fee, they will place your kayak on their tour boat and fly you out to Rudyerd Bay, and then return you to Ketchikan on the tour boat. They also have one-way fares for those who want to paddle all the way back to town.

Outdoor Alaska rents single kayaks at $35 per day for 1 to 3 days and $30 per day for longer trips. Doubles are $40 per day for 1 to 3 days and $35 for longer rentals. You can also rent single and double kayaks from Southeast Exposure for similar prices. Both companies have a limited number of boats so if possible plan ahead and reserve them before the summer. Contact Southeast Exposure (tel (907) 225-8829) at PO Box 9143, Ketchikan, Alaska 99901. Outdoor Alaska (tel (907) 225-6044) is at PO Box 7814, Ketchikan, Alaska 99901.

You cannot do this trip without good rain gear or a backpacker's stove, as wood in the monument is often too wet for campfires. Be prepared for extended periods of rain and have all gear sealed in plastic bags. Either order your maps ahead of time or hope that the sections you want are in stock at the Tongass Trading Company, 203 Dock St in Ketchikan. Then take the maps to the USFS office and have somebody point out the camping spots in the area where you are going to paddle. Since much of the monu-

ment is steep-sided fjords, good campsites are scarce in many areas.

More Information

For information or hand-outs on the monument, either visit the USFS office in the Federal Building in Ketchikan or contact the monument office at Misty Fjords National Monument (tel (907) 225-2148), 1817 North Tongass Highway, Ketchikan 99901.

Section	miles	km
Ketchikan to Thorne Arm	13.0	20.9
Thorne Arm to Point Alava	9.0	14.4
Point Alava to Stanley Island	21.0	33.8
Winstanley Island to Rudyerd Bay	9.0	14.4
Rudyerd Bay to Walker Cove	10.0	16.0

TRACY ARM

Tracy Arm, like Glacier Bay, is another fjord in the Southeast that features tidewater glaciers rumbling and calving icebergs into the water. Unlike Glacier Bay, this wilderness area is not nearly as popular during the summer. It combines steep 2000 foot (600 metre) granite walls rising straight out of the water with cascading waterfalls and a pair of glaciers that sparkle like diamonds on a ring.

The 30 mile (48 km) arm is no more than 0.5 mile (0.8 km) wide at its upper end – ideal conditions for the novice kayaker. Calm water is the norm in Tracy Arm as the steep and narrow fjord walls provide protection from stormy weather and strong winds. Wildlife includes bald eagles, mountain goats, seals, brown and black bears and an occasional whale. Even more interesting is the gallery of icebergs that float past you out to sea.

Adjoining Tracy Arm, just to the south, is Endicott Arm, a 30 mile (49 km) fjord that was carved by Dawes and North Dawes glaciers. It is icebergs from these glaciers, some as large as three-storey buildings, that often make it into the main shipping lanes of Stephens Passage, creating navigation hazards and delighting travellers on the state ferries.

Extending from Endicott Arm is Fords Terror. This narrow water chasm was named after a US sailor who in 1889 found himself battling surging rapids, whirlpools and

Tracy Arm

Kayak Route

grinding icebergs for 6 terrifying hours when he tried to row out against the incoming tide. Endicott Arm, Tracy Arm and Fords Terror together make up the Tracy Arm-Fords Terror Wilderness Area, a 653,000 acres (261,200 hectares) preserve and a great place for a week's paddling.

Getting Started

The departure point for Tracy Arm is Juneau. Kayaks can be rented for $30 a single and $40 a double per day from Alaska Discovery (tel 586-1911) and placed on the tour boat *Glacier Seal* (tel 789-7429), which offers drop-offs and pick-ups at the entrance of the arm for $85 per person. This makes the trip considerably easier as it is a 2 or 3 day paddle in open water to the mouth of Tracy Arm.

It is a pleasant 2 to 3 day paddle from one end of the arm to the other. Most kayakers camp on Harbor Island, near the entrance of Tracy and Endicott arms, at least 1 night even though level ground for a tent is difficult to find. The only other camping spots in the first half of Tracy Arm are two valleys almost across from each other, 8 miles (13 km) north along the arm.

Purchase topographic maps from the Big

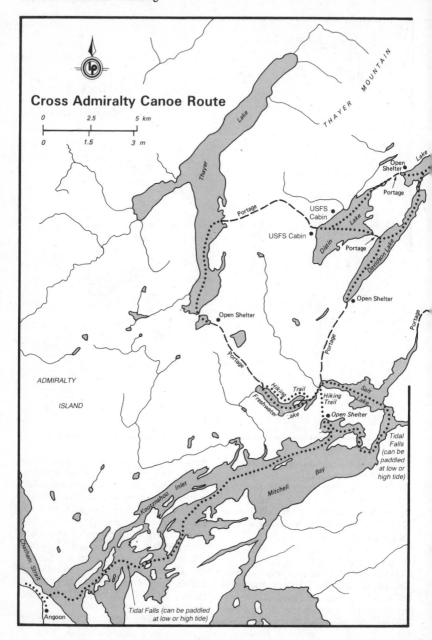

Cross Admiralty Canoe Route

0   2.5   5 km

0   1.5   3 m

THAYER MOUNTAIN

Thayer Lake

Portage

USFS Cabin

USFS Cabin

Distin Lake

Open Shelter

Portage

Davidson Lake

Portage

Open Shelter

Open Shelter

Portage

Portage

ADMIRALTY ISLAND

Portage

Hiking Trail

Freshwater Lake

Hiking Trail

Open Shelter

Salt Lake

Tidal Falls (can be paddled at low or high tide)

Kootznahoo Inlet

Mitchell Bay

Chatham Strait

Angoon

Tidal Falls (can be paddled at low or high tide)

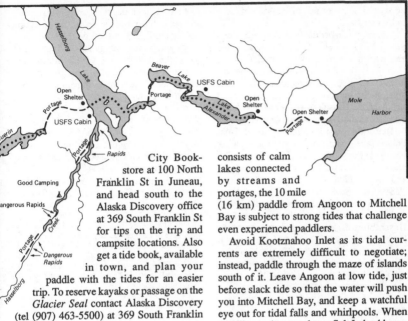

City Bookstore at 100 North Franklin St in Juneau, and head south to the Alaska Discovery office at 369 South Franklin St for tips on the trip and campsite locations. Also get a tide book, available in town, and plan your paddle with the tides for an easier trip. To reserve kayaks or passage on the *Glacier Seal* contact Alaska Discovery (tel (907) 463-5500) at 369 South Franklin St, Juneau, Alaska 99801.

More Information

Tracy Arm Wilderness Area is managed by the US Forest Service, which can be contacted for more information or hand-outs at USFS Juneau District (tel (907) 789-3111), PO Box 2097, Juneau, Alaska 99801.

CROSS ADMIRALTY ISLAND

Admiralty Island National Monument, 50 miles (80 km) south-west of Juneau, is the site of one of the few canoe routes in the Southeast. This preserve is a fortress of dense coastal forest, ragged peaks and brown bears, which outnumbers anything else on the island including humans. The island also supports one of the largest bald-eagle nesting areas, and Sitka black-tail deer can be seen throughout the monument.

The Cross Admiralty Canoe Route is a 32 mile (51 km) paddle that spans the centre of the island from the village of Angoon to Mole Harbor. Although the majority of it

consists of calm lakes connected by streams and portages, the 10 mile (16 km) paddle from Angoon to Mitchell Bay is subject to strong tides that challenge even experienced paddlers.

Avoid Kootznahoo Inlet as its tidal currents are extremely difficult to negotiate; instead, paddle through the maze of islands south of it. Leave Angoon at low tide, just before slack tide so that the water will push you into Mitchell Bay, and keep a watchful eye out for tidal falls and whirlpools. When paddling to Angoon, leave Salt Lake 4 hours before the slack tide, after high tide.

From the west end of Salt Lake there is a 3.5 mile (5.6 km) portage to Davidson Lake, which is connected to Lake Guerin by a navigable stream. Between Lake Guerin and Hasselborg Lake is a 1.7 mile (2.7 km) portage followed by a 0.5 mile (0.8 km)

Bald Eagle

portage on the east side of Hasselborg Lake to Beaver Lake.

Canoeists can paddle from Beaver Lake to the east end of Lake Alexander, where they can take a 2.5 mile (4 km) trail to Mole Harbor. This is the most common route followed, but there are numerous trails in the area, including portages to Thayer Lake and a route along Hasselborg Creek that connects Salt Lake with Hasselborg Lake.

There are good camping spots at Tidal Falls on the eastern end of Salt Lake, on the islands at the south end of Hasselborg Lake and on the portage between Davidson Lake and Distin Lake. The US Forest Service (USFS) also maintains three-sided shelters (no reservations or rental fee) at the south end of Davidson Lake, at the east end of the Hasselborg Lake portage and at Mole Harbor. Finally, for those who can plan in advance, there are several USFS cabins (reservations needed, $20 per night) along the route, including those on Hasselborg Lake, Lake Alexander and Distin Lake.

Getting Started

Juneau is the departure point for this 4 to 7 day trip, though you will probably pass through the small village of Angoon, a port-of-call on the State Marine Highway, which greatly reduces your transport costs as the one-way fare between Juneau and Angoon is $20. The problem is what to do at Mole Harbor, the east end of the trail. You can charter a bush plane to pick up both your party and the boats, but that is an expensive exercise for those on a tight budget.

One alternative is to backtrack to Angoon and return to Juneau on the state ferry, which charges only $6 for canoes or kayaks that are carried on. This means setting up your trip around the ferry schedule, but the savings are enormous.

Check with Alaska Discovery (tel (907) 586-1911) in Juneau, 369 South Franklin St, about canoe rentals. In Angoon, this guide company rents canoes for $40 per day at the Angoon Trading Company (tel (907) 788-3111) on Kootznahoo Rd. Alaska Discovery also have some canoes cached along the

route for their guided trips, and during spring and autumn canoes can be picked up at one side of the island and left on the other. Purchase your topographic maps in Juneau and then take them to the USFS information centre in Centennial Hall or to the Alaska Discovery office to have someone point out where strong tidal currents exist.

More Information

This is a USFS-maintained preserve and information can be obtained from the information centre in the Juneau Centennial Hall or by writing to the Admiralty Island National Monument (tel (907) 789-3111), 8465 Old Dairy Rd, Juneau, Alaska 99802.

Section	miles	km
Angoon to Salt Lake Tidal Falls	10.0	16.0
Tidal Falls to Davidson Lake portage	2.5	4.0
portage to Davidson Lake	3.5	5.6
Davidson Lake to		
Hasselborg Lake portage	6.0	9.6
portage to Hasselborg Lake	1.7	2.7
Hasselborg Lake to		
Beaver Lake portage	2.0	3.2
portage to Beaver Lake	0.5	0.8
Beaver Lake to Mole Harbor portage	3.0	4.8
portage to Mole Harbor	2.5	4.0

HOONAH TO TENAKEE SPRINGS

This 40 mile (64 km) paddle follows the shorelines of Port Frederick and Tenakee Inlet from Hoonah to Tenakee Springs and includes a short portage of a 100 yards/ metres or so. You might pass an occasional clear cut, but there are few other signs of civilisation along the route once you are beyond the two villages. The area is part of the Tongass National Forest and consists of rugged and densely forested terrain populated by brown bears, which are often seen feeding along the shoreline.

It is important to carry a tide book and to reach the portage at high tide. Boot-sucking mud will be encountered along the portage, but take heart, it is just a short walk over a low ridge to the next inlet. Highlights of the trip include the scenic south shore of Tenakee Inlet with its many bays and coves. The village of Tenakee Springs has a public bath house around its natural hot springs that

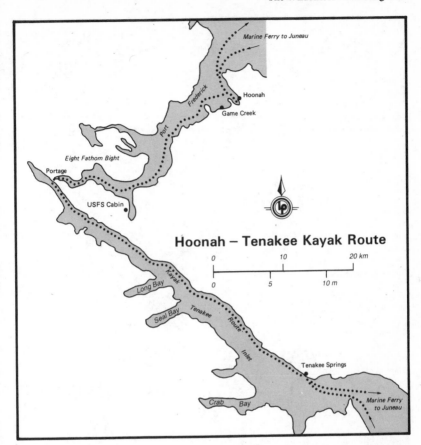

Hoonah – Tenakee Kayak Route

will soothe any sore muscles resulting from the paddle.

Getting Started

This adventure is within the grasp of many backpackers on a budget as there is a state ferry service to both Hoonah and Tenakee Springs from Juneau. The one-way fare from Juneau to Hoonah is $16 (to Tenakee Springs $18), with a $6 charge for kayaks.

The best way to start the paddle is from Hoonah in order to end the trip in Tenakee Springs, a charming village. However, this has to be planned carefully, as there is only

one ferry every 4 days to Tenakee Springs. Kayaks, $30 a single and $40 a double per day, can be rented at Alaska Discovery (tel (907) 586-1911), 369 South Franklin St in Juneau. Plan to purchase all supplies and topographic maps in Juneau, although there is food and lodging in both villages (see the Southeast chapter).

More Information

For more information about the route or the surrounding area, contact the USFS office in the Hoonah Ranger District (tel (907) 945-3631), PO Box 135, Hoonah, Alaska 99829.

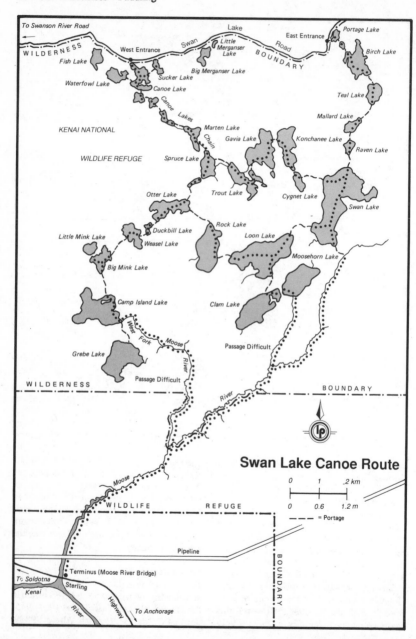

To Swanson River Road
Lake
Swan
Road
East Entrance
Portage Lake
WILDERNESS
BOUNDARY
West Entrance
Little
Merganser
Lake
Birch Lake
Fish Lake
Big Merganser Lake
Sucker Lake
Waterfowl Lake
Canoe Lake
Teal Lake
Canoe
Lakes
Mallard Lake
KENAI NATIONAL
Marten Lake
Chain
Gavia Lake
Konchanee Lake
WILDLIFE REFUGE
Spruce Lake
Raven Lake
Otter Lake
Trout Lake
Cygnet Lake
Swan Lake
Duckbill Lake
Rock Lake
Little Mink Lake
Weasel Lake
Loon Lake
Big Mink Lake
Moosehorn Lake
Camp Island Lake
Clam Lake
West
Fork
Moose
Passage Difficult
Grebe Lake
River
WILDERNESS
Passage Difficult
BOUNDARY
River
Moose
Swan Lake Canoe Route

0   1   2 km
0   0.6   1.2 m

= Portage

WILDLIFE   REFUGE
BOUNDARY
Pipeline
Terminus (Moose River Bridge)
To Soldotna
Sterling
Kenai
River
Highway
To Anchorage

SWANSON RIVER & SWAN LAKE

In the northern lowlands of the Kenai National Wildlife Refuge there is a chain of rivers, lakes, streams and portages, of course, that make up the Swanson River and nearby Swan Lake canoe routes. The trips are perfect for novice canoeists as rough water is rarely a problem and the portages do not exceed 0.5 mile (0.8 km) on the Swan Lake system or 1 mile (1.6 km) in the Swanson River area.

Fishing is good for rainbow trout in many of the lakes and wildlife is plentiful; a trip on either route could result in sightings of moose, bear, beaver or a variety of waterfowl. Both routes are popular trips among Anchorage canoeists as they are well marked and maintained, with open shelters along the way.

The Swanson River system links more than 40 lakes and 46 miles (74 km) of river, and a one-way trip is 80 miles (128 km). It can be a more challenging trip than the Swan Lake paddle, especially when the water is low. The easier Swan Lake route connects 30 lakes with forks of the Moose River; the one-way trip is 60 miles (96 km). A common 4 day trip on Swan Lake begins at the west entrance of the canoe route and ends at Moose River Bridge on the Sterling Highway.

Getting Started

To reach either the Swan Lake or Swanson River canoe routes, travel to *Mile 84* (135 km) of the Sterling Highway east of Soldotna and turn north on Robinson Lake Rd, just west of Moose River Bridge. Robinson Rd turns into Swanson River Rd and leads to Swan Lake Rd 17 miles (27 km) north from the Sterling Highway. East on Swan Lake Rd are the entrances to both canoe systems, with the Swanson River route beginning at the very end of the road. The west entrance for Swan Lake is at Canoe Lake and the east entrance is another 6 miles (9.8 km) beyond at Portage Lake; both are well marked.

During the summer, the Great Alaska Fish Camp, a lodge at *Mile 81.7* (131.5 km) of the Sterling Highway where it crosses the Moose River, rents out canoes and runs a shuttle bus service to the head of Swan Lake Canoe Trail. You conveniently end up back at Moose River Bridge and the camp to eliminate any need for a pick-up. The rental fee for a canoe is $25 per day, and it costs $50 to have your boat and yourself shipped to the western entrance of the trail. Contact the Great Alaska Fish Camp (tel (907) 262-4515; (800) 544-2261 – toll free), PO Box 218, Sterling, Alaska 99672.

You can also rent canoes in Soldotna from Ronland's Sports Den (tel (907) 262-7491), PO Box 2861, Soldotna, Alaska 99669; or in Anchorage from Hugh Glass Backpacking Company (tel (907) 344-1340), PO Box 110796, Anchorage, Alaska 99511.

More Information

The visitor centre for the Kenai National Wildlife Refuge is at *Mile 97.9* (157.6 km) of the Sterling Highway, 2 miles (3.2 km) south of Soldotna. You can also get information before your trip from the Refuge Manager, Kenai National Wildlife Refuge (tel (907) 262-7021), PO Box 2139, Soldotna, Alaska 99669.

BAY OF ISLANDS CIRCUIT – KATMAI NATIONAL PARK

This route begins and ends at Brooks Camp (the summer headquarters of Katmai National Park) and takes paddlers into seldom-visited sections of the preserve, offering the ultimate in wilderness adventures. The complete circuit is an 80 mile (128 km), 7 to 10 day paddle, depending on weather and wind conditions.

The trip is long but not difficult, as no white water is encountered and boats only have to be carried across one portage, 1 mile (1.6 km) long. The first section from Brooks Camp to the Bay of Islands is especially scenic and offers calm water flanked by mountains. Here the water is deep and clear and the offshore islands provide superb campsites.

It takes 2 to 3 day to paddle through Naknek Lake and the Bay of Islands to the 1 mile (1.6 km) Lake Grosvenor portage. From

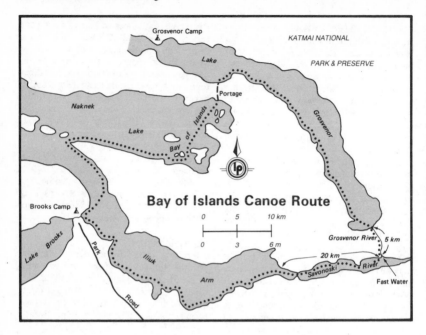

Grosvenor Camp

KATMAI NATIONAL

PARK & PRESERVE

Lake

Portage

Naknek

Grosvenor

Lake

Bay of Islands

Bay of Islands Canoe Route

0   5   10 km

0   3   6 m

Brooks Camp

Grosvenor River   5 km

20 km

Lake Brooks

Park

Iliuk

Savonoski   River

Arm

Fast Water

Road

this portage, it is a 14 mile (22 km) paddle along the south shore of Lake Grosvenor to the Grosvenor River. The Grosvenor is a slow-moving clear-water river where paddlers often spot moose, bears, beavers and river otters. It flows into the Savonoski River, a prime brown-bear habitat, especially when the salmon are running. For this reason, park rangers often recommend paddling the 12 miles (19 km) of the Savonoski in a single day and not camping along the river.

Canoeists also have to keep a sharp eye out for obstructions and sand bars that may develop in the river. The last leg is the 20 mile (32 km) paddle along the south shore of the Iliuk Arm back to Brooks Camp.

Getting Started
See the Katmai National Park section in the Bush chapter for information on getting to and from the park; also check the section on the Valley of 10,000 Smokes in this chapter

for the special backcountry needs of the preserve. Paddlers have to remember that Katmai is famous for its sudden and violent storms, some that last for days. Good waterproof clothing is essential and all gear should be sealed in plastic bags. It is unwise to paddle too far from shore, as it leaves you defenceless against sudden storms or high winds.

Getting a canoe or hard-shell kayak into the park can be an expensive ordeal for backpackers. Most visitors rent a canoe from the lodge in Brooks Camp for $30 per day; if possible, call a of couple weeks before your arrival at Katmai to reserve one. For advance reservations or rental information write to Katmailand Inc (tel (800) 544-0551 – toll free), 455 H St, Anchorage, Alaska 99501.

More Information
For more information about the park or hand-outs covering backcountry travel,

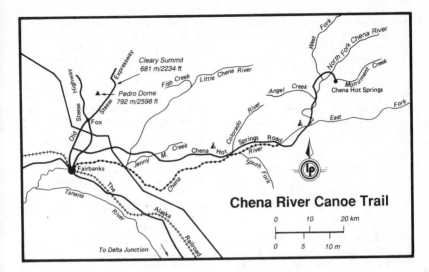

Chena River Canoe Trail

contact the park headquarters at Katmai National Park (tel (907) 246-3305), PO Box 7, King Salmon, Alaska 99613.

Section	miles	km
Brooks Camp to		
Lake Grosvenor portage	30.0	48.0
portage	1.0	1.6
Lake Grosvenor to Grosvenor River	14.0	22.5
Grosvenor River to Savonoski River	3.0	4.8
Savonoski River to Iliuk Arm	12.0	19.3
along Iliuk Arm to Brooks Camp	20.0	32.0

CHENA RIVER

The Chena River is one of the finest rivers for canoeing in the Fairbanks area and a long-time favourite among local residents. It flows through a landscape of rolling forested hills with access to alpine tundra above 2800 feet (850 metres). The river features no white water and paddlers only have to watch out for the occasional sweeper or log jam.

Wildlife in the area includes brown bears, moose, red foxes, beavers and river otters, while the fishing is excellent for grayling and northern pike. With the Interior's long, hot summer days, this trip can be an outstanding wilderness adventure.

Getting Started

Chena Hot Springs Rd provides access to the river at *Mile 27.9* (44.9 km) east of Fairbanks, *Mile 28.6* (46 km), *Mile 29.4* (47.3 km), *Mile 33.9* (54.6 km) at Fourmile Creek and *Mile 39.6* (63.7 km) at North Fork Chena River where there is a state campground (20 sites, $5 fee). From *Mile 39.6* of Chena Hot Springs Rd, the paddle along the river to Fairbanks is a 70 mile (113 km) trip that can be done comfortably in 4 to 5 days.

Beaver Sports (tel (907) 479-2494) at 2400 College Rd in Fairbanks has a few canoes for rent at $120 per week. The store is across the road from Noyes Slough, which can be paddled to from the Chena River, solving the problem of picking up the canoe. Now you just have to worry about getting to the trailhead.

Hitchhiking with a canoe is tough, though I've seen several backpackers be successful at it. One way around this is to rent a boat from CanoeAlaska (tel (907) 479-5183), PO Box 81750, Fairbanks, Alaska 99708 – a company which mainly caters for canoe instruction and organising group trips, not rentals. However, they will provide you with a boat for $50 the first day and $20 per day after that, along with a shuttle run up Chena Hot Springs Rd for $75; transport has to be arranged around their outings.

The other alternative is to rent a used car in Fairbanks (see the Getting Around section in the Fairbanks chapter), drop off the canoe and hitchhike back to the trailhead after returning the car to Fairbanks.

More Information

Much of the river lies in the Chena River State Recreation Area, which is administered by the Alaska Division of State Parks. Contact the Fairbanks office for more information at the Division of Parks (tel (907) 451-2695), 3700 Airport Way, Fairbanks, Alaska 99709.

BEAVER CREEK

Travellers with lots of time, a yearn to paddle through a roadless wilderness but not a lot of funds for bush-plane travel, will find Beaver Creek the ultimate adventure. The moderately swift stream, characterised by long clear pools and frequent rapids, is rated Grade I in difficulty and can be handled by novice canoers with pervious expedition experience. The Bureau of Land Management (BLM) manage the 111 mile (178 km) creek as part of the White Mountains National Recreation Area, where it flows through rolling hills forested in white spruce and paper birch and past the jagged peaks of the White Mountains.

The scenery is spectacular, the chances of seeing another party remote and you'll catch so much grayling you'll probably never want to eat another one after the trip. If you take a day off at Victoria Creek and scale the 5000 feet (1500 metre) high Victoria Peak, you should see wildlife such as moose, bears and mountain sheep. You can also spend a night in the Borealis-Le Fevre Cabin, a BLM cabin on the banks of Beaver Creek.

The trip begins from *Mile 58* (92 km) of the Steese Highway at Nome Creek where nine times out of 10, due to low water, you'll be forced to line your boat 10 miles (16 km) to its confluence with Beaver Creek. Most paddlers then plan on 7 to 10 days to reach

Victoria Creek, a 127 mile (207 km) trip, where gravel bars nearby are used by bush planes to land and pick paddlers up.

You can avoid the air fare by continuing along Beaver Creek which spills out of the White Mountains into Yukon Flats National Wildlife Refuge where it slows down and meanders through a marshy area. Eventually it flows north into the Yukon River where after 2 or 3 days you'll pass under the Yukon River Bridge over Dalton Highway. This is a 395 mile (644 km) paddle and a 3 week expedition; the stuff great Alaska adventures are made of. See the White Mountain Trail & Beaver Creek Canoe Route map in the Trekking section of this chapter (page 83).

Getting Started

You can rent a canoe at either Beaver Sports or CanoeAlaska, see the Chena River Canoe Route in this chapter for details. The trick is to arrange transport out to the Steese Highway and be picked up on the Dalton Highway; either one is a challenge in logistics. The start of the paddle is at *Mile 58* (92 km) of the Steese Highway where a rough 4WD track, US Creek Rd, leads down to Nome Creek. The Yukon River Bridge on the Dalton Highway is about 175 miles (280 km) north of Fairbanks.

You can try to arrange transport with Spell of the Yukon Tours (tel (907) 455-6128) at PO Box 72964, Fairbanks, Alaska 99707-2964, who run overnight tours up the Steese Highway to the Arctic Circle Hot Springs. Or try Backcountry Logistical Services (tel (907) 457-7606) at PO Box 82265, Fairbanks, Alaska 99708-2265, where you can also rent canoes.

Another way to arrange transport is to visit the student centre at the Univeristy of Alaska (Fairbanks), the above sport shops or the Fairbanks Visitor Center and seek out a high school or college student looking to earn a few dollars. Even if you have to pay them $75 to drop you off on the Steese Highway and $100 to haul you out from the Yukon River, it would still be a fraction of a bush-plane fare.

If you do find transport, keep in mind that

Steven's Village is half a day's paddle from the Yukon River Bridge on the banks of the river. Spending a night in this small village is a cultural experience in itself and you could use its one radio/telephone to contact your driver and arrange an exact pick-up time for the next day.

You can also check with the Fairbanks Visitor Center for any tour company running trips up the Dalton Highway. The Northern Alaska Tour Company (tel (907) 479-3825), PO Box 82991, Fairbanks, Alaska 99708, runs such a trip.

More Information

For more information contact the Steese-White District of the BLM (tel (907) 474-2200) at 1150 University Ave, Fairbanks, Alaska 99709.

TOURS
Guide Companies

Most of Alaska's wilderness is not accessible to the first-time visitor; travellers either don't know about wilderness areas or don't know how to get to them. This is where guide companies are very useful.

Guides are not only for novice, never-put-on-a-backpack campers. Their clients can be experienced backpackers who want to explore the far reaches of Alaska's wilderness but don't have the time or money to put together an expedition on their own. Guides can arrange the many details of a large-scale trip into the backcountry – everything from food and equipment to air charter. They work on the principle that a group of 10 or 12 can explore an area cheaper than one or two.

Trips can range from a 1 day hike on a glacier to a 12 day raft trip or a 3 week ascent of Mt McKinley, and costs from $125 to more than $200 per day, depending upon the amount of air travel involved. Expeditions usually have five to 12 clients; guide companies are hesitant to take larger groups because of their environmental impact. The tour season is from late May to September, while a select group of companies specialise in winter expeditions of Nordic skiing or dog-sledding.

Guided expeditions cost money, and most budget travellers prefer unguided trips. However, many guide companies offer adventures to areas that are only visited by a few people each year; there is something inviting about that. Although most guide companies begin taking reservations in April, don't hesitate to call one after you've arrived in Alaska. Often you can score a hefty discount of 30% to 50% in the middle of the summer as guide companies are eager to fill any remaining places on a scheduled trip.

The following is a list of recreational guide companies in Alaska. Don't get them confused with hunting or fishing guides whose main interest is to make sure that their client gets a trophy to hang on the wall of the family room. Also be careful not to confuse expeditions with fishing camps or wilderness lodges. The camps and lodges are established rustic resorts in the wilderness where you spend a week with many of the comforts of home, but see little beyond the immediate area

Southeast Outdoor Alaska (tel (907) 225-6044), PO Box 7814, Ketchikan, Alaska 99901, is a Ketchikan guide company that provides a variety of tours and services to Misty Fjords National Monument, including guided kayaking trips. A 3 day paddle to the heart of Rudyerd Bay, the most scenic part of Misty Fjords, is $380 per person and includes float plane and boat transport from Ketchikan. Outdoor Alaska also have vessel-supported kayak trips where you paddle and camp on your own but return to the tour boat for hot meals and assistance if needed. A 3 day supported trip to Rudyerd Bay is $235 per person.

Alaska Discovery (tel (907) 586-1911), 369 South Franklin, Juneau, Alaska 99801, is one of the oldest and largest guide companies in Alaska. They mainly operate in the Southeast with kayak trips in Glacier Bay, canoe trips across Admiralty Island and raft trips down the Tatshenshini River being their specialty. Among their expeditions are a 4 day paddle in Glacier Bay for $800 per person and a spectacular 7 day Hubbard

Glacier adventure for $1000 per person. The company also rents kayaks ($40 per day) in Juneau and canoes at Angoon on Admiralty Island.

Chilkat Guides (tel (907) 766-2409), PO Box 170, Haines, Alaska 99827, offer a handful of raft trips from its base in Haines, including a 4 hour float down the Chilkat River, an area with many bald eagles. The trip departs twice a day during the summer and costs $45 per person. The company also runs tours to the Tsirku and Tatshenshini rivers.

Ice Field Ascents, PO Box 449, Haines, Alaska 99827, a small guide company, offer mountaineering trips that allow clients to view the wonders of the Haines-Skagway region and to learn the art of glacier travel and alpine survival. Expeditions of 10 to 14 days include Glacier Bay Boundary Peaks, a Haines to Skagway Mountain Trek and the Mendenhall Towers Rock Climbing Adventure. The company also offers a weekend ice-climbing trip to Davidson Glacier, south of Haines.

Alaska Cross Country Guiding & Rafting (tel (907) 767-5522), PO Box 124, Haines, Alaska 99827, is based in Haines and runs trips around the Chilkat Bald Eagle Preserve. Wildlife photography and hiking trips are supported by raft, canoe and at times air boats; they will accommodate groups as small as two people.

Anchorage Area & Southcentral Alaska Float Trips (tel (907) 333-4442), PO Box 140264, Anchorage, Alaska 99514, utilise rafts or fold boats for river trips such as the John and Kobuk rivers in the Brooks Range, the Kisaralik and Aniakchak rivers in Western Alaska, and Swan Lake and Lake Creek closer to Anchorage. They also rent rafts.

Hugh Glass Backpacking Co (tel (907) 344-1340), PO Box 110796, Anchorage, Alaska 99511, is a long-established guide company which offers a wide range of trips into Prince William Sound, Kenai Fjords National Park, the Arctic National Wildlife Refuge, Katmai National Park, Brooks Range, and the Wrangell and St Elias mountains. Trips may include trekking, canoeing, rafting or sea kayaking, and can be designed as photography or fishing adventures. The company also rents canoes in Anchorage.

Alaska Sea Kayaking (tel (907) 745-3487), 211 South Bailey, Palmer, Alaska 99645 , offers a variety of sea kayaking trips among the many fjords and coves in western Prince William Sound. They utilise a charter boat out of Whittier to ship kayaks and clients to and from wilderness areas.

Alaska Treks & Voyages (tel (907) 224-3960 in summer, (907) 584-5414 in winter), PO Box 625, Seward, Alaska 99631, offer a wide range of adventures, including a Ruth Glacier ski tour near Mt McKinley, sea kayaking in Kenai Fjords National Park, a trail-and-tundra trek in the Kenai Mountains and 1½ day kayak trips out of Seward. They also rent sea kayaks from the boat harbour in Seward.

Alaska River Adventures (tel (907) 276-3418), 1831 Kuskokwim St, Anchorage, Alaska 99508 offer guided tours all year round. In summer, they run boating trips from a 1 day outing along the Kenai River to 3 days of white-water paddling through the Talkeetna Canyon and 5 days on Lake Creek, south of Mt McKinley. There are also longer expeditions to the Alagnak River and the Kanektok River in the Bristol Bay region.

CampAlaska (tel (907) 376-9438), PO Box 872247, Wasilla, Alaska 99687, is not quite a true wilderness guide company. They offer van tours that combine camping with day hikes, rafting, canoeing and, of course, sightseeing, from the Alaskan highways. CampAlaska also runs a 7 day trip along the George Parks and Richardson highways that includes Denali National Park, Fairbanks and Valdez for $525 per person. A 10 day 'Arctic Quest' trip from Anchorage to Prudhoe Bay is $925 per person.

Mt McKinley & the Interior St Elias Alpine Guides (tel (907) 277-6867), PO Box 111241, Anchorage, Alaska 99511, specialises in mountaineering and glacier skiing adventures at Wrangell-St Elias

Rafting on the Copper River (SEAG)

National Park. They also offer a 12 day trip down the Copper River to Cordova for $1595 per person, and a variety of 1 day and half-day hikes around the historic Kennecott Copper Mines and nearby glaciers from $25 to $75 per person. All trips begin in the remote village of McCarthy.

Denali Raft Adventures (tel (907) 683-2234), PO Box 190, Denali Park, Alaska 99755, offer a variety of 1 day rafting trips down the Nenana River near Denali National Park; some are in calm waters while others involve 2 hours of white-water rafting. Prices range from $30 to $50 per person for 2 to 5 hour trips.

Nova (tel (907) 745-5753), PO Box 1129, Chickaloon, Alaska 99674, specialises in river rafting. Their trips range from a 1 day run down the Matanuska River for $40 per person to a 3 day journey along the Talkeetna River that involves flying to the heart of the Talkeetna Mountains and grade IV white water for $555 per person.

Alaska Back Country Guides Co-op (tel (907) 479-2754), PO Box 81533, Fairbanks,

Alaska 99708, is based in Fairbanks and offers a variety of backpacking, glacier trekking, rafting and canoeing trips. Among them are canoe trips in the Wrangell-St Elias National Park and throughout the Kenai Peninsula.

Fairbanks & Brooks Range Alaska Fish & Trails Unlimited (tel (907) 479-7630), 1177 Shypoke Drive, Fairbanks, Alaska 99701, runs backpacking trips in the Gates of the Arctic National Park, a late-autumn photography trip, spring Nordic ski tours and fishing adventures that include rafting out of the Brooks Range to Bettles.

Arctic Treks (tel (907) 455-6502), PO Box 73452, Fairbanks, Alaska 99707, specialise in treks and boating in the Gates of the Arctic National Park and the Arctic National Wildlife Refuge. A 15 day trip combining backpacking and rafting in the Gates of the Arctic costs $1825.

Sourdough Outfitters (tel (907) 692-5252), PO Box 90, Bettles, Alaska 99726, run canoe, kayak and backpacking trips to the Gates of the Arctic National Park, Noatak and Kobuk rivers and other areas. It also provides unguided trips for individuals who have the experience to make an independent journey but want a guide company to handle the logistics, such as trip planning, transport and canoe or raft rental, of a major expedition.

Unguided trips throughout the Brooks Range are priced from $300 to $700 per person. Guided trips range from an 8 day backpacking trek in the Gates of the Arctic National Park for $1200 per person to a 22 day canoe trip along the Noatak River for $2500 per person.

Alaska Wilderness Expeditions (tel (907) 479-5496), PO Box 73297, Fairbanks, Alaska 99707, specialises in boating trips in the region around Fairbanks. Their more popular outings are the 2 day run of the Chena or Chatanika rivers, 5 days on the Gulkana River and 7 days along the Fortymile River.

General Bullmoose Canoe Tours (tel (907) 479-4061), 1437 Ithaca, Fairbanks, Alaska 99709, is another one-person operation which takes no more than than five clients

per trip and specialises in 2 to 4 day trips along the Chena River; the basic daily rate is $80 per day.

Brooks Range Expeditions (tel (907) 692-5333), PO Box 9, Bettles, Alaska 99726, operate trips to the Brooks Range by canoe, raft, inflatable canoe and foot during the summer. The following two expeditions are very popular because they combine hiking and boating: backpacking in the Gates of the Arctic and the North Fork River Float, a 10 day adventure for $1500 per person; and 10 days on the Noatak headwaters with numerous day hikes for $1750. The company also rents canoes for those who want to venture into the Brooks range on their own.

CanoeAlaska (tel (907) 479-5183), PO Box 81750, Fairbanks, Alaska 99708, specialises in canoeing trips that teach boating skills and explore scenic rivers. Classes are limited to eight people and rafts are used to support and assist paddlers. Throughout the summer, the guide company runs 2 day trips on the Chena River and 3 day outings on the Gulkana River. The cost is $125 per person and includes instruction, canoe and paddling equipment, meals and transport.

Brown Bear

Southeast Alaska

The north country begins in Southeast Alaska, as do the summer adventures of many visitors to the state, and for good reasons. The Southeast is the closest part of Alaska to the continental USA; Ketchikan is only 90 minutes away by air from Seattle or 2 days on the State Marine Ferry from Bellingham.

The Southeast, affected greatly by warm ocean currents, has the mildest climate in Alaska and offers warm summer temperatures averaging 69°F (20°C), with an occasional heat wave that sends temperatures to 80°F (26°C). Similarly, the winters are equally mild and subzero day temperatures are rare. Residents who have learned to live with an annual rainfall of 60 to 200 inches (1500 to 5000 mm) call the frequent rain 'liquid sunshine'. The heavy precipitation creates the dense, lush forests and numerous waterfalls most travellers come to cherish.

Travel to and around the Southeast is easy. The Alaska State Marine Ferry system connects this roadless area to Bellingham in the US state of Washington and provides transport around the area, making it the longest (and many think the best) public ferry system in North America. Relaxing 3 day cruises through the maze of islands and coastal mountains of the Southeast's Alexander Archipelago is a pleasant alternative to the long and often bumpy Alcan (Alaska Highway). The state ferry connects 15 ports and services 64,000 residents, of which 75% live in Juneau, Ketchikan, Sitka, Petersburg and Wrangell.

However, the best reason to begin and end your trip in the Southeast is its scenery. Few places in the world have the spectacular views found in the Southeast. Rugged snow-capped mountains rise steeply from the water to form sheer-sided fjords, decorated by cascading waterfalls. Ice-blue glaciers that begin among the highest peaks, fan out into a valley of dark-green Sitka spruce trees, and

wilderness waters support whales, sea lions, harbour seals and huge salmon runs.

At one time the Southeast was the heart and soul of Alaska, and Juneau was not only the capital but the state's major city. However, WW II and the Alcan shifted the state's growth to Anchorage and Fairbanks. Today, much of the region lies sleepily in the Tongass National Forest, at 16 million acres (6.5 million hectares) it is the largest national forest in the USA.

In recent years, the Southeast has experienced an incredible boom in summer tourism, but there is still room to breathe. The population density is about 2½ people per sq mile and will probably stay that way as much of the region is federal monuments and preserves such as the spectacular Glacier Bay National Park & Preserve, Admiralty Island and Misty Fjords national monuments, Klondike National Historical Park, Tracy Arm and Fords Terror Wilderness.

More than anywhere else in Alaska, each community in the Southeast clings to its own character, colour and past. There is Norwegian-influenced Petersburg and Russian-tinted Sitka. You can feel the gold fever in Skagway, see lumberjacks and fishers in Ketchikan or venture to Juneau for a hefty dose of government, glaciers and uncontrolled growth.

The best way to visit the Southeast is to purchase a ferry ticket from Bellingham to Skagway ($218 one way) with no itinerary and plenty of time. Stop at each town,

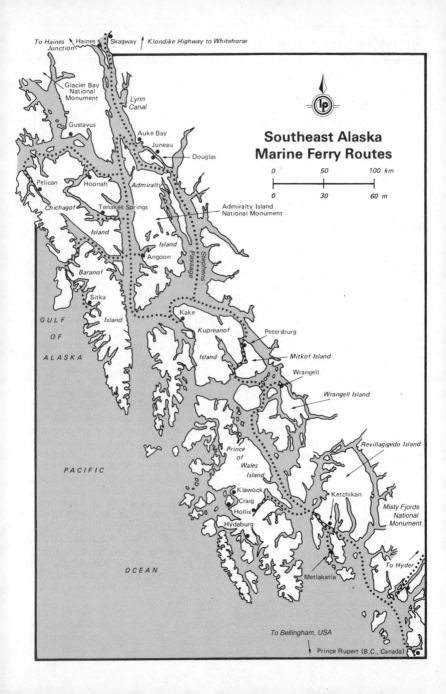

**Southeast Alaska
Marine Ferry Routes**

0   50   100 km

0   30   60 m

explore it and then hop back on the ferry to the next one. To rush from the Lower 48 to Juneau and then fly to Anchorage is to miss some of the best things that Alaska has to offer.

Ketchikan

Ketchikan, otherwise known as the First City, has a population of 13,000 and is located on the south-west side of Revillagigedo (ra-vee-ah-ga-GAY-doh) Island, only 90 miles (144 km) north of Prince Rupert. It is the first stop the state ferry makes in Alaska so tourists pile off the boat for their first look at the north country, and rarely does Ketchikan disappoint them.

The town grew around salmon canneries and sawmills. The first cannery was built in 1883, and at one time Ketchikan was proclaimed the 'Salmon Capital of the World', a title which has since disappeared. A sawmill was built in the centre of Ketchikan in 1903, and in 1954 the huge Ketchikan Pulp Mill was constructed at Ward Cove. However, in the 1970s over-fishing nearly collapsed the salmon fisheries while strikes began to mar the logging industry.

Just as Ketchikan began to recover from hard times, the sawmill in the city centre was hit by a strike in 1983 that resulted in Louisiana-Pacific closing the mill. Two years later the historical downtown mill was razed for a parking lot. In 1984, Louisiana-Pacific shut down the Ward Cove Pulp Mill, the area's major employer, for 6 months, and Ketchikan's population actually decreased during the hard times of the early 1980s.

The city and the people survive, a credit to their frontier image. Although the First City's industries now include government services and tourism, fishing and timber are still its trademark. Fishing provides almost 20% of the city's economy and 230 commercial fishers are based in Ketchikan. The timber industry (consisting of logging, a sawmill and a pulp mill) account for another 14.5% of the jobs. These industries have given the city its rough-and-tumble character and on a Saturday night Ketchikan bars are full, loud and lively.

If you stay in Ketchikan longer than an hour, chances are good that it will rain at least once, if not several times; average annual rainfall is 162 inches (4110 mm), but it has been known to be more than 200 inches (5000 mm). Despite all the rain, the only people with umbrellas are tourists. First City residents never seem to use them, nor do they let the rain interfere with their daily activities, even outdoor ones, whether it be fishing, hiking or having a softball game. If they stopped every time it drizzled, Ketchikan would cease to exist.

Orientation
The city is spread out – it is several miles long and never more than 10 blocks wide. Ketchikan is centred around one road, Tongass Ave, which runs along the shores of Tongass Narrows and sometimes over it, supported by pillars. Crossroads appear mostly in the city centre and the area surrounding the state ferry terminal known as West End. There were no traffic signals in Ketchikan until 1984, and the first one was installed despite the objections of many residents. Many businesses and homes are suspended above the water or cling to the hillside and have winding staircases or wooden streets leading to their front doors.

On a clear day – and there are a few during the summer – Ketchikan is a bustling community. It is backed by forested hills and surrounded by a waterway that hums with float planes, fishing boats, ferries and large cruise ships; to the south is the distinctively shaped Deer Mountain. Whether basked in sunshine or painted with a light drizzle, it is an interesting place to start an Alaskan summer.

Information
Tourist Offices The Ketchikan Visitor Bureau (tel 225-6166) on the City Dock can supply general information about Ketchikan and the city bus system. The bureau is open Monday to Friday from 8 am to 6 pm,

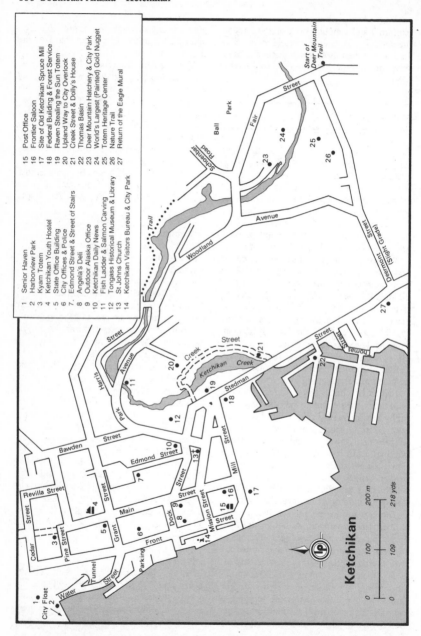

1   Senior Haven
2   Harborview Park
3   Kyam Totem
4   Ketchikan Youth Hostel
5   State Office Building
6   City Offices & Police
7   Edmond Street & Street of Stairs
8   Angela's Deli
9   Outdoor Alaska Office
10 Ketchikan Daily News
11 Fish Ladder & Salmon Carving
12 Tongass Historical Museum & Library
13 St Johns Church
14 Ketchikan Visitors Bureau & City Park

15 Post Office
16 Frontier Saloon
17 Site of Old Ketchikan Spruce Mill
18 Federal Building & Forest Service
19 Raven Stealing the Sun Totem
20 Upland Way to City Overlook
21 Creek Street & Dolly's House
22 Thomas Basin
23 Deer Mountain Hatchery & City Park
24 World's Largest (Painted) Gold Nugget
25 Totem Heritage Center
26 Nature Trail
27 Return of the Eagle Mural

Ketchikan

0   100   200 m
0   109   218 yds

Creek Street, Ketchikan

Saturday from 8 am to 5 pm and Sunday from 8 am to 6 pm.

For information about hiking trails, cabin reservations or other outdoor opportunities, contact the US Forest Service (USFS) information centre (tel 225-2148) in the Federal Building on the corner of Stedman and Mill streets. It is open from 7.30 am to 5 pm weekdays and has information and handouts on activities in the Ketchikan area and a list of cabins still available during the summer. There is also an interesting slide presentation and other displays.

Laundromats The Highland Cafe & Laundromat (tel 225-5308) is at 2703 Tongass Ave. The laundromat closest to the Ketchikan Youth Hostel is Suds & Duds at 825 Bawden St, just off Park Ave, which is open daily from 8 am to 9 pm.

Things to See
The best way to explore Ketchikan is on foot with a 3 hour, 2 mile (3.2 km) walk around the city centre. Start at the visitor bureau, a brown building on the busy City Dock, and pick up a free city map or a copy of the *Ketchikan Daily News Visitors Guide* which has the walking tour in it. Begin by heading south on Front St, which changes to Mill St when it swings sharply east past the site of the Ketchikan Spruce Mill which was demolished in 1985.

Within three blocks, at the corner of Mills and Stedman streets, is the distinctive white **Federal Building** where the US Forest Service maintains its Tongass National Forest Visitor Center on the 1st floor.

By turning right (south-west) on Stedman St, you cross Ketchikan Creek and come to **Creek St**, not so much a street as a boardwalk built on pilings. This was the famed red-light district in Ketchikan for half a century until prostitution became illegal in 1954. During its heyday, Creek St supported up to 30 brothels. The first house, with its bright red doors and windows, is **Dolly's House**, the parlour of the city's most famous madam, Dolly Arthur.

The house has since been turned into a museum dedicated to this infamous era and is open from 9 am to 4 pm daily except Sunday. For a $2 admission fee you can see the brothel, including its bar that was placed over a trapdoor to the creek for quick disposal of bootleg whiskey. There are another 20 buildings on Creek St including small shops, the Morning Raven Artists Gallery and a restaurant. Perhaps the best attraction on this unusual street is free – watching the salmon swim up Ketchikan Creek to spawn.

Across from Creek St is **Thomas Basin**, one of three boat harbours in the city. It is impossible to stay in Ketchikan and not spend any time at the waterfront. The lifeblood of this narrow city is found in its collection of boat harbours, float planes and fishing fleets that stretch along the lapping waters of the Tongass Narrows.

Thomas Basin, along with Thomas Street (another boardwalk built on pilings) is the most picturesque harbour. An hour or so spent at the docks will acquaint you with Ketchikan's fishing fleet and the three kinds of fishing boats – gillnetters, power trollers and seiners. You may even end up at the colourful Potlatch Bar on Thomas St having a brew with someone from the fishing fleet.

Continuing south on Stedman St, you'll pass the large mural, *Return of the Eagle*, on the Ketchikan Community College's Robinson Building. Turn left (east) onto Deermont St. At the beginning of the street is a steep hill, the first of many you will tackle in the Southeast, and at the end is the trailhead for the 3.1 mile (5 km) climb to Deer Mountain (see the Trekking section in the Wilderness chapter). About halfway up the street to the left is a short road that swings to the **Totem Heritage Center**, where totem poles salvaged from deserted Tlingit communities are brought to be restored to their original condition.

The total collection, the largest in Alaska, numbers more than 30, and five of the poles are on display in the central gallery along with indigenous art and artefacts. There are also lectures, films and a 15 minute guided tour during the summer, usually scheduled around the times when the large cruise ships are in port. The centre is open Monday to Saturday from 8 am to 5.30 pm and Sunday from 9 am to 5 pm in the summer; admission is $1.50 but it is free on Sunday afternoon.

A bridge from the Totem Heritage Center crosses Ketchikan Creek to the **Deer Mountain Hatchery**, a fascinating place where biologists annually raise 150,000 king salmon and an equal number of coho salmon and then release them into the nearby stream. Observation platforms, outdoor displays and friendly workers provide an interesting lesson in the salmon's life cycle. In July or later, you'll see not only the salmon fry but returning adult fish swimming upstream to spawn.

Next to the hatchery is **City Park**, a quiet spot with numerous small streams, each, it seems, with its own wooden bridge and bench. The park is a pleasant place to escape the bustling crowds and tour groups that fill the city when a cruise ship is in town.

From the hatchery head down Park Ave, cross Ketchikan Creek again and on the other side of the road you will soon see the Upland Way stairs. A climb up the stairs takes you to a viewing platform overlooking the city centre, Thomas Basin and Creek St. Beyond Upland Way on Park Ave you will arrive at another bridge crossing Ketchikan Creek, with a wooden salmon mounted over a fish ladder at the creek's falls. The ladder enables salmon to reach upstream spawning gravels; it's a magnificent sight when these fish leap against the current during the late-summer migration.

Park Ave curves south towards the city centre and ends at Dock St. Near the corner of Park Ave and Dock St is the Centennial Building which houses the **Ketchikan Public Library** and the **Tongass Historical Museum**. The museum features a small collection of local and indigenous artefacts, many of them tied in with Ketchikan's fishing industry; entry costs $1 but is free on Sunday.

Among the more interesting displays is the model of the *Ketchikan Queen*, a seine boat. The museum is open Monday to Saturday from 8.30 am to 5 pm and Sunday from 1 to 5 pm during the summer. The library is open Monday to Thursday from 10 am to 8 pm, Friday and Saturday from 10 am to 6 pm and from Sunday 1 to 5 pm. Just outside the Centennial Building is the *Raven Stealing the Sun* totem, which was commissioned by the city in 1983.

Head west along Dock St, and alongside the Ketchikan Daily News Building is Edmond St. This is the 'Street of Stairs', as it leads to a system of long staircases. The next crossroad on Dock St is Main St which leads north to the Ketchikan Youth Hostel on the corner of Grant St and to the huge Kyan Totem another block beyond that. If you stay on Dock St you will return to the City Dock.

Festivals

Ketchikan has three major festivals during the summer, of which the Fourth of July celebration is the biggest and the best. It includes a parade, contests and softball games, an impressive display of fireworks over the channel and a logging show sponsored by the Alaska Loggers Association.

On a smaller scale is the Blueberry Festival that takes place in the lower floor and basement of the State Office Building towards the end of August. The festival consists of an arts & crafts show, singers and musicians, and food stalls that serve blueberries in every possible way.

Places to Stay

Camping There are four public campgrounds in Ketchikan and all of them are $5 per night for a site and have a 14 day limit. Unfortunately, none of them are close to town.

Settler's Cove (nine sites) is 16 miles (26 km) north of the ferry terminal and the other three campgrounds are on Ward Lake Rd. Take North Tongass Highway 4 miles (6.4 km) north of the ferry terminal to the pulp mill on Ward Cove and then turn right onto Ward Lake Rd. The first campground is *Signal Creek* (24 sites), 1 mile (1.6 km) up the road. It is followed by *CCC Campground* (four sites) 0.25 mile (0.4 km) further up and *Last Chance Campground* (22 sites), another 1.8 miles (2.9 km) along Ward Lake Rd.

The entire area is known as the Ward Lake Recreational Area and a night spent here is worth all the effort it takes to reach it. Along with the campgrounds there are four scenic lakes and three trails that dip back into the surrounding lush rainforest.

If you are camping and need a shower in town, you can head to one of Ketchikan's two public pools at the Valley Park Elementary School (tel 225-5720), south-east of the city centre, or Ketchikan High School (tel 225-2010) on Baranof Rd in the the West End area. Call for opening times and rates. There are also showers at the Highland Cafe & Laundromat (tel 225-5308), 2703 Tongass Ave.

Hostels The *Ketchikan Youth Hostel* (tel 225-3780) is in the basement of the United Methodist Church on the corner of Grant and Main streets in the centre of the city. It's open from Memorial Day (25 May) to Labor Day (7 September) and provides kitchen facilities (50c extra per meal), showers and a space on the floor with a mat to sleep on.

The hostel is interesting because it always seems full with travellers heading north for a long trip. Since Ketchikan is their first Alaskan stop, they fill the recreation room with travel talk and much excitement in the evenings, and often depart the hostel with a travelling partner or warm friendships. The fee is $4 per night for youth hostel members and $7 per night for nonmembers. If you're arriving at night, call the hostel to check whether space is available.

The *Rain Forest Inn* (tel 225-9500) is at 2311 Hemlock St, 0.7 mile (1.1 km) from the state ferry terminal and half a block from the bus stop at the corner of Tongass Ave and Jefferson St. The Inn offers dormitory bunks for $17 per night and provides showers, laundry facilities and a guest lounge. There are also eight rooms for rent (rates vary with size) that accommodate two to four guests.

Bed & Breakfast Check with Ketchikan Bed & Breakfast (tel 225-8550) to arrange a stay in a private home. Rates begin at $40 for a single and $50 a double, and include breakfast and usually transport from the ferry terminal or airport. You might consider *The Great Alaska Cedar Works* (tel 247-8287) which at one time was the foreman's house of a salmon cannery. Eleven miles (18 km) north of the city, it offers two bedrooms and a sleeping loft with a great view of the Inside Passage; rates are $35 for a single, $55 for a double.

Hotels There is a wide range of hotels in Ketchikan from those catering to cruise-ship tourists to the more dilapidated ones that survive on the flood of summer workers. The *Union Rooms Hotel* (tel 225-3580) at 319 Mill St, one of the more run-down hotels, has rooms with shared baths for $26 per night or $84 per week. The *Gilmore Hotel* at 326 Front St used to be another run-down place before undergoing major renovations recently, giving it a historical flavour. They still have studio rooms with shared baths but the rates now range from $52 to $70 per night. From here, the prices at better hotels jump to $60 per night or more.

Places to Eat

There's a good choice of places to eat in Ketchikan, but all reflect the expensive Alaskan prices that usually send the newly arrived visitor into a 2 day fast. If this is your first Alaskan city, don't fret – it gets worse as you go north!

For breakfast in the city centre, there is the *Pioneer Pantry* at 124 Front St, where two eggs, potatoes and toast is $6. There are also several good sandwich places in the city centre including *Angela's Delicatessen* across from the City Dock, an excellent deli with sandwiches priced from $5 to $7. Similar is *Aardvarks'* in the back of the Gilmore Mall on Front St, with soup and a small sandwich for under $5.

During the summer, the City Dock has several food vendors serving everything from shish kebabs and clam chowder to halibut sandwiches and crepes; most items are under $6 and can be enjoyed while watching the busy waterway and without having to leave a tip.

The best eatery in town is *Kay's Kitchen* at 2813 Tongass Ave, overlooking the Bar Boat Harbor. Kay's menu is limited to sandwiches, thick soups and home-made pies that could very well be the best in the Southeast. This small restaurant is 10 minutes south of the ferry terminal but unfortunately it is only open Tuesday to Saturday from 11 am to 4 pm. It's more expensive than the other sandwich shops but it's worth the extra.

Ketchikan finally received a *McDonald's* in 1985; it's in Port West Plaza on Tongass Ave between the ferry terminal and the tunnel. *Pizza Mill* at 808 Water St and *Harbor Lights Pizza*, 2531 Tongass Ave, are the places to go for a large pizza with everything on it and a pitcher of beer.

For a good Alaskan seafood dinner, try the *Gilmore Garden* in the Gilmore Hotel, which offers abalone, prawns, salmon and halibut fresh from the fleet. Plan on spending at least $15 in this quiet and quaint restaurant. If you want cheaper Alaskan seafood, stop at the *Silver Lining* store at 1705 Tongass Ave, where you can purchase fresh seafood and then cook it yourself at the youth hostel.

Entertainment

After hiking all day, if you're still raring to go, try the *Frontier Saloon* on 127 Main St. The split-level bar has entertainment and dancing nightly during the summer and can be an exceptionally lively place in the true 'bottoms up' fashion.

Another lively place with dance music is the *Sourdough Bar* at the north end of City Dock. The walls of the bar are covered with rows of photos, all of fishing boats, while ship bells, ring floats and other fishing memorabilia hang from the ceiling.

The long-time fisher's pub is the *Potlatch Bar* on Thomas St just above the Thomas Basin Boat Harbor. Just before you enter the tunnel you'll see the *Arctic Bar*, a quiet little place where you can go for an afternoon brew on a hot summer day. The bar is built on pillars above the water and has an open deck that overlooks Tongass Narrows. Here you can enjoy the sea breeze while watching the float planes take off and land, as Taquan Air is next door and moors its planes at the dock right below the deck.

Hiking

There is a variety of hiking adventures in the Ketchikan area, but the majority are either out of town or the trailhead must be reached by boat. The one exception is the Deer Mountain Trail, a 3.1 mile (5 km) climb which begins near the city centre and provides access to two free-use US Forest Service (USFS) cabins and two other alpine trails (see the Trekking section in the Wilderness chapter).

Ward Lake Nature Walk This is an easy trail around Ward Lake that begins near the shelters at the far end of the lake. The trail is 1 mile (1.6 km) of flat terrain and information signs. To reach the lake, follow North Tongass Highway 7 miles (11 km) out of the city to the pulp mill on Ward Cove, turn right

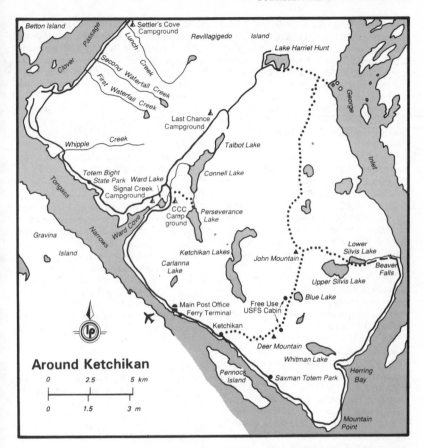

Around Ketchikan

0   2.5   5 km

0   1.5   3 m

on Ward Lake Rd and follow it for 1 mile (1.6 km).

Perseverance Trail This trek is a 2 mile (3.2 km) walk from Ward Lake Rd to Perseverance Lake through mature coastal forest and muskeg. The view of the lake with its mountainous backdrop is spectacular, while the hiking is easy as the trail consists mainly of boardwalks and steps. The trailhead is 1.5 miles (2.4 km) from the start of Ward Lake Rd.

Talbot Lake Trail This trail starts from Connell Lake Rd which is a gravel road that heads east, 3 miles (4.8 km) from the start of Ward Lake Rd. The 1.6 mile (2.6 km) trail is a mixture of boardwalk and gravel surface and leads north from the Connell Lake Dam to Talbot Lake, where it ends at private property. This path will eventually be connected to the Perseverance Trail.

Paddling

Many short and long-term kayak trips begin in Ketchikan and range from an easy paddle in well-protected waters to a 2 week trip to Misty Fjords National Monument and back (see the Paddling section in the Wilderness chapter). Kayaks can be rented from Southeast Exposure (tel 225-8829) or Outdoor Alaska (tel 222-6044). Both businesses have singles and doubles for $30 to $40 per day and can assist you with transport to the end of the road where most paddlers begin. Before any trip, purchase the topographical map that covers the area from Tongass Trading Company at the north end of City Dock.

Naha River Trail From the end of the North Tongass Highway, it's an 8 mile (13 km) paddle to the trailhead for the Naha River Trail, a 6.5 mile (10.4 km) path that follows the river and leads to three USFS cabins and two lakes. The trailhead is on Naha Bay, a body of water that leads into Roosevelt Lagoon through a narrow outlet. Kayakers trying to paddle into the lagoon must enter it at high slack tide, as the narrow pass becomes a frothy, roaring chute when the tide is moving in or out. The current in the salt chuck actually changes directions depending on the tide.

The trail is a combination of boardwalk, swing bridges and an uphill walk to Naha River, Jordan and Heckman Lake cabins. All three cabins ($20 per night) must be reserved in advance at the USFS office in Ketchikan. This is an interesting side trip as locals fish these waters for salmon and trout while in August it's often possible to see bears catching salmon at a small waterfall 2 miles (3.2 km) up the trail from the Roosevelt Lagoon.

Wolf Creek Trail An even easier paddle is the 5 mile (8 km) trip from the end of North Tongass Highway to the trailhead for the Wolf Lake Trail at Moser Bay. The 2.5 mile (4 km) trail passes through timber slopes and over muskeg to a three-sided shelter (no reservation or rental fee) at the outlet of Wolf Lake. A steep hill is encountered near the salt water but this should not discourage the average hiker.

George & Carroll Inlets At the end of South Tongass Highway past Herring Bay, you are

already in George Inlet, which makes this 3 to 4 day paddle an easy one in water that is calm most of the time. North winds do occasionally whip down George Inlet but both waterways are protected from southwesterlies, the prevailing winds in the Ketchikan area.

While not on the same dramatic scale as Misty Fjords, the two inlets are scenic and it's an easy way to explore some of Ketchikan's backcountry. The return trip from Herring Bay to the end of George Inlet is a 25 mile (40 km) paddle.

USFS Cabins

There are 30 cabins in the Ketchikan area; most need to be reserved in advance and cost $20 per day. The following cabins are close to the city, which reduces air-charter time, the biggest cost factor in using them. There are numerous bush-plane operators in Ketchikan; two of the more reliable ones are Temscoir (tel 225-9810), 1249 South Tongass Ave, Ketchikan, Alaska 99901 and Ketchikan Air Service (tel 225-6608), 1600 International Airport, Ketchikan, Alaska 99901.

Alava Bay Cabin This cabin is on the southern end of Behm Canal. It provides ample opportunity for hiking and beachcombing along the coast, freshwater fishing and viewing wildlife such as black bear and Sitka deer. The cabin is 20 air miles (32 km) from Ketchikan.

Fish Creek Cabin A short trail connects Thorne Bay with the Fish Creek Cabin. You can either paddle to it (a 3 to 4 day trip) or fly in, as it is only 18 air miles (29 km) from Ketchikan. There is a trail to nearby Low Lake, while fishing for cutthroat trout, rainbow trout and Dolly Varden is possible in the creek.

Patching Lake Cabins There are two cabins on Patching Lake, 20 air miles (32 km) from Ketchikan. At either one there is good fishing for cutthroat trout and grayling.

Other cabins in the area include three on the Naha River Trail (see the Ketchikan Paddling section in this chapter) and the two free-use cabins on the Deer Mountain and Blue Lake trails that require no reservations.

Getting There & Away

Air Alaska Airlines (tel 225-2141) flies to Ketchikan with stops at other major Southeast communities as well as Anchorage and Seattle. There are several flights between Ketchikan and Juneau, including one that locals call the 'milk run', as it stops at Petersburg, Wrangell and Sitka and is little more than a series of take-offs and landings. One-way fares from Ketchikan to Juneau and Sitka are $100, and $85 to Petersburg.

Boat It's an exceptional day when there isn't a ferry departing from Ketchikan for other Southeast destinations or Bellingham. One-way fares from Ketchikan to Wrangell are $20, Petersburg $32, Juneau $66, Sitka $48 and Haines $78.

The state ferry *Chilkat* used to make several runs a day to Metlakatla from Ketchikan but now it only sails during the winter when the other boats are in dry dock. The service to Metlakatla has since been added to the *Aurora* on its trip to Hollis on Prince of Wales Island. The trip runs several times a week and the one-way fare to Hollis is $16 and to Metlakatla $12.

For exact sailing times call the ferry terminal (tel 225-6181).

Getting Around

Airport Transport The Ketchikan airport is on one side of Tongass Narrows and the city is on the other. Years ago there was talk of building a bridge from the airport across the channel to town. That was only talk, and today you hop on the airport ferry that leaves the airport every half hour and departs from next to the state ferry terminal on the quarter hour. The fare is $2 one way or return if you travel both ways in a single day.

Bus The city bus system consists of small buses that hold up to 30 passengers and follow a circular route from the ferry terminal in the West End of town to the area south of Thomas Basin, circling back by the Totem Heritage Center and the trailhead to Deer Mountain. The route does not include Saxman Totem Park or anything north of the state ferry terminal. Buses return to each stop every hour; the fare is $1.

The drivers are exceptionally friendly and can often be coaxed into pointing out the town's highlights and giving you titbits of Alaskan lore. The city buses are a cheap alternative to the expensive Gray Line bus tours of the city.

Bicycle & Car Rental Another way to get around the city – an alternative to hitching – is to rent a bicycle at People Power Bike Shop (tel 225-2488) at 1920 Tongass Ave. Then there is always All Star Car Rental, which rents vehicles for $40 a day with unlimited mileage. For two to four people, this is a good way to spend a day seeing the sights out of town. The rental company operates two offices, one in the airport (tel 225-2232) and a second in the city centre (tel 225-5123).

AROUND KETCHIKAN
Saxman Totem Park

For a look at the world's largest standing collection of totem poles, head 2.3 miles (3.7 km) south of Ketchikan on South Tongass Highway to Saxman Totem Park. The park's 24 poles were bought here from abandoned villages around the Southeast and were restored or recarved in the 1930s.

At the entrance to the park is the impressive *Sun & Raven* totem, probably the most photographed one in Alaska, and the rest of the park is uphill from there. Among the collection is a replica of the Lincoln Pole; the original is in the Alaska State Museum in Juneau. This pole was carved in 1883 to commemorate the first sighting of white people, using a picture of Abraham Lincoln.

Saxman Totem Park, an incorporated Indian village of more than 300 residents, also has a community hall and theatre where you can see a slide and sound show about the park and Tlingit culture. This cultural centre (tel 225-9038) is open daily in the summer from 8.30 am to 5 pm. There is also a gift shop, of course, and a recently completed tribal house with indigenous artists working on various projects. Dance performances are given regularly at Saxman during the summer; call the cultural centre for details.

North Tongass Highway

Mud Bight is 9.5 miles (15.3 km) north of Ketchikan along North Tongass Highway, past the Ward Creek Recreation Area. This community of float houses is an interesting spot as the dwellings rise and fall with the water to the extent that they are left high on the mud at low tide.

Totem Bight, 10 miles (16 km) north of Ketchikan, is a state historical park (no entry fee) that contains 14 restored or recarved totems and a colourful community house. Just as impressive as the totems is the park's wooded setting and the coastline. A viewing deck overlooks the Tongass Narrows. The North Tongass Highway ends 18 miles (29 km) north of Ketchikan at Settler's Cove State Campground, another scenic coastal area with a lush rainforest bordering a gravel beach and rocky coastline.

Misty Fjords National Monument

This spectacular national monument, which begins just 22 miles (35 km) east of Ketchikan, is best noted for its sea cliffs, steep-sided fjords and rock walls that jut 3000 feet (900 metres) straight out of the ocean. Walker Cove, Rudyerd Bay and Punchbowl Cove, the most picturesque areas of the preserve, are reached via Behm Canal, the long, deep inlet that separates Revillagigedo Island from the Coast Mountains on the mainland.

Wildlife at Misty Fjords includes brown or black bears, mountain goats, Sitka deer, bald eagles and a variety of marine mammals. As the name suggests, the monument can be a drizzly place with an average annual rainfall of 150 inches (3810 mm), but many people think the real beauty of Misty

Mountain Goat

Fjords lies in the granite walls and tumbling waterfalls wrapped in a veil of fog and mist.

The preserve is popular with kayakers (see the Paddling section of the Wilderness chapter), while less adventurous visitors view it on day cruises or sightseeing flights. Viewing Misty Fjords from a charter plane costs $110 per hour or so with either Misty Fjords Air Outfitters (tel 225-5155) or Temsco Air Service (tel 225-9810). The time actually spent viewing the monument is short however, and the area's peaceful setting is lost when the pilot has to yell at you over the roar of the bush plane.

Tour ships offer a more dramatic perspective of the preserve while letting you view it at a more leisurely pace. Outdoor Alaska (tel 225-6044) offers an 11 hour cruise for $120 that departs from Ryus float at the foot of Dock St, Ketchikan. The boat leaves at 8.30 am every Friday, Wednesday, Saturday and Sunday, and the cruise includes a small breakfast, sandwich buffet lunch and dinner. A shorter 8 hour trip in which you return aboard a bush plane costs $175. If you can plan ahead, the best way to experience Misty

Fjords is to rent one of the 15 US Forest Service cabins (reservations needed, $15 per night) in the area.

Metlakatla

This small Indian community used to be a common day trip out of Ketchikan until the state ferry *Chilkat* was taken out of service. Metlakatla is now served four times a week by the *Aurora*; on Saturday the ferry visits the community twice, making it possible to do a day trip from Ketchikan. The rest of the week the ferry stays in port only as long as it takes to unload, generally half an hour, which means viewing the town requires either staying overnight or flying back to Ketchikan.

Metlakatla, 12 miles (19.5 km) south-west of Ketchikan on the west coast of Annette Island, is a well-planned community in the heart of the Annette Island Indian Reservation, the only reservation in Alaska. The village (pop 1500) bustles during the summer as its boat harbour overflows with fishing vessels and its cold- storage plant & cannery, which has been operating continuously since 1901, is busy handling the catch of the fleet.

Things to See While on board the ferry or from shore near the terminal, you can see one of the community's four fish traps, a large collection of logs and wire with a small hut off to one side. The fish traps, illegal everywhere else in Alaska, catch salmon by guiding the fish through a series of funnels, keeping them alive until ready to harvest.

The main attraction in town is **Father Duncan's Cottage**, now preserved as a museum. Metlakatla was founded when William Duncan, a Scottish-born minister, led several hundred Tsimshian Indians here from British Columbia in 1887 after a dispute with church authorities. In 1891, Congress granted reservation status to the entire island and under Duncan's supervision the tribe prospered after building a salmon cannery and sawmill. Duncan lived in the cottage until his death in 1918 and it now features the minister's personal artefacts and

photographs of turn-of-the-century Metlakatla. The museum is open Monday to Friday from 10 am to 5 pm; admission is $1.

A traditional **Tribal Loghouse**, down by the small boat harbour, houses displays of log carvings and indigenous art, and is the site of the community salmon bake whenever a cruise ship is in port. The Annette Island Cannery (tel 886-4661) used to offer tours but call them first as there were plans to discontinue them.

Places to Stay & Eat There is accommodation at the *Taquan Inn* (tel 886-6112) for $30 a single, and in the back a small cafe overlooks the cannery. Keep in mind the town is dry and they discourage camping on the island. In the end, it's better and much cheaper to visit Metlakatla on Saturday, bring your own lunch and plan on spending the night back in Ketchikan.

Hiking The hike to Yellow Hill provides good views of the western side of the island. Walk south along Airport Rd for 1.5 miles (2.4 km) and look for the boardwalk on the right; it's an easy 30 minute walk to the top. Another hike in the area is the 3 mile (4.8 km) Purple Lake Trail, 1.8 miles (2.9 km) down Purple Mountain Rd. You can reach Purple Mountain Rd by travelling 2.7 miles (4.3 km) south on Airport Rd. This trail involves a steep climb to the mountainous lake area.

Getting There & Away Three days a week the state ferry *Aurora* makes a single run to Metlakatla but on Saturday it visits the community twice. The first run departs Ketchikan at 9.15 am, arriving in Metlakatla in about an hour. The second run leaves Metlakatla at 6.30 pm, giving you almost 8 hours on the island. Since the ferry terminal is only 1 mile (1.6 km) east of town, there's enough time to walk to Metlakatla for an interesting and cheap trip. The one-way ferry ticket from Ketchikan to Metlakatla is $12.

You can also fly to Metlakatla – Temsco Airlines (tel 225- 9810) provide daily, regularly scheduled flights for around $20 one way.

Hyder

Hyder is a state ferry port at the head of Portland Canal on the fringe of Misty Fjords National Monument. Nass Indians regularly visited the area to hunt birds, pick berries and more often than not to hide from the aggressive Haida tribes. In 1896, Captain D D Gailland explored the Portland Canal for the US Army Corps of Engineers and built four stone storehouses, the first masonry buildings erected in Alaska, which still stand today.

But Hyder and its British Columbia neighbour Stewart, didn't boom until Yukon gold-rush prospectors began settling in the area at the turn of the century. Major gold and silver mines were opened in 1919 and Hyder, enjoying its heyday, became the supply centre. It's been downhill ever since and the population has now shrunk to around 40 to 60 year-round residents, leading to its title 'the friendliest ghost town in Alaska'.

Because of Hyder's isolation from the rest of the state, and the country for that matter, residents are almost totally dependent on the much larger Stewart (pop 900) just across the Canadian border. They use Canadian money in Hyder, set their watches to Pacific time (not Alaska time), use a British Columbia area code and the children go to school in Canada. All this can make a side trip here a little confusing.

The most famous thing to do in Hyder is drink at one of it's 'friendly saloons'. The historic *Glacier Inn* is the best known and features an interior papered in signed bills, creating the '$20,000 Walls' of Hyder. The *First and Last Chance Saloon* is also well known and both bars hop at night.

Stewart has a museum or you can head 3 miles north of town to Fish Creek and watch bears feed on chum salmon runs from late July to September. If you want to kill a day, hitchhike 30 miles (49 km) east of Stewart on Highway 37A in British Columbia to Bear Glacier; it can be viewed without even getting out of the car.

Places to Stay In Stewart, there's the *Rainey Creek Campsite* ($9 per night) or the *King Edward Hotel*, the *King Edward Motel* and the *Alpine Hotel*. Single rooms for each of the hotels are $45, and doubles are $52.

Getting There & Away Hyder is a possible side trip from Ketchikan because the ferry *Aurora* departs Ketchikan at 12.30 am on Friday and reaches Hyder at 11.45 am. It then departs Hyder at 3 pm on Friday and reaches Ketchikan at 1.45 am on Saturday, giving you 3 hours to explore the town (or drink in the bars). The one-way fare is $32 and the trip includes cruising scenic Portland Canal. If you want to stay overnight call Temsco Airlines (tel 225-9810 in Ketchikan) which has a schedule service once a week between Ketchikan and Hyder.

Prince of Wales Island

If time is no problem and out-of-the-way places or different lifestyles intrigue you, then this accessible island with Indian villages and logging camps can be an interesting jaunt. At 135 miles (220 km) long and covering more than 2230 sq miles (5775 sq km), Prince of Wales Island is the third largest island in the USA after Kodiak and Hawaii.

The island's landscape is characterised by steep forested mountains, deep U-shaped valleys, lakes, salt-water straits and bays that were carved out by glaciers long ago. The mountains rise to 3000 feet (900 metres) and the spruce-hemlock forest is broken up by muskegs and, unfortunately, many clear cuts. The 900 mile (1450 km) coastline has numerous bays, coves, inlets and protective islands, making it a kayaker's delight.

You can take the state ferry from Ketchikan to Hollis; from this village (pop 475) there is access to a 500 mile (800 km) network of rough dirt roads, the most extensive network in the Southeast – in fact more roads than the rest of Southeast put together. The logging roads connect Hollis with remote backcountry and the villages of Craig, Klawock, Thorne Bay and Hydaburg. For someone carrying a bicycle through

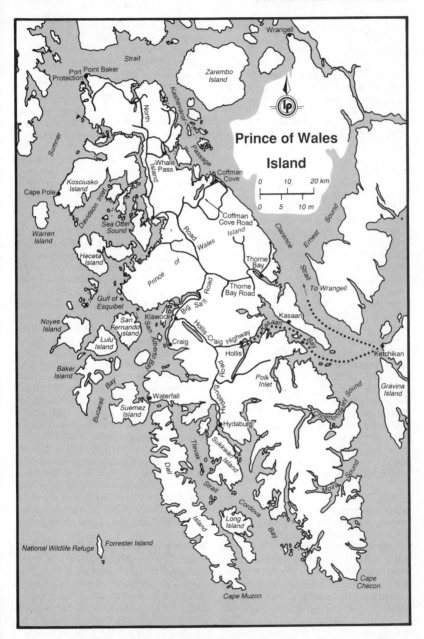

Alaska, especially a mountain bike, a week on Prince of Wales Island is worth all the trouble of carting it around.

Getting There & Away The state ferry *Aurora* makes a daily Ketchikan to Hollis run during the summer, including two trips on Saturday. The one-way fare from Ketchikan to Hollis and from Metlakatla to Hollis is $16. Once at Hollis, where there are few visitor facilities and no stores or restaurants, getting around the island is a little more difficult.

Prince of Wales Transporter (tel 755-2348) runs a minivan between Hydaburg and Klawock, stopping at Craig along the way, for $15 one way. Ask the ticket agent at the state ferry terminal as soon as you arrive for information on minivan departures. You can always hitchhike as there is a small amount of traffic to Craig and Klawock after the arrival and departure of each ferry, but keep in mind that almost half the boats arrive after 9 pm and some at 3.30 am.

If there are three or four of you, an ideal way to get around is to rent a vehicle at Ketchikan's All Star Rental (tel 225-2232 in Ketchikan) and take it over on the state ferry for an additional $17 one way. This allows you to explore the far reaches of the island and to fish the highly productive streams (accessible by road) for cutthroat trout, Dolly Varden and salmon. Two of the 22 US Forest Service cabins, Stanley Creek Cabin and Red Bay Lake Cabin (reservations needed, $20 rental fee), can be reached from the road; check with the USFS information centre in the Ketchikan Federal Building for availability.

With a mountain bike you can explore the island and its network of logging roads; there are only 30 miles (49 km) of gravel surface roads which stretch from Hollis to Klawock and then south to Craig. The rest are logging roads and their condition depends on the weather and the amount of traffic on them. It's not unusual to find a culvert missing or a section washed out completely and passable only by 4WD vehicles – in other words, a mountain biker's dream come true. The

fare to carry a bike over on the ferry is $5 one way but invest another $2 for a copy of the *Prince of Wales Road Guide* that can be purchased at the US Forest Service office in Ketchikan or Craig.

Craig Craig (pop 1167), 31 miles (50 km) north-west of Hollis, is the most interesting community to visit, and on a Saturday night you can rub elbows with loggers and fishers in lively Alaskan fashion at the Craig Inn. The town was founded as a salmon canning and cold storage site in 1907 and today fishing still accounts for more than half of its employment. Most of the rest are employed in the logging industry which explains the clear cuts around Craig.

Other than a totem pole that washed up on a beach and was erected in front of the old school gym, there are no 'attractions' in Craig. The reason you come here is to experience an Alaska town that doesn't turn itself inside out for tourists every summer. For information on fishing, hiking and paddling trips, contact the US Forest Service office (tel 826-3271) on 9th St near the boat harbour; it's open Monday to Friday from 8 am to 4.30 pm.

Camping is permitted in the city park overlooking the ocean. The park is a short hike from town and can be reached by following Hamilton Drive onto Graveyard Island, or just ask any local for directions to the ball field. Other accommodation includes a lodge and *Ruthann's Hotel* (tel 826-3377) which has 10 rooms from $50 to $60 per night. There are also dour restaurants, including *Lacey's Pizza* in the Thibodeau Mall, closed Monday and Tuesday but open to 9 pm the rest of the week, and *Thompson House Grocery*. Like any other remote village in Alaska, food prices are very high.

Klawock Klawock (pop 760) is a Tlingit village 24 miles (39 km) north-west of Hollis and only 6 miles (10 km) north of Craig. The town was the site of the first cannery in Alaska built in 1878 but is better known today for its collection of 21 totem poles. Totem Park, in the centre of the village,

Top: Cruise ship pulling into Juneau (ADT)
Bottom: Commercial fishing boats in Southeast Alaska harbor (USFS)

Top: Hiking in the lush rainforests of Southeast Alaska (USFS)
Left: Totem pole in Southeast Alaska (CAT)
Right: Totem poles in Sitka National Historical Park (ADT)

features both replicas and originals that were found in the abandoned Indian village of Tuxekan in the 1930s.

The best place to stay is half a mile up Big Salt Road at *Log Cabin Campgrounds* (tel 755-2205) which offer tent space and showers for $15 per night and rustic cabins along the beach for $35 per night. They also rent canoes for $18 per day that can be used in either Big Salt Lake or Klawock Lake. Within town there is a city-operated campground (12 sites, fee) while *Dave's Diner* (tel 755-2986) has the cheapest meals.

Thorne Bay Thorne Bay (pop 518) was established in 1962 when Ketchikan Pulp Company moved its main logging camp here from Hollis. Some say the town still looks like a logging camp but it lies in a picturesque setting 59 miles (95 km) north-east of Hollis.

Just 6 miles (10 km) north of Thorne Bay on Forest Rd 30 is the *Sandy Beach Picnic Area* with tables, pit toilets and fireplaces. It's a great place to set up camp as there are spectacular views of Clarence Strait. Another scenic spot is the *Gravely Creek Picnic Area*, 4 miles (6.5 km) north-west of the village on Thorne Bay Road. The facility has fireplaces, pit toilets and an open shelter. Less than 1 mile (1.6 km) away, the Thorne River offers excellent fishing for cutthroat trout, Dolly Varden, rainbow trout and steelhead.

In Thorne Bay, supplies can be obtained at *Clear Cut Market* while *Gallagher's Galley* (tel 828-3955) offers meals. *McFarland's Floatel* (tel 828-3335), an unusual place to stay, offers rooms in a large float house that rises and falls with the tides from $55 for a single. They also have beach-front log cabins for $100 a day that sleep four. There is a US Forest Ranger Office (tel 828-3304) in town for recreational information on the area.

Hydaburg This town (pop 475) was founded in 1911 when three Haida villages were combined. Today, most of the residents are commercial fishers but subsistence is still a necessary part of life. Located 36 miles (58 km) south-west of Hollis, Hydaburg was only connected to the rest of the island by road in 1983.

This scenic village is known for an excellent collection of restored totems in a park that was developed in the 1930s. It also provides easy access for paddlers into the South Prince of Wales Wilderness, a 90,000 acre (36,000 hectares) preserve. Lodging and meals are available at *Sanderson's Boarding House* (tel 285-3244) while *Tide's Inn* (tel 285-3292) also serves meals. There is also a grocery store and gasoline station in town.

Wrangell

The next major town north along the state ferry route is Wrangell, a cluster of canneries, shipping docks, lumber mills and logging tugs. The community's claim to history is that it is the only Alaskan fort to have existed under three flags – Russian, British and American. Its strategic location near the mouth of the Stikine River has given it a long and colourful history.

The Russians founded the town when they arrived in 1834 and built a stockade they called Redoubt St Dionysius. Its purpose then was to prevent encroachment by the Hudson Bay traders working their way down the Stikine River. But in 1840, the Russians leased it to the British, who renamed it Fort Stikine.

The Americans gained control of the centre when they purchased Alaska, and in 1868 changed the name to Fort Wrangell. Wrangell thrived as an important supply centre for fur traders and later for gold miners, who used the Stikine River to reach gold rushes in both British Columbia and the Klondike fields in the Yukon.

Today, the town is still considered colourful by Southeast residents but for different reasons. Wrangell is a proud, traditional and sometimes stubborn community that clings to age-old Alaskan beliefs of independence

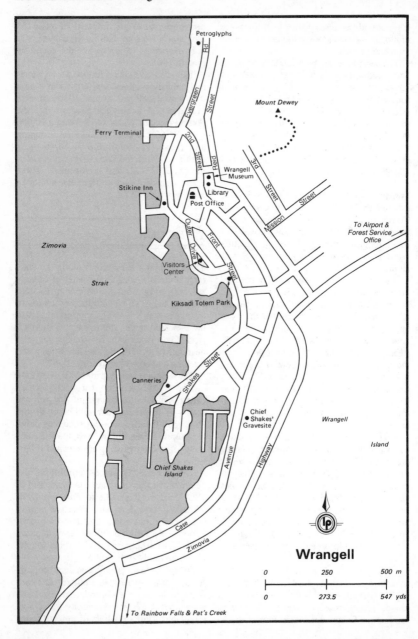

Petroglyphs

Evergreen Rd

2nd Street

Reid Street

Mount Dewey

Ferry Terminal

Wrangell Museum

3rd Street

Stikine Inn

Library

Post Office

Mission Street

Zimovia

Outer Drive

Front Street

To Airport & Forest Service Office

Strait

Visitors Center

Kiksadi Totem Park

Shakes Street

Canneries

Chief Shakes' Gravesite

Wrangell

Case Avenue

Chief Shakes Island

Zimovia Highway

Island

Wrangell

0	250	500 m
0	273.5	547 yds

To Rainbow Falls & Pat's Creek

from excess government and of using the land and natural resources to earn a living.

As the rest of the state is pushed into the 21st century with heavy regulations on industries such as mining, logging and fishing, Wrangell often finds itself lagging behind economically while resisting the new ideas of preserving and setting aside the wilderness. It's not that the town lynches environmentalists every Saturday night, but the issues surrounding the Alaska Lands Bill, or 'd-2', were not easy ones for Wrangell residents to accept.

Wrangell (pop 3100) has an economy still based heavily on a lumber mill, 6 miles (9.6 km) south of town, and on a fishing fleet that supports a cannery and a cold-storage plant along the waterfront. The boat harbour in town is busy during the summer, but it is nowhere near as large as those in Ketchikan or Petersburg.

Information

The Wrangell Visitor Center (874-3901) is an A-frame hut on Outer Drive in front of City Hall. It is open on a part-time basis that usually coincides with the cruise ship schedule. Nearby is the Wrangell Sentinel on Lynch St, which publishes the free *Wrangell Visitors Guide*, the best source of information for the area.

The US Forest Service (USFS) office (tel 874-2323), 0.75 miles (1.2 km) north of town at 525 Bennett St, is open from 8 am to 5 pm Monday to Friday. It is the source of information for USFS cabins, trails and campgrounds in the area.

Things to See

Wrangell is one of the few places in the Southeast where the ferry terminal is in the heart of town. If you're not planning to spend a night here, you can still disembark for a quick look around. To get a good view of Wrangell, including a stroll out to the petroglyphs along the shoreline, you'll need about 2 hours.

Beginning at the state ferry terminal, you can reach the **Wrangell Museum** by going up 2nd St to the large white building on the left. The museum is housed in the town's first schoolhouse, built in 1906 and later used as a morgue and city hall, among other things. The collection features indigenous artefacts, petroglyphs, local relics and photographs from Wrangell's past. There is also a room devoted to the town's artists. The museum is open Monday to Saturday from 1 to 4 pm or whenever a cruise ship is in port; it charges $1 for admission.

Next door to the museum is the **Wrangell Public Library** with several totems in front of it, while diagonally opposite is the US Customs office and the post office. There is a good view of Zimovia Strait from the post-office lawn.

By heading south down the hill from the post office, you come to Front St and the beginning of Wrangell's business district. The eastern (uphill) side of Front St is the historical section with each building featuring its distinctive false front. The other side of the street is a land-fill area, as a fire ravaged the centre of town in 1952, destroying docks and buildings originally built on pilings over the water. Also on Front St is **Kiksadi Totem Park**, which was dedicated in 1987 by Sealaska Native Corporation with the first traditional totem raising in Wrangell in more than 40 years. Four totems are now in place.

Continue south along Front St and you will pass the former mill site of the Alaska Pulp Company. The mill still stands but operations have been moved to another mill 6 miles (9.6 km) south along the Zimovia Highway. At the old mill, Front St flows into Shakes St, which ends with the cannery and freezing factory of Wrangell Fisheries Inc and Wrangell Fresh Seafood. No tours are available at either place.

Across from the cannery is the bridge to **Chief Shakes Island**, Wrangell's most interesting attraction, about 1 mile (1.6 km) from the ferry terminal. The island, in the town's Inner Boat Harbor, features an impressive collection of totem poles (duplicates of the originals that were carved in the late 1930s) and the **Shakes Community House** (tel 874-3770). The community house is an excellent example of a high-caste tribal house and contains tools, blankets and other cultural items. It is open at various times to accommodate the cruise ships in town (call them for details), and there is a $1 donation to see it. Just as impressive as the tribal house is the view of bustling Wrangell Harbor from the island.

From Shakes St you can turn right onto Case Ave and follow it for two blocks to Hansen's Boat Shop. Across the street on the hillside is Chief Shakes' gravesite enclosed by a Russian-style picket fence topped by two killer-whale totems.

Festivals

The only major event during the summer, other than the local salmon derby, is the Fourth of July celebration. All of Wrangell, like most small Alaskan communities, gets involved in the festival, which features a parade, fireworks, logging show, street games, food booths and a salmon bake in town.

Places to Stay

Camping The nearest campground to town is the *City Park*, 1.8 miles (2.9 km) south of the ferry terminal on Zimovia Highway. This waterfront park is immediately south of the cemetery and city ball field and provides picnic tables, shelters and rest rooms. Camping is free but there is a 2 day limit.

Further out of town is the *Shoemaker Bay Recreation Area*, 4.7 miles (7.5 km) south of the ferry terminal on Zimovia Highway and across from the trailhead to the Rainbow Falls Trail. Camping is provided in a wooded area near a creek, and there is a 10 day limit but no fees.

Still further south is *Pat's Creek* at *Mile 10.8* (17 km) of Zimovia Highway where it becomes a narrow Forest Service road. There are two dirt roads heading off to the left; the first is to the lake and the second is to the campground, basically just a clear spot that is no longer maintained by the US Forest Service. Near the campground there is a trail along the creek that leads back to Pat's Lake

where you'll find good fishing for cutthroat trout and Dolly Varden.

Bed & Breakfast If staying in a private home interests you, there is *Clarke Bed & Breakfast* (tel 874-2125 day, 874-3863 evening) at 732 Case Ave. A bed and a meal in the morning costs $35 for singles and $45 for doubles. You should call ahead as their rooms are limited. There's also *Barton's by the Sea* (tel 874-3045) near Petroglyph Beach which features two rooms with an ocean view. Rates are $40 for a single and $45 for a double.

Hotels There is no youth hostel and only three hotels in town; the cheapest is the *Thunderbird Hotel* (tel 874 3322) at 110 Front St with rooms from $45 per night.

Places to Eat

The cheapest place for a meal is *The Wharf* on Front St, across from the laundromat. The restaurant is open daily and has the usual fare of eggs, sandwiches and hamburgers. Nearer to the ferry terminal and open later at night is *J&W's* at the City Dock, which sells hamburgers and hot dogs. The same menu can be found at the *Snack Shack* on Front St.

The town's best place to eat, featuring local shrimp and other seafood, is at the *Dockside Restaurant* in the Stikine Inn, with its excellent view of the boat harbour; dinners range from $15 to $20. *Benjamin's* on Outer Drive is the largest supermarket and carries ready-to-eat items in its deli. Also, fishermen often sell their catch to residents and visitors down at the boat harbours. Shrimp and salmon are the delicacy of the Wrangell fleet.

Entertainment

It is often in the town's bars that the true spirit of Wrangell comes shining through. Mingle with locals at the *Totem Bar* on Front St or with people from the fishing industry at the *Marine Bar* on Shakes St near Chief Shakes Island. During a night run on the ferry, you have time to get off for a beer at the *Stikine*

Inn Lounge, which has live music and the only dance floor in Wrangell.

Hiking

Petroglyphs An interesting afternoon can be spent looking for petroglyphs – primitive rock carvings believed to be 8000 years old. The best set lie 0.75 miles (1.2 km) from the ferry terminal and can be reached by heading north on Evergreen Rd or, as the local call it, Old Airport Rd. Walk past Stough's Trailer Court and proceed to a marked wooden walkway. Follow the boardwalk to the beach and then turn right and start walking north toward the end of the island. With your back to the water, look for the carvings on the large rocks.

Many of the petroglyphs are spirals and faces, and there are about 20 in the area but most are submerged during high tide. Check a tide book before you leave and remember that the entire walk takes 1 to 2 hours – too long for the state ferry stopover. Several gift shops in town sell 'rubbing kits' that allow you to take images of the carvings home on rice paper.

Mt Dewey Trail This 0.5 mile (0.8 km) trail winds its way up a hill to an observation point overlooking Wrangell and the surrounding waterways. From Mission St, walk a block and turn left at the first corner, 3rd St. Follow the street past a brown and red A-frame house with a white balcony. The trail, marked by a white sign, begins 50 yards (45 metres) past the house on the right. Once you're at the trailhead, the hike is a short one, 15 minutes or so to the top, but it is often muddy.

Rainbow Falls Trail This old trail was rebuilt and extended in 1985 by the US Forest Service (USFS). The trailhead for the Rainbow Falls Trail is signposted 4.7 miles (7.5 km) south of the ferry terminal on the Zimovia Highway. The trail begins directly across from the Shoemaker Bay Recreation Area and just before the Wrangell Institute Complex.

From the trailhead it is a 1 mile (1.6 km) hike to the waterfalls and then another 2.5 miles (4 km) to an observation point overlooking Shoemaker Bay on Institute Ridge, where the USFS has built a three-sided shelter. The lower section can be soggy at times so it is best hiked in rubber boots, while upper sections are steep. The views are worth the hike and a pleasant evening can be spent on the ridge. A return trip to the ridge takes 4 to 6 hours.

Thoms Lake Trail At the end of the paved Zimovia Highway is a dirt road, known officially as Forest Rd 6290, that extends 30 miles (48 km) south along Wrangell Island. On this road, 23 miles (37 km) south of Wrangell, is the Thoms Lake Trail, which leads 1.2 miles (1.9 km) to a state park recreation cabin and a skiff on the lake. Since there is no state park office in Wrangell, you have to reserve the cabin through the Divison of Parks office in Juneau (tel 465-4563). Keep in mind that this trails cuts through muskeg and during wet weather can get extremely muddy. It is a 1½ hour hike to the cabin.

Long Lake Trail The trailhead for the Long Lake Trail is 27 miles (44 km) south-east of Wrangell on Forest Rd 6270. This pleasant hike is only 0.6 mile (0.9 km) and planked the entire way. It leads to a shelter, skiff and outhouses on the shores of the lake.

Paddling

The beautiful and wild Stikine River is characterised by a narrow and rugged shoreline and the mountains and hanging glaciers that surround it. It is the fastest navigable river in North America and is highlighted by the Grand Canyon, a steep-walled enclosure of the waterway where churning white water makes river travel impossible. Trips from below the canyon are common among rafters and kayakers; they begin with a charter flight to Telegraph Creek in British Columbia and end with a 160 mile (256 km) float back to Wrangell.

Travellers who arrive at Wrangell with their own kayak but not enough funds for the expensive charter of a bush plane can undertake a trip from the town's harbour across the Stikine Flats, where there are several US Forest Service (USFS) cabins, and up one of the three arms of the Stikine River. By keeping close to shore and taking advantage of eddies and sloughs, experienced paddlers can make their way 30 miles (49 km) up the Stikine River to the Canadian border or even further, passing 12 USFS cabins and the two bathing huts at Chief Shakes Hot Springs along the way. But you must know how to line a boat upstream and navigate a highly braided river.

The USFS office in Wrangell can provide information on the Stikine River, including a very helpful brochure and map entitled *Stikine River Canoe and Kayak Trips*. There are no places in Wrangell to rent a canoe or kayak. If you are without a boat but are still intrigued by the Stikine River, plan to rent one in Juneau.

Guide companies no longer offer boat trips down the Stikine, probably due to a lack of demand. Several charter captains will run up the river but usually only for a day of fishing or sightseeing; inquire at the visitor centre for further details.

USFS Cabins

The 20 USFS cabins in the Wrangell Ranger District are not usually as busy as those around Juneau or Ketchikan. Six of them (Binkley Slough, Koknuk, Little Dry Island, Sergief Island and two on Gut Island) lie in the Stikine River Flats, 12 to 15 miles (19 to 24 km) from Wrangell. The cabins can be paddled to or are a 30 minute bush-plane flight.

The most interesting cabin in the area, however, is on the mainland at Anan Bay, 28 air miles (45 km) from Wrangell. Near the Anan Bay Cabin is a 1 mile (1.6 km) trail that leads to a bear observation & photography platform. The observatory is on the creek from Anan Lake and in July and August can be used to safely watch black bears feeding on the salmon runs. The cabin is a 50 minute flight from Wrangell or a 31 mile (50 km) paddle.

Getting There & Away

Air Alaska Airlines (tel 874-3308) provides a year-round jet service to Wrangell with a daily northbound and southbound flight. Many claim that the flight north to Petersburg is the 'world's shortest jet flight', since the 11 minute trip is little more than a take-off and landing with the huge aircraft seeming to skim the waterway.

Boat There is an almost daily northbound and southbound ferry service from Wrangell in the summer. The next stop north is Petersburg via the scenic Wrangell Narrows. The ferry terminal in Wrangell is open 1½ hours before each ferry arrival and from 2 to 5 pm on weekdays. There is also a recorded message (tel 874-3711) for 24 hour ferry information.

Petersburg

When the state ferry heads north from Wrangell, it begins one of the most scenic and exciting sections of the Inside Passage. After crossing over from Wrangell Island to Mitkof Island, the ferry threads its way through 46 turns of Wrangell Narrows, a 22 mile (27 km) narrow channel that is only 300 feet (91 metres) wide and 19 feet (6 metres) deep in places. At one point the sides of the ship are so close to the shore that you can almost gather firewood for the evening.

At the other end of this breathtaking journey through the Wrangell Narrows lies Petersburg, one of the hidden gems of Southeast Alaska. This busy little town, an active fishing port during the summer, is decorated by weathered boathouses on the waterfront, freshly painted homes along Nordic Drive (Main St) and the distinctive Devil's Thumb peak and other snow-capped mountains on the horizon.

Peter Buschmann arrived in the area in 1897 and found a fine harbour, abundant fish and a ready supply of ice from nearby Le Conte Glacier. He built a cannery and enticed his Norwegian friends to follow him there,

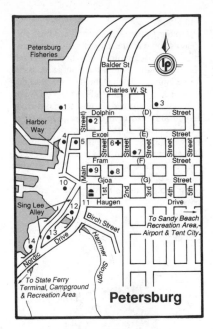

1   Petersburg Fisheries
2   Harbor Bar
3   Swimming Pool
4   Harbormaster & Visitors Bureau
5   Pilot Newspaper
6   Hospital
7   Clausen Memorial Museum
8   Alaska State Troopers
9   Scandia House
10 Kito's Kave
11 Forest Service & Post Office
12 Municipal Building
13 Sons of Norway Hall
14 Harbor Lights Pizza

772-3646) in the Harbormaster's Building at the head of North Boat Harbor on the waterfront. The office doubles up as the visitor centre and has free maps of Petersburg and other hand-outs. Summer hours are 7.30 am to 5 pm on weekdays.

For information about hiking, paddling, camping or reserving cabins, head over to the US Forest Service office (tel 722-3871) upstairs in the post office on Nordic Drive (Main St). The office is open weekdays from 8 am to 5 pm and the entrance is at the rear of the building. Hikers attempting to cross to Kupreanof Island to tackle Petersburg Mountain or the Petersburg Lake trails should seek a ride at the Skiff Float near the end of the North Boat Harbor.

A few years ago the city changed many of its street names from simple letters to full names that represent fishing boats of the past. Both names will be given here, with the new one appearing in parentheses.

Across the street from the Harbormaster's Building is the office of the Petersburg Pilot, which publishes the free *Viking Visitor Guide* every summer.

Things to See

On the waterfront near the corner of D St (Dolphin St) and Nordic Drive (Main St) is **Petersburg Fisheries**, founded in 1900 by Peter Buschmann and today a subsidiary of Icicle Seafoods of Seattle. On Harbor Way, at the end of G St (Gjoa St), is the long pier

and the resulting town was named after Buschmann. Today, a peek into the local phone book will reveal evidence of the strong Norwegian heritage which unifies Petersburg.

Petersburg (pop 3282) is the youngest community in the Southeast but boasts of having the largest home-based halibut fleet in Alaska, and some say the world. The economy has blossomed on fishing and the town's four canneries and two cold-storage plants draw an army of summer workers from the Lower 48.

Petersburg has several canneries sitting above the water on pilings, boat harbours bulging with vessels and a constant flow of barges, ferries and sea planes. Even at night you can see small boats trolling the nearby waters for somebody's dinner.

Information & Orientation

For general information about Petersburg, go to the Chamber of Commerce office (tel that leads out to **Chatham Strait Seafoods**. The canneries, the backbone of the Petersburg economy, are not open to the public and do not offer tours.

Continuing south, Harbor Way passes Middle Boat Harbor and turns into **Sing Lee Alley** (Indian St). This was the centre of old Petersburg and much of the street is built on pilings over Hammer Slough. The **Sons of Norway Hall**, begun by Buschmann in 1897 and finished in 1912, is the predominant large white building with the colourful rosemaling, a flowery Norwegian art form.

Hammer Slough provides photographers with the most colourful images of Petersburg. Both Sing Lee Alley (Indian St) and Birch St follow the tidal area and wind past clusters of weathered homes and boathouses suspended on pillars above a shoreline of old boats, nets and crab pots. Sing Lee Alley (Indian St) crosses Hammer Slough and then joins Nordic Drive (Main St). To the south, Nordic Drive turns into Mitkof Highway and heads out past the state ferry terminal; to the north Nordic Drive heads back into the centre of Petersburg.

Turn east up F St (Fram St) from Nordic Drive (Main St) to the **Clausen Memorial Museum** on the corner of 2nd St. Outside the museum is the *Fisk* , an 11 foot (3.3 metre) bronze sculpture commemorating the town's life by the sea. Inside the museum is an interesting collection of local artefacts and relics, most tied in with the history of fishing in Petersburg. Included in the back room is the largest king salmon ever caught, 126 lb (57 kg). You'll also see the giant lens from the old Cape Decision Lighthouse. The museum is open daily during the summer from 1 to 4 pm. There is no admission charge but donations are welcome.

From the museum, follow 2nd St north for three blocks to reach the Petersburg High School. Within the same complex is the **Roundtree Swimming Pool** (tel 772-3392), a large white building attached to the rear of Stedmen Elementary School up the hill. A swim at the pool is $1.50 per person, or use of the showers and locker room is 75 cents; contact the pool for opening hours.

Festivals

Petersburg puts on its own Fourth of July celebration with the usual small-town festivities. The community's best event, and one that is famous around the Southeast, is the Little Norway Festival, held on the weekend closest to Norwegian Independence Day on 17 May, usually before most tourists arrive. If you are even near the area, hop over to Petersburg for it. The locals dress in old costumes, Nordic Drive (Main St) is turned into a string of booths and games, and several dances are held in local halls. The best part of the festival is the fish feed, when the town's residents put together a pot-luck feast.

Little Norway Festival, Petersburg

Places to Stay

Petersburg is a hard-working fishing community that concentrates on the present rather than trying to package its past for a ship full of visitors. This explains why budget accommodation is nonexistent here.

There is no youth hostel in Petersburg, although the town desperately needs one, and the one cheap hotel recently underwent major renovation and increased its prices. *Scandia House* (tel 772-4281), on Nordic

Drive (Main St) in the centre of town, now has a 'European' style and charges $45 for a single without a bath. Even *Narrows Inn* (tel 772-3434), across from the ferry terminal and supposedly the 'budget-conscious' lodge, charges $40 a night for just a bunk.

Camping It is difficult to camp near town. Petersburg has *Tent City* on Haugen Drive, 0.5 mile (0.8 km) or a 10 minute walk northwest of the airport. The city-operated campground provides wooden pads, each holding three to five tents, to avoid the wet muskeg. However, the facility was designed primarily for young cannery workers who arrive in early summer and occupy an entire pad by building plastic shelters around them. By the time you come along, there are few, if any, spaces available to pitch a tent.

If you can stake out an area, head down to the police station in the Municipal Building on Nordic Drive (Main St) and pay the officer in charge your user fee. The cost is $3 per night plus a $25 deposit, although during the last few summers city officials have been rather loose about collecting the deposit.

The other organised campgrounds are designed for motorhomes & campervans and are located out of town. At *Mile 22* (35 km) of the Mitkof Highway is the *Ohmer Creek Campground* (15 sites, no fee) with a 14 day limit, and at *Mile 26.8* (43 km) is the *Sumner Strait Campground* (no fee).

Backpackers have a couple of ways to avoid the lack of budget accommodation in Petersburg. There is no camping within the city limits, and if you pitch a tent at the Sandy Beach Recreation Area, on the corner of Sandy Beach Rd and Haugen Drive 3 miles (4.8 km) north of town, local police will most likely kick you out in the middle of the night.

However, by hiking 0.5 (0.8 km) beyond the Sandy Beach picnic area & shelter along the shoreline, you can camp on the scenic beach. Bring drinking water and pitch your tent above the high-tide line. You can also camp up the Ravens Roost Trail which begins near the airport, but you will have to walk more than 1 mile (1.6 km) uphill before finding a site that isn't muskeg.

Another way to avoid expensive accommodation is to rent a used car at All Star Rental (tel 772-4424) and drive to a campground out of town. The agent for this state-wide car rental company is in Scandia House on Nordic Drive (Main St), but during the summer it pays to call ahead and reserve a vehicle. Rates are $32 per day with a 100 free miles (160 km).

Places to Eat
Even if you're trying to survive the summer on a bag of rice and a bottle of soy sauce, splurge on a seafood dinner in Petersburg, a town that makes a living from what it catches. Just about every eatery in Petersburg serves seafood, but the best by far is the *Petersburg Fish Company* just north of the ferry terminal on Nordic Drive, a 15 minute walk from the centre of town. Dinners of halibut, clams, oysters, salmon or stuffed prawns range from $7 to $10 while a big bowl of clam chowder and bread is less than $4. There are half a dozen tables inside and a few more outside where, if it isn't raining, you can enjoy your meal while watching float planes take off and land. Petersburg Fish Company also sells fresh seafood, including cooked crab that you can crack open yourself.

For breakfast, there's the *Homestead Cafe* on Nordic Drive (Main St), a long-time favourite. A plate of eggs, potatoes and toast costs $6 while hamburgers are $5 and up. *Harbor Lights Pizza* is diagonally opposite the Sons of Norway Hall on Sing Lee Alley (Indian St) and offers pizza, beer and wine along with a good view of the busy boat harbour below it. *Beach Boy*, the snack shack of Petersburg, is in the centre of town on Nordic Drive (Main St) but it only has a few tables outside.

Two more interesting places in town are *Helse Health Foods* and the *Tantes Kitchen*, both near the beginning of Sing Lee Alley (Indian St). Helse is a health-food store and restaurant, and a pleasant place for tea during a rainy afternoon if the place is open; hours tend to be irregular. Tantes (closed Mondays) is a bakery that sells fresh pastries, cookies and croissants. It's in the rear of the Biblio-mania Bookstore, one of Petersburg's more interesting shops.

Entertainment
To listen to the fisher's woes or to meet cannery workers, there is the *Harbor Bar* on Nordic Drive (Main St). For something a little livelier try *Kito's Kave* on Sing Lee Alley (Indian St). This bar and liquor store has live music and dancing most nights after 9 pm. When the boats are in it can be a rowdy place that hops until 2 or 3 am. *The Spa* in Scandia House has hot tubs for two, saunas and a tanning booth.

Hiking
Raven's Roost Trail This 4 mile (6.5 km) trail begins at the water tower on the south-east side of the airport, accessible from Haugen Drive. A boardwalk crosses muskeg areas at the start of the trail, while much of the route is a climb to beautiful open alpine areas at 2013 feet (610 metres); some of it is steep and requires a little scrambling. A two-storey US Forest Service (USFS) cabin (reservations needed, $15 per night) is above the tree line in an area that provides good summer hiking and spectacular views of Petersburg, Frederick Sound and Wrangell Narrows.

Petersburg Mountain Trail On Kupreanof Island, this trail ascends 2.5 miles (4 km) from Wrangell Narrows behind Sasby Island to the top of Petersburg Mountain. There are outstanding views from here, the best in the area, of Petersburg, the Coastal Mountains, glaciers and Wrangell Narrows. Plan on 3 hours to the top of the mountain and 2 hours for the return. To get across the channel, go to the skiff float at the North Boat Harbor (Old Boat Harbor) and hitch a ride with somebody who lives on Kupreanof Island. From the Kupreanof Public Dock, head right on the overgrown road towards Sasby Island.

Petersburg Lake Trail This 6.5 mile (10.5 km) trail, just one of a trail system in the Petersburg Creek-Duncan Salt Chuck Wil-

derness on Kupreanof Island, leads to a USFS cabin (reservations needed, $20 per night). See the Trekking section in the Wilderness chapter for further details.

Three Lakes Trails These four short trails, connecting three lakes and Ideal Cove, are located off Three Lakes Rd, a Forest Service road that heads east off Mitkof Highway at *Mile 13.6* (22 km) and returns at *Mile 23.8* (38 km). Beginning at *Mile 14.2* (23.1 km) of Three Lakes Rd is a 3 mile (4.8 km) loop with boardwalks leading to Sand, Crane and Hill lakes, known for their good trout fishing.

On each lake there is a skiff and a picnic platform. Tennis shoes are fine for the trail but to explore around the lakes you need rubber boots. There is a free-use shelter on Sand Lake. From the Sand Lake Trail there is a 1.5 mile (2.4 km) trail to Ideal Cove on Frederick Sound.

Paddling
There is a variety of interesting trips in the Petersburg area, most of which are blue-water paddles requiring a week or more to undertake. Kayaks are difficult to come by in Petersburg, and if you're planning a major expedition from this port, you may want to obtain one in Juneau or Ketchikan. You can try Deb Hurley who runs Helse Health Foods (tel 772-3444) in town but lives on Kupreanof Island, and rents out the kayaks she uses to paddle across the channel to her shop.

You can purchase topographic maps at Diamante (tel 772-4858) on Nordic Drive (Main St), but often in a town this size the map you want is gone. It's best to obtain them in Ketchikan or Juneau before you arrive. Within Petersburg there are a dozen charter boats that deal mostly in fishing trips, but they can also provide drop-off and pick-up services to remote areas. Contact the visitor centre for a current list of them.

Le Conte Glacier The most spectacular paddle in the region is to Le Conte Glacier, 25 miles (40 km) east of Petersburg, the

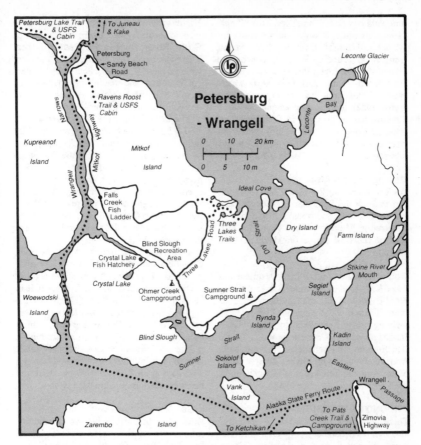

Petersburg Lake Trail & USFS Cabin

To Juneau & Kake

Petersburg

Sandy Beach Road

Leconte Glacier

Petersburg - Wrangell

Ravens Roost Trail & USFS Cabin

Narrows

Kupreanof Island

Mitkof Highway

Wrangell

Mitkof Island

0   10   20 km

0   5   10 m

Leconte Bay

Ideal Cove

Dry Island

Farm Island

Falls Creek Fish Ladder

Three Lakes Trails

Dry Strait

Stikine River Mouth

Blind Slough Recreation Area

Crystal Lake Fish Hatchery

Crystal Lake

Three Lakes Road

Ohmer Creek Campground

Sumner Strait Campground

Segief Island

Woewodski Island

Blind Slough

Rynda Island

Kadin Island

Strait

Sumner

Sokolof Island

Eastern

Wrangell

Passage

Vank Island

Alaska State Ferry Route

To Pats Creek Trail & Campground

Zimovia Highway

Zarembo   Island

To Ketchikan

southernmost tidewater glacier in North America. From town, it takes 3 to 4 days to reach the frozen monument, which includes crossing Frederick Sound north of Coney Island. The crossing should be done at slack tide as winds and tides can cause choppy conditions. If the tides are judged right, it is possible to paddle far enough into Le Conte Bay to camp within view of the glacier.

Thomas Bay Almost as impressive is Thomas Bay, 20 miles (32 km) from Petersburg and north of Le Conte Bay on the east side of Frederick Sound. The bay features a

pair of glaciers, including Baird Glacier where many paddlers spend a day hiking. The mountain scenery surrounding the bay is spectacular and there are three USFS cabins (reservations needed, $20 per night): Swan Lake Cabin, Spurt Cove Cabin and Cascade Creek Cabin. Consult the local USFS office (874-2323) about crossing Frederick Sound and the availability of cabins. Paddlers need 4 to 7 days for the round trip out of Petersburg.

Kake to Petersburg Backpackers can take the state ferry to the Indian village of Kake and paddle back to Petersburg. This 90 mile (144 km) route follows the west side of Kupreanof Island through Keku Strait, Sumner Strait and up Wrangell Narrows to Petersburg. The highlight of the trip is Rocky Pass, a remote and narrow winding waterway in Keku Strait that has almost no boat traffic other than the occasional kayaker. Caution has to be used in Sumner Strait, which lies only 40 miles (64 km) away from open ocean and has its share of strong winds and waves. Plan on 7 to 10 days for the trip.

Getting There & Away

Air The Alaska Airlines (tel 772-4255) milk run through the Southeast provides a daily northbound and southbound flight out of Petersburg. The airport is 1 mile (1.6 km) east of the post office on Haugen Drive (Airport Rd).

Boat The State Marine Ferry terminal (tel 772-3855) is about 1 mile (1.6 km) along Nordic Drive from the southern edge of town. There is usually one northbound ferry arriving daily. Travellers continuing onto Juneau should consider taking the *Le Conte* if it fits into their schedule. This ship sails from Petersburg to Juneau but stops at Kake, Sitka, Angoon, Tenakee and Hoonah along the way; the one-way fare is $36.

AROUND PETERSBURG

There are a few sights around Petersburg, although it's debatable whether it's worth the hassle of getting out to see them. Those without transport can either rent a vehicle or contact Tongass Traveler (tel 772-4837) which offers a 2 hour van tour. For $25, Patti Norheim takes you to a shrimp cannery, fish hatchery and a tree farm among other things, and then returns you to her home in town where you sit on her deck enjoying wine and a shrimp cocktail. Travellers with their own vehicle who plan to spend some time around Petersburg should pick up a copy of the *Mitkof Island Road Guide* from the US Forest Service office for $1.

One of the best fishing spots in the area is at *Mile 14.5* (23.3 km) of the Mitkof

Highway where a 0.3 mile (0.5 km) boardwalk leads through a muskeg meadow to the **Blind River Rapids Recreation Area**. There is a small trail shelter along the river where anglers come to catch Dolly Varden, cutthroat trout and steelhead from mid-April to mid-May, king salmon in June and July and coho salmon after mid-August.

The **Crystal Lake Fish Hatchery** at *Mile 17.5* (28 km) of the Mitkof Highway is a $2.2 million facility used to stock coho, king salmon and trout throughout the Southeast. No formal tours are offered, but hatchery personnel are pleasant and informative. It is open weekdays from 8 am to 4 pm. Nearby in Blind Slough Recreation Area is the **Trumpeter Swan Observatory**, designed to permit sheltered photography and viewing of this majestic bird.

On the way back to town, stop at the **Falls Creek Fish Ladder** at *Mile 13.7* (22 km) of the Mitkof Highway, an impressive sight in August when coho and pink salmon leap along its steps. At *Mile 9* (14 km) of the highway is the **Heintzleman Nursery** operated by the US Forest Service, which includes six greenhouses that produce a million seedlings of Sitka spruce per year. It is open to the public on an informal basis on weekdays from 8 am to 4.30 pm. Like the hatchery, there is no admission charge.

Kake

Kake is an Indian beach-front community (pop 700) on the north-west coast of Kupreanof Island. It is the traditional home of the Kake tribe of the Tlingit Indians and today the community maintains subsistence rights while also running commercial fishing, fish processing and logging enterprises to supplement its economy. Kake is known for having the tallest totem pole in Alaska (and some say the world), a 132 foot (39 metre) carving that was first raised at Alaska's pavilion in the 1970 World's Fair in Osaka, Japan.

The state ferry *Le Conte* stops twice a week at Kake on its run between Petersburg and Sitka. The one-way fare from Petersburg to Kake is $16. Within town, 1.5 miles (2.4

km) from the ferry terminal, are three general stores, a laundromat and the *New Town Inn*, where rooms begin at $50 for singles. Rough logging roads lead south from town and eventually reach scenic Hamilton Bay, 20 miles (32 km) south-east of Kake.

Tebenkof Bay Wilderness Kake serves as the departure point for blue-water trips into Tebenkof Bay Wilderness, a remote bay system composed of hundreds of islands, small inner bays and coves. The return paddle is a scenic 10 day adventure that can lead to sightings of bald eagles, black bears and a variety of marine mammals. Paddlers should have experience in ocean touring and be prepared to handle a number of portages. Kayaks can be rented in either Juneau, Sitka or Petersburg and then carried on board the state ferry to Kake.

The most common route is to paddle south from Kake through Keku Strait into Port Camden, where at its western end there is a 1.3 mile (2 km) portage trail to the Bay of Pillars. From the Bay of Pillars you encounter the only stretch of open water as you paddle 3 miles (4.8 km) around Point Ellis into Tebenkof Bay. The return east follows Alecks Creek from Tebenkof Bay into Alecks Lake, where there is a 2.3 mile (3.7 km) portage trail to No Name Bay. From here paddlers can reach Keku Strait and paddle north to Kake via the scenic Rocky Pass.

Sitka

In a region of Alaska strong in colour and history, Sitka (pop 8400) is the gem in a beautiful setting. Facing the Pacific Ocean, the city is overshadowed to the west by Mt Edgecumbe, the extinct volcano with a cone similar to Japan's Mt Fuji. The waters offshore are broken up by a myriad of small, forested islands that are ragged silhouettes during the sunsets, while to the east the town is flanked by snow-capped mountains and sharp granite peaks. On a clear day Sitka rivals Juneau for the sheer beauty of its surroundings.

Along with its natural beauty, Sitka is steeped in history. It became the first non-Indian settlement in the Southeast when Alexander Baranof established a Russian fort near the present ferry terminal in 1799. Three years later, Tlingit Indians, armed with guns from British and American traders, overwhelmed the fort, burned it to the ground and killed most of its inhabitants.

Baranof returned in 1804 and after destroying the Tlingit fort, established a settlement called New Archangel at the present site of Sitka, making it the headquarters of the Russian-American Company. Sitka flourished both economically and culturally on the strength of the fur trade; it was known as the 'Paris of the Pacific' in its golden era.

In 1867, Sitka picked up its present name after the USA took control of the town following the purchase of Alaska. After the territorial capital was transferred to Juneau in 1900, the city fell upon some hard times but boomed again during WW II when a military base was built on nearby Japonski Island. At one time during the war, Sitka had a population of 37,000 military and civilian residents. Today, the city is supported by a pulp mill, fishing fleet, cold-storage plants and several federal agencies that have offices in the area.

However, the town clings to its strong Russian heritage and prides itself on being the cultural centre of the Southeast, if not all of Alaska. It seemed only natural to those living in Sitka that when author James Michener decided to write his epic novel *Alaska* he chose their town as his home base to conduct research.

When arriving in Sitka by state ferry, you will sail through the Sergius Narrows, a tight waterway that ships must follow at slack tide. Any other period is too hazardous for vessels to negotiate the fierce currents caused by the changing of the tides. This often forces the state ferry to take a 3 hour stop at Sitka while waiting for the tide and allows travellers a quick view of the city even if they're not disembarking.

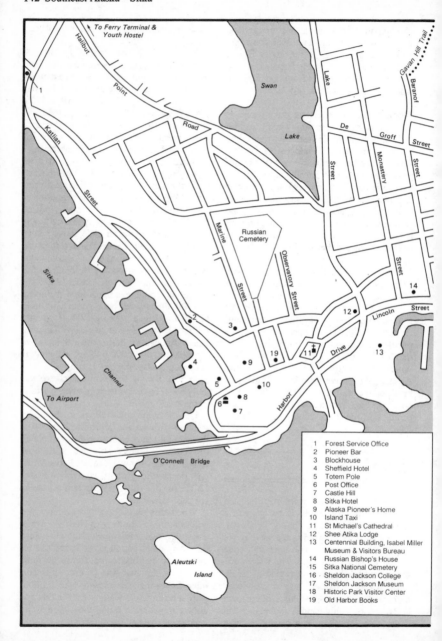

1   Forest Service Office
2   Pioneer Bar
3   Blockhouse
4   Sheffield Hotel
5   Totem Pole
6   Post Office
7   Castle Hill
8   Sitka Hotel
9   Alaska Pioneer's Home
10 Island Taxi
11 St Michael's Cathedral
12 Shee Atika Lodge
13 Centennial Building, Isabel Miller
    Museum & Visitors Bureau
14 Russian Bishop's House
15 Sitka National Cemetery
16 Sheldon Jackson College
17 Sheldon Jackson Museum
18 Historic Park Visitor Center
19 Old Harbor Books

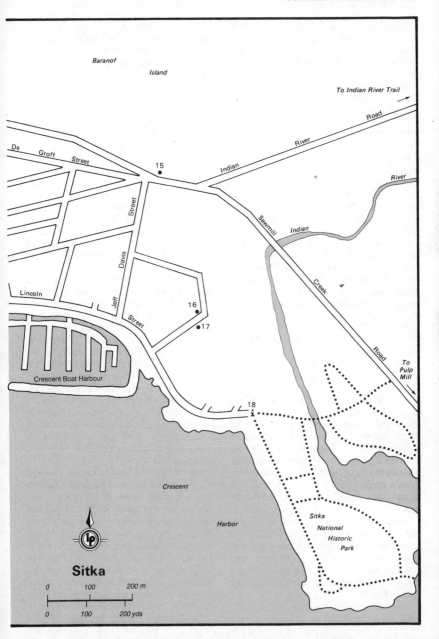

The ferry terminal is 7 miles (11 km) north of town, too far to see anything on foot, but Sitka Tours does run a bus tour for those waiting for the ferry to depart. The tour briefly covers the major sites: Sitka National Historical Park, St Michael's Cathedral and Sheldon Jackson College. The cost is $8 per person.

Information

The Sitka Visitor Bureau (tel 747-8604), in the Centennial Building off Harbor Drive next to the Crescent Boat Harbor, is open daily from 9 am to 5 pm. The US Forest Service office (tel 747-6671), the place to go for trail information, cabin reservations and hand-outs about enjoying the wilderness, is in a three-storey red building on the corner of Siginaka and Katlian streets, across from the Thomas Boat Harbor. The office is open on weekdays from 8 am to 5 pm. Sitka has three state recreation areas; information about their use or any Alaskan state park can be obtained from the Division of Parks office (tel 747-6249) at Old Airport Turnaround on Halibut Point Rd. The office is open from 8 am to 4.30 pm weekdays.

Things to See

Contact the Sitka Visitor Bureau in the Centennial Building for a map of the city listing the points of interest. Also inside the building is the **Isabel Miller Museum** which has a collection of relics from the past, along with a model of the town as it appeared in 1867. One is a hand-carved Tlingit canoe made from a log. The Centennial Building is open from 8 am to 5 pm and 7 to 10 pm.

Next to the Centennial Building is the impressive **Public Library**, an excellent spot when they kick you out of the hostel. The library is open Monday to Thursday from 10 am to 9 pm, Saturday from 10 am to 5 pm and Sunday from 1 to 5 pm.

At the heart of the city centre is **St Michael's Cathedral** in Lincoln St, two blocks west from the Centennial Building. Built between 1844 and 1848, the church stood for over 100 years as the finest Russian Orthodox cathedral in Alaska until fire destroyed it in 1966. The priceless treasures and icons inside were saved by Sitka's residents, who built a replica of the original cathedral. The church is open daily from noon to 4 pm during the summer for visitors, even earlier if there is a cruise ship in port. Donations of $1 are requested upon entering.

Continue west on Lincoln St and next to the post office is the walkway that leads to **Castle Hill**. This was the site of an early stronghold of the indigenous Kiksadi clan and later the foundation of a succession of Russian buildings including Baranof's Castle, which housed the governor of Russian America in 1837. It was here on 18 October 1867 that the official transfer of Alaska from Russia to the USA took place.

More Russian cannons can be seen in **Totem Square** across from the post office on Lincoln St. Next to it is the prominent, yellow **Alaska Pioneers Home**. Built in 1934 on the old Russian Parade Ground, the home is for elderly Alaskans. Visitors are welcome to meet the 'old sourdoughs' and listen to their fascinating stories of gold-rush days or homesteading in the wilderness. There is a gift shop in the basement that sells handicrafts made by the residents. The 13 foot (4 metre) bronze Prospector statue in front of the state home was dedicated on Alaska Day in 1949 and is modelled on long-time Alaskan resident William 'Skagway Bill' Fonda.

Another part of Sitka's Russian past can be seen on the hill west of the Alaska Pioneer Home. On the corner of Kogwanton and Marine streets is the replica **Blockhouse** of the type the Russians used to guard their stockade and separate it from the Indian village. Originally, there were three on a wall that kept the Tlingits restricted to an area along Katlian St. Adjacent to the wooden blockhouse is the **Russian Cemetery**. There are more old headstones and Russian Orthodox crosses at the end of Observatory St.

The **Russian Bishop's House**, the only

original Russian building still standing in Sitka, is the first of many sights at the east end of town. The soft-yellow structure on Lincoln St across from the west end of Crescent Harbor was built in 1842 and is one of the few surviving examples of Russian colonial architecture in North America. Bishop Ivan Veniaminov, who eventually was canonised St Innocent, was the first resident of the home which was later used as a school, chapel and office.

The National Park Service which purchased the building in the early 1980s has been restoring it to its 1853 setting. The 1st floor is now a museum dedicated to the building and its Russian occupants, while work continues on the restoration of the 2nd floor with the Bishop's personal quarters and the Chapel of the Annunciation.

Further east along Lincoln St, past the boat harbour, is **Sheldon Jackson College**, where Michener stayed and worked for much of the three summers he spent in Alaska. Among the buildings on campus is the octagonal **Sheldon Jackson Museum**. Constructed in 1895, it's the oldest cement building in Alaska and today houses one of the best indigenous-culture collections in the state.

The artefacts were gathered by Dr Sheldon Jackson, general agent for education, from 1880 to 1900, making the collection the oldest in the state. It features an impressive display of indigenous masks, hunting tools and baskets from such tribes as the Eskimo, Tlingit, Haida and Aleut. Hanging from the ceiling, and equally impressive, is the collection of boats and sleds used in Alaska, from reindeer sleds and dog sleds to kayaks and umiaks. The museum (tel 747-5237) is open daily from 8 am to 5 pm in the summer; admission is $1.

Sitka's most noted attraction lies further east at the end of Lincoln St, where the National Park Service maintains the **Sitka National Historical Park**. The 107 acre (43 hectare) park, 0.5 mile (0.8 km) east of the city centre, features a trail that winds past 15 totem poles moved here from the Louisiana Exposition in St Louis in 1904 and now standing in a beautiful forest setting next to the sea.

The park is at the mouth of the Indian River where the Tlingit Indians were finally defeated by the Russians in 1804 after defending a wooden fort for a week. The Russians had arrived with a gunboat and three other ships to revenge a Tlingit Kiksadi clan raid on a nearby outpost 2 years earlier. But despite their cannons, they did little damage to the walls and when they stormed the structure with the help of Aleuts, they were repulsed in a bloody battle. It was only when the Tlingits ran out of gunpowder and flint and slipped away at night that the Russians were able to enter the now deserted fort.

Begin at the park's visitor centre (tel 747-6281) where there are displays of Russian and indigenous artefacts, and where carvers demonstrate traditional arts. A 1 mile (1.6 km) self-guided loop leads past the totems to the site of the Tlingit fort near the Indian River. The fort is long gone but its outline can still be seen and is marked by posts. Admission is free and the visitor centre is open daily from 8 am to 5 pm in the summer.

Also at the east end of town and a place of interest mostly to history buffs is the **Sitka National Cemetery**. The plot is off Sawmill Creek Rd, just west of the Public Safety Academy, and can be reached from Sheldon Jackson College along Jeff Davis Rd. The area was designated a national cemetery by past president Calvin Coolidge and includes headstones of Civil War veterans, members of the Aleutian Campaign in WW II and many notable Alaskans.

For a lot of visitors, Sitka's most colourful area is **Katlian St**, which begins off Lincoln St at the west end of town, next to the Sheffield Hotel. The road is a classic mixture of weather-beaten houses, docks and canneries where there always seems to be fishing boats unloading their catch. Katlian St portrays the sights and sounds of the busy Southeast fishing industry. Even the vacant yards along it reflect dependence on the sea, as they have discarded fishing nets or stacks of crab pots. In short, it is a colourful, bustling place and a photographer's delight.

Festivals

Extending its reputation as the cultural centre of the Southeast, the city sponsors the Sitka Summer Music Festival over 3 weeks in June at the Centennial Building. The emphasis of the festival is on chamber music and brings together professional musicians for concerts and workshops. The highly acclaimed event is popular so it can be hard to obtain tickets to the twice-weekly evening concerts. However, rehearsals, open to the public, are easier to attend and usually free.

Sitka highlights its Fourth of July celebration with the All-Alaska Logging Championships. The event brings loggers from around the state and the Pacific Northwest to compete in a variety of contests, including axe throwing and tree topping.

On the weekend nearest 18 October, the city holds its Alaska Day Festival by re-enacting the transfer of the state from Russia to the USA with costumes (and even beards) of the 1860s. A parade highlights the 3 day event.

Places to Stay

Camping The nearest campground to the centre of town is *Sealing Cove* (tel 747-3439), a new commercial campground ($5 per night) at Sealing Cove Harbor on Japonski Island. There are two US Forest Service (USFS) campgrounds in the Sitka area but neither is close to town.

Starrigavan Campground is a 0.7 mile (1.1 km) walk north of the ferry terminal at *Mile 7.8* (12.4 km) of Halibut Point Rd. The campground (29 sites, $5 per night) is in a scenic setting and adjacent to a saltwater beach and hiking trails. On your way to the area you'll pass Old Sitka State Park, which features lighted trails and interpretive displays dedicated to the site of the original Russian settlement.

Sawmill Creek Campground (seven sites) is 6 miles (9.6 km) east of Sitka on Blue Lake Rd off Sawmill Creek Rd and past the pulp mill. Although the area is no longer maintained by the USFS, it provides mountain scenery with an interesting trail to Blue Lake, a good fishing spot.

Showers in town can be obtained for $1.25 at the Sitka Public Pool (tel 747-5677) in Riatchley Junior High School on Halibut Point Rd; call them for opening hours. You can also get a shower for $2 at Homestead Laundromat, 621 Katlian St.

Youth Hostel The *Sitka Youth Hostel* (tel 747-8356) is in the basement of the Methodist Church at 303 Kimsham Rd. Follow Halibut Point Rd north-west out of town and then turn right onto Peterson Rd, a quarter of a mile (0.4 km) past the Lakeside Grocery Store. Once on Peterson Rd you immediately veer left onto Kimsham Rd. Registration is from 6 to 10 pm and check-out time is 8 am. There are no kitchen facilities, but there is an eating area. The cost is $5 for youth hostel members and $7 for nonmembers.

Bed & Breakfast There are a number of B&Bs in the Sitka area that offer singles with a good meal in the morning for around $40 a single and $50 a doubles. Stop at the visitor bureau for an updated list of them or try *Creek's Edge Guest House* (tel 747-6484) which overlooks Sitka Sound and Mt Edgecumbe and provides a shuttle service. *Helga's Bed & Breakfast* (tel 747-5497), right on the beach at 2821 Halibut Point Rd, has five rooms. The ferry bus will drop you off here on the way to town.

If you have some extra funds and want a unique experience, book a room at the *Rockwell Lighthouse* (tel 747-3056), the last lighthouse built in Alaska. They will provide the 3 minute skiff ride from town and you not only get to stay in a lighthouse but you will enjoy an excellent view of town and the rugged coastline around it. It's not cheap though, the rates are $125 per day.

Hotels There are five hotels in Sitka. The cheapest is the *Sitka Hotel* (tel 747-3288) at 118 Lincoln St where single rooms with common bath are $35. A step up is *Potlatch House* (tel 747-8611) at the end of Katlian St, near the intersection with Halibut Point

Rd; the motel has 30 rooms from $45. The rates at other hotels begin at $90.

Places to Eat

Sitka has a restaurant for everybody's budget and desire. The breakfast places in town are *Lory's Sitka Cafe* at 166 Lincoln St and *Revard's* at 324 Lincoln St, two restaurants that have been pouring the morning coffee for locals for years. Both have eggs, potatoes and toast for around $5. The Sitka Cafe's best bargain is its huge bowl of home-made clam chowder for $3. For just coffee in the morning, there is the *Coffee Express* on Lake St, next door to the fire station. It has limited seating inside, opens at 7 am on weekdays and offers a choice selection of coffees and teas.

For dinner, try *Los Amigos*, 1305 Sawmill Creek Rd, for Mexican dishes. The *Bayview*, upstairs in the Bayview Trading Centre across from Crescent Harbor, has the best hamburgers in Sitka. Although the service can be slow at times, their menu lists 26 varieties of hamburgers ranging from $6 to $9. The Bayview also serves beer and wine in a setting which offers every table a view of the boat harbour across the street.

Along Katlian St there is the *Twin Dragon* and *Sitka Sound Seafood*. Twin Dragon is a Chinese restaurant with greasy decor but good food, especially their fried beef in hot sauce and Mongolian beef. Sitka Sound Seafood sells smoked salmon, fresh halibut, prawns and crab, as well as seafood dinners from $6 to $10. The city's *McDonald's* is 1 mile (1.6 km) out of town on Halibut Point Rd.

For those who like to make an evening out of their meal, there's the *Strawberry Patch* on Siginaka Way, a short walk from the junction with Katlian St where the USFS office is located. The restaurant offers great views of the Sitka coastline and Thomas Harbor. It specialises in freshly baked breads and pastries, and has a good salad bar. The *Shee Atika Lodge* has a fine restaurant but meal prices are high. Head here in the morning, however, as it is a great place to sip a cup of coffee while watching the sunrise over Crescent Boat Harbor.

Entertainment

Sitka's most interesting night spot is the *Pioneer Bar*, the classic fisher's pub on Katlian St down by the waterfront. The walls are covered with photos of fishing boats and the score board for the pool table often has 'help wanted' messages scrawled across it from fishers looking for black-cod crew or notes from somebody seeking work on a troller. Above the long wooden bar is a large brass bell, but put off the urge to ring it unless you want to buy a round of drinks for the house. Just as crowded after work but with a different clientele is the lounge in the *Shee Atika Lodge*, which draws professionals and office workers for music, dancing and drinking.

Another option at night is to book a passage on the 2½ hour night cruise offered by Silver Bay Harbor Tours (tel 747-8941). Their boat departs from Crescent Harbor daily at 7 pm for a view of Sitka and its waterfront at night; the fare is $20 per person.

Hiking

Sitka offers superb hiking in the beautiful but tangled forest that surrounds the city. Second only to Juneau for the variety and number of trails that can be reached on foot, Sitka has 11 trails which start from its road system and total over 40 miles (64 km) through the woods and mountain areas. If you're planning to spend time in Sitka, stop at the US Forest Service (USFS) office and ask for a copy of *Sitka Trails* which provides information and rough maps to 30 trails in the area.

Indian River Trail This easy trail is a 5.5 mile (8.8 km) walk along a clear salmon stream to the Indian River Falls, an 80 foot (24 metre) waterfall at the base of the Three Sisters Mountains. The hike takes you through a typical Southeast rainforest and offers the opportunity to view black bears, deer and bald eagles. The trailhead, a short walk from the centre of town, is off Sawmill

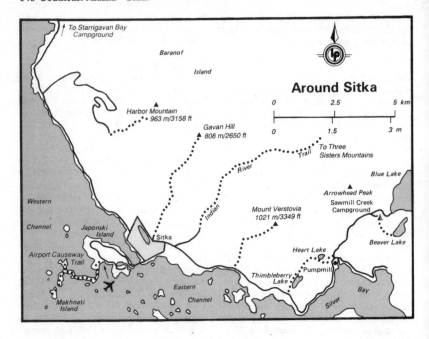

Creek Rd just east of the National Cemetery. Pass the driveway leading to the Public Safety Academy parking lot and turn up the dirt road with a gate across it. This leads back to the city water plant where the trail begins left of the pump house. Plan on 4 to 5 hours for a round trip to the falls.

Gavan Hill Trail Also close to town is the Gavan Hill Trail which ascends 3 miles (4.8 km) and 2500 feet (762 metres) to the Gavan Hill alpine summit. The trail provides excellent views of Sitka and the surrounding area. From the end of the trail, the adventurous hiker can continue onto the peaks of the Three Sisters Mountains.

From Lincoln St, head north up Baranof St for six blocks to the house at 508 Baranof St past Merrill St. The trail begins just beyond this house and heads to the northeast, reaching Cross Trail within three-quarters of a mile (1.2 km). There is good camping in the alpine regions of the trail, but

bring water and a camp stove, as wood and drinking water are not available above the tree line. Plan on 3 to 4 hours to hike the trail one way.

Airport Causeway Hike This hike begins in Sitka city centre with a 1.8 mile (2.9 km) walk across O'Connell Bridge and past the boat harbours on Japonski Island to the airport. From the high arch of the bridge, you get some of the best views of Sitka and the mountains that flank it to the east. At the airport, the hike continues along the airport causeway and extends 1.5 miles (2.4 km) into Sitka Sound across Sasedni, Kirushkin and Makhnati islands.

It was built during WW II when the army wanted to provide harbour protection for the naval air station and the city. Along the causeway there is fascinating beachcombing for shells and driftwood, and interesting tidal pools to investigate. You can also view the underground bunkers, personnel quarters and gun emplacements on Makhnati Island that were left over from Sitka's military build-up during WW II.

Most people reach the trailhead by boat, and travellers can rent a kayak in Sitka (see the Sitka Paddling section for more details). At times it is also possible to arrange an escort across the airport runway to the beginning of the causeway. When you get to the airport you must contact the airport manager (tel 966-2960) during work hours, simply scampering across the runway is illegal. Plan on 2 to 3 hours for the round trip.

Mt Verstovia Trail This 2.5 mile (4 km) trail is a challenging climb of 2550 feet (777 metres) to the 'shoulder', a small summit that is the most common end of the trail, although it is possible to climb to 3349 feet (1021 metres), the actual peak of Mt Verstovia. The view from the 'shoulder' on clear days is spectacular, undoubtedly the best in the area.

The trailhead is 2 miles (3.2 km) east of Sitka along Sawmill Creek Rd. Once you reach the Kiksadi Club on the left, look for the trailhead marked Mount Verstovia Trail. The Russian charcoal pits (signposted) are reached within quarter of a mile (0.4 km) and shortly after that the trail begins a series of switchbacks. Plan on a 4 hour round trip to the 'shoulder'. From the 'shoulder', the true peak of Mt Verstovia lies to the north along a ridge that connects the two. Allow an extra hour each way to hike to the peak.

Harbor Mountain Trail This trail is reached from Harbor Mountain Rd, the only road in the Southeast that provides access to a sub-alpine area. Head 4 miles (6.4 km) north-west from Sitka on Halibut Point Rd to the junction with Harbor Mountain Rd. It is 4.5 miles (7.2 km) up the rough dirt road to a parking area and nearby picnic shelter.

After another 0.5 mile (0.8 km) you reach the parking area at the end of the road and an unmarked trail begins on the east side of the lot. The trail ascends 1.5 miles (2.4 km) to the alpine meadows, knobs and ridges above the road from where the views are spectacular. Plan on spending 2 to 4 hours scrambling

through the alpine area, or better still, camp up there.

Beaver Lake Hike This short trail starts from Sawmill Creek Campground, which is reached from Sawmill Creek Rd, 5.5 miles (8.8 km) east of Sitka. Across from the pulp mill on Sawmill Creek Rd, turn left onto Blue Lake Rd for the campground; the trailhead is on the southern side of the campground.

Although steep at the beginning, the 0.8 mile (1.3 km) trail levels out and ends up as a scenic walk through open forest and along muskeg and marsh areas to Beaver Lake which is surrounded by mountains. Vandals have made the skiff at the lake unsafe to use. Plan on an hour hike for the round trip.

Mt Edgecumbe Trail The 6.7 mile (11 km) trail begins at Fred's Creek USFS Cabin (reservations needed, $20 per night), and ascends to the top of the summit crater of this extinct volcano. Needless to say, the views from the summit are spectacular on a clear day. About 3 miles (4.8 km) up the trail is a free-use shelter (no reservations required).

Mt Edgecumbe lies on Kruzof Island, 10 miles (16 km) west of Sitka, and can only be reached by boat because large swells from the ocean prevent float planes from landing. Explore Alaska Charters (tel 747-3465) is a booking agency for charter boats in town and can arrange to drop off and pick up hikers for $70 one way per party. Actual hiking time is 5 to 6 hours one way, but by securing Fred's Creek USFS Cabin you can turn the adventure into a pleasant 3 day trip with nights spent in two shelters.

Paddling

Sitka also serves as the departure point for numerous blue-water trips along the protected shorelines of Baranof and Chichagof islands. Baidarka Boats (tel 747-8996), PO Box 6001, Sitka, Alaska 99835, is owned and managed by Larry Edwards and rents kayaks in town. Contacting Larry to reserve boats or set up a trip is highly recommended. Rigid single kayaks are $30 a day or $110 a week with a $50 deposit. Rigid doubles are $40 a day and $145 a week, and folding doubles are $55 a day and $250 a week. You can purchase topographic maps at Old Harbor Books (tel 747-8808), 201 Lincoln St in Sitka.

Katlian Bay This 45 mile (72 km) round trip, beginning from Sitka Harbor and ending at scenic Katlian Bay on the northern end of Kruzof Island, is one of the most popular paddles in the area. The route follows narrow straits and well-protected shorelines which are marine traffic channels, making it an ideal trip for less experienced blue-water paddlers who will never be far from help.

A fish buyer is usually anchored in Katlian Bay and has limited groceries for sale. A scenic side trip is to hike the sandy beach from the Katlian Bay around Cape Georgiana to Sea Lion Cove on the Pacific Ocean. Catch the tides to paddle the Olga and Neva straits on the way north and return along Sukot Inlet, spending a night at the USFS cabin on Brent's Beach, if you can reserve it. Plan on 4 to 6 days for the paddle.

Shelikof Bay You can combine a 10 mile (16 km) paddle to Kruzof Island with a 6 mile (9.6 km) hike across the island from Mud Bay to Shelikof Bay along an old logging road and trail. Once on the Pacific Ocean side you'll find a beautiful sandy beach providing lots of beachcombing and the Shelikof USFS Cabin (reservations needed, $20 per night).

West Chichagof The western shoreline of Chichagof Island is one of the best blue-water trips in Southeast Alaska for experienced kayakers. Unfortunately, the trip involves a float-plane charter, as few paddlers have the experience to paddle the open ocean around Khaz Peninsula that forms a barrier between the north end of Kruzof Island and Slocum Arm. The arm is the southern end of a series of straits, coves and protected waterways that shield paddlers from the ocean's swells and extend over 30 miles (48 km) north to Lisianski Strait.

With all its hidden coves and inlets, the trip is a good 2 week paddle. Those with even more time and a little adventure in their hearts could continue another 25 miles (40 km) through Lisianski Strait to the fishing village of Pelican, where the state ferry stops twice a month in the summer. Such an expedition would require at least 2 to 3 weeks but would keep the air charter costs down to a 30 minute flight to Slocum Arm.

USFS Cabins

There are a number of USFS cabins close to Sitka which require less than 30 minutes of flying time to reach. The following cabins, which cost $20 per night, should be reserved ahead of time through the USFS office in Sitka.

For information on Fred's USFS Cabin, Brent's Beach USFS Cabin and Shelikof USFS Cabin on Kruzof Island, the site of Mt Edgecumbe, see the Sitka Hiking and Paddling sections. Local air-service operators who can handle chartering requests are Bell Air (tel 747-8636) at 475 Katlian St, and Mountain Aviation (tel 966-2288) in the airport terminal.

Redoubt Lake Cabin This A-frame cabin is at the north end of Redoubt Lake, a narrow body of water south of Sitka on Baranof Island. The cabin is a 20 minute flight from Sitka. You can also reach it by paddling to the head of Silver Bay from town and then hiking a 5 mile (8 km) trail south to the cabin.

Baranof Lake Cabin This cabin is a favourite among locals, as it has a scenic, mountainous setting on the east side of Baranof Island with a 1 mile (1.6 km) trail to Warm Springs Bay. At the bay there is a bathhouse constructed around the natural hot springs which costs $2.50 to use. The cabin is a 20 minute flight from Sitka.

Lake Eva Cabin Located on Baranof Island, this cabin has a skiff with oars, an outdoor fire pit and a wood stove inside. A trail from the lake outlet, which can be fished for Dolly Varden, cutthroat trout and salmon in late summer, leads down to the ocean. The cabin is a 20 minute flight from Sitka.

White Sulphur Springs Cabin A 45 minute flight to the western shore of Chichagof Island, this cabin is popular with Southeasterners because of the hot springs bathhouse in front of it. The free hot springs are used by cabin renters as well as fishers and kayakers passing through.

Getting There & Around

Air Sitka is served by Alaska Airlines (tel 966-2266) with flights to Juneau and Anchorage. It is part of the milk run that connects the city to Wrangell, Petersburg and Ketchikan. The airport is on Japonski Island, 1.8 miles (2.9 km) west of the town centre. On a nice day, it can be a scenic 20 minute walk from the airport terminal over the O'Connell Bridge to the heart of Sitka. Otherwise, the white Airporter minibus of Sitka Tours meets all jet flights and charges $2.50 for a ride to the city hotels; it does not go to the youth hostel.

Regularly scheduled flights among the small air charter companies include Sitka to Pelican for $85 one way with Bellair (tel 747-8636) at 475 Katlian St, and Sitka to Tenakee Springs with Mountain Aviation (tel 966-2288), in the airport terminal, for $55 one way.

Boat The State Marine Ferry terminal is 7 miles (11.2 km) north of town on Halibut Point Rd, and there are northbound or southbound departures almost daily. Because of the unusual route the boats must follow to Sitka, it's a good idea to call the ferry terminal (tel 747-8737) to double-check sailings and departure times.

Passage from Sitka to Juneau is $20, Sitka to Angoon $16, Sitka to Petersburg $20 and Sitka to Tenakee Springs $18. The Airporter minibus meets all ferries and charges $2.50 for a trip into town. You can also catch the minibus out to the ferry terminal from the major hotels (Shee Atika Lodge, Sheffield House) when it picks up hotel guests.

Car & Bicycle Rental All-Star Rental (tel 966-2552) can provide a compact vehicle for $29.95 per day with unlimited mileage. The dealer is adjacent to the airport terminal. Sitka Tool Shed (tel 747-3900) at 245 Katlian St has bicycles for rent.

TENAKEE SPRINGS

What began in the late 1800s as a winter retreat for fishers and prospectors on the east side of Tenakee Inlet has today evolved into a rustic village known for its slow and relaxed pace of life. Tenakee Springs (pop 150) has no roads, cars or running water, and consists mainly of a ferry dock, a row of houses, cabins on pilings and the dirt path behind them.

The town's main attraction is the natural hot springs that send 106°F (41°C) water bubbling out of the ground. The alternative lifestyle is centred around the public bathhouse at the end of the ferry dock. The building there encloses the principal spring which flows through the concrete bath at 7 gallons (27 litres) per minute. Bath hours, separate for men and women, are posted and most locals take at least one good soak per day, if not two.

The Thanksgiving Storm of 1984 hit the Tenakee Springs waterfront hard and demolished a dozen of the buildings on pilings and damaged others. The community has since patched itself up and the relaxed atmosphere has returned to this quaint Chichagof Island hamlet. Tenakee Springs is an interesting and inexpensive side trip, especially by using the state ferry *Le Conte's* Friday night run from Juneau, thus saving accommodation expenses.

Places to Stay & Eat

Opposite the bathhouse at the foot of the ferry dock is the *Snyder Mercantile Company* (tel 736-2205), where the town's first phone was installed in 1976. The store sells limited supplies and groceries, and also rents cabins for $25 per night plus $5 for each additional person. To be sure of getting a cabin, you have to reserve them in advance

(PO Box 505, Tenakee Springs, Alaska 99841) and check in during store hours, Monday to Saturday from 9 am to 5 pm. Relatively new in town is the *Tenakee Inn* (tel 736-9238), a Victorian-style lodge that has beds in a bunkroom for $15 a night and rooms with private baths from $45 to $50 a night.

Your ferry will most likely arrive in the middle of the night, in which case it's best to plan on camping out for the first evening. Since much of the land around town was purchased through the Alaska Lands Lottery in the late 1970s, you have to hike out of town a fair way before finding an available spot to camp.

The best place to pitch a tent, if you are planning to stay a few days, is at the rustic campground 1 mile (1.6 km) east of town at the mouth of the Indian River. It's quiet, picturesque and equipped with several tables and a covered picnic shelter. Keep the camp clean, however, to discourage brown bears from investigating your site, especially during the salmon runs in late August.

The town's restaurant is the *Blue Moon Cafe*. Further down the path towards the boat harbour is the *Tenakee Tavern*, the spot to have a brew after your evening soak.

Hiking & Paddling

There is good fishing in the local streams for trout, salmon and Dolly Varden, and day hikes begin at each end of town. The dirt path, dubbed Tenakee Ave, extends 8 miles (13 km) east of town, where it ends at an old cannery on Coffee Cove, and more than 7 miles (11.4 km) to the west of town, passing a few cabins in either direction.

Tenakee Springs is one end of a common blue-water paddle from Hoonah (see the Paddling section in the Wilderness chapter); obtain supplies and a kayak from Juneau. If, however, you just want to paddle in the inlet for a day, rent kayaks from the Tenakee Inn (tel 736-9238) for $20 a day.

Whether paddling or hiking along the shore, always keep an eye out for marine mammals such as humpback whales which are commonly sighted in Tenakee Inlet along

with orcas, or killer whales, and harbour porpoises. You may also see brown bears while paddling or hiking in the area as Chichagof Island is second only to Admiralty Island in the Southeast for the highest density of bears.

Getting There & Around

The ferry *Le Conte* stops at Tenakee Springs three to four times a week, connecting it to Angoon, Hoonah, Sitka, Juneau and occasionally even Haines and Skagway. Study the ferry schedule carefully to make sure you don't have to stay in the town longer than you want.

For the true budget traveller, the best deal is to take a late Friday night ferry out of Juneau, saving on a night's accommodation and arriving in Tenakee Springs at 6 or 7 am on Saturday. It's then possible to catch a middle-of-the night ferry the following morning that reaches Juneau on Sunday morning, making for a rather unusual 2 day but no nights (at least none that you have to pay for) side trip. The one-way fare from Tenakee Springs to Juneau or Sitka is $18.

Channel Flying (tel 789-3360) has daily flights from Juneau to Tenakee Springs at 9.30 am, and Wings of Alaska (tel 789-0790) has flights from Juneau to Tenakee Springs at 7.30 am and 4.30 pm. The one-way fare is about $50. For getting around the town, you can rent a bicycle at the Tenakee Inn.

HOONAH

As you head north on board the state ferry *Le Conte*, the next stop after Tenakee Springs before reaching Juneau is Hoonah. It is the largest Tlingit village in Southeast Alaska, with a population of almost 900. The Huna, a Tlingit tribe, have lived in the Icy Strait area for hundreds of years and legend tells of them being forced out of Glacier Bay by an advancing glacier. A store was built at the present day Hoonah site in 1883 and an established community has existed there ever since.

Hoonah has an indigenous population of roughly 80%. It lacks the charm and friendliness – as well as the public bathhouse – of Tenakee Springs, but it does offer spectacular scenery in the surrounding mountains. The lifestyle is mainly subsistence while the occupation of most residents involves fishing and logging, as evident by the clear cuts seen from the roads.

The town serves as the beginning of the kayak trip down Port Frederick to Tenakee Inlet (see the Paddling section in the Wilderness chapter).

Things to See

The most photogenic area lies 1 mile (1.6 km) north-west of Hoonah, where the faded red buildings of the old **Hoonah Packing Cannery** serenely guard Port Frederick. There is good fishing for Dolly Varden from this point.

In town, or actually on a hill overlooking Front St, is the **Cultural Center & Museum** which displays indigenous art and artefacts. The centre, open Monday to Friday from 9 am to 3 pm, has no admission charge.

Places to Stay & Eat

There is a small grocery store in Hoonah. You can occasionally purchase fresh seafood directly from the *Cold Storage Plant*. You'll find showers and a laundromat at the marina, and accommodation and meals at the *Huna Totem Lodge* (tel 945-3636), 1.4 miles (2.3 km) from the ferry terminal. In town, meals are available at *Mary's Inn Cafe*, open from 8 am to 10 pm Monday to Saturday.

There are no official campgrounds but backpackers do not have to walk far out of town to find a suitable spot to pitch a tent. The high school also has a pool with showers; admission is $1.

Hiking & Paddling

Hoonah lies south-east of Glacier Bay National Park across Icy Strait, but the paddle to the preserve is an extremely challenging trip for advanced kayakers only. An overnight kayak trip can be made to the Salt Lake Bay USFS Cabin, 14 miles (22.4 km) from Hoonah on Port Frederick.

The cabin is rented out for $20 per night and needs to be reserved, but it is not heavily used. Originally a trapper's cabin, the structure is small but can still sleep four. There is active logging in the area so be ready for clear cuts.

The **Spassky Trail**, a 3.3 mile (5.2 km) walk, begins 3.5 miles (5.6 km) east of Hoonah and winds to Spassky Bay on Icy Strait.

For more information about paddling or hiking in the area, contact the USFS office (tel 945-3631) at PO Box 135, Hoonah, Alaska 99829.

Getting There & Away

The *Le Conte* docks in Hoonah 4 days a week on its route between Tenakee Springs and Juneau. The ferry terminal (tel 945-3292), 0.5 miles (0.8 km) from town, is open 2 hours before the ferry arrives. Wings of Alaska (tel 945-3275) and LAB Flying Service (tel 945-3661) also maintain offices in Hoonah and provide daily services to Juneau.

PELICAN

If you time it right, you can catch a ferry to Pelican, a lively little fishing town on Lisianski Inlet on the north-west coast of Chichagof Island. The *Le Conte* makes a special run to the town twice a month, providing transport from Juneau for only $28 one way.

The town was established in 1938 by a fish packer and named after his boat. Fishing is Pelican's reason for being as it is the closest harbour to the rich Fairweather salmon grounds. Its population of 200 doubles during the summer when commercial fishers and cold-storage workers arrive for the trolling season from June to mid-September.

The town is a photographer's delight as

most of it is built on pilings over tidelands and its main street is a wooden boardwalk; there are only 2 miles (3.2 km) of gravel road beyond that. There's a bed & breakfast place here and *Rosie's Bar & Grill* (tel 735- 2265) where you can get a burger, a beer or even a bed – there are four rooms for rent upstairs for around $70.

The reason for visiting Pelican is to get a good view of the Southeast's fishing industry and to mingle with trollers and cold-storage workers at Rosie's at night. If you plan to stay over (and don't want to wait 2 weeks for the next ferry), Channel Flying (tel 789-3331 in Juneau) and Wings of Alaska (tel 789-0790 in Juneau) both have daily scheduled flights to Juneau.

Juneau

First appearances are often misleading, and Juneau is a case in point. Over half the north-bound state ferries arrive in the capital city between midnight and 6 am at the Auke Bay Ferry Terminal, 14 miles (22 km) from the city centre, leaving disgruntled backpackers to sleepily hunt for transport and lodging. At this point you might be unappreciative of Juneau, but give it a second chance. Few cities in the USA and none in Alaska are as beautiful as Juneau; residents claim it is the most scenic capital in the country, while others describe it as a 'little San Francisco'.

The city centre, which hugs the side of Mt Juneau, has many narrow streets running past a mixture of new structures, old store-fronts and slanted houses, all held together by a network of staircases. The bustling waterfront features cruise ships, tankers, fishing boats, a few kayakers and a dozen float planes buzzing in and out like flies. Overhead are the snow-capped peaks of Mt Juneau and Mt Roberts, which provide just a small part of the superb hiking found in the area.

The city (pop 30,000) was born in the 1880s when gold was found in a local stream, and today Juneau still holds much of its frontier appearance. Joe Juneau and Dick Harris, two vagabond prospectors, stumbled onto the precious metal at Gold Creek in 1880 and almost overnight a tent city appeared. The post office was established 2 years later and the capital of Alaska was moved to Juneau in 1900 after the declining whaling and fur trade reduced the import-ance of Sitka.

Almost 75 years later in 1974, Alaskans voted to move the state's capital again, this time to a small highway junction called Willow that lay in Anchorage's strong sphere of influence. The so-called 'capital move' issue hung over Juneau like a dark cloud, restricting its growth and threatening to turn the place into a ghost town, as 65% of the residents work for the state government.

The issue became a political tug-of-war between Anchorage and the Southeast until the voters, faced with a billion-dollar price tag to reconstruct a capital at Willow, defeated the funding in 1982. Although the conflict will probably never go away, the state-wide vote gave Juneau new life and the town boomed in typical Alaskan fashion, literally bursting at its seams.

McDonald's and Wendy's fast-food chains appeared, new office buildings sprang up and apartments and condominiums mush-roomed. The sudden growth was too much too soon for many of the residents, who were disgusted at the sight of wooded hillsides being bulldozed for yet another apartment complex.

The city entered the 1990s with new con-cerns as a Canadian mining company prepared to reopen the Alaska-Juneau Mine for gold production. Environmental con-cerns are sweeping through the town as plans call for disposing the tailings of the mine in Sheep Creek Valley, site of a popular hiking trail. Others are pushing for the project to proceed, seeing the new interest in mining as a way for Juneau to lessen its dependency on the government.

Travellers will find Juneau to be a fine city offering a variety of accommodation, good restaurants and transport services. It also serves as the departure point for several wilderness attractions, including Glacier Bay National Park and Admiralty Island National Monument.

Orientation

While the city centre clings to a mountainside, the rest of the city 'officially' sprawls over 3100 sq miles (5000 sq km) to the Canadian border, making it one of the largest cities, area-wise, in the USA. There are five sections to Juneau, with the city centre being the busiest and most popular area among visitors during the summer. From here, Egan Drive, the only four-lane highway in the Southeast, heads north-west to Mendenhall Valley.

Known to locals as simply 'The Valley', this area contains a growing residential section, much of Juneau's business district and the world-famous Mendenhall Glacier. In the Valley, Egan Drive turns into Glacier Highway, a two-lane road that takes you to Auke Bay, the site of the State Marine Ferry terminal, more boat harbours and the last spot to purchase food or gas to the end of the road at Echo Cove.

Across the Gastineau Channel is Douglas, a small town south-east of Juneau, which at one time was the area's major city. The road north out of this sleepy little town is Douglas Highway which runs around Douglas Island to the fifth area of Juneau known to locals as North Douglas. Located here are the Eagle Crest Ski Area, many scenic turn-offs and a lot of cabins and homes half hidden in the trees which are owned by people who work in Juneau but don't want to live in its hustle-bustle atmosphere.

Information

The main visitor centre is the Davis Log Cabin at 134 3rd St (tel 586-2201), open from 8.30 am to 5 pm Monday to Friday, and from 10 am to 5 pm Saturday and Sunday. There are also smaller visitor information booths at the Juneau Airport terminal out in the Valley and at the Marine Park on the city waterfront.

For information about cabin rentals, hiking trails, Glacier Bay, Admiralty Island or any outdoor activity in the Tongass National Forest, stop at the information centre (tel 586-8751) in the Centennial Hall at 101 Egan Drive. The centre is staffed by both US Forest Service (USFS) and National Park personnel and is open from 8.30 am to 6 pm daily in the summer.

For current fishing conditions and local hot spots, the Alaska Fish & Game Department has a fishing hotline on 465-4116. The Alaska Division of State Parks (tel 465-4563) also has an office in Juneau on the 3rd floor, 400 Willoughby Ave, which is open from 8 am to 4.30 pm Monday to Friday.

Things to See

Much of your sightseeing time will be spent in the city centre, where nothing more than a good pair of walking shoes is needed. Start at the **Marine Park**, a delightful waterfront park across from the Sealaska Building at the southern end of Egan Drive, where there is an information kiosk, open daily from 9 am to 6 pm. Among the hand-outs they offer is a walking-tour map.

The tour leads from the park along Ferry Way to **South Franklin St**, a historical district that underwent major renovation in 1985. The buildings along this stretch, many dating back to the early 1900s, have since been turned into bars, gift shops and restaurants and are stormed by mobs of visitors every time a cruise ship docks. Heading north-west you will pass two excellent bookstores, Hearthside and Big City. Both are good sources of Alaskan literature and material.

At the Baranof Hotel, the tour turns left (south-west) onto 2nd St and then quickly right (north-west) onto Seward St, where it passes the **Davis Log Cabin**, a replica of the first church in Juneau. The cabin is another information centre and houses a small collection of local historical relics and objects.

The next building up Seward St is the **Court Building**; from here you proceed to the corner of North Franklin and 5th streets, a block to the north-east and then a block to the north-west. Just down 5th St to the right (north-east) is the **St Nicholas Russian**

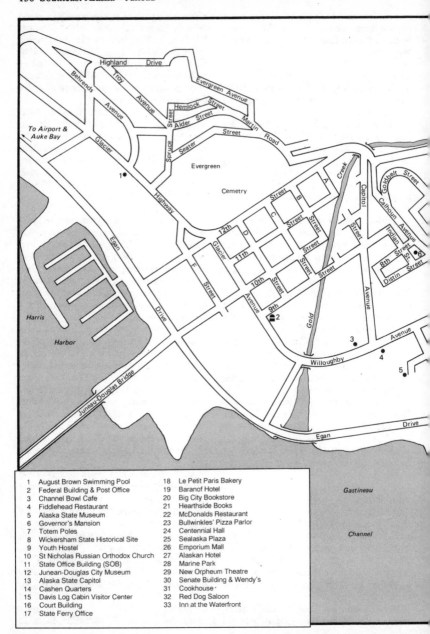

1   August Brown Swimming Pool
2   Federal Building & Post Office
3   Channel Bowl Cafe
4   Fiddlehead Restaurant
5   Alaska State Museum
6   Governor's Mansion
7   Totem Poles
8   Wickersham State Historical Site
9   Youth Hostel
10 St Nicholas Russian Orthodox Church
11 State Office Building (SOB)
12 Junean-Douglas City Museum
13 Alaska State Capitol
14 Cashen Quarters
15 Davis Log Cabin Visitor Center
16 Court Building
17 State Ferry Office

18 Le Petit Paris Bakery
19 Baranof Hotel
20 Big City Bookstore
21 Hearthside Books
22 McDonalds Restaurant
23 Bullwinkles' Pizza Parlor
24 Centennial Hall
25 Sealaska Plaza
26 Emporium Mall
27 Alaskan Hotel
28 Marine Park
29 New Orpheum Theatre
30 Senate Building & Wendy's
31 Cookhouse ·
32 Red Dog Saloon
33 Inn at the Waterfront

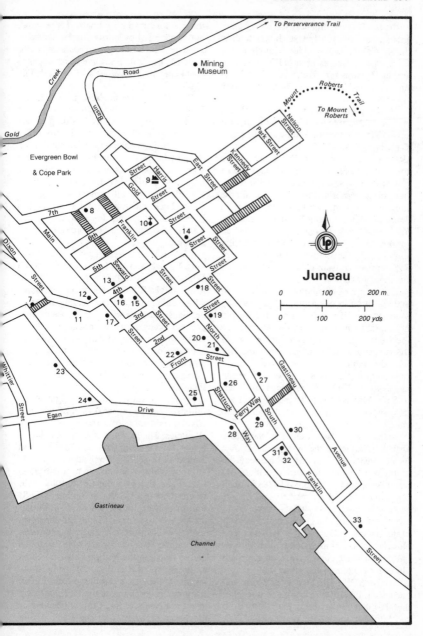

Orthodox Church, probably the most photographed structure in Juneau. It was built in 1894, making it the oldest church in the Southeast, and has exhibits of Russian icons, original vestments and religious relics. Tours are conducted daily during the summer for a $1 donation.

Heading back south-west on 5th St, descend Seward St and then turn south-west on 4th St to the Court Building and the **State Capitol** (tel 464-4565), though you might not recognise it at first. The capitol looks more like a school than the Alaskan seat of government. Inside are the legislative chambers, the governor's office and offices for the hundreds of staff members who arrive in Juneau for the winter legislative session. Within the lobby is a visitors desk where free tours of the building are offered daily during the summer. The 30 minute tours start every 1½ hours or so from 8.30 am to 5 pm; call for exact times.

Continue a block south-west along 4th St and you'll reach the **Juneau-Douglas City Museum** (tel 586-3572). Housed in the old Memorial Library building, the museum has local artwork, a large custom relief map of the area and audio-visual presentations. But it's best exhibits are interpretive displays covering the gold-mining history of Juneau and Douglas. The museum is open from 9 am to 5 pm Monday to Friday and from 11 am to 5 pm Saturday and Sunday; the admission charge is $1.

Across from the museum is the **State Office Building,** or the SOB as it is known locally. Inside the SOB on the 8th floor is the grand court which features a century-old totem pole and a restored 1928 Kimball organ played for office workers and visitors each Friday at noon. The **Alaska State Library** is also off the grand court. The panoramic view of Juneau's waterfront and Douglas Island from the adjoining outdoor balcony is most impressive – an excellent place to have lunch on a sunny day.

At the SOB, 4th St curves north and becomes Calhoun Ave; in a block it reaches the six-pillar **Governor's Mansion.** Built and furnished in 1912 at a cost of $44,000,

the structure has a New England appearance but is accented by a totem pole, carved in 1940 by Tlingit Indians and presented to the governor as a gift. Tours can be arranged by contacting the Governor's office (tel 465-3500).

Behind the Governor's Mansion is Indian St which curves sharply into 9th St. Follow 9th St west to the **Federal Building,** where the main post office is on the 1st floor. The Federal Building sits on the junction of 9th St and Glacier Ave, a major bus stop where you can pick up buses to the Valley or Douglas. Following Glacier Ave back towards town you will arrive at a bridge over Gold Creek where a memorial plaque has been placed to honour Joe Juneau and Dick Harris, who stumbled upon gold in the icy stream.

Glacier Ave curves east and becomes Willoughby Ave, and in a few blocks you reach Whittier St. Turn right (south) on Whittier St to the **Alaska State Museum,** an impressive white building. This outstanding museum provides Alaskans with a showcase of their past, including artefacts from all four indigenous groups: Athabascan, Aleut, Eskimo and those on the north-west coast. There are also displays relating to the Russian period, major gold strikes in the state and the Alaska Pipeline.

By far the most impressive sight is the full-size, two-storey eagle's nest where a circular staircase allows you to view it from all angles. The museum is open Monday to Friday from 9 am to 6 pm and Saturday and Sunday from 11 am to 6 pm; admission is $1.

From Whittier St you can turn left (east) onto Egan Drive to the **Centennial Hall,** where there is a US Forest Service (USFS) information centre (tel 586-8751). During the summer a variety of films and slide presentations are given in the adjoining theatre.

Continue east on Egan Drive, and just before reaching the Marine Park you come to the **Sealaska Building,** the headquarters for one of the state's most successful Indian corporations. Step inside the 1st floor lobby to view a Haida canoe, Chilkat blankets or the beautiful tapestry in the Bank of the

North that was designed by Rie Munoz, a well-known Juneau artist.

Another attraction in the city centre is at the top (northern end) of Main St. After climbing the steep street, catch your breath and turn right (west) on 7th St to the **Wickersham State Historical Site**, the historical home of Judge James Wickersham, the pioneer judge and statesman of Alaska. The house was built in 1898 and occupied by the Judge who also served as Alaska's first delegate to Congress from 1928 to 1939. For years it was maintained by his granddaughter but in 1985 the state took over the historical site. Inside are photographs, books and other memorabilia from the Judge's colourful career. The house is open daily from 1 to 4 pm and guided tours can be arranged; there is no admission charge.

Gold

Gold fever and gold mines built Juneau and today mining companies are staging a resurgence in and around the city. There are several interesting and free places to view what must have been an incredible era in Alaska's history. First head to the Juneau-Douglas City Museum for their exhibit and pick up the *Last Chance Basin Walking Tour* and *Treadwell Mine Historic Trail* brochures.

The **Last Chance Mining Museum** is at the end of Basin Rd, a 2 mile (3.2 km) walk from the city centre. The museum was originally the old compressor house for the Alaska-Juneau Mine on Gastineau Channel, and today it houses tools, machinery, ore samples, mine cars and other relics of the golden past. It closed in 1986 but there are plans to reopen it in the future.

Even if the museum itself is not open, you can still view the impressive complex of railroad lines, ore cars and buildings. To reach the area follow North Franklin St up the hill to its end and turn right (south-east) onto 6th St. Turn immediately left (northwest) on Gold St which turns into Basin Rd. The ruins are 0.5 mile (0.8 km) down this scenic road.

At the end of nearby Perseverance Trail

(see the Juneau Hiking section) is the **Glory Hole**, a caved-in mine shaft that was connected to the Alaska-Juneau Mine, along with the remains of the **Silver Bowl Basin Mine**.

Perhaps the most interesting areas to explore are the **Treadwell Mine** ruins across the Gastineau Channel near Douglas. From the Capital Transit bus turnaround in Douglas, continue south towards the Sandy Beach Recreation Area, past the softball fields and Douglas Boat Harbor. The beach was made from the tailings of the Treadwell Mine and the old pilings from its shipping dock still stand.

Take one of the staircases from the beach to St Ann's St right above Sandy Beach and follow the street further south to Old Treadwell Rd. The dirt road leads to old foundations, the shells of boarding houses and the mine shaft, another glory hole, of the Treadwell Mining Community. The operation closed down in 1922 after a 1917 cave-in caused the financial collapse of the company. During its heyday at the turn of the century, the mine made Douglas the major city on the channel with a population of 15,000.

Across the channel from Treadwell is the **Alaska-Juneau Mine** on the side of Mt Roberts. The mine closed down in 1944 after producing more than $80 million in gold when it was valued at $20 to $35 an ounce. Today, it is the centre of a controversial plan to reopen it by a Canadian mining company.

Gold Panning There is a natural fascination among visitors passing through the Southeast about gold-rush history and even an interest among many to try panning themselves. It has turned out to be quite a recreational activity throughout much of the state the past few years, even giving rise to commercial gold-panning tours.

They're not really necessary. Any hardware store in Juneau will sell you a gold pan (black plastic ones are the cheapest and easiest to see those flecks of gold) and at the US Forest Service information centre you can get all the 'dos and don'ts' to avoid trespassing and jumping any claims. Those really serious about panning for gold bring a short shovel, boots, rubber gloves and a small bottle to hold all that gold.

The best public creeks to pan in Juneau are Bullion Creek in the Treadwell Mine area, Gold Creek up by the Last Chance Basin, Sheep Creek on Thane Rd and Salmon, Nugget and Eagle creeks off Egan Drive and Glacier Highway north of the city centre. To spend a day with an 'old sourdough' try the Thane Orehouse (tel 586-3442) where equipment, hands-on instruction and access to an ore-bearing creek are $6 per person for a whole day of panning.

Glaciers

Juneau is also known as the 'Gateway to the Glaciers'. There are several in the area including the Mendenhall Glacier, Alaska's famous drive-in glacier. The flow of ice is 13 miles (21 km) from the city centre at the end of Glacier Spur Rd. Head out along Egan Drive and at *Mile 9* (14.4 km) turn right onto Mendenhall Loop Rd, staying on Glacier Spur Rd when the loop curves north to head back to Auke Bay.

Today, the Mendenhall Glacier flows 12 miles (19 km) from its source, the Juneau Icefield, and has a 1.5 mile (2.4 km) face. On a sunny day it's beautiful, with blue skies and snow-capped mountains in the background. On a cloudy and drizzly afternoon it can be even more impressive, as the ice turns shades of deep blue.

There is an interesting visitor centre at the glacier with a large relief map of the ice field and glaciers, and audio-visual room with slide presentations and films, and an information desk. There are several hiking trails in the area, including a 0.5 mile (0.8 km) nature trail, the East Glacier Trail or the Nugget Creek Trail (see the Juneau Hiking section).

The cheapest way to see the glacier is to hop on a Capital Transit bus in the city centre and get off at the corner of Mendenhall Loop and Glacier Spur roads. The fare is 75c and buses depart from the State Capitol and the Federal Building every half an hour or so.

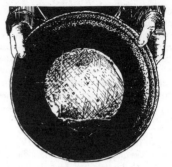

Gold Panning

From the Loop Rd, it is another 1 mile (1.6 km) to the visitor centre. Then there is always hitchhiking, a relatively easy method of travel in Juneau.

On your way out to Mendenhall Valley, look to your right high in the mountains when you pass Lemon Creek to see the remains of the Lemon Creek Glacier. By hiking, you can get a close and uncrowded look at Herbert Glacier on *Mile 27.5* (43 km) of Galcier Highway or Eagles Glacier at *Mile 28.4* (45 km) (see the Juneau Hiking section).

One way to see all the glaciers and the ice field is to splurge on a sightseeing flight. They're not cheap, most cost around $80 per person for a 45 minute flight, but on a clear day it can provide a spectacular overview of the ice field. All the air charter companies run them. Wings of Alaska (tel 789-0790) offer scenic flights during the summer from the International Airport and the Marine Park at the city waterfront when there is a cruise ship in.

You can also view the ice field and glaciers from a helicopter which includes landing on the sea of ice and spending a few minutes walking around. Gray Line (tel 586-3773) offers such a tour that lasts 90 minutes. The price to stand on ice? How about $115 per person.

Festivals

Juneau's main festival during the summer is on the Fourth of July when the celebrations

Top: Mendenhall Glacier (ADT)
Left: Walking at the top of Mendenhall Glacier near Juneau (JD)
Right: Glacier Bay National Park (ADT)

Top: Salmon fishing in Southeast Alaska (USFS)
Bottom: US Forest Service Cabin in Tongass National Park (USFS)

include a parade, a carnival, fireworks over the channel and a lot of outdoor meals from Sandy Beach in Douglas to Juneau's city centre. In mid-April there is the week-long Alaska Folk Festival.

Places to Stay

Camping There are some fine campgrounds beyond Mendenhall Valley and a dozen unofficial ones near the city centre. *Mendenhall Lake Campground*, one of the most beautiful US Forest Service (USFS) campgrounds in Alaska, is 13 miles (21 km) from the city centre and 5 miles (8 km) south of the Auke Bay Ferry Terminal. The campground (60 sites) is on Montana Creek Rd, a dirt road that runs off Mendenhall Loop Rd. The tent sites are alongside a lake and many have spectacular views of the nearby glacier. There is a 14 day limit and the nightly fee is $5 per site.

The other USFS campground, *Auke Village*, is 2 miles (3.2 km) north of the ferry terminal on Glacier Highway. The area (11 sites) provides shelters, tables, wood and an interesting beach to walk along. The fee is also $5 per night with a 14 day limit.

Many backpackers prefer to stay close to the city centre and end up hiking along Basin Rd. Where the road crosses Gold Creek there are some flat areas in the bush that serve as good spots to pitch a tent. If you have some time, it is even better to hike the Perseverance Trail off Basin Rd to the Granite Creek Trail and camp in the bowl at the end of this footpath (see the Juneau Hiking section).

Glacier Highway ends 41 miles (66 km) north of Juneau at a pleasant spot called Echo Cove. There are no developed facilities here, but it's a nice spot to camp for a while and a favourite among locals. There is usually good offshore salmon fishing in August. Other scenic but undeveloped areas are Eagle Beach on Glacier Highway, and Fish Creek on North Douglas Highway.

Hostels In the autumn of 1985, the *Juneau Youth Hostel* (tel 586-9559) went from being just another church basement to being one of the best hostels in Alaska. The large yellow house is on the corner of Harris and 6th streets in the colourful Starr Hill neighbourhood. Its location is ideal – five blocks from the State Capitol, four blocks from the Mt Roberts Trail and two blocks from Basin Rd and the beginning of the scenic Gold Creek area.

The hostel has cooking facilities, showers and a common room with a fireplace. Check-in time is from 5 to 11 pm, check-out is 9 am and reservations are accepted if accompanied by the first night's fee and sent with a self-addressed, stamped envelope. Fees are $7.50 for youth hostel members and $9.50 for nonmembers. For reservations contact the Juneau Youth Hostel, 614 Harris St, Juneau, Alaska 99801.

Bed & Breakfast Juneau has exploded with bed & breakfast lodging. There are more than two dozen B&Bs and most have rates that range from $30 to $40 for singles and from $50 to $60 for a double. The only problem is securing a room after stepping off the ferry late at night. For that reason, it's wise to book ahead, even a day or two while travelling through the region. An easy way to do this is to contact the Alaska Bed & Breakfast Association (tel 586-2959) which covers most of the Southeast, including Juneau, of course.

When looking for a B&B, keep in mind that the city-centre places will be booked solid for months in advance. But you might find a room and even have a more enjoyable stay at one outside of the city. The *Lost Cord Bed & Breakfast* (tel 789-7296) has its own beach on Auke Bay. Rooms cost from $20 to $55 but include a courtesy pick-up at the ferry terminal or airport. In Douglas, the *Windsock Inn* (tel 364-2431) near the bus stop to Juneau has rooms for $35 a single and $40 a doubles.

Hotels Most hotels, especially the city-centre ones, tend to be heavily booked during the summer tourist season. The cheapest hotel is the *Inn at the Waterfront* (tel 586-2050), a small hotel across from the cold-storage plant on South Franklin St. The owners recently redecorated the rooms, but it would still be wise to look before you rent. Rooms range from $28 for a single with a shared bath all the way up to $115.

Cashen Quarters (tel 586-9863) is a small hotel at 303 Gold St with only four rooms to rent. Each room has a three-quarter size bath and costs $35 a single.

On South Franklin St is the *Alaskan Hotel* (tel 586-1000) with charming historical decor in its lobby and rooms dating back to 1913 when it was first opened. Singles without bath are $36 a night and the hotel features private sauna rooms and an interesting bar in the back. Out of town there is the *Tides Motel* (tel 780-4622) on Glacier Highway in the Lemon Creek area with singles from $40.

Places to Eat

Juneau's size allows it to have an excellent cross section of restaurants that no other Southeast town could possibly support. If you're really hungry, the best bargain for a full dinner during the summer is one of the town's two salmon bakes. The *Gold Creek Salmon Bake* is held in the Last Chance Basin on Basin Rd and is a pleasant walk from the youth hostel. The salmon bake costs $17 for an all-you-can-eat affair that includes salad, bread, your first beer and salmon that is cooked with a tangy brown sugar sauce. At the outdoor tables you can enjoy the spectacular mountain scenery and there is usually nightly entertainment. You can also catch a free bus to the bake which departs from the Baranof Hotel daily beginning at 6 pm.

Four miles (6.5 km) south of town on Thane Road is the *Thane Ore House Salmon Bake* (tel 586-3442). The dinner is basically the same and the price is $15 per person. Near the remains of the Alaska Gastineau Mine, the Ore House has a small mining museum and is where *Gold Rush Days Review* is performed by the Janice Holst Dancers (for an additional charge). For times and pick-up points of its free transport vehicle, call the Ore House.

City Centre The cheapest place for breakfast or lunch is the *Federal Building Cafeteria* on the 2nd floor of the Federal Building, which also provides a nice view of the Gastineau Channel for its diners. Open from 7 am to 3.30 pm, the restaurant offers eggs, potatoes, toast and bacon for around $3, and hamburgers and sandwiches for under $2. The nearby *Channel Bowl Cafe*, a local hang-out on Willoughby Ave across from the Foodland Supermarket, is known for large portions and reasonable prices, especially for breakfast.

McDonald's and *Wendy's*, two fast-food chains that also serve breakfast, are near each other. McDonald's is at the corner of 2nd and Seward streets diagonally opposite the Sealaska Building, while Wendy's is in the Senate Building on South Franklin St.

Closer to the youth hostel at 299 North Franklin St is *Le Petit Paris*, which offers excellent croissants for 90c and croissant sandwiches from $4. The small corner bakery has limited seating inside and is open from 7.15 am to 6 pm.

Cheap dinners of pizza or sandwiches can be obtained at *Bullwinkle's Pizza Parlor* across from the State Office Building on Willoughby Ave. Good-sized sandwiches cost between $4 and $7, while 9 inch (22 cm) pizzas begin at $5. There is also wine, a large selection of imported beer and silent movies on the back wall at night.

The best Mexican restaurant in the city centre is *Armadillo Tex-Mex Cafe* at 431 South Franklin St, where you can fill up on huge tostada compuesta. Almost across the street on the 1st floor of the Emporium Mall is the *Heritage Coffee Co & Cafe*, a good spot for an afternoon break, as it serves various coffees, cappuccino, steamed milk and croissants.

Next door to the Red Dog Saloon on South Franklin St is the *Cookhouse* with a soup and salad bar, and an early bird special from 4 to 6 pm. For $10 you get a full dinner with a choice of salmon or ribs, a trip to the salad bar and home-made ice cream. For a quick lunch, the street vendors, selling everything from hot dogs to bagel sandwiches, are probably the cheapest way to go. Look for them along Marine Park and in the city centre.

For a complete dinner, if you're not worrying about paying for your ferry ticket to Haines, try the *Fiddlehead Restaurant* on Willoughby Ave. The food is excellent but dinners are priced from $16. The place is another good spot for afternoon tea and freshly baked foods. They occasionally have live folk music at night.

Bellezza Ristorante is Juneau's finest Italian restaurant. It is at 240 Main St in the Court Plaza Building, better known throughout town as the 'Spam Can' Building, where the Alaska State Ferry has a ticket office.

The *Summit Restaurant* (tel 586-2050) on the main floor of the Inn on the Waterfront has a menu of gourmet dishes from $14 which are served in a tiny dining room that holds perhaps 15 people. It's an interesting little restaurant, but you have to call ahead to reserve a table.

Juneau's fishing fleet is nowhere near the size of those in Ketchikan or Petersburg, but there are still a number of places to obtain Alaska's delicacies from the sea. In the city centre, *Foodland Supermarket* on Willoughby Ave across from the Federal Building has a good selection of local seafood, including salmon, halibut, prawns and crabs' legs. The *Alaska Smoked Salmon Co* at 230 South Franklin St in the Marine View Center specialises in shipping seafood home with visitors.

Finally, as you are strolling around town, look for the occasional fisher selling prawns, crabs and halibut from boats at several spots along the waterfront, including the City Dock on South Franklin St and the Auke Bay Harbor out of town.

Douglas The best restaurant in Douglas is *Beauty & the Feast* next to the Billiken Bar at 916 3rd St. The pub-like restaurant has excellent salads and omelettes.

The Valley A second *McDonald's* is on the corner of Egan Drive and Old Glacier Highway across from the Nugget Mall. In the Mendenhall Mall, on Mendenhall Loop Rd a short way from the Egan Drive junction, there is a *Taco Bell* and another *Bullwinkle's*

Pizza Parlor which has a lunch buffet with all the pizza and salad you can eat.

Jerry's Meats across from McDonald's has a fine selection of seafood at reasonable prices.

Entertainment

With a population that is larger, younger and a little more cultured than most other Southeast towns, Juneau is able to support a great deal more nightlife. The most famous nightspot is the *Red Dog Saloon*, which is mentioned in every travel brochure and the final destination of every tour bus. In 1987, the bar moved to a new location on the corner of Marine Way and South Franklin St but has still managed to retain its Alaskan decor. The bar is interesting with its sawdust floor and relics covering the walls, but the Red Dog is not a place to spend an entire evening drinking unless you can put up with instamatic cameras flashing at the stuffed bear. The best time to go is after 11 pm.

South Franklin St as a whole is Juneau's drinking section. Many places are local hang-outs that will undoubtedly turn you off, which is fine with those leaning against the bar inside. The *Triangle Club*, however, is a pleasant little spot on the corner of Front and South Franklin streets. Although there is limited seating inside, the bar offers widescreen television and a good hot dog to go along with a mug of beer.

Hidden in the back of the *Alaskan Hotel* is a unique bar with an interior and cash register that matches the rest of the hotel's historical setting. Often there is folk or jazz music. Just down the street at the top of the Senate Building where Wendy's is, you'll find *The Penthouse*. The bar, which was the first in Juneau to enforce a dress code after 7 pm, has music, dancing and a huge video screen. Many locals beat the code and high prices by stopping by in the afternoon to enjoy a drink and the fine views of Juneau.

A little quieter and at the west end of the city centre is the *Breakwater Inn* on Glacier Ave, past the high school. The bar is on the 2nd floor and overlooks the Aurora Basin Boat Harbor, an active place in the summer.

On the other side of the channel in Douglas, there are two bars across the street from each other and similar in atmosphere. *Billikens* and *Louie's* on Douglas Highway are favourites with locals, especially softball players who hold their games at nearby Sandy Beach Recreational Area.

Juneau also supports a unique movie theatre which on nice summer days doubles as an outdoor cafe. The *New Orpheum Theatre & Cafe*, off Marine Way near Marine Park, specialises in classic movies in a small, 30 seat theatre. The other half of the place is a cafe and local artist gallery that stays open until midnight and serves cappuccino and espresso coffee along with pastries, ice-cream pies, salads and soups.

Another way to spend an evening is soaking in a hot tub or sweating in a sauna, a favourite activity among all Alaskans. The Augustus Brown Pool (tel 586-2055) next to the high school on Glacier Ave has a large 20 person sauna along with a pool and exercise area. There are various opening hours, including one at night from Monday to Thursday. Admission costs range from $1 to $3 per session.

For a more private evening, rent out one of the hot-tub rooms at the Alaskan Hotel (tel 586-1000) which are designed for two or three people and include a sauna and shower. The cost is $10 per person per hour and you should call ahead to reserve it.

Hiking

Few cities, if any, in Alaska have the many diverse hiking trails that Juneau has. To spend time here without taking at least a 1 day hike is to miss the area's top attraction. The US Forest Service (USFS) maintains 20 trails which are described in its booklet *Juneau Trails* ($2), available from the information centre in the Centennial Hall.

For those who don't feel up to walking the trails on their own, Juneau Parks & Recreation (tel 586-5226) hold adult hikes every Wednesday and family hikes along easier trails every Saturday. The hikes begin at the trailhead at 10 am; on Wednesday there is often car-pooling to the trail with hikers

meeting at Cope Park, a short walk from the youth hostel. Call Juneau Parks & Recreation for more details.

Perseverance Trail This trail system off Basin Rd is the most popular one in Juneau and includes the Perseverance, Mt Juneau and Granite Creek trails. Together, the trails can be combined into a rugged 10 hour walk for hardy hikers or an overnight excursion into the mountains that surround Alaska's capital city. To reach the trailhead from the youth hostel, take 6th St one block southwest to Gold St which turns into Basin Rd, a dirt road that curves away from the city into the mountains as it follows Gold Creek. After crossing a bridge over the creek look for the posted trailhead on the left.

From the Perseverance Trail it is possible to pick up the Granite Creek Trail and follow the path to the creek's basin, a beautiful spot to spend the night. From here, you can gain access to Mt Juneau by climbing the ridge and staying left of Mt Olds, the huge rocky mountain. Once on the summit of Mt Juneau, you can complete the loop by descending along the Mt Juneau Trail, which joins Perseverance Trail a mile (1.6 km) from its beginning.

The hike to the 3576 foot (1090 metre) peak of Mt Juneau along the ridge from Granite Creek is an easier but longer trek than the ascent from the Mt Juneau trail. The alpine sections of the ridge are peacefully serene and on a clear day in the summer there are outstanding views. At the end of the Perseverance Trail, there are gold-mine ruins and the steep-sided Glory Hole. From the trailhead for the Perseverance Trail to the upper basin of Granite Creek is a 3.3 mile (5.3 km) one way hike; it is then another 3 miles (4.8 km) along the ridge to Mt Juneau.

Mt Roberts Trail This is the other hike that starts close to the youth hostel. The trail is a 4 mile (6.4 km) ascent to the mountain above the city. The trail begins at a marked wooden staircase at the north-eastern end of 6th St and consists of a series of switchbacks with good resting spots. When you break out of

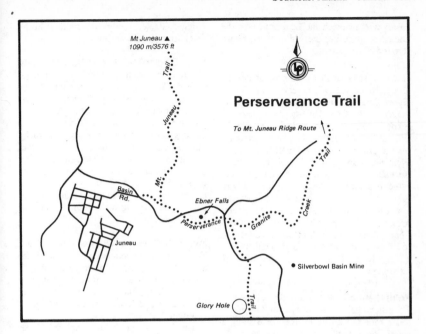

Mt Juneau ▲
1090 m/3576 ft

Perserverance Trail

To Mt. Juneau Ridge Route

Basin Rd.

Ebner Falls

Juneau

Perserverance

Granite

Creek Trail

Mt. Juneau Trail

● Silverbowl Basin Mine

Glory Hole

Trail

the trees at Gastineau Peak you come across a wooden cross and good views of Juneau, Douglas and the entire Gastineau Channel. The Mt Roberts summit is a steep climb through the alpine brush to the north of the city.

Dan Moller Trail This 3.3 mile (5.3 km) trail leads to an alpine bowl at the crest of Douglas Island where there is a USFS cabin (reservations needed, $20 per night). See the Trekking section in the Wilderness chapter for further details.

Treadwell Ditch Trail Also on Douglas Island, this trail can be picked up either 1 mile (1.6 km) up the Dan Moller Trail or just above D St in Douglas. The trail stretches 12 miles (19 km) north from Douglas to Eagle Crest, although most people only hike to the Dan Moller Trail and then return to the road, a 5 mile (8 km) trip. The path is rated as easy and provides views of the Gastineau Channel

while winding through scenic muskeg meadows.

Mt Bradley Trail This 2.6 mile (4.2 km) trail begins in Douglas through a vacant lot behind section 300 of 5th St and is a much harder climb than the hikes up Mt Roberts or Mt Juneau. Both rubber boots and sturdy hiking boots are needed as the trail can be muddy in the lower sections before you reach the beautiful alpine areas above the tree line. The climb to the 3337 foot (1017 metre) peak should only be attempted by experienced hikers.

Cropley Lake Trail Another trail on Douglas Island is the 1.5 mile (2.4 km) route to Cropley Lake. The trail was built primarily for Nordic skiing but in the summer it can be hiked to the alpine lake, which provides good scenery and camping. The start is up Fish Creek Rd, a short way past the Eagle Crest Ski Lodge in a creek gully to the right. An easier way to reach the lake is to take the chair lift up during the summer; the return fare is $10 per person.

Sheep Creek Trail South-east of Juneau along Thane Rd is the very scenic Sheep Creek Trail, a 3 mile (4.8 km) walk into the valley south of Mt Roberts where there are many historical mining relics. The trailhead is 4 miles (6.4 km) from Juneau at a staircase on the gravel spur to a Snettisham Power Plant substation. The trail is relatively flat in the valley, from where you scramble up forested hillsides to the alpine zone. Many hikers follow the power line once they are above the tree line to reach the ridge to Sheep Mountain. It is possible to continue from Sheep Mountain over Mt Roberts and return to Juneau along the Mt Roberts Trail. This is a very long 10 to 12 hour day hike, if attempted.

Point Bishop Trail At the end of Thane Rd, 7.5 miles (12 km) south-east of Juneau, is this 8 mile (13 km) trail to Point Bishop, a scenic spot that overlooks the junction between Stephens Passage and Taku Inlet. The trail is flat but can be wet in many spots, making waterproof boots the preferred footwear. The hike makes for an ideal overnight trip as there is good camping at Point Bishop.

East Glacier Trail This trail, the first of several near the Mendenhall Glacier, is a 3 mile (4.8 km) round trip that provides good views of the glacier from a scenic lookout at the halfway point. The trail begins off the 0.5 mile (0.8 km) nature walk near the Mendenhall Glacier Visitor Center.

Nugget Creek Trail Just beyond the East Glacier Trail's scenic lookout is the start of the 2.5 mile (4 km) Nugget Creek Trail to the Vista Creek Shelter, a free-use shelter that doesn't require reservations. The total round trip to the shelter from the Mendenhall Glacier Visitor Center is 8 miles (13 km). Hikers who plan to spend the night at the shelter can continue along the creek towards

Nugget Glacier, though the route is bushy and hard to follow at times.

West Glacier Trail This is one of the most spectacular trails in the Juneau area. The 3.4 mile (5.4 km) trail begins off Montana Creek Rd past Mendenhall Lake Campground and hugs the mountainside along the glacier, providing exceptional views of the icefalls and other glacial features. It ends at a rocky outcrop but a rough route continues from here to the summit of Mt McGinnis, another 2 miles (3.2 km) away. Plan on 4 to 5 hours for the West Glacier Trail, an easy hike that can be done in tennis shoes; or plan on a long day if you want to tackle the difficult Mt McGinnis route.

Montana Creek & Windfall Lake Trails These two trails connect at Windfall Lake and can be combined for an interesting 13 mile (21 km) overnight trip. It is easier to begin at Montana Creek and follow the Windfall Lake Trail out to the Glacier Highway.

The 9.5 mile (15.3 km) Montana Creek Trail, known for its high concentration of bears, begins near the end of Montana Creek Rd, close to the rifle range. The 3.5 mile (5.6 km) Windfall Lake Trail begins off a gravel spur that leaves the Glacier Highway just before it crosses Herbert River, 27 miles (43 km) north-west of Juneau. Wear rubber boots as either trail can be muddy during the summer, although the worst parts are planked.

Spaulding Trail This trail's primary use is for Nordic skiing, but it can be hiked in the summer if you're prepared for some muddy sections. The 3 mile (4.8 km) trail provides access to the Auke Nu Trail that leads to the John Muir USFS Cabin (reservations needed, $20 per night). The trailhead for the Spaulding Trail is at Glacier Highway just past and opposite the Auke Bay Post Office, 12.3 miles (20 km) north-west of Juneau. Check at the information centre in the Centennial Building about the availability of the cabin.

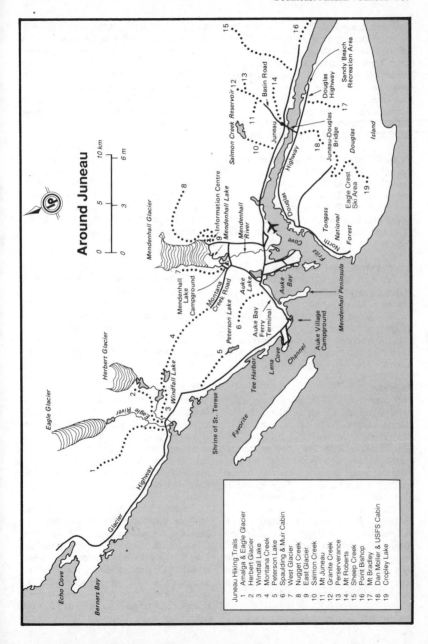

Around Juneau

0 5 10 km

0 3 6 m

Eagle Glacier

Echo Cove

Berners Bay

Herbert Glacier

Eagle River

Glacier Highway

Highway

1

2

Windfall Lake

3

Herbert Glacier

4

Montana Creek Road

Mendenhall Glacier

7

Mendenhall Lake Campground

9 Information Centre

Mendenhall Lake

Mendenhall River

8

Peterson Lake

5

6

Auke Lake

Auke Bay Ferry Terminal

Auke Bay

Fritz Cove

Shrine of St. Terese

Tee Harbor

Favorite Channel

Lena Cove

Auke Village Campground

Mendenhall Peninsula

North Tongass National Forest

Salmon Creek Reservoir

10

11

Basin Road

12

13

14

15

16

Juneau

Douglas Highway

Juneau-Douglas Bridge

18

Douglas

17

Eagle Crest Ski Area

19

Sandy Beach Recreation Area

Douglas Island

Juneau Hiking Trails
1 Amalga & Eagle Glacier
2 Herbert Glacier
3 Windfall Lake
4 Montana Creek
5 Peterson Lake
6 Spaulding & Muir Cabin
7 West Glacier
8 Nugget Creek
9 East Glacier
10 Salmon Creek
11 Mt Juneau
12 Granite Creek
13 Perseverance
14 Mt Roberts
15 Sheep Creek
16 Point Bishop
17 Mt Bradley
18 Dan Moller & USFS Cabin
19 Cropley Lake

Peterson Lake Trail This 4 mile (6.4 km) trail provides access to good Dolly Varden fishing in both Peterson Creek and Peterson Lake. The trailhead has been moved to avoid private property and is now located 20 feet (6 metres) before the *Mile 24* marker on Glacier Highway, north of the Shrine of St Terese. Wear rubber boots as it can be muddy during the summer. A USFS cabin (reservations, $20) is located at Peterson Lake.

Herbert Glacier Trail This level trail extends 4.6 miles (7.4 km) along the Herbert River to Herbert Glacier. The trail is easy, though wet in some places, and the round trip takes 4 to 5 hours. The trail begins just past the bridge over Herbert River at *Mile 28* (45 km) of Glacier Highway in a small parking lot to the left.

Amalga Trail Also known as the Eagle Glacier Trail, this level route winds 5.5 miles (8.8 km) one way to the lake formed by Eagle Glacier, 0.8 mile (1.3 km) from its face. The trailhead is just beyond the Glacier Highway bridge across Eagle River, 0.4 mile (0.6 km) past the trailhead for the Herbert Glacier Trail. Plan on a round trip of 7 to 8 hours to reach the impressive Eagle Glacier.

Paddling
Both day trips and extended 3 to 5 day paddles are possible out of Juneau in sea-touring kayaks. Boats can be rented from Alaska Discovery (tel 586-1911) at 369 South Franklin St for $40 a double and $30 a single per day, with discounts for rentals of 5 days or more. Topographical maps can be obtained in Juneau at the Foggy Mountain Shop (tel 586-6780) in the Emporium Mall off Shattuck Way, or Big City Books (tel 586-1772) at 100 North Franklin St. The bulletin boards at Foggy Mountain and Alaska Discovery are good places to check for used kayaks or canoes for sale. If you have the funds, purchasing and reselling a boat in Juneau is a cheap alternative to renting one for long-term paddles.

Taku Inlet This waterway is an excellent 4

to 5 day trip highlighted by close views of Taku Glacier. Total paddling distance is 30 to 40 miles (48 to 64 km) depending on how far you travel up the inlet. It does not require any major crossing, though rounding Point Bishop can be rough at times. It is possible to camp at Point Bishop and along the grassy area south-west of the glacier, where brown bears are occasionally spotted.

Berners Bay At the western end of Glacier Highway, 40 miles (64 km) from Juneau, is Echo Cove where kayakers put in for paddles into the protected waters of Berners Bay. The bay, which extends 12 miles (19 km) north to the outlets of the Antler, Lace and Berners rivers, is ideal for an overnight trip or longer excursions up Berners River.

Oliver Inlet On the north-east coast of Admiralty Island is Oliver Inlet, where a 0.8 mile (1.3 km) portage trail connects it to scenic Seymour Canal. The paddle to Oliver Inlet is 18 miles (29 km) and involves crossing Stephens Passage, a challenging open-water crossing for experienced kayakers only. At the south end of the portage trail from Oliver Inlet is the Seymour Canal USFS Cabin (reservations needed, $20 per night).

USFS Cabins
Numerous USFS cabins are accessible from Juneau but all are heavily used, requiring reservations as much as 180 days in advance. If you're just passing through, however, check with the USFS information centre in the Centennial Building, where staff members maintain a cabin update listing that shows which units are still available and when.

The John Muir, Peterson Lake and Dan Moller cabins, accessible by foot from the Juneau road system, and Seymour Canal Cabin, at the southern end of the portage from Oliver Inlet, have already been mentioned in the Juneau Hiking and Paddling sections. The following cabins are within 30 minutes flying time from Juneau; the air charter costs range from $150 to $200 per person for return transport. Both Channel

Flying (tel 586-3331) and LAB Flying Service (tel 789-9160) can provide air services on short notice.

West Turner One of the most scenic and by far the most popular cabin in the Juneau area, this unit is a 30 minute flight from Juneau on the western end of Turner Lake, where there is good fishing for trout, Dolly Varden and salmon. A skiff is provided.

Admiralty Cove This cabin on a scenic bay has access to Young Lake along a very rough 4.5 mile (7 km) trail. The unit is a 30 minute flight from Juneau in a tidal area where float planes can land only during high tide. Brown bears frequent the area.

Young Lake There is a USFS cabin at each end of Young Lake, and both are provided with a skiff. The lake offers good fishing for cutthroat trout and land-locked salmon. An overgrown trail connects North Young Lake Cabin with Admiralty Cove. There is no trail between South and North Young Lake cabins.

Getting There & Around
Airport & Ferry Terminal Transport Transport can be a problem when you arrive at Juneau Airport or the Auke Bay Ferry Terminal. Late-night arrivals heading for the city centre are best off getting the Mendenhall Glacier Transport bus that meets all ferry arrivals and the Eagle Express Line bus (tel 586-2660) that provides a service from the airport. Fares to the city centre are $6 from the airport and $9 from Auke Bay Ferry Terminal. For more information about pick-up points in the city centre, call 780-4677.

During the day, travellers have more of an option. Hitchhiking is easy in the area, as long as you're not trying to catch a ferry and avoid thumbing along the four-lane Egan Drive. It is also possible to walk to the nearest public bus stop for a 75c ride into town. From the ferry terminal, walk south along the Glacier Highway for a little over 1 mile (1.6 km) to Dehart's Grocery Store near

the Auke Bay terminal. From the airport, just stroll from the terminal to Airport Mall on Old Glacier Highway.

Air Alaska Airlines (tel 789-0600) has scheduled services to Seattle, all major Southeast communities, Glacier Bay, Anchorage, and Cordova from Juneau daily during the summer. The one-way fare from Juneau to Anchorage is $196. Even better is the $141 fare from Juneau to Cordova which allows you to continue travelling on the state ferries to Valdez, Seward, Homer and Kodiak. Delta Airlines (tel 789-9771) has daily scheduled flights from Juneau to Anchorage, Fairbanks and Seattle. Both airlines have a ticket office in the Baranof Hotel on South Franklin St.

The smaller air-service companies have a number of scheduled flights to small communities in the area that are considerably cheaper than chartering a plane there. LAB Flying Service (tel 789-9160) flies to Hoonah for $40 one way and Haines for $50. Channel Flying (tel 789-3331) offers a $50 flight to Tenakee Springs, $76 to Pelican and $65 to Angoon.

On Friday, Tuesday and Sunday evenings, Skagway Air (tel 789-2006) flies to Skagway for $65 one way and $110 return. Also check with Wings of Alaska (tel 789-0790) when shopping around for scheduled flights to other Southeast communities.

Bus Capital Transit, Juneau's public bus system, runs every half an hour during the week with alternating local and express services from 7 am until 6 pm. After 6 pm and on Saturdays, only hourly local services are available. The main route circles the city centre, stopping at the City Dock Ferry Terminal, Capitol Building, the Federal Building, and then heading out to the Valley and Auke Bay Boat Harbour via the Mendenhall Loop Rd, where it travels close to the Mendenhall Lake Campground. There is also a minibus that runs every hour from city stops to Douglas. Fares are 75c each way.

There is no public bus service on Sunday. Grab a route map at the city offices or the visitor centre; call 789-6901 for more information.

Boat The state ferry no longer uses the city terminal and now arrives and departs from the Auke Bay Ferry Terminal (tel 789-7453). This is a hassle for budget travellers but it made the city businesses happy as it opened up another dock to large 'Love Boat' cruise ships, the real money spenders.

There are daily state ferry departures during the summer from Juneau to Sitka for $22, Petersburg $38, Ketchikan $66, Haines $18 and Skagway $22. A smaller ferry, the *Le Conte*, connects Juneau to Hoonah, Angoon and Tenakee Springs. The city ferry ticket office (tel 465-3941) is on the ground floor of the silver Court Plaza Building on Main St near the State Office Building. You can either call that office or the Auke Bay terminal for ferry information.

Car Rental There are several car rental places in Juneau for those needing a vehicle – a great way for two or three people to see the sights out of the city or to reach a trailhead. Late model cars cost around $29 per day and 20 cents per mile but you usually get 100 free miles. Considering all the roads in Juneau don't total much more than 100 miles (160 km), you don't need to worry too much about the mileage charge. For car rentals call either All Star Rental (tel 789-9000) near the Airport or Rent-A-Wreck (tel 789-4111) at 8600 Airport Blvd.

Tours Tracy Arm is a steep-sided fjord, highlighted by a pair of tidewater glaciers and a gallery of icebergs that float down the length of it. Located 50 miles (80 km) south-east of Juneau, the fjord makes an interesting day trip. Alaska Seal (tel 789-7429) offers 2 day cruises to both Tracy Arm and Endicott Arm. The boat departs from the Auroa Basin Boat Marina across from the Breakwater Inn on Saturday and Wednesday. The fare is $178 per person and includes a bunk on the ship and meals.

The company also offers a 10 hour dinner cruise to Tracy Arm for $75 per person and

a kayaker's special for those who want to be dropped off for a few days for some scenic paddling (see the Paddling section in the Wilderness chapter).

A number of companies offer city tours through Juneau and the surrounding area for those travellers with limited time. Gray Line (tel 586-3773) departs from the Baranof Hotel at 127 North Franklin St and offers a 2½ hour Mendenhall Glacier tour for $22. Even better is Mendenhall Glacier Transport (tel 789-5460) which has a $9, 2½ hour glacier tour that includes a few city and Douglas Island sights.

Alaska up Close (tel 789-9544) offers an Art Alaska Tour in which visitors are taken into the private studios and galleries of Juneau artists. The 2½ hour tour costs $20 per person. The company, which caters to small groups and uses a van for transport, also has bird-watching tours and trips out to Mendenhall Glacier.

AROUND JUNEAU

Other sights outside the city include the **Chinook Alaska Brewing Company** (tel 780-5866) on Shaune Drive in the Lemon Creek area. Juneau's only brewery, in fact Alaska's only brewery, offers tours on Tuesday and Thursday and a free glass of suds at the end. Call for current tour times or go into any liquor store and purchase its pale ale or amber beer. Beware, although brewed locally it's not cheap at $7 for a six pack.

The **Auke Bay Marine Lab** is 12.5 miles (20 km) north-west of Juneau and 1 mile (1.6 km) south of the State Marine Ferry terminal. The research facility has a self-guided tour of displays and saltwater tanks and is open from 8 am to 4.30 pm on weekdays. South of the lab on the shores of Auke Lake is the **University of Alaska (Juneau Campus)**, a small college in a beautiful setting. Among the many buildings are a student union and a bookstore.

At *Mile 23.3* (37 km) of Glacier Highway is the **Shrine of St Terese**, a natural stone chapel on its own island that is connected to the shore by a stone causeway. As well as being the site of numerous weddings, the island is situated along the Breadline, a well-known salmon fishing area in Juneau. This is perhaps the best place to fish for salmon from the shore.

Scenic viewing points include North Douglas Rd for a look at Fritz Cove and Mendenhall Glacier from afar, and **Eagle Beach Recreation Area** at *Mile 28.6* (46 km) of Glacier Highway for stunning views of the Chilkat Mountains and Lynn Canal. Bird enthusiasts should stop at the scenic lookout at *Mile 6* (9.6 km) of Egan Drive, which overlooks the **Mendenhall Wetlands & Refuge**. A viewing platform is located there with signboards that explain the natural history of the refuge.

If the temperatures soar above 80°F (26.6°C), head over to **Sandy Beach** and watch the pale locals cram in as much sun-tanning as they can under the midnight sun.

Admiralty Island

Only 15 miles (24.4 km) south-east of Juneau is Admiralty Island National Monument, a 955,747 acre (382,299 hectare) preserve, most of which has been designated as a wilderness area. The Tlingit Indians who know the island as Xootsnoowu, 'the Fortress of Bears' (the name was well chosen), have resided on the island for more than 1000 years

Admiralty Island has a wide variety of wildlife. Bays like Mitchell, Hood, Whitewater and Chaik contain marine mammals such as harbour seals, porpoises and sea lions. Seymour Canal, the island's largest inlet, has one of the highest densities of nesting eagles in the world, and humpback whales often feed in the waterway. Sitka black-tailed deer are plentiful and the streams choke with spawning salmon during August. But more than anything else Admiralty Island is known for its bears.

The island has one of the highest densities of bear in Alaska; it supports more brown bears than people. On Admiralty Island, the bears enjoy a good life. The animals roam the

drainages, searching for sedges, roots and berries much of the year. During August, they feast on salmon and then settle into dens on the upper slopes to sleep away most of the winter.

Admiralty is a rugged island. The coastal rainforest of Sitka spruce and western hemlock cover the island, broken up only by numerous lakes, rivers and open areas of muskeg. Around 2500 feet (750 metres), the tree line is reached and beyond that you'll find alpine-tundra and eventually rock outcrops and even permanent ice fields.

Although you can fly in for a stay at a US Forest Service (USFS) cabin or an expensive lodge, most visitors to the monument are people looking for a wilderness experience and who take the Cross Admiralty Island Canoe Route (see the Paddling section in the Wilderness Chapter) or spend time paddling Seymour Inlet and Mitchell or one of many other bays.

Before arriving, secure supplies and information in Juneau. Most visitors arrive from Juneau and information can be obtained from the USFS office at Centennial Hall on Egan Drive, the Alaska Discovery office on South Franklin St (they rent the canoes on the island) or the Admiralty Island National Monument office (tel 789-3111) at 8465 Old Dairy Road out in Mendenhall Valley.

ANGOON

The lone settlement on Admiralty Island is Angoon, a predominantly Tlingit community of 650 residents. Tlingit tribes occupied the site for centuries, but the original village was wiped out in 1882 when the US Navy, sailing out of Sitka, bombarded the Indians after they staged an uprising against a local whaling company.

Today, the economy is a mixture of commercial fishing and subsistence, while in town the strong indigenous heritage is evident in the painted fronts of the 16 tribal community houses. The old lifestyle is still apparent in this remote community and time in Angoon is spent observing and understanding the Tlingit culture. Tourism seems to be tolerated only because the village is a port-of-call for the state ferry.

Angoon only has 3 miles (4.8 km) of road. The village itself is at one end, perched on a strip of land between Chatham Strait on the west coast of Admiralty Island and turbulent Kootznahoo Inlet that leads into the interior of the national monument. The community serves as the departure point for many kayak and canoe trips into the heart of the monument, including the 32 mile (51 km) Cross Admiralty Canoe Route to Mole Harbor.

Many people are content to just spend a few days paddling and fishing Mitchell Bay and Salt Lake. Alaska Discovery rents canoes for $40 a day in Angoon from the Angoon Trading Company (tel 788-3111) on Kootznahoo Rd. Before undertaking such an adventure, stop at the US Forest Service office (tel 788-3166) in the Old City Office Building on Flagstaff Rd in Angoon for information on the tides in Kootznahoo Inlet and Mitchell Bay. The office is open from 8 am to 5 pm Monday to Friday. The tides here are among the strongest in the world; the walk between the airport and the town allows you to view the turbulent waters at mid-tide.

Places to Stay & Eat

By far the best place to stay in Angoon is the *Favorite Bay Inn* (tel 788-3123) in Dick Powers' large, rambling home 2 miles (3.2 km) from the ferry terminal. A bed and a hearty breakfast is $42 for a single room and $50 for a double. *Kootznahoo Lodge* (tel 788-3501), a few dollars more, has 10 rooms and is on Kootznahoo Rd.

Angoon is a dry community and the only cafe in town is a hang-out for teenagers at night. Groceries and limited supplies can be picked up at the *Angoon Trading Company* (tel 788-3111) on Kootznahoo Rd. It is also the place to rent canoes. There are also supplies at the *Seaside Store* on Chatham St but it's best to come with a full supply of your own food.

Getting There & Away

There are approximately two southbound and two northbound ferries a week stopping at Angoon on the run from Sitka to Juneau during the summer. The one-way fare to Angoon is $20 from Juneau and $18 from Sitka. The ferry terminal is 3 miles (4.9 km) from town.

Channel Flying (tel 788-3641 in Angoon) has daily flights to Juneau for $65. Bellair, the Sitka air charter company, also has an office in Angoon and has scheduled flights between the two towns for $66 per person.

PACK CREEK BEAR REFUGE

On the eastern side of Admiralty Island, spilling into Seymour Canal, is Pack Creek. To the north of it is Swan Cove and to the south is Windfall Harbor. All three areas have extensive tide flats that draw a large number of bears to feed, thus making them favorite spots to observe and photograph the animals.

As Pack Creek has been closed to hunting since the mid-1930s, several bears have become used to the presence of humans. The only resident in the area is the legendary Stan Price, who has lived on a float house near the Pack Creek estuary since the late 1950s.

The bears are most abundant in July and August when the salmon are running, and most visitors are boaters who go ashore to view the animals and then camp somewhere else. At Pack Creek, you watch the bears from the Viewing Sand Spit near Price's residence, while a 1 mile (1.6 km) trail leads back to an old observatory. There are campsites south of a small boat outhaul or, better yet, on the east side of Windfall Island. There is also a free three-sided shelter at Windfall Harbor.

If you're contemplating this trip, first check with the USFS office in Juneau. The number of bear/human incidents has increased in the last few years along with the number of visitors to the refuge. In 1981, 100 people visited the area; in

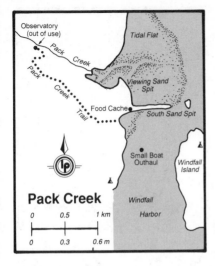

Pack Creek

Observatory (out of use)

Pack Creek

Tidal Flat

Viewing Sand Spit

Food Cache

South Sand Spit

Pack Creek Trail

Small Boat Outhaul

Windfall Island

Windfall

Windfall Harbor

| 0 | 0.5 | 1 km |
| 0 | 0.3 | 0.6 m |

weather. From the inlet, the Alaska Division of Parks & Outdoor Recreation operate the Oliver Inlet tramway that can be used to cross the 1 mile (1.6 km) portage into Seymour Canal. At the south end of the portage is the Seymour Canal Cabin (reservations needed) that can be rented for $20 per night by calling the State Division of Parks office (tel 465-4563) in Juneau.

You can also arrange to be dropped off and picked up by any of the air charter companies in Juneau (see the Juneau Getting There & Around section); it's about a 30 minute flight from Juneau. There is one campsite south of Pack Creek from where it is possible to hike north to the Viewing Sand Spit area. Alaska Discovery does offer a guided trip into the area but it's only part of an Alaska photo expedition that also includes Glacier Bay kayaking and whale watching. The 8 day trip is $1800 per person.

1987, visitors topped 900. There has been talk of either curtailing people in the area or going to a permit system such as the one used at McNeil River State Game Sanctuary, Alaska's most famous bear watching area.

Pack Creek is an adventure for experienced backpackers who are used to encountering bears in the wilderness. The bears may be used to humans but they are far from tame. Reportedly a few of them have been fed human food and they occasionally approach visitors in search of more. A food cache is provided near the South Sand Spit as you should never enter the area with food in your pack. Do not leave the Viewing Sand Spit into the meadow to get closer to the bears. Stay on the spit, wait for the bears to move into range and use a telephoto lens for close-up shots.

Getting There & Away

Experienced kayakers can rent a boat from Alaska Discovery (tel 586-1911) in Juneau and paddle to the refuge. The run down Gastineau Channel and around Douglas Island isn't bad, but the Stephens Passage crossing to reach Oliver Inlet has to be done with extreme care and a close eye on the

Glacier Bay

Sixteen tidewater glaciers spilling out of the mountains and filling the sea with icebergs of all shapes, sizes and shades of blue have made Glacier Bay National Park & Preserve an icy wilderness renowned throughout the world.

When Captain George Vancouver sailed through the ice-choked waters of Icy Strait in 1774, Glacier Bay was little more than a dent in a mountain of ice. Less than a century later, John Muir made his legendary discovery of Glacier Bay and found that the end of the bay had retreated 20 miles (32 km) from Icy Strait. Today, the glacier that bears his name is 60 miles (96 km) from Icy Strait and in its rapid retreat has revealed plants and animals which have fascinated naturalists since 1916.

Apart from having the world's largest concentration of tidewater glaciers, Glacier Bay is the habitat for a variety of marine life, including whales – the humpbacks being by far the most impressive and acrobatic as they heave their massive bodies out of the water

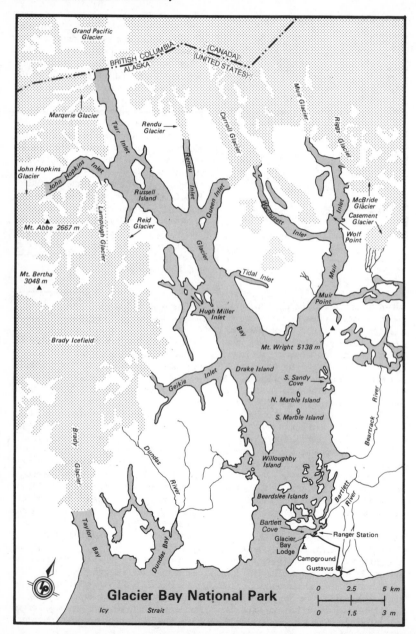

Glacier Bay National Park

in leaps known as breaching. Adult humpbacks can often reach 40 to 50 feet (12 to 15 metres) and weigh up to 9 tons (8163 kg). Other marine life include harbour seals, porpoises, killer whales and sea otters, while other wildlife include brown and black bears, wolves, moose, mountain goats and over 200 species of birds.

Glacier Bay is a park of contrasts. It is lush spruce/hemlock forests, bare shores recently exposed by glaciers, steep fjords up bay, the flat terrain around Gustavus and an inlet full of icebergs.

The park is many things to many people, but it is not a cheap side trip. Of the 130,000 annual visitors, over 100,000 arrive aboard a cruise ship and never leave the boat. The rest are a mixture of tour-group members who head straight for the lodge and backpackers who wander towards the free campground. Plan on spending at least $200 for a trip from Juneau to Glacier Bay, but remember that the cost per day drops quickly after you've arrived.

GUSTAVUS

The park is serviced by a small settlement called Gustavus, an interesting backcountry community of 220 residents. Among the citizens of Gustavus are a mixture of professional people – doctors, lawyers, former government workers and artists – who have decided to drop out of the city rat race and live on their own in the middle of the woods. Electricity only arrived in the early 1980s, and in most homes you still have to pump the water at the sink or build a fire before you can have a hot shower.

There is no 'town centre' in Gustavus; the town is merely an airstrip left over from the military build-up of WW II and a road to Bartlett Cove, known to locals as 'The Road'. They refer to every other road and dirt path in the area as 'The Other Road' regard-

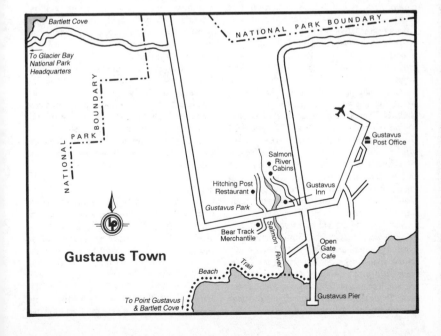

less of which one they are talking about. Along the Road there is little to see, as most cabins and homes are tucked away behind a shield of trees. The heart of Gustavus is the bridge over the Salmon River; near it is the town's park, the Gustavus Inn and the only grocery store in the area.

Places to Stay & Eat

The Gustavus Inn (tel 697-2254) is a charming family homestead lodge that recently added six more rooms; they now have 16 rooms and space for 26 people. The inn is mentioned in every travel book and brochure on Alaska and rooms are hard to obtain at the last minute. Nightly rates are $100 per person and include meals. The inn is really known for its gourmet dinners which including home-grown vegetables and entrees of local seafood such as salmon, crab, halibut and trout served family style. Dinners cost $25 per person and you have to call ahead for a space at the table.

Another fine place is the *Glacier Bay Country Inn* (tel 697-2288) which offers a room and three meals a day for $80. A cheaper alternative for lodging in Gustavus is the *Salmon River Cabins* (tel 697-2245) on a road that heads north-east just before you cross the Salmon River Bridge from the airport. Cabins are $40 per night and can accommodate up to four people. Each has a wood-burning stove and a gas camp stove for cooking. Bicycles can be rented for $5 a day.

Puffin Bed & Breakfast (tel 697-2260) and *Goode River Bed & Breakfast* (tel 697-2241) offer rooms from $35 a night. The Puffin B&B has cabins with wood heaters, and Goode River B&B has rooms in a spacious log home. To rent a rustic log cabin out in the woods (how Alaskan can you get!) call *Beyond Goode River* (tel 697-2241).

Just north of the Salmon River Bridge is the *Hitching Post*, with a limited menu of hamburgers and sandwiches. Or head south on the road to the dock to reach the *Open Gate Cafe* with a deli-style bakery and sandwiches. Try to avoid buying too much from *Bear Track Merchantile*, the small grocery near the bridge.

BARTLETT COVE

Bartlett Cove is the park headquarters and includes the Glacier Bay Lodge, a restaurant, a visitor centre, a campground and the main dock where the tour boats depart for excursions up the bay. The cove lies within the Glacier Bay Park but is still 40 miles (65 km) south (and another high-priced trip) of the nearest glacier. At the foot of the dock is the park's visitor centre where you can obtain backcountry permits, seek out information or purchase a variety of books or topographic maps that cover the park.

Places to Stay

Glacier Bay Lodge (tel (800) 622-2042) has 55 rooms that cost $126 per night for a double. They also offer dormitory bunks at $20 a night but the campground is still a better place to spend the night. In the evening, there is a crackling fire in the lodge's huge stone fireplace while the adjoining bar usually hums with an interesting mixture of park employees, visitors, backpackers and locals from Gustavus. Nightly slide presentations, ranger talks and movies held upstairs cover the natural history of the park.

The campground is free and always seems to have space. It is a quarter of a mile (0.4 km) south of the Glacier Bay Lodge in a lush forest just off the shoreline. It provides a bear cache, eating shelter and pleasant surroundings in which to pitch a tent. Showers are available in the park at $2.50 a turn, but there is no place that sells groceries or camping supplies.

Hiking

Glacier Bay is a trail-less park, and in the backcountry foot travel is done along river banks, on ridges or across ice remnants of glaciers. The only developed trails are in Bartlett Cove. For a hiking adventure up the bay see the Wolf Point Route in the Trekking section of the Wilderness chapter.

Forest Trail This 1 mile (1.6 km) nature walk begins and ends near the Bartlett Cove

John Hopkins Inlet

Dock and winds through the pond-studded spruce/hemlock forest near the campground. There are daily ranger-led walks along this trail; inquire at the lodge.

Bartlett River Trail This 1.5 mile (3.2 km) trail begins just up the road to Gustavus, where there is a posted trailhead, and ends at the Bartlett River estuary. Along the way it meanders along a tidal lagoon and passes through a few wet spots. Plan on 2 to 4 hours for the 3 mile (4.8 km) return trip.

Pt Gustavus Beach Walk This walk along the shoreline south of Bartlett Cove to Pt Gustavus and Gustavus provides the only overnight trek from the park headquarters. The total distance is 12 miles (19 km) while the walk to Pt Gustavus, an excellent spot to camp, is 6 miles (9.6 km). Plan on hiking the stretch from Pt Gustavus to Gustavus at low tide, which will allow you to ford the Salmon River as opposed to swimming across it. Pt Gustavus is an excellent place to sight killer whales in Icy Strait.

Paddling
Glacier Bay offers an excellent opportunity for inexperienced kayakers. By utilising the tour boat it is possible to skip the long and open paddle up the bay and enjoy only the well-protected arms and inlets where the glaciers are located.

Kayaks with skirts, paddles, life vests and foot-controlled rudders can be rented from Glacier Bay Sea Kayaks (tel 697-2257), but reservations are strongly recommended for trips in July and August. Write to them before you leave at: Glacier Bay Sea Kayaks, PO Box 26, Gustavus, Alaska 99826. The rigid double kayaks cost $40 per day up to 3 days, $35 a day up to 6 days and $30 a day for longer rentals.

Transport is on the *Spirit of Adventure* which departs daily at 7 am and will put you ashore at Muir Point, Ptarmigan Creek (near the entrance of John Hopkins Inlet) or Blue

Mouse Cove on the west side of the bay. The most dramatic glaciers are in the West Arm, but surprisingly many paddlers prefer Muir Inlet due to the lack of cruise ships and tour boats in that arm. Plan on a week to paddle from Muir Point up the arm and return to the pick-up point; 8 to 10 days for a drop-off in the West Arm with a return paddle to Bartlett Cove.

Transport fares for kayakers (above and beyond your boat rental) are $93.50 per person for a one-way drop-off and $158.50 return. If you're going to spend this much money, purchase the multidrop pass where for an additional $22 you can be picked up and dropped off at another location. Then make sure you have enough time to enjoy this wonder in ice.

For paddlers who want to avoid the tour boat fares but still long for a kayak adventure, there are the Beardslee Islands. While there are no glaciers to view, the islands (a day's paddle from Bartlett Cove) offer calm water, protected channels and pleasant beach camping. Wildlife includes black bears, seals and bald eagles, while the tidal pools burst with activity at low tide. The islands make for an ideal and easy 3 day paddle.

Getting There & Around

The only way to get to Glacier Bay from Juneau is to fly. There is no state ferry terminal at Gustavus and the commercial cruise ship service was discontinued in 1990. The cheapest flight is the Alaska Airlines flight that departs Juneau daily around 5 pm for the 15 minute trip to Gustavus; the one-way fare is $50.

The *Glacier Express* that used to run from Juneau to Gustavus is no longer in service but check around at the visitor centre to see if somebody else hasn't picked up the service. Glacier Bay Airways (tel 697-2249 in Gustavus, 789-9009 in Juneau) also flies daily to Glacier Bay.

Once at Gustavus Airport, you are still 10 miles (16 km) from Bartlett Cove, the park headquarters. The Glacier Bay Transportation Company has a bus service that meets all airline flights, but at $7.50 a seat you

might consider hitchhiking. Thumbing along the road is not too bad as there is always a small stream of traffic shuffling between Gustavus and the park headquarters.

The other way to reach Glacier Bay is to book a total package tour out of Juneau, which usually includes return air fares and boat passage up the bay to view the glaciers. Such packages are offered by Glacier Bay Yacht Tours (tel 586-6835), but tend to be expensive for the short time you are in the park. They charge $614 per person for a package that includes air fare to Gustavus, 2 nights lodging and meals on their *Executive Explorer* that cruises both the West Arm and Muir Inlet.

Tour Boats In preparation for the day when Muir Inlet will no longer have any true tide-water glaciers, the *Glacier Bay Explorer* was withdrawn from service in 1989 and is unlikely to return. The other park tour boat, *Spirit of Adventure*, was switched to a day trip up the West Arm of Glacier Bay as opposed to Muir Inlet. It's a little ironic, perhaps, but Glacier Bay's most famous tourist attraction, the glacier Muir made famous, is slowly melting back into the mountains.

The *Spirit of Adventure*, a 220 passenger catamaran, departs Bartlett Cove for an 8 hour trip up the West Arm daily at 7 am. It returns at 4.30 pm where a waiting bus will whisk you away in time to catch the Alaska Airlines flight back to Juneau. The tour of the West Arm glaciers, the reason you've spent so much money to get here, is another $142. But that includes lunch – what a deal!

Haines

Haines (pop 1150) lies in the upper (northern) reaches of the Inside Passage and is an important access point to the Yukon Territory (Canada) and Interior Alaska. While the town itself may lack the charm of Sitka or Petersburg, the surrounding scenery is stunning. Travellers who arrive on the state ferry will see Lynn Canal, the longest and deepest fjord in North America, close in on them; there's a mad scramble to the left side of the boat when the US Forest Service (USFS) guide on board announces the approach of Davidson and Rainbow glaciers to the west.

Once in town, mountains seem to surround you on all sides. To the west, looming over Fort Seward, are the jagged Cathedral Peaks of the Chilkat Mountains; to the east is the Chilkoot Range; and standing guard behind Haines is Mt Ripinsky.

Haines is 75 miles (120 km) north of Juneau on a wooded peninsula between the Chilkat and Chilkoot inlets. Originally it was a stronghold of the wealthy Chilkat Tlingit Indians who called the settlement Dtehshuh, meaning 'end of the trail'. The first White person to settle was George Dickinson of the Northwest Trading Company who arrived in 1878 and was followed by missionaries and a trickle of other settlers. Eventually, of course, the gold prospectors stampeded through the town.

In 1897, Jack Dalton, a gun-toting entrepreneur, turned an old Indian trade route into a toll road for miners seeking an easier way to reach the Klondike. He charged $2 per head of cattle. The Dalton Trail quickly became a heavily used pack route to mining districts north of Whitehorse, and Dalton himself reaped the profits until the White Pass & Yukon Railroad in Skagway put him out of business in 1900.

The army established Alaska's first permanent post at Haines in 1903 and named it Fort William H Seward after the secretary of state who negotiated the purchase of the state. The fort was used as a rest camp during WW II and was closed in 1946. World War II also led to the construction of the Haines Highway, the 159 mile (254 km) link between the Southeast and the Alcan (Alaska Highway).

Logging and fishing have been the traditional industries of Haines, but in the 1970s the town became economically depressed as the lumber industry fell on hard times. The town's remaining sawmill filed for bankruptcy in 1984, but by then Haines' residents had already begun to swing their economy towards tourism. Haines survived and will probably become a major Southeast tourist destination in the future. The town has spectacular scenery with comparatively dry weather, only 53 inches (1346 mm) of rain annually, and is accessible by road.

Information

The Haines Visitor Center (tel 766-2202) is on the corner of 2nd Ave and Willard St in Haines and is open from 8 am to 8 pm daily during the summer. The centre has racks of free information, along with rest rooms, a small message board and a used-book exchange. For information on the town's three state parks, head to the Alaska Division of State Parks office (tel 766-2292) on Main St above Helen's Shop. The office is open Monday to Friday from 8 am to 4.30 pm.

Things to See

The **Sheldon Museum** (tel 766-2366) is near the waterfront at the eastern end of Main St, just off Front St. It features a collection of indigenous artefacts and relics from Haines' pioneer and gold-rush days, including the sawn-off shotgun Jack Dalton used to convince travellers to pay his toll. The museum also shows *Last Stronghold of the Eagles*, an excellent movie by Juneau filmmaker Joel Bennett about the annual gathering of bald eagles, twice a day at 1.30 and 3.30 pm. Admission is $2 and the museum is open from 1 to 4 pm daily.

Across Front St from the museum, the **Small Boat Harbor** bustles during the summer with fishers and pleasure boats. A walk up Main St will take you through the heart of the Haines' business district. A block north of Main St on 2nd Ave is **The Gutenberg Dump**, an unusual bookstore in a large rambling house where the owner lives upstairs. It is open from 10 am to 6 pm Monday to Saturday, but a sign on the door says: 'If you need something, knock'. South along 3rd Ave from Main St is the post office, and across the street is the public library, open Monday to Friday from 11 am to 4.30 pm and Saturday from 1 to 4 pm.

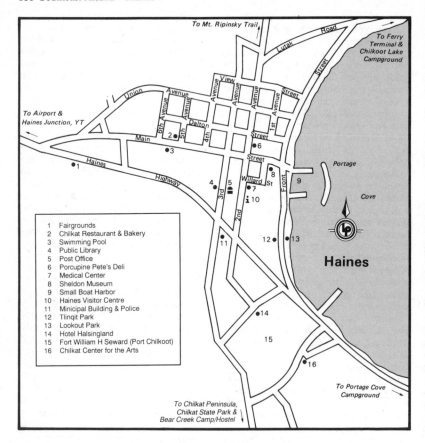

To Mt. Ripinsky Trail

Lutak Road

To Ferry
Terminal &
Chilkoot Lake
Campground

View Avenue

Union Avenue

Street

To Airport &
Haines Junction, YT

Dalton

Main

Haines

Highway

Street

Street

Willard St

Portage

Cove

Haines

1 Fairgrounds
2 Chilkat Restaurant & Bakery
3 Swimming Pool
4 Public Library
5 Post Office
6 Porcupine Pete's Deli
7 Medical Center
8 Sheldon Museum
9 Small Boat Harbor
10 Haines Visitor Centre
11 Minicipal Building & Police
12 Tlinqit Park
13 Lookout Park
14 Hotel Halsingland
15 Fort William H Seward (Port Chilkoot)
16 Chilkat Center for the Arts

To Portage Cove
Campground

To Chilkat Peninsula,
Chilkat State Park &
Bear Creek Camp/Hostel

Follow 3rd Ave south and turn left (south-east) onto the first road past the post office to **Tlingit Park** near Portage Cove. Between the park and Front St is an old **cemetery** with many of the headstones dating back to the 1880s, marking the graves of Haines' pioneers. Across Front St along the shoreline is **Lookout Park,** a vantage point where you can get good views of the boat harbour to the left (north), Port Chilkoot Dock to the right (south) and the Coastal Mountains all around. A display points out the various peaks that rise above Haines.

Follow Front St south as it curves around

Portage Cove and turn uphill (east) at the Port Chilkoot Dock to reach **Fort Seward**. The old army fort was designated a national historical site in 1972 and is slowly being renovated. In the centre of the fort are the parade grounds, while to the north is Building No 53, formerly the Commanding Officers' quarters and today the Hotel Halsingland. A walking-tour map of the fort is available in the lobby of the hotel.

In the centre of the parade ground is **Totem Village**. Although not part of the original fort, it provides an interesting view of a tribal house, totem poles and a Yukon trapper's cabin. Also in Fort Seward is the **Alaskan Indian Arts Skill Center** (tel 766-2160) in the former post hospital and the **Chilkat Center for the Performing Arts** – a refurbished cannery building and the site of nightly productions from the Chilkat Dancers and Lynn Canal Community Players. The skill centre features indigenous artists carving totems, masks and war clubs or weaving Chilkat blankets; many of them are available for purchase. The centre is open from 9 am to noon and from 1 to 5 pm Monday to Saturday during the summer.

Art Galleries In the past few years, Haines has slowly become a commune for artists in the same way that Homer attracts the creative souls of Southcentral Alaska. With Haines spectacular surroundings, it is not hard to understand why. The *Haines Sentinel* publishes an annual visitors' guide which includes descriptions of 30 local artists and a handful of small galleries that display and sell their work.

In the middle of Fort Seward's parade ground is **Sea Wolf Art Studio** (tel 766-2266), which features the work of Tresham Gregg, one of Haines' better-known indigenous artists who is involved mostly in wood carving and prints of Tlingit designs.

Nearby on Beach Rd is the **Art Shop** (tel 766-2284), a small red gallery that was formerly the Port Chilkoot telegraph office and now holds an impressive display of art. These include the prints of John Svenson, known throughout the Northwest as Alaska's foremost mountain illustrator. Other galleries worth stopping at are **Chilkat Valley Arts** (tel 766-2990) on the corner of 2nd Ave and Willard St and the **Northern Arts Gallery** (tel 766-2850) opposite.

Festivals
Like every other Alaskan town, Haines has a Fourth of July celebration, but its biggest festival is the Southeast Alaska State Fair. Held in mid-August, the event includes parades, dances, livestock shows and exhibits that draw participants from all Southeast communities.

Places to Stay
Camping Haines has several state campgrounds ($5 per night); the closest to town is *Portage Cove* (nine sites). This scenic beach campground for backpackers and cyclists is only 0.5 mile (0.8 km) south-east of Fort Seward or 2 miles (3.2 km) from the centre of town and has water and pit toilets. Follow Front St south (which becomes Beach Rd as it curves around the cove near Fort Seward) and the campground is at the end of the gravel road. Five miles (8km) north of the ferry terminal on Lutak Rd is *Chilkoot Lake State Park* (32 sites). The campground, which offers picnic shelters and good fishing for Dolly Varden, is on Chilkoot Lake, a turquoise-blue lake surrounded by mountain peaks.

If you have some spare time in Haines, spend the night at *Chilkat State Park* (32 sites), 7 miles (11.2 km) south-east of Haines on Mud Bay Rd. The park, situated towards the end of the Chilkat Peninsula, has good views of Lynn Canal and of the Davidson and Rainbow glaciers that spill out of the mountains into the canal. There are hiking trails and fishing nearby. Within town, you can pitch your tent at *Port Chilkoot Camper Park* (tel 766-2755) for $3 a night. The private campground is in Fort Seward behind the Hotel Halsingland and has showers for $1.50.

For a shower in town, head to Susie Q's Laundromat near the eastern end of Main St by the boat harbour; showers cost $1.50. There is also the Haines Public Pool (tel 766-2666) open for various sessions, including early-bird swims that begin at 6.30 am and late-night sessions from 7 to 9 pm; the cost per session is $4.

Hostels *Bear Creek Camp & Hostel* (tel 766-2259) is 2.5 miles (4 km) south of town. From the post office, follow 3rd Ave south onto Mud Bay Rd near Fort Seward. After 0.5 mile (0.8 km) veer left onto Small Tract Rd and follow it for 1.5 miles (2.4 km) to the hostel. There is room for 22 in the hostel's dorms; the cost is $8 per night for youth-hostel members and $12 for nonmembers.

There are also tent sites for $3.25 per night and cabins that sleep up to four people for $30 per night. Open year round, the camp has a sauna, wood stoves and cooking facilities.

Bed & Breakfast The *Summer Inn Bed & Breakfast* (tel 766-2970) has a number of bedrooms from $35 per night, most with a good view of Lynn Canal. It's at 247 2nd Ave, 4 miles (6.4 km) from the ferry terminal. Within the military complex, there's *Fort Seward Bed & Breakfast* (tel 766- 2856) in the the former home of the army's surgeon.

Hotels In Haines there are seven hotels and lodges of which the *Cache Inn Lodge* (tel 766-2910) at *Mile 1* (1.6 km) of Mud Bay Rd is probably the cheapest. The lodge offers rustic cottages for 'old-Alaska living', whatever that means, for $30 per night and $35 for two or more. In town, check out the *Hotel Halsingland* (tel 766-2000) which has some rooms from $35 per night and *Fort Seward Lodge* (tel 766-2009) with 10 rooms from $30 per night. Both are in the historical buildings of Fort Seward. The rates at most other motels in town begin at $50 a night.

Places to Eat
The popular place for breakfast among locals is the *Chilkat Restaurant & Bakery* on the corner of Main St and 5th Ave, which opens at 7 am. A plate of eggs, potatoes and toast is $5.50, and you can get coffee and a warm muffin for under $2 or a loaf of freshly baked bread.

The *Commander's Room* in Fort Seward's Hotel Halsingland provides a historical setting in which to eat, with a nice view of the surrounding mountains. The cost of breakfast is similar to the Chilkat Restaurant & Bakery and the portions are filling. At night, the restaurant serves a variety of seafood including prawns, scallops and salmon, with dinners costing from $16 to $19. The best breakfast value in town is at the *Bamboo Room* on the corner of 2nd Ave and Main St, where a plate of pancakes and coffee costs $4.

For deli-type sandwiches or pizza by the slice try *Porcupine Pete's* across from the Bamboo Room on 2nd Ave, while the best pizza in town is at the *Pizza Cutter* within the Fogcutter Bar, near the eastern end of Main St. Locally caught seafood ends up on a variety of menus in Haines. The town's salmon bake, *Port Chilkoot Potlatch*, takes place nightly from 5 to 8 pm at Totem Village in the centre of Fort Seward. For $18 per person you can enjoy all the grilled salmon, salad and baked beans you can handle in one sitting.

Haines' most unique restaurant is the *Catalyst* (tel 766-2670) in the heart of Main St. The small eatery has limited seating, so parties of more than four should call for reservations. The food is excellent, and along with seafood the restaurant offers a salad bar and freshly baked pastries and desserts.

To take some salmon or crab back to your campsite, go to *Howsers Supermarket*, a distinctive store front with the large moose antlers on Main St. The food market, which is open daily, usually has a good selection of whatever is being caught in the area.

Entertainment
For beer on tap and to rub elbows with the locals, stop at the *Fogcutter* on Main St or the *Pioneer Bar* next to the Bamboo Room on the corner of 2nd Ave and Main St. Both spots can get lively and full at night as Haines is a hard-drinking town. For someplace a little quieter where you can watch the traffic in the bay, there is the *Harbor Bar* next to the Small Boat Harbor at the eastern end of Main St.

Other activities at night include performances by the Chilkat Dancers in full Tlingit costume at the Chilkat Center for the Performing Arts in Fort Seward. The performances start at 7 pm and 8.30 pm on Monday and 8.30 pm only on Wednesday, Thursday and Saturday; the admission charge is $5. On Friday and Sunday at 8.30 pm you can see the melodrama *Lust for Dust*, performed by the Lynn Canal Community Players during the summer; tickets are $5.

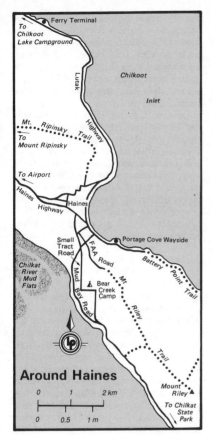

Ferry Terminal
To
Chilkoot
Lake Campground

Lutak

Chilkoot

Inlet

Mt.
Ripinsky
Trail
To
Mount Ripinsky

Highway

To Airport

Haines
Highway

Haines

Small
Tract
Road

FAA Road

Portage Cove Wayside

Chilkat
River
Mud
Flats

Mud Bay Road

Bear Creek
Camp

Battery Point Trail

Mt Riley Trail

Around Haines

0   1   2 km

0   0.5   1 m

Mount
Riley
To Chilkat
State
Park

Hiking

There are two major trail systems near Haines: south of town are the Chilkat Peninsula trails which include the climb to Mt Riley; north of Haines is the path to the summit of Mt Ripinsky. Stop at the visitor centre in town before hiking and pick up its brochure, *Haines is for Hikers*, which describes the trails in more detail.

For those who want to venture into the remote mountainous regions that surround Haines, Ice Field Ascents, PO Box 449, Haines, Alaska 99827, runs a weekend Davidson Glacier ice-climbing expedition.

The company provides transport across Lynn Canal, equipment and instructions in ice-climbing techniques.

Mt Ripinsky Trail The trip to the 3563 foot (1068 metre) summit of Mt Ripinsky (also known as the South Summit) is an all-day hike (6 to 8 hours) with a sweeping, uninterrupted view almost from Juneau to Skagway. The route which includes Peak 3920 and a descent from 7 Mile Saddle to Haines Highway is either a strenuous 10 hour journey for experienced hikers or an overnight trip.

To reach the trailhead, follow 2nd Ave north to Lutak Rd (the road to the ferry terminal) and past the fire station. Leave Lutak Rd when it curves right and head up the hill on Young St. Turn right along an old, buried pipeline and follow it for 1 mile (1.6 km) to the start of the trail, just as the pipeline heads downhill to the tank farm.

The trail crosses a pair of streams, passes by an old reservoir and then ascends steadily through spruce and hemlock, reaching open muskeg at 1300 feet (390 metres). After a second climb you come to Johnson's Creek at 2500 feet (750 metres) where there is drinking water and impressive views of the Southeast's snowcapped mountains all the way to Admiralty Island. From here, the route goes from dwarfed hemlock to open slope where there is snow until late summer.

The North Summit has a benchmark and a high wooden surveyor's platform. You can camp in the alpine area between the two peaks and then continue the next day by descending the North Summit and hiking west along the ridge to Peak 3920. From here you can descend to 7 Mile Saddle and then the Haines Highway, putting you 7 miles (11.4 km) north-west of town. This is a 10 miles (16 km) loop and a challenging overnight hike where the trail is steep in places and easily lost. The views, however, are spectacular.

Battery Point Trail This 2.4 mile (3.8 km) trail is a flat walk along the shore to Kelgaya Point where there is a primitive campsite and a vault toilet. At Kelgaya Point, you can cut across to a pebble beach and follow it to Battery Point. The trail begins a quarter of a mile (0.4 km) beyond Portage Cove Campground at the end of Beach Rd. Plan on about 2 hours for the return hike.

Mt Riley Trails This climb to a 1760 foot (537 metre) summit is considerably easier than the one to Mt Ripinsky, but it still provides good views in all directions, including Rainbow and Davidson glaciers. One trail up the mountain begins at a junction almost 2 miles (3.2 km) up the Battery Point Trail out of Portage Cove Campground. From here, you hike 5.5 miles (8.8 km) over Half Dome and up Mt Riley.

Another route, closer to town, begins at the end of FAA road which runs behind the Officers' Row in Fort Seward. From the road's end, follow the water supply access route for 2 miles (3.2 km) to a short spur that branches off to the right and connects with the trail from Mud Bay Rd. The hike is 3.8 miles (6 km) one way and prevents you from having to find the 3 mile (4.8 km) ride out to Mud Bay Rd, the site of the third trailhead to Mt Riley. The trailhead off Mud Bay Rd is posted and this route is the steepest but most direct to the summit. Plan on 5 to 6 hours for a return hike to the summit.

Seduction Point Trail The trail begins at Chilkat State Park Campground and is a 6.5 mile (10.6 km) one-way hike to the point that separates Chilkoot and Chilkat inlets. The trail swings between inland forest and beaches and provides excellent views of Davidson Glacier.

It can be turned into an excellent overnight hike if you have the equipment by setting up camp at the cove east of Seduction Point. Carry in water and check the tides before departing as the final stretch along the beach after David's Cove should be walked at low or mid-tide. The entire round trip takes most hikers 9 to 10 hours.

Rafting

Haines is also the departure point for numer-

ous raft trips in the area. Chilkat Guides (tel 766-2409) offer a 4 hour float down the Chilkat River that provides plenty of opportunity to view bald eagles and possibly brown bears; there is little white water. The guide company runs the trip twice daily at 9 am and 2 pm beginning at the Art Shop on Beach Rd in Fort Seward.

On a much greater scale of adventure is the 11 day raft trip down the Tatshenshini/Alsek River system from Yukon Territory to the coast of Glacier Bay. Haines serves as the departure point for this river trip which is unmatched by any other Alaskan raft trip for its scenic mix of rugged mountain ranges and dozens of glaciers. Both Chilkat Guides and Alaska Discovery (tel 586-1911) run the trip which is priced at around $1400 per person.

Getting There & Around

Air There is no jet service to Haines, but several charter companies run regularly scheduled north and southbound flights. The cheapest service, Wings of Alaska (tel 766-2030), has four daily flights to Juneau for $50, and four flights to Skagway for $35. Also check with Haines Airways (tel 766-2646) or LAB Flying Service (tel 766-2222). Any of them will arrange a sightseeing flight over Glacier Bay National Park; the park is only a 10 minute flight from Haines. Most planes hold five passengers and an hour's flight is $225, or $45 per person, for a quick view of the glaciers.

Bus From Haines you can catch buses north to Whitehorse, Anchorage or Fairbanks. Alaskon Express has a bus departing Haines at 8.15 am Friday and Tuesday that stops overnight at Beaver Creek and then continues onto Anchorage, reaching the city at 6.15 pm the following day. The fare from Haines to Anchorage is $173 and does not include lodging.

On the same runs you can also make connections at either Haines Junction or Beaver Creek for Fairbanks, Whitehorse or Skagway, though why anybody would want to ride a bus to Skagway instead of a ferry is beyond me. The one-way fare to Fairbanks is $149, Glennallen $134 and Whitehorse $71. The bus picks up passengers at Hotel Halsingland and the Wings of Alaska office (tel 766-2030) on 2nd Ave.

Alaska-Denali Transit offers a once-a-week service between Haines and Anchorage, departing the Southeast town every Tuesday at 8.00 am. This 2 day journey ($115) includes stops at Fairbanks and Denali National Park, and an overnight stop at Tok. Contact the visitor centre in Haines for the company's pick-up points.

Boat State ferries arrive and depart almost everyday from the terminal (tel 766-2111) in Lutak Inlet north of town. The one-way fare north to Skagway is $12 and south to Juneau is $18.

The Haines Street Car (tel 766-2819), a large blue bus, meets all state ferry arrivals and for $4 will take you the 4 miles (6.4 km) into town. The bus also departs town 30 minutes before each ferry arrival and stops at the Hotel Halsingland, the Art Shop in Fort Seward and near the visitor centre in town before heading out to the ferry terminal.

AROUND HAINES
Alaska Chilkat Bald Eagle Preserve
In 1982, the state reserved 48,000 acres (19,200 hectares) along the Chilkat River to protect the largest known gathering of bald eagles in the world. Each year from October to January, more than 3500 eagles congregate here to feed on chum salmon. They come because an upswelling of warm water prevents the river from freezing and encourages the late run of salmon. It's a remarkable sight, hundreds of birds along the banks of the river sitting in the bare trees that line the river, often six or more birds to a branch.

The eagles can be seen from the Haines Highway, where lookouts allow motorist to park and view the birds. The best view is between *Mile 18* (29 km) and *Mile 22* (35.2 km) of the Haines Highway and you really have to be here after November to enjoy the birds in their greatest numbers. Unfortunately, most travellers have long departed

Alaska by then. There are resident eagles which can be spotted throughout the summer but their numbers are not nearly as great as the winter gathering.

The state park office in Haines can provide a list of state-permitted guides who conduct tours into the preserve. Among them is Alaska Nature Tours (tel 766-2876) which conducts 3 hour tours in the morning and afternoons, based on the cruise-ship schedules. The tours cover much of the scenery around the Haines area but often concentrate on the river flats and river mouths where the eagles gather during the summer. You won't view thousands of them, but groups generally see several dozen birds during the day. The tour is $45 per person.

Kluane National Park
Kluane National Park, 120 miles (192 km) north of Haines, is one of Canada's newest and most spectacular parks. The preserve encompasses 8649 sq miles (22,000 sq km) of rugged coastal mountains in the southwestern corner of the Yukon Territory. There are no roads in this wilderness park but the Haines Highway runs along its eastern edge, providing easy access to the area. The 150 mile (240 km) Haines Highway, which follows Jack Dalton's gold-rush toll road, was recently paved, which now makes it an extremely scenic and smooth drive ending at the Alcan (Alaska Highway) in Haines Junction.

Amid the lofty mountains of Kluane National Park lies Mt Logan, Canada's highest peak at 19,636 feet (5950 metres) and the most extensive nonpolar ice field in the world from which glaciers spill out onto the valley floors. Wildlife is plentiful and includes Dall sheep, brown bears, moose, mountain goats and caribou.

The park's visitor centre, in Haines Junction on the Alcan (Alaska Highway), is open from 9 am to 8 pm daily in the summer. Along with displays and a free slide show covering the area's natural history, the centre can provide you with information, back-country permits and topographic maps for overnight hikes into the park.

The main activity in Kluane is hiking, and trails consist primarily of old mining roads, animal trails or natural routes along river beds or ridges. The trailheads for eight routes are located along the Haines and Alaska highways. For those who want to view the park but not hike it, Burwash Lodge, near the north end of Kluane Lake, offers 1 hour sightseeing flights for groups of four at $60 per person.

Alsek Pass Trail This 15 mile (24 km) trail is a flat walk along an old abandoned mining road most of the way. It begins 6 miles (9.6 km) west of Haines Junction at Mackintosh Lodge and ends at Sugden Creek.

Auriol Trail This 12 mile (19 km) loop which begins 3.8 miles (6 km) south of Haines Junction is a good day hike. The trail passes several vantage points which provide sweeping views of the area. A primitive campground along the way can be used to turn the walk into an overnight excursion.

Cottonwood Trail This 53 mile (85 km) loop begins at the Kathleen Lake Campground, 12 miles (19 km) south of Haines Junction. It ends at Dezadeash Lodge off the Haines Highway. The route runs along old mining roads that require some climbing and fording of streams. Wildlife, especially brown bears, is plentiful on this 4 day hike.

Slims River Trail This 16 mile (25.5 km) trail is one of the most scenic in the Kluane National Park as it passes old mining relics and ends at Observation Mountain, which you can scramble up for a view of the spectacular Kaskawulsh Glacier. The trailhead is 40 miles (64 km) west of Haines Junction near a park information centre.

Skagway

Skagway, a place of many names, much history and little rain, is the northern terminus of the state ferry. The town (pop 700) lies

1	Railway Station
2	White Pass & Yukon Railway Depot & NPS Office & Vistor Center
3	Arctic Brotherhood Hall
4	Golden North Hotel
5	Sweet Tooth Saloon
6	Sports Emporium
7	Fairway Market
8	Moe's Frontier Bar
9	Laundromat
10	Moore's Cabin
11	Eagle's Hall
12	Post Office
13	Skagway Inn
14	City Hall & Trail of '98 Museum
15	Air Terminal
16	Hanousek Park Campground

in the narrow plain of the Skagway River at the head of the Lynn Canal and, at one time or another, has been called Skaguay, Shkagway and Gateway to the Golden Interior. It is also known as the Home of the North Wind, and residents tell visitors that it blows so much here you'll never breathe the same air twice.

But Skagway is also one of the driest places in what is often the soggy Southeast. While Petersburg averages over 100 inches (2500 mm) of rain a year and Ketchikan a drenching 154 inches (3910 mm), Skagway only gets 26 inches (660 mm) of rain annually.

Much of Skagway is within the Klondike Gold Rush National Historical Park which extends from Seattle to Dawson in the Yukon Territory. The National Park Service is constantly restoring the old shop fronts and buildings so the town looks similar to the boom town it was in the 1890s, when the gold rush gave birth to Skagway.

The town and the nearby ghost town of Dyea were the start for over 40,000 goldrush stampeders who headed to the Yukon by way of either the Chilkoot Trail or the White Pass Trail. The Chilkoot Trail, which started from Dyea, was the most popular as it was several miles shorter. The White Pass Trail, which began in Skagway and was advertised as a 'horse trail', was brutal. In the winter of

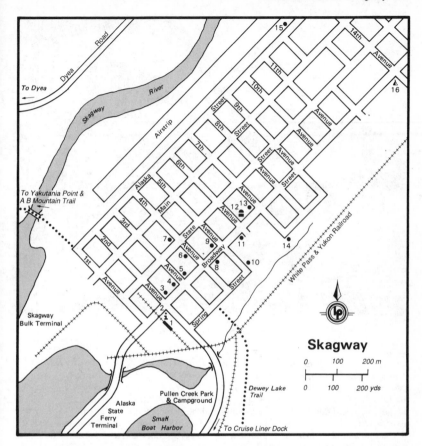

1897-98, some 3000 pack animals were driven to death by over-anxious owners and the White Pass was called the 'Dead Horse Trail'.

In 1887, the population of the town was two; 10 years later the population was 20,000 people and the gold-rush town was Alaska's largest city and a centre for saloons, hotels and dance halls. Skagway became infamous for its lawlessness. For a time, the town was held under the tight control of Jefferson Randolph 'Soapy' Smith and his gang who conned and swindled naive newcomers out of their money and stampeders out of their

gold dust. Soapy Smith was finally removed from power by a mob of angry citizens in a gunfight between him and city engineer Frank Reid. Both men died in the fight and Smith's reign as the 'uncrowned prince of Skagway' ended, having lasted 9 months.

In the height of the gold rush, Michael J Heney, an Irish contractor, convinced a group of English investors that he could build a railroad over the White Pass Trail to Whitehorse. Construction began in 1898 with little more than picks, shovels and blasting powder, and the narrow-gauge railroad reached Whitehorse, the Yukon capital, in

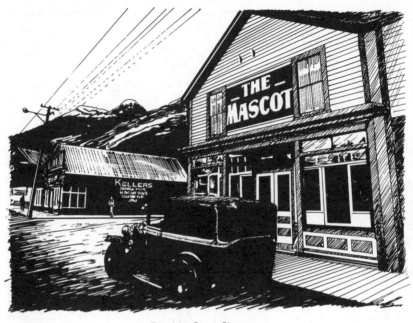

Broadway Street, Skagway

July 1900. The construction of the White Pass & Yukon Railroad was nothing short of a superhuman feat, and the railroad became the focal point of the town's economy after the gold rush and during the military build-up of WW II.

The line was shut down in 1982 but was revived in 1988 to the delight of backpackers walking the Chilkoot Trail and cruise-ship tourists. Although the train hauls no freight, its rebirth was important to Skagway as a tourist attraction. Today, Skagway survives almost entirely on tourism as bus tours and more than 200 'Love Boat' cruise ships visit this modern-day boom town every summer.

Information

For information on the Chilkoot Trail, local trails and camping, contact the National Park Service Visitor Center on the corner of Broadway St and 2nd Ave. For any other information, visit the Skagway Visitor

Bureau (tel 938-2854) in the City Hall on the corner of Spring St and 7th Ave.

Things to See

Unlike most Southeast towns, Skagway is a delightful place to arrive at aboard the state ferry. The dock and terminal are at the south-west end of Broadway St, the main avenue in town. You step off the ferry right into a bustling town where half the people are dressed as if they are trying to relive the gold-rush days while the other half are obviously tourists off the luxury liners.

Near the dock, at the corner of Broadway St and 2nd Ave, is the **National Park Service** (NPS) office and visitor centre in the White Pass & Yukon railroad depot. The visitor centre is open from 8 am to 8 pm daily and features displays, slide shows and the movie *Days of Adventure, Dreams of Gold*, shown every hour. The 30 minute movie is narrated by Hal Holbrook and is the best way to slip back into the gold-rush days; other gold-rush programmes begin at 10 am. The centre also has walking tours of the historical city centre daily at 11 am and 3 pm.

A seven-block corridor along Broadway St, part of the historical area, contains the restored buildings, false fronts and wooden sidewalks of Skagway's golden era. Diagonally opposite the NPS office is the **Arctic Brotherhood Hall**. The hall is hard to miss as there are about 20,000 pieces of driftwood tacked to the front of it, making it one of the most distinctive buildings in Alaska. A 25 minute film, *The White Pass & Yukon Route Story*, is shown in the hall throughout the day from 9 am to 5 pm; admission is $2.50.

On the corner of 5th Ave and Broadway St is the **Corrington Museum of Alaska History** (tel 983-2580). This new museum is private and features 40 exhibits covering the state's history, beginning with the Bering Land Bridge, displayed on scrimshaw, hand-carved ivory from walrus tusks. There is an admission fee.

A block south-east of the museum on 5th Ave is **Moore's Cabin**, the oldest building in Skagway. Captain William Moore and his son built it in 1887 when they staked out their homestead as the founders of the town. Moore had to move his home to its present location, however, when gold-rush stampeders overran his homestead. The National Park Service has since renovated the building.

On the corner of Broadway St and 7th Ave is the **City Hall**; upstairs is the **Trail of '98 Museum**. They are housed in a granite building that was built in 1900 as McCabe College and later served as a US Court until the city obtained it in 1956. The museum is open daily in the summer from 8 am to 8 pm and charges $2 for admission. The money is well spent however, as it is jammed with gold-rush relics, including many items devoted to the town's two leading characters, 'Soapy' Smith and Frank Reid. You can purchase a copy of the 15 July 1898 *Skagway News* that described all the details surrounding the colourful shoot-out.

For visitors who become as infatuated as the locals over Smith and Reid, there is the walk out to the **Gold Rush Cemetery**. From the ferry terminal, it is a 2.5 mile (4 km) stroll to the graveyard north-east along State St, which runs parallel to Broadway St. Follow State St until it curves into 23rd Ave and look for the sign to Soapy's grave across the railroad tracks. A wooden bridge along the tracks leads to the main part of the cemetery, the site of many stampeders' graves and the plots of Reid and Smith. From Reid's gravestone, it is a short hike uphill to the lovely **Reid Falls** which cascade 300 feet (90 metres) from the mountainside.

In 1898, Skagway's rival city, **Dyea**, located at the foot of the Chilkoot Trail, was the shortest route to Lake Bennett where stampeders began their float to Dawson City. After the White Pass & Yukon Railroad was completed in 1900, Dyea quickly died. Today it is little more than a few old cabins, the pilings of Dyea Wharf and Slide Cemetery, where 47 men and women were buried after perishing in an avalanche on the Chilkoot Trail in April 1898.

Dyea Rd, a scenic drive, winds 9 miles (14.4 km) from Skagway to the ghost town but it is filled with hairpin turns that are a headache for drivers of campervans. **Skagway Overlook**, a scenic turn-off with a viewing platform, is 2.5 miles (4 km) out of town along the Dyea Rd. The overlook offers an excellent view of Skagway, its waterfront and the peaks above the town. Just before crossing the bridge over the Taiya River, you pass the Dyea Camping Area (22 sites), a free campground where a NPS ranger is stationed in the summer to assist hikers on the Chilkoot Trail which starts near the campground.

Festivals & Events

Skagway's Fourth of July celebrations feature a foot race, parade and fish feed. The town holds an equally entertaining Solstice Party of 21 June, highlighted by a street dance on Broadway. The Hug & Kisses Road Run, held on the last Saturday in August, is from Dyea to Skagway. It ends with each finisher receiving a hug, a kiss and a T-shirt.

Places to Stay

Camping The city manages two camp-grounds that serve campervaners and backpackers. On the corner of Broadway St and 14th Ave is *Hanousek Park*, which provides tables, pit toilets and water for $6 per tent site. Near the ferry terminal is *Pullen Creek Park Campground* (33 sites) on the waterfront by the Small Boat Harbor. Designed primarily for campervaners, sites without electricity are $10 per night. This is also the place to go for a shower ($1).

For an informal but scenic campsite, go to the picnic area along Yakutania Point, 2 miles (3.2 km) from the ferry terminal. Head north-west (left) on 1st Ave, cross the air strip and suspension bridge over Skagway River and then head west (left) along the path on the other side of the river. The path follows the river and leads to a picnic area that includes tables, grills and even a covered shelter. Nine miles (14.4 km) north of Skagway is the free *Dyea Camping Area* (22 sites) which is operated on a first-come first-to-set-up basis. There's vault toilets, tables and fire places but no water.

Hostels The *Home Youth Hostel* (tel 983-2131), a very pleasant and friendly place to stay, has recently opened in Skagway. It's about 0.5 mile (0.8 km) from the ferry terminal on 3rd Ave near Main St. Reservations are advised and can be made by calling the hostel or writing to the Home Youth Hostel, Box 231, Skagway, Alaska 99840. The hostel has 10 beds ($10 for member, $15 for nonmembers) and check-in time is from 5 to 10 pm; they will also pick you up from the ferry terminal.

Hotels *Irene's Inn* (tel 983-2521) on Broadway St at 6th Ave is the cheapest place with singles (shared baths) from $30 per night. The *Golden North Hotel* (tel 983-2294), on the corner of Broadway St and 3rd Ave, has some rooms for $35, but not many. *Sergeant Preston's Lodge* (tel 983-2521) on 6th Ave between Broadway and Main streets and *Skagway Inn* (tel 983-2289) on Broadway St between 6th and 7th avenues have rooms

from $40 a night. Keep in mind that getting a hotel room in Skagway during the summer is extremely difficult without advance reservations.

Places to Eat

For breakfast and sandwiches there is the *Northern Lights Cafe* on Broadway St between 4th and 5th avenues and the *Sweet Tooth Saloon* closer to the ferry terminal on Broadway St. A full breakfast at either place ranges from $5 to $7. The Sweet Tooth is the place to go for coffee and a fresh doughnut. The best spot for dinner is *Mary's B&B Cafe* on the corner of State St and 10th Ave. If you haven't had your fill of grilled salmon yet there's always *Jo-Dee's Salmon Bake* on 2nd Ave across from the railroad depot; salmon dinners are $14 per person.

The cheapest way to eat, however, is to buy your food at the *Fairway Market* on the corner of 4th Ave and State St and cook it over a fire at your campsite. The *Skagway Sports Emporium* on 4th Ave between Broadway and State streets sells freeze-dried food for hiking trips, along with topographic maps and limited camping equipment.

Entertainment

For a town with only 700 permanent residents, there's a lot to do in Skagway at night. On the corner of Broadway St and 2nd Ave is the town's most unique bar, the *Red Onion Saloon*, which frequently features folk music. This historical establishment doubles as a gold-rush saloon in the tradition of Juneau's Red Dog Saloon. The place really hops when cruise ships are in, as the ships' bands often hold a jam session for locals in the bar.

Moe's Frontier Bar down the street can be a lively spot, especially late at night, as can the *Golden North Hotel Lounge*, which offers the cheapest way to drink – beer by the pitcher.

Skagway has the best melodrama in the Southeast. Gambling for prizes and drinking begins in the back room of the *Eagle's Hall* on the corner of Broadway St and 6th Ave every night at 8 pm. This is followed at 9 pm

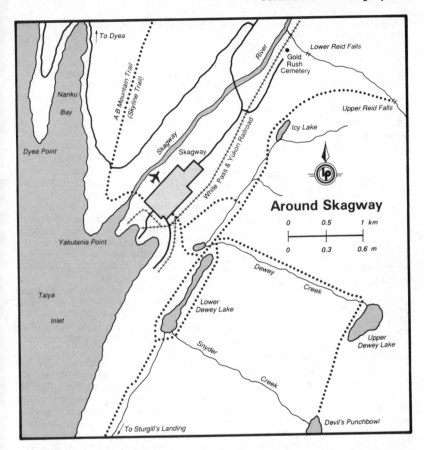

by the lively production of *Skaguay in the Days of '98* which covers the gold-rush days of the town and the full story of 'Soapy' Smith in a truly entertaining manner. It is $10 for both the play and preshow entertainment.

Hiking

The Chilkoot Trail (see the Trekking section in the Wilderness chapter) is probably the most popular hike in Alaska, but there are other good treks around Skagway. There is no US Forest Service (USFS) office in Skagway, so for trail conditions and other information contact the National Park Visitor

Center (tel 983-2921) at the corner of Broadway St and 2nd Ave.

Dewey Lake Trail System This series of trails leads east of Skagway to a handful of alpine and subalpine lakes, waterfalls and historical sites. From Broadway St follow 3rd Ave south-east to the railroad tracks. On the east side of the tracks are the trailheads to Lower Dewey Lake, 0.7 mile (1.1 km); Icy Lake, 2.5 miles (4 km); Upper Reid Falls, 3.5 miles (5.6 km); and Sturgill's Landing, 4.5 miles (7.2 km).

Plan on taking an hour for the return hike

to Lower Dewey Lake where there are picnic tables, camping spots and a trail that circles the lake. At the northern end of the lake is an alpine trail that ascends steeply to Upper Dewey Lake, 3.5 miles (5.6 km) from town, and Devil's Punchbowl another 0.7 mile (1.1 km) south of the upper lake. The hike to Devil's Punchbowl is an all-day trip or an ideal overnight excursion, as the views are excellent and there is a free-use USFS shelter that does not require reservations.

A B Mountain Trail Also known as the Skyline Trail, this route ascends 5.5 miles (8.8 km) to the 5100 foot (1555 metre) summit of A B Mountain, named for the A B that appears on its south side in the form of a snow-melt every spring. The trailhead is on Dyea Rd about 1 mile (1.6 km) from Skagway via the Skagway River footbridge off the north-west end of 1st Ave. The trail is steep and requires a full day to complete.

Denver Glacier Trail This trail takes you along the right-of-way of the White Pass & Yukon Railroad for 3 miles (4.8 km) before turning onto the marked Denver Glacier Trail for another 2 miles (3.2 km) to the glacier itself. Near the glacier is an old rustic hunter's cabin that can be slept in.

Laughton Glacier Trail An even more strenuous hike along the railroad tracks is to continue 9 miles (14.4 km) past the Denver Glacier Trail to Glacier Station. Here, at the old rail depot, is the start of a 2 mile (3.2 km) trail to Laughton Glacier where there is a USFS cabin (reservations needed, $15 per night). Check with the White Pass & Yukon Railroad to see if transport is offered to the old depot. The alpine setting around the cabin is extremely scenic, with the impressive glacier nearby.

Getting There & Around
There is a taxi and bus service out to Dyea and the trailhead for the Chilkoot Trail (see the Trekking section in the Wilderness chapter), or you can hitchhike to the trail,

which is possible because of the stream of hikers that go out there daily in the summer.

Air There are regularly scheduled flights from Skagway to Juneau, Haines and Glacier Bay with LAB Flying Service (tel 983-2471), Wings of Alaska (tel 983-2442) and Skagway Air (tel 983-2218), which generally offers the cheapest fares.

Bus Northbound travellers will find that scheduled buses are the cheapest way to travel other than hitchhiking. Alaskon Express has a bus departing at 7.30 am Sunday, Tuesday, Wednesday and Friday that arrives in Whitehorse at noon. On the Friday and Tuesday bus, you can continue to Beaver Creek where the bus stops overnight and connections can be made to Anchorage or Fairbanks. There is also a 9 am bus that departs Skagway on Saturday, Monday and Thursday for Whitehorse.

Purchase tickets and board the bus at the Westmark Hotel (tel 983-2241) on 3rd Ave between Broadway and Spring streets. The one-way fare from Skagway to Anchorage is $185, Fairbanks $169 and Whitehorse $51.

Train It is now possible to travel to Whitehorse on the White Pass & Yukon Railroad with a bus connection at Fraser (British Columbia). The northbound train departs the Skagway depot daily during the summer (late May to September) at 1 pm, reaching Fraser at 2.35 pm. You then board a bus and arrive in Whitehorse at 6.30 pm. The one-way fare is $89, quite a bit more than the bus but the ride on the historic, narrow-gauge railroad is worth it. Purchase tickets at the railroad depot (tel 983-2217).

Boat The state ferry (tel 983-2229) departs daily during the summer from the terminal and dock at the south-west end of Broadway St. There are lockers in the terminal but the building is only open 3 hours prior to the arrival of a ferry and while the boat is in port.

Hitchhiking Hitchhiking, the cheapest form of transport, is possible along the Klondike

Highway if you are patient and are hitching when a state ferry pulls in. Backpackers contemplating hitchhiking north would do better, however, if they buy a $12 ferry ticket to Haines and hitchhike the Haines Highway instead as it has considerably more traffic.

Tours Without a doubt the most spectacular tour from Skagway is the Summit Excursion on the White Pass & Yukon Railroad. The 3 hour journey begins at the railroad depot where you board the 1890 parlour cars for the trip to White Pass along the narrow-gauge line built during the height of the 1898 Klondike gold rush.

This is only a small portion of the 110 mile (177 km) route to Whitehorse but it contains the most spectacular scenery including crossing Glacier Gorge and Dead Horse Gulch, viewing Bridal Veil Falls and then making the steep climb to White Pass at 2885 feet (870 metres), 20 miles from Skagway. The tour is offered twice a day at 9 am and 1.30 pm. Tickets are $67 per person and can be purchased at the railroad depot (tel 983-2217).

Both Alaska Sightseeing (tel 983-2828) and Gray Line (tel 983-2241) offer 2 hour tours of the city that include Gold Rush Cemetery, the historical district and Skagway Overlook; tickets are $15 per person. For those leaving the Southeast without seeing Glacier Bay, Skagway Air (tel 983-2218) offers 1 hour sightseeing flights of the bay and the Chilkoot Trail for $45 per person.

Mountain Goat

Southcentral Alaska

Upon reaching Haines, most independent travellers continue their Alaskan adventure by heading north through Canada's Yukon Territory to the Alcan (Alaska Highway). They drive, hitchhike or bus the famous highway to the state's Interior, viewing Denali National Park and possibly Fairbanks before heading south towards Anchorage (see the Getting Around chapter).

For travellers who were enchanted by the Southeast and the Alaska Marine Highway and want to avoid the long days on the Alcan (Alaska Highway), there is a pleasant and cheaper alternative from Juneau. For less than the cost of a Haines to Anchorage bus ticket, you can fly on Alaska Airlines from Juneau to Cordova ($141), another remote coastal fishing town.

From Cordova you can jump on the southwest system of the Alaska Marine Ferry to explore Southcentral Alaska to the west. Known by many as the Gulf Coast region, this area is really a continuation of Alaska's rugged coastal playground that begins in Ketchikan.

Both Southeast and Southcentral Alaska boast spectacular scenery with glaciers, fjords and mountain ranges half buried by ice fields and covered at the base by lush forest; both areas are also affected by the Japanese Current causing a wet but mild climate. Fishing is an important industry to these regions and the state ferry is one of the main modes of transport.

However, Southcentral (the region around Prince William Sound and the Gulf of Alaska) has one important feature that the Panhandle (Southeast) doesn't – roads and traffic between many of the towns. This alone makes the Southcentral one of the cheapest, most accessible and most popular areas in the state to visit.

With half of the state's population just to the north in Anchorage, the Southcentral's Kenai Peninsula is a haven for campervaners, anglers and tour groups. There are dozens of trails and water routes throughout the peninsula, but because of its accessibility you may have to hike a little longer or climb a little higher to achieve the wilderness solitude so easily obtained in the Southeast.

Southcentral can be divided into three main areas. Prince William Sound, with its communities of Cordova, Valdez and Whittier, is characterised by towering mountains, glaciers and abundant marine wildlife. To the west of the sound is the Kenai Peninsula and the towns of Seward, Kenai, Soldotna and Homer. This great forested plateau, bounded by the Kenai Mountains and the Harding Ice Field to the east, is broken up by hundreds of lakes, rivers and streams, making it an outdoor paradise for hikers, canoeists and anglers.

To the south-west is Kodiak Island and the city of Kodiak, the home of the largest fishing fleet in Alaska. Though often caught in the rainy and foggy weather created on the Gulf of Alaska, Kodiak has a rugged beauty and isolated wilderness areas few visitors make an effort to venture into.

YAKUTAT

On the flight to Cordova there is a stopover at Yakutat, the most northern Southeast community. The town (pop 450) is isolated from the State Marine Ferry because of the turbulent nature of the Gulf of Alaska. For travellers on a tight schedule, there is no reason to stop over in Yakutat but those who do will find the scenic setting of the Tlingit village stunning, even if the visitor facilities are limited and expensive.

The town is surrounded by lofty peaks, including Mt Elias at 18,114 feet (5489 metres) to the west and Mt Fairweather at 15,388 feet (4663 metres) to the east. Northwest of Yakutat is the large Malaspina Glacier.

Yakutat has three lodges, the cheapest being the *Ponderosa Inn* (tel 443-2368) with rooms from $65, a handful of restaurants and cafes, and two grocery stores. Camping is possible at *Cannon Beach*, a picnic area near town that is administered by the US Forest Service (USFS). The main attraction in the area is the Malaspina Glacier, which can be viewed from sightseeing flights offered by Gulf Air Taxi (tel 784-3240), the local air-charter operator based at the airport. Other visitors come to beachcomb the miles of sandy beach that surround Yakutat, searching for Japanese glass balls blown onshore by the violent Pacific storms.

USFS Cabins

The USFS, which maintains an office at Yakutat Airport, administers 11 cabins in the area along with the Russell Fjord Wilderness to the north-east. None of the cabins are on the fjord or near Hubbard Glacier – the advancing ice flow that made world news when it reached Gilbert's Point in June 1986 and basically turned Russell Fjord into a freshwater lake by cutting it off from Disenchantment Bay. Within a few months the pressure of the rising water broke the ice dam and Hubbard Glacier began to retreat. Other than a quick sightseeing flight, the only way to see the glacier and the amazing scene of it calving during mid-tide is through an Alaska Discovery guided expedition.

Of the 11 USFS cabins in the area, five of them can be reached from Forest Highway 10 that extends east from Yakutat. It is best to rent the cabins from the USFS office in the Juneau Centennial Hall (tel 586-8751 in Juneau) when you pass through the capital city. Rental information can also be obtained at the Yakutat USFS office (tel 784-3359) in the Flight Service Building at the airport in

Yakutat or by contacting USFS, PO Box 327, Yakutat, Alaska 99689.

Situk Lake This cabin is on the forested south-eastern shore of the lake and provides excellent fishing for salmon and steelhead trout as well as good viewing of brown bears, moose, otters and bald eagles. It can be reached by a 5 mile (8 km) trail that begins east of the bridge at *Mile 9* (14.4 km) of Forest Highway 10.

Situk Weir Travellers who raft down the the Situk River end up at Situk Landing, a large parking lot 8 miles (12.8 km) from town along Lost River Rd. A quarter of a mile (0.4 km) trail leads from the parking area to the Situk Weir USFS Cabin. The cabin provides excellent fishing for salmon, Dolly Varden and trout in the mouth of the Situk River. For some good beachcombing, the beaches along the Gulf of Alaska can be reached along a 2 mile (3.2 km) path.

Harlequin Lake This cabin is a 30 mile (48 km) drive from Yakutat along Forest Highway 10. The unit offers excellent fishing and views of Harlequin Lake and the massive icebergs from Yakutat Glacier. A trail leads south 4 miles (6.4 km) from the cabin to Middle Dangerous USFS Cabin.

Prince William Sound

Prince William Sound, the northern extent of the Gulf of Alaska, rivals the Southeast for the steepest fjords and the most spectacular coastlines and glaciers. The sound is a marvellous wilderness area of islands, inlets, fjords, lush rainforests and towering mountains. Flanked to the west by the Kenai Mountains and to the north and east by the Chugach Mountains, Prince William Sound covers 15,000 sq miles (38,000 sq km) and has abundant wildlife, including whales, sea lions, harbour seals, otters, eagles, Dall sheep, mountain goats and, of course, bears.

Another trait the sound shares with the

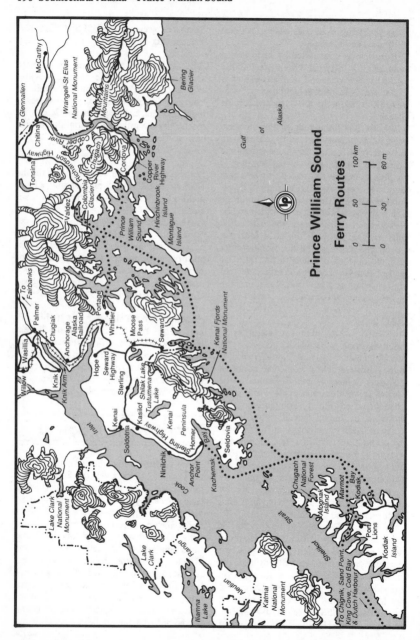

Prince William Sound

Ferry Routes

Southeast is rain – lots of rain. It averages well over 100 inches (2500 mm) of rain per year, with the fishing town of Cordova receiving 167 inches (4240 mm) annually. Summer temperatures range from 54°F (12°C) to a high of 70°F (21°C).

At centre stage of Prince William Sound is the Columbia Glacier. The bluish wall of ice, named after New York's Columbia University, is one of the most spectacular tidewater glaciers on the Alaska coast, as it covers 440 sq miles (1126 sq km). The glacier's face is 3 miles (4.8 km) wide and in some places it is 262 feet (80 metres) high.

When passing the glacier by boat, the stunning scene includes hundreds of seals sunning on the ice pack, a backdrop of mountains and usually the thunder of ice calving off its face – sometimes induced by the ship's captain who sounds the horn in front of it. When the Columbia Glacier calves icebergs into the sea, there's an explosion of ice and water that few onlookers ever forget.

Travellers who take the Alaska Airlines jet to Cordova can continue their journey across Prince William Sound by the Alaska Marine Ferry. At Valdez, you have the option of returning to the road, but most travellers elect to stay on the state ferry to Whittier on the west side of the sound as this section of the marine highway includes passing the Columbia Glacier. From Whittier, there is a rail service to Anchorage (see the Getting Around chapter), and from Valdez you can reach Anchorage by bus.

CORDOVA

Nestled between Orca Inlet and Lake Eyak and overshadowed by Mt Eccles, Cordova is a beautiful little fishing town on the east coast of Prince William Sound and a place worth taking the extra time and expense to visit. The community has 2600 permanent residents but doubles its population during the summer with fishers and cannery workers as the town's economy is centred around its fishing fleet and fish-processing plants. The area around Cordova is an outdoor paradise, and the town is a jumping-off point to 14 USFS cabins, some good

alpine hiking and the Copper River Delta, a staging and nesting area for millions of birds each year.

Modern-day Cordova was born when Michael J Heney, the builder of the White Pass & Yukon Railroad from Skagway to Whitehorse, arrived in 1906 and decided to transform the summer cannery site into the railroad terminus for his line from the Kennecott Copper Mines near McCarthy. Construction of the Copper River & Northwestern Railroad began that year and was completed in 1911 – another amazing engineering feat by the 'Irish Prince' that cost $23 million to build.

Within 5 years, Cordova was a boom town where more than $32 million worth of copper ore passed through its docks. The railroad and town prospered until 1938, when labour strikes and the declining price of copper permanently closed the Kennecott Mines. The railroad ceased operations and Cordova turned to fishing, its main economic base today, which is why the 1989 Exxon oil spill devastated the town.

Although most of the halibut and salmon swimming beneath the oil appear to have survived, the mishap cancelled or postponed the fishing seasons in 1989. Commercial fishing boats were left idle, while there were stories of lifelong fishers breaking down in tears as they steered their boats through the slick were common. The only saving grace for the industry was that Exxon was forced to lease many of the commercial fishing boats to assist with the clean-up at $3400 a day or more.

Information

General information about Cordova can be obtained from the Chamber of Commerce (tel 424-7260) on 1st St next to the National Bank of Alaska; it is open Tuesday and Thursday from 1 to 4 pm.

Things to See

On the corner of Adams Ave and 1st St is the **Cordova Museum & Library** in the Centennial Building. The small but interesting museum has displays on marine life, includ-

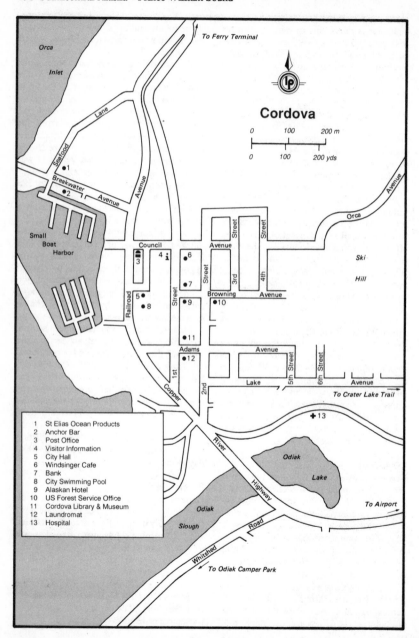

Orca
Inlet

To Ferry Terminal

Cordova

0   100   200 m

0   100   200 yds

Seafood   Lane

1

Breakwater
2

Avenue

Avenue

Small
Boat
Harbor

Orca   Avenue

Council   Avenue

Street   Street

Ski
Hill

Railroad

3   4   i   6

7

Street

3rd   4th

Street

5   9   Browning   Avenue

8   10

11

Adams

1st   12

Street

Avenue

5th Street   6th Street

2nd   Lake   Avenue

Copper   To Crater Lake Trail

+ 13

River   Odiak

Odiak
Lake

Highway   To Airport

1 St Elias Ocean Products
2 Anchor Bar
3 Post Office
4 Visitor Information
5 City Hall
6 Windsinger Cafe
7 Bank
8 City Swimming Pool
9 Alaskan Hotel
10 US Forest Service Office
11 Cordova Library & Museum
12 Laundromat
13 Hospital

Odiak
Slough

Road

Whitshed   To Odiak Camper Park

ing a rare leatherback turtle caught nearby, relics from the town's early history, Russian artefacts and a three-seater bidarka (kayak-type boat).

When the state ferry is in port, they show an excellent film on the history of the town. There is also a visitor centre at the entrance of the museum. Admission to the museum is free and it is open daily from 1 to 5 pm, except Wednesday and Sunday, and in the evening on Saturday. The library has more extended hours in the evening.

The **City Swimming Pool** (tel 424-7200) is on Railroad Ave in a brown building next to City Hall. Built in 1974, the Olympic-size pool is open to the public at various times. Call for a list of the session times and activities.

North on Railroad Ave from the pool is the **Small Boat Harbor**, the real centre of activity in Cordova during the summer. In 1984, the harbour was doubled in size, and it is now one of the five largest in the state and hums with boats and fishers between season openings and when the fleet is in town on the weekends. Cordova's fleet is composed primarily of salmon seiners and gillnetters, and the season runs from mid-May into September. Dungeness and Tanner crabs are harvested for a few months during the summer and later in the winter.

Festivals

Because of the economic importance of the fishing season, no events are planned during the summer in Cordova other than a small Fourth of July celebration. The town's biggest event is its Iceworm Festival in mid-February, when there is little else to do.

Places to Stay

Camping There is no youth hostel in Cordova. The closest campground is the *Odiak Camper Park* (tel 424-6200), 0.5 mile (0.8 km) from town on Whitshed Rd next to the recently covered and landscaped dump site. The gravel campground is primarily for campervans and charges $5 per night, but water, showers and rest rooms are available. Unofficial spots for pitching a tent are on the

bluffs across from the ferry terminal or up 6th St at the ski hill.

Bed & Breakfast Quite a few B&Bs have popped up in the past few years; when researching this book there were five operating around town. Check with the visitor centre for a current list of them as they often change, and expect to pay between $45 and $50 per person for a room. One of the oldest B&Bs, *Oystercatcher* (tel 424-5154), is at the corner of 3rd St and Council Ave. You might also try the *Fathom Inn* (tel 424-3116) on Breakwater Ave and the *Harborview Guesthouse* (tel 424-5356) on Observation Ave.

Hotels Of the four hotels in town, the *Alaskan Hotel & Bar* (tel 424-3288) on 1st St is the cheapest. A single room with a shared bath costs $35 a night, while singles with a bathroom are $45. The Alaskan, like all hotels in Cordova, is booked solid through most of the summer. The *Cordova Hotel* (tel 424-3388) has slightly higher rates, while the *Prince William Sound Motel* (tel 424-3201) has rooms from $60.

Places to Eat

The *Windsinger Cafe* on 1st St behind the Club Bar has breakfast, home-made soups and quick bites to eat (they have a takeaway window). Try the *OK Restaurant* near the museum for Chinese food and *Taco Loco*, on Nicoloff Ave near the new boat harbour, for Mexican food. The *Ambrosia*, also on 1st St, specialises in pizza and Italian food, while the *Killer Whale Cafe* in the Orca Book & Sound Store is a delicatessen with good desserts.

For a meal with a view, try the restaurant in the *Reluctant Fisherman* which overlooks the harbour and specialises in seafood. *The Powder House*, a little way from town at *Mile 1.5* (2.4 km) of the Copper River Highway, is a bar that serves sandwiches and has a deck overlooking a lake.

Places to pick up your own supplies include *Davis Super Foods*, a supermarket on 1st St; *Hometown Bakery* on 2nd St for fresh bread and pastries; and *St Elias Ocean Products* on Seafood Lane near the Small Boat Harbor for seafood.

Entertainment

The Powder House Bar, which earns its name because it lies on the site of the original Copper River & Northwestern Railroad powder house, is a fun place that features folk, bluegrass and country music at night. If you happen to be there on a rare evening when it isn't raining, there is a deck outside overlooking Eyak Lake.

In town, there is the *Club Bar* on 1st St with music nightly or the *Anchor Bar* on Breakwater Ave across from the Small Boat Harbor, for those who want to mingle with the fishers.

Hiking & USFS Cabins

There are a number of hikes and cabins (reservations needed, $20 per day) accessible from the Cordova road system. Before venturing into the surrounding area, hikers should first stop at the US Forest Service office (tel 424-7661) on the corner of Browning Ave and 2nd St to pick up an assortment of free trail maps. Seaman's Hardware on 1st St sells topographic maps of the area.

Crater Lake Trail This 2.5 mile (4 km) hike begins on Lake Eyak, about 0.5 mile (0.8 km) beyond the Municipal Airfield on Eyak Lake Rd. The trail ascends steeply but is easy to follow as it winds through lush forest. At the top, it offers panoramic views of both the Copper River Delta and Prince William Sound. Plan on 2 to 4 hours for the round trip from the road to the open country around Crater Lake.

Mt Eyak Ski Hill A quick scramble up the ski hill at the end of 6th Ave. Hardy hikers can spend a day climbing from here to the top of Mt Eyak and down the other side to Crater Lake.

Lydic Slough Trail & Eyak River Cabin At *Mile 7.1* (11.4 km) of Copper River Highway is Lydic Slough Trail, which leads 3 miles

(4.8 km) along the Copper River Flats to a cabin on Eyak River. The Eyak River offers excellent trout and salmon fishing as well as opportunities to view moose, brown bear and a wide range of waterfowl.

McKinley Lake Trail The 2.5 mile (4 km) McKinley Lake Trail begins at *Mile 21.6* (34.8 km) of Copper River Highway and leads to the head of the lake and the remains of the Lucky Strike gold mine. Two cabins, McKinley Lake and McKinley Trail, are on this path, making them accessible by foot from the highway.

Pipeline Loop Trail At *Mile 21* (33.6 km) of Copper River Highway is this 2 mile (3.2 km) trail past several small lakes. The trail provides access to good fishing holes for grayling and trout, and merges into the McKinley Trail that can be followed back to form something of a loop. The entire walk provides excellent views of the surrounding mountains.

Sheridan Mountain Trail This trail starts at the end of Sheridan Glacier Road, 17 miles (27.7 km) south-east of town. Most of the 2 mile (3.2 km), one-way trail is a moderate climb that passes through mature forests before breaking out into an alpine basin. The view of mountains and Sheridan and Sherman glaciers from the basin is a stunning sight, and it only gets better when you start climbing the surrounding rim. During a dry spell, hiking boots are fine for the walk, otherwise you might want to tackle this one in rubber boots.

Getting There & Around

Airport Transport All jets arrive and depart from Cordova Airport, 12 miles (19.4 km) from town on Copper River Highway. The Airporter bus greets all arrivals and charges $8 for the trip into town. You can catch the bus at the major hotels in town for a ride out to the airport.

Air Alaska Airlines (tel 424-7151) makes a daily stop at Cordova on its run from Seattle to Anchorage. The one-way fare for the short flight to Anchorage is $72. Wilbur's Flight Service (tel 424-5695) provides a daily commuter service from Cordova to Valdez and Anchorage as well as the usual sightseeing flights and transport to USFS cabins. Wilbur also runs the airport bus.

Boat During the summer, the MV *Bartlett* stops twice a week at Cordova and the MV *Tustumena* once, providing a ferry service to Valdez and then onto Whittier, Seward, Homer and Kodiak. The fare from Cordova to Valdez is $26, and $54 to Whittier and Seward. On Wednesdays, the MV *Bartlett* makes a direct run from Cordova to Whittier, skipping the Columbia Glacier, for only $32. The ferry terminal (tel 424-7333) is north of town on Railroad Ave.

AROUND CORDOVA
Copper River Highway

There is more than 50 miles (80 km) of road extending out from Cordova, most of it centred around the Copper River Highway. Built on the old railroad bed to the Kennecott Mines, the road was originally going to connect Cordova with the Richardson Highway and the rest of Alaska. Construction was halted in 1964 after the Good Friday Earthquake damaged the existing roadbeds and bridges, knocking out the fourth span of the famous Million Dollar Bridge in front of Childs Glacier.

Things to See Today, the highway provides access to the **Copper River Delta**, a huge area of tidal marshes and outwashes, and a bird-watcher's paradise. Millions of birds and water fowl use it as a nesting and staging area during the summer, including arctic terns, dusty Canada geese, trumpeter swans, great blue herons and bald eagles. A drive along the highway at dawn or dusk can provide views of moose, brown bears, beavers and porcupines, while on rare occasions a lynx or wolverine can be seen from the roadside.

The wildlife is so abundant in this area that in 1962, the US Forest Service (USFS), the

Beaver

US Fish & Wildlife and the state agreed to manage 33,000 acres (13,200 hectares) of the delta as a game and fish habitat. The refuge has since been enlarged to 2.3 million acres (920,000 hectares) and in 1972 the delta on the east side of the Copper River Highway was closed to off-road vehicles.

The area provides access to hiking (see the Cordova Hiking & USFS Cabins section), wildlife, bird watching, rafting on swift glacial rivers and angling. The streams and rivers along the highway are renowned for their fishing and can provide the ultimate angling experience – fishing an isolated stretch of river with mountains around you and wildlife just beyond the next bend. Sockeye salmon fishing begins in mid-June and peaks around the Fourth of July. Coho salmon run from August to September, and cutthroat trout and Dolly Varden can be caught throughout the summer and autumn.

The highway also provides access to a handful of glaciers that flow out of the Chugach Mountains. The first is the **Sheridan Glacier**, which you can view from the bridge over the Sheridan River 15 miles (24 km) from Cordova or 3 miles (4.8 km) beyond the Cordova Airport. One mile (1.6 km) before the bridge, the Sheridan Glacier access road leads 4.3 miles (6.9 km) to the north, ending at a picnic table with a partial view of the ice floe. From here there is a 1 mile (1.6 km) trail to the dirt-covered glacial moraine.

Several other glaciers can be seen spilling

out of the mountains; by far the most impressive is **Childs Glacier** to the west of the Million Dollar Bridge, 48 miles (77 km) from Cordova. A short side road leads from the highway to within 200 yards/metres of the spectacular glacier's face. Periodical calving from the glacier almost stops Copper River's downstream momentum. From the Million Dollar Bridge you can view Childs Glacier, less than 1 mile (1.6 km) downstream or **Miles Glacier**, 5 miles (8 km) upstream.

At least 1 day should be spent exploring the Copper River Highway, or more if you want to include time fishing and hiking. Stop at the USFS office in Cordova and pick up a copy of the brochure *Copper River Delta* which includes a map and milepost listings of every trailhead, undeveloped campsites, wildlife viewing areas and streams to toss a lure into.

Getting Around The only problem in experiencing this area is transport. Hitching Copper River Highway is slow going and renting a car in Cordova is expensive, if you can even obtain one. Both the Imperial Cab Company (tel 424-3201) and the Reluctant Fisherman Inn (tel 424-3272) rent vehicles for $55 per day and 50 cents a mile, making a single-day journey to Childs Glacier a $105 affair – worth it if there are three or more people sharing the expenses.

Alaska Seacoast Charters (tel 424-7742) offer a 6 hour tour that includes a view of Cordova and then a ride out to the Million Dollar Bridge for $25 per person, by far the most reasonable way to see this road. They need at least four people before the van will depart. Also check with the Whiskey River Cycle Shop (tel 424-3354) on Breakwater Ave. They rent bicycles for $8 a day.

Many guide companies offer trips down the Copper River, including two local companies in Cordova. Contact Cordova Rafting (tel 424-3533) or American Raft & Trail (tel 424-3939, summers only) about their trips. Single-day trips, with a ride out to Childs Glacier and a float back, may be possible.

VALDEZ

In the heart of Prince William Sound and less than 25 miles (40 km) east of the Columbia Glacier is Valdez, the most northerly ice-free port in the western hemisphere and the southern terminus of the Alaska Pipeline. The town and port were named after a Spanish naval officer by Spanish explorer Don Salvador Fidalgo in 1790. Valdez boomed at the turn of the century when thousands of gold-seekers stampeded through the town on their way to Alaska's Interior and the Klondike gold fields.

They followed the Valdez Trail, a route that included a trek over the Valdez Glacier where hundreds of lives were lost due to falls in crevasses, snowblindness and hypothermia. After the town lost the Copper River & Northwestern Railroad in a bitter fight to Cordova, the old gold-rush trail was rerouted and improved into a wagon trail which was paved to become the Richardson Highway in the 1920s.

In 1964, Valdez lost its role as the main cargo route to Interior Alaska. In 4 short minutes, the Good Friday Earthquake demolished the city. All of Valdez's history is dated either before or after the devastating catastrophe, as the city was one of the worse hit in Alaska. The earthquake caused the land to ripple like water and produced massive tidal waves that destroyed most of the harbour and left few buildings undamaged.

Afterwards, the residents voted to rebuild their city at a new site on more stable ground. The old town lies 4 miles (6.4 km) east of Valdez on Richardson Highway, but all that remains today is a vacant field and a plaque dedicated to those who lost their lives during the frightful event.

Valdez regained its role as the gateway to the Interior when it was chosen as the terminus of the Trans-Alaska Pipeline. Work began in 1974 and the $9 billion project was completed in 1977; the first tanker was filled with the black gold on 1 August 1977. Today, the city's economy depends heavily on oil and the taxes the oil company pay out.

Fishing and tourism also contribute to the economy, but oil has clearly made Valdez a rich city. Major projects completed in the early 1980s include a $50 million container terminal to enhance the city's reputation as the 'Gateway to the North' and the $7 million Civic Center. With oil money, the Chugach Mountains as a beautiful backdrop and an ideal location in the middle of the Prince William Sound playground, Valdez and its 3700 residents seemed to have all a city could want.

However, a price was paid for the city's involvement in the oil industry when the *Exxon Valdez* rammed a reef and spilt 11 million gallons (42 million litres) of oil into Prince William Sound in 1989. It was the worst oil spill in US history, and Valdez became the centre of an environmental storm. Exxon directed the oil clean-up from Valdez during the first summer after the spill and created a money rush that hadn't been seen since the pipeline was built.

Thousands of people flocked to Valdez from all over the country in search of clean-up jobs that paid $10 to $15 an hour. Within a month, the oil company had created an army of 9000 workers; many spent their days at the oil-soaked beaches on Prince William Sound but their nights in Valdez, whose population jumped from 3000 to 12,000. As it was during the pipeline construction, available lodging became nonexistent and prices in restaurants and supermarkets skyrocketed. Despite a caravan park set up near the airport, people spent the summer living out of tents or in the back of pick-up trucks.

Amazingly, the tourist still arrived that summer, many eager to witness the mishap. After the summer of 1989, Exxon shifted its operation and workers to Seward, Homer and Kodiak to concentrate on the shoreline that experienced the worst oil damage. You will, most likely, see little damage from the oil spill in the sound around the Valdez.

Information
The Valdez Visitor Centre (tel 835-4836, summer only) is at 200 Chenega Ave near the City Hall and is open daily from 9 am to 9 pm in the summer. Along with the usual hand-outs and city maps, the centre houses the first barrel of oil from the Alaska Pipeline and a cross-section of the pipeline. They also show films on the pipeline and the 1964 earthquake daily during the summer.

Things to See
Valdez's bustling **Small Boat Harbor** is south of North Harbor Drive which ends opposite the corner of Fidalgo Drive and Clifton Court, near **Point of View Park**. The observation platform on the knoll is a good spot to view the old town site to the east, the pipeline terminal to the south and Valdez Narrows to the west. Next door to the park is the **US Coast Guard Headquarters** which offer free tours of its Vessel Traffic Center and daily slide presentation every 30 minutes from 9.30 to 11 am and 1.30 to 3 pm. West of the Coast Guard Headquarters is the **Civic Center** and more panoramas of the area.

From the Civic Center, head two blocks north on Robe River Drive and turn right (east) on Egan Drive to the **Valdez Museum** (tel 835-2764) in the Centennial Building. The museum is packed with displays that include a model of the Trans-Alaska Pipeline, a 19th century saloon bar, old mining equipment and an exhibit and photographs of how the 1964 earthquake changed the town. In the summer, the museum is open daily from 9 am to 8 pm; a donation of $1 is encouraged.

Diagonally opposite the museum is the **Valdez Library** which among other things runs a book and magazine swap for travellers. The library is open from 10 am to 8 pm Monday to Thursday and from 10 am to 6.30 pm Friday and Saturday. To reach **Prince William Sound Community College**, follow Chenega Ave north from the museum and turn right (east) on Pioneer Drive. The small campus, a division of the University of Alaska, has huge wooden carvings that are part of Peter Toth's collection of 50 sculptures dedicated to the American Indian.

Pioneer Drive runs east into Richardson Highway, and 0.5 mile (0.8 km) to the north is the **Salmon Spawning View Point** on Crooked Creek. The wooden platform, the

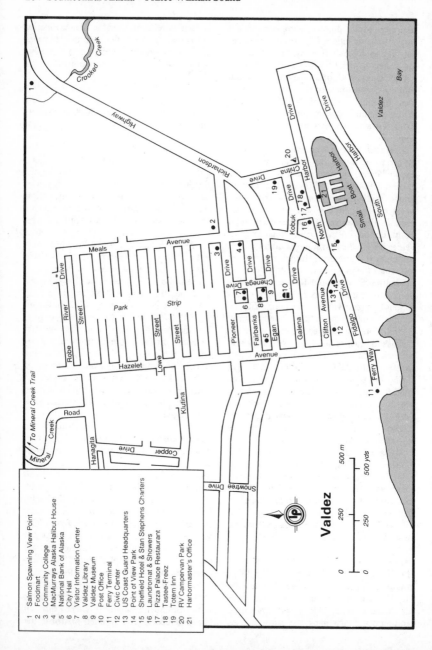

1   Salmon Spawning View Point
2   Foodmart
3   Community College
4   MacMurrays Alaska Halibut House
5   National Bank of Alaska
6   City Hall
7   Visitor Information Center
8   Valdez Library
9   Valdez Museum
10 Post Office
11 Ferry Terminal
12 Civic Center
13 US Coast Guard Headquarters
14 Point of View Park
15 Sheffield Hotel & Stan Stephens Charters
16 Laundromat & Showers
17 Pizza Palace Restaurant
18 Tastee-Freez
19 Totem Inn
20 RV Campervan Park
21 Harbormaster's Office

Valdez

site of the old hatchery, is a good spot to watch salmon spawn in July and August.

Festivals

Valdez has both a Fourth of July celebration and an end-of-summer festival called 'Gold Rush Days'. The 5 day festival takes place in mid-August and includes a parade, bed races, dances, a free fish feed and a portable jailhouse that is pulled throughout town by locals who go about arresting people without beards and other innocent bystanders.

Places to Stay

Camping Valdez, the city of wealth and beauty, desperately lacks cheap accommodations for backpackers, and good public campgrounds are also scarce. The nearest one is the *Valdez Glacier Campground* (101 sites) almost 6 miles (9.6 km) from town past the airport on Airport Rd. Although the campground is free, scenic and offers outhouses and water, it is hardly convenient for those on foot.

While there are only expensive private campgrounds catering for campervans in town, Valdez does not have any ordinances restricting camping within the city. It is a common and accepted practice for backpackers to pitch their tents in a number of places around town, including across Chitna St on the hill overlooking the waterfront, along Mineral Creek Rd and down by the city dock, especially when waiting for an early-morning state ferry.

Bed & Breakfast There are a number of B&Bs in town that charge around $50 for a single and $60 for a double. They change often, so call or stop at the visitor centre for the latest list. Try *Mineral Creek Bed & Breakfast* (tel 835-4205), a cedar log cabin with a sauna and mountain bikes to ride back into town. There's also the *Lake House* (tel 835-4752) away from town and near an alpine lake with rooms for $60 a single and $70 a double.

Hotels Rates in the city's six motel/hotels range from $80 a night for singles in the *Valdez Motel* (tel 835-4444) at 112 Egan Drive to $115 at the top-of-the-range *Westmarks*. No room in town is cheap nor easy to obtain for anybody who has just stepped off the ferry. Call ahead, and if there is a group of you, try one of the cottages at *The Village Inn* (tel 835-4445) for $70 a night.

Places to Eat

The *Tastee-Freez* on North Harbor Drive across from the Small Boat Harbor is a fast-food place with hamburgers and fries; it even has a salad bar. During the summer it also serves breakfast. Another fast-food place in town is *MacMurray's Alaska Halibut House* on the corner of Meals Ave and Fairbanks Drive across from Village Inn, which offers good halibut & chips, a salad bar, clam chowder and seafood dinners from $14.

A little classier than the local hamburger joint is *Pizza Palace* on North Harbor Drive, with views of the harbour from its bar. The place specialises in pasta and local seafood, and dinners cost $14 to $19. *Totem Inn* (tel 835-4443) at the corner of Kobuk Drive and Chitna Drive runs a salmon bake if you haven't had your fill of them yet.

Foodmart on the corner of Pioneer Drive and Meals Ave has the cheapest supermarket prices in town and its own bakery. At *Valdez Market* on Egan Drive you can buy ready-made sandwiches from the deli inside, along with groceries.

Entertainment

Among the places you may want to try are *Sugarloaf Saloon* at the Village Inn on the corner of Meals Ave and Richardson Highway, or the *Harbor Club Bar* in the Pizza Palace, where you can view the pipeline terminal while ordering your brew.

Eagle Hall (tel 835-4460) shows historical films on eagles and the Good Friday Earthquake twice a night during the summer; admission is $2.50. There are usually numerous activities, including plays performed by local groups or travelling theatre groups, at the Civic Center (tel 835-4440) during the summer. Contact the centre for a list of current events.

Hiking

In an area surrounded by mountains and glaciers, you would think that there is good hiking around Valdez, but this is not the case. There are few developed trails in the area (though many are now being proposed), so reaching much of the surrounding alpine country requires considerable hacking through thick bush. There is no US Forest Service office in Valdez and no nearby cabins.

Mineral Creek Trail The best walk away from town is the old road along Mineral Creek and the 1 mile (1.6 km) trail from its end to the old Smith Stamping Mill. The road is no longer maintained and is in poor condition, suitable only for those on foot or in a 4WD vehicle.

To reach the trailhead, follow Hazelet Ave north 10 blocks from Egan Drive to Hanagita St and turn left (west); then turn right (north) onto Mineral Creek Rd. The road bumps along for 5.5 miles (8.8 km) and then turns into a 1 mile (1.6 km) trail to the old stamping mill. Following the trail beyond the mill at Brevier Creek also requires considerable bush hacking. If you are hiking the entire road, the trip up the lush green canyon can be a pleasant all-day adventure.

Solomon Gulch Trail A newer trail is located across from the Solomon Gulch Fish Hatchery on Dayville Rd, off the Richardson Highway. This 1 mile (1.6 km) trail is a steep, uphill hike that quickly leads to splendid views of the Valdez Port and the city below. It ends at Solomon Lake.

Rafting

Lowe River, a glacial river that cuts through the impressive Keystone Canyon, is a few miles outside of Valdez and has become a popular float trip during the summer. Keystone Raft & Kayak (tel 835-2606) offers day trips on the river, carrying passengers 6 miles (9.6 km) through white water and past the cascading waterfalls that have made the canyon famous. The guide company runs the 1½ hour trip five times daily and charges $25 per person for the scenic adventure.

Getting There & Around

Air Alaska Airlines, through its contract carrier ERA Aviation (tel 835-2595), provide two daily flights (three during the summer) between Valdez and Anchorage from the Valdez Airport, 5 miles (8 km) from town on Airport Rd; the one-way fare is $88.

Bus The bus service out of Valdez, like much of Alaska, always seems to be in a constant state of change. Recent reports suggest that the Valdez-Anchorage Bus Line was out of business but check this out first. That leaves Gray Line (tel 835-2357) operating the run between Valdez and Anchorage. Buses depart from the Westmark Hotel at 8 am daily except Sunday and reach Anchorage around 6 pm; the one-way fare is $58.

Alaska-Yukon Motorcoaches (tel 835-4391) also depart from the Westmark Hotel and can provide transport to Fairbanks; buses leave Tuesday, Thursday and Sunday, and the one-way fare is $80.

Boat The Alaska Marine Ferry is by the far the cheapest way to view the Columbia Glacier but keep in mind that the ferry stays 3.5 miles (5.6 km) from the glacier's face, while private tours will pass within 0.5 mile (0.8 km) of it.

The one-way Valdez to Whittier fare is $54. The state ferry also connects Valdez to Cordova ($26), Seward ($54), Homer ($126) and Kodiak ($86), since both the MV *Bartlett* and MV *Tustumena* call at Valdez. Between the two ships there are runs to Whittier six times a week, three weekly sailings to Cordova and a weekly run to Seward, Homer and Kodiak. The ferry terminal (tel 835-4436) in Cordova is at the southern end of Hazelet Ave and reservations for these popular runs are strongly recommended.

AROUND VALDEZ

The **oil pipeline terminal**, the heart and soul

of Valdez, lies across the bay on Dayville Rd, 8 miles (13 km) from town along Richardson Highway. Dayville Rd is interesting as it branches off the highway and hugs the mountainside passing several eagle nests and the scenic Solomon Gulch.

The Copper Valley Hydro Project which supplies power for both Valdez and Glennallen was recently completed at Soloman Gulch. Across the road is the new Solomon Gulch Hatchery, which has a self-guided interpretive walk open to visitors from 8 am to 5 pm daily. Dayville Rd ends at the terminal's visitor centre and bronze monument dedicated to the construction workers who built the pipeline.

The terminal is nothing short of remarkable as it contains over 15 miles (24 km) of pipeline, 18 oil storage tanks and four tanker berths. Oil is pumped out of Prudhoe Bay on the Beaufort Sea in northern Alaska and travels 800 miles (1300 km) south through the pipeline to the terminal, where it is either stored or loaded into tankers. It is estimated that there are 9.6 billion barrels of oil under the North Slope, of which 1.7 million barrels flow out of the pipeline into tankers every day at the terminal.

Displays at the visitor centre explain all this, and for many it's enough to stare at the facility from the entrance gate and then head back. If you want a closer look at the place, a Gray Line bus departs from the visitor centre in Valdez twice daily for a 2 hour tour. You never leave the bus except for one viewpoint above the terminal, and the fare is $18 per person.

COLUMBIA GLACIER

Most travellers view this magnificent tidewater glacier while crossing Prince William Sound to or from Valdez. The State Marine Ferry is the cheapest way to sail between Whittier and Valdez but it stays a good 3.5 miles (5.6 km) from the glacier's face, giving passengers a wider view of the glacier as it winds back into the Chugach Mountains.

Privately run cruise ships sail considerably closer to the face after threading their way through almost 3 miles (4.8 km) of icebergs, where you can often observe seals basking under the sun. At one time the private tour boats were able to get within a quarter of a mile (0.4 km) of the glacier's 3 mile (4.8 km) wide face, but that is difficult today as the glacier has begun receding rapidly, discharging much more ice. Tour boats can still get within 0.5 mile (0.8 km) to 1 mile (1.6 km) at most times, and from this close the ongoing show of ice calving off the 300 foot (90 metre) wall of ice into the sound is an awesome sight and a photographer's delight.

The *Glacier Spirit* and *Vince Peede*, operated by Stan Stephens Charters (tel 835-4731), depart daily from Valdez at 10 am and 1.30 pm respectively from the dock in front of the Sheffield Hotel. The 9 hour cruise to the glacier and back, salmon bake included, is $75 per person. There is also a 6 hour morning trip that departs at 7 am and costs $50; the difference is you get a danish instead of a salmon bake.

Tickets can be purchased at the Westmark Hotel or the Bear Paw RV Park at the Small Boat Harbor in Valdez. Also check with Glacier Charter Service (tel 835-5141) which runs the *Lu-Lu Belle* daily, while Alaska Waterways (tel 835-5151) run a pontoon boat out to Shoup Bay where you can view wildlife, experience Shoup Glacier and have a beach barbecue with shrimp netted that day. The full-day excursion is $70 per person.

RICHARDSON HIGHWAY TO GLENNALLEN

The section of the Richardson Highway from Valdez to Glennallen is an incredibly scenic route that includes canyons, mountain passes, glaciers and access to the massive Wrangell-St Elias National Park. Hitchhiking is fairly easy during the summer, making it convenient to stop often and enjoy the sights and campgrounds along the way.

The highway begins in the centre of Valdez, but *Mile 0* is near the site of old Valdez, as the mileposts were erected before the Good Friday Earthquake and were never changed. The junction with Dayville Rd, which leads to the pipeline terminal, is 6.9 miles (11.1 km) from town, and at this point Richardson Highway swings north.

At *Mile 13* (21 km) you reach **Keystone Canyon** with its many waterfalls and unusual rock formations high above the road. In the next 1 mile (1.6 km) two magnificent waterfalls appear, first the Horsetail and then the Bridal Veil 0.5 mile (0.8 km) down the highway. The canyon wall is so sheer that the waterfalls appear to be cascading straight down and actually spray the road with mist.

At *Mile 14.8* (23.8 km) of Richardson Highway, the northern end of the canyon, there is an abandoned hand-drilled tunnel that residents of Valdez began but never finished when they were competing with Cordova for the railroad to the Kennecott Mines. A historical marker briefly describes how nine companies fought to develop the short route from the coast to Kennecott Copper Mines, leading to the 'shootout in Keystone Canyon'.

The **Trans-Alaska Pipeline** can be seen at *Mile 20.4* (32.8 km). The short loop road to the first camping area, *Blueberry Lake Wayside*, is at *Mile 24* (38.4 km) of Richardson Highway. The state recreational area offers 10 sites and four covered picnic shelters in a beautiful alpine setting with lofty peaks surrounding it. There's good fishing in the nearby lakes, but beware if you are spending the night here because the site is above the tree line and the weather can be windy and foul at times.

The highway continues to ascend until it reaches **Thompson Pass** at *Mile 26* (41.8 km). There are several scenic turn-offs near the pass, elevation 2771 feet (845 metres), which in early summer is covered by wildflowers. This spot also holds most of Alaska's snowfall records, including 62 inches (157 cm) of snow in a 24 hour period in December 1955.

At *Mile 28.6* (46 km) of Richardson Highway is the turn-off to the **Worthington Glacier State Recreation Area**, where it is possible to drive to the glacier's face on a short access road. Within this state recreation area are outhouses, picnic tables and a large covered viewing area.

A 1 mile (1.6 km) trail begins at the crest of the moraine on the left side of Worthington Glacier from the parking lot. It's a scenic hike that follows the edge of the glacier, and the walk should be done with caution. Never hike on the glacier itself. Thompson Pass and the surrounding area above the tree line are ideal for tramping, as hikers will have few problems climbing through the heather.

The pipeline continues to pop into view as you travel north on Richardson Highway and at one point it passes beneath the road. The next campground, the *Little Tonsina River State Wayside* (10 sites, $5 per night), appears at *Mile 65* (104 km). The *Squirrel Creek State Campground* (14 sites, $5 per night) is at *Mile 79.4* (127.8 km) of Richardson Highway and offers a scenic little camping area on the banks of the creek. There is good fishing for grayling and rainbow trout in Squirrel Creek. The Edgerton Highway junction that leads to the heart of the Wrangell-St Elias National Park is 3 miles (4.8 km) past the campground.

A lookout over **Willow Lake** is at *Mile 87.6* (141 km). The lake can be stunning on a clear day with the water reflecting the Wrangell Mountains, the 100 mile (160 km) chain that includes 11 peaks over 10,000 feet (3048 metres). The two most prominent peaks visible from the lookout are Mt Drum, 28 miles (45 km) to the north-east, and Mt Wrangell, Alaska's largest active volcano, to the east. Mt Wrangell is 14,163 feet (4317 metres) and on most days a plume of steam is visible from its crater.

At *Mile 91* (145.6 km) of Richardson Highway, a gravel road leads east and intersects with the Edgerton Highway. **Copper Center** (pop 220) is at *Mile 101* (161.6 km). At the turn of the century, the town was an important mining camp for the thousands of prospectors eyeing the gold fields in the Yukon and later in Fairbanks. Near the bridge over the Klutina River is the *Copper Center Lodge* (tel 822-3245), which began in 1897 as the Blix Roadhouse and was the first lodge built north of Valdez. The lodge still serves as a roadhouse today and a place where you can get a delicious plate of sourdough pancakes; rooms range from $35 to $50.

Just north of the town on Richardson Highway is the **Chapel on the Hill**, built in 1942. During the summer, the log chapel features a short slide presentation on the history of the Copper River Basin area; admission is free.

At *Mile 115* (185 km) is the major junction between the Glenn and Richardson highways. The Richardson Highway continues north to Delta Junction and eventually Fairbanks (see the Interior chapter). The Glenn Highway (see the Interior chapter) heads west to Glennallen, a short distance away, and onto Anchorage.

WRANGELL-ST ELIAS NATIONAL PARK

This national park, created in 1980, stretches north 170 miles (270 km) from the Gulf of Alaska. It encompass 13.2 million acres (5.3 million hectares) of mountains and forelands bounded by the Copper River on the west and Canada's Kluane National Park to the east. Together, Kluane and Wrangell-St Elias national parks make up 19 million acres (7.7

million hectares) and the greatest expanse of valleys, canyons and towering mountains in North America, including the continent's second and third highest peaks.

This area is an intersection of mountain ranges. To the north are the Wrangell Mountains, to the south the Chugachs and thrusting from the Gulf of Alaska and clashing with the Wrangells are the St Elias Mountains. There are so many mountains and so many summits in this rugged land that, as the park brochure says, 'you quickly abandon the urge to learn their names'.

Spilling out from the peaks are extensive ice fields and over 100 major glaciers – some of the largest and most active in the world. The Bagley Ice Field near the coast is the largest subpolar mass of ice in North America. The Malaspina Glacier, which spills out of the St Elias Range between Ice Bay and Yakutat Bay, is larger than the US state of Rhode Island.

Wildlife in Wrangell-St Elias National Park is more diverse and plentiful than in any other Alaska park. Species in the preserve include moose, black and brown bears, Dall sheep, mountain goats, wolves, wolverines, beavers and three of Alaska's 11 caribou herd.

Wolf

The Richardson Highway borders the north-west corner of the park and two rough dirt roads lead into its interior. However, Wrangell-St Elias is a true wilderness park with few visitor facilities or services beyond the highway. An adventure into this preserve requires time and patience rather than money, but it can lead to a once-in-a-lifetime experience.

Information

The park's main headquarters (tel 822-5235) is at *Mile 105* (168 km) of Richardson Highway, 10 miles (16 km) before the junction with the Glenn Highway. The office is open daily during the summer and rangers can answer questions about the park as well as supply various hand-outs and rough maps of the area. They also schedule daily tours and interpretive programmes. During the summer, rangers are stationed in Chitina (tel 823-2205), at the end of Edgerton Highway, and in Nabesna (tel 822-5238).

McCarthy

The mountainous hamlet of McCarthy is near the ruins of the famous Kennecott Copper Mines. Once you're across the Kennicott River, follow the road up a small rise to the **McCarthy & Kennicott Museum**, an old railroad depot that features old photographs and historical artefacts. From the museum take the right fork into McCarthy, an extremely scenic village of 16 or so residents.

St Elias Alpine Guides, which run the B&B in town, will also arrange a guided tour up to the **Kennecott Mines** (the miners never corrected their misspelling of Kennicott) where 700 men worked in 1917. The mines were in operation for almost 30 years and produced more than 590,000 tons (535 million kg) of copper ore. When world copper prices crashed in 1938, the mines closed and today there are still 40 buildings in this ghost town of mining history and lore. The tour lasts 2 to 3 hours and costs $25 per person. The guides also have a half-day walk on the Root Glacier for $55.

Places to Stay The cheapest accommodation in McCarthy is at the *McCarthy Lodge* (tel 373-3357) which is full of mining relics and photographs of the era, and is a place to get a bed, meal, shower or ride to the Kennecott Mines. The lodge was built in 1916 as a hotel and has bunkhouse accommodation for $12.50 and double rooms for $75.

There is also *McCarthy Wilderness Bed & Breakfast* (tel 277-6867 in Anchorage), a log cabin with no telephone, electricity or running water. Bathing is done in a log sauna and reading is by kerosene lamp; rooms are $55 for two people. They also offer a 3 day/3 night package that includes a tour of the mines and a half-day raft or glacier hiking trip for $265 per person. It sounds like a lot but this would surely be the highlight of your Alaskan adventure.

Hiking

Root Glacier From McCarthy, it's a 16 mile (26 km) round trip past the Kennecott Mine ruins to Root Glacier. This is a long day hike or a pleasant overnight excursion. Begin at the McCarthy Museum and take the left fork, a gravel road that leads 5 miles (8 km) to the village of Kennicott (pop eight). From Kennicott, the trail continues for another 4 miles (6.5 km) along the moraine of the Kennicott and Root glaciers. You cross three streams along the way, including Jumbo Creek in 2 miles (3.2 km) where extreme caution should be used. You should also be careful around the edge of Root Glacier where there is rotting ice.

Haley Creek Another overnight hike begins in the O'Brien Creek Campground, 3 miles (4.8 km) south of Chitina. The scenic trail follows the old bed of the Copper River & Northwestern Railroad 5 miles (8 km) through Woods Canyon to Haley Creek. Just before reaching Haley Creek you pass through a tunnel. The creek offers superb camping on a sandy strip with a roaring waterfall nearby.

Getting There & Around

Driving Edgerton Highway and McCarthy Rd combine to provide a 92 mile (147 km) route into the heart of Wrangell-St Elias National Park, ending at the mountainous hamlet of McCarthy near the ruins of the famous Kennecott Copper Mines.

The 32 mile (51 km) Edgerton Highway, partly paved and partly gravel, begins at *Mile 82.6* (133 km) of Richardson Highway and ends at Chitina. The town, which has 42 permanent residents, is the last place to purchase food or gas. Backpackers can camp along the 3 mile (4.8 km) road south to O'Brien Creek or beside Town Lake within Chitina. There is also a small campground with eight free sites next to the Copper River Bridge that is maintained by the Alaska Department of Transportation. Travellers staying in Chitina should stop at the ranger station, which is open from 8 am to 5 pm daily during the summer.

From Chitina, McCarthy Rd – a rough dirt road that is not regularly maintained – follows the abandoned Copper River & Northwest Railroad bed. It leads 60 miles (96 km) further east to the two forks of the Kennicott River. Two-wheel vehicles can usually travel this stretch during the summer, but plan on 3 to 4 hours for the trip.

You pass a couple of commercial campgrounds along the way and at *Mile 13.5* (22 km) come to the access road to the trailheads for the Dixie Pass, Nugget and Kotsina trails (see the Hiking section in the Wilderness chapter). At *Mile 17* (27.7 km) of McCarthy Rd is the Kuskulana River Bridge. This historic railroad bridge was built in 1910 and has a 525 foot (157 metre) span, 238 feet (71 metres) above the river.

To continue the final 1 mile (1.6 km) to McCarthy you have to use the hand-pulled trams erected by locals. The two trams are open platforms large enough to carry two people and their backpacks. Use gloves and make sure you have enough strength to pull your load several hundred feet to the other side of the river.

Bus Hitching McCarthy Rd is tough (but always possible) which is why Wrangell Mt Bus Adventures (tel 822-5519) was established. The bus company departs from The Hub service station at the junction of the Richardson and Glenn highways in Glennallen at 1 pm and arrives in McCarthy at 6 pm after stopping in Chitina and three scenic pullovers. On Monday, Wednesday and Friday, a bus departs McCarthy at 7 am for Glennallen. The return trip between the two towns is $80.

Tours St Elias Alpine Guides (tel 277-6867) based in Anchorage run the most extensive trips into the national park. They offer 4 days of climbing Root Glacier for $528 per person as well as glacier skiing in the summer and other mountaineering expeditions. They also run several backpacking and raft trips, including a 14 day float down the Copper River from McCarthy to Cordova for $1595 per person.

WHITTIER

On the day the military was cutting the ribbon that marked the completion of the Alcan (Alaska Highway), the army was also having a tunnel 'holing through' ceremony outside of Whittier. World War II and the Japanese invasion of the Aleutian Islands brought the US military searching for a second warm-water port in Southcentral Alaska, one that would serve as a secret port. Whittier was chosen because it was well hidden between the high walls of the Passage Canal Fjord in which it lies, and for the consistently bad weather that hangs over it.

Work began immediately on two tunnels through the Chugach Mountains that would connect the port to the main line of the Alaska Railroad. The tunnels, though overshadowed by the Alcan, were another amazing feat of engineering. The first was drilled through almost 1 mile (1.6 km) of solid rock, while the second, begun simultaneously from the other side of the mountain, required carving a route 2.5 miles (4 km) long. When General Simon Buckner blasted open the second tunnel during the 'holing through' ceremony in 1942, the two tunnels

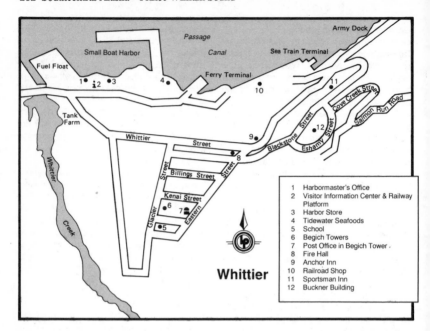

missed perfect alignment by an eighth of an inch (0.3 cm).

Whittier owes both its existence and its skyscraper appearance to the military. After WW II, the port became a permanent base, and tall concrete buildings were constructed to house and service the personnel. One building, the Begich Towers, is 14 storeys tall. Nearby, the massive Buckner Building once housed 1000 people and had a bowling alley, a theatre, cafes, a hospital and a jail.

Today, the Begich Towers have been converted into condominiums where 60% of Whittier's 344 residents live. Military and government activities ceased in 1963 but the small town continues to exist on fishing and tourism, and as a port of call for both the Alaska Marine Ferry and the Alaska Railroad.

Things to See

The vast majority of travellers stay in Whittier only long enough to board the train to Anchorage or the ferry to Valdez. However, it is one of the more interesting towns in Alaska and on a clear day it is a beautiful spot to be. The town is nestled at the base of the mountains that line Passage Canal, and the surrounding peaks are capped with snow for much of the year. To the west of town a glacier spills out of the mountains.

As soon as you disembark from the train, you will spot the new **Whittier Visitor Center**, housed in a railcar donated by the Alaska Railroad. Due north is the **Small Boat Harbor** that contains fishing boats, private craft and the numerous tour vessels that work the Columbia Glacier route between Whittier and Valdez.

There is also a small museum in town on the 1st floor of the Begich Towers, down the hall from the post office. The **Whittier Historical & Fine Arts Museum** is open from 1 to 5 pm daily. It contains strips of sperm-whale bone, ivory carvings, and displays on Prince William Sound marine life and the

1964 earthquake which killed 13 people in town but did little damage to the concrete buildings or nearby tunnels; donations are accepted.

Also in the Begich Towers is the **Whittier Library**, open afternoons from Monday to Friday, featuring a small collection of books and local memorabilia. From the south-west corner of the Begich Towers, a track leads west to Whittier Creek, while above it, falling from the ridge of a glacial cirque, is the picturesque **Horsetail Falls**.

Places to Stay & Eat

There are two hotels in Whittier. The *Anchor Inn* (tel 472-2354) is the cheapest with rooms from $35, while the *Sportsman Inn* (tel 472-2352) has singles from $40. The Sportsman Inn, north-east of the Buckner Building, also sells groceries and has a dining room, public laundry, bar and a three-person sauna which is rented out by the hour.

There is a campervan facility behind the Begich Towers where you can set up a tent, but the gravel surface is not worth the $5 per night charge. The best place to camp is at the *First Salmon Run* (see the Whittier Hiking section), a scenic spot with a shelter, picnic tables and outhouses. Or you can pitch a tent just about anywhere near town by walking into the bush and away from the road.

For hamburgers, there is the *Hobo Bay Trading Company*, while the *Dog House* has hot dogs, milkshakes etc. Both are near the Small Boat Harbor. You can also purchase some of the day's catch from *Tidewater Seafoods* next to the ferry dock. Groceries are available at either of the hotels.

Hiking

Portage Pass Trail This makes a superb afternoon hike as it provides good views of Portage Glacier, Passage Canal and the surrounding mountains and glaciers. Even better, hike up in the late afternoon and spend the evening camping at Divide Lake.

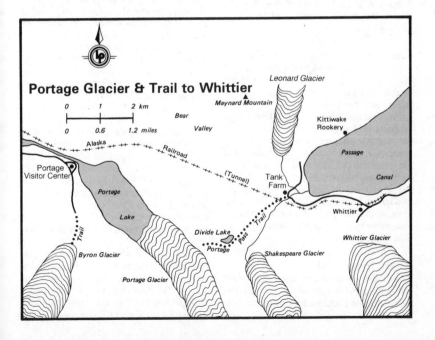

Portage Glacier & Trail to Whittier

To pick up the trailhead, walk west along the gravel road from the train platform as it parallels the tracks. Follow it 1.3 miles (2 km) to the tank farm and the tunnel at Maynard Mountain, and turn left onto a road that crosses the tracks. Follow the right fork as it begins to climb steeply along the flank of the mountain, until it goes through a small pond. Here you can climb a promontory, elevation 750 feet (229 metres), for views of Portage Glacier or Passage Canal to the east.

Divide Lake is another 0.5 mile (0.8 km) south-west and by travelling left (south) around it you can head down the slope to the glacier. Plan on 2 hours to reach Divide Lake. The trip to the glacier and back to Whittier is an 8 mile (12.8 km) hike.

Smitty's Cove From the front of the Sportsman Inn, Smitty's Cove lies a quarter of a mile (0.4 km) down the road to the right (north-east). At low tide you can beachcomb all of the cove to the point east of it. Smitty's Cove is a favourite haunt of Alaska scuba divers and is occasionally referred to as Diver's Cove.

First Salmon Run This is a 0.8 mile (1.3 km) walk along a dirt road to the First Salmon Run Picnic Area, so named because of the large king and silver salmon runs in the creek in June and late August.

From the north-east corner of the Buckner Building behind the Sportsman Inn, follow the road that leads up the mountain, staying to the right at the first fork and to the left at the second fork. The road leads into the picnic area, where you can cross a bridge over the stream and continue another 3 miles (4.8 km) to Second Salmon Run. This walk, along what is known as Shotgun Cove Rd, is exceptionally scenic as you can see Billings Glacier most of the way.

Getting There & Away

There are two ways of getting out of Whittier and neither one is by road. To go west you take the Alaska Railroad; to head east you take a boat.

Train There are four trains departing Whittier on Tuesday and Wednesday, and six trains the rest of the week, but only the 3.30 pm run takes you all the way to Anchorage, via a bus connection at Portage. The one-way fare from Whittier to Anchorage is $18 and from Whittier to Portage is $7.50. If arriving by ferry, you have a 5½ hour break before the last train, the daily 8.30 pm run, pulls out of Whittier. That's enough time to see the town or tackle the Portage Pass Trail (see the Whittier Hiking section).

Boat The state ferry MV *Bartlett* goes east six times a week at 3 pm from the ferry dock. All departures go to Valdez and cruise near the impressive Columbia Glacier; the one-way fare from Whittier to Valdez is $54.

The other alternative to Valdez is the charter vessels that depart from the Small Boat Harbor and usually include lunch and a closer view of the glacier than the state ferry provides. The *Glacier Seas* costs $110 one way and makes the Whittier to Valdez run on Monday, Wednesday and Friday. Either book a ticket when you're in Anchorage by calling Alaska Sightseeing (tel 276-1305) or search out the boat in the harbour the night before you wish to go, and purchase a ticket from the captain. The *Glacier Queen II* also makes the trip out of Whittier and is managed by Westour (tel 277-5581).

Tours College and Harriman fjords, north of Whittier, contain not one but 26 glaciers with such academic names as Harvard, Dartmouth, Yale and Vassar, after the Eastern colleges in the USA that supported the expedition leading to their discovery. On the way to Harriman Fjord, cruise ships pass so close to a Kittiwake rookery that you can see the eggs of the black-legged birds in their nest.

Various tour boats which sail out of the Small Boat Harbor in Whittier offer day cruises to this icy world (including the *Klondike*, a 212 passenger vessel operated by Phillips Tours). The 110 mile (179 km) return trip lasts almost 6 hours and costs $99 per person, including lunch. Contact the visitor centre in Whittier for tickets and names of other tour boats operating.

Kenai Peninsula

Because of its diverse terrain, easy accessibility and close proximity to Alaska's largest city (Anchorage), the Kenai Peninsula has become the state's top recreational area. It is well serviced, well developed and, unfortunately, well used during the summer. Although some trails are very popular all summer and many campgrounds are always filled near capacity, if you hike a little further or climb a little higher you can find a tent space with only nature around you.

The area is serviced by two major highways and one minor one. From Anchorage, the Seward Highway follows the Turnagain Arm where the road has been carved out of mountains, and then turns south at Portage to the picturesque community of Seward on Resurrection Bay.

The Sterling Highway heads west from the Seward Highway 90 miles (144 km) out of Anchorage at Tern Lake Junction. When it reaches the crossroad town of Soldotna, near Cook Inlet, it turns south, follows the coast past some great clam-digging beaches and ends up at Homer, the most delightful town on the Peninsula. The third road is Hope Highway, which heads north from Seward Highway, 70 miles (113 km) out of Anchorage, to the small historical mining community of Hope, 16 miles (26 km) from the junction.

Traffic is heavy on the main highways, making hitchhiking an easy form of travel during the summer. The area is connected to the rest of Prince William Sound by the state ferry MV *Tustumena* which runs from Cordova and Valdez across the sound to Seward, over to Homer and then south to Kodiak. Alaska Airlines, through its contract carrier, also provides regularly scheduled services between Anchorage and Kenai, Homer and Kodiak.

SEWARD HIGHWAY

Travellers from Whittier should think twice before purchasing a train ticket to Anchorage. For half the fare you can get off at Portage, where there is easy hitchhiking down the Seward Highway into the heart of the Kenai Peninsula, Alaska's outdoor playground. The highway stretches for 127 miles (204 km) and is another scenic gem in the state's fledgeling system of roads.

The first section of the Seward Highway from Anchorage, *Mile 127* (204 km), to Portage Glacier, *Mile 79* (127 km), is covered in the Anchorage chapter. When heading south, keep in mind that the mileposts along Seward Highway show distances beginning from Seward, *Mile 0*, to Anchorage, *Mile 127* (204 km).

Near *Mile 68* (109 km) the highway begins climbing into the alpine region of **Turnagain Pass**, where there is a roadside stop with litter barrels and toilets. In early summer, this area is a kaleidoscope of wildflowers that range from purple violets to reds. Just past *Mile 64* (103 km) is the US Forest Service (USFS) sign pointing to the northern trailhead of **Johnson Pass Trail** (see the Trekking section in the Wilderness chapter), a 23 mile (37 km) route over an alpine pass.

The USFS *Granite Creek Campground* (18 sites, $5 fee) is at *Mile 63* (101.4 km) of the Seward Highway and provides tables, water and a place to camp for hikers coming off the Johnson Pass Trail at its northern end. This campground, roughly halfway between Anchorage and Seward, is a nice place to spend the evening. Most of the sites are along the creek which can be fished for Dolly Varden.

The junction to Hope Highway (see the Hope Highway section in this chapter) is at *Mile 56.7* (91 km). From here the paved Hope Highway heads 18 miles (28.8 km) north, and 1 mile (1.6 km) past the small hamlet of Hope. Seward Highway continues south of this junction, and at *Mile 46* (73.6 km) you cross the Colorado Creek Bridge and the short side road to the USFS *Tenderfoot Creek Campground* (27 sites, $5 fee).

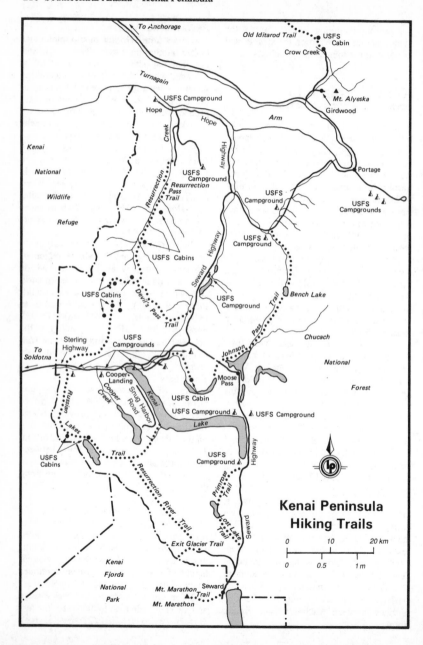

Kenai Peninsula
Hiking Trails

This scenic campground lies on the shores of Upper Summit Lake and provides good fishing in the spring and autumn for landlocked Dolly Varden.

The **Devil's Pass Trail** (see the Resurrection Pass Trail in the Trekking section of the Wilderness chapter), a 10 mile (16 km) hike over a 2400 foot (732 metre) gap to Resurrection Pass Trail, is at *Mile 39.4* (63.4 km) of the Seward Highway. Tern Lake Junction, the beginning of the Sterling Highway, is at *Mile 37* (59.5 km). By driving 0.5 mile (0.8 km) west from the junction you will reach the USFS *Tern Lake Campground* (33 sites, $5 fee).

At *Mile 33* (53 km) of the Seward Highway is the **Carter Lake Trail**, a 2.3 mile (3.7 km) trail that provides quick (but steep) access into subalpine terrain. The path, an old jeep trail, starts from a parking area on the west side of the highway and ascends steeply almost 1000 feet (305 metres) to Carter Lake.

From the lake, a trail continues another 1 mile (1.6 km) around the west side of the lake to Crescent Lake. There is good camping at the end of Carter Lake. Half a mile (0.8 km) south of the Carter Lake trailhead on the other side of the highway is the southern trailhead to the Johnson Pass Trail (see the Trekking section in the Wilderness chapter).

The Seward Highway continues south and at *Mile 29.4* (47.3) passes through the village of **Moose Pass** (pop 200). This small town has a general store, post office, two restaurants and sponsors the Moose Pass Summer Festival on the weekend nearest the summer solstice on 21 June. At *Mile 25* (40 km) of the Seward Highway is an obscure dirt road that leads west to the USFS *Trail River Campground* (63 sites, $5 fee), featuring many campsites among the tall spruce along Kenai Lake and the Lower Trail River.

Ptarmigan Creek Bridge is at *Mile 23* (37 km) of the Seward Highway. Right before it on the east side of the highway is the entrance to the USFS *Ptarmigan Creek Campground* (26 sites, $5 fee). The 3.5 mile (5.6 km) **Ptarmigan Creek Trail** begins in the campground and ends at Ptarmigan Lake, a

beautiful body of water that reflects the mountains surrounding it. A 4 mile (6.4 km) trail continues around the north side of the lake, which offers good fishing for Dolly Varden at its outlet to the creek. Plan on 5 hours for a return hike to the lake, as some parts of the trail are steep.

The **Victor Creek Trail**, at *Mile 19.7* (31.7 km) on the east side of the highway, is the trailhead for a fairly difficult path that ascends 3 miles (4.8 km) to good views of the surrounding mountains.

After crossing the bridge over South Fork Snow River at *Mile 17.2* (27.7 km), look to the west for the road that leads 1 mile (1.6 km) to the USFS *Primrose Landing Campground* (10 sites, $5). This scenic campground is on the east end of the beautiful Kenai Lake and contains the trailhead to the Primrose Trail (see the Lost Lake Trail in the Seward Hiking section).

The **Grayling Lake Trail**, a 2 mile (3.2 km) hike to Grayling Lake, has side trails that connect it to Meridian and Leech lakes, a beautiful spot with good views of Snow River Valley. All three lakes have good fishing for grayling. The trailhead is in a paved parking lot at *Mile 13.2* (21.2 km) on the west side of the Seward Highway.

SEWARD

Seward (pop 2500) is a pretty little town flanked by rugged mountains on one side and the salmon-filled Resurrection Bay on the other. It is the only town on the eastern side of the Kenai Peninsula. It was founded in 1903 by Alaska Railroad surveyors who needed an ice-free port to serve as the ocean terminal for the rail line. The first spike was driven in during 1904 and the line was completed in 1923.

During that time, Seward prospered as it served as the beginning of the Iditarod Trail to Nome and thousands of prospectors stampeding their way through town. Dog teams were used to haul supplies, mail and gold along this 958 mile (1533 km) route.

Like most towns in Southcentral Alaska, Seward began a new era of history in 1964 after the Good Friday Earthquake (or Black

1 Kenai Fjords National Park Visitor Center
2 Christiaan's
3 Railroad Car & Tourist Information Cache
4 Resurrection Bay Historical Museum
5 Post Office
6 Forest Service Office
7 St Peter's Episcopal Church
8 Van Guilder Hotel
9 City Hall & State Park Office
10 New Seward Hotel
11 Library
12 Rest Rooms
13 Pavilion
14 Ferry Office
15 Pioneer Bar
16 Laundromat
17 Seward Marine Center

Seward

0   100   200 m

0   100   200 yds

Friday as Alaskans call it) caused fires and tidal waves that destroyed 90% of the town. At one point, a 3500 foot (1050 metres) stretch of waterfront slid into the bay and Seward was completely cut off from the rest of the state.

Today, the only reminder of the natural disaster is at the public library (tel 224-3646) on the corner of 5th Ave and Adams St across from City Hall, where the slide show, *Seward is Burning*, is shown from Monday to Saturday at 2 pm. It covers the earthquake through the eyes of residents who witnessed it.

The town has completely rebuilt its fine Small Boat Harbor and waterfront facilities with a $10 million dock designed to be earthquake proof. Most of the area's residents either work at Seward Fisheries, the largest halibut receiving station on the US west coast, fish or are connected with the Seward Marine Center, a ship-repair facility, and the town's growing maritime industry.

Information

Your first stop in Seward should be at the Seward Railroad Car on the corner of 3rd Ave and Jefferson St. At one time, the Pullman dining car carried President Warren G Harding to the place where he drove in the golden spike that completed the Alaska Railroad. Today, it houses the Chamber of Commerce Information Cache (tel 224-3094), where you can pick up maps, information or a walking-tour map of the city. The centre is open daily in the summer from 9 am to 5 pm.

The Kenai Fjords National Park Visitor Center in the Small Boat Harbor (tel 224-3175) has displays, information and a slide show on the nearby park. The centre is open daily during the summer from 8 am to 7 pm. For information on Chugach National Forest trails, cabins and campgrounds, go to the US Forest Service information centre (tel 224-3374) at 344 4th Ave. And for information on Caines Head State Park, head to the Alaska Division of Parks & Outdoor Recreation office (tel 224-3434) on the 2nd floor of the City/State Building at the corner of 5th Ave and Adams St. Both the state parks and

US Forest Service (USFS) offices are open Monday to Friday from 8 am to 5 pm.

Things to See

The walking tour begins north of the Seward Railroad Car on 3rd Ave, where the houses on the left are known as **Millionaires Row**. They were built around 1905 by railroad officials and bankers who had just arrived in the newly created town. Nearby at the corner of Jefferson St and 3rd Ave is the **Resurrection Bay Historical Museum**, open daily from 11 am to 4 pm. The museum features artefacts and photographs of the 1964 earthquake, including a clock that stopped the instant the disaster struck. There are also exhibits on the Russian era in Resurrection Bay when a shipyard was established in 1793, and Seward's role in the Iditarod Trail. The admission charge is 50 cents.

The tour heads west to 1st Ave and follows it south to Lowell St and the start of the trail to Mt Marathon (see the Seward Hiking section). The walk continues east onto Adams St, where at the corner of 2nd Ave is **St Peter's Episcopal Church**, built in 1906. Inside is the famous mural of the Resurrection by Dutch artist Jan Van Emple who used Alaskan models and the nearby bay as the backdrop.

Head south on 3rd Ave until Railway Ave to view the **Seward Marine Center**, operated by the University of Alaska. The centre is open to the public Monday to Friday from 1 to 5 pm and has tanks holding live Alaska marine specimens, displays, films and tours of the facility. The walking tour continues north on 4th Ave where many of the businesses have restored the pioneer look to their buildings. Turn onto 5th Ave at Jefferson St and then head south to the **Seward Library** on the corner of Adams St.

Not on the tour but equally interesting is the **Small Boat Harbor** at the northern end of 4th Ave. The place hums during the summer with fishing boats, charter vessels and a large number of sailboats. Often it is possible to view sea otters in the surrounding waters. Nearby is the Kenai Fjords National

Park Visitor Information Center. You can get a shower at the Harbormaster's office for $1.

Festivals

Seward holds two events each summer that have become popular with Alaskans throughout the Southcentral. The Fourth of July celebration is a big event in Seward, highlighted by the annual Mt Marathon Race, which pulls runners from around the state. The city's most famous event, however, is the Silver Salmon Derby on the second Saturday of August. First prize is $10,000 for the largest salmon caught. Other events on derby weekend include the Silver Salmon Run and softball tournaments.

Places to Stay

Camping There are two city campgrounds in the Seward area. In town, you can camp on the shore of the bay along 7th Ave (also known as Ballaine Blvd) from the Small Boat Harbor south to the State Marine Ferry office. Referred to as the *City Greenbelt Campground*, it has outhouses along the strip and a picnic pavilion at the corner of Railway and 7th avenues. At night an attendant comes by to collect $4.25 per site.

Forest Acres Campground is 2 miles (3.2 km) north of town on the west side of Seward Highway and also has a $4.25 fee. Camping is not allowed in the small city park near the ferry terminal.

Youth Hostel If you don't have a tent and sleeping bag, cheap accommodation can be tough to find in Seward. The *Snow River Youth Hostel*, which was off Seward Highway near Primrose State Campground 16 miles (25.6 km) north of Seward, was closed in 1990. You might want to check to see if it has since been reopened but don't bet on it.

Bed & Breakfast You might do better with B&Bs. There are almost a dozen of these places in the Seward area, including *Seward Waterfront Lodging* (tel 224-5563) which has rooms for $30 and *White House Bed & Breakfast* (tel 224-3614) with singles for

$25. Stop at the visitor centre for the latest list.

Hotels None of the hotels in town are cheap. *Murphy's Motel* (tel 224-8090) near the boat harbor has singles for $52 a night, and the *Marina Motel* (tel 224-5518) just up the highway offers rooms from $45. The *Van Guilder Hotel* (tel 224-3525), which was built in 1916 and has been operating as a hotel since 1921, is at 307 Adams St and has some 'efficiency rooms' for $50 a night. The *New Seward Hotel* (tel 224-8001) has singles for $40. After that, rates zoom into the $70 range. Also keep in mind that a last-minute room is hard to secure in Seward at the height of the summer season.

Places to Eat

Christiaan's at the corner of 3rd Ave and Monroe St probably has the cheapest fare, including 97 cent hamburgers and a $1.99 breakfast, something that is almost unheard of anywhere else in the state. The restaurant also features outdoor seating and is open to 11 pm daily.

For something a little more healthier than milkshakes and fried food, try *Le Barn Appetit* on Resurrection Rd past the first bridge. This health food store, B&B and bakery has deli sandwiches, crepes, fresh baked bread, quiche and other good things to eat.

Want Chinese? The *Peking Chinese Restaurant* is at the corner of 4th Ave and Jefferson St and is open until 10 pm daily. For a Mexican burrito, a pizza with everything or fish & chips, head to *Niko's* at 133 4th Ave. Finally, *Ray's Waterfront* overlooking the boat harbour is good for local seafood but plan on spending a bundle for dinner.

Entertainment

Seward's oldest drinking hole, the *Pioneer Bar* on the corner of 5th Ave and Washington St, is a fun place where someone is usually bashing on the honky-tonk piano. *Niko's Night Club* near the ferry dock features live music and a rosewood bar that the owner claims is 120 years old. There are also lounges in the *Van Guilder Hotel* and the *Breeze Inn* overlooking the Small Boat Harbor.

Hiking

For information on the hikes in and around the Seward area, stop at the US Forest Service (USFS) office (tel 224-3374) on 4th Ave between Adams and Jefferson streets. The office is also the place to check out the availability of cabins in the Seward area.

Race Point Trail The most popular trail near the town centre is the trek towards the top of Mt Marathon, the mountain that sits behind the city. The route is well known throughout Alaska. In 1909, two sourdough miners wagered how long it would take to run to the top and back and then dashed off for the peak.

After that, it became an official event at the Seward Fourth of July celebrations and today attracts hundreds of runners with an equal number of spectators who line the streets to watch them race. The fastest time is 43 minutes and 23 seconds, set in 1981. Most runners come down the mountain in less than 10 minutes, usually by sliding halfway on their behinds.

Hikers can take their time and enjoy the spectacular views of Seward and Resurrection Bay. The hiker's trail begins at the end of Monroe St but is overgrown and hard to find at times. The runner's trail begins at the west end of Jefferson St (also known as Lowell St) up the Lowell Canyon. The trailhead is marked and is in a small gravel pit just past a pair of water tanks.

Scramble up the ridge to the right of the gully; for fun return through the gully's scree. You never really reach Mt Marathon's summit, though you do reach a high point of 3022 feet (921 metres) known as Race Point on the broad east shoulder. Plan on 3 to 4 hours for the 3 mile (4.8 km) round trip.

Two Lakes Trail This easy 1 mile (1.6 km) loop goes through a wooded area and passes two small lakes at the base of Mt Marathon. Begin the hike near the first lake behind the

Alaska Vocational & Training Center on the corner of 2nd Ave and B St. Near the start of the trail is a scenic waterfall.

Resurrection River Trail This 16 mile (25.6 km) trail, built in 1984, is the last link in a 70 mile (112 km) system across the Kenai Peninsula from Seward to Hope. This continuous trail is broken only by the Sterling Highway and provides the best long-term wilderness adventure on the Peninsula, leading hikers through a diversity of streams, rivers, lakes, wooded lowlands and alpine areas.

The southern trailhead for the Resurrection River Trail is 8 miles (12.8 km) up the Exit Glacier Rd that leaves the Seward Highway at *Mile 3.7* (6 km) (see the Kenai Fjords section in this chapter). The northern trailhead joins the Russian Lakes Trail (see the Trekking section in the Wilderness chapter), 5 miles (8 km) from Cooper Lake or 16 miles (25.6 km) from the Russian River Campground off Sterling Highway. The hike from Seward Highway to Sterling Highway is a 40 mile (64 km) trip, including walking up Exit Glacier Rd.

There are two USFS cabins (reservations needed, \$20 per night) along the trail; the Resurrection River USFS Cabin is 6.5 miles (10.4 km) from the southern trailhead and the Fox Creek USFS Cabin is another 1.5 miles beyond it. Check with the USFS office in Seward about availability of the cabins and the best places to camp along the trail, as good sites are scarce.

Lost Lake Trail At *Mile 5.2* (8.4 km) of Seward Highway, this 7 mile (11.2 km) trail to the alpine lake is one of the most scenic hikes the Kenai Peninsula has to offer in mid-summer. The trailhead is marked in a parking area west of the highway and the beginning of the trail is a rough logging road. At 1.5 miles (2.4 km), a winter trail, designed primarily for snowmobiles, branches off to the right. The final 2 miles (3.2 km) of the trail are above the tree line and the lake is a glorious place to spend a night.

An option to returning is to continue

around the east side of Lost Lake to the Primrose Trail, another USFS-maintained route. This 8 mile (12.8 km) trail leads through alpine country and ends at Primrose Campground at *Mile 17.2* (27.7 km) of Seward Highway. Plan on 7 to 10 hours for the return trip to Lost Lake and bring a camp stove because there is no wood near the lake.

Caines Head State Recreation Area This 6,000 acre (2400 hectare) preserve lies along the shore of Resurrection Bay, 5.5 miles (9 km) south of Seward. It's the scenic site of an abandoned WW II fort and includes military ruins and 650 feet (196 metres) headlands that rise above the water for sweeping views of the bay and the mountains around it.

Facilities around the North Beach include shelters, toilets, campsites and a ranger station that is staffed through most of the summer. You can explore this coastline either by boat, kayak or on foot beginning at the end of Lowell Rd (see the Coastal Trail in the Trekking section of the Wilderness Chapter for more information).

Getting There & Around
Bus Seward Bus Lines (tel 224-3608) provides a daily service to Anchorage during the summer, with a bus departing from 550 Railroad Ave at 9 am. The bus departs Anchorage at 2.30 pm for the return trip to Seward; the one-way fare is $25. The bus company also has connections with Intercity Lines to Soldotna, Kenai and Homer. To get around town, the Trolley (tel 224-8075) has a service that extends from the ferry terminal north past the railroad terminal for $1 per ride.

Train The Alaska Railroad resumed passenger services to Seward in 1987 for the first time since the 1950s and now makes a daily run to the city from Anchorage. Trains leave Seward at 6 pm Thursday to Monday and reach Anchorage at 10 pm after travelling a spectacular route that includes glaciers, steep gorges and rugged mountain scenery. Even when departing at 6 pm, you can still view the scenery thanks to those long Alaskan

days. The one-way fare is $35 and the service is offered from late May to early September. Call the terminal (tel 224-5550) at the northern end of 4th Ave for tickets and more information.

Boat The state ferry terminal (tel 224-5485) is on the waterfront near the corner of 5th and Railroad avenues. Ferries arrive in Seward twice a week from Kodiak or Valdez and depart for the same communities before continuing onto other Southcentral ports. The fare to Valdez is $54, to Kodiak $48 and to Homer $86. The trip to Valdez includes passing the Columbia Glacier. The boat to Kodiak Island passes the Stellar sea lions on the Chiswell Islands near the mouth of Resurrection Bay and nearby Bear Glacier.

KENAI FJORDS NATIONAL PARK
Seward serves as the departure point for most trips into the Kenai Fjords National Park. The park, created in 1980, was thrust into the news during the Exxon oil spill. It covers 587,000 acres (238,000 hectares) and consists mainly of the Harding Ice Field, the rugged coastline where tidewater glaciers calve into the sea, and the offshore islands.

The Exxon oil spill had an impact on the park 2 weeks after the tanker struck the reef in Prince William Sound. But much of the coastline was spared from heavy damage as favourable winds kept the bulk of the initial oil from striking the shore. Still, there was damage and the park staff, determined not to let the public forget the heavy price of our oil dependency, has since created a series of oil spill exhibits for their visitor centre on 4th Ave in Seward. Despite the world's worst oil spill, Kenai Fjords is still a major tourist attraction, with the abundance of wildlife and Exit Glacier its main attractions.

For the adventurous, there is Harding Ice Field. One of the largest ice fields in North America, it remained undiscovered until earlier this century when a map-making team realised several coastal glaciers belonged to the same massive system. The ice field is 35 miles (57 km) long and 20 miles (32 km) wide and eight glaciers reach the sea from it, while Exit Glacier is a remnant of a larger glacier that once extended into Resurrection Bay.

Experienced mountaineers, equipped with skies, ice axes and crampons, are the only ones who can explore the 300 sq mile (768 sq km) ice field. The many deep fjords, broken coastline and rich marine life also make the park a blue-water paddler's dream, though kayakers have to be cautious and experienced in rough water to handle the sections exposed to the Gulf of Alaska.

Information

The Kenai Fjords National Park Visitor Center (tel 224-3874) is on 4th Ave in Seward near the Harbormaster's office and the Small Boat Harbor. It is open daily from 8 am to 7 pm and has exhibits and slide programmes as well as hand-outs on the park. There is also a ranger station at Exit Glacier, which is staffed and open daily during the summer.

Hiking

Besides the nature trail from the ranger station to Exit Glacier, the only other developed hike in the glacier area is the trek to Harding Ice Field. The hike to the ice field is a difficult ascent which follows a steep, roughly cut and sometimes slippery route on the north side of Exit Glacier, beginning at its base. It's a 6.5 miles (10.6 km) one-way hike to the ice field at 3500 feet (1050 metres) and for reasonably fit trekkers a good 4 hour hike/climb.

The all-day trek is well worth it for those with the stamina, as it provides spectacular views of not only the ice field but of Exit Glacier and the valley below. The upper section of the route is snow covered for much of the year. A ranger-led hike to the ice field departs the ranger station on Saturdays at 10 am. Bring a lunch and good boots if you plan to join in.

Kayaking

Blue-water paddles out of Resurrection Bay along the coastline of the park are challenges for experienced kayakers only, but they reward those who undertake such an adventure with daily wildlife encounters and close-up views of the glaciers from a unique perspective. *Alaska Treks & Voyages* (tel 224-3960) rent out both rigid and inflatable kayaks from the Small Boat Harbor in Seward; singles are $30 a day and doubles $60. The guide company also runs a 10 day trip along the park's coastline or overnight and weekend tours.

One way to get around the guide company's fee, for those experienced at kayaking but unsure about the Gulf of Alaska, is to be dropped off and picked up in one of the many protected fjords. Contact the National Park Service for information on such bays, and then make arrangements with Alaska Treks & Voyages for transport out to the area.

Getting There & Around

Most of the park and all but one of its 36 named glaciers are inaccessible to visitors except through expensive sightseeing flights or on charter boats. The lone exception is Exit Glacier, which can be reached by a 10 mile (16 km) gravel road. The road leaves the Seward Highway at *Mile 3.7* (6 km) on a well-posted junction and winds back almost 8 miles (12.8 km) to a bridge and parking area where the trailhead for the Resurrection River Trail is located.

In 1985, the footbridge over the river was replaced by a vehicle bridge and the road was extended another 2 miles (3.2 km) to the ranger station and visitor centre near the glacier. From the ranger station, a 0.5 mile (0.8 km) nature trail leads to Exit Glacier and you can actually touch the dense, blue-tinged glacial ice and view ice towers that loom 150 feet (46 metres) above you.

The rangers schedule a variety of activities during the summer, most of them on Saturday and Sunday, that include campfire talks, walks to the glacier and all-day hikes to the Harding Ice Field. There is also a walk-in campground (10 sites, free) just after crossing the bridge.

Tours For the best view of the Harding Ice

Field and the glaciers it fans out of, contact Harbour Air (tel 224-3133) in Seward about their daily sightseeing flights. The other approach is to view the park's rugged coastline and tidewater glaciers on a tour boat.

Kenai Fjords Tours (tel 224-8068) runs an 8 hour tour of the park with boats departing at 8 am daily. The fare is $70 per person and tickets may be purchased at their office on the boardwalk in Seward's Small Boat Harbor. Quest Tours (tel 224-3025) offer a similar tour for the same price. Despite the oil spill, this cruise rates right up there with those to College Fjord and Glacier Bay. One of these three trips into the world of ice and marine wildlife is a must during any stay in Alaska.

If there is a group of you Trails North (tel 224-3587) will arrange a charter van to take you out to Exit Glacier from Seward. The cost is $77 for 2 hours and the van holds up to 14 passengers.

HOPE HIGHWAY

This paved road leads almost 18 miles (28.8 km) north to the historical community of **Hope** and the northern trailhead for the Resurrection Pass Trail. Hope experienced a minor stampede in 1896 when news of a gold strike bought over 3000 prospectors to the cluster of cabins and to nearby Sunrise, a tent city. Within a few years the majority had left to look for gold elsewhere and today Hope is a small village with a summer population of 225. Nothing remains of Sunrise.

Even if you are not planning to hike the Resurrection Pass Trail, Hope is a great side trip; the town is tucked away in a very scenic area and lets you step back in time. Hitchhiking is not hard, but plan on 2 to 3 days for this trip rather than a rushed overnight stop.

At *Mile 16* (25.6 km) of the Hope Highway is the junction to Palmer Creek and Resurrection Creek roads. Turn left (south) onto Resurrection Creek Rd and in 0.7 miles (1.1 km) Palmer Creek Rd branches to the left. Near the junction is the unattended Hope Airstrip. Four miles (6.4 km) down Resurrection Creek Rd is the northern trailhead of the Resurrection Pass Trail.

Palmer Creek Rd is a scenic drive that leads 7 miles (11.2 km) to the USFS *Coeur d'Alene Campground* (six sites, free use). Beyond the campground, the road is not maintained but leads another 5 miles (8 km) to alpine country above 1500 feet (457 metres) and ends at the ruins of the abandoned Swetmann mining camp. From the old mining buildings it is easy to scramble through the tundra to several small alpine lakes.

Hope

To reach Hope town centre, turn right on Hope Rd at *Mile 16.5* (26.6 km) of Hope Highway. Hope Rd leads to the waterfront and passes many of the town's historical buildings and abandoned log structures that have become favourites among photographers.

Places to Stay & Eat Hope has a post office, general store, laundromat and a couple of lodges and cafes. Within town, there is *Henry's One Stop* (tel 782-3222) on Hope Rd where you can get a meal, a beer, a shower or even a room. Just before entering the old mining community, you pass *Bear Creek Lodge* (tel 782-3141) where it is possible to rent restored hand-hewn log cabins along the creek. Rates begin from $50 a night for a cabin but the lodge is a scenic resort in the woods with a small restaurant, a scattering of cabins and even a replica of an old log cache.

Camping sites abound all around Hope but the USFS maintains the *Porcupine Campground* (24 sites, $5 fee), 1.3 miles (2 km) beyond Hope at the end of Hope Highway. Near the campground is *Davidson Enterprises*, a general store that sells groceries, gasoline and liquor.

Gold Panning

There are about 125 mining claims throughout the Chugach National Forest but most of today's prospectors are recreational miners out there for the fun, searching their pans or sluice box for a little colour. Some of the more serious ones actually make money from their time spent along the creeks, but

Top: Cruise ship in Prince William Sound (AVB)
Bottom: Alaska Highway (CAT)

Top: Nugget Pond at Camp Denali with Mt McKinley behind (CD)
Bottom: Horned Puffins, Kenai Fjords National Park (NPS)

most are happy to take home a bottle with a few flakes in it.

The Hope area provides numerous opportunities for the amateur panner, including a 20 acre (8 hectare) claim that the USFS has set aside near the Resurrection Pass trailhead for recreational mining. There are usually some regulars out there who don't mind showing newcomers how to swirl the pan. Other panning areas include Sixmile Creek between *Mile 1.5* (2.4 km) and *Mile 5.5* (8.8 km) of Hope Highway, and many of the creeks along the Resurrection Pass Trail.

Panning Technique The only piece of equipment that is absolutely necessary is a gravity-trap pan, one that measures 10 to 20 inches (25 to 50 cm) across and can usually be bought at any good Alaskan hardware or general store. Those who have panned for a while also show up with rubber boots and gloves to protect hands and feet from icy waters, a garden trowel to dig up loose rock, a pair of tweezers to pick up gold flakes and a small bottle to hold their find.

Panning techniques are based on the notion that gold is heavier than the gravel it lies in. Fill your pan with loose material from cracks and crevices in streams or around large boulders where gold might have washed down and become lodged. Add water to the pan and rinse and discard larger rocks, keeping the rinsing in the pan. Continue to shake the contents towards the bottom by swirling the pan in a circular motion and wash off the excess sand and gravel by dipping the front into the stream.

You should be left with heavy black mud, sand, and if you are lucky, a few flakes of gold. Use tweezers or your fingernail to transfer the flakes into a bottle filled with water.

Hiking

Gull Rock Trail From Porcupine Campground there are two fine trails to scenic points overlooking the Turnagain Arm. The first is an easy 5.1 mile (8.3 km) walk to Gull Rock, a rocky point 140 feet (43 metres) above the Turnagain shoreline. The trail

follows an old wagon road built at the turn of the century, and along the way there are the remains of a cabin and a sawmill to explore. You also view Turnagain Arm most of the time and even Mt McKinley on a clear day during this extremely scenic trek. The round trip to Gull Rock takes 4 to 6 hours.

Hope Point This is not a trail but more of a route that follows an alpine ridge for incredible views of Turnagain Arm. Begin at the entrance sign to Porcupine Campground and follow an unmarked trail along the right-hand side of the small Porcupine Creek. After 0.3 mile (0.5 km), the trail leaves the side of the creek and begins to ascend a bluff to the right, reaching an outcropping with good views of Turnagain Arm in 45 minutes or so. From here, you can follow the ridge above the tree line to Hope Point, elevation 3708 feet (1131 metres). Other than an early summer snowfield, there is no water after Porcupine Creek.

STERLING HIGHWAY TO KENAI

It is only 58 miles (93 km) from Tern Lake Junction to Soldotna along the Sterling Highway, not much more than a 1 hour drive. Yet the stretch contains so many hiking, camping and canoeing opportunities that it would take you a month to enjoy them all. Surrounded by the Chugach National Forest and Kenai National Wildlife Refuge, Sterling Highway and its side roads pass a dozen trails, 20 campgrounds and an almost endless number of lakes, rivers and streams in which to fish or paddle.

Do not rush through this area just to reach Kenai or Soldotna. If you are driving, make good use of your freedom to explore the handful of back roads. If you are hitchhiking, don't hesitate to give up a ride to spend a day camping or hiking somewhere. There will always be another ride once you are ready to return to the road.

Mileposts along the highway show distances from Seward, making Tern Lake Junction, the start of the Sterling Highway, *Mile 37* (59.5 km). The first campgrounds are 8 miles (12.8 km) west from the junction at *Mile 45* (72.4 km). Just past the Sunrise Motel is the Quartz Creek Rd. Follow the road south 0.3 mile (0.5 km) to the USFS *Quartz Creek Campground* (41 sites, $6 fee) on the shores of Kenai Lake or 3 miles (4.8 km) to the USFS *Crescent Creek Campground* (13 sites, $5 fee).

The **Crescent Creek Trail**, about 0.5 mile (0.8 km) beyond the Crescent Creek Campground, has a marked trailhead and leads 6.5 miles (10.4 km) to the outlet of Crescent Lake and a USFS cabin (reservations needed, $15 per night). The trail is an easy walk and beautiful in September during the autumn colours; from the cabin there is access to the high country. Anglers can fish for arctic grayling in the lake during the summer and autumn. Make cabin reservations at the Chugach National Forest office (tel 271-2500) in Anchorage. At the east end of the lake is the Carter Lake Trail to Seward Highway, but no path connects the two trails.

Another 0.5 mile (0.8 km) west on Sterling Highway is a large lookout and observation point for Dall sheep in the Kenai Mountains and mountain goats in the Cecil Rhode Mountains directly across Kenai Lake. Displays explain the life cycle of the animals. The Kenai River Bridge is at *Mile 47.8* (77 km) and immediately after it is Snug Harbor Rd, which leads south 12 miles (19.3 km) to Cooper Lake and the eastern trailhead

to the Russian Lakes Trail (see the Trekking section in the Wilderness chapter).

The Kenai River parallels the highway for the next 10 miles (16 km) where several gravel lookouts offer good views. At *Mile 48.7* (79 km) you pass through **Cooper Landing** (pop 400). This service centre was named after Joseph Cooper, a miner who worked the area in the 1880s. A school was built here in 1929 and the first post office was established in 1937, a year before the town was connected by road to Seward.

There is now a five-building national historic district, which includes the colourful

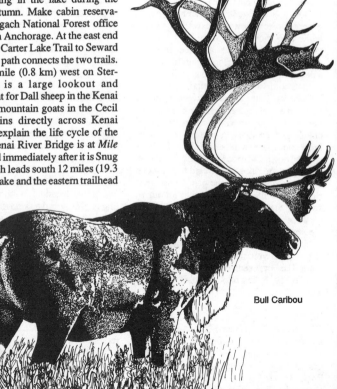

Bull Caribou

Old Copper Landing Store. But this town is best known as the starting point for half-day raft trips down the Kenai River. A number of companies run the trip, including Osprey Outfitters (tel 595-1265) and the Alaska River Co (tel 595-1226). Expect to pay about $35 for the 4 hour trip.

At *Mile 50.7* (81.6 km) of the Sterling Highway is the USFS *Cooper Creek Campground* (27 sites, $5 fee) where there are camping sites on both sides of the highway. Several of those on the north side of the highway are scenically located on the Kenai River.

The final USFS campground is at *Mile 52.8* (85 km), 16 miles (25.6 km) west of Tern Junction. The *Russian River Campground* (84 sites, $6) is a beautiful spot where the Russian and Kenai rivers merge. Both the Cooper Creek and Russian River campgrounds lie on prime red salmon spawning areas and the campsites tend to fill up by noon in late summer. The Russian River Campground is so popular that they charge you $2 just to park and fish.

One mile (1.6 km) down Russian River Campground Rd is the trailhead and parking area for the Russian Lakes Trail, while a quarter of a mile (0.4 km) west of the campground on Sterling Highway is the well-marked entrance to the Resurrection Pass Trail (see the Trekking section in the Wilderness chapter).

Once west of the Resurrection Pass trailhead, you leave Chugach National Forest, administered by the Forest Service, and enter the **Kenai National Wildlife Refuge**, managed by the US Fish & Wildlife Service. The impressive populations of Dall sheep, moose, caribou and bear found here have attracted hunters from around the world since the early 1900s. In 1941, President Roosevelt set aside 1.73 million acres (692,000 hectares) as the Kenai National Moose Range and the 1980 Alaska Lands Act increased it to almost 2 million acres (800,000 hectares).

Along with an abundance of wildlife, good fishing and great mountain scenery, the refuge offers some of the least used trails within the Kenai Peninsula. Hikers who want to spend a few days trekking here should first go the Kenai National Wildlife Refuge Visitor Station at *Mile 57.8* (93 km) of Sterling Highway or the visitor centre in Kenai and pick up a copy of the booklet *Kenai National Wildlife Refuge Hiking Trails*.

The first campground in the refuge is *Kenai-Russian River Recreational Area* (10 sites, fee) at *Mile 55* (88.5 km) of Sterling Highway. West of the confluence of these two salmon-rich rivers, this campground is heavily used from mid to late summer by anglers. A privately owned ferry carries anglers to the opposite bank of the Kenai River here, using cables and the current to propel it across the river in both directions. During the height of the salmon season a couple of hundred anglers will be lined up at 5 am to catch the first trip across the river.

The 3 mile (4.8 km) **Fuller Lake Trail** begins at *Mile 57.2* (92.1 km) of the Sterling Highway and ends at Fuller Lake just above the tree line. The trail, an old road blocked by logs, is marked. Halfway up the trail you reach Lower Fuller Lake, where you cross a stream over a beaver dam and continue over a low pass to Fuller Lake. At the lake, the trail follows the east shore and then branches; the fork to the left leads up a ridge and becomes the **Skyline Trail**. This trail is not maintained and is unmarked above the bush line. It follows a ridge for 6.5 miles (10.4 km) and descends to *Mile 61* (97.6 km) of Sterling Highway. Those who want to hike both trails should plan to stay overnight at Fuller Lake.

Just past the Fuller Lake trailhead on Sterling Highway is the **Skilak Lake Loop Rd** junction at *Mile 57.8* (93 km) and the **Kenai National Wildlife Refuge Visitor Station**. The log cabin is open daily from 10 am to 7 pm and is the source of hand-outs, maps and brochures on the refuge. The 19 mile (30.4 km) loop road, a scenic side trip to an already scenic highway, is a popular and often crowded recreational avenue. There are seven USFS campgrounds along the road and all are free and well marked. The campgrounds from east to west are:

Campground	No of Sites	Location
Jim's Landing	5	near the junction
Hidden Lake	40	*Mile 3.6* (5.8 km)
Upper Skilak Lake	10	*Mile 8.4* (13.5)
Lower Ohmer	4	*Mile 8.6* (13.8 km)
Engineer Lake	8	*Mile 9.7* (15.6 km)
Lower Skilak Lake	14	*Mile 14* (22.5 km)
Bottinentnin Lake	3	*Mile 19* (30.6 km)

The **Kenai River Trail**, 0.6 mile (0.9 km) past the visitor station on the Skilak Lake Loop Rd, winds 6.3 miles (10 km) to Skilak Lake and then turns into the **Hidden Creek Loop**. The 1.4 mile (2.2 km) loop trail curves back to its beginning at *Mile 4.6* of Skilak Lake Loop Rd. Both trails are easy walks along level terrain.

The **Skilak Lookout Trail** begins at *Mile 5.5* (8.8 km) of Skilak Lake Rd and ascends 2.6 miles (4.1 km) to a knob at 1450 feet (442 metres) that offers a panoramic view of the surrounding mountains and lakes. Plan on 4 to 5 hours for the round trip and bring water as there is none on the trail.

The **Seven Lakes Trail**, a 5 mile (8 km) hike to the Sterling Highway, begins at *Mile 9.7* (15.6) of Skilak Lake Loop Rd, at the spur to Engineer Lake. The trail is easy walking over level terrain and passes Hidden and Hikers lakes before ending at *Kelly Lake Campground* on a side road off Sterling Highway. There is fair to good fishing in Kelly and Engineer lakes.

If you choose to stay on the Sterling Highway past the Skilak Lake Rd junction, you pass the small *Jenny Lake Campground* at *Mile 60* (96 km) and a side road at *Mile 69* (110.4 km) that leads south to the *Peterson Lake Campground* (three sites, free) and *Kelly Lake Campground* (three sites, free) near one end of the Seven Lakes Trail. The west junction with Skilak Lake Rd is at *Mile 75.3* (121.2 km) of the Sterling Highway.

At *Mile 81* (130.3 km) of Sterling Highway you arrive in the small town of **Sterling** (pop 2800). Sterling meets the usual travellers' needs with restaurants, lodges, gas stations and grocery stores. Check out *Moose River Bed & Breakfast* (tel 262-5670), 0.5 mile (0.8 km) past town, for

everybody's vision of typical Alaskan accommodation – log cabins and a lodge on the banks of a river.

Also beyond the town is the *Izaak Walton Recreation Site* (17 sites, $5 fee) at the confluence of the Kenai and Moose rivers. A display explains the nearby archaeological site where excavations suggest that the area was used by Eskimos 2000 years ago. The recreational area is heavily used all summer, as anglers swarm here for the salmon runs, while paddlers end their Swan Lake canoe trip at the Moose River Bridge. Canoe rentals and transport are available at the bridge for the Swan Lake and Swanson River canoe trails (see the Paddling section in the Wilderness chapter).

At *Mile 85* (136 km) of the Sterling Highway, Swanson River Rd turns north for 18 miles (29 km), with Swan Lake Rd heading east for 3 miles (4.8 km) at the end of it. The roads are accesses to the Swanson River and Swan Lake canoe routes and three campgrounds: *Dolly Varden Lake Campground* (15 sites, free) 14 miles (22 km) up Swanson River Rd; the *Rainbow Lake Campground* (three sites, free) another 2 miles (3.2 km) beyond; and the *Swanson River Campground* (eight sites, free) at the very end of the road. Even without a canoe, this is a good area to spend a day or two as there are trails to many of the lakes which offer superb fishing.

Across Sterling Highway from Swanson River Rd is the entrance to Scout Lake Loop Rd, where the *Scout Lake Campground* (14 sites, free) is located. The **Alaska Division of Parks Office** (tel 262-5581), also off Scout Lake Loop Rd, has hand-outs, displays and information on the remote Kachemak Bay State Park to the south.

KENAI

Kenai (pop 6000) is the second-oldest permanent settlement in Alaska as it was established by Russian fur traders in 1791. It offers good views of the active volcanoes across the inlet and a little Russian history and colour that often get lost in the town's

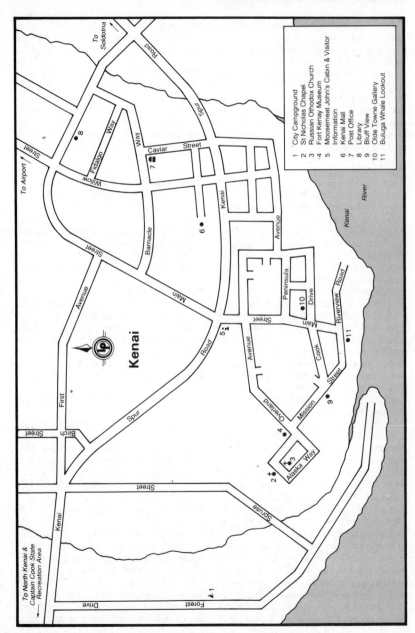

massive oil industry. It doesn't, however, have the charm of Seward or Homer.

The town is at the mouth of the Kenai River on Cook Inlet, where you can view Mt Redoubt to the south-west, the volcano that erupted stream and ash in December 1989, Mt Iliamna at the head of the Aleutian Range and the Alaska Range to the north-west. You reach the heart of the city by going north on Kenai Spur Rd at *Mile 94.2* (151.6 km) of Sterling Highway.

Information
Kenai Spur Rd leads to Moosemeat John's Cabin at the corner of Main St, which is the Kenai Visitor Center. Built in the 1920s, the cabin was moved to its present location in 1976 and is the source of hand-outs and maps on the Kenai area. It is open Monday to Friday from 9 am to 5 pm and Saturday from 10 am to 4 pm.

Things to See
From the visitor centre, follow Overland Ave to **Fort Kenay**, two blocks west towards Cook Inlet. Inside the fort is the **Kenai Historical Museum** with a collection of artefacts dating back to the town's Russian origins and its gold-mining days. Around the fort (constructed as part of the Alaska Centennial in 1967) are several old homes moved there for restoration. The fort and museum are open Monday to Saturday from 10 am to 5 pm; donations are accepted.

Across Mission St from the fort is the **Russian Orthodox Church**, built in 1896 and today the oldest Orthodox church in Alaska. West of the church is the blue-domed **St Nicholas Chapel**, built in 1906 on the burial site of Father Igumen Nicolai, Kenai's first resident priest. There are no regularly scheduled tours of either building but both are a photographer's delight.

Head south-east on Mission St and you will be travelling along **The Bluff**, a good vantage point from which to view the mouth of the Kenai River or the mountainous terrain on the west side of Cook Inlet. At the corner of Main and Mission streets is the **Beluga Whale Lookout**. From here it is possible to

see groups of white whales in the late spring and early summer as they ride the incoming tides into the Kenai River to feed on salmon.

Places to Stay & Eat
Hotels in Kenai are expensive and tend to be filled during the king salmon runs in June and July; most rooms cost from $50 a night for a single. Either plan on camping in this area or head south-east to Soldotna where there is more competition among motels and thus slightly lower rates.

To camp within Kenai, the *City Campground* (30 sites, free) is in a pleasant wooded area near the bluffs overlooking Cook Inlet. The campground is within walking distance of town; you follow Kenai Spur Rd through the city centre and then turn left (south) on Forest Drive. For cheap food, there's *Kentucky Fried Chicken* at the Kenai Mall on Kenai Spur Rd in the centre of town.

Getting There & Away
Intercity Bus Lines has a connecting van from a bus on the Sterling Highway that arrives at from 12.30 pm Sunday to Friday at the Uptown Motel (tel 283-3660) on Spur View Drive. Call the hotel about transport onto Homer or Anchorage. The one-way fare from Anchorage to Kenai is $27.50.

CAPTAIN COOK STATE RECREATION AREA
By following the Kenai Spur Rd north for 36 miles (57.6 km), you will reach this uncrowded state recreation area that encompasses 4000 acres (1600 hectares) of forests, lakes, rivers and beaches along Cook Inlet. The area offers swimming, camping and the beauty of Cook Inlet in a setting that is unaffected by the stampede for salmon to the south.

Kenai Spur Rd ends in the park after first passing Stormy Lake, where there is a bathhouse and a swimming area along the water's edge. Also within the park is the *Bishop Creek Campground* (12 sites, $5) and the *Discovery Campground* (57 sites, $5). Both camping areas are on the bluff overlooking the Cook Inlet where some of the world's greatest tides can be seen ebbing and flowing.

The best hiking in the park is along the saltwater beach, but don't let the high tides catch you off guard. Those paddling the Swanson River Canoe Route (see the Paddling section in the Wilderness chapter) will find the park an appropriate place to end the trip.

SOLDOTNA

Soldotna (pop 3000) is strictly a service centre at the junction of the Sterling Highway and Kenai Spur Rd. The town was born when both roads were completed in the 1940s. Today, it is little more than a hub for the anglers and guides who work the Kenai River in hope of catching an 80 lb plus (36 kg plus) king salmon. The Alaska Department of Fish & Game report the Kenai River to be the most heavily fished stream in the state, as hundreds of thousands of anglers

flood the area annually and congest the waterway with powerboats.

Information

Information on the town can be obtained at the Soldotna Visitor Center (tel 262-9814) in the town centre on the Sterling Highway, just south of the Kenai River Bridge. The impressive centre is built in a wooded setting along the banks of the river and outside there is a series of steps and landings that lead down to the water.

How important is sport fishing to this town? If you're unsure, go inside the visitor centre where among the stuffed and mounted animals is a 94 lb (42.3 kg) king salmon that was caught in 1987 and is the fifth largest sport-caught salmon in the world. You can picnic on the decks, fish in the river or gather information on the surrounding area at the centre; it is open from 9 am to 6 pm daily during the summer.

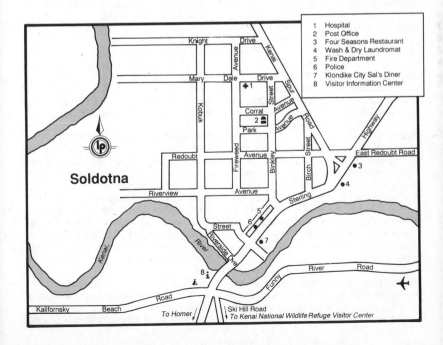

1	Hospital
2	Post Office
3	Four Seasons Restaurant
4	Wash & Dry Laundromat
5	Fire Department
6	Police
7	Klondike City Sal's Diner
8	Visitor Information Center

Opposite the Kalifornsky Beach Rd near the Kenai River is the junction to Funny River Rd. Turn left (east) here and turn right (south) immediately onto Ski Hill Rd, following it for 1 mile (1.6 km) to reach the Kenai National Wildlife Refuge Visitor Center (tel 262-7021). Open from 8 am to 4.30 pm weekdays and from 10 am to 6 pm weekends, the centre features a good series of wildlife displays, daily slide shows in its theatre and naturalist-led outdoor programmes on the weekends. There are also three short trails (maps available) that begin at the visitor centre and wind into the nearby woods and lakes.

Things to See & Do

The most interesting thing to do in Soldotna is to drive onto Kalifornsky Beach Rd just after passing the bridge over the Kenai River. The road heads north at first and passes Centennial Park Campground and then the Kenai campus of the **University of Alaska**. The **Damon Memorial Museum**, a log cabin with a small collection of artefacts, is 1.5 miles (2.4 km) past the university.

Eventually the road heads west, then south after passing a junction to Kenai. It continues south for 16 miles (26 km) along the Cook Inlet and offers some splendid views on the waterway and the Alaska Range before rejoining Sterling Highway at the small settlement of Kasilof.

Places to Stay

Camping There is the *Centennial Park Campground* (108 sites, $6 per night) at the corner of Sterling Highway and Kalifornsky Beach Rd (near the visitor centre) and the *Swiftwater Park Campground* (20 sites, $6) on East Redoubt Ave at *Mile 94* (151.2 km) of the Sterling Highway. Both are on the Kenai River which means from late June to mid-August you better be there before noon to stake out a site.

Youth Hostel Unfortunately, Soldotna is the site of another youth hostel that closed recently. Check at the visitor centre to see if it has been resurrected.

Hotels Most of hotels are geared up for campervaners and anglers and are lined up along Sterling Highway and Kenai Spur Rd – take your pick. The *Riverside Inn* (tel 262-4451) has rooms from $50 which seems to be the competitive rate here. You might do better with a B&B, contact the visitor center for the latest list as they change with the seasons.

Places to Eat

Fast (and cheap) restaurants include *Dairy Queen* on the corner of Kenai Spur Rd and Sterling Highway, which serves hamburgers, and Alaska's latest *McDonald's* 0.5 mile (0.8 km) down the Sterling Highway. *Sal's Klondike Diner* on the Sterling Highway in the city centre is open 24 hours for a breakfast that costs $5 for two eggs, toast and potatoes. For something to savour between bites, try the *Four Seasons* (tel 262-5006) at 43960 Sterling Highway. The restaurant has a variety of seafood, home-made desserts and a Sunday breakfast buffet for $6.95 that is served from 9 am to 1 pm.

Getting There & Away

Intercity Bus Lines stops at Sal's Diner in Klondike City along the Sterling Highway in the town centre from Sunday to Friday at noon. You can then pick up a bus heading south to Homer ($10) or make arrangements for transport to Anchorage ($27.50).

STERLING HIGHWAY TO HOMER

From Soldotna, the Sterling Highway rambles south, hugging the coastline and opening up to grand views of Cook Inlet every so often. This stretch is 78 miles (126 km) long and passes through a handful of small villages near some great clamming areas, ending at the charming village of Homer. Take your time in this area; the coastline and Homer are worth every day you decide to spend here.

Kasilof

Kasilof, a fishing village (pop 1200), is at *Mile 108.8* (175 km) of Sterling Highway. Turn west on Kalifornsky Beach Rd and travel 3.6 miles (5.8 km) to reach the Small Boat Harbor on the Kasilof River, the heart of the town. Sterling Highway crosses a bridge over the Kasilof River 1 mile (1.6 km) south of the Kalifornsky Beach Rd turn-off. On the other side of the bridge is the *Kasilof River State Wayside* (11 sites, $5 fee) on the riverbank. At *Mile 111.5* (179.4 km) of the Sterling Highway, the Coho Loop Rd heads north-west towards the ocean, and the Tustumena Lake Access Rd heads southeast.

Just east on the Tustumena Lake Access Rd from the Sterling Highway is the **Kasilof Incubation Facility**, a state-owned salmon hatchery open to the public from 8 am to 4.30 pm daily. The hatchery handles silver and king salmon and steelhead trout. If you're here at the right week in July you can watch the 'egg take' (biologists removing eggs from female kings). Another 0.3 mile (0.5 km) down the access road is the *Johnson Lake Recreation Area* (43 campsites, $5 fee) with entry into the lake which has rainbow trout. At the end of the 7 mile (11.2 km) access road is the *Tustumena Lake Campground* (10 sites, $5 fee), which really lies on the Kasilof River, 1 mile (1.6 km) from the large Tustumena Lake.

Clam Gulch

At *Mile 117.4* (188.9 km) of Sterling Highway, before reaching the hamlet of Clam Gulch (pop 120), you pass the junction of a 2 mile (3.2 km) gravel road. Just west on the road is *Clam Gulch State Recreation Area* which has covered picnic tables, outhouses and a campground (116 sites, $5 fee). More importantly, the road provides access to the beaches along the Cook Inlet and the start of the area's great clam digging. The village of Clam Gulch is less than a mile (1.6 km) south of the gravel road on Sterling Highway and has a post office, gasoline station and lodge.

Clam Digging Almost all of the beaches on the west side of the Kenai Peninsula have a good supply of razor clams, considered by locals to be a true delicacy from the sea. You

first have to purchase a sport-fishing licence (a 1 day visitor's licence is $5, and a 10 day licence is $15), then obtain a shovel and a large bucket to carry your bag limit of 60 clams.

There is good clamming from April to August, though the best time is July, right before spawning. Wait for the tide to drop at least 1 foot (30 cm) from the high water mark, or better still to its lower levels 4 to 5 feet (1.5 metres) down. Look for the clam's footprint in the sand, a dimple mark left behind when it withdraws its neck. Shovel a scoop or two next to the mark and then reach in the sand for the clam. You have to be quick, since a razor clam can bury itself and be gone in seconds.

The best way to cook clams is right on the beach over an open fire while soaking in the mountain scenery across Cook Inlet. Use a large covered pot and steam them in salt water or, better still, in white wine with a clove of garlic. For those who want their clams without the fuss, the *Clam Shell Lodge* (tel 262-4211) at *Mile 118.3* (193 km) of the Sterling Highway sells clam chowder and clam dinners in its restaurant. They even arrange clamming charters.

Ninilchik

Ninilchik has a camping area and good clamming beach. Sandwiched around the town at *Mile 134.4* (216.3 km) of the Sterling Highway is the Ninilchik State Recreation Area which includes three campgrounds, a day-use area and access to the clamming beaches. North of the Ninilchik River is the *Ninilchik Campground* (43 sites, $5 fee) while the most scenic camping is south of the bridge.

Head west on Ninilchik Beach Access Rd to reach the day-use area which has a trail to the river. Further along the access road are two undeveloped campgrounds (100 sites, $5 fee) adjacent to the clamming beds. Back on Sterling Highway, just south of the beach access road, is the *Ninilchik View Campground* (13 sites, $5 fee) which has campsites on a bluff. A stairway leads down the bluff to the beach, the river and the village of Ninilchik.

Before crossing the bridge over the Ninilchik River, you pass Coal St. The short access road leads to the town's **Russian Orthodox Church** which was built in 1901. The historic church, topped with the unique spires and crosses of the Russian Orthodox faith, is on a wide bluff and commands an unbelievable view of Cook Inlet and the smoking volcanoes on the other side. Historic signs along the beach access road south of the bridge point the way to **Old Ninilchik Village**, which includes several log buildings and a trail up to the church.

Present-day Ninilchik (pop 450) is 0.5 mile (0.8 km) further south on the Sterling Highway at *Mile 135.5* (218 km). It was moved after the Good Friday Earthquake sank the original town 3 feet (1 metre). The Kenai Peninsula State Fair, the 'biggest little fair in Alaska' is held annually in town at the end of August.

At *Mile 137.2* (221 km) of Sterling Highway is the *Deep Creek State Recreation Area* (300 undeveloped campsites) on the beach near the mouth of the creek. It is used for beach camping, surf fishing and clamming. Further on is the *Stariski Creek State Recreation Site* (12 campsites, $5 fee) on a bluff overlooking Cook Inlet at *Mile 152* (244.4 km) of Sterling Highway.

Anchor Point

The town of Anchor Point (pop 1500) is another 5 miles (8 km) south on the highway and a monument here notes that this is 'the most westerly point on the North American continent accessible by a continuous road system'. Anchor Point is a fishing hot spot during the summer. Within town are gasoline stations, a post office, grocery stores and the *Anchor River Inn* (tel 235-8531), which has single rooms from $36. Next to the inn is the visitor centre, which is staffed by volunteers and open from 10 am to 4 pm weekdays during the summer.

Anchor River Rd, which begins behind the Anchor River Inn, leads to the Anchor

River State Recreation Area. Entrance into the state area is by a beach access road on the south side of Anchor River which leads past five campgrounds ($5 fee). The last one, *Halibut Campground*, has 30 sites and is near Cook Inlet. The road ends at a beautiful stretch of beach with good views of Mt Redoubt and Mt Iliamna across the inlet and interesting tidal pools to explore.

Anchor River is renowned for its salmon, steelhead and Dolly Varden fishing. If you're packing along your rod and reel, make sure you pick up an Anchor River State Recreation Area brochure which lists the seasons and even shows the favourite fishing holes along the river.

The Old Sterling Highway continues south in the state recreation area and rejoins the new highway at *Mile 164.8* (265.3 km). From Anchor Point, Sterling Highway ascends the bluffs overlooking Homer and Kachemak Bay, about 5 miles (8 km) from Homer. If you are driving, take this section slowly as there are some great viewing points that will be missed by the hasty. One of the best is 3.2 miles (5.1 km) north of Homer.

HOMER

Arriving in Homer (pop 3600) is like opening one of those pop-up greeting cards – it's an unexpected thrill. A couple of miles before town, the Sterling Highway provides a few teasers that whet your appetite but never fully prepare you for the charming, colourful fishing village that lies ahead. As the road makes a final turn east along the bluffs, Homer unfolds completely. It's an incredible panorama of mountains, white peaks, glaciers, and the beautiful Kachemak Bay into which stretches Homer Spit, a long strip of land.

The community is supported by its fishing industries and the influx of tourists that arrive each summer. It's recognised around the state as the arts capital of Southcentral Alaska because of the large number of artists and galleries in the area. It is little wonder that they choose Homer; the scenery is inspiring and the climate exceptionally mild.

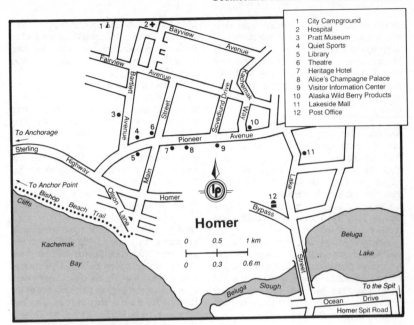

1 City Campground
2 Hospital
3 Pratt Museum
4 Quiet Sports
5 Library
6 Theatre
7 Heritage Hotel
8 Alice's Champagne Palace
9 Visitor Information Center
10 Alaska Wild Berry Products
11 Lakeside Mall
12 Post Office

Homer is protected from the severe northern cold by the Kenai Mountains to the north and east. Summer temperatures rarely go above 70°F (21°C) nor fall much below 0°F (-17.8°C) in winter. Annual rainfall is only 28 inches (710 mm), much of it snow.

It may be an artist colony in Alaska, but around the USA, Homer is best known as the home of Tom Bodett. The humorist grew up in the US state of Michigan, attended Michigan State University for awhile and somehow ended up living in Homer. He is famous for his *End of the Road* radio show, his best selling book of the same title but mostly for his Motel 6 ads and its closing line 'and we'll leave the light on for ya'. The radio show is broadcast from Homer and between Bodett's fame and the natural beauty of the area, the town has rapidly developed in the 1980s from a quaint fishing village to a major tourist destination complete with tour buses arriving almost daily from Anchorage.

Information

Information, hand-outs and maps on the Homer area can be obtained from the Homer Visitor Center (tel 235-7740) in the small log cabin on Pioneer Ave diagonally opposite Alaska Wild Berry Products. The centre is open daily in the summer from 10 am to 6 pm.

On West Pioneer Ave is the main office of the Alaska Maritime National Wildlife Refuge, which features information, maps and exhibits on the wildlife in its preserve. The centre is open from 8 am to 5 pm weekdays.

Things to See

West from the Homer Visitor Center on Pioneer Ave and north on Bartlett St is the **Pratt Museum** (tel 235-8635), which features Eskimo and Indian artefacts, historical displays and exhibits on marine life in Kachemak Bay. By far the most intriguing aspect of the museum are the aquariums which house octopuses, sea anemones and other marine life. The museum is open daily in the summer from 10 am to 5 pm and charges $3 for admission. Films on Alaska are shown from June to August on Thursdays at 7 pm; call the museum for programme details.

Art Galleries The beautiful scenery has inspired numerous artists to gather here, and the handful of galleries in town display more than the usual ivory carvings and gold nugget jewellery you see everywhere else. The oldest gallery is the 8 x 10 Studio in a log cabin at 581 Pioneer Ave. The gallery houses Toby Tyler's oil, water colour and pastel works of local scenery.

A few doors down Pioneer Ave is Ptarmigan Arts, which features a variety of works from more than 40 artists in the area. A few of the galleries even have workshops in the back. The Pratt Museum also has an art gallery that exhibits work by artists from around the Kenai Peninsula.

The Spit This long needle of land is a 5 mile (8 km) sand bar which stretches into Kachemak Bay; during the summer it is the centre of activity in Homer and the heart of its fishing industry. It draws thousands of tourists and backpackers every year, making the spit not only a scenic spot but an interesting mecca of fishers, cannery workers, visitors and charter-boat operators.

The hub of all this activity is the Small Boat Harbor at the end of the spit, one of the best facilities in Southcentral and home base for over 700 boats. On each side of the harbour's entrance is a cannery. Nearby are rows of gray Cape Cod buildings that house charter-boat operators, a small visitor centre, gift shops and a couple of eateries, all connected by wooden sidewalks.

The favourite activity on the Homer Spit, naturally, is beachcombing, especially at dawn or dusk while viewing the sunset or sunrise. You can stroll for miles along the beach, where the marine life is as plentiful as the driftwood, or you can go clamming at

Mud Bay, on the east side of the spit. Blue mussels, an excellent shellfish overlooked by many people, are the most abundant. Locals call the clams and mussels 'Homer grown'.

Another popular activity on the spit is a shrimp, clam or crab boil. Grab your camp stove and large metal pot, purchase some fresh seafood from the Icicle Seafood Market across from the campground and buy a can of beer from Homer Liquor & Wine at the end of the spit. Then head down to the beach and enjoy your Alaskan feast while watching the tide roll in and the sun set. No beach fires are allowed between Land's End and the Whitney Fidalgo Access Rd.

Skyline Drive North of town are bluffs, referred to by locals as 'the Hill', that rise gently to 1100 feet (335 metres). These green slopes, broken up by colourful patches of wildflowers, provide excellent views on a clear day of the glaciers that spill out of the Harding Ice Field across the bay. The best views are from Skyline Drive, which runs along the bluff above Homer.

Follow Pioneer Ave east out of town where it turns into East End Rd and then turn north onto East Hill Rd up the bluffs to Skyline Drive. At the west end of Skyline Drive is Ohlson Mountain Rd which ascends 1513 feet (454 metres) to the peak of Ohlson Mountain. Many roads, including East End Rd, are paved and ideal for cycling (see the Homer Getting There & Around section).

Kachemak Bay This beautiful body of water extends 30 miles (48 km) into the Kenai Peninsula and features a coastline of steep fjords and inlets with the glacier-capped peaks of the Kenai Mountains in the background. Marine and bird life are plentiful in the bay, but it is best known for its rich fishing grounds, especially halibut. Over 20 charter fishing boats operate out of the Small Boat Harbour and charge from $80 to $125 for a day of fishing.

For those who have no desire to hook an 80 lb (36 kg) halibut but still want to see the bay, there is the Gull Island trip offered by

Rainbow Tours (tel 235-7272). The 1½ hour tour departs daily at 9 am, noon and 4 pm from Homer Spit and cruises across the bay to view the Gull Island bird rookery, which includes puffins among the nine nesting species. The fare is $20 per person.

Another interesting cruise is to Halibut Cove, a small village of 50 people on the south shore of Kachemak Bay. In the early 1920s, the cove supported 42 herring salteries and a population of more than a 1000. Today, the quaint community has a pair of art galleries that produce 'octopus ink paintings', the noted Saltry Restaurant, some cabins for rent and boardwalks to stroll.

Kachemak Bay Ferry Tours run the *Danny J* out to the artist colony at 1 and 5 pm, returning at 4 and 9 pm; the return fare is $40. You can make arrangements for tickets or reserve a table on the deck of the *Saltry Restaurant* by contacting Central Charters (tel 235-7847) in Homer. For accommodation at the *Halibut Cove Cabins*, which offer a pair of cosy cabins that sleep four (bring your own sleeping bags), call Halibut Cove Experiences (tel 235-8110), a community information office on the Homer Spit.

Festivals
Summer events in Homer begin in May with the almost month-long Spring Arts Festival. This event began as an outlet for local artists to display their work and has since evolved into a festival with dancers, musicians and craftspeople.

The Fourth of July celebration is usually a 3 day event that includes a parade, a foot race, various local contests such as a grease-pole climb, and art & craft booths.

Places to Stay
Camping Beach camping is allowed along the entire west side of Homer Spit, a beautiful spot to pitch a tent. The nightly fee is $4 if you are pitching your tent in the city-controlled sections near the end of the spit; there are toilets next to the Harbormaster's office, the place to check in.

The *City Campground* is on a hill overlooking the town and can be reached by

Puffin

following the signs north up Bartlett Ave. There is a $4 nightly fee at the City Campground, and a 14 day limit applies at both campgrounds. You can take a shower ($2.50) and wash your clothes at the same time in Washboard Laundromat on Ocean Drive.

Bed & Breakfast Bed & breakfast places have popped up in Homer like mushrooms in the spring. At last count there were more than a dozen. Some interesting ones include the *Seaside Farm Bed & Breakfast* (tel 235-7850) whose cabins provide beach access; doubles are $40 per night. *Homer Bed & Breakfast* (tel 235-8996), 2 miles (3.2 km) up East Hill Rd, overlooks Kachemak Bay and features an outdoor sauna; rooms cost $45 to $60. *Beach House Bed & Breakfast* (tel 235-5945) also has good views of the bay and a jacuzzi.

Hotels There are seven hotels in the area but most single rooms cost from $50 to $60. All hotels are heavily booked during the summer. At the *Driftwood Inn* (tel 235-8019) on the corner of Olson Lane and Bunnell Ave near Bishop Beach, there are some single rooms without bath for $28; rates climb to

$65 from there. The *Heritage Hotel* (tel 235-7787), the historic log hotel in the middle of Pioneer Ave, has three-person rooms without bath for $58.

Places to Eat

At the end of the spit you'll find a couple of fast-food places: *Addies's Big Paddies*, which serves local halibut, seafood chowder and hamburgers; and *Casa di Pizza* where you can get a beer and a slice of pizza and still have enough money left for the ferry out of town. There is also the *Land's End Restaurant* at the end of the spit, a good place for breakfast with a great view, and the *Porpoise Room* which overlooks the Small Boat Harbor and has a seafood buffet nightly for $17.

In town, there is an assortment of cafes and bakeries, while on Ocean Drive, a short way from the spit, is the *Fresh Sourdough Express Bakery*. The cafe bakes breads, bagels and sourdough pizza daily as well as featuring seafood. Of course, it was inevitable that a boom town like Homer would finally get its own *McDonald's*. I wonder if Tom Bodett ever has Chicken McNuggets for lunch.

Entertainment

Homer's most famous drinking hole is on the spit. The *Salty Dawg Saloon*, a log cabin bar with a lighthouse tower over it, has the same claim to fame as Juneau's Red Dog Saloon, right down to the sawdust on the floor and an amazing collection of local artefacts (junk?) on the walls. Actually the saloon is three small log structures, including a tower that was originally a water tank, relocated here after the Good Friday Earthquake of 1964. The place is worthy of at least a look at the collection, if not a few beers while you study them. Nearby are other hang-outs for fishers. In town, on Pioneer Ave, is *Alice's Champagne Palace*, which has live music almost nightly.

Homer is also blessed with entertainment that doesn't require a bar stool. *Pier One Theatre* (tel 235-7333 or 235-7951) performs live drama and comedy in a 'come as

you are' warehouse next to the fishing lagoon on the spit. Plays are performed on Friday, Saturday and Sunday from Memorial Day (25 May) to Labor Day (7 September). In July, the theatre also has additional activities (one-act plays, readings etc). The Kenai Peninsula Symphony also gives concerts in Homer during August.

Hiking

For all its natural beauty, Homer lacks good public trails. The best hiking is along the beaches, while most trails off the road system are private paths that usually lead to somebody's homestead or cabin.

Bishop Beach Hike This hike, which begins at the southern end of Main St near Olson Ave, makes either an excellent afternoon stroll or a 10 mile (16 km) trek north of Homer. The views of Kachemak Bay and the Kenai Mountains are superb, while the marine life seen scurrying along the sand at low tide is fascinating.

Check a tide book, available from most gasoline stations or sports stores, and leave before low tide and return before high tide. High tides cover most of the sand, forcing you to scramble onto the base of the nearby cliffs. Within 2 miles (3.2 km) of Homer is a rocky spit that extends far out at low tide, and within 5 miles (8 km) from the foot of Main St is Diamond Ridge Rd off Sterling Highway, where you can hitchhike back to town.

Homer to Anchor River Bishop Beach can also be hiked all the way to Anchor River, an 8 mile (12.8 km) walk. From there you can hitchhike north through the rest of the Kenai Peninsula.

Getting There & Around

Air ERA Aviation (tel 235-5205), the contract carrier for Alaska Airlines, provides eight daily flights between Homer and Anchorage from the Homer Airport, 1.7 miles (2.7 km) east of town on Kachemak Drive. The one-way fare is $81. Homer Air (tel 235-8591) provides an air-taxi service to Seldovia.

Bus Intercity Bus Lines depart from the Heritage Hotel (tel 235-7783) from Sunday to Friday at 3.30 pm for Anchorage. The one-way fare between the two cities is $37.50.

Boat The state ferry MV *Tustumena* provides a twice-weekly service from Homer to Seldovia and Homer to Kodiak, where once a week it continues onto Seward and the rest of the Southcentral ports. The ferry terminal (tel 235-8449) is at the end of Homer Spit. The one-way fare from Homer to Seldovia is $14 and from Homer to Kodiak $42.

Rainbow Tours depart daily from the spit at 11 am to Seldovia, and return at 4 pm. The trip takes 1½ hours and the fare is $40 return or $25 one way.

Bicycle The best way to get around Homer or to tackle Skyline Drive is to rent a bicycle from Quiet Sports (tel 235-8620) at 140 West Pioneer Ave. The shop has mountain bikes for $10 (4 hours) or $15 (a full day).

KACHEMAK BAY STATE PARK
This park, along with the adjoining Kachemak Bay State Wilderness Park to the south, is 350,000 acres (142,000 hectares) of mountainous and glacial wilderness that is only accessible by bush plane or boat. Visitor facilities include primitive campsites, a seasonal ranger station at the head of Halibut Cove Lagoon and almost 20 miles (32 km) of trails. For information on the park, contact the Alaska Division of Parks & Outdoor Recreation office (tel 235-7024) at *Mile 168.5* (271 km) of Sterling Highway, 4 miles (6.4 km) north of Homer.

Hiking
Grewingk Glacier Trail The most popular hike in the park is this 3.5 mile (5.7 km), one-way trail from near *Rusty Lagoon Campground* (five sites), across the glacial outwash to superb views of Grewingk Glacier. The easy walk is over level terrain

and through stands of spruce and cottonwood. Rock cairns point the way across the open outwash.

Lagoon Trail Departing from the Grewingk Glacier trail is the 1 mile (1.6 km) Saddle Trail which leads to the trailhead for the Lagoon Trail. This 5.5 mile (9 km) route leads to the ranger station at the head of Halibut Cover Lagoon, passing the the community of Halibut Cove along the way. At one point you cut across the wet, boggy area around the mouth of Halibut Creek and then climb to the junction with Goat Rope Spur Trail at 1200 feet (360 metres). At the ranger station, more trails extend south to several lakes, Poot Peak and the Wosnesenki River.

Getting There & Around
The state park makes an excellent side trip for anybody who has a tent, a spare day and wants to escape the overflow of campervaners on Homer Spit. Rainbow Tours (tel 235-7272) provide a drop-off and pick-up service for backpackers who want to stay overnight at Glacier Spit and spend a day hiking up to the nearby glacier. Also contact Halibut Cove Experiences (tel 235-8110) for transport to other sections of the park.

You can also spend 3 or 4 days paddling the many fjords of the park, departing from Homer and making overnight stops at Glacier Spit or Halibut Cove. A strong paddler, using the tides, can reach Glacier Spit in half a day. Kayaks can be rented from Quiet Sports (tel 235-8620) on Pioneer Ave in Homer, where double kayaks cost $90 for 2 days or $190 for the week and singles are $65 for 2 days, $140 for the week.

SELDOVIA
Across Kachemak Bay from Homer and in a world of its own is Seldovia (pop 600), a small fishing village. The town is slow moving, sleepy and lives up to its nickname, 'City of Secluded Charm'. Although in recent years tour boats have made it a regular stop, the village has managed to retain much of its old Alaskan charm and can be an

Seldovia

interesting and inexpensive side trip away from Alaska's highway system.

Seldovia is one of the oldest settlements along Cook Inlet and may have been the site of the first coal mine in Alaska when the Russians began operating one in the late 1700s. They also used the town as a year-round harbour and gathered timber here to repair their ships. By the 1890s, Seldovia was an important shipping and supply centre for the region and the town boomed right into the 1920s with salmon canning, fur farming and a short-lived herring industry. After the Sterling Highway to Homer was completed

in the 1950s, Seldovia's population and importance as a supply centre began to dwindle but it was the 1964 earthquake that caused the most rapid change in the community.

The Good Friday Earthquake caused the land beneath Seldovia to settle 4 feet (1.2 metres), allowing high tides to flood much of the original town. In the reconstruction of Seldovia, much of it's waterfront and beloved boardwalk were torn out while Cap's Hill was levelled to provide fill material.

Today, a small remnant of the early boardwalk can be seen if you walk a short distance to the east of the ferry terminal. The town's most popular sight is the **St Nicholas Russian Orthodox Church**. Built in 1891, the church was recently restored and is open to visitors between 1 and 2 pm on weekdays. It is just off Main St, overlooking the town.

An information cache is located within the Synergy Art Works on Main St across from the boat harbor.

Places to Stay & Eat

The town's hotel, *Annie McKenzie's Boardwalk Hotel* (tel 234-7816), is on Main St across from the Small Boat Harbour and charges $58 for a single and $78 for a double. *Seldovia Lodge* (tel 234-7654), which consists of old trailer units, has rooms from $36.

The best option for accommodation is to camp for free on spectacular Outside Beach, where there are picnic tables and pit toilets. The stretch, known for good silver salmon surf fishing and great sunsets, is 1.9 miles (3 km) north from town; follow Seldovia St towards Jakalof Bay.

On Main St, there is the *Kachemak Cafe*, three bars and the *Stampers Family Market* for groceries and supplies. Public rest rooms, showers and water are available at the Harbormaster's office at the Small Boat Harbor.

Hiking

For those who have a spare day in Seldovia, two trails start from Jakalof Bay Rd. The first is a privately built trail that ascends steeply above the tree line to Gunsight Mountain. It leaves the road 8 miles (12.8 km) east of town but is unmarked, making it wise to inquire locally about its exact location. The second trail is a 2 mile (3.2 km) path to the Tutka Lagoon salmon-rearing facility. It departs from Jakalof Bay Rd 12 miles (19.2 km) east of town and is signposted.

Getting There & Around

The state ferry stops at Seldovia twice a week on a round trip from Homer. The ferry terminal (tel 234-7886) is at the north end of Main St and the one-way fare from Homer

to Seldovia is $14. Rainbow Tours (tel 235-7272 in Homer) sail daily from Homer to Seldovia, departing Homer at 11 am; the fare is $40 return.

You can also fly to Seldovia; a scenic 12 minute flight from Homer passes over the Kenai Mountains and Kachemak Bay. Homer Air (tel 235-8591) offers several flights daily to Seldovia.

Bicycles can be rented from Josh's Bikes & Fishing (tel 234-7603), and the Boardwalk Hotel rents out skiffs.

Kodiak Island

KODIAK

South-west of the Kenai Peninsula in the Gulf of Alaska is Kodiak (pop 12,000). The city is on the eastern tip of Kodiak Island, the largest island in Alaska at 3670 sq miles (9542 sq km) and the second largest in the USA after the Big Island of Hawaii. Kodiak can claim the largest fishing fleet in the state, with over 2000 boats, and it is the second largest commercial fishing port in the USA. Residents proudly call their city the 'King Crab Capital of the World'.

Kodiak Island is home for the famed Kodiak brown bear, the largest terrestrial carnivore in the world. There is an estimated 2400 of them on the island and some males have reached 1500 lb (675 kg) in weight.

Kodiak has some of the foggiest weather in Southcentral Alaska. Greatly affected by the turbulent Gulf of Alaska, the city is often rainy and foggy with occasional high winds. The area receives 80 inches (2000 mm) of rain per year and has an average temperature of 60°F (16°C) during the summer. On a clear day, however, the scenery is equal to that in any other part of the state. Mountains, craggy coastlines and some of the most deserted beaches accessible by road are Kodiak's most distinctive features.

The island, especially the city of Kodiak, can also claim some of the most turbulent history in Alaska. The Russians first landed on the island in 1763 and made the settlement

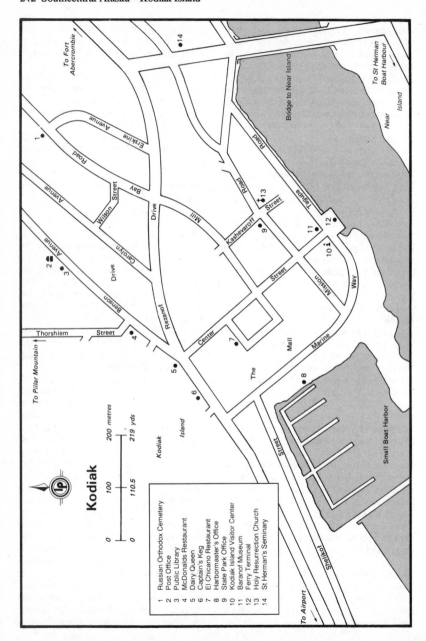

Kodiak

0   100   200 metres

0   110.5   219 yds

To Pillar Mountain

To Fort Abercrombie

To St Herman Boat Harbour

Near Island

Bridge to Near Island

Small Boat Harbor

To Airport

1   Russian Orthodox Cemetery
2   Post Office
3   Public Library
4   McDonalds Restaurant
5   Dairy Queen
6   Captain's Keg
7   El Chicano Restaurant
8   Harbormaster's Office
9   State Park Office
10   Kodiak Island Visitor Center
11   Baranof Museum
12   Ferry Terminal
13   Holy Resurrection Church
14   St Herman's Seminary

of Kodiak the capital of Russian-America in 1792 before moving it to Sitka 12 years later.

In 1912, Kodiak had its first disaster when Mt Katmai on the nearby Alaska Peninsula erupted. The explosion not only created the Valley of 10,000 Smokes in Katmai National Park, but it blanketed the then sleepy fishing village with 18 inches (45 cm) of ash causing great harm to wildlife, fish and homes. The ash can still be seen today at Fort Abercrombie on the ground or when you lift up the moss growing on trees.

The second disaster was worse. The Good Friday Earthquake in 1964 shook the entire island, and the following tidal wave levelled Kodiak city centre, destroying the boat harbour and wiping out the local fishing fleet. Processing plants, canneries and 158 homes were lost; damages totalled $24 million.

The natural disasters, however, are now part of Kodiak's turbulent history and today the city thrives as the fishing capital of Alaska with 15 fish-processing plants employing thousands of people during the summer. Kodiak Island is also the site of Alaska's largest Coast Guard station, which occupies the old US naval base. Four large Coast Guard cutters patrol out of Kodiak, seizing foreign vessels that illegally fish in US waters and assisting distressed ships caught in the violent storms of the North Pacific. The island was also affected by the Exxon oil spill, although it took a while for the spill to reach its shorelines.

Information
You'll reach the Kodiak Island Visitor Center (tel 486-4782) as soon as you leave the state ferry terminal. On the corner of Center St and Marine Way, the centre is open weekdays from 8 am to 5 pm and is the source of many free hand-outs, including a good map of the city.

The Alaska Division of Parks & Outdoor Recreation office (tel 486-6339) is on the corner of Mission Rd and Kashevaroff St, north-east of the visitor centre. The office is open weekdays from 8 am to 5 pm and is the place to go for information on hiking trails,

state campgrounds or renting recreation cabins.

The Kodiak National Wildlife Refuge office (tel 487-2600) is 4 miles (6.4 km) south-west of the city on Chiniak Rd. Open from 8 am to 4.30 pm weekdays and from noon to 4.30 pm weekends, the centre has information on their public-use cabins.

Things to See
Across the street from the visitor centre is the **Baranof Museum** in Erskine House, built by the Russians between 1792 and 1799 as a storehouse for precious sea otter pelts. The museum contains many items from the Russian period of Kodiak's history and many fine examples of Aleut basketry. The museum is open from 10 am to 3 pm weekdays and noon to 4 pm weekends; admission is $1.

Near the museum on Mission Rd is the **Holy Resurrection Church**, which serves the oldest Russian Orthodox parish in the New World – it was established in 1794. One of the original clerics was Father Herman, who was elevated to sainthood at Kodiak in 1970 during the first canonisation ever performed in America. His relics are kept in a carved wooden chest near the altar. Also within the church are polished brassware, several icons and rare paintings. The church doesn't keep set opening hours; inquire at the visitor centre about tours inside. Its blue and white onion-domed features make a great photograph, if you can squeeze out the huge gas storage tank that flanks it.

More Russian Orthodox history can be explored at **St Herman's Theological Seminary** which opens its Veniaminov Research Institute Museum to the public from 1 to 4.30 pm daily. On display inside the museum are indigenous artefacts, icons and bibles used by Orthodox missionaries on the Yukon River in the 1800s. The seminary, founded in 1973 to train orthodox readers and priests, is on Mission Rd north-east of the church.

Follow Marine Way left (west) from the ferry terminal as it curves past the **Small Boat Harbor**, the heart and soul of Kodiak. Crab boats, salmon seiners and halibut schooners cram the city docks, while more boats dock across the channel at **St Herman Harbor** on Near Island. An afternoon on the docks can lead to friendly encounters with fishers and the chance to see catches unloaded or nets being repaired. Although no tours are available, canneries can be seen clattering and steaming around the clock during the summer on nearby Shelikof St, or you can take the bridge across the channel to St Herman Harbor to view more boats.

Fort Abercrombie State Historical Park

This military fort was built in 1941. Its two 8 inch (20 cm) guns, left over from WW II, were installed by the US Army in preparation for a Japanese invasion that never came. Today, it is a state historical park, sitting majestically on the cliffs over wooded Monashka Bay. Restoration of the fort has begun with remounting of the guns and repair of the bunkers.

A self-guided tour winds through the WW II relics on Miller Point and past the beautiful views of ocean and rocky shorelines where inviting tidal pools are fun to explore. The park, 4.5 miles (7.2 km) north-east of Kodiak off Monashka Bay Rd, has 14 camping sites. Nearby is the Frank Brink Amphitheatre.

Pillar Mountain

The placement of a Distant Early Warning (DEW)-line site and later a communications saucer on top of this 1270 foot (387 metre) mountain has resulted in a road that climbs to a scenic overlook behind the city and provides excellent views of the surrounding mountains, ocean, beaches and islands. One side seems to plunge straight down to the harbour below, while the other overlooks the green interior of Kodiak Island. Pick up the bumpy dirt road to Pillar Mountain by heading north up Thorsheim St and turning left on Maple Ave, which runs into Pillar Mountain Rd.

Buskin River State Recreation Site

Four miles (6.4 km) south-west of the city on Chiniak Rd is this 90 acre (36 hectare) state recreation area, containing 18 camping sites and access to the Buskin River. Anglers flock here for the salmon fishing, the best on this part of Kodiak Island, while nearby is the US Fish & Wildlife Service visitor centre. The centre has numerous exhibits and displays as well as films on the island's wildlife, including the brown bears that live there. The centre is open from 8 am to 4.30 pm weekdays and from noon to 4.30 pm weekends.

Places to Stay

Camping There are no campgrounds in Kodiak and camping within the city limits is illegal. The closest campground is *Gibson Cove City Campground*, 2.5 miles (4 km) south-west of Kodiak. Sites are $2 per person per night but there are showers and rest rooms.

The *Buskin River State Recreation Site* (18 sites, $5 fee) is 4 miles (6.4 km) south-west of town on Chiniak Rd, along the way to the airport. The spot provides picnic shelters, pit toilets, trails through nearby wooded areas and good fishing on Buskin River or surf fishing in the ocean. Nearby is the Kodiak National Wildlife Refuge headquarters and visitor centre.

There is also camping at *Fort Abercrombie State Historical Park* (14 sites, $5 fee) north-east of Kodiak, the most scenic campground in which to pitch a tent, and at *Pasagshak River State Recreation Site*. All campgrounds have a 7 day limit.

Bed & Breakfast There are some B&Bs in Kodiak but most have rates ranging from $45 to $60; not exactly budget accommodation. Contact Kodiak Bed & Breakfast Service (tel 486-5367) to see if anything is available. One alternative is renting a car and heading out of the city to a place like *Kalsin Inn Ranch* (tel 486-2695) with rooms from $35 or *Road's End* (tel 486-2885), 42 miles (68 km) out of Kodiak on Chiniak Rd with rooms from $25 to $40.

Hotels There is no youth hostel in Kodiak and hotels in the city are expensive. The *Kodiak Star Motel* (tel 486-5657) on 119 Yukon St has rooms from $51 while the *Shelikof Lodge* (tel 486-4141) at 211

Thorsheim St is slightly cheaper with singles beginning at $49. All hotels tend to be heavily booked during the summer.

Places to Eat

McDonald's has reached Kodiak and you can now head up Thorsheim St near the police station and fire department for a cheap but filling dinner of Big Macs, shakes and fries. For mexican food, there's *El Chicano* on the 2nd floor of the Center Street Plaza. Open until 9.30 pm from Monday to Thursday and until 10 pm from Friday and Saturday, the restaurant has good food, large portions and 'grande' margaritas. Further up the price range is the *Captain's Keg* next door to the Dairy Queen on Rezanof Drive. The restaurant has a huge salad bar and features chicken, ribs and pizza.

For local seafood or to rub elbows with fishers over early morning coffee, try the *Kodiak Cafe* next to the Small Boat Harbor on Marine Way, or the *Cooper Room Restaurant* nearby in the Solley's Building for a bowl of prawns. Heading out to a campground for the night? Purchase fresh seafood from the *East Point Seafood Company* at 420 Marine Way.

Entertainment

Clustered around the city waterfront and Small Boat Harbor are a handful of bars that cater to Kodiak's fishing industry. At night they are interesting places, overflowing with fishers, deck hands and cannery workers drinking hard and talking lively. The *B&B Bar* across from the harbour claims to be Alaska's oldest bar, having served its first beer in 1899. Another is the *Anchor Bar* on Shelikof Ave, which also has washers and dryers and sells laundry supplies. At this unique pub, you can order a beer while waiting for your wash to finish.

For music at night, there is *Solly's Office* in the mall which is a restaurant & lounge featuring country music, while *Mecca* nearby has rock & roll booming across its dance floor.

Festivals

Kodiak's best event, if you happen to be around in late May, is its week-long Crab Festival, featuring a parade, foot and kayak races, fishers' skills contests and a lot of cooked king crab.

There is also the State Fair & Rodeo held in mid-August at the Bell Flats rodeo grounds, a Fourth of July celebration and the Great Buskin Raft Race in June that combines a raft race with five mandatory beer stops.

If you enjoy local pageantry, make an effort to see *Cry of the Wild Ram*, which depicts Kodiak's Russian days in a high-spirited manner complete with cannons roaring and a wooden stockade bursting into flames. It is held during the first 2 weeks of August in the Frank Brink Amphitheatre, a magnificent outdoor theatre near Fort Abercrombie. The play takes place rain or shine and tickets are $12 to $15 per person. Contact Kodiak-Baranof Productions (tel 486-5291) for ticket information.

Hiking

There are dozens of hiking trails in the Kodiak area but unfortunately very few are maintained and the trailheads are not marked along the roads. Once on the path, windfall can make following the track difficult or even totally conceal it. Still, hiking trails are the best avenue to the natural beauty of Kodiak Island. Before starting out, contact the Kodiak area ranger of the Alaska Division of Parks (tel 486-6339) for exact location and condition of trails.

Pillar Mountain Two trails depart from Pillar Mountain Rd. The first begins near the KOTV satellite receiver near the lower city reservoir and provides an easy walk north to Monashka Bay Rd. The second begins at the communications tower at the top of the mountain and is a descent of the south-west side. It ends at the Tie Substation, where a gravel road leads out to Chiniak Rd about 1 mile (1.6 km) north-east of the Buskin River State Recreation Site. Plan on an afternoon for either trail.

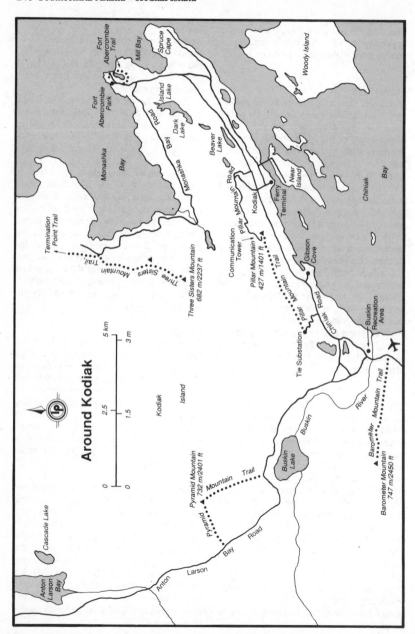

Around Kodiak

Barometer Mountain Trail This trail is popular but there's a steep climb of 5 miles (8 km) to the 2452 foot (748 metre) summit. To reach the trailhead, follow Chiniak Rd south of the Buskin River Campground and turn right on the first road immediately after passing the end of the airport's runway. Look for a well-worn trail on the left. The trek begins in thick alder before climbing the hogback ridge of the mountain to provide spectacular views of Kodiak and the bays south of the city.

Termination Point Trail This is another popular hike along a 5 mile (8 km) trail that starts at the end of Monashka Bay Rd and branches into several trails near Termination Point. Most of the hiking is done in virgin spruce forest.

Getting There & Around
Air MarkAir in conjunction with Alaska Airlines provides five daily flights between Kodiak and Anchorage for $138 one way. The airport is 5 miles (8 km) south of Kodiak on Chiniak Rd.

Boat The state ferry MV *Tustumena* stops at Kodiak three times a week from either Seward or Homer, stopping first at Port Lions, a nearby village on Kodiak Island. The ferry terminal (tel 486-3800) is in the city centre. The one-way fare to Homer is $42 and to Seward $48.

Car Rental There are four car-rental companies in Kodiak, including Rent-A-Heap (tel 486-5200) that will provide you with wheels to explore the island's outer edges. The used cars cost $24 a day plus 24 cents a mile for a small two-door compact.

Bicycle Cyclists will find Kodiak's roads interesting to ride around, especially the 12 mile (19.2 km) Anton Larsen Bay Rd that leads north-west from near Buskin River State Campground over the mountainous pass to the west side of the island, where you will find quiet coves and shorelines to explore. Plan on 2 hours for the ride to Anton

Larsen Bay. The ride down Chiniak Rd can be equally impressive. The Elkay Bicycle Shop (tel 486-4219) on Malutin Lane just off Mill Bay Rd in Kodiak handles repairs and parts or will rent you used cycles or mountain bikes for $10 to $15 a day.

AROUND KODIAK
Kodiak Island Roads
Over 100 miles (160 km) of paved and gravel roads head from the city into the wilderness that surrounds Kodiak. Some are rough jeep tracks, manageable only by 4WD vehicles, but many can be driven or hitched along to isolated stretches of beach, great fishing spots and superb coastal scenery.

To the south of Kodiak, Chiniak Rd winds 47.6 miles (76.6 km) to Cape Greville, following the edge of three splendid bays along the way. The road provides access to some of the best coastal scenery in Alaska and opportunities to view sea lions and puffins offshore, especially at Cape Chiniak near the road's southern end.

Just past *Mile 30* (48 km) of Chiniak Rd you arrive at the junction with Pasagshak Bay Rd that winds 16.4 miles (26.4 km) due south to the *Pasagshak River State Recreation Site*. This small campground (seven sites, free) is famous for its silver and king salmon fishing as well as for a river that reverses its flow four times a day with the tides. These scenic areas, and not the city, are the true attractions of Kodiak Island. Anybody who has the time (and patience) to hitchhike or the money to rent a car (see the Kodiak Getting There & Around section) should explore these roads.

Kodiak National Wildlife Refuge
This 1.8 million acre (754,700 hectare) preserve which covers the majority of Kodiak Island is the chief stronghold of the Alaska brown bear. An estimated 2400 bears reside in the refuge and the surrounding area. The refuge is known worldwide for brown bear hunting and to a lesser degree for salmon and steelhead fishing. There are no maintained trails within the preserve and cross-country hiking is extremely hard due to thick bush.

Access into the park is by charter plane or boat out of Kodiak – both are expensive.

The US Fish & Wildlife Service administers nine free-use cabins in the refuge that should be reserved in advance. Cabin reservations are selected by four annual lotteries, each covering usage for certain months. Cabins that are not reserved can be obtained on a first-come first-serve basis. The closest units to Kodiak, Uganik Island Cabin and Veikoda Bay Cabin, are both on the ocean with good beaches nearby. If you are planning your trip, write to the Kodiak National Wildlife Refuge (PO Box 825, Kodiak, Alaska 99615) about reserving a cabin. If you're already in Kodiak, call the refuge headquarters (tel 487-2600) to check if any cabins are available.

Shuyak Island State Park

Covering almost a quarter of the most northern island in the Kodiak Archipelago, this park, 54 air miles (88 km) north of Kodiak, features a unique rain forest of virgin Sitka spruce, rugged coastline, beaches and protected waterways. Shuyak is not large, the island measures only 12 miles (19 km) long and 11 miles (18 km) wide, yet it contains more sheltered waterways than any other part of the archipelago, making it a kayaker's delight. Wildlife includes otters, sea lions, dall porpoises offshore and a modest population of the famous Kodiak brown bear.

The park's four cabins are on inlets and bays, and the cedar structures have bunks for eight, a wood stove, propane lights, a cooking stove but no running water. The cabins cost $15 per person per day. It's best to write for reservations before your trip (Alaska State Parks, SR Box 3800, Kodiak, Alaska 99615). But if you are passing through Kodiak give the Alaska Division of Parks (tel 486-6339) a call to see if any of them happen to be free.

Wolf

Anchorage

Anchorage, the hub of Alaska's road system, an international air junction and home for half of the state's residents, is a city of prosperity and much debate.

Those who live in the Anchorage area claim there is no other city like it in the world. It's Alaska's Big Apple and the state revolves around it. Everything you could possibly want is only a short hop away from the urban area which houses 219,000 people. Glaciers, mountains, hiking trails or white-water rivers to raft are only 20 minutes away from the city. Within a couple of hours drive is the recreation paradise of the Kenai Peninsula and a handful of state and national preserves which offer unlimited camping, hiking and fishing.

Yet in Anchorage you can enjoy all the comforts and attractions offered by any large US city, including a modern performing arts centre, enclosed shopping malls, and bars and nightclubs that buzz late into the night.

But many of the state's residents look at the city, shake their heads and say, 'Anchorage is great. It's only 20 minutes from Alaska'. To them, everything that Alaska is, Anchorage isn't. The city is a mass of uncontrolled urban sprawl or, in down-to-earth terms, a beer can in the middle of the woods. It has billboards, traffic jams and dozens of fast-food restaurants. Its trees are being ripped out for caravan parks and shopping centres. If you visit Alaska, it is inevitable that you pass through Anchorage at least once, if not several times; you'll either hate the city or love it.

Anchorage has the advantage of being north of the Kenai Mountains, which shield the city from the excess moisture experienced by Southcentral Alaska. The Anchorage Bowl – the city and surrounding area – receives only 14 inches (355 mm) of rain annually. Nor does the area have the extreme temperatures of the Interior. The average temperature in January is 13°F (-11°C), while at the height of the summer

it's only 58°F (14°C). The area does, however, have more than its fair share of overcast days, especially in early and late summer.

Although Captain James Cook sailed up Cook Inlet in 1778 looking for the mythical Northwest Passage, Anchorage wasn't settled until 1914 when surveyors chose the site as the work camp and headquarters for the Alaska Railroad; by 1915 it was a tent city of 2000. The area's growth occurred in sudden spurts, caused by increased farming in the Matanuska Valley to the north in the 1930s, the construction of military bases during WW II, and the discovery of oil in Cook Inlet in the late 1950s.

Two events literally reshaped the city. The Good Friday Earthquake devastated much of Anchorage city centre and resulted in the rebuilding of entire sections of town with the aid of low interest loans from the government. Later, the city prospered when oil was discovered in Prudhoe Bay, and Anchorage served as the headquarters for much of the Trans-Alaska Pipeline construction.

Today, Anchorage is truly the heart of Alaska and the centre of the state's commerce and financial communities. Though the wide Anchorage Bowl is boxed in by the Chugach Mountains to the east and Cook Inlet to the west, the city continues to sprawl and seems to be in a constant state of rebuilding. Although the decline of oil prices in the late 1980s has slowed its economy, Anchorage is still the fastest growing city in Alaska, and little wonder. Almost two-thirds of the state's population lives in the greater Anchorage trading area, making them the recipients of the greatest proportion of the state's oil royalties.

What oil has done to Anchorage in the last decade is amazing; the state legislature spent tax dollars to build the city a performing arts centre, a convention centre, a sports arena, a beautiful library and a major expansion to the Anchorage Museum of History & Art. The price of gasoline at the pump will surely fluctuate in the 1990s but one thing is certain, as long as oil gushes from Prudhoe Bay or anywhere in Alaska, Anchorage will prosper.

Orientation

If you fly into Anchorage, you'll arrive at the airport in the south-west corner of the city. If you drive in from the south on Seward Highway or from the north on Glenn Highway, the roads lead you through the city toward Cook Inlet. Whichever way you arrive, it's best to head for the city centre. There is bus transport from the airport and where both highways end (or begin if you are leaving), less than 1 mile (1.6 km) from each other.

Anchorage city centre is a somewhat undefined area boxed in by 3rd Ave to the north, 10th Ave to the south, Minnesota Drive to the west and Ingra St (Seward Highway) to the east.

Information

There are three visitor centres in Anchorage. The main one is in the log cabin (tel 274-3531) on the corner of 4th Ave and F St, open daily from 7.30 am to 7 pm June to August, 8.30 am to 6 pm May and September, and 9 am to 4 pm the rest of the year. Along with many services and hand-outs, this centre operates an Emergency Language Bank of 27 languages designed to help foreign travellers in distress. They also have the 24 hour All About Anchorage recording (tel 276-3200) that lists current events taking place in the city that day.

The other two information centres are at the domestic and overseas terminals of the International Airport and are staffed for most incoming flights.

Backpackers and hikers should contact the Alaska Public Lands Information Center (tel 271-2737) at the corner of 4th Ave and F St (diagonally opposite the Log Cabin Information Center) for information and hand-outs on any national park, federal refuge or state parks in Alaska. This is where to head for help planning wilderness adventures and to purchase topographic maps and books. The centre is like 'one-stop shopping' for information on outdoor activities and trips; 99% of your questions will be answered here. The centre is open daily from 9 am to 7 pm.

If the Public Lands office can't help you, there are several other centres that you can contact. Information on state parks can also be obtained from the Alaska Division of Parks & Outdoor Recreation (tel 561-2020) at 3601 C St. The Chugach National Forest office (tel 271-2500) at Suite 206, 201 East 9th St, has details on any US Forest Service national forest, trail or cabin.

The Bureau of Land Management (for the Pinnell Mountain Trail) also maintains an office (tel 271-5555) at 701 C St, as does the US Fish & Wildlife Service (for the Kenai National Wildlife Refuge) at 1011 East

Anchorage Convention & Visitors Bureau

Tudor Rd (tel 786-3487). If Anchorage is your first stop in Alaska, make good use of these agencies to gather the latest information for the rest of your trip. If somebody in Anchorage doesn't have the brochure, no one in Alaska will.

Things to See

Begin any visit to the city at the **Log Cabin Information Center** (tel 274-3531) on the corner of 4th Ave and F St. The centre is housed in a log cabin complete with a sod roof and is open from 7.30 am to 7 pm during the summer. Among the hand-outs and maps they provide is the *Anchorage Visitors Guide*, which describes among other things a 3 to 4 hour walking tour of the city centre.

Those not up to walking the tour can catch the double-decker bus provided by People Mover. The route provides a good orientation to the city for new arrivals and allows you to see many of the following attractions without having to hoof it. The bus doesn't stop at the visitor centre, however, so you have to walk one block west on 4th St and two blocks south on G St to catch it at the Transit Center (tel 343-6543 for Rideline). The No 10 bus passes the Transit Center every 90 minutes. The ride lasts 30 minutes and the fare is 80c.

The beautiful thing about getting around Anchorage is the simplicity of the street layout, especially in the city centre. Numbered avenues run north to south and lettered streets east to west. The city walking tour begins by heading north on E St, where on the corner of 2nd Ave it passes the **Cadastral Survey Monument** and then the **Alaska Railroad Depot**.

The monument notes the original 1915 town-site survey and has four etchings that trace Anchorage from its first auction of public land to a current city map. The railroad depot, at the base of the hill, features historical photos in its lobby, totem poles outside and Engine No 1 on a platform. The small locomotive was built in the 1900s for construction of the Panama Canal and was later shipped to Alaska for use on the railroad.

The tour continues west on 2nd Ave and then swings onto Christensen Drive, where at the corner of 3rd Ave it comes to the **Port of Anchorage Observation Deck**. From here you can view the mouth of Ship Creek and the Port of Anchorage, which handles more than 400 tankers and cargo ships annually.

Turn east on 3rd Ave and then south on F St until you reach the **Old Federal Building** on the corner of 4th Ave. Built in the 1930s, the building is on the National Register of Historic Places and was the focal point of celebrations following the passage of the Alaska Statehood Act in 1958. Today, it houses the **Alaska Public Lands Information Center**, where exhibits, films and hand-outs covering all of Alaska's public parks, preserves and wilderness areas are available. There's even a trip-planning computer to assist you backpacking in the woods. On the front lawn stands *The Northern Lights* as depicted by a local sculptor.

West on 4th Ave and half a block north on K St is the eye-catching large statue entitled *The Last Blue Whale*. Inside the adjoining building is Fred Machetanz's famous painting *The Hunt*.

Nearby at the west end of 3rd Ave is **Resolution Park** and the **Captain Cook Monument**, which honours the English captain's 200th anniversary when he sailed into Cook Inlet with officers George Vancouver and William Bligh at his side.

From the viewing deck you have an excellent view of the surrounding mountains, including the Talkeetnas to the north-east and the snow-covered Alaska Range to the west. On a clear day you can see Mt McKinley and Mt Foraker to the north, while to the west is Mt Susitna, known as 'The Sleeping Lady', which marks the south-west end of the Alaska Range. There is also a panorama of Cook Inlet; often the large white caps you see are beluga whales feeding on salmon fry or smelt.

The tour continues east down to 6th Ave, and near the corner of H St is the **Oomingmak Musk Ox Producers Co-op**. The co-operative handles a variety of garments

made of arctic musk-ox wool, hand knitted in isolated Eskimo villages. Outside, a mural depicts a herd of musk oxen, while inside the results of this cottage industry are sold. Those interested in the unusual garments should consider the co-op's farm tour in Palmer. East on 6th Ave at the corner of G St is the **People Mover Transit Center**, where you can pick up a local bus to any section of the city (see the Anchorage Getting Around section).

At 725 5th Ave, near the bus station, is **Imaginarium** (tel 276-3179), a hands-on science museum and a place to go if you have children tagging along. The award-winning centre features more than 20 exhibits that explain the northern lights, earthquakes, oil exploration, bears and other Alaskan topics. You can even enter a polar bear's den. The museum is open daily during the summer and admission is $4 for adults and $2 for children.

Diagonally across from the transit centre on the north side of 6th Ave is the new **Performing Arts Center**, one of only 18 in the country, and the equally new **Egan Civic & Convention Center**. Eventually, the tour leads to the **Anchorage Historical & Fine Arts Museum** (tel 343-4326) near the corner of 7th Ave and A St. In 1984, the museum was expanded to triple its original size and now is an impressive centre for displays on

Alaskan history and indigenous culture as well as an art gallery that features work by regional, national and international artists. The Alaska Gallery upstairs traces the history and people of this land in large, three-dimensional exhibits. The museum is open Monday to Saturday from 10 am to 6 pm and Sunday from 1 to 5 pm; admission is $2. Ask about the Alaskan films shown daily at 3 pm during the summer.

Another museum worth passing through is the **Heritage Library Museum** in the National Bank of Alaska building on Northern Lights Blvd and C St. It features a small but impressive collection of native tools, costumes and weapons plus there's no admission charge. It's open weekdays from 1 to 4 pm.

Less impressive is Anchorage's other museum, the **Alaska Wilderness Museum** (tel 274-1600) at the corner of 5th Ave and I St, which contains 30 exhibits, including a series of dioramas recreating Alaska wildlife habitat. Somehow, going indoors to view displays of wilderness, complete with stuffed animals, seems a little ironic in this state. Opening hours are from 8 am to 6 pm daily in the summer and admission is $5.

If you are into art, head over to the **Visual Arts Center** (tel 274-9641) at 713 West 5th Ave. Its galleries feature contemporary works from both Alaska and national artists.

It's open from noon to 6 pm Tuesday to Saturday and they ask for a donation of $2. The lobby of the Federal Building on the corner of 7th Ave and C St often has an artwork collection on display.

Parks For a view of the Anchorage skyline there is Earthquake Park at the west end of Northern Lights Blvd on the Knik Arm (take bus No 93 from the youth hostel). There is little evidence of the 1964 disaster, but an interpretive sign details the powerful force that shook Anchorage and killed 115 people.

The best part of the park is the excellent panorama of the city skyline set against the Chugach Mountains; on a clear day you can see Mt McKinley and Mt Foraker to the north. The view is best seen from the Coastal Trail at the lower area of the park. Someday this bike trail will extend from Anchorage city centre south to Girdwood along Turnagain Arm.

Within the city centre there is Delaney Park, known locally as 'The Park Strip' because it stretches from A to P streets between 9th and 10th avenues. The green strip, the site of the 50 ton (45,350 kg) bonfire that highlighted statehood in 1959 and later where Pope John Paul II gave an outdoor mass in 1981, is a good place to lie down on a hot afternoon.

For information and a program of activities in Anchorage's parks, call the city's Department of Parks & Recreation (tel 343-4474).

Lakes If the weather is hot enough, several lakes in the area offer swimming. The closest one to the city centre is Goose Lake, 2 miles (3.2 km) south-east of the city centre on Northern Lights Blvd (take bus Nos 2, 45 or 93). Before or after your dip, take a stroll through the **University of Alaska** at Anchorage, the largest campus in the state university system. It is connected to Goose Lake Park by footpaths. There is also swimming at Spenard Lake, 3 miles (4.8 km) south of the city centre on Spenard Rd and then west on Lakeshore Drive (take bus Nos 6, 7 or 93), and at Jewel Lake, 6.5 miles (10.4 km) south-west of the city centre on Dimond Blvd (take bus No 7).

Military Bases Elmendorf Air Base and Fort Richardson were established during WW II as the major northern military outposts for the USA, and continue today to contribute to Anchorage's economy. In the early 1940s, Elmendorf Air Force Base (tel 552-5755) housed one of the nation's strongest air stations and is now home base for F-15 Eagles, T-33s and other huge aircraft.

The base offers a weekly summer tour that allows you to view the hangars and planes along with the rest of the facility. Call ahead to find out times and reserve a seat on the bus. There is also a log cabin wildlife museum with over 200 Alaskan mammals, fish and birds (ask the guard for directions) that is open from 10 am to 5 pm weekdays and from 10 am to 4 pm Saturday during the summer (take bus No 14 from the Transit Center).

Fort Richardson (tel 863-8113) also has a wildlife museum with 250 specimens, along with a golf course and a salmon hatchery. The museum, Building 600, is open from 9 am to 5 pm weekdays, from 10 am to 4 pm Saturday and from noon to 4 pm Sunday (take bus No 75). Both museums are free.

Lake Hood Air Harbor Those enchanted by Alaska's bush planes and small air-taxi operators will be overwhelmed by Lake Hood, the world's busiest float-plane base (and ski-plane base in the winter). Almost every type of small plane imaginable can be seen flying onto and off the lake's surface. The float-plane base can be reached by bus No 93 from the youth hostel and makes an interesting afternoon trip when combined with a swim in adjoining Lake Spenard.

You may also want to stop in at the **Reeve Aviation Picture Museum**, dedicated to Alaska pioneer aviator Robert Reeve. Located in the city centre at the corner of 6th Ave and D St, the museum has more than 1100 photos and prints of the state's famous bush pilots.

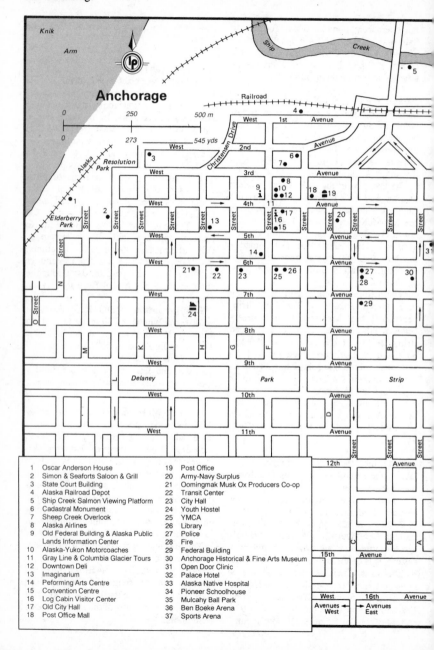

Anchorage

Knik
Arm

Ship Creek

Railroad

0   250   500 m

0   273   545 yds

West   1st   Avenue

West   2nd   Avenue

Resolution Park

West   3rd   Avenue

West   4th   Avenue

West   5th   Avenue

Elderberry Park

West   6th   Avenue

West   7th   Avenue

West   8th   Avenue

West   9th   Avenue

Delaney   Park   Strip

West   10th   Avenue

West   11th   Avenue

West   12th   Avenue

15th   Avenue

West   16th   Avenue

Avenues West ← ← Avenues East

1	Oscar Anderson House
2	Simon & Seaforts Saloon & Grill
3	State Court Building
4	Alaska Railroad Depot
5	Ship Creek Salmon Viewing Platform
6	Cadastral Monument
7	Sheep Creek Overlook
8	Alaska Airlines
9	Old Federal Building & Alaska Public Lands Information Center
10	Alaska-Yukon Motorcoaches
11	Gray Line & Columbia Glacier Tours
12	Downtown Deli
13	Imaginarium
14	Peforming Arts Centre
15	Convention Centre
16	Log Cabin Visitor Center
17	Old City Hall
18	Post Office Mall
19	Post Office
20	Army-Navy Surplus
21	Oomingmak Musk Ox Producers Co-op
22	Transit Center
23	City Hall
24	Youth Hostel
25	YMCA
26	Library
27	Police
28	Fire
29	Federal Building
30	Anchorage Historical & Fine Arts Museum
31	Open Door Clinic
32	Palace Hotel
33	Alaska Native Hospital
34	Pioneer Schoolhouse
35	Mulcahy Ball Park
36	Ben Boeke Arena
37	Sports Arena

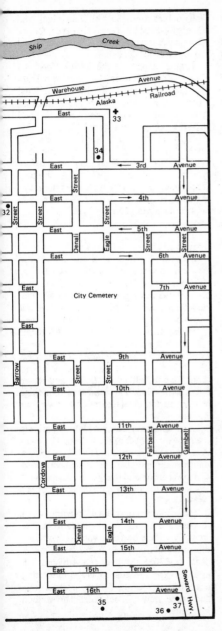

Ship Creek From mid to late summer, king, coho and pink salmon spawn up Ship Creek, the historical site of Tanaina Indian fish camps. There is a good viewing platform on the creek, 0.5 mile (0.8 km) east from the Railroad Depot, where you can watch the return of the salmon. Follow C St north as it crosses Ship Creek Bridge and then turn right on Whitney Rd.

Festivals
Summer festivals include a large Fourth of July celebration, a Renaissance Faire with Shakespeare-type costumes and plays in early June at the Tudor Center, and an Octoberfest in mid-September. Smaller events worth seeing are Kite Day in early June, when kite flyers show up in full force in Delaney Park – a colourful scene; and the city's summer solstice in mid-June, which includes the Mayor's Midnight Sun Marathon and the Campbell Creek Classic (during which anything that floats is paddled down the local river).

Places to Stay
Camping The Anchorage Parks & Recreation Department maintains two parks where there is overnight camping. The closest one to the city centre is *Lion's Camper Park* in Russian Jack Springs Park, south of Glenn Highway on Boniface Parkway. The campground has 10 tent sites, 50 campervan spaces, hot showers and rest rooms. The surrounding park features tennis courts, hiking trails and a picnic area. The campground, 2.5 miles (4 km) from the city centre, can be reached by bus No 8; it is also within walking distance of bus route No 12.

Centennial Park has 83 sites, showers and rest rooms but is 4.6 miles (7.4 km) from the city centre on Glenn Highway. Take the Muldoon Rd exit south of the highway and turn west onto Boundary Ave for half a block. Bus Nos 3 and 75 run past the corner of Muldoon Rd and Boundary Ave. The cost is $12 per night for either campground and there is a limit of 7 days.

Youth Hostel The *Anchorage Youth Hostel*

(tel 276-3635), one of the main youth hostels in the Alaska Council, is in the city centre, one block south of the Transit Center at 700 H St. The cost is $10 per night for members and $13 for nonmembers; there is a 3 night maximum stay unless special arrangements are made with the house parents. Check-in is from 5 to 9 pm and check-out time is 9 am.

Along with sleeping facilities, there is a common room, kitchen, showers and even double rooms. Laundry facilities are available and you can store extra bags here for $1 per day. From the airport, take bus No 6 for the 5.7 mile (9.2 km) trip into the Transit Center. This hostel is busy during the summer, so many travellers reserve a bunk ahead of time by mailing a money order for the first night's stay along with number and gender of people arriving to: Anchorage AYH, 700 H St, Anchorage, Alaska 99501.

Bed & Breakfast A large number of Anchorage residents have organised B&B accommodation by opening up their spare bedrooms for summer travellers. Most places are on the fringes or in the suburbs of the city and provide a clean bed, a good breakfast and local insight into both the city and the Alaskan way of life. Call either Alaska Private Lodging (tel 258-1717) or Stay with a Friend (tel 355-4006) to arrange such accommodation.

Hotels Anchorage has more than 35 hotels and motels and 3700 rooms for rent, so late arrivals and independent travellers with no reservations have few problems finding an available bed. However, trying to find a single room under $40 and a double under $50 is often tricky.

One of the cheaper hotels in the city centre is the *Palace Hotel* (tel 277-6313) on the corner of 4th Ave and Barrow St, which offers singles from $25 and doubles from $30. A much better place to stay for only a few dollars more is the *Midtown Hotel* (tel 258-7778) at 604 West 26th St, just off Arctic Blvd between Fireweed Lane and Northern Lights Blvd (bus No 9 from the Transit Center). The Midtown has singles from $30

and doubles from $35 with shared bath, and is eight blocks from Chester Creek Greenstrip, the beautiful series of parks that divides Anchorage in half.

Higher in price is the *Kobuk Hotel* (tel 274-1650) at 1104 East 5th Ave near Ingra St. For late arrivals at the International Airport there is the *Spenard Motel* (tel 243-6917) 1 mile (1.6 km) away at 3960 Spenard Rd with single rooms from $30.

If you are driving in late from the north, there is *John's Motel* (tel 277-4332) at 3543 Mt View Drive off Glenn Highway before you begin to enter the heart of Anchorage. This small motel, which also has hook-ups for campervans, has single rooms from $40 and doubles from $50.

Places to Eat

City Centre For those on a strict budget you have a choice of fast-food places: *McDonald's* on the corner of 4th Ave and E St, *Wendy's* down the street at 239 4th Ave, and *Burger King* at 520 West 5th Ave. All now compete for the breakfast trade as well as for the lunch and dinner crowd looking for a quick burger. Just as easy on the money pouch is the *Federal Building Cafeteria* off C St between 7th and 8th avenues. It's open from 7 am to 1.30 pm weekdays and serves breakfast and lunch in pleasant surroundings where you don't feel like gulping down your food.

More notable and a little higher in price is the *Downtown Deli* near McDonald's on 4th Ave, unquestionably the city's best known delicatessen and also one of its best. Good Chinese cuisine and spicy Szechwan food is available at the *Tea Leaf* on the corner of 3rd Ave and E St.

Those looking to make an evening out of dinner have a long list of places to choose from. One of the best that won't set you back too much is *Simon & Seafort's Saloon & Grill* at 420 L St between 4th and 5th avenues. The restaurant has the interesting decor of a turn-of-the-century grand saloon and a nice view of Cook Inlet. The seafood is excellent.

Top: Russian church in Ninilchik on the Kenai Peninsula (ADT)
Bottom: View of Homer Spit, Homer (ADT)

Top: Interior Alaska lake with canoe (ADT)
Bottom: The coastline near Kodiak on Kodiak Island (ADT)

Midtown The area roughly from Debarr Rd to Tudor Rd east of Minnesota Drive is occasionally referred to as 'midtown' and any fast-food restaurant you're craving for is here. *McDonald's* is at 800 West Northern Lights Blvd, the *Burger King* is just down the road while nearby is *Kentucky Fried Chicken, Taco Bell*, etc. At the corner of Spenard Rd and Minnesota Drive is *Skipper's* for all the fish, salad and chowder you can consume for $7. There is also a Skipper's at 5668 Debarr Rd.

A step up from fast food is *Hogg Brothers Cafe* at 2421 Spenard Rd near Chilkoot Charlie's. The restaurant has very good breakfasts in the $4 to $5 range and a lunch menu with sandwiches priced around $6. Occasionally there is even live music before it closes at 4 pm.

To the south in the Plaza Mall, on the corner of 36th Ave and C St, is *Natural Pantry* (tel 563-2727), a health food store and a restaurant. The restaurant is excellent (and healthy for you) as well as being affordable. The extensive salad bar is $4.25 for all you can eat, and most sandwiches are under $4. The restaurant is open from 10 am to 7 pm weekdays and from 10 am to 6 pm Saturday; it's closed on Sunday.

Harry's at 101 West Benson Blvd is a good old Irish pub dedicated to Harry Truman, the man who refused to move from his home on the side of Mt St Helens when the volcano began erupting in 1980. The decor is dedicated to him, with a statue of the old-timer and walls of photos of his mountain home. The place is also a good restaurant, where you can get sandwiches, hamburgers and salad meals for under $9.

Entertainment
Anchorage is a city where you can hike all day in the mountains and dance all night in the bars. One of the more colourful places is *Chilkoot Charlie's*, or 'Koots' as the locals call it, at 2435 Spenard Rd in the midtown area. The bar hops at night and features a band and dancing in one room, a long bar in the other, sawdust on the floor and rusty artefacts all over the walls. Liquor prices are reasonable and even better at happy hour from 4 to 8 pm, when drinks are two for the price of one.

Other places for music are *Midnight Express* at 2612 Spenard Rd, which features live music, usually country rock; *The Cattle Company* on the corner of C St and Tudor Ave; and the *Fly By Nite Club* at 4811 Spenard Rd, which draws an older crowd in their late 20s and 30s for blues and jazz music. Nearby, *Harry's* at 101 West Benson Blvd has entertainment and delicious ice-cream drinks that can be enjoyed from its 'step-down bar'.

In Anchorage city centre, you have the *Great Alaskan Bush Co*, the city's notorious strip joint on 4th Ave. Great views of the area can be obtained for the (steep) price of a drink in the *Crow's Nest* at the top of the Captain Cook Hotel on the corner of 5th Ave and K St; or at the *Penthouse Lounge* at the top of the Sheffield House Hotel at 720 West 5th Ave, where floor-to-ceiling windows let you marvel at Mt McKinley on a clear day.

Noteworthy bars on the fringes of the city include the *Peanut Farm* (tel 563-3283) at 5227 Old Seward Highway. It's a good old bar with bowls of peanuts on the tables for those who prefer drinking to dinner. The *Upper 1* at the International Airport is for travellers waiting for their flight or for anyone who enjoys watching jumbo jets land and take-off.

Anchorage has a civic opera, a symphony orchestra, several theatre groups and a concert association that brings a number of dance companies and art groups to the city every year. Big-name performers arrive more frequently now that the Performing Arts Center has been completed. For a daily report on all cultural events around the area, call the All About Anchorage phone line (tel 276-3200) for its recorded message.

Those watching their funds carefully should keep in mind the free films offered around town. The Anchorage Historical & Fine Arts Museum shows Alaska films daily at 3 pm while the Alaska Public Lands Information Center has daily showings of wildlife movies. The *ACRO Theater* (tel 263-4545) on G St between 6th and 7th avenues presents two films, the first is on Alaska's development from the gold-rush era and the second is about indigenous art and culture. They are shown on Tuesday and Thursday at 2 and 3 pm.

The city has numerous movie theatres, including *Capri Cinema* (tel 272-3211), take bus No 75; *Denali Theatre* (tel 279-2332), take bus Nos 3 and 7; *Fireweed Theatre* (tel 277-3825), take bus No 60; *Fourth Avenue Theatre* (tel 272-1024) in the city centre; and *Totem Theatre* (tel 333-8222), take bus Nos 5 and 75.

Or for something different, head to the *Alaska Experience Theatre* (tel 272-9076) at the corner of G St and 6th Ave. The theatre shows a 40 minute, 70 mm film that is projected on a huge domed screen and is entitled *Alaska the Great Land*. There is an admission charge for this travelogue but you also get to watch a second film about the 1964 Good Friday Earthquake.

Hiking
With the Chugach Mountains at its doorstep, Anchorage has many excellent day hikes that begin on the outskirts of the city and quickly lead into the beautiful alpine area to the east. Most of them begin in the Hillside area of the city that borders Chugach State Park, the second largest state preserve at 495,000 acres (198,000 hectares), and can be reached on the People Mover bus system.

For trail information, contact the Chugach State Park office (tel 345-5014) in Anchorage or stop in at the new visitor centre in the historic Potter Section House at *Mile 115* (187.4 km) of Seward Highway. Park rangers also lead hikes throughout the area on Saturday and Sunday during the summer, and the park office maintains a recorded message (tel 694-6391) listing what hikes are planned and where to gather. If you want to head into the park on an overnight trip and need backpacking gear, call Alaska Sports Rental (tel 562-2208) at 300 West 36th Ave to rent the basics.

Flattop Mountain Trail Because of its easy

access, this trail is the most popular hike near the city. The path to the 4500 foot (1372 metre) peak is not difficult and from the summit there are good views of Mt McKinley to the north and most of Cook Inlet. The trail begins at the Glen Alps entrance to the Chugach State Park.

Catch bus No 92 to the corner of Hillside Rd and Upper Huffman Rd. Walk 0.7 mile (1.1 km) east along Upper Huffman Rd and then turn right on Toilsome Hill Drive for 2 miles (3.2 km). This switchback road ascends steeply to the Glen Alps park entrance, a parking lot where trailhead signs point the way to Flattop Mountain, the upper trail of the two that begin here. The round trip is 4 miles (6.4 km) with some scrambling over loose rock up steep sections near the top of the mountain. Plan on 3 to 5 hours for the entire hike.

Rabbit Lake Trail People Mover bus No 92 also provides transport to this trail, which leads to the beautiful alpine lake nestled under 5000 foot (1525 metre) Suicide Peak. Leave the bus at the corner of Hillside Drive and De Armoun Rd. Extending to the east here is Upper De Armoun Rd. Follow it 1 mile (1.6 km) and then turn right onto Lower Canyon Rd for 1.2 miles (1.9 km) to reach the trailhead parking lot.

The trail begins by paralleling Upper Canyon Rd, a rough jeep track, for 3.5 miles (5.6 km) and then continues another 2 miles (3.2 km) from its end to the lake. The return trip from the corner of Hillside Drive and De Armoun Rd is 15.4 miles (24.6 km), or a 6 to 9 hour hike. You can camp on the lake's shore for a scenic evening in the mountains.

Wolverine Peak Trail This path ascends to the 4455 foot (1358 metre) triangular peak that can be seen to the east of Anchorage. It makes for a strenuous but rewarding full-day trip resulting in good views of the city, Cook Inlet and the Alaska Range.

Take bus No 92 to the intersection of Hillside Drive and O'Malley Rd. Head east up Upper O'Malley Rd for 0.5 mile (0.8 km) to a 'T' intersection and turn left (north) onto

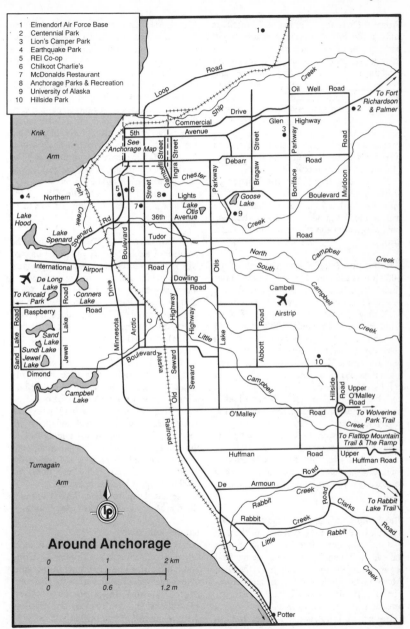

1 Elmendorf Air Force Base
2 Centennial Park
3 Lion's Camper Park
4 Earthquake Park
5 REI Co-op
6 Chilkoot Charlie's
7 McDonalds Restaurant
8 Anchorage Parks & Recreation
9 University of Alaska
10 Hillside Park

Around Anchorage

0   1   2 km

0   0.6   1.2 m

Prospect Drive for 1.1 miles (1.7 km). This ends at the Prospect Heights entrance and parking area of the Chugach State Park. The marked trail begins as an old homesteader road that crosses South Campbell Creek and passes junctions with two other old roads in the first 2.3 miles (3.7 km).

Keep heading east, and the old road will become a footpath that ascends above the bush line and eventually fades out. Make sure to mark its whereabouts in order to find it on the way back. From here it is 3 miles (4.8 km) to the Wolverine Peak.

The return trip from the corner of O'Malley Rd and Hillside Drive is 13.8 miles (22 km), a 9 hour hike. Many people just trek to the good views above the bush line, shortening the trip to 7.8 miles (12.5 km).

Rendezvous Peak Route The trek to the 4050 foot (1235 metre) peak is an easy 5 hour round trip, less from the trailhead, and rewards hikers with incredible views of Mt McKinley, Cook Inlet, Turnagain and Knik arms, and the city far below. Take bus No 75 for 6.5 miles (10.4 km) north-east on Glenn Highway to Arctic Valley Rd. Turn right (east) on Arctic Valley Rd (this section is also known as Ski Bowl Rd) and head 7 miles (11.2 km) to the Arctic Valley Ski Area at the end. From the parking lot, a short trail leads along the right-hand side of the stream up the valley to the north-west. It ends at a pass where a short ascent to Rendezvous Peak is easily seen and climbed.

The round trip from the ski area parking lot is only 3.5 miles (5.6 km), but it is a much longer day if you can't thumb a ride up Arctic Valley Rd.

The Ramp This is another of the many alpine summit hikes from the east side of the city that includes hiking through tranquil tundra valleys with good chances of seeing Dall sheep during the summer. Begin at the Glen Alps entrance to the state park (see the previously mentioned Flattop Trail for directions to the entrance).

Instead of following the upper trail to

Flattop Mountain at the parking lot, hike the lower one as it extends 0.5 mile (0.8 km) to the power line. Turn right and follow the power line for 2 miles (3.2 km), past 13 power poles, to where an old jeep trail crosses over from the left and heads downhill to the south fork of Campbell Creek.

The trail then crosses the creek and continues up the hill beyond it to a valley on the other side. Hike up the alpine valley to Ship Lake Pass, which lies between The Ramp at 5240 feet (1598 metres) to the north, and The Wedge at 4660 feet (1421 metres) to the south. Either peak can be climbed.

The round trip from the Glen Alps entrance is 14 miles (22.4 km), or an 8 to 10 hour hike.

Williwaw Lakes Trail This hike leads to the handful of alpine lakes found at the base of Mt Williwaw. The trail makes a pleasant overnight hike and many trekkers consider it the most scenic outing in the Hillside area of Chugach State Park. The hike begins on the same lower trail as The Ramp does, from the Glen Alps entrance parking lot (see the previously mentioned Flattop Trail for directions to the entrance).

Walk 0.5 mile (0.8 km) to the power line and then turn right. This time walk only about 300 yards/metres and then turn left on a trail marked by a Middle Fork Loop Trail sign. This trail leads down and across the south fork of Campbell Creek and then north for 1.5 miles (2.4 km) to the middle fork of the creek. Here you reach a junction; continue on the right-hand trail and follow the middle fork of Campbell Creek until you reach the alpine lakes at its end.

The round trip from Glen Alps is 16 miles (25.6 km), or 7 to 9 hours of easy hiking.

Guide Companies
Anchorage is home base for a large number of guide companies that run hiking, kayaking and rafting trips to every corner of the state. Check the Wilderness chapter for the complete list and descriptions of their expeditions, and don't be shy about calling them at the last minute. Often you not only

get a place in the group but get a hefty discount as well for filling up a leftover spot. Those who don't have the time or the money for a 10 day float or a trek in the Brooks Range should not overlook the day trips out of the city.

Camp Alaska Tours (tel 376-2353), based in Wasilla, offer tours by van, as opposed to tours by bus, where travellers sleep in a tent and donate to a food kitty. Although not quite a wilderness guide company, they are definitely a lot more personal and affordable than a Gray Line tour.

Among the trips they offer are a 7 day journey that includes Valdez, Columbia Glacier, Fairbanks and Denali National Park for $550 per person, and a 6 day adventure through the Kenai Peninsula and Kodiak Island for $525. The nice thing about the Kodiak trip is that a van allows the group to see parts of the island most travellers miss.

Alaska Sea Kayak Adventures (tel 276-3418) have been around for a while and can meet the needs of anybody who wants to try sea kayaking. The guide company can supply all the gear and offers a wide range of outings from 1 to 7 days.

Alaska Alpine School (tel 277-6867) offers glacier trekking, mountaineering, ski touring or outings as uncomplicated as nature hikes and backpacking trips. The cost of joining a nature hike begins at $50, while your first ascent of a mountain might cost $2100.

The ultimate in white-water rafting lies 80 miles (128 km) north-east of Anchorage in the Matanuska River. The Lions Head portion of the river is rated Class IV and V on the International White Water Scale and is an exhilarating, drenching experience. Nova Riverrunners (tel 745-5753) in Chickaloon run a 4 hour float down the Matanuska River and provide transport if you need it. They also have 2 day helicopter/raft trips on the Chickaloon River and 3 day adventures on the Talkeetna River; guided raft trips cost from $40 per person.

Other rafting companies to check into are Knik Glacier Raft Tours (tel 745-1577), which have an easy-paddling raft trip on the Knik River for $30, and Alaska Whitewater Wilderness Raft Trips (tel 338-0471), which offer half-day to 5 day expeditions.

Getting There & Away

Air Anchorage International Airport, 6.5 miles (10.5 km) west of the city centre, is one of the busiest airports in the country, handling 130 flights daily from the 16 major airlines that serve it. From here you can catch a flight to anywhere in Alaska. Alaska Airlines (tel 243-3300) and its system of contract carriers provide the most intrastate routes to travellers, with flights departing daily.

Samples of one-way fares from Anchorage are: $116 to Fairbanks, $192 to Juneau, $79 to Cordova and $231 to Nome. Far cheaper flights are available if you book return tickets 2 weeks in advance. ERA provides flights to Valdez ($88 one way) and you book them through Alaska Airlines.

MarkAir (tel 243-1414) provides services to Katmai, Barrow, Denali National Park and Kodiak among other places. A one-way ticket to Kodiak is $138 and you can also book that through Alaska Airlines. There is often information about plane tickets for sale in the classified pages of the *Anchorage Times*.

Bus Alaska-Denali Transit (tel 561-1078) has a weekly van during the summer that departs Anchorage on Saturday at 8 am for a 2 day trip to Haines via Denali National Park and Fairbanks. They stop overnight in Tok and then reach Haines on Sunday evening in time for you to catch the state ferry on Monday back to Bellingham.

The one-way fare from Anchorage to Haines is $115, to Fairbanks $55 and to Denali National Park $35. The return trip leaves Haines at 8.00 am Tuesdays, and arrives in Anchorage around 9.30 pm on Wednesday evening. The company has recently overhauled its routes and schedules so contact them at 701 West 58th Ave in Anchorage to double-check timetables and departure points.

The Alaska-Yukon Motorcoaches (tel

276-1305), which picks up passengers at the Sheffield Hotel on the corner of 5th Ave and G St, offer a daily run to Valdez for $75, and by way of Prince William Sound for $140. It also offers services to Haines three times a week for $250. The Haines run is a 3 day trip with overnight stops (at your own expense) at Glennallen and Destruction Bay. You can also catch a daily bus to Glennallen for $45.

Gray Line's Alaskon Express (tel 227-5581) departs from its office on 547 West 4th Ave as well as a handful of major hotels on Saturday and Tuesday at 7 am for Palmer, Glennallen, Tok and Beaver Creek in the Yukon Territories where the bus stops overnight. From Beaver Creek you can make connections to Whitehorse, Haines or Skagway. The overnight stop is at your own expense and the one-way fare to Haines is $173, Skagway $185, Tok $77 and Glennallen $48.

Seward Bus Lines (tel 224-3608) takes on passengers at the Samovar Inn on the corner of 7th Ave and Gambell St and departs daily at 2.30 pm for Seward, reaching the town at 5.30 pm. The one-way fare is $25.

Also working the Kenai Peninsula is Alaska Intercity Lines (tel 279-3221) which departs Anchorage Sunday to Friday at 7 am and reaches Soldotna at noon and Homer at 3.30 pm. The buses depart from various hotels, including the Westmark Anchorage at 720 West 5th Ave, the Sheraton Anchorage at 401 East 6th Ave and Days Inn at 321 East 5th Ave. The one-way fare to Soldotna is $27.50 and $37.50 to Homer.

Train The Alaska Railroad (tel 265-2494) maintains its office in the depot at 421 West 1st Ave and provides services both north and south of Anchorage. To the north, the Denali Express departs Anchorage daily at 8.30 am, reaching Denali Park at 3.45 pm and Fairbanks at 8 pm. The one-way fare to Denali is $62 and to Fairbanks is $88. On Wednesday, Saturday and Sunday a local train departs Anchorage at 8.30 am and makes an all stops trip to Hurricane Gulch; the return fare to Hurricane Gulch is $88.

To the south, a bus departs Anchorage Rail Depot at 11.45 am daily which connects with the 1.30 pm Whittier Shuttle. This train arrives at Whittier in time to connect with the 3 pm sailing of the MV *Bartlett* past the Columbia Glacier to Valdez. The service is provided from late May to mid-September; the one-way fare to Whittier is $18.

From late May to the first week of September you can also catch a rail diesel car to Seward from Thursday to Monday. The trip is a scenic one along the Turnagain Arm and through the mountains of the Kenai Peninsula where you pass three glaciers and cross steep gorges. The train departs Anchorage at 7 am and arrives in Seward at 11 pm. There is also a special run on the Fourth of July holiday. The one-way fare is $35, and the round trip is $60.

Boat The State Marine Ferry (tel 272-4482) doesn't service Anchorage but does have an office in the city at 213 West 5th Ave. Here you can obtain information, make reservations or purchase advance tickets. If you know the dates on which you want to make the Columbia Glacier cruise, it is highly recommended that you purchase your ticket as far in advance as possible for this popular trip.

Hitchhiking Hitching out of Anchorage can be made a lot easier by first spending 80 cents and hopping on a People Mover bus. Travellers heading north should take bus Nos 76, 78, 93 or 102 to Peter's Creek Trading Post on Glenn Highway. If you're heading to Portage, Seward or the rest of the Kenai Peninsula, take bus Nos 92 or 101 and get off at the corner of De Armoun Rd and Seward Highway.

Getting Around
Airport Transport People arriving at the International Airport have a couple of ways to reach the city. Ace Airporter (tel 694-6484) is a limousine service which leaves every half an hour from 5.30 am to 8 pm daily from the baggage claim area to major hotels in the city centre; plan on $7 one way.

Even cheaper is to wait a little and catch

the People Mover bus No 6, which departs roughly every hour Monday to Saturday from the lower level near gate 33. The fare is 80 cents and the bus ends up at the Transit Center which is only a block from the youth hostel.

Bus Anchorage has a good public bus system in the People Mover. All buses, except No 93, begin at the People Mover's terminal in the Transit Center at the Municipal Building near the corner of 6th Ave and G St in the city centre. The fare is 80 cents or $15 for 20 tokens, and drivers do not carry any change. If the trip requires more than one bus, ask the driver for a transfer, which allows you to ride on the connecting bus for only an additional 10 cents.

A full service operates from Monday to Friday, with a reduced service on Saturday; 10 buses run on Sunday, none of which go to the International Airport. For information on any route call the Ride Line on 343-6543.

If you are planning to spend some time in the Anchorage area there are two things worth investing in. Pick up a copy of the *People Mover Timetable* for 50 cents at the Transit Center which details all the routes and bus times. You might also want to purchase a monthly bus pass which provides unlimited travel for $25.

Car Rental When there are three or more of you, renting a used car is often an affordable and ideal way to see Anchorage, the surrounding area or the Kenai Peninsula. You may be able to find a used compact for $20 a day plus 20 cents a mile at some of the small independent dealers (service stations that rent cars between oil changes).

Try Road Ready (tel 279-7287) or check the yellow pages for others. Also reasonably priced is Rent-A-Wreck (tel 561-2218) which has an office at the International Airport. A step up in price is All-Star Rental (tel 243-2271) with compacts for $29.95 per day and 25 cents a mile with 150 free miles. If you can, try to reserve a vehicle in advance as car rentals in Anchorage can be heavily booked.

Bicycle Anchorage has 120 miles (196 km) of paved bicycle paths that parallel major roads or wind through many of its parks and green-belt areas. One of the more popular routes is the 4 mile (6.4 km) path through the Chester Creek Green Belt from the University of Alaska and Goose Lake Park to Westchester Lagoon overlooking Knik Arm.

Or try the exceptionally beautiful Coastal Trail, which begins at Elderberry Park, at the western end of 5th Ave, and winds 11 miles (17.7 km) west of Anchorage around Point Woronzof to Point Campbell in Kincaid Park. Along the way you are treated to good views of Knik Arm where occasionally you can spot the backs of beluga whales. On clear days you can see the Alaska Range.

During the summer, Earth Cycles loans out fat-tyre, single-speed bicycles at the corner of 4th Ave and F St near the Log Cabin Visitor Center. The bikes are free as long as you supply a $5 deposit and photo identification. The bikes are available Monday to Saturday from 9 am to 5 pm. Trail maps are available at the nearby visitor centre.

Tours

City Tours The cheapest tour of the city is on board the People Mover's double-decker bus that departs from the Transit Center every hour or so and heads down Spenard Rd to the airport and returns back up A St, passing the Alaska History & Fine Art Museum along the way – all for just 80 cents.

For the deluxe bus tour of Anchorage, contact either Gray Line (tel 277-5581) at the corner of 4th Ave and F St, or Alaska Sightseeing (tel 276-1305) in the Sheraton Hotel on 4th Ave. Gray Line has a 4 hour tour for $20 that departs daily at 8 am and 3 pm and includes the Alaska History & Fine Arts Museum and Lake Hood among other sights. Alaska Sightseeing has a full-day bus tour for $48 which also includes the military bases, Portage Glacier and the Alyeska Ski Resort.

Area Tours Gray Line offers a daily 6 hour Portage Glacier/Turnagain Arm tour for $28 which departs at 8.30 am and noon. Gray

Line also operates the *Ptarmigan* which cruises past the Portage Glacier; the 4 hour trip from Anchorage that includes an hour on the boat is $32. It departs daily at 7.15 am and 3.30 pm. They also have a Matanuska Valley tour that includes Palmer and a visit to an Alaskan farm. You have to be hard pressed for something to do to take the farm tour, but it departs on Monday, Wednesday and Saturday during the summer and the fare is $26.

A better and much cheaper way to spend an afternoon is to hop on People Mover bus Nos 74, 76 or 78 for the scenic trip north of Anchorage along Eagle River, through Chugiak and to Peter's Creek. The 48 mile (77 km) round trip takes about 2 hours and costs a mere 80 cents. Those who take the first bus out in the morning have been known to occasionally spot moose between Fort Richardson and Eagle River.

Package Tours Travellers on a tight schedule will find a variety of package tours available in Anchorage to other areas of the state. They include accommodation, transport and meals, and are a way to cover a lot in a day or two if you are willing to pay the price.

The most popular trip out of the city is the cruise past Columbia Glacier to Valdez and returning to Anchorage along the scenic Richardson and Glenn highways. Both Gray Line (tel 277-5581) and Alaska Sightseeing (tel 276-1305) offer the tour as a 2 day/1 night package with a night at a hotel or a 1 day trip where you fly back to Anchorage. American Sightseeing's 2 day trip is $295 per person, based on shared accommodation, the 1 day rush is $285 per person. Gray Line is slightly cheaper with $259 for the 2 day trip and $255 for the 1 day excursion.

Grey Line and Alaska Sightseeing, along with a few other large tour companies, have package tours everywhere, shuffling tour groups to such unlikely places as Barrow and Kotzebue. If you only have a day left in Alaska and are just dying to see Kotzebue, Gray Line will take you there and back in only 11 hours for $315.

Also offering a variety of package tours is Alaska Railroad (tel 265-2494). Three are worth considering for those short on time. The Denali Overnight tour includes a return train trip to Denali National Park and 1 night's lodging in the park for $189 per person, based on double occupancy. But maybe the best deal is the 'Seward Sampler' where $109 gets you a return trip to the Kenai Peninsula town, a half-day cruise on Resurrection Bay and the possibility of stopping at Portage Glacier if you take a bus back.

For $219 per person, based on double occupancy, you can get lodging in Seward, an 8 hour Kenai Fjords cruise and a tour to Exit Glacier. If you can't spend at least a week in the Kenai Peninsula, this might be the best alternative.

Around Anchorage – South

Travellers who arrive in Anchorage and head south to the Kenai Peninsula will immediately be struck by Alaska's splendour; they no sooner leave the city limits than they find themselves following the edge of the spectacular Turnagain Arm. An extension of Cook Inlet, the arm is known for having some of the highest tides in the world while giving way to constant views of the Kenai Mountains to the south.

SEWARD HIGHWAY
The Seward Highway, which runs along Turnagain Arm south of Anchorage, hugs the water and at times has been carved out of the mountainside; it runs side by side with the Alaska Railroad. A bike path shoulders much of the road and when completed will connect the bike trails in Anchorage with those in Girdwood.

The Seward Highway begins as New Seward Highway in Anchorage on the corner of 5th Ave and Gambell St at a junction with the Glenn Highway. It heads south and reaches the coast near Rabbit Creek Rd.

From here the mileposts on the road measure the distance to Seward.

At *Mile 118* (190 km) or 9 miles (14.4 km) south of Anchorage city centre, the highway passes the first of many gravel Turnagain Arm lookouts. In 1 mile (1.6 km), the highway reaches two small lookouts over the **Potter Marsh Waterfowl Nesting Area**, a state game refuge. There are display signs at the lookouts where you can often marvel at arctic terns and Canada geese nesting nearby. Some 130 species of birds and waterfowl have been spotted in this refuge at Anchorage's back door.

Two miles (3.2 km) to the south you enter Chugach State Park and pass the **Potter Section House**. Renovated and re-opened in 1986, the house used to be home for a crew of railroad workers who maintained the tracks when locomotives were powered by coal. Now the house is a state historic site and museum featuring displays and railroad exhibits, including a vintage snowblower and working model train. It's open daily from May to September and has information on outdoor activities in Chugach State Park. There is no admission charge.

Across the street is the posted northern trailhead for the **Old Johnson Trail**, an 11 mile (17.6 km) path. The route was originally used by Indians and later by Russians, trappers and gold miners at the turn of the century. Today, it provides you with an easy hike and a 'mountain-goat's eye view' of Turnagain Arm, alpine meadows and beluga whales feeding in the waters below. From Potter, the trail heads south-east and reaches McHugh Picnic Area in 3.5 miles (5.6 km); Rainbow (with access to Seward Highway) in 7.5 miles (12 km); and Windy Corner at its southern end in 9.5 miles (15.2 km). Plan on 5 to 7 hours for the entire walk.

In the next 10 miles (16 km), the highway passes numerous lookouts, many with scenic views of Turnagain Arm. Just beyond *Mile 112* (179.2 km) of Seward Highway is McHugh Creek Picnic Area (30 picnic tables) and the second access to the Old Johnson Trail followed by **Beluga Point**. The point has a commanding view of the Turnagain Arm and features telescopes and interpretive displays to assist travellers in spotting the white whales in May and August. At *Mile 103.6* (166.7 km) is **Indian**, consisting mainly of a couple of bars and a restaurant.

Just west of Turnagain House and Indian Creek is a gravel road that leads 1.3 miles (2 km) past a pump station and ends near Indian Creek, where there is parking space and the posted trailhead for the **Indian Valley Trail**, a 6 mile (9.6 km) path to Indian Pass. The trail is easy, with only an occasional ford of Indian Creek, and leads to the alpine setting of the pass. In the alpine areas of the pass, more experienced hikers can continue north to eventually reach the Ship Creek Trail which ends at Ski Bowl Rd north of Anchorage. Plan on 5 to 7 hours for the 12 mile (19.2 km) round trip on the Indian Valley Trail.

The **Bird Ridge Trail** starts near *Mile 102* (164 km) of Seward Highway, look for a large marked parking area to the north. From here the trail to the ridge begins with an uphill climb to a power line access road, follows it for 0.3 mile (0.5 km) and then turns left and climbs Bird Ridge, which runs along the valley of Bird Creek. The hike is steep in many places but quickly leaves the bush behind for the alpine beauty above. You can hike over 4 miles (6.4 km) on the ridge itself, reaching views of the headwaters of Ship Creek below. Viewing points of Turnagain Arm are plentiful and make the trail a good mountain hike.

The *Bird Creek State Campground* (19 sites, $5) is just beyond *Mile 101* (161.6 km). The campground is scenic and known for its fine sunbathing, but is often full by early afternoon during the summer, especially on weekends. The next 10 miles (16 km) after Bird Creek Campground contains 16 turn-offs, all good spots to watch the **tidal bores**. Bores, barrelling walls of water that often exceed 10 feet (3 metres) in height as they rush 15 miles (24 km) an hour back across the mud flats, are created twice a day by the powerful tides in Turnagain Arm.

There are more than 60 places around the world where tidal bores occur (the highest are the 25 foot (7 metre) bores on the Amazon basin) but the Turnagain and Knik arms are the only places in the USA where they take place on a regular basis. To avoid missing the turbulent incoming waves, get the time of low tide from either of Anchorage's daily newspapers and add two hours and 15 minutes. At that time the bore will be passing this point along the highway. Arrive early and then continue down the road after the bore passes your lookout to view it again and again.

Alyeska Access Rd

Girdwood At *Mile 90* (144.9 km) of Seward Highway is the junction with the access road which goes to Girdwood, a small hamlet of 300 residents, 2 miles (3.2 km) north-east up the side road. Girdwood has a post office, restaurants, grocery store and Kinder Park, site of the town's annual Forest Fair usually held in the first week of July. The 2 day event features a variety of entertainment, art & craft booths, contests and food in a delightful small-town atmosphere.

Alyeska Ski Area Another mile (1.6 km) east of Girdwood is the Alyeska Ski Area. The ski resort hums during the winter and is also a busy place during the summer, when tour groups leave the buses to wander through the gift shops and expensive restaurants or participate in hot-air balloon flights and horse-drawn carriage rides. The best thing about the resort is the scenic chair-lift ride to the Skyline Restaurant, 2000 feet (612 metres) above the valley floor. The 20 minute ride costs $15 per person but the views of the surrounding area and Turnagain Arm are incredible; it's a lazy person's way to good alpine hiking.

A small but charming youth hostel in the area can be reached by turning right onto Timberline Drive before the ski lodge and then turning right again on Alpine Rd for 0.4 mile (0.6 km). The *Alyeska Youth Hostel* (tel 277-7388) is in a cabin with wood heat, gas lighting and a kitchen area, and includes the use of a wood-burning sauna.

Unfortunately, the hostel only has six beds, so you might want to make reservations by sending the first night's fee, name, time and date of arrival to the Alyeska Hostel, PO Box 10-4099, Anchorage, Alaska 99510, or call ahead to try and secure space. The hostel is only open from Wednesday to Sunday and nightly fees are $8 for members and $10 for nonmembers.

Begin the **Alyeska Glacier View Trail** by taking the chair lift to the Skyline Restaurant and then scrambling up the knob behind the sun deck. From here, you follow the ridge into an alpine area where there are views of the tiny Alyeska Glacier. The entire return hike is less than 1 mile (1.6 km). You can continue up the ridge to climb the so-called summit of Mt Alyeska, a high point of 3939 feet (1201 metres). The true summit lies further to the south but is not a climb for casual hikers.

Crow Creek Rd Two miles (3.2 km) up the Alyeska Access Rd and just before Gird-wood is the junction with Crow Creek Rd, a bumpy gravel road. It extends 5.8 miles (9.3 km) to a parking lot and the marked trailhead to the **Crow Creek Trail**, a short but beautiful alpine hike. It is 4 miles (6.4 km) to Raven Glacier, the traditional turn-around point of the trail, and with transport, hikers can easily do the 8 mile (12.8 km) round trip in 4 to 8 hours.

The trail is a highly recommended trek as it features gold-mining relics, an alpine lake and usually Dall sheep on the slopes above. There are also many possibilities for longer trips and a US Forest Service (USFS) cabin 3 miles (4.8 km) up the trail ($20 per night) which can be reserved in advance through the USFS office in Anchorage. You can also camp around Crow Pass, turning the walk into a pleasant overnight trip. Or, you can continue and complete the 3 day, 25 mile (40 km) route along the Old Iditarod Trail to the Chugach State Park Eagle River Visitor Center (see the Around Anchorage – North section in this chapter).

From the Alyeska Access Rd, Seward Highway continues south-east and at *Mile 81*

(129.6 km) reaches the **Wetland Observation Platform** constructed by the Bureau of Land Management. The platform features interpretive plaques on the ducks, arctic terns, bald eagles and other wildlife that can often been seen from it.

Portage

Portage, the departure point for passengers and cars going to Whittier on the Alaska Railroad, is passed at *Mile 80* (128 km) of Seward Highway. There is not much left to Portage, which was destroyed by the Good Friday Earthquake, other than a few structures sinking into the nearby mud flats. During the summer, the shuttle train departs the loading ramp six times from Thursday to Monday at 8 and 10.45 am and 1.30, 5, 7.30 and 9.30 pm. On Tuesday and Wednesday it just departs on the four afternoon runs. The daily 1.30 pm trip connects with the MV *Bartlett*, the state ferry that cruises from Whittier to Valdez. The one-way fare from Whittier to Portage is $7.50 per adult and $32 for a car.

Portage Glacier

A mile (1.6 km) south of the loading ramp in Portage is the junction with Portage Glacier Access Rd. The road leads 5.4 miles (8.7 km) past three campgrounds to a visitor centre overlooking Portage Glacier, which recently surpassed Denali National Park as Alaska's most visited attraction. More than 600,000 people view it annually with the number raising sharply each year. This is evident during the summer as a stream of tour buses and cars pass through. The magnificent ice floe is 5 miles (8 km) long and 1 mile (1.6 km) wide at its face and is the Southcentral's version of the drive-in glacier.

However, even if crowds are what you're trying to avoid, Portage Glacier is not to be missed. The glacier, with its lake and icebergs, is classic Alaskan imagery, while the **Begich-Boggs Visitor Center**, completed in 1986, is well worth viewing. The $8 million centre houses, among other things, a simulated ice cave you can walk through, an

iceberg taken from Portage Lake that you can touch, a 200 seat theatre with free films shown regularly, and an enclosed observation deck.

For those who want to get even closer to the glacier, Gray Line recently began 1 hour cruises on board it's tour boat, *Ptarmigan*. Don't get this cruise confused with any glacier cruise along Tracy Arm in the Southeast or College Fjord in Prince William Sound; you simply motor around the lake and it's $18.50 per person.

If you're planning to camp in the area, take in some of the activities sponsored by the centre. They include nature walks, gold-panning demonstrations and a hike to Byron Glacier to search for iceworms.

There are only two campgrounds in the area now as Beaver Pond was flooded when nature's little engineers built additional dams. Try either the *Black Bear Campground* (12 sites, $5 fee) or *Williwaw Campground* (38 sites, $5).

Williwaw is particularly pleasant as there is a salmon-spawning observation deck near it and a 1 mile (1.6 km) nature walk through beaver and moose habitat. Keep in mind, you never get a site late in the day at these campgrounds. With more than half a million people coming to see Portage Glacier annually, these facilities always seem to be full.

Check with rangers about a planned trail to the face of Portage Glacier. Otherwise, hiking in the area consists of the **Byron Glacier Trail**, an easy 1 mile (1.6 km) path to the base of Byron Glacier that begins near the visitor centre (see the Portage Glacier map on page 213). Once you reach the permanent snow in front of the glacier, look for iceworms in it. The worms, immortalised in a Robert Service poem, are black, thread-like and less then an inch (2.5 cm) long. They survive by consuming algae and escape the heat of the sun by sliding between ice crystals of glaciers and snowfields.

From Portage, Seward Highway turns south and heads for the scenic town of Seward on Resurrection Bay, 128 miles (205 km) from Anchorage (see the Southcentral chapter).

Around Anchorage – North

GLENN HIGHWAY

The 189 mile (304 km) Glenn Highway begins at the corner of Medfra St and 5th Ave (*Mile 0*), just west of Merrill Field Airport in Anchorage, and extends to Glennallen and the Richardson Highway. The first 42 miles (68 km) heads north-east to Palmer, the trade centre of the Matanuska Valley, where the highway connects with the George Parks Highway which goes to Fairbanks. From here, the Glenn Highway curves north-east to Glennallen (see the Interior chapter). Mileposts on the highway show distances from Anchorage.

On the first 8 miles (12.8 km) north-east from Anchorage, you pass the exits to Elmendorf Air Force Base, Centennial Campground and Arctic Valley Rd to Fort Richardson (see the Anchorage Things to See section). At *Mile 11.5* (18.5 km) of Glenn Highway is the turnoff to *Eagle River State Campground* (50 sites, $10 fee), just up Hiland Rd. The scenic campground is in a wooded area on the south bank of the Eagle River. The spot is popular and has a 4 day limit. Don't drink the glacier-fed water of the Eagle River. Also, don't plan on getting a tent space if you arrive late.

At *Mile 13.6* (22 km) of Glenn Highway is the exit to Eagle River (pop 9000) and Eagle River Rd. This 12.7 mile (20.4 km) road ends at the **Eagle River Visitor Center** for Chugach State Forest. The log cabin centre (tel 694-2108) is open daily, except Wednesday, from 11 am to 7 pm and features wildlife displays, hand-outs for hikers, naturalist programmes and telescopes with which to view Dall sheep in the surrounding mountains.

The visitor centre also serves as the northern trailhead for the **Old Iditarod Trail**, a 25 mile (40 km) historical trail. The route was used by gold miners and dog-sled teams until 1918, when the Alaska Railroad was completed from Seward to Fairbanks. Today, it is

a 3 day hike through excellent mountain scenery and up to Crow Pass, where you can view nearby Raven Glacier and Crystal Lake. From here you hike down the Crow Creek Trail and emerge on Crow Creek Rd, 7 miles (11.2 km) away from the Seward Highway (see the Around Anchorage – South section in this chapter).

Although this route involves fording several streams, including Eagle River itself, and some climbing to Crow Pass, it is an excellent hike – one of the best in the Southcentral and Anchorage regions. It is also a way to bypass Anchorage for those who want to avoid big-city hassles and head straight for the Kenai Peninsula. Backpackers in Anchorage can reach the junction of Eagle River Rd on People Mover bus Nos 74, 76 and 78 and from there hitch to the visitor centre. Bring a stove as campfires are not allowed in the state park.

Northbound on Glenn Highway, the Thunderbird Falls exit is reached at *Mile 25.2* (40.6 km) and leads 0.3 mile (0.5 km) to a parking area and the trailhead for the **Thunderbird Falls Trail**. The 1 mile (1.6 km) trail is a quick and easy hike to the scenic falls formed by a small, rocky gorge.

Eklutna

The Indian village of Eklutna (pop 25 or so) is reached by taking the Eklutna Rd exit at *Mile 26.5* (42.6 km) of Glenn Highway. The village is west of the highway and contains the **St Nicholas Russian Orthodox Church** (built in the 1830s), a hand-hewn log chapel, and brightly coloured spirit houses in a cemetery nearby.

Eklutna Rd bumps and winds east for 10 miles (16 km) to the west end of Eklutna Lake, the largest body of water, 7 miles (11.2 km) long, in Chugach State Park. Here you'll find the *Eklutna Lake State Recreation Area* (50 sites, $5 fee). The road continues east past the campground and around the lake, but vehicles are prohibited due to numerous washouts. Motorcycles and bicycles may be used along this section, however.

From the campground parking lot, head across a bridge to the picnic area and look for

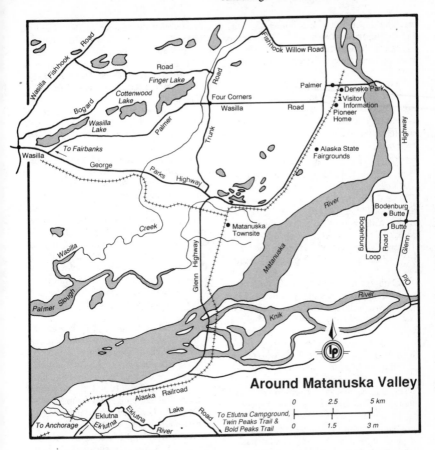

Around Matanuska Valley

0	2.5	5 km
0	1.5	3 m

the marked trailhead to **Twin Peaks Trail**. The trail is an abandoned road that heads 4 miles (6.4 km) above the tree line to the passes between Twin Peaks. It is well marked in the beginning and forks after a quarter of a mile (0.4 km), rejoining the spur 0.5 mile (0.8 km) later. Above the tree line, the road turns into a hard-to-follow trail. At this point, scrambling in the alpine area is easy and the views of Eklutna Lake below are excellent. Plan on several hours for the hike, depending on how far you go above the tree line, and keep a sharp eye out for Dall sheep.

The **Bold Peak Trail** is another good hike

from the lake shore to the alpine area below Bold Peak, 7522 feet (2294 metres). The drawback is that you have to walk (or bike) 5.5 miles (8.8 km) from the Eklutna Lake picnic area to the trailhead due to washouts that have closed the remainder of Eklutna Lake Rd to vehicles.

Heading east around the lake and look for a large stream that flows underneath the road through four large culverts. After crossing it, walk another 150 yards (136 metres) and turn sharply left (north) on an old road. The trailhead is posted 50 yards (45 metres) up the road. From here, the trail ascends steeply, reaching the bush line in 1.5 miles (2.4 km) and ending in another mile (1.6 km). Great views are obtained here, while those people with the energy can scramble up nearby ridges.

To actually climb Bold Peak requires mountaineering skill and equipment. The Bold Peak Trail round trip, from the campground and picnic area, is a 16 mile (25.6 km) hike and takes 8 to 10 hours.

PALMER

From Eklutna Lake Rd, the Glenn Highway continues north, crosses bridges over the Knik and Matanuska rivers at the northern end of Cook Inlet, and at *Mile 35.3* (56.8 km) reaches a major junction with the the George Parks Highway. At this point, Glenn Highway curves sharply to the east and leads into Palmer (pop 3000), 7 miles (11.2 km) away.

Although a railroad station was built here in 1916, the town was really born in 1935, when it was selected for an unusual social experiment during President Franklin Roosevelt's New Deal relief programmes. Some 200 farming families, hit hard by the Great Depression in the US Midwest, were moved north to raise crops and livestock in the Matanuska and Susitna valleys.

The failure rate was high within this transplanted agricultural colony, but somehow Palmer survived and today it is the only community whose economy is based primarily on farming. The farms of the Matanuska Valley grow the 60 lb (27 kg) cabbages and 7 lb (3.1 kg) turnips as a result of the midnight sun that shines up to 20 hours a day during the summer.

Things to See

Stop at the **Palmer Visitor Center** (tel 745-2880), a rustic log cabin near the corner of Fireweed Ave and South Valley Way in the centre of town. Open from 9 am to 6 pm daily, the centre has a small museum in the basement with relics from its 'colony' era. Outside is its Agricultural Showcase, a garden of flowers and the area's famous

oversized vegetables such as 50 lb (22 kg) cabbages and 100 lb (45 kg) pumpkins.

More farming relics and an odd assortment of planes, cars and trucks can be viewed at the **Alaska Historic & Transportation Museum** on the state fairgrounds 1 mile (1.6 km) south of town off Glenn Highway. The museum is open Tuesday to Saturday from 8 am to 4 pm and has outdoor exhibits and displays in three railroad cars. There is also a building which contains bush-pilot portraits and aircraft engines among other things, and is named after noted pilot Don Sheldon. The admission charge is $3.

Also in the state fairgrounds is the **Colony Village**, which began in 1975 as a Bicentennial project. The village attempts to preserve buildings from the area's 'colony' days of the late 1930s. Of the five buildings, four of them, two houses, a barn and a church, were part of the original Matanuska Valley Colony and built in either 1935 or 1936. Admission into the village is free, and it is open from 10 am to 4 pm Monday to Saturday.

Farms If you have a vehicle, a drive through the back roads of the Palmer area and past the farms makes an interesting afternoon. To view a few of the colony farms that survived along with the original barns they built, head north-east 9 miles (14.4 km) on Glenn Highway and exit onto Farm Loop Rd.

Old Glenn Highway, which departs from the present highway right before the bridges across the Knik and Matanuska rivers and rejoins it in Palmer, can also provide views of the area's farms, especially on Bodenberg Loop Rd that runs off it, west from Butte. Keep an eye out for vegetable stands if you're passing through the area during mid to late summer.

At *Mile 50* (80 km) of Glenn Highway, just east of Palmer, is the **Musk Ox Farm**, where you can see the only domestic herd of these prehistoric beasts in the world. Tours allow you to view and photograph more than 100 shaggy musk oxen while the guide explains how their qiviut (down hair) is combed and woven into the world's rarest cloth, and probably one of the most expen-

Palmer

sive at more than $60 per oz (28.4 g). The farm is open daily from June to mid-September from 10 am to 6 pm and admission is $5. Tours are given every half-hour and a gift shop displays the finished products.

Riding Stables With all the farms in the valley, it shouldn't be surprising that the Palmer area boasts a number of riding stables and horse ranches. The Silver Bullet Ranch (tel 745-8646) is south-east of Palmer off the Old Glenn Highway (call to get exact turn-by-turn directions) and offers unguided horseback rides through wooded trails along the Knik River. Rates range from $15 an hour per person to $60 for a 5 hour ride; they will also arrange overnight rides. Also check with Hatcher Pass Trail Rides (tel 745-2789) which has half-day guided rides in the Hatcher Pass area north of Palmer for $50 per person.

Festivals
The best reason to stop in Palmer is the Alaska State Fair, an 11 day event that ends on Labor Day (7 September). The fair features produce and livestock from the surrounding area, horse shows, a rodeo, a carnival and the largest cabbages you'll ever see. Within the state fairgrounds is the outdoor Borealis Theatre and during the third week of July it is the site of a bluegrass festival, worth attending if you are passing through. Those in Anchorage should check with the Alaska Railroad (265-2494) which occasionally runs special trains to Palmer for these events.

Places to Stay
Camping Camping in town is possible at *Deneke Park*, where there is a large grassy area for people to pitch tents. The park also has tables and coin-operated showers. The nightly fee is $4.40. From the visitor centre,

head north along South Valley Way and turn right into East Cottonwood Ave just past the Alaska State Troopers office. The park is on the corner of East Cottonwood and South Denali streets.

Bed & Breakfast Contact Mat-Su Valley Bed & Breakfast Association (tel 376-7662) or pick up their brochure at the visitor centre. The brochure lists 10 B&Bs with rates from $20 per person. Most of them, however, are outside of town.

Hotels There is no youth hostel in Palmer. The cheapest hotel in town is the *Pioneer Motel* (tel 745-3425) at the corner of North Alaska and Arctic streets, where a single room is $40 per night. Also in Palmer is the *Fairview Motel* (tel 745-1505) across from the state fairgrounds which has singles for $46 and doubles for $56.

Hiking

The best hike near Palmer is the climb to the top of Lazy Mountain, elevation 3720 feet (1134 metres). The 2.5 mile (4 km) trail is steep at times, but makes for a pleasant trek that ends in a alpine setting with good views of the Matanuska Valley and its farms below. From the Glenn Highway in Palmer, head east on Arctic Ave, the third exit into town, which turns into Old Glenn Highway. After crossing the Matanuska River, turn left onto Clark-Wolverine Rd and then left in 0.5 mile (0.8 km) at a 'T' junction. This puts you onto the unmarked Huntly Rd, and you follow it for 1 mile (1.6 km) to the Equestrian Center parking lot at its end. The trailhead, marked Foot Trail, is on the north side of the parking lot. Plan on 3 to 5 hours for the return hike.

Rafting

Knik Glacier Raft Tours (tel 745-1577) operates out of Palmer and has a raft trip down the Knik River past the 5 mile (8 km) wide Knik Glacier. This is a float down a river not a heart-throbbing white-water adventure, but the scenery is spectacular. Trips depart daily at noon and 6 pm. The cost is $30 per person with transport from Palmer.

Caribou

The Interior

Between Anchorage and Fairbanks is an area commonly referred to as the Interior and affectionately referred to as the 'Golden Heart of Alaska'. This 'great, big, broad land way up yonder' has been searched over by miners, immortalised by poets such as Robert Service and is immediately visualised when somebody says 'the Last Frontier'.

The Golden Heart is bordered by dramatic mountain chains, with the Alaska Range lying to the south and the Brooks Range to the north. In between is the central plateau of Alaska, a vast area of land that gently slopes to the north and is broken up by awesome rivers such as the Yukon, Kuskokwim, Koyukuk and Tanana. It is the home of Mt McKinley, the highest peak in North America (20,320 feet, 6194 metres), and of Denali National Park & Preserve, the best known attraction in the state, which offers superb hiking, camping and fishing. It is the stomping grounds for brown bear, moose, caribou and Dall sheep, whose numbers are unmatched anywhere else in the USA.

The Interior can be enjoyed by even the most impecunious traveller because it's accessible by road. The greater part of Alaska's highway system forms a triangle which includes the state's two largest cities, Anchorage and Fairbanks, and allows cheap travel by bus, train, car or hitchhiking.

The George Parks Highway leaves Anchorage and winds 358 miles (573 km) to Fairbanks, passing Denali National Park along the way. The Glenn Highway spans 189 miles (302 km) between Anchorage and Glennallen and then continues another 125 miles (200 km) to Tok in a section known as the Tok Cutoff. The Richardson Highway passes Glennallen from Valdez and ends at Fairbanks, 368 miles (589 km) away. Dividing the triangle from east to west is the Denali Highway, 136 miles (218 km) long and at one time the only road to Denali National Park.

All four roads are called highways, though they are rarely more than two-lane roads. All of them pass through spectacular scenery, offer good possibilities of spotting wildlife and are lined with turn-offs, campgrounds and hiking trails. For the most part, the towns along them are small, colourless service centres with gasoline stations, motels and cafes, although a few have managed to retain their rustic gold-rush and frontier flavour. The real attraction of the Interior is not these service centres but what lies in the hills and valleys beyond the highway.

In this region of mountains and spacious valleys, the climate varies greatly and the weather can change appreciably from 1 day to the next. In the winter, the temperatures drop to -60°F (-51°C) for days at a time. In the summer, they can soar above 90°F (32°C). The norm for the summer is long days with warm temperatures from 60°F to 70°F (15°C to 21°C). However, it is common for Denali National Park to experience at least one snowfall in the lowlands between June and August.

Here, more than anywhere else in the state, it is important to have warm clothes while still being able to strip down to a T-shirt and hiking shorts. Most of the area's 10 to 15 inches (250 to 380 mm) of annual precipitation comes in the form of summer showers, with cloudy conditions common, especially north of Mt McKinley. In Denali National Park, Mt McKinley is hidden by the weather for 2 days out of 3.

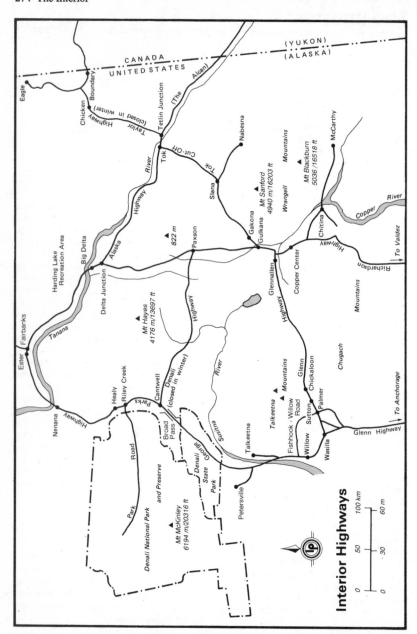

Interior Highways

Getting Around

Bus transport is available on every highway except the Denali, and there is a train service between Anchorage and Fairbanks (see the Getting Around chapter or the Getting There sections in this chapter). Bus routes and even the companies themselves change often in Alaska, so it pays to double-check bus departures with a phone call.

The hitchhiking is surprisingly good during the summer, as the highways are cluttered with the stream of campervans and summer tourists arriving from down south. Avoid backtracking if you can, even if it means going out of your way on an alternative route. All the highways offer their own roadside scenery that is nothing short of spectacular.

George Parks Highway

Many travellers and most overseas visitors arrive in Alaska through Anchorage and venture north along the George Parks Highway. The road, which was opened in 1971, provides a direct route to Denali National Park while passing through some of the most rugged scenery Alaska has to offer. The road begins at a junction with the Glenn Highway 35.3 miles (56.8 km) north of Anchorage. Mileposts read distances from Anchorage and not from the junction.

WASILLA

From its junction with Glenn Highway, the George Parks Highway heads north and passes numerous roadside stands selling fresh produce from the Matanuska Valley farms before reaching the town of Wasilla (pop 3700) in 7 miles (11.2 km).

At one time, this community was a mining supply centre and in the 1970s was little more than a sleepy little town servicing local farmers. From 1980 to 1983, the population of Wasilla doubled when Alaskans who wanted to work in Anchorage but live elsewhere began moving into the town making it an Anchorage dormitory community.

There was even talk of building a bridge across the Knik Arm to shorten the drive to Anchorage, while shopping malls and businesses have mushroomed along the highway. This is all a bit ironic because many feel Wasilla, with its strip malls and convenience stores, is now just a slice of the big city that many were trying to escape.

Things to See

The **Wasilla Museum** doubles as the visitor centre (tel 376-2005) and is in a historical park on Main St just off the highway. The centre is open daily year-round from 10 am to 6 pm and admission to the museum and **Frontier Village** is $1. The museum is packed with artefacts, including tools and other relics from the early farmers, and mining displays in the basement. In the historical village, there are half a dozen buildings; it's the place to go if you want to see Alaska's first public sauna or an historic ferris wheel.

Wasilla serves as the second starting point for the famous 1049 mile (1678 km) Iditarod race to Nome, while Knik, the home for many Alaskan mushers, is checkpoint number four on the route. For more on this uniquely Alaskan race, stop in at the **Iditarod Headquarters** (tel 376-5155) at *Mile 2.2* (3.5 km) of Knik Rd. The office is open daily during the summer from 8 am to 5 pm and has historical displays, a video of the race and a gift shop with an assortment of race paraphernalia.

If you want more information on dog mushing and racing, continue south along Knik Highway to *Mile 13.7* (22 km) and the **Knik Museum & Sled Dog Musher's Hall of Fame**. The museum is open from noon to 6 pm Wednesday to Sunday and you'll find more displays on the Iditarod Trail, Alaskan mushers and, of course, the Canine Hall of Fame.

Places to Stay & Eat

There are quite a few hotels and B&Bs in the Wasilla area but the best place to stay is the *Mat-Su Resort* (tel 376-2228) on the shores of Wasilla Lake. The resort has rooms from

$25 per person as well as bigger rooms with kitchenettes and even cabins. The resort also has a restaurant, lounge and an assortment of rowboats and paddleboats for rent on the lake. You can also try the *Windbreak Hotel* (tel 376-4484), 1 mile (1.6 km) south of town on George Parks Highway, which has singles for $35 and doubles for $45.

The nearest place to camp is *Lake Lucille Park*, a Matanuska-Susitna Borough park near the Iditarod Headquarters on Knik Highway. The park has a campground (46 sites, $5 fee) along with rest rooms, a shelter and a network of trails. There is also access to the lake which is stocked annually with silver salmon and rainbow trout.

For a more unusual side trip, spend a night or two in the Hatcher Pass area, near the Independence Mine State Historical Park on Fishhook-Willow Rd. Book your own cabin at *Hatcher Pass Bed & Breakfast* at the base of the pass on Fishhook-Willow Rd for $55 per night for two people. There is also the *Hatcher Pass Lodge* (tel 745-5897) further up the Fishhook-Willow Rd at *Mile 17* (27.7 km) with cabins, a restaurant and an outdoor sauna. Rooms begin at $40 per person.

It's mind boggling the variety of restaurants found in Wasilla, most surviving from highway trade. For a town of under 4000 residents, you'll find a *Shakey's Pizza*, *Wendy's*, *McDonald's*, *Burger King* and *Popeye's Chicken*. The only one missing in this group is the Colonel.

AROUND WASILLA
Independence Mine State Park

This fascinating 272 acre (110 hectare) state historical park, 21 miles (31.5 km) north of Wasilla, is entirely above the tree line. Within the beautiful bowl-shaped valley of the park are the remains of 16 buildings that were built in the 1930s by the Alaska-Pacific Mining Company which for 10 years were second only to Juneau's A-J Mine as the leading gold producer in Alaska. Today, it looks like a ghost town, with weather-beaten buildings surrounded by the craggy Talkeetna Mountains.

The Alaska Division of Parks administers and staffs the site and is busily restoring the old mess halls, bunkhouses and mills that still stand. Facilities include a museum and visitor centre (tel 745-2827), originally the manager's home, which has a hard-rock display and a simulated mining tunnel. Pick up maps and follow the walking tour of the area where interpretive signs explain the history and use of the remaining structures. Or join a guided tour ($2) that is given several times daily. You can even try your hand at gold panning with a pan from the visitor centre.

To reach the park, follow Wasilla's Main St east as it turns into Wasilla-Fishhook Rd and extends 10.5 miles (16.8 km) to a junction with Fishhook-Willow Rd. Turn left on this road; the park is another 10.5 miles (16.8 km) along the road. Hitchhiking is better than on most backcountry roads in Alaska, as more than 150,000 visitor annually endure the bumps and dust to view the mining relics. You can also join a guided tour in Palmer through Frontier Tours (tel 745-2880) which offer a 4 hour tour for $25 per person, or rent a vehicle for the day through National Car Rental (tel 373-7368), the only car rental company in Wasilla.

Big Lake

From Wasilla, the George Parks Highway continues in a westerly direction for the next 10 miles (16 km) and then curves north, reaching Willow at *Mile 69* (111 km). Before entering the small village, you pass two side roads to the west that lead to state recreation areas offering lakeside campgrounds and canoe trails.

At *Mile 52.3* (84.2 km), where the George Parks Highway curves north, is the junction with Big Lake Rd. Head 3.3 miles (5.3 km) down the road and turn right at the gasoline station; in 0.5 mile (0.8 km) you will reach the *Rocky Lake State Campground* (10 sites, $5 fee). A few hundred yards further along Big Lake Rd is a fork known as 'Fisher's Y' where the town of Big Lake (pop 2,300) has sprung up. The right fork leads 1.6 miles (2.6 km) to the *Big Lake North State Campground* (150 sites, $5), the left fork 1.7 miles

(2.7 km) to the *Big Lake South State Campground* (13 sites, $5 fee).

Big Lake is connected to several smaller lakes by dredged waterways, making it possible to paddle for miles, though you have to share the lake with powerboats. Another possible trip (if you can figure out how to get back) is to paddle Fish Creek, which begins in Big Lake and flows into the Knik Arm. The start of this canoe trail is where the left fork of Big Lake Rd crosses the creek. The trip is a 13 mile (21 km) paddle and ends at the Knik Rd bridge west of Knik (see the following Nancy Lake State Recreation Area section for information on canoe rental).

Nancy Lake State Recreation Area
The George Parks Highway continues northwest from Big Lake Rd, passes the village of Houston (pop 800) and *Little Susitna River City Campground* (86 sites, $5 fee), and reaches the junction with Nancy Lake Parkway at *Mile 67.2* (108 km). The parkway leads to the northern portion of the Nancy Lake State Recreation Area, a lake-studded park that offers camping, fishing, canoeing and hiking.

Although it lacks the dramatic scenery of the country to the north, the state park with its 130 lakes is still a scenic spot and one worth stopping at for a couple of days if you have the time. Within a mile or so on the parkway you come to the State Recreation Area office (tel 496-6273), the place to stop for information or to reserve a cabin. Nancy Lake Parkway extends 6.6 miles (10 km) to the west and ends at the *South Rolley Lake Campground* (106 sites, $5 fee).

Hiking For those without a canoe, you can still reach the backcountry by one of two trails. The **Chicken Lake Trail** begins at *Mile 5.7* (9.2 km) of the parkway and extends 3 miles (4.8 km) south to the lake and another 2.5 miles (4 km) to the east shore of Red Shirt Lake. A round-trip hike on the trail is an 11 mile (17.6 km) overnight trek but count on wet conditions at times.

More popular, and drier, is the **Twin Shirt Lakes Trail** that begins near the campground

at the end of the parkway. Built in 1986, the trail leads 3.5 miles (5.6 km) south primarily on high ground and ends at the northern end of Red Shirt Lake. Along the way you pass Red Shirt Overlook with its scenic views of the surrounding lake country and the Chugach Mountains on the horizon.

Paddling The most popular canoe trail is the **Lynx Lake Loop**, a 2 day, 16 mile (26 km) trip that passes through 14 lakes and over an equal number of portages. The trail begins and ends at the posted trailhead for the Milo Lakes Canoe Route on *Mile 4.7* (7.6 km) of the parkway. The portages are well marked and many of them are planked where they cross wet sections. The route includes nine primitive campsites, accessible only by canoe, but bring a camp stove because campfires are prohibited in the backcountry.

The largest lake on the route is Lynx Lake and you can extend your trip by paddling south on it where a portage leads off to six other lakes and two more primitive campsites in Skeetna Lake. You can rent canoes at Tippecanoe Rentals (tel 495-6688) in Willow. Rates begin at $5 an hour or $60 for 4 to 7 days. They will also arrange drop-off and pick-up transport for an additional fee.

Cabins The state recreation area has 12 cabins scattered along the shorelines of four lakes. They can be rented for up to 3 nights and most hold six people and cost $20. A few are larger and cost $25 a night. Four of the cabins are on Nancy Lake, and three of these can be reached after a short hike in from the Nancy Lake Parkway. Four more cabins are on Red Shirt Lake which requires a 3 mile (4.8 km) hike in and then a short canoe paddle. The other four cabins are on the Lynx Lake Canoe Route with three on Lynx Lake and one on James Lake.

The cabins are relatively new, most of them were built in 1988, and have plywood sleeping platforms, a wood stove and screens on the windows. As you can imagine, they are very popular. Try to reserve them ahead of time by writing to: Division of Parks & Outdoor Recreation, PO Box 107001,

278 The Interior – George Parks Highway

Anchorage, Alaska 99510; or call (907) 561-2020.

Getting There & Away The state recreation area can be reached from the Alaska Railroad by taking the local train from Anchorage to Willow and then hitchhiking or walking 1.8 miles (2.9 km) south on George Parks Highway to the junction of the Nancy Lake Parkway.

WILLOW
Willow (pop 500) at *Mile 69* (111 km) of the George Parks Highway is a small village that became famous in the 1970s as the place selected for the new Alaskan capital that was to be moved from Juneau. The capital-move issue was put on the back burner in 1982, however, when funding for the immense project was defeated in a general state election.

The Alaska Railroad stops in Willow, and it is a small service centre with the usual visitor facilities such as gasoline station, restaurant and grocery store. Two miles (3.2 km) north of Willow is the junction to Fishhook-Willow Rd that leads 31.6 miles (51 km) to the Independence Mine State Park and eventually to Glenn Highway by way of Hatcher Pass. By driving just 1.3 miles (2.1 km) up this road you reach the *Willow Creek State Campground* (17 sites, $5 fee).

To spend a night in a rustic cabin or for a great piece of home-made pie, stop at the *Sheep Mountain Lodge* (tel 745-5121) at *Mile 88* (143 km) of the George Parks Highway. The lodge has four log cabins, some with private baths and some without, that cost around $50 a night. Inside the main lodge is a restaurant, lunch counter and a bar.

TALKEETNA
At *Mile 98.7* (158.8 km) of George Parks Highway, a side road heads off to the north and leads 14.5 miles (23.3 km) to Talkeetna (pop 400), the most interesting and colourful town along the highway.

The village was once a pioneer mining and trapping settlement that was established in 1901, and today it retains much of that early Alaskan flavour along its narrow dirt roads lined with log cabins and clapboard businesses. Main St, the only paved road in the village, begins with a 'Welcome to beautiful downtown Talkeetna' sign at the town park and ends at the banks of the Susitna River. From here, it is possible to hike along the gravel banks of the river to camp, fish or take in the scenic views of the surrounding mountains.

Things to See & Do
On Main St is the **Talkeetna Museum** (tel 733-2571) in the old schoolhouse built in 1936. It is open daily during the summer from 10 am to 6 pm and can provide a walking-tour map of the town's historical buildings, of which many are being restored. Inside the museum are displays which cover Talkeetna's early history and two of its more famous characters – Ray Genet and Don Sheldon. Genet was an Alaskan mountain climber who made a record 25 climbs to the summit of Mt McKinley before dying near the summit of Mt Everest in Nepal. Sheldon was a bush pilot who pioneered many of the routes used today to carry climbers to Mt McKinley. There is also a rather impressive 12 foot (4 metre) high model of Mt Mckinley.

The High One (as Athabascan Indians referred to Mt McKinley) and the colourful legends of both men add considerably to the mountaineering atmosphere that is felt, seen and heard in Talkeetna during the summer. The town, though small, is the jumping-off spot for most climbing expeditions to North America's highest peak, and the scores of climbers from around the world give the place an international feel.

The vast majority of climbers use the West Buttress route, developed by Bradford Washburn, which means flying in ski planes from the town's airstrip to the Kahiltna Glacier. From here, at 7000 feet (2134 metres), they begin climbing for the South Peak, elevation 20,320 feet (6193 metres). There is a **National Park Service Ranger Station** (tel 733-2231) in town to handle the numerous expeditions during the summer;

they even have a slide and tape presentation on climbing North America's highest peak. Climbers themselves are often encountered in the local bars, hotels and roadhouses, and conversations with them make for an intriguing evening.

Other attractions in Talkeetna include the town's Moose Dropping Festival, held on the second Saturday in July. It features, among other things, a moose-dropping throwing contest. Several air-taxi operators run sightseeing flights to Mt McKinley that can be expensive but an awe-inspiring experience on a clear day. At times, it is possible to see climbing parties en route to the summit.

Check around with the handful of charter companies, but plan on spending from $60 to $85 for a flight, depending if you want to land on a glacier or not. If the day is nice, you'll be waiting in line at the airport but this flight is worth it. Offering such trips are K2 Aviation (tel 733-2291), Talkeetna Air Taxi (tel 733-2218) and Doug Geeting Aviation (tel 733-2366).

Another way to enjoy the mountain if the day is clear is to join a raft trip run by Talkeetna Rafting (tel 733-1045). The outfitters offer a 4 hour float down the Susitna River that includes a sand-bar fish fry and the possibility of seeing the peaks of the Alaska Range along with wildlife such as bald eagles and moose. The cost is $35 per person, and there is a four person minimum.

Places to Stay & Eat

There was once talk of opening up a youth hostel in Talkeetna while another one was located just a few miles north of town on the George Parks Highway. Neither made it into the 1990s. There are six hotel/lodges in town, of which the best is the *Fairview Inn* (tel 733-2423). The historical hotel was built in the early 1920s and was visited by President Harding in 1923 during his golden spike ceremony that completed the Alaska Railroad. Singles are $20 per night and doubles $25, but there are only six rooms which are heavily booked most of the summer. The inn also has a lively bar that is a good place to

meet climbers, w...
strums away on the...

There is the *City* ...
of Main St on the ban...
spots to pitch a tent can...
river's gravel bars a short ...

The best place for a hea...
Talkeetna Roadhouse (tel 733... the centre of town, where dinners ... served family style and you eat with lodge guests and the family that runs the place. You must contact them before 3 pm so they can set a place for you at dinner; it's an all-you-can-eat meal for only $10. Better still, go there in the morning for coffee and the best home-baked cinnamon rolls found on the George Parks Highway. The roadhouse also has rooms ranging from $27 for a single (shared bath) to $36 for a double.

Getting There & Away

The express train of the Alaska Railroad stops daily in Talkeetna from late May to mid-September on both its northbound and southbound runs from Anchorage to Fairbanks. The northbound train from Anchorage, heading for Denali National Park, arrives at 11.20 am; the southbound train arrives at 4 pm and reaches Anchorage that night at 8 pm. On Wednesday, Saturday and Sunday during the summer, the local train passes through Talkeetna before it turns around at Hurricane Gulch. Drop by the museum, the town's unofficial visitor centre, for more information.

Hitching along the spur road from Talkeetna to the George Parks Highway can be slow going at times, especially early in the morning for travellers in a rush to reach Anchorage or Denali National Park.

DENALI STATE PARK

This 324,420 acre (129,768 hectare) reserve, the second largest state park in Alaska, is entered when you cross the southern boundary at *Mile 132.2* (213 km) of the George Parks Highway. The park covers the transition zone from low coastal environment to the spine of the Alaska Range and provides numerous views of towering peaks, includ-

McKinley and the glaciers on its northern slopes. The park is largely undeveloped but does offer a handful of turn-offs, trails and one campground that can be reached from the George Parks Highway which runs through the preserve.

It may share the same name and a border with the renown national park to the north, but Denali State Park is an entirely different experience. Because of it's lack of facilities, you need to be more prepared when you arrive for hiking and backpacking adventures. There are no rangers here describing routes or an information centre selling maps and guidebooks. But this may be the park's blessing for this preserve also lacks the crowds, long waits and tight regulations that irk many backpackers to the north in Denali National Park. At the height of the summer season, experienced backpackers may want to consider the state park as a hassle-free and cheaper alternative to the national park.

Less than 3 miles (4.8 km) from the southern boundary of the park at *Mile 135.2* (217.6 km) of George Parks Highway is **Ruth Glacier Overlook**, where the glacier is less than 5 miles (8 km) to the north-west. Displays at the paved lookout also point out Mt McKinley, Mt Hunter, Moose Tooth and several glaciers. *Byers Lake State Campground* (66 sites, $5 fee) at *Mile 147* (236.6 km) of George Parks Highway provides tables, an outhouse and access to Byers Lake.

Hiking

There are currently several trails under consideration or construction in the park and interested hikers should contact the Alaska Division of Parks office in Anchorage (tel 561-2020) about the status and location of them. Keep in mind that no fires are allowed in the backcountry so you must pack a stove.

Byers Lake Trail This is an easy 5 mile (8 km) trek around the lake. It begins at the Byers Lake State Campground and passes six hike-in campsites on the other side of the lake that are 1.8 miles (2.9 km) from the posted trailhead.

Cascade Trail This 7 mile (11.4 km) route at the north-east end of the lake departs from the Byers Lake Trail. It ascends Curry Ridge to Tarn Point, providing spectacular views of the area.

Troublesome Creek Trail The trailhead is posted and in a parking area at *Mile 137.7* (224 km) of the George Parks Highway. The trail ascends along the creek until it reaches the tree line where you move into an open area dotted with alpine lakes and surrounded by mountainous views. From here, it becomes a route marked only by rock cairns as it heads north to intersect the Cascade Trail.

Either follow the Cascade Trail to Byers Lake Campground for a 15 mile (24.4 km) backpacking trip or, for the more adventurous, continue onto the Little Coal Creek Trail, a 32 mile (52 km) trek above the tree line. The views from the ridges are spectacular but keep in mind numerous black bears feeding on salmon is the reason for the creek's name.

Little Coal Creek Trail At *Mile 163.8* (263.6 km) of the George Parks Highway, there is the trailhead and parking area for the Little Coal Creek Trail, which ascends to the tree line of Indian Ridge. From there, you continue to the summit of Indian Mountain, an elevation gain of about 3,300 feet (990 metres). It's a 9 mile (14.7 km) round-trip trek but again the views are well worth the effort.

BROAD PASS TO DENALI NATIONAL PARK

The northern boundary of the Denali State Park is at *Mile 168.6* (271.3 km) of George Parks Highway, and 9 miles (14 km) beyond that is the bridge over Honolulu Creek where the road begins a gradual ascent to **Broad Pass**. Within 18 miles (29 km) of the creek you begin viewing the pass and actually reach it at *Mile 203.6* (327.7 km), where there is a paved parking area.

Broad Pass, elevation 2300 feet (701 metres), is the point of divide where rivers to the south drain into Cook Inlet and those to the north empty into the Yukon River. The area is worth stopping at in order to spend some time hiking. The mountain valley, surrounded by white peaks, is unquestionably one of the most beautiful spots along the George Parks Highway or the Alaska Railroad line, as both use the low gap to cross the Alaska Range.

From the pass, the George Parks Highway begins a descent and after 6.3 miles (10 km) comes to the Cantwell Post Office just before *Mile 210* (336 km) at the junction with Denali Highway. The rest of **Cantwell** (pop 100) lies 2 miles (3.2 km) west on the Denali Highway. Another scenic spot is reached at *Mile 234* (377 km) on the east side of the highway, where there are fine views of **Mt Fellows**, elevation 4476 feet (1364 metres). The mountain is well photographed because of the constantly changing shadows on its sides. The peak is especially beautiful at sunset.

The entrance to Denali National Park & Preserve is at *Mile 237.3* (382 km) of George Parks Highway and just inside the park are two campgrounds. The next public campground is in Fairbanks. The highway before and after the park entrance has become a tourist strip of private campgrounds, lodges, restaurants and other businesses, all feeding off Alaska's most famous drawing card.

Snowshoe Hare

Denali National Park

The name has been changed and the boundaries altered, but the park is still unquestionably Alaska's best known and probably most-loved attraction. Few people leave Denali National Park disappointed. Most visitors, especially backpackers, depart amazed at what they saw and loaded with canisters of exposed film.

Situated on the northern and southern flanks of the Alaska Range, 237 miles (382 km) from Anchorage and about half that distance from Fairbanks, Denali is the nation's first subarctic national park and a

wilderness that can be enjoyed by those who never sleep in a tent. As a result of the 1980 Alaska Lands Act, the old Mt McKinley National Park was enlarged by 4 million acres (1.6 million hectares), redesignated and renamed.

Today, the park comprises 6 million acres (2.4 million hectares) or an area slightly larger than the US state of Massachusetts. Within it roam 37 species of mammals, ranging from moose, caribou, Dall sheep and brown bears to foxes and snowshoe hares, while 130 different bird species have been spotted.

The park's main attraction is Mt McKinley, an overwhelming sight if you catch it on a clear day. At 20,320 feet (6194 metres), the peak of this massif is almost 4 miles high, but what makes it stunning is that it rises from an elevation of 2000 feet (610 metres). What you see from the park road is 18,000 feet (5490 metres), almost 3 miles, of rock, snow and glaciers reaching for the sky. In contrast, Mt Everest, the highest mountain in the world at 29,028 feet (8848 metres), only rises 11,000 feet (3353 metres) from the Tibetan Plateau.

Combine the park's easy viewing of wildlife and the grandeur of Mt McKinley with the free shuttle-bus system and the fine accommodation at the park entrance and you have the source of its only complaint – crowds. The park attracted more than 650,000 people in 1989; a decade earlier only a fifth of that number visited it. From late June to early September, Denali National Park is a busy and popular place. Riley Creek Campground overflows with campervans, nearby Morino Campground is crowded with backpackers, and the park's hotel is bustling with large tour groups. The pursuit of shuttle-bus seats, backcountry permits and campground reservations at the visitor centre often involves long, Disneyland-type lines.

Although crowds disappear once you are hiking in the backcountry, many people prefer to visit the park in early June or late September to avoid them. Mid to late September can be particularly pleasant, for not only are the crowds gone but so are the bugs. This is also when the area changes colours and valleys go from a dull green to a fiery red, while the trees turn every shade of yellow and orange.

It is wise to arrive at the park early in the day if possible, as all the campgrounds are filled on a first-come first-serve basis. In the middle of the tourist season, campgrounds are often full by 10 am and there is little you can do but look for accommodation outside the park. Except for the Morino Campground near the entrance, which is a walk-in campground for backpackers, sites at all park campgrounds are obtained by registering first at the Riley Creek Visitor Center. Popular sites like Wonder Lake are booked solid for days at a time.

The same holds true for backcountry permits. The park is divided into 37 zones and only a regulated number of backpackers are allowed into each section at a time. You have to obtain a permit for the zone you want to stay overnight in, and that usually means waiting a day or two at Riley Creek until one opens up. Denali National Park cannot be a quick side trip in the middle of the summer. Plan to spend at least 3 days or more if you want to spend a night in one of its campgrounds and a day riding the shuttle bus to Wonder Lake.

There is also an admission fee now, though it should hardly stop anybody from visiting the park. A $3 per person fee is charged to all visitors travelling beyond the check point at Savage River Campground. The fee is collected when you obtain a shuttle bus token at the Riley Creek Visitor Center, making some complain that the shuttle bus really isn't free after all. It all depends on how you view it, I guess.

Information

The Riley Creek Visitor Center near the entrance of the park can supply information and hand-outs as well as permits, and also sells topographic maps and publications relating to Denali National Park. Outside the centre, there is a 24 hour recorded weather report, worth listening to if you have just obtained your backcountry permit. The centre is open daily during the summer from 5.30 am to 7 pm.

The Eielson Visitor Center at *Mile 66* (106.2 km) of the park road is also a source of information, hand-outs, topographic maps and backcountry permits. The ranger staff hold their own hikes and naturalist programmes. Eielson Visitor Center is open daily during the summer from 9.30 am to 7.30 pm.

Along the Park Road

The park road begins at George Parks Highway and winds 91.6 miles (147.4 km) through the heart of the park, ending at Kantishna, an old mining settlement and the site of two wilderness lodges. Travellers with vehicles can only drive to Savage River Campground at *Mile 12* (19.2 km) of the park road during the summer unless you have a special permit, which for anybody not related to the park superintendent is impossible to obtain.

Half of the free shuttle buses run from Riley Creek to the Eielson Visitor Center at *Mile 66* (106.2 km) and then turn around; the round trip takes 7½ hours. The rest drive all the way to Wonder Lake Campground, *Mile 84* (135.2 km), a 10 hour round trip.

Mt McKinley is not visible from the park entrance or the nearby campgrounds and hotel. Your first glimpse of it comes between *Mile 9* (14.4 km) and *Mile 11* (17.6 km) of the park road, if you are blessed with a clear day. The park's weather, despite its Interior location, is cool, with long periods of overcast conditions and drizzle during the summer. The rule of thumb stressed by the National Park Service rangers is that Mt McKinley is hidden 2 out of 3 days.

From Savage River, the road dips into the Sanctuary and Teklanika river valleys, and Mt McKinley disappears behind the foothills. Both these rivers make for excellent hiking areas, and three of the five backcountry campgrounds are situated along them. Sanctuary River Campground is the most scenic of the three and at *Mile 22* (35.8 km) it is a good base camp to explore Primrose Ridge, an excellent hiking area.

Equally scenic and just as small (seven sites) is the Igloo Creek Campground at *Mile 34* (55.4 km) of the park road in a spruce woods along the creek. This camp allows you to make an easy day hike into the Igloo and Cathedral mountains to spot Dall sheep.

After passing through the canyon formed by the Igloo and Cathedral mountains, the road ascends to **Sable Pass**, elevation 3880 feet (1183 metres) at *Mile 38.5* (62 km). The canyon and surrounding mountains are excellent places to spot Dall sheep, while the pass is known as a prime habitat for Toklat brown bears. From here, the road drops to the bridge over the East Fork Toklat River at *Mile 44* (71 km). Hikers will enjoy treks that lead from the bridge along the river banks both north and south. By hiking north, you can complete a 6 mile (9.6 km) loop that ends at the **Polychrome Pass Overlook** at *Mile 46.3* (74.5 km) of the park road.

The pass is a rest stop for the shuttle buses and a popular spot for visitors. This scenic area has an elevation of 3500 feet (1067 metres) and gives way to views of the Toklat River to the south. The alpine tundra above the road is good for hiking and an excellent place to photograph Dall sheep.

The park road then crosses two single-lane, wooden bridges over the Toklat River and ascends near **Stony Hill**, elevation 4508

feet (1374 km) at *Mile 61* (98 km). This is the first spot for an exceptional view of Mt McKinley, while another quarter of a mile (0.4 km) down the road is a lookout for viewing caribou. From the lookout, a short scramble north takes you to the summit of Stony Hill. After climbing through Thorofare Pass, elevation 3900 feet (1189 metres), the road descends to the **Eielson Visitor Center** at *Mile 66* (106.2 km).

The centre is known for its excellent views of Mt McKinley, the surrounding peaks of the Alaska Range and Muldrow Glacier. It offers interpretive displays and conducts a series of its own programmes, including hikes, afternoon naturalist talks and demonstrations. One programme worth sticking around for is the hour-long Tundra Walk that takes place daily at 1 pm and again at 3 pm. Catch a shuttle bus by 11 am at Riley Creek to make it to the centre for the walk. Several day and overnight hikes are possible from the centre, including one around Mt Eielson (see the Trekking section in the Wilderness chapter) and another to Muldrow Glacier.

Past the Eielson Visitor Center the park road drops to the valley below, passing at *Mile 74.4* (119.7 km) of the park road a sign for **Muldrow Glacier**. At this point, the glacier lies about 1 mile (1.6 km) to the south, and the terminus of the 32 mile (51 km) ice floe is clearly visible, though darkened by a blanket of vegetation.

Wonder Lake Campground is at *Mile 84* (135.2 km) of the park road. Here the beauty of Mt McKinley is doubled on a clear day, with the mountain's reflection in the lake's surface. Ironically, the heavy demand for the 20 sites at Wonder Lake and the numerous overcast days caused by Mt McKinley itself prevent the majority of visitors from ever seeing this remarkable panorama. If you do experience the reddish sunset on the summit reflecting off the still waters of the lake, cherish it as a priceless moment.

Places to Stay

Those opposed to sleeping in a tent have few alternatives at the main entrance of the park. The *Denali National Park Hotel* (tel 683-

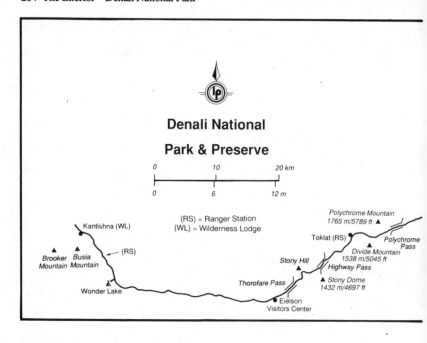

Denali National

Park & Preserve

(RS) = Ranger Station
(WL) = Wilderness Lodge

Kantishna (WL)

Brooker   Busia
Mountain Mountain

(RS)

Wonder Lake

Polychrome Mountain
1765 m/5789 ft ▲

Toklat (RS)

Polychrome
Pass

Divide Mountain
1538 m/5045 ft

Stony Hill

Highway Pass

Thorofare Pass

▲ Stony Dome
1432 m/4697 ft

Eielson
Visitors Center

2215 in the summer) only offers rooms at $100 or more per night. There used to be inexpensive compartments in original Pullman sleepers of the Alaska Railroad but the National Park Service condemned them in 1987. They also ruled out the youth hostel situated nearby in railroad cars, which means if you want go cheap inside the park you have to camp.

Camping The campgrounds at the main entrance of the park are the *Riley Creek Campground* and the *Morino Campground*. First, stop at the nearby visitor centre to be assigned a site in Riley Creek, the largest and nicest campground in the park. There are 102 sites (of which most are gone before noon), piped-in water and flush toilets; the nightly fee is $10.

The Morino is a free walk-in campground for backpackers without vehicles, providing only a metal cache to keep your food away from the bears. Though it is listed as having only 10 sites, there is usually a spot to pitch a tent. The other five campgrounds are spread along the park road, four of them within the first 34 miles (54.4 km). They are:

Savage River (34 sites, $10) at *Mile 12* (19.3 km)
Sanctuary River (7 sites, $10) at *Mile 22* (35.4 km)
Teklanika River (50 sites, $10) at *Mile 29* (46.6 km)
Igloo Creek (7 sites, $10) at *Mile 34* (54.4 km)
Wonder Lake (20 sites, $10) at *Mile 84* (135.2 km)

You may have to spend a day or two waiting for an open campsite somewhere, and there is a 14 day limit on staying in one campground or a combination of them.

Wilderness Lodges At the western end of the park road are two places that are as close to wilderness lodges as you'll ever find on a road. *Camp Denali* (tel 683-2290) offers several different types of accommodation, most with fixed arrival and departure dates.

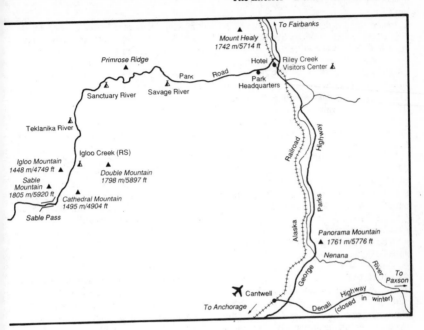

But they do have Hawk's Nest cabins for $200 a night that will hold up to four people. Camp Denali is more than just a place to stay as they offer a wide range of activities including wildlife observation and photography, rafting, fishing, gold panning and, of course, hiking. Plus your best view of the High One (Mt McKinley) is obtained from here.

Nearby is the *Kantishna Roadhouse* (733-2535) with cabin accommodation that start over $100 a night. The wilderness resort also has gold panning, hiking, photography activities during the day and a hot tub and sauna to enjoy at night. Keep in mind that these places will most likely be booked long before you arrive in Alaska. If you want to treat yourself (and escape the crowds at Riley Creek), write to the lodges in advance, 6 months in advance is not over doing it. Write to: Camp Denali, PO Box 216, Cornish, New Hampshire 03746, (603) 675-2248; or Kantishna Roadhouse, PO Box 130, Denali National Park, Alaska 99755.

Outside the Park For a park of 6 million acres (2.4 million hectares), Denali occasionally stuns visitors who arrive late in the afternoon or the early evening to find that there is no place to stay. They are informed by National Park Service rangers of private accommodation outside the park, and these people make a good living from the overflow.

Included among these are several private campgrounds where you can expect to pay from $10 to $15 for a campsite. The closest is the *Lynx Creek Campground* (tel 683-2548) 1 mile (1.6 km) north of the park entrance on George Parks Highway. *Canyon Campground* (tel 683-2379) is 3 miles (4.8 km) north of the park.

Six miles (9.6 km) south of the park entrance is the *Denali Grizzly Bear Campground* (tel 683-2696) which offers campsites, tents for rent and cabins with cooking facilities. Near Healy, a small town 11 miles (17.6 km) north of the park entrance, there is the *KOA Campground* (tel 683-2379), which provides free bus rides to the Riley Creek Visitor Center.

If there are three or four in your party, consider *Denali Cabins* (tel 683-2643 during the summer), where you can get a large cedar cabin with outdoor hot tub for $70 per night. The cabins are 6 miles (9.6 km) south of the park entrance at *Mile 231* (369.6 km) of George Parks Highway but there is a shuttle bus service to the entrance.

There's also *Denali Bed & Breakfast* (tel 683-2258) which offers tent cabins for $35 a night for two and is across from the Lynx Creek Campground north of the park entrance. At *Mile 238.5* (388.7 km) of the George Parks Highway is *Denali Crow's Nest Log Cabins* (tel 683-2723), looking like a Swiss alpine village on the edge of Horseshoe Lake; a cabin for four is $75.

Places to Eat

There are two restaurants and one bar in the park, all located off the lobby of the Denali National Park Hotel. The *Denali Dining Room* serves full meals in pleasant surroundings but is overpriced for most budget travellers. Breakfast after 8 am, however, can be a leisurely and reasonable $7 affair; it is pleasant to sit around drinking the fresh coffee for a spell. The *Whistle Stop Snack Shop*, also off the lobby, is open from 11 am until midnight and serves hamburgers and sandwiches.

The *Gold Spike Saloon*, two lounge cars side by side, is the hotel's bar that hops at night with an interesting mixture of climbers, hikers, visitors and park employees. An even more interesting gathering of travellers can be found in the hotel lobby itself, where around the giant stone fireplace you'll find retired couples dragging large suitcases, foreign tour groups being herded here and there, and backpackers munching on dried banana chips from their day pack.

McKinley Mercantile, a block from the hotel, sells a variety of fresh and dried food, some canned goods and other supplies. The selection is limited and highly priced. Your best bet is to stock up on supplies in Fairbanks or Anchorage before leaving for the park. The small park grocery store is open daily from 8 am to 8 pm and has coin-operated showers behind it. Once you leave the main entrance area, there are no more visitor services in the park.

Activities

Riley Creek Visitor Center offers a variety of programmes during the summer, all of them free. One of the most popular is the dog-sled demonstration. The park keeps the dogs for winter maintenance of the park and holds demonstrations daily at 11 am, 3 and 4 pm behind park headquarters, 3.5 miles (5.6 km) west of the entrance on the park road. The 30 minute talks explain the current and historical use of the dogs, and the teams pull a ranger on a wheeled sled. A free bus leaves the visitor centre half an hour before each demonstration.

The centre also offers daily nature walks from the park hotel and longer hikes throughout the park. Check the centre's bulletin board for the time and place of the day hikes. The auditorium behind the park hotel is the site of a daily slide programme at 7 and 9 pm that covers the history, wildlife or mountaineering aspects of the park. There are also daily campfire programmes at Riley Creek Campground, and at Savage River and Teklanika River campgrounds various nights of the week.

Hiking

Even for those who have neither the desire nor the equipment for an overnight trek, hiking is still the best way to enjoy the park and to obtain a personal closeness with the land and its wildlife. The best way to undertake a day hike is to ride the shuttle bus and get off at any valley, river bed or ridge that takes your fancy. There are few trails in the park as most hiking is done across open terrain. When you've had enough for one day, return to the road and flag down the first bus going in your direction.

You can hike virtually anywhere in the park that hasn't been closed because of the impact on wildlife. Popular areas include the

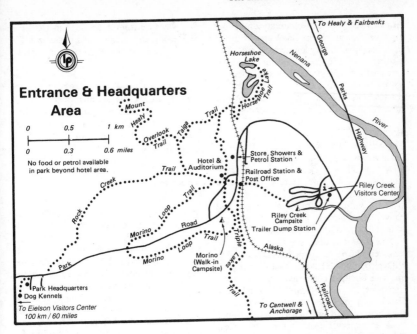

Entrance & Headquarters Area

No food or petrol available in park beyond hotel area.

Teklanika River south of the park road, the Toklat River, the ridges near Polychrome Pass and the tundra areas near the Eielson Visitor Center. On a day hike, always take piped water with you, as water found in the park must be boiled or treated before drinking (see the Health Section in the Facts for the Visitor chapter for information on water purification). The few maintained trails in the park are found around the main entrance area.

Horseshoe Lake Trail This trail is a leisurely 0.5 mile (0.8 km) walk from the Denali National Park Hotel to an overlook of the lake. An additional 0.7 mile (1.2 km) takes you down a steep trail to the lake. At the Riley Creek Visitor Center, trail guides are available to describe plants and animals seen along the way.

Triple Lakes Trail A moderate 9 mile (14.4 km) hike that starts from the railroad depot,

runs along the train tracks and ends at the George Parks Highway. After crossing Riley Creek train trestle, the trail skirts off the tracks, follows the creek drainage and passes Triple Lakes. The trail emerges on the George Parks Highway just north of McKinley Village, 7 miles (11.2 km) south of the park entrance.

Morino Loop Trail This leisurely walk of 1.5 miles (2.4 km) begins off the road through Riley Creek Campground and offers good views of Hines and Riley creeks. Eventually the trail swings through the Morino Campground and back to the Riley Creek Campground.

Mt Healy Trail Behind the west wing of the park hotel is the trailhead for the steep hike up Mt Healy. The trail is 3 miles (4.8 km) long, ascends 1700 feet (518 metres) and offers fine views of the Nenana Valley. Plan on 5 to 6 hours for the round trip.

Rock Creek Trail This moderate 2 mile (3.2 km) walk connects the hotel area with the park headquarters & dog kennels area. The trail passes Rock Creek near the headquarters and then passes through mixed aspen and spruce forest before emerging on the service road behind the hotel. This is a pleasant way to arrive at the sled-dog demonstrations.

Rafting

The Nenana River and the impressive gorge it carves is a popular white-water rafting area. Several rafting companies offer daily floats here during the summer. The most exciting run, called the Healy Express, consists of 22 miles (35 km) of white water and canyon, ending near the town of Healy, 10 miles (16 km) north of the park.

This float runs often every day during the summer. The departure point is at McKinley Village, 7 miles (11.2 km) south of the park entrance but most companies run shuttle bus transport from the Denali National Park Hotel. The going rate is $30 per person for the 2 hour run and $45 for a 4 hour trip. Either book at the travel desks in the hotel or call Denali Raft Adventures (tel 683-2234), McKinley Raft Tours (tel 683-2392) or Owl Rafting (tel 683-2215).

Getting There & Away

Air ERA Aviation (tel 248-4422 in Anchorage) has an office in the railroad depot and offers a daily flight to Anchorage that departs the Denali Park Airstrip at 3 pm; the one-way fare is $98. From Anchorage, a flight departs to the park from the International Airport at 1.30 pm. There is no break in price for a round-trip ticket.

Bus Both north and southbound bus services are available from Denali National Park. Alaska-Yukon Motorcoaches has a daily bus from Anchorage to Fairbanks which reaches Denali at 1.45 pm and then departs an hour later. There is also a southbound bus that arrives at the park at noon and then continues onto Anchorage at 2 pm. But keep in mind that this company wants to sell package tours not a bus seat, so their prices are steep. The one-way fare from Anchorage to Denali is $95; from Anchorage to Fairbanks is $120. Check at the park hotel for departure points and tickets.

Alaska-Denali Transit, a budget bus company, has a weekly Anchorage to Haines service during the summer that runs via Denali, Fairbanks and Tok (see the Bus section in the Getting Around chapter). The one-way fare from Anchorage to Denali National Park is $35; the bus leaves Anchorage 8.00 am on Saturdays. Call (907) 273-3331 for reservations, schedule information and pick-up points.

Train The most enjoyable way to arrive at the park is aboard the Alaska Railroad (see the Train section in the Getting Around chapter) with its viewing-dome cars that provide sweeping views of Mt McKinley and the Susitna and Nenana river valleys along the way. All trains arrive at the railroad depot between the Riley Creek Campground and the park hotel, and only stay long enough for passengers to board. Within the depot is a post office, some lockers and the offices for local air-taxi operators.

You can only arrive at Denali on the express train; the northbound train leaves Anchorage at 8.30 am daily from late May to mid-September arriving in Denali at 3.45 pm and reaching Fairbanks at 8 pm. The southbound train leaves Fairbanks at 8.30 am, arrives in Denali at 12.15 pm (or so they say) and arrives in Anchorage at 8 pm. The one-way fare from Denali National Park to Anchorage is $62; the fare to Fairbanks is $33.

Getting Around

Shuttle Bus What makes the park and its wildlife so accessible is the park road that runs the length of the preserve and the free shuttle buses that use it. Buses leave the Riley Creek Visitor Center every half an hour from 6 am to 2 pm and then every hour until 6 pm. Between 6 and 7 pm an overnight bus departs for Wonder Lake, returning the next morning. The buses either head out to the

Top: Anchorage skyline (ADT)
Bottom: Floatplane in Anchorage (AVB)

Top: Dog sledding (ADT)
Bottom: The Nenana River Gorge and the Alaska Railroad en route to Denali National Pa[r]k
and Preserve (JD)

Red Fox

the wildlife is accustomed to the rambling yellow school buses and rarely stop their activities when one passes by. The naturalist on board can't guarantee it, but it's a pretty sure bet that passengers will be able to spot some wildlife on any trip. The most common are brown bears, moose, Dall sheep, red foxes and ptarmigans.

You have to use the bus system to go from one campground to the next as in 1987 officials put a ban on campers from driving to their reserved sites. The buses also provide access to the best day hikes for which back-country permits are not needed. Once in the backcountry, you can stop a bus in either direction on the park road by flagging it down for a ride back, if they are not full.

Passengers armed with binoculars and cameras scour the terrain for wildlife. When something is spotted, the name of the animal is called out, prompting the driver to slow down and sometimes stop for viewing and picture taking. The driver also doubles as a park guide and naturalist for a more interesting trip. Some visitors never put on hiking boots, but just ride the shuttle bus.

Eielson Visitor Center or to Wonder Lake before turning around.

Use of the buses is free, but there is a heavy demand for the 40 seats on each one. So heavy, that park officials have begun handing out bus tokens the day before their date of use. The token guarantees you a seat on a particular bus and by all means try to obtain them the night before. If you are part of a group, you can pick up tokens for every-body, while people with campsite permits can register for a special bus.

If you didn't obtain a token the day before, get to the Riley Creek Visitor Center at 5 am or so for a 6 am bus token. It's worth losing a little sleep to make it to the first runs of the day, as the wildlife is superb in the early morning and competition for the buses between 8 and 10 am is fierce. Also keep in mind that competition for late afternoon buses is not as heavy and they return in the early evening, another prime time to spot wildlife.

The free bus system was put into effect in 1972 to prevent the park road from becoming a busy highway of cars and trailers. Today,

Tour Bus The park concessionaire operates a bus tour along the park road. The bus departs from the Denali National Park Hotel at 6 am and 3 pm daily. The 6 hour tour, designed primarily for package-tour groups, costs $35 per person and doesn't even go as far as the Eielson Visitor Center. Reserve a seat the night before at the Denali National Park Hotel reservation desk.

NORTH OF DENALI NATIONAL PARK

For 50 miles (80 km) north of the Denali National Park entrance, the George Parks Highway parallels the Nenana River, provid-ing many viewing points of the scenic river. One of them is the June Creek Rest Area at *Mile 269* (433 km), where a gravel road leads down to the small creek and a wooden stair-case takes you up to fine views of the area. Also provided are outhouses, picnic tables and shelters.

Nenana

The only major town between Denali National Park and Fairbanks is Nenana (pop 540) which you reach at *Mile 305* (488 km) of George Parks Highway before crossing the Tanana River. Originally a construction camp for the Alaska Railroad, the town made history on 5 July 1923 when President Warren G Harding arrived and drove the golden spike that completed the railroad on the north side of the Tanana River.

Today, the community is more famous for the Nenana Ice Classic, a lottery event in which Alaskans try to guess the exact time of the ice break-up. The first movement of river ice in April or May is determined by a tripod which the surging ice dislodges. The movement stops a clock and the official winner is announced. Excitement swells in the small town, and through most of the state for that matter, as break-up time nears in Nenana.

Stop at the **Nenana Visitor Center** (tel 832-9453), a log cabin with a sod roof at the junction of the George Parks Highway and A St, to see a replica of the tripod and the 1974 book of guesses – a 12 by 18 inch (30.5 by 45.7 cm) volume that is almost 4 inches (10 cm) thick. Outside the visitor centre is the *Taku Chief* river tug, which once pushed barges along the Tanana River. The centre is open daily during the summer from 8 am to 6 pm.

Travel down Front St, parallel to the river in town, or cross to the north side of the bridge to view **fish wheels** at work, best seen in late summer during the salmon runs. The wheels, a traditional fish trap, scoop salmon out of the water as they move upstream to spawn.

Nenana was little more than the site of a roadhouse until it was chosen as the base to build the northern portion of the Alaska Railroad. Its depot was built in 1923, extensively restored in 1988 and is now on the National Register of Historic Places. It's an impressive building and includes the **Alaska Railroad Museum**. East of the depot, a monument commemorates when President Harding drove in the gold spike marking the completion of the Alaska Railroad.

Ester

From Nenana, the George Parks Highway shifts to a more easterly direction, passes a few more scenic turn-offs and arrives at the old mining town of Ester (pop 200) at *Mile 351.7* (566 km). The town was established in 1906 when a sizeable strike was made at Ester Creek, and at one time Ester was a thriving community of 15,000.

Today, Ester is the home of the *Cripple Creek Resort* (tel 479-7274 in the summer) and its Malemute Saloon, the restored mess hall and bunkhouse of the mining camp and a regular stop for every tour bus out of Fairbanks. Rooms at the resort range from $33 for a single to $38 a double and $43 for a triple. The saloon, with its rustic mining-days atmosphere and daily recitals of Robert Service poetry, can be a fun place at night. Shows begin nightly at 8 pm and are $5 per person. If you're hungry, check out their *Bunkhouse Restaurant* where they charge $12 for a plate at their all-you-can-eat buffet and $18 for all the Alaskan Dungeness crab you can feast on.

From Ester, it is 7 miles (11.2 km) to Fairbanks, the second largest city in Alaska, at the end of George Parks Highway at *Mile 358* (576 km) (see the Fairbanks chapter).

The Alcan

Travellers heading north along the Alcan (also called the Alaska Highway) reach the USA/Canadian border at *Mile 1189.5* (1914.3 km) from Dawson Creek in British Columbia. The spot is marked by a lookout and plaque, while 0.5 mile (0.8 km) further along the highway is the US Customs border station. On the USA side of the highway you will notice mileposts at almost every mile. These posts were erected in the 1940s to help travellers know where they were on the new wilderness road. Today, they are a tradition throughout Alaska and are still used for mailing addresses and locations of businesses. They measure the mileage from Dawson Creek, *Mile 0* on the Alcan.

Once in Alaska, two US Fish & Wildlife campgrounds (free!) are passed along the Alcan before you reach Tok. At *Mile 1249.4* (2010.7 km) is the *Deadman Lake Campground* (15 sites). At *Mile 1456.7* (2022.5 km) is the *Lakeview Campground* (eight sites) on beautiful Yager Lake where on a nice day you can see the St Elias Range to the south.

TOK

Although you enter Alaska just north of Beaver Creek in the Yukon, Tok serves as the gateway to the 49th State. The town of 1200, 125 miles (200 km) beyond the USA/Canadian border, is at the major junction between the Alcan (Alaska Highway) that heads north-west to Fairbanks 206 miles (329.6 km) away, and the Tok Cutoff, an extension of the Glenn Highway that ends in Anchorage 328 miles (528 km) to the south-west.

Tok was born in 1942 as a construction camp for the Alcan. Originally, it was called Tokyo Camp near Tokyo River, but WW II sentiment caused locals to shorten it to Tok. Today, the town is a trade and service centre for almost 4000 residents in the surrounding area. If arriving into Alaska, this is your first chance to gather up information and brochures for around the state.

Information

Near the corner of the Tok Cutoff and the Alcan is the Tok Visitor Center & Alaska Public Lands Information Center (tel 883-5667), open daily in the summer from 7 am to 10 pm. The centre offers a mountain of travel information and hand-outs along with free coffee, a large floor map and rest rooms. There is also a small museum in the timberline room and wildlife displays consisting of mounted heads and skins. The most important item in the centre for many backpackers is the message board. Check out the board or display your own message if you are trying to hitch a ride through Canada along the Alcan. It is best to arrange a ride in Tok and not wait until you reach the international border.

Directly across the highway from the visitor centre is the **Tetlin National Wildlife Refuge office** (tel 883-5312). The US Fish & Wildlife office is open from 8 am to 4.30 pm Monday to Friday and has films on Alaskan wildlife that are usually shown in the Public Lands Information Center at 10 am, 11 am, 3 pm and 6 pm; there is no admission charge.

Things to See

You can hop on the **Red Shuttle Bus** for $1 which departs the visitor centre from 4 to 9 pm for a tour of the area. Tok is the Sled Dog Capital of Alaska as it is estimated one of every three people in the area is involved with the sport in one way or another. Most of them by raising dogs. Ask at the visitor centre about local dog-sled demonstrations that are usually held in town throughout the summer.

If you are staying overnight in Tok, by all means don't miss the showing of *Spirit of the Wind*, a movie that was made and produced in Alaska which covers the life of one of the state's most famous dog-sled racers. The music in this film, alone, is worth the $3.95 admission. It's shown nightly at 8.30 pm in the Westmark Inn.

Places to Stay

Camping The closest private campground is the *Golden Bear Motel* (tel 883-2561) just 0.3 mile (0.5 km) south of town on Tok Cutoff. The motel has tent spaces for $8 a night and coin-operated showers, but it is the first of many tourist traps in the state set up to catch the steady stream of campervans passing through. Among the things it uses as bait is a sad-looking moose called Bucky that is saddled so tourists can have their picture taken on it. Wouldn't the gang back home love that? The closest public campground is the *Tok River State Recreation Site* (25 sites, $5 fee), a scenic spot with access to the river.

Youth Hostel Probably the best accommodation in town is at the *Tok International Youth Hostel*, a mile south on a side road at *Mile 1322.5* (2116 km) of the Alcan. That puts it 9 miles (14.4 km) west of the town, but it provides 10 beds in a big army tent along with tent sites in a pleasant wooded area. Those biking it to Alaska should note that Tok's bike trails pass near the hostel before ending at Tanacross Junction at *Mile 1325.8* (2133.7 km) of the Alcan. The rate per night at the hostel is $6 for members and $9 for nonmembers. There is no phone at the youth hostel, but the Tok Visitor Center can supply information on it.

Hotels Those travellers bussing up north from Haines or Skagway will find themselves stopping overnight in Tok. There are nine hotel/motels in the area; many of them are around the junction of the two highways. The cheapest one is the *Gateway Motel* (tel 883-4511) across the Alcan from the visitor centre. The motel has rooms with shared baths from $25 a single. Just about everything else in town begins at $45 for a single.

Getting There & Away

Tok can be difficult for hitchhikers. If you can't score a ride, even after pleading with motorists at the visitor centre, keep in mind that Alaskon Express has a bus headed where you most likely want to go. The buses leave from the Westmark Inn (tel 883-2291). On Saturday and Tuesday a bus arrives at 3 pm, leaves an hour later and overnights in Beaver Creek, reaching Whitehorse, Haines or Skagway the next day. On Saturday and Wednesday a bus departs at 10 am and reaches Anchorage by 6.15 pm that day. And most importantly, on Saturday at 4 pm and Wednesday at 10 am a bus departs for Fairbanks. The one-way fare from Tok to Anchorage is $77, to Fairbanks $40, to Glennallen $33, to Haines $109 and Skagway $129.

The Alaska-Denali Transit van passes through Tok twice a week. Once on its way to Haines and once on the westbound run to Anchorage via Fairbanks and Denali National Park. The one-way fare from Tok to Anchorage is $75, to Fairbanks $40, to Haines $65 and to Denali $65. Contact them at 701 West 58th Ave in Anchorage (tel 273-3331) for schedules, reservations and pick-up points.

TOK TO DELTA JUNCTION

Within 10 miles (16 km) west of Tok on the Alcan you are greeted with views of the Alaska Range which parallels the road to the south. The *Moon Lake State Campground* (15 sites, $5 fee) is at *Mile 1332* (2144 km), 18 miles (29 km) west of Tok. This state wayside offers tables, outhouses and a swimming area in the lake where it is possible to do the backstroke while watching a float plane land nearby.

Although there are no more official campgrounds until Delta Junction, travellers often stop overnight at the *Gerstle River State Wayside*, a large lookout at *Mile 1393* (2242 km) of the Alcan. The scenic spot provides covered tables and outhouses but no piped-in drinking water. Nearby is the trailhead for the **Donna Lakes Trail**, a trek of 3.5 miles (5.6 km) to Big Donna Lake and 4.5 miles (7.2 km) to Little Donna Lake. Both are stocked with rainbow trout.

DELTA JUNCTION

This town (pop 1300) is known as the 'End of the Alcan' as the famous highway joins the existing Richardson Highway here to complete the route to Fairbanks. The community began as a construction camp and picked up its name from the junction between the two highways. Delta Junction is a service centre not only for travellers but also for the growing agricultural community in the surrounding valleys and the 1200 military personnel and their families stationed at nearby Fort Greely.

Information

The log cabin which houses the Delta Junction Visitor Center is in the 'Triangle', the area where the Alcan merges into the Richardson Highway. Just outside the visitor centre is the large white milepost for *Mile 1422* (2288.4 km) of the Alcan, marking the end of the famous highway.

This causes much confusion for travellers, as Fairbanks has an even larger milepost at *Mile 1523* (2437 km), proclaiming it to be the end of the road. The debate will never end, but in Delta Junction they argue that the larger city to the north is nothing more than the terminus for the Richardson Highway. The community itself is spread out considerably on both highways, with the 'Triangle' as the town's unofficial centre.

The visitor centre, open daily from 9 am to 6 pm in the summer, is the usual source of local information, hand-outs and free coffee. Those who have just completed the Alcan from Dawson Creek can also purchase an End-of-the-Highway certificate for $1, or else wait until Fairbanks.

Things to See
There isn't a lot to do in Delta Junction unless you wander in during the **Deltana Fair** (giant vegetables, livestock shows and parades) on the first weekend in August. If you have the time, head 3 miles (4.8 km) south of Delta Junction down Richardson Highway to the scenic lookout across from the FAA facility. The mountainous panorama with the Delta River in the foreground is spectacular from this spot. On a clear day you can easily spot Mt Hayes, 13,832 feet (4218 metres), in the centre and Mt Moffit, 13,020 feet (3971 metres), to the left, as well as several other peaks.

Check out the **Delta Junction Public Library** behind the City Hall in the centre of town if you have run out of reading material after the long haul on the Alcan. The library is open afternoons until 4 pm from Monday to Saturday in the summer and runs a paperback swap for travellers.

Places to Stay
Camping There are two public campgrounds in the area. The closest is the *Delta State Campground* (22 sites, $5 fee), 1 mile (1.6 km) north of the visitor centre. The other is the *Clearwater State Campground* (18 sites, $5 fee), 13 miles (21 km) north-east of town. Follow the Richardson Highway and turn right on Jack Warren Rd, 2.4 miles (3.8 km) north of the visitor centre. Head 10.5 miles (16.8 km) east along the road and look for signs to the campground, which is along Clearwater Creek; the creek has good fishing for grayling.

Youth Hostel The *Delta Youth Hostel* is a unique log cabin in a wooded retreat 9 miles (14.4) north of Delta Junction on the way to Fairbanks. Although it is hassle to get out there without your own vehicle, the hostel is worth finding and is a pleasant place to spend a day or two. Follow Richardson Highway 6 miles (9.6 km) to *Mile 272* (435 km) as measured from Valdez, and turn right onto Tanana Loop Rd. Head 1 mile (1.6 km) down the road, turn right onto the Tanana Loop Extension and then look for the unmarked dirt road that leads left to the hostel; the building is 3 miles (4.8 km) from the highway.

The hostel offers 10 beds and kitchen facilities but has no phone. You can however call 895-5074 for more information. Rates are $4.75 for members and $6.75 for non-members.

Hotels There are a number of hotel/motels within Delta Junction. The *Evergreen Inn* (tel 895-4666) is across from the visitor centre and has rooms from $35 to $40. *Kelley's Motel* (tel 895-4667) is nearby, on the west side of the highway, and offers singles for $35 and doubles for $40. Also consider the *Silver Fox Roadhouse* (tel 895-4157), 18 miles (29 km) south-east of Delta Junction on the Alcan, where there are cabins for $30.

Richardson Highway

The Richardson Highway, Alaska's first highway, begins in Valdez and extends north 266 miles (428 km) to Delta Junction, where the Alcan (Alaska Highway) joins it for the final 98 miles (158 km) to Fairbanks. The road was originally scouted in 1919 by Captain W R Abercrombie of the US Army, who was looking for a way to link the gold town of Eagle with the warm-water port of Valdez. At first it was a telegraph line and footpath, but it quickly turned into a wagon trail following the gold strikes at Fairbanks around the turn of the century.

Today, the road is a scenic wonder; it

passes through the Chugach Mountains and the Alaska Range while providing access to Wrangell-St Elias National Park. Along the way it is highlighted by waterfalls, glaciers, five major rivers and the Alaska Pipeline, which parallels the road most of the way.

VALDEZ TO DELTA JUNCTION

The first section of the Richardson Highway from Valdez, *Mile 0*, to the junction with the Glenn Highway, *Mile 115* (185 km), is covered in the Richardson Highway to Glennallen section in the Southcentral chapter. The next 14 miles (22.4 km) from Glennallen to the junction of the Tok Cutoff, which includes the campgrounds at the Dry Creek State Recreation Site and Gulkana, is covered in the Tok Cutoff section in this chapter. Mileposts along the highway show distances from old Valdez, 4 miles (6.4 km) from the present city which is the new beginning of the Richardson Highway.

Glennallen to Sourdough Creek

At *Mile 112.6* (181.2 km) of the highway, just north of Glennallen, is a turn-off with an interpretive display on the development of transport in Alaska. Even more appealing is the view from a bluff nearby where you can view several peaks of the Wrangell Mountains which lie in Wrangell-St Elias National Park. The highest mountain is Mt Blackburn at 16,300 feet (4996 metres).

Once past Gulkana, the highway parallels the Gulkana River for the next 35 miles (56 km) through land that is owned by the Ahtna Native Corporation. Fishing for king and red salmon is excellent in this river from mid-June to mid-July and for rainbow trout and grayling most of the summer. In order to fish off the shore, you must have a permit ($10), issued at the Ahtna Corp Building in Gulkana. During the popular salmon runs the permits are also sold along the highway.

At *Mile 147.4* (237.2 km) the road reaches the Bureau of Land Management (BLM) *Sourdough Creek Campground* (15 sites, free), which provides access into the Gulkana River for canoeists and rafters. Also

in the campground is the trailhead for the 1.4 mile (2.2 km) path to Sourdough Creek.

On the other side of the highway and to the north is the *Sourdough Roadhouse* (tel 822-3355), established in 1903 when the old Valdez Trail to Eagle ran behind it. Today, it is a national historical site and, its owners claim, the oldest existing roadhouse in Alaska. Its dining room is open from 6 am to midnight and anybody passing through in the morning should stop for its famous sourdough breakfast: two eggs, bacon or ham and all the sourdough pancakes you can eat. The roadhouse has bunkhouse accommodation for $15 and cabins from $35.

Gulkana Canoe Route

This trip along the Gulkana River from Paxson Lake, *Mile 175* (281.6 km) of the Richardson Highway, to where the highway crosses the river at Gulkana is a popular canoe, kayak and raft route of 80 miles (128 km). The first 45 miles (72 km) is only for experienced white-water paddlers or rafters, as it involves several challenging rapids, including Canyon Rapids, Class IV white water. Although there is a short portage around Canyon Rapids, rough Class III waters follow. The final 35 miles (56 km) from Sourdough Creek BLM Campground to Gulkana is a pleasant 1 or 2 day paddle in mild water that can be enjoyed by less hardcore canoeists.

All land from the Sourdough Creek Campground south is owned by the Ahtna Native Corporation, which charges boaters to camp on it. The exception, three single-acre sites, are signposted along the river banks and have short trails leading back to the highway.

Alaska Range Foothills to Black Rapids Glacier

Ten miles (16 km) north of Sourdough Creek, the Richardson Highway enters the foothills of the Alaska Range. Gradually there are sweeping views of not only the Alaska Range to the north but the Wrangell Mountains to the south and the Chugach

Mountains to the south-west. More splendid views follow; you can see the large plateau to the west where the headwaters of the Susitna River form and the Glennallen area to the south. At *Mile 175* (281.6 km) of Richardson Highway is the gravel spur that leads 1.5 miles (2.4 km) west to the *Paxson Lake BLM Campground* (20 sites, free).

The junction with the Denali Highway is at *Mile 185.5* (298.5 km), where the small service centre of **Paxson** is located. Five miles (8 km) north of Paxson, look for the parking area by the Gulkana River on the west side of the highway, where there are litter barrels and picnic tables. This scenic spot provides views of Summit Lake and the Alaska Pipeline. From mid to late summer this is also a good spot to watch the salmon spawn.

After passing Summit Lake, the bridge over Gunn Creek is reached at *Mile 196.7* (316.5 km) of Richardson Highway and provides views of **Gulkana Glacier** to the north-east. From here, the highway begins climbing to its highest point at **Isabel Pass**, elevation 3000 feet (914 metres). The pass is at *Mile 197.6* (318 km) and is marked by a historical sign dedicated to General Wilds Richardson, after whom the highway is named. From this point you can view Gulkana Glacier to the north-east and Isabel Pass pipeline camp below it.

Three miles (4.8 km) north of the pass at *Mile 200.5* (322.7 km) of Richardson Highway, a gravel spur leads 1.5 miles (2.4 km) to *Fielding Lake Wayside*, where you can camp (seven sites, free) in a scenic area above the tree line at 2973 feet (893 metres). This high up in the Alaska Range, the ice often remains on the lake until July. The highway and the pipeline parallel each other north from Fielding Lake, and there are several lookouts to view the monumental efforts to move oil. One of the best is at *Mile 205.7* (331 km), where the pipeline can be photographed on an incline up a steep hill.

At *Mile 225.4* (362.7 km) of Richardson Highway, there is a viewpoint with picnic tables and a historical marker pointing out what little ice remains of **Black Rapids**

Glacier to the west. The glacier is known as the 'Galloping Glacier' for its famous 3 mile (4.8 km) advancement in the winter of 1936 when it almost engulfed the highway. Across from the marker, the easy **Black Rapids Lake Trail**, 0.3 mile (0.4 km) long, winds through wildflowers to Black Rapids Lake.

Donnelly Creek to Delta Junction

The last public campground before Delta Junction is just before *Mile 238* (383 km) of Richardson Highway, where a short loop road leads west of the highway to the *Donnelly Creek State Campground* (12 sites, $5 fee). This is a great place to camp as it is seldom crowded and is extremely scenic with good views of the towering peaks of the Alaska Range. Occasionally, the Delta bison herd can be seen from the campground.

Two interesting turn-offs are passed in the final 25 miles (40 km) before reaching the Alcan. The first is at *Mile 241.3* (388.3 km) and overlooks the calving ground of the Delta buffalo herd to the west. In 1928, 23 bison were transplanted here from Montana for the pleasure of sportsmen, and today they number almost 400. The animals have established a migratory pattern in the area which includes summering and calving along the Delta River. There is an interpretive display at the turn-off where often you can spot up to 100 animals. Since the herd is 2 to 3 miles (3.2 to 4.8 km) away, binoculars are needed for clear views.

The other turn-off is just before *Mile 244* (390.4) and has spectacular views of the pipeline and three of the highest peaks in the Alaska Range to the south-west. From south to west you can view Mt Deborah, 12,339 feet (3761 metres); Hess Mountain, 11,940 feet (3639 metres); and Mt Hayes, 13,832 feet (4216 metres).

The highway passes Fort Greely just beyond *Mile 261* (417.6 km) and then arrives at the Delta Junction Visitor Center on the 'Triangle', where the Alcan merges with the Richardson Highway at *Mile 266* (428 km). From here it is 98 miles (157.7 km) to Fairbanks.

DELTA JUNCTION TO FAIRBANKS

From Delta Junction, the Richardson Highway merges with the Alcan for the remaining 98 miles (157 km) to Fairbanks and passes the most interesting attraction in the Delta Junction area at *Mile 275* (442.6 km). **Big Delta State Historic Park**, a 10 acre (4 hectares) park, preserves Rika's Landing, an important crossroad for travellers, miners and the military on the Valdez to Fairbanks Trail from 1909 to 1947.

Centerpiece of the park is Rika's Roadhouse (tel 895-4201) which has been renovated and now contains historical displays and a gift shop. Guides in period dress lead tours through the complex which includes a blacksmith shop museum, Signal Corp station, and the Packhouse Pavilion where local artisans work on spinning, weaving, quilting and willow carving. The roadhouse is open daily during the summer from 9 am to 5 pm. There is also a restaurant in the Packhouse Pavilion.

Just beyond the state historical site, you pass through the farming village of **Big Delta** (pop 300) at *Mile 275.3* (443 km). From the town's bridge across the Tanana River you can look east for an impressive view of the Alaska Pipeline suspended over the water or look west for equally impressive views of the Alaska Range.

The junction to the *Quartz Lake State Campground* (16 sites, $5 fee) is at *Mile 278* (445 km) of Richardson Highway. Turn east at the posted road and head 2.8 miles (4.5 km) to the campground along the shores of the scenic lake which provides good fishing for rainbow trout. A trail from the campground leads over to nearby Lost Lake, where there are two more campsites.

For the next 20 miles (32 km), the highway passes a handful of lookouts where there are spectacular views of both the Tanana River in the foreground and the Alaska Range behind it.

The spur that leads to *Harding Lake State Campground* (89 sites, $5 fee) is at *Mile 321.5* (517.4 km). The campground, which has a ranger office near the entrance, has picnic shelters and drinking water as well as

swimming and canoeing opportunities in the lake.

From the campground, it is 43 miles (69 km) to Fairbanks, and there are two public campgrounds along the way. At *Mile 346.7* (558 km) of Richardson Highway is *Chena Lakes Recreation Area* (78 campsites, fee), and 3 miles (4.8 km) north of here is the *North Pole Public Park* with a few tent sites. The Richardson Highway reaches Fairbanks at *Mile 363* (580 km).

Tok Cutoff

The Tok Cutoff is often considered to be the northern half of the Glenn Highway, but mileposts along the road show distances from Tok and not from Anchorage, as they do once you pass Glennallen.

TOK TO GLENNALLEN

From Tok, it is 328 miles (528 km) to Anchorage, which is reached by first travelling the Tok Cutoff 139 miles (224 km) south-west to Glennallen on the junction of Richardson and Glenn highways. From there, it is another 189 miles (304 km) to Anchorage via the Glenn Highway.

The first of only two public campgrounds on the Tok Cutoff is reached at *Mile 15.7* (25.3 km). The *Eagle Trail State Campground* (40 sites, $5 fee) is near Clearwater Creek and provides drinking water, toilets, rain shelter and fire pits. The historical **Eagle Trail**, which at one time extended to Eagle on the Yukon River, can still be hiked on a 1 mile (1.6 km) section from the campground. Look for the posted trailhead near the covered picnic shelters.

The second campground is another 45 miles (72 km) south-west along the highway just before *Mile 61* (97.6 km). The *Porcupine Creek State Campground* (12 sites, $5 fee) is set in a scenic spot along the creek and provides tables, toilets and drinking water. An historical marker and splendid views of Mt Sanford, a dormant volcano with an elevation of 16,237 feet (4949 metres), is 1 mile (1.6 km) north along the highway.

Nabesna Rd

At *Mile 65.2* (105 km) of Tok Cutoff is the junction with Nabesna Rd. The 45 mile (72.4 km) side road extends into the Wrangell-St Elias National Park (see the Wrangell-St Elias National Park section in the Southcentral chapter) and ends at Nabesna, a mining community of less than 25 residents.

The side trip is a unique experience off the highways; the road is only one of two that lead into the heart of the national park. At the beginning of the road is **Slana**, a small village of 40 residents or so. Slana has an Indian settlement on the north banks of the Slana River and fishing wheels can still be seen working during the salmon runs. There is also a National Park Service ranger station (tel 822-5238) that can assist with information on Wrangell-St Elias National Park.

The first 30 miles of Nabesna Rd is manageable gravel road but after that the surface is extremely rough with several streams flowing over it. There are no tourist facilities in **Nabesna** and no campgrounds along the way. Good camping spots, however, along with scenic lakes and inviting ridges for backpackers, lie from one end of this road to the other.

One of the most unique youth hostels in Alaska, and maybe the USA, is 5 miles (8 km) south-west of the Nabesna Rd junction at *Mile 72.1* (117.5 km) of Tok Cutoff. The *Mentasa Mountains Home Hostel* is a wilderness hostel. In other words, the only way to reach it is on foot during the summer and by plane in the winter. Clearly posted on the highway, you follow trail markers for 6 miles (9.8 km) up the Suslositna Valley to the lodge. The home has four beds and charges $5.25 per night for members. Coy Brown, who runs the lodge, offers special programs, lectures and tours in a spectacular mountain setting where wildlife is abundant. This lodge is well worth the hike in.

Gakona Junction

Officially, Tok Cutoff ends at Gakona Junc-

tion, 125 miles (201 km) south-west of Tok, where it merges with the Richardson Highway. The village of **Gulkana** (pop 100) is 2 miles (3.2 km) to the south and you can camp (voluntary fee) along the Gulkana River by the bridge in town. The eastern end of the Glenn Highway is 14 miles (22.4 km) south from Gakona Junction.

Glenn Highway

The Glenn Highway runs west from Glennallen to Anchorage with the mileposts along the road showing the distance from Anchorage, *Mile 0*.

GLENNALLEN

Glennallen (pop 500), referred to by some as 'The Hub' of Alaska's road system, is a service centre on Glenn Highway, 2 miles (3.2 km) west from the junction with the Richardson Highway. Because of its strategic location, the town provides a wide range of facilities and services, and serves as the major departure point to the Wrangell-St Elias National Park. It is also the home base for many fishing and hunting guides; otherwise, there is little reason to linger here.

Places to Stay

Camping The closest public campground is the *Dry Creek State Campground* (58 sites, $5 fee), 5 miles (8 km) north-east of town on the Richardson Highway between the junction with the Glenn Highway and the Tok Cutoff to the north. Hitchhikers who get caught in Glennallen overnight, however, never have to walk far to find a place to pitch a tent.

Motels Of the handful of motels, *Caribou Motel* (tel 822-3302) on Glenn Highway in the heart of town is the cheapest. Singles with shared baths are $35, and doubles are $48.

Getting There & Away

Bus Glennallen is notorious among hitchhikers as a place for getting stuck in, especially at the Glenn Highway junction when trying to thumb a ride north to the Alcan.

The *Hub of Alaska* (tel 822-3555), a Tesoro service station at the junction of the Richardson and Glenn highways, serves as a visitor centre for the area and bus information can be obtained here.

It's wise to double-check with the centre as the meagre system of buses is always in a constant state of flux. However, you can count on Gray Line's Alaskon Express passing through twice a week. On Saturday and Wednesday, the westbound bus departs Glennallen at 1.30 pm and reaches Anchorage at 6.15 pm. On Saturday and Tuesday, the eastbound bus departs the town at 12.30 pm for Tok; the bus then stops overnight at Beaver Creek in the Yukon where connections to Haines and Skagway can be made.

These buses stop at the Caribou Cafe (tel 822-3656), next door to the Caribou Hotel in Glennallen, and the one-way fare to Anchorage is $48, to Tok $33 and to Haines $134.

Alaska-Yukon Motorcoaches provide a service from Valdez to Fairbanks if their package tours haven't claimed all the seats on the bus. The bus runs to Fairbanks on Tuesday, Thursday and Saturday and to Valdez on Monday, Wednesday and Friday.

You can also take a Wrangell Mt Bus Adventures (tel 822-5519) van from Glennallen to McCarthy, home of the Kennecott Mine in Wrangell-St Elias National Park. It departs Glennallen Monday, Wednesday and Friday at 1 pm and arrives at McCarthy at 6 p.m. The return fare to McCarthy is $80.

GLENNALLEN TO PALMER

The Glenn Highway runs west from Glennallen through a vast plateau bordered by the Alaska Range to the north and the Chugach Mountains to the south. This is an incredibly scenic section that extends for almost 150 miles (241.4 km) west; it is also a good area for spotting wildlife. The lowlands are roamed by moose and caribou, and the timbered ridges are prime habitat for black bears and grizzlies. On the slope of both mountain ranges, and often visible from the highway, are flocks of Dall sheep.

Tolsona Creek to Little Nelchina River

The first public campground west from Glennallen is the *Tolsona Creek State Campground* (10 sites) at *Mile 172.7* (278 km) on the south side of the Glenn Highway. There is no fee for staying in this state campground, but there's no drinking water either. The creek is a good spot to fish for grayling.

Nearby is the *Tolsona Wilderness Campground* (tel 822-3865), a private facility with 45 sites that border the river. The fee is $6 a night for a site but here you have water, coin-operated showers and laundry facilities. In the morning, if you're really hungry, stop at the *Tolsona Lake Lodge* (tel 822-3433) at *Mile 170.5* (274.4 km) of Glenn Highway for their all-you-can-eat sourdough-pancake breakfast.

The next public campground along the highway is the *Lake Louise State Recreation Area* (46 sites, $5 fee) which provides shelters, tables, water and swimming in the lake. The scenic campground is 17 miles (27 km) up Lake Louise Rd which leaves the Glenn Highway at *Mile 160* (256 km).

Nearby is the *Evergreen Lodge* (tel 822-3250), with rustic cabins that sleep four from $25 a night per person. The lodge overlooks Lake Louise and the meals, served family-style in a large dining room, are excellent, especially when topped off by home-made blueberry ice cream. A mile up Lake Louise Rd from the Glenn Highway is a turn-off with good views of Tazlina Glacier and Carter Lake.

The *Little Nelchina River Campground* (11 sites, free) is just off Glenn Highway at *Mile 137.5* (221.3 km).

The 35 miles (56 km) between these three campgrounds is a hiker's delight, as several trails go from the highway to the nearby mountains and lakes.

A lookout with litter barrels marks the trailhead for the **Mae West Lake Trail**, a short hike at *Mile 169.3* (272.3) of Glenn Highway. This 1 mile (1.6 km) trail leads to a long, narrow lake fed by Little Woods Creek.

The trailhead for the **Lost Cabin Lake Trail** is on the south side of the highway at *Mile 165.8* (266.8 km), where a pair of litter barrels have been placed. The trail winds 2 miles (3.2 km) to the lake and is a berry picker's delight from late summer to early autumn.

At *Mile 138.3* (222.6 km) of Glenn Highway, or 0.8 mile (1.3 km) east of the Little Nelchina River Campground for those camping there, is the trailhead for the **Old Man Creek Trail**. This trail leads 2 miles (3.2 km) to Old Man Creek and 9 miles (14.4 km) to Crooked Creek, where you can fish for grayling. It ends at the old mining area of Nelchina, 14.5 miles (23 km) from the highway. Here it merges into the old Chickaloon-Knik-Nelchina Trail, a gold miner's route used before the Glenn Highway was built.

Today, the Chickaloon-Knik-Nelchina route is an extensive system of trails that extend beyond Palmer, with many posted access points along the north side of the highway. The system is not maintained regularly and hikers attempting any part of it should have good outdoor experience and the right topographic maps.

Eureka Summit to Palmer

From Little Nelchina River, the Glenn Highway begins to ascend, and views of Gunsight Mountain (you have to look hard to see the origin of its name) come into sight. At **Eureka Summit**, you can not only see Gunsight Mountain but the Chugach Mountains to the south, the Nelchina Glacier spilling down in the middle and the Talkeetnas to the north. This impressive unobstructed view is completed to the west, where the highway can be seen dropping into the river valleys separating the two mountain chains. Eureka Summit, elevation 3322 feet (1013 metres), is at *Mile 129.3* (208 km) of the Glenn Highway; it is the highway's highest point.

The trailhead for the **Belanger Pass Trail**, at *Mile 123.3* (198.4 km) on Martin Rd

across from the Tahneta Lodge, is marked by a Chickaloon-Knik-Nelchina Trail sign. For the most part it is used by miners and hunters in off-road vehicles for access into the Talkeetna Mountains, and at times the mining scars are disturbing.

The views from Belanger Pass, a 3 mile (4.8 km) hike, are excellent and well worth the climb. From the 4350 foot (1326 metre) pass, off-road-vehicle trails continue north to Alfred Creek, another 3.5 miles (5.6 km) away, and eventually they lead around the north side of Syncline Mountain past active mining operations.

Two miles (3.2 km) west of the Belanger Pass trailhead is **Tahneta Pass** at *Mile 121* (194.7 km) of the Glenn Highway. Half a mile (0.8 km) west of Tahneta Pass is a scenic turn-off where you can view the 3000 foot (914 metre) pass. To the east of the turn-off lies Lake Liela, and Lake Tahneta beyond it.

The **Squaw Creek Trail** is another miner and hunters' trail that begins at *Mile 117.6* (189.3 km) of Glenn Highway and merges into the Chickaloon-Knik-Nelchina Trail. It begins as an off-road-vehicle trail marked by a Squaw Creek Trail sign. It extends 3.5 miles (5.6 km) to Squaw Creek and 9.5 miles (15 km) to Caribou Creek after ascending a low pass between the two. Although the trail can be confusing at times, the hike is a scenic one with the Gunsight, Sheep and Syncline mountains as a backdrop.

From here, the Glenn Highway begins to descend and the scenery becomes stunning as it heads towards the Talkeetna Mountains, passing an oddly shaped rock formation at *Mile 114* (183.5 km) known as the Lion's Head. About 0.5 mile (0.8 km) beyond it, the highway reaches the first view of Matanuska Glacier. To the north is Sheep Mountain, properly named as you can often spot Dall sheep on its slopes.

At *Mile 113.5* (182.7 km) of Glenn Highway is the *Sheep Mountain Lodge* (tel 745-5121), which is affiliated with Alaska Youth Hostels. The lodge is 70 miles east of Palmer and has no kitchen facilities but does feature a cafe, bar and liquor store. There is also a sauna, hot tub and great hiking nearby.

The youth hostel charges $8 a night for a bunk.

There is also inexpensive lodging just 2 miles (3.2 km) west down the road at *Mile 111.5* (181.7 km) of the Glenn Highway, which raises the question why good accommodation is always next door to each other? The *Bunk 'N Breakfast* (tel 745-5143) offers a bunk for $10 per night and a bunk & breakfast for $15. Bring your sleeping bag and your binoculars to search for Dall sheep on Sheep Mountain just across the highway.

At *Mile 101* (162.5 km) you reach the *Matanuska Glacier State Campground* (12 sites, $5 fee). The area has sheltered tables, water and trails along a nearby bluff that provide good viewing points of the glacier. It is a beautiful campground but, for obvious reasons, a popular one so there is a 3 day limit here.

Matanuska Glacier is a stable ice floe that is 4 miles wide (6.4 km) at its terminus and extends 27 miles (43.5 km) back into the Chugach Mountains. Some 18,000 years ago, it covered the area where the city of Palmer is today. If you want to drive near the glacier's face, stop at the Glacier Park Resort (tel 745-2534), *Mile 102* (166 km) of Glenn Highway, and pay $5 to follow its private road for the closest view of Matanuska Glacier.

The **Puritan Creek Trail** is just before the bridge over the creek (also known as Purinton) at *Mile 89* (143 km) of the Glenn Highway. There is a short dirt road that heads north of the highway and then east, passing an off-road-vehicle trail that ascends a steep hill to the north. The trail is a 12 mile (19.2 km) walk to the foot of Boulder Creek, though the final 7 miles (11.2 km) consist mainly of trekking along the gravel bars of the river. The scenery of the Chugach Mountains is excellent and there are good camping spots along Boulder Creek.

From Boulder Creek, it is possible to climb to Chitna Pass and down to Caribou Creek and more sections of the Chickaloon-Knik-Nelchina Trail, a system that parallels the Glenn Highway. The adventurous backpacker who is experienced with a map and compass could hike for days, exiting at a number of trailheads, including Belanger Pass and Squaw Creek.

In the next 13 miles (20.8 km), the Glenn Highway passes three public campgrounds. The first is *Long Lake State Campground* (nine sites, free) at *Mile 85.3* (137.3 km). Along with toilets and fire pits, the campground offers access to a grayling fishing hole that is a favourite among Anchorage's residents.

Two miles (3.2 km) west of the Long Lake Campground is a gravel spur road that leads to the *Lower Bonnie Lake State Campground* (eight sites, free), a 2 mile (3.2 km) side trip from the highway. The third campground is the *King Mountain State Recreation Site* (22 sites, $5 fee) at *Mile 76* (121.6 km) of the Glenn Highway. This scenic campground is on the banks of the Matanuska River, with a view of King Mountain to the south-east.

After passing through **Sutton** (pop 850) at *Mile 61* (98.2 km), you come to the last public campground before Palmer. The *Moose Creek State Campground* (12 sites, $5 fee) is a small site on the creek at *Mile 54.5* (87.2 km) of Glenn Highway which has sheltered tables, outhouses and drinking water. Five miles (8 km) beyond Moose Creek is the junction to the Fishhook-Willow Rd which provides access to the Independence Mine State Park (see the Around Wasilla section in this chapter). The highway then descends into the agricultural centre of Palmer.

From Palmer, Glenn Highway merges with the George Parks Highway and continues south to Anchorage, 43 miles (67 km) away (see the Anchorage chapter).

Denali Highway

With the exception of 21 miles (33.6 km) that is paved at its east end, the Denali Highway is a gravel road extending from Paxson on the Richardson Highway to Cantwell on the George Parks Highway, just south of the main entrance to Denali National Park.

When the 135 mile (216 km) route was opened in 1957 it was the only road to the national park, but it became a secondary route after the George Parks Highway was completed in 1972. Today, the Denali Highway is only open from mid-May to October. Most of it runs along the foothills of the Alaska Range to the north and through glacial valleys where you can see stretches of alpine tundra.

There are numerous trails into the surrounding backcountry but none of them are marked. Also in the area are two popular canoe routes. Ask locals at the roadhouses for information and take along topographic maps that cover the areas you intend to trek or paddle.

There are no established communities along the way, but a few roadhouses provide food, lodging and gasoline. If driving, it is best to fill up with gasoline at Paxson or Cantwell.

From Paxson, *Mile 0*, the highway heads west and passes the 1 mile (1.6 km) gravel road to Sevenmile Lake at *Mile 7* (11.2 km). From here, the terrain opens up and provides superb views of the nearby lakes and peaks of the Alaska Range. Most of the lakes, as many as 40 in the spring, can be seen from a lookout at *Mile 13* (21 km) of the Denali Highway.

The **Swede Lake Trail** is near *Mile 17* (27.3 km) of the highway and leads south 3 miles (4.8 km) to Swede Lake after passing Little Swede Lake in 2 miles (3.2 km). Beyond here, it continues to the Middle Fork of the Gulkana River but the trail is extremely wet at times and suitable only for off-road vehicles. Anglers fish the lakes for trout and grayling. Inquire at the Tangle River Inn (tel 895-4356) at *Mile 20* (32.2 km) for directions to the trail and an update on its condition.

The paved portion of the Denali Highway ends just beyond *Mile 21* (33.6 km), and in another 0.5 mile (0.8 km) the highway reaches the Bureau of Land Management (BLM) *Tangle Lakes Campground* (13 sites, free) to the north, on the shores of Round Tangle Lake. A second BLM campground,

Upper Tangle Lakes (seven sites, free), is 0.2 mile (0.3 km) down the road on the south side. Both campgrounds serve as the departure point for two scenic canoe routes and nearby Tangle River Inn provides canoe rentals. Caribou are occasionally spotted in the surrounding hills.

The **Delta River Canoe Route** is a 35 mile (56 km) paddle which begins at the Tangle Lakes BLM Campground north of the highway and ends a few hundred yards from *Mile 212.5* (340 km) of Richardson Highway. Begin the canoe route by crossing Round Tangle Lake and continuing to Lower Tangle Lake, where a waterfall must be portaged around. Following the waterfall is a set of Class III rapids that must either be lined for 2 miles (3.2 km) or paddled with an experienced hand. Every year, the BLM reports numerous canoeists who damage their boats beyond repair on these rapids and are forced to hike 15 miles (24 km) back out to the Denali Highway. The remainder of the trip is a much milder paddle.

The **Upper Tangle Lakes Canoe Route** is easier and shorter than the Delta River route but requires four portages, none of which are marked but are easy to figure out in the low bush tundra. All paddlers attempting this route must have topographic maps. The route begins at Tangle River and passes through Upper Tangle Lake before ending at Dickey Lake, 9 miles (14.4 km) to the south. There is a 1.2 mile (1.9 km) portage into Dickey Lake.

From here, experienced paddlers can continue by departing Dickey Lake's outlet to the south-east into the Middle Fork of the Gulkana River. For the first 3 miles (4.8 km), the river is shallow and mild but then it plunges into a steep canyon where canoeist have to contend with Class III and IV rapids. Most canoeists choose to either carefully line their boats or portage. Allow 7 days for the entire 76 mile (123.9 km) trip from Tangle Lakes to Sourdough Campground on the Gulkana River off Richardson Highway.

At *Mile 25* (40 km), the Denali Highway crosses Rock Creek Bridge, where the **Landmark Gap Trail** leads north 3 miles (4.8 km)

to Landmark Gap Lake, elevation 3217 feet (981 metres). You can't see the lake from the highway but you can spot the noticeable gap between the Amphitheatre Mountains.

A parking lot on the north side of the highway at *Mile 32* (51.2 km) is the start of the 3 mile (4.8 km) **Glacier Lake Trail**.

From here, the highway ascends **MacLaren Summit**, elevation 4086 feet (1245 metres), one of the highest highway passes in the state. The summit is reached at *Mile 35.2* (56.6 km) and has excellent views of Mt Hayes, Hess Mountain and Mt Deborah to the west and MacLaren Glacier to the north.

The MacLaren River is crossed at *Mile 42* (67.6 km) of Denali Highway on a 364 foot (111 metre) multiple-span bridge. Another bridge crosses Clearwater Creek at *Mile 56* (89.6 km), where nearby there are campsites and outhouses. Beginning at *Mile 69* (110.4 km) is the first of many hiking trails in the area; all are unmarked and many are nothing more than old gravel roads. Inquire at the Gracious Lodge, a roadhouse at *Mile 82* (132 km), for the exact location of the trails.

The **Hatchet Lake Trail**, a 5 mile (8 km) walk, begins near Raft Creek just before *Mile 69* (110.4 km) of Denali Highway.

Denali Trail begins on the north side of the highway at *Mile 79* (126.4 km), 0.5 mile (0.8 km) before the road crosses the Susitna River on a multiple-span bridge. It winds for 6 miles (10 km) to the old mining camp of Denali, first established in 1907. A few of the old buildings still remain. Today, gold mining has resumed in the area. Several old mining trails branch off the trail, including an 18 mile (29 km) route to Roosevelt Lake from Denali Camp. The area can provide enough hiking for a 2 or 3 day trip, but only tackle these trails with a map and compass in hand.

The **Snodgrass Lake Trail** leads 2 miles (3.2 km) south of the highway to Snodgrass Lake, known among anglers for its good grayling fishing. The trail starts at a parking area between *Mile 80* and *Mile 81* (128 and 129.6 km) of the Denali Highway.

The **Butte Lake Trail**, an off-road-vehicle track, leads 5 miles (8 km) south to Butte Lake, known for its large lake trout, often weighing over 30 lb (13.5 kg). The trailhead is at *Mile 94* (150.4 km). Motorised transport can be arranged through *Adventures Unlimited*, a roadhouse with lodging and food at *Mile 100* (160 km).

At *Mile 104.3* (167.8 km) of Denali Highway is the *Brushkana River BLM Campground* (17 sites, free), which provides a shelter, drinking water and a meat rack for hunters who invade the area in late summer and autumn. The river, which the campground overlooks, can be fished for grayling and Dolly Varden. From here, it is another 20 miles (32 km) to where the Denali Highway merges with the George Parks Highway; the entrance to Denali National Park is 17 miles (27 km) north of this junction on George Parks Highway.

Taylor Highway

The scenic Taylor Highway extends 161 miles (259 km) north from Tetlin Junction, 13 miles (21 km) east of Tok on the Alcan (Alaska Highway), to the historic town of Eagle on the Yukon River. It is a beautiful but rough drive as the road is narrow, winding and ascends Mt Fairplay, Polly Summit and American Summit, all over 3500 feet (1067 metres) in elevation.

The highway is the first section to Dawson City in the Yukon and offers access to the popular Fortymile River Canoe Route and much off-road hiking. As with the Denali Highway, the problem of unmarked trailheads exists, making it necessary to have the proper topographic maps in hand. Many trails are off-road-vehicle tracks used heavily in late summer and autumn by hunters.

By Alaskan standards there is light to moderate traffic on Taylor Highway during the summer, until you reach Jack Wade Junction, where the majority of vehicles continue east to Dawson City. Hitchhikers going to Eagle have to be patient in the final 65 miles (105 km) north of Jack Wade Junction, but the ride will come. If you're driving, leave Tetlin Junction with a full tank of gasoline because roadside services are limited along the route.

From Tetlin Junction, *Mile 0*, the highway heads north, and within 9 miles (14.4 km) begins to ascend towards Mt Fairplay, elevation 5541 feet (1689 metres). A lookout near the summit is reached at *Mile 35* (56 km) and is marked by litter barrels and an interpretive sign describing the history of Taylor Highway. From here, you are rewarded with superb views of Mt Fairplay and the valleys and forks of the Fortymile River to the north. The surrounding alpine area offers good hiking for those who need to stretch their legs.

The first Bureau of Land Management (BLM) campground is at *Mile 49* (78 km) on the west side of the highway. *West Fork BLM Campground* (27 sites, free) has outhouses but no drinking water; all water taken from nearby streams should be boiled or treated first (see the Health section in the Facts for the Visitor chapter for information on water purification). Travellers packing along their gold pans can try their luck in West Fork River which is the first access point for the paddle down Fortymile River.

CHICKEN

After crossing a bridge over the Fortymile River's Mosquito Fork at *Mile 64.4* (103.6 km), the Taylor Highway passes the old **Chicken Post Office** on a hill beside the road, at *Mile 66.2* (106.5 km). The post office, still operating today, was originally established when Chicken was a thriving mining centre.

The community of Chicken itself (pop between 30 and 50) is 0.5 mile (0.8 km) to the north on a spur road that leads to an airstrip, grocery, restaurant and gasoline station. The town's name, according to one tale, originated at a meeting of the resident miners in the late 1800s. When trying to come up with a name for the new tent city, somebody suggested Ptarmigan, since the chicken-like bird existed in great numbers throughout the area. All the miners liked it but none of them could spell it. The town's name has been Chicken ever since.

Just north of the spur to the village is Chicken Creek Bridge, built on tailing piles from the mining era. If you look back to the left, you can see the **Chicken Dredge** which was used to extract gold from the creek between 1959 and 1965. Most of the forks of the Fortymile River are virtually covered from one end to the other by active mining claims and often you can see suction dredging for gold from the highway.

Views of the old town site of Chicken, now in the hands of a mining company, can be obtained at *Mile 67.3* (108.3 km) by looking to the west. At *Mile 75.3* (121.2 km) is the bridge over South Fork and the most popular access point for the Fortymile River Canoe Route.

FORTYMILE RIVER CANOE ROUTE

The historic Fortymile River, designated as the Fortymile National Wild River, offers an excellent escape into scenic wilderness for paddlers experienced in lining their canoes around rapids. It is also a step back into the gold-rush era of Alaska as paddlers will view such abandoned mining communities as Franklin, Steele Creek and Fortymile while undoubtedly seeing some present-day mining. The best place to start is the bridge over South Fork, because access points south of here on Taylor Highway often are too shallow for an enjoyable trip.

A common trip is to paddle the 40 miles (64 km) to the bridge over O'Brien Creek at *Mile 113* (181 km) of Taylor Highway. This 2 to 3 day trip involves three sets of Class III rapids. A greater adventure is to continue past O'Brien Creek and paddle the Fortymile River into the Yukon River and from here head north to Eagle at the end of the Taylor Highway. This trip is 140 miles (224 km) long and requires 7 to 10 days to cover, along with lining several sets of rapids in the Fortymile River. The planning and organising for such an expedition has to be done carefully before you leave for Alaska (see the Eagle section in this chapter about paddling the Yukon River).

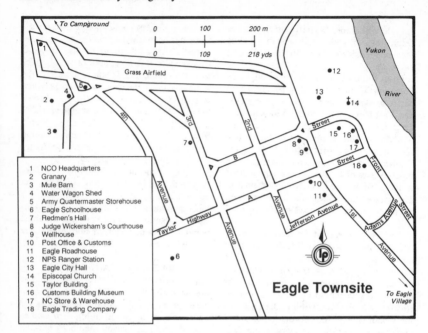

1 NCO Headquarters
2 Granary
3 Mule Barn
4 Water Wagon Shed
5 Army Quartermaster Storehouse
6 Eagle Schoolhouse
7 Redmen's Hall
8 Judge Wickersham's Courthouse
9 Wellhouse
10 Post Office & Customs
11 Eagle Roadhouse
12 NPS Ranger Station
13 Eagle City Hall
14 Episcopal Church
15 Taylor Building
16 Customs Building Museum
17 NC Store & Warehouse
18 Eagle Trading Company

Eagle Townsite

WALKER FORK TO AMERICAN CREEK

At *Mile 82* (132 km) of Taylor Highway is the *Walker Fork BLM Campground* (18 sites, free) which lies on both sides of the highway and has tables, firewood and a short trail to a limestone bluff overlook.

A lookout is reached at *Mile 86* (144.7 km) of the highway, where you can view the **Jack Wade Dredge**, which operated from 1900 until 1942. For most of its working days the dredge was powered by a wood-burning steam engine which required 10 to 12 cords of wood per day. The old Jack Wade mining camp is passed 4 miles (6.4 km) north of the dredge; after being abandoned for 30 years the mine is now being reworked as the result of higher gold prices.

The Jack Wade Junction is at *Mile 95.7* (154 km) of Taylor Highway, and here the Top of the World Highway (also known as the Dawson Highway) winds 3.5 miles (5.6 km) to the Canadian/US border and another 75 miles (120 km) east to Dawson City. The

Taylor Highway continues north from the junction and ascends **Polly Summit**, elevation 3550 feet (1083 metres). The summit is reached at *Mile 105* (168 km), and 5 miles (8 km) beyond it is a scenic lookout where you can view the Fortymile River.

From the summit, Taylor Highway begins a steep descent; drivers must take this section slowly. Along the way there are numerous lookouts with good views as well as a variety of abandoned cabins, old gold dredges and mine tailings. *Liberty Creek BLM Campground* (seven sites, free) at *Mile 132* (211 km) of Taylor Highway is on King Solomon Creek. This campground used to provide tables, outhouses and firewood but has not been maintained in recent years. Holiday prospectors should try their luck in the nearby creek.

The last campground before Eagle is the *American Creek BLM Wayside* at *Mile 154* (247.8 km). The wayside is interesting as there are usually some miners and prospectors staying there. Eagle is another 6 miles (9.4 km) to the north.

EAGLE

The historic town of Eagle (pop 160) had its beginnings in the late 1800s and today is one of the best-preserved boom towns of the mining era in Alaska.

The original community, today called Eagle Village, was established by the Athabascan Indians long before Francois Mercier arrived in the early 1880s and built a trading post in the area. A permanent community of miners was set up in 1898. A year later, the US Army decided to move in and build a fort in its effort to maintain law and order in the Alaskan Interior. A federal court was established at Eagle in 1900 by Judge Wicker sham, and the next year President Theodore Roosevelt issued a charter that made Eagle the first incorporated city of the Interior.

Eagle reached its peak at the turn of the century when it had a population of over 1500 residents and the overland telegraph wire was completed from Valdez in 1903. Some residents even went as far as to call their town the 'Paris of the North', though that was hardly the case.

Other gold strikes in the early 1900s, most notably at Fairbanks, began drawing residents away from Eagle and caused the removal of Judge Wickersham's Court to the new city in the west. The army fort was abandoned in 1911, and by the 1940s Eagle's population had dwindled to 10. When the Taylor Highway was completed in the 1950s, however, the town's population increased to its present levels.

Things to See

If you're spending a day in Eagle, the best way to see the town and learn its history is to be in front of **Judge Wickersham's Courthouse** at the corner of B St and 1st Ave at 10 am. The courthouse, now a museum managed by the Eagle Historical Society, offers a free walking tour of the town daily during the summer, beginning at the front porch. The tour covers such historical and

renovated buildings as the **Eagle City Hall**, where the city council continues to hold regular meetings, the **Customs Building Museum** and the **Eagle Post Office** on the corner of A St and 1st Ave, where a plaque commemorates explorer Roald Amundsen's visit to Eagle.

The Norwegian explorer hiked overland to Eagle in 1905 after his ship froze in the Arctic Sea off Canada. From the town's telegraph office he sent word to the waiting world that he had just navigated the Northwest Passage. Amundsen stayed 2 weeks in Eagle and then mushed back to his sloop. Nine months later, the ship reached Nome completing the first successful voyage from the Atlantic to the Pacific Ocean across the Arctic Ocean.

To the north of town is **Fort Egbert**, which can be reached from Taylor Highway via 4th Ave. The Bureau of Land Management has been involved in restoring the old army fort, which once contained 37 buildings; several are now open to visitors during the summer. The restored mule barn, carriage house, dog house and officers' quarters are clustered together in one section of the fort.

Places to Stay

The *Eagle Trading Co* (tel 547-2220) has rooms along with groceries, a cafe, a coin-operated laundry and public showers. The one-stop business is on Front St, overlooking the Yukon River. Most people camp at the *Eagle BLM Campground* (13 sites, free). To reach it, follow 4th Ave north 1.5 miles (2.4 km) through Fort Egbert to the campground.

Paddling

Yukon River Float During its heyday, Eagle was an important riverboat landing for traffic moving up and down the Yukon River. Today, it is still an important departure point for the many paddlers who come to float the river through the Yukon-Charley Rivers National Preserve. The 150 mile (240 km) Yukon River trip extends from Eagle to Circle at the end of Steese Highway northeast of Fairbanks; most paddlers plan on 6 to 10 days for the float.

It is not a difficult paddle, but it must be planned carefully with air-taxi operators in order to shuttle boats, equipment and people from Circle. Floaters and paddlers should come prepared for insects and can usually camp on open beaches and river bars where winds keep the bugs down. Paddlers also need to be prepared for extremes in weather; freezing nights can be followed by daytime temperatures of 90°F (32°C).

Tatondak Outfitters (tel 547-2221) in Eagle rent rafts for $70 per day; the rafts will easily hold four people and their gear. The guide company also run an air service that picks up rafters in Circle and returns them to Eagle. Budget around $250 for the flight if you and your party can return in a Cessna 185.

For more information on rentals and air services in the area before you depart for Alaska, write to Tatondak at PO Box 55, Eagle, Alaska 99738. The National Park Service maintains an Eagle office (tel 547-2233) on the banks of the Yukon River in Fort Egbert. The office has maps and books for sale and on request will show a video on the preserve. Write to the National Park Service (PO Box 64, Eagle, Alaska 99738) in advance for more information on travelling the Yukon River.

Snowshoe Hare

Fairbanks

Everyone agrees that Fairbanks (pop 72,000) is 'extremely Alaska'. The Fairbanks Visitor Bureau made that expression the city's official slogan one summer in an ad campaign, but Alaskans had already been saying it for years. Extremes are a way of life in the state's second largest city. On first glance, Fairbanks appears to be a spread-out, low-rise city with the usual hotels, shopping malls, McDonald's and a university tucked away on the outskirts of town. A second look reveals that this community is different, that the people and the place are one of a kind.

Fairbanks has log cabins, lots of them, from the heart of town to those hidden among the trees on the back roads. It has a semiprofessional baseball team that plays games at midnight without the aid of artificial lights. It also has a golf course that claims to be the 'world's most northernest', and a college campus where students and staff ski from classroom to classroom much of the year.

Extremely Alaska is the only way to describe Fairbanks' weather. During the summer, it is pleasantly warm with an average temperature of 70°F (21°C) and an occasional hot spell in August where the temperature breaks 90°F (32°C). The days are long with more than 20 hours of light from June to August, peaking at almost 23 hours on 21 June.

In the winter, however, Fairbanks is very cold. The temperature stays below 0°F (-18°C) for months and can drop to -60°F (-51°C) or even lower for days at a time. The days are short, as short as 3 or 4 hours, and the nights are cold. It's so cold in the winter that parking meters come equipped with electric plugs because cars have heaters around their engines to prevent freezing. Beards and moustaches freeze into icicles in only minutes at -60°F (-51°C), and a glass of water thrown out of a second-storey window shatters as ice when it hits the ground.

Consider the city's boom-or-bust economy for extremes. Fairbanks was founded in 1901 when E T Barnette was heading up the Tanana River with a boat load of supplies and was swept up by the fast waters of the Chena River. When he stepped ashore at the present site of 1st Ave and Cushman St, he decided to stay. Fairbanks really came into its own when gold, the metal that gave birth to so many other Alaskan towns, was discovered by Italian prospector Felix Pedro 12 miles (19 km) north of Barnette's trading post in 1902. In the next 2 years, a boom town sprang to life amid the hordes of miners stampeding into the area.

After the gold was panned and the mines were shut down, Fairbanks' growth slowed to a crawl. The Alaska Railroad and then WW II and the construction of the Alcan (Alaska Highway) produced the next booms in the city's economy, but neither affected Fairbanks like the Alaska Pipeline. After oil was discovered in Prudhoe Bay in 1968, Fairbanks was never the same. For 4 years, from 1973 to 1977, the town burst at its seams as the principal gateway to the North Slope, where construction of the Alaska Pipeline was at its height.

Workers, who came from all over the USA and the world looking for four-digit weekly pay cheques, filled every hotel room and tent site for miles around. Prices soared, lines at the supermarket became unbearable, and suddenly there were traffic jams in a town that had had none before. During this boom everybody tried to profit; this was truly a 20th century gold rush.

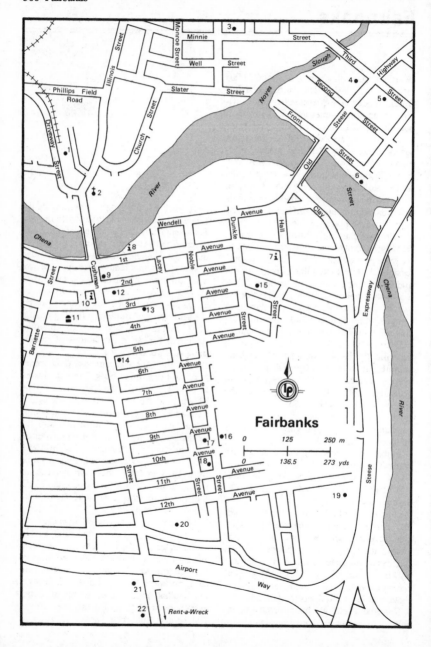

Fairbanks

1	Railroad Depot
2	Immaculate Conception Church
3	Tamarac Inn
4	Burger King
5	Wendy's Restaurant
6	Graehl Landing
7	Arctic Wildlands Information Center
8	Visitor Bureau Log Cabin
9	Yukon Quest General Store & Museum
10	Alaska Public Lands Information Center
11	Post Office
12	Co-op Restaurant & Fountain
13	Fairbanks Hotel
14	Transit Park
15	Royal Fork Restaurant
16	Westmark Fairbanks
17	Grayline Office
18	Golden Nugget Motel
19	Federal Building
20	Foodland
21	El Sombrero
22	Kentucky Fried Chicken

The aftermath of the pipeline construction was just as extreme. The city's population shrank and unemployment crept towards 25%. But like the weather, Fairbanks residents endured all this, and will endure in the future if a proposed gas line is constructed. Fairbanks' residents are a hardy and independent breed because they have to be. That, more than the log cabins or the midnight sun, is the city's trademark. The residents tend to be more colourful than most Alaskans, maybe a bit louder, a degree more boastful. They exemplify to the fullest the Alaskan theme of 'work hard, play hard, drink hard'.

Orientation

Fairbanks, the transport centre for much of the Interior and Arctic Alaska, is a spread-out town that covers 31 sq miles (80 sq km). The city centre is hard to describe and even harder to recognise. Generally, it is considered to be the area bounded by Airport Way to the south, Steese Highway to the east, Cowles St to the west and the banks of the Chena River to the north. Running from north to south through the city centre is

Cushman St, the closest thing Fairbanks has to a main street.

The best way to get oriented in Fairbanks is to begin at the visitor bureau. A guided walking tour departs the centre daily during the summer at 10 am and 3 pm, if the weather is nice. Tours last about an hour and provide a good insight into the city's history and development. Best of all, they're free.

Information

The main source of information is the Visitor Bureau Log Cabin (tel 456-5774) which overlooks the Chena River near the corner of 1st Ave and Cushman St. The many services offered include a recorded telephone message (tel 456-INFO) that lists the daily events and attractions in town; a language bank for foreign travellers who need assistance from an interpreter; and an 80 page brochure with accommodation and restaurants written in German, French and Japanese as well as English.

The log cabin is open daily during the summer from 8.30 am to 5 pm. Other visitor centres are located in Alaskaland (tel 452-4529), open daily from 11 am to 9 pm, and near the baggage claim of the Fairbanks International Airport, open daily from 1.30 to 10.30 pm.

Head to the Alaska Public Lands Information Center (tel 451-7352) on Cushman St, two blocks south of the Chena River, for brochures, maps and information on state and national parks, wildlife refuges and recreation areas. The centre also has exhibits and video programmes on a variety of topics along with a small theatre that shows films. Opening hours are 8.30 am to 9 pm daily during the summer but there is also a 24 hour recorded message (tel 452-PARK) for those in a hurry to get to Denali National Park.

Things to See

Next to the visitor bureau is the **Golden Heart Plaza**, a riverside park which features the bronze statue, *The Unknown First Family*, that was dedicated in 1986.

A cure for those with gold fever is to head

across the street to the **Key Bank** which has a display of large gold nuggets along with mounted animal trophies and Mt McKinley artwork.

The **Immaculate Conception Church**, just across the Chena River Bridge from the visitor bureau, was built in 1904 and was moved to its present location in 1911. The church is a national historic monument and features beautiful stained glass windows. **St Matthew's Episcopal Church** at 1035 1st Ave is a unique log church built in 1905 and rebuilt in 1947 immediately after it burned down.

The **Yukon Quest General Store & Museum** (tel 451-8985) is just south of the visitor bureau on the corner of Cushman St and 2nd Ave. The Iditarod, the best known dog-sled event in Alaska, is only one of two long-distance races. The other is the Yukon Quest, a 1000 mile (1600 km) run between Fairbanks and Whitehorse that was organised in the mid-1980s along many of the early trails used by trappers, miners and the postal service. The museum has a variety of displays that include sleds, harnesses and even the booties dogs wear while running. It is open from 10 am to 5 pm daily during the summer.

The excellent **Noel Wien Library** (tel 452-5177) on the corner of Airport Way and Cowles St is a long walk from the visitor bureau (take the Metropolitan Area Commuter Service (MACS) Blue Line bus). Along with a large Alaskan section, the library features an art exhibit and a stone fireplace, so it can be a warm place to be on a rainy day. Opening hours are Monday to Wednesday from 10 am to 9 pm, Thursday and Friday from 10 am to 6 pm, Saturday from 10 am to 5 pm and Sunday from 1 to 5 pm.

Don't overlook Fairbanks' outdoor art as you walk around town. In 1979, local artists painted murals, ranging from abstract art to wildlife scenes, on 20 buildings as part of a beautification programme. Most of them can be seen in a four-block section beginning at the visitor bureau, which has a free hand-out identifying the murals.

Alaskaland The city's largest attraction is this 44 acre (18 hectare) pioneer theme park created in 1967 to commemorate the 100th year of American possession of Alaska. Inside are such historical displays as the *Nenana*, a former sternwheeler of the Yukon River fleet, Gold Rush Town, a street of log cabins relocated from the city centre, the Pioneers of Alaska Museum and the Wickersham House Museum.

At the back of the park, you'll find the Native Village Museum and Mining Valley, with displays of gold-mining equipment. A miniature 30 gauge train, the Crooked Creek & Whiskey Island Railroad, will take you around the park, while at night there's entertainment at the Palace Saloon and one of the best salmon bakes in the state.

The entrance to Alaskaland is off Airport Way near Peger Rd. A free shuttle bus, made to look like a train, makes hourly runs each day between the visitor bureau and the park from 11 am to 9.30 pm. You can also reach the park on a MACS Blue Line bus. Alaskaland (tel 452-4244) is open daily from 11 am to 9 pm. Some visitors find a theme park in Alaska a little corny, while others think it is an enjoyable step back into Alaska's history. Whatever you may think, you can't beat the price – there is no admission fee.

University The University of Alaska, Fairbanks (UAF), is the original and main campus of the state-wide college and an interesting place to wander around for an afternoon. The school is 4 miles (6.4 km) west from the centre of Fairbanks in a beautiful and unusual setting for a college; it is on a hill that overlooks the surrounding area, and on a clear day it is possible to view Mt McKinley from marked vantage points. Stop at the Wood Center in the middle of campus first to pick up a map of the college. The building is the student centre and general meeting place on campus, as it provides a cafeteria, pub, games rooms, outdoor patio, showers and a laundry service in the basement. There is also a ride board here for those trying to hitchhike to other parts of the state or the Alcan.

The main attraction of UAF is the excellent University Museum, which houses indigenous and pioneer artefacts as well as Blue Babe, a 36,000 year old preserved bison, the state's largest public gold display and the northern lights as shown on a huge video screen. The museum is open daily in the summer from 9 am to 9 pm and the admission fee is $3. On the outskirts of the campus is the Agricultural Experiment Farm, where the university dabbles in growing vegetables of mythical proportions.

Because of its lofty perch, the campus is the best place in Fairbanks to view Mt McKinley on a clear day. A turn-off and marker defining the mountainous horizon is at the south end of Yukon Drive. UAF is also a good spot to view another polar phenomenon – the northern lights. The amazing colours that snake across the sky are best seen away from the centre of town in early or late summer. If you have never seen the northern lights before arriving in Fairbanks, be prepared. This far north they are so vivid and active that they are bound to keep you up half the night watching them.

Reach the campus by taking MACS Red or Blue Line buses right to Wood Center. Free tours of the experimental farm are offered on weekdays from 8 am to 4.30 pm, every half hour during the summer. There are also tours of the campus, offered weekdays during the summer, that include the museum, library and Geophysical Institute. The 2 hour tour begins at 10 am from the museum.

You can also tour the university's Large Animal Research Station (known simply as the musk-ox farm) or attend special shows at the Geophysical Institute if you're curious about the centre of the earth. The musk-ox farm also has herds of caribou and reindeer, and tours are offered twice a week during the summer on Tuesday and Saturday at 1.30 and 2.30 pm. The admission charge is $3. Call the UAF Relations office (tel 474-7581) for more information and details.

Pipeline The closest spot to view the Trans-Alaska Pipeline, where some 1.5 million barrels of oil flow daily on their way to

Valdez, is 8 miles (12.8 km) north of the city on Steese Highway. The turn-off is at Goldstream Rd.

Sled Dogs Fairbanks is the home of the North America Sled Dog Championships, a 3 day event where mushers, some with teams as large as 20 dogs, compete in a series of races. This is not the Iditarod or Yukon Quest. Speed, not endurance, is the key as the races range from 20 to 30 miles (32.6 to 49 km). The Alaska Dog Mushers Association, which hosts the championships, also maintains the Dog Mushers' Museum (tel 455-6528) at *Mile 4* (6.4 km) of Farmers Loop Rd. Open daily during the summer, the museum features displays on sled dog racing, of course, slide shows, videos of races and even live demonstrations throughout the summer. Call the museum for information and times of the dog demonstrations.

Festivals & Events
Golden Days has grown to be Fairbanks' largest celebration of the summer. Staged

during the third week of July, the festival commemorates Felix Pedro's discovery of gold with parades, games, booths, a boat parade on the Chena River and numerous special events such as the Hairy Legs Contest and locking up unsuspecting visitors in the Golden Days Jail. The summer solstice is also well celebrated on the 21 June, when the sun shines gloriously for almost 23 hours. Called Sunfest, events include foot races, speedboat races, art & craft booths and the traditional Midnight Sun baseball game pitting the Goldpanners against another Alaska rival.

Around the second week in August, the Tanana Valley Fair is held at the fairgrounds on College Rd. It features sideshows, a rodeo, entertainment, and the usual livestock shows and large produce.

Places to Stay

Camping The only public campground in the Fairbanks area is the *Chena River State Campground* (51 sites, $10 fee) off University Ave just north of Airport Way. The campground has tables, toilets, fireplaces and water, and can be reached by MACS Blue Line bus.

The other campgrounds in the city are private and charge from $10 to $15 per night to camp. They are the *Tanana Valley Campground* (tel 456-7956) near the fairgrounds on College Rd, and the *Norlite Campground* (tel 474-0206) on Peger Rd just south of Airport Way and the entrance to Alaskaland. Both have showers and laundry facilities, but Tanana Valley provides more natural wooded surroundings for campers. Norlite is little more than an open field.

Youth Hostel The *Fairbanks Youth Hostel* has been on the move ever since the local chapter was opened in the early 1980s. Last reports have it at the Tanana Valley Fairgrounds (MACS Red Line bus) north of town off College Rd, where it consists of an old military hut with an addition. Nightly rates are $6.50 for members and $9 for non-members. Long range plans call for another move someday, possibly closer to Alaska-

land. When arriving in town, call the Alaska Division of Parks on 479-4114 to make sure of the hostel's location.

Another alternative to expensive hotel rooms or staying at the youth hostel is the *Fairbanks Shelter & Shower* (tel 479-5016) at 248 Madcap Lane near the university; it offers simple dormitory accommodation for $15

Bed & Breakfast The Fairbanks Bed & Breakfast (tel 452-4967) is a reservation service for a number of private homes around the city that rent spare rooms to travellers. Plan on $35 to $60 per night for singles or doubles, and call ahead for reservations. The host will often meet you at the railroad depot or airport.

Hotels Hotel/motel rooms in Fairbanks are expensive even by Alaskan standards with most offering rooms from $60 or $70 per night during the summer. The few with reasonable rates are less than desirable or are a considerable distance from the city centre. Check out the room before handing over your money.

The cheapest and closest hotel to the railroad depot is the *Fairbanks Hotel* (tel 456-6440) at 517 3rd Ave. Singles without bath are $35 per night, and doubles cost $42. The *Tamarac Inn* (tel 456-6406), close to the city centre, is north of the Chena River at 252 Minnie St. Single rooms cost $44 and doubles are $56; some units come with cooking facilities.

Other places with good rates and clean rooms are some distance from the city centre. The *Monson Motel* (tel 479-6770), near the International Airport on 1321 Karen St, has rooms and sleepers from $30 and campsites for $10 a night. Two other places under $60 are the *Alaska Motel* (tel 456-6393) at 1546 Cushman St in the city centre with rooms from $40 to $65 and the *Golden North Motel* (tel 479-6201) at 4888 Airport Way with rooms from $40.

Places to Eat

City Centre Nothing is cheap in Fairbanks

but a relatively inexpensive breakfast and lunch are offered at the *Co-op Restaurant & Fountain* at 535 2nd Ave and the grill in *Woolworth* at 302 Cushman St. For a moderately priced dinner with beer and wine, try *The Pantry* in the Great Land Hotel at 723 1st Ave.

The best Chinese food in the city centre is at *Tiki Cove* in the Polaris Hotel where dinners begin at $12; the cheapest Chinese food is at *Wong's Kitchen* in the Rampart Mini-Mall. Other then Taco Bell, the closest Mexican restaurant to the city centre is *El Sombrero* at 1420 South Cushman St but it is a bit expensive. Nearby and cheaper is *Los Amigos* at 636 28th Ave.

Around Town Hungry souls should take in the *Alaskaland Salmon Bake* (free shuttle bus from the visitor bureau), where for $15 you not only get grilled salmon but halibut, spareribs and salad. Pricewise, a better deal is available at the *Royal Fork Buffet Restaurant* at 414 3rd St off Steese Expressway. You can gorge on their buffet at lunch (11 am to 4 pm); for only $5.50 you can have all the fried chicken, desserts and salad you want.

In Bentley Mall and at 1705 South Cushman St is the *Food Factory* which has cheap submarines and other sandwiches that can be enjoyed with your favourite beer. Chain and fast food restaurants such as *Dairy Queen*, *Big Boys*, *Taco Time* and *McDonald's* can be found along University Ave and Airport Way. It's a little unbelievable but this city has five, count'em five, *Pizza Huts* scattered around.

The best place around town to turn dinner into an evening is the *Pumphouse*, 2 miles (3.2 km) from the city centre on Chena Pump Rd. The Pumphouse, once used in the gold-mining era, is now a national historical site that houses a restaurant and saloon. The atmosphere is unique; inside and out there are artefacts and relics from the golden past. Dinners cost from $15 to $22, or you can go there simply to enjoy a drink while taking in the boat traffic on the Chena River. The MACS Blue Line bus includes the restaurant

in its run in the early evening from 5 pm to 6.30 pm.

Entertainment

The barrooms are the best place to meet locals in Fairbanks, and it seems you never have to travel far to find one. Rowdy saloons that are throwbacks to the mining days are the area's specialty. The *Palace Saloon* (tel 456-5960) at Alaskaland is alive at night with honky-tonk piano, turn-of-the-century can-can dancers and other acts on its large stage. The saloon presents two shows nightly during the summer; a musical comedy entitled *Good as Gold* and an after-hours burlesque show. The admission charge is $5

The *Malemute Saloon*, 7 miles (11.2 km) west of Fairbanks in Ester, also offers ragtime piano and vaudeville acts, and it has made a ritual out of reading Robert Service poetry. There are two shows nightly from Monday to Saturday at this tour-bus haven; the admission charge is $5.

Other lively establishments on the outskirts of Fairbanks are *Senator's Saloon* at the Pumphouse on Chena Pump Rd, *Ivory Jack's* on Goldstream Rd, and the *Howling Dog Saloon* in Fox at the intersection of the Steese and Elliott highways 12 miles (19.2 km) north of the city centre. All have live music or entertainment. The Howling Dog has rock & roll bands and an occasional volleyball game played out the back under the midnight sun.

Live music and a college atmosphere are found at the *University Pub* in the Wood Center at UAF. In the city centre, try *The Big I Bar*, the local hang-out for city workers and reporters from the *Daily News-Miner*. The bar is north of the Chena River near the railroad depot on North Turner Rd.

The Goldpanners are Fairbanks' entry in a semipro league made up of teams of top college and amateur players from around the country which compete each summer. More then 80 professionals, including Tom Seaver and Dave Winfield, have played in what began as an all-Alaska baseball league but now includes teams from Hawaii and other states as well. Games are played at Growden

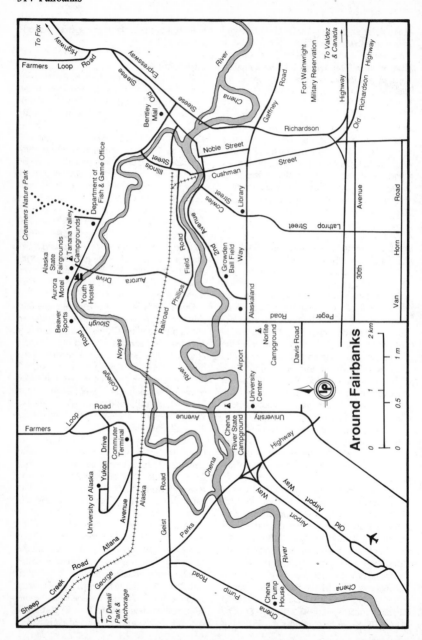

Around Fairbanks

Memorial Park West on 2nd Ave; most games start at 7.30 pm.

A variety of free summer concerts take place in Bicentennial Park on Cushman Ave. Call the visitor bureau 24 hour message on current events (tel 456-4636) for dates of concerts or home baseball games. A quieter and more relaxing evening can be had at the *Three-D Steam Bath* (tel 456-6740) at 308 Wendell St, where you'll find old-fashioned steam rooms for two. The place is open until 10 pm daily and 11 pm on Friday and Saturday; the cost is $6 per person or $10 per couple.

Hiking

Two of the best trails in the state are north of Fairbanks and are administered by the Bureau of Land Management (BLM). At *Mile 27* (43 km) of Elliott Highway is the 4 to 5 day **White Mountain Trail**. The trailheads for the even more impressive **Pinnell Trail** are at *Mile 85.5* (137 km) and *Mile 107.3* (172 km) of Steese Highway (see the Trekking section in the Wilderness chapter for information on both these trails). Contact the BLM office in Fairbanks (tel 474-2200) for trail conditions and availability of the three public-use cabins they rent out.

Creamer's Field Trail A self-guided, 2 mile (3.2 km) trail winds through Creamer's Field Migratory Wildlife Refuge, an old dairy farm that has since become an Audubon bird-lover's paradise, as more than 100 species of bird pass through each year. The refuge is at 1300 College Rd (MACS Red Line bus) and the trailhead is in the parking lot adjacent to the Alaska Department of Fish & Game office (tel 452-1531), where trail guides are available. The trail is mostly boardwalk with an observation tower along the way and lots of bugs. The flocks of geese, ducks and swans move onto nesting grounds by late May but sandhill cranes can be spotted throughout the summer.

Chena Lakes Recreation Area This facility opened in 1984 as the last phase of an Army Corps of Engineers flood control project prompted by the Chena River flooding of Fairbanks in 1967. Two separate parks, Chena River and Chena Lakes, make up the recreational area which is 18 miles (28.8 km) south-east from Fairbanks past North Pole, off the Laurance Rd exit of Richardson Highway. The Chena River park contains a 2.5 mile (4 km) self-guided nature trail. The Chena Lake park offers swimming and canoe, sailboat and paddleboat rentals. Between the two parks there are three campground loops providing 78 sites. The day-use fee is $3 and the overnight camping fee is $5.

Paddling

Fairbanks offers a wide variety of canoeing opportunities, both leisurely afternoon paddles and overnight trips, into the surrounding area. There are also many places to rent boats; single-day rates range from $30 to $40 per boat. For travellers without transport, Beaver Sports (tel 479-2494) at 2400 College Rd is conveniently located near water, avoiding problems of how to get the boat from the store to the dock. Wilderness Canoe Adventures (tel 452-8968) at 316 Front St rents canoes and provides drop-off and pick-up services as well.

Also check into Backcountry Logistical Services (tel 457-7606) at 469 Goldmine Trail and CanoeAlaska (tel 479-5183), which rent out boats and even supply transport when they're not running a trip.

Around Town An afternoon can be spent paddling the Chena River; the mild currents let you paddle upstream as well as down. You can launch a canoe from almost any bridge crossing the river, including the Graehl Landing near the north side of Steese Highway where locals like to paddle upstream and then float back down.

From Beaver Sports on College Rd, you can put your rented canoe in quiet Noyes Slough and paddle east to Graehl Landing, then west along the Chena River through the city centre before paddling back up the slough. The round trip is a 13 mile (21 km) paddle.

Chena & Tanana Rivers Those looking for an overnight or even longer paddle should check into a float down the Chena River from the Chena River Hot Springs Rd east of Fairbanks (see the Paddling section in the Wilderness chapter) or a pleasant 2 day trip down the Tanana River. The popular Tanana River trip usually begins from the end of Chena Pump Rd and finishes in the town of Nenana, where it is possible to return with your canoe to Fairbanks on the Alaska Railroad. This 60 mile (100 km) trip can be done in a single day but would require 10 to 12 hours of paddling.

Chatanika River The Chatanika River can be paddled for 28 miles (45 km) west from Cripple Creek BLM Campground at *Mile 60* (96.6 km) of Steese Highway. The river parallels the road to Chatanika River State Campground at *Mile 39* (62.8 km). From here, the trip can be extended another 17 miles (27 km) to a bridge at *Mile 11* (17.7 km) of Elliott Highway.

The river is not a difficult paddle but it requires considerable driving because you have to shuttle boats and people between Fairbanks and the two highways. Many locals get around this by only paddling the upper portion of the river that parallels Steese Highway and chaining a bicycle at the end of the route so they can get back to their car.

Cabins

Fred Blixt Cabin This public-use cabin is off *Mile 62* (99 km) of Elliott Highway, 10 miles (16 km) before the junction with Dalton Highway. A short spur leads from the road to the cabin, which should be reserved in advance through the BLM office (tel 474-2200) in Fairbanks. The rental fee is $15 per night.

Cripple Creek Cabin This old trapper's cabin, renovated by the BLM in 1972, is at *Mile 60.5* (96.8 km) of Steese Highway. It is between the highway and the Chatanika River and is reached by a short trail. The cabin, available only from mid-August to

mid-May, does not offer a truly isolated setting because Cripple Creek Campground and a YCC Camp are nearby. Still, the surrounding area is scenic. The rental fee is $15 and the cabin should be reserved in advance through the Fairbanks BLM office.

Guide Companies

Check the Wilderness chapter for a list of the many outfitters based in the Fairbanks area. CanoeAlaska offers trips and canoeing classes from mid-May to early August and are limited to eight people in four boats. Outings include 2 days on the Chena River or 3 days on the Gulkana River. The cost, $125 per person, covers the boat, transport, food and guide.

Getting There & Away

Air The Fairbanks International Airport was expanded in 1984 and serves as the gateway for supplies and travellers heading into the Brooks Range and Arctic Alaska. The airport is almost 4 miles (6.4 km) south-west of the city off Airport Way. The terminal is impressive inside, with wall hangings, wildlife displays and Ben Eielson's bi-plane hanging from the ceiling.

Alaska Airlines (tel 452-1661) provides five daily flights to Anchorage, where there are connections to the rest of the state, as well as a direct flight from Fairbanks to Seattle. The one-way standard fare (the most expensive) to Anchorage is $116.

The other intrastate airline is MarkAir (tel 474-9166), which has three direct flights daily to Anchorage for the same fare as well as flights to Barrow. Delta Air Lines (tel 474-0238) and Air North Canada (tel 452-5555), among others, also fly out of Fairbanks. A number of air-taxi operators have regularly scheduled flights and also make mail flights to small communities in the Bush. Frontier Flying Service (tel 474-0014) has flights almost daily to Eagle, Bettles and Anaktuvuk Pass.

Bus From Fairbanks, Alaskon Express (tel 456-5816) stops at Delta Junction, Tok and then overnights at Beaver Creek in the

Yukon. The next day you can make connections onto Haines or Whitehorse. Buses depart from the Westmark Inn at 1521 Cushman St in the city centre at 10 am Tuesday and Saturday during the summer. The one-way fare from Fairbanks to Delta Junction is $20, to Tok $40 and to Haines $149 (lodging at Beaver Creek is not included).

Alaska-Yukon Motorcoaches (tel 452-8518) depart from the Captain Bartlett Hotel, 1411 Airport Way, at 8.30 am daily during the summer for a package tour to Denali National Park but you can also secure just a seat if you bug them enough. Obviously they don't want independent travellers, however, as the one-way fare to Anchorage is $120.

Alaska-Denali Transit has a weekly service from Fairbanks to Anchorage via Denali National Park and a weekly service to Haines via Delta Junction and Tok. The fare to Anchorage is $55, to Denali $25, to Tok $40 and to Haines $99. For information on schedules and pick-up points call (907) 273-3331.

Train The Alaska Railroad (tel 456-4155) has an express train that departs Fairbanks daily at 8.30 am from late May to mid-September. The train reaches Denali National Park around noon and Anchorage at 8 pm. The railroad depot is at 280 North Cushman St, a short walk from the Chena River. The one-way fare to Denali National Park is $33 and to Anchorage $88.

Hitchhiking Thumbing is made much easier by jumping on a MACS bus first. Hitchhikers heading towards Denali National Park and Anchorage on George Parks Highway should take the Blue Line bus and get off at the corner of Geist St and the George Parks Highway. To head down Richardson Highway towards Delta Junction and the Alcan, the best bet is to jump on the Red Line bus and get off at the corner of South Cushman St and 30th Ave about 3 miles (4.8 km) south of the city centre.

Getting Around

Airport Transport There's no Metropolitan Area Commuter Service (MACS) bus to the airport; the closest stop is a 1.5 mile (2.4 km) hike to the University Center at the corner of Airport Way and University Ave. There are limousine services from the airport which costs $6 per person for a trip into the city centre.

Bus MACS provides local bus transport in the Fairbanks area from 6.45 am to 7.45 pm Monday to Friday with limited services on Saturday and none on Sunday. There is now only two runs due to a city budget cut in 1986. The Blue Line runs from the city centre west via Airport Way and the university. The Red Line goes from the hospital on the south side of Airport Way, through the city and to the university via College Road. Together they form a convenient loop that meets most travellers' needs.

The fare is $1.50, although a token can be purchased in advance for $1 from a variety of businesses or at the Transit Park on the corner of Cushman St and 5th Ave. The Transit Park is the central terminal for the system as all buses pass through here. For more information contact the MACS office (tel 452-6623) at 3175 Peger Rd or call their Transit Hotline (456-EASY) that gives daily bus information.

There is also the Alaskaland Tram which runs daily from 11.30 am to 9 pm and passes the visitor centre and a few of the major hotels (Westmark Inn, Golden Nugget) every hour. It heads west along 1st Ave to Alaskaland before heading back to the city centre along Airport Way and Cushman St. It's limited transport but it's free.

Car Rental For a small group of travellers, splitting the cost of a used-car rental is the best and often the cheapest way to see the outlying areas of Fairbanks or to venture to such places as the Arctic Circle Hot Springs, Circle on the Steese Highway or Manly Hot Springs at the end of Elliott Highway.

Rent-A-Wreck (tel 452-1606) at 2105 Cushman St, south of Airport Way, has used cars for $30 per day and 25 cents a mile. All Star Rental (tel 456-3213) has cars for $32.95 per day and 25 cents a mile with 100 free miles. At these prices, a 3 day drive to Arctic Circle Hot Springs would cost around $140 (including insurance and mileage) that can be divided by up to four people. You might also want to check with Arctic Rent-A-Car (tel 451-0111) and Rainbow Rent-A-Car (tel 457-5900) before calling the expensive national companies. Like most other cities in Alaska, it's hard to score a rental car in Fairbanks at the last minute.

Bicycle Bicycles can be rented from the Lucky Sourdough Tourist Trap (tel 456-2522) at 402 Barnette St, west of Cushman St. One of the better day trips on a bike is to peddle Farmer's Loop Rd from University Ave north of the university to Steese Highway for scenic views of the city and the surrounding valley.

Tours
Both Gray Line, which leaves from the Westmark Fairbanks (tel 274-6631), and Alaska Sightseeing, which departs from the Captain Bartlett Hotel (tel 452-8518), offer a 3 hour city tour for $20 that includes the university, Gold Dredge No 8 on Steese Highway and the Trans-Alaska Pipeline. The tour is scheduled twice daily at 9.30 am and 2.30 pm in small minibuses. Gray Line also offers just a gold-dredge tour where they take you out to the huge Gold Dredge No 8, a national historic landmark, which was in operation until 1959. The 2 hour tour is $14, leaves daily at 9.15 am and 2.45 pm and you get to try your hand at gold panning.

You can travel the Chena River on the historic sternwheeler *Discovery* if you're up to parting with $25 for the 4 hour trip. The boat departs twice daily at 8.45 am and 2 pm in the summer from Discovery Landing, located off the Dale Rd exit at *Mile 4.5* (7.2 km) of Airport Way. American Sightseeing also has a riverboat trip for $35 as does Red Hat Tours (tel 457-3000), whose city tour at $18 is probably the best one for your money.

If for some strange reason you're not

heading south but still want to experience Denali National Park, the Alaska Railroad (tel 456-4155) has an overnight excursion to the park. The fare is $179 per person, based on double occupancy, and includes a return ticket, accommodation for 1 night and a 6 hour tour along the park road.

Around Fairbanks

HOT SPRINGS
Back around the turn of the century, when gold prospectors were stooping in near-freezing creeks panning for gold, there was one saving grace in the area – the hot springs. There are three of them around Fairbanks and all were quickly discovered and used by the miners as a brief escape from Alaska's ice and cold. Today, the same mineral water, ranging in temperature from 120°F to 150°F (50°C to 65°C), soothes the aches and pains of frigid travellers passing by.

The hot springs include Chena Hot Springs, 56 miles (90 km) east of Fairbanks, Arctic Circle Hot Springs, 135 miles (216 km) north-east of Fairbanks on Steese Highway, and Manley Hot Springs, 152 miles (245 km) west of Fairbanks on Elliott Highway. Hitchhiking Chena Hot Springs Rd isn't bad but the other two are a challenge. The cheapest way to get there, even if there are only two of you, is to rent a used car and drive yourself (see the Fairbanks Getting Around section in this chapter).

CHENA HOT SPRINGS ROAD
Chena Hot Springs Rd extends 56 miles (90 km) east off Steese Highway to the hot springs of the same name. The road is paved and in good condition. The resort, the closest of the three hot-spring resorts to Fairbanks, is also the most developed as it has been turned into a year-round facility offering downhill skiing in the winter.

From *Mile 26* (41.6 km) to *Mile 51* (81.6 km), the road passes through the middle of the **Chena River State Recreation Area**, a 254,080 acre (102,823 hectare) preserve containing the river valley and the surrounding alpine areas. This is a scenic park that offers good hiking (see the Fairbanks Hiking section), fishing and two public campgrounds. The first is *Rosehip State Campground* (25 sites, $5 fee) at *Mile 27* (43.5 km) of Hot Chena Springs Rd, while further to the east is *Tors Trails State Campground* (20 sites, $5 fee) near the trailhead for the Granite Tors Trail. Both campgrounds are scenic and provide canoe access to the river.

The trailhead for the **Granite Tors Trail** is across the road from the Tors Trails Campground and can be reached by following the levee for a short distance on the west side of the stream. Tors are isolated pinnacles of granite popping out of the tundra. The first set of tors is 6 miles (9.6 km) from the trailhead; the best group lies a further 2 miles (3.2 km) along the trail.

Just before the fifth bridge over the Chena River at *Mile 49* (79 km) of Chena Hot Springs Rd is the turn-off for the 3.5 mile (5.6 km) Angel Rocks Trail. The trail begins along the river and then turns inland to swing past spectacular rock outcrops. This is not an easy hike; plan on 3 hours or more to complete it.

The trailhead for the **Chena Dome Trail** is at *Mile 50.5* (81.6 km) of Chena Hot Springs Rd. The trail follows the ridge for almost 30 miles (48 km) around the Angel Creek Drainage. It makes an excellent backpacking trip that provides good alpine hiking with scenic views. On the ridge, the route is mostly marked by rock cairns.

Chena Hot Springs

At the end of the Chena Hot Springs Rd is the *Chena Hot Springs Resort* (tel 452-7867), which offers a variety of accommodation and activities during the summer. The most popular activity is hot-tub soaking, done indoors where there are two jacuzzis, a pool and a hot (very hot) tub. The resort has a restaurant, bar and a huge fireplace in the lounge. Hotel rooms begin at $56 for singles and $86 for a double; rustic cabins begin at $70 per couple.

If the accommodation seems highly priced, take heart. If there is a lot of you, large cabins with sleeping lofts holding up to 10 people are $95 a night. If there is only one or two of you, head for the campground. It's not the most scenic in Alaska but the resort recently turned it into a free facility. The use of the hot tubs is $5.50 per day for each camper.

Getting There & Away

Hitchhiking is not the grand effort it is on the Steese Highway because of the heavy summer usage of the Chena River State Recreation Area. You can also call Goldline Express (tel 474-0535) which runs vans or a bus out to the Chena Hot Springs Resort for $50 per person return.

STEESE HIGHWAY

The Arctic Circle Hot Springs lies off the 162 mile (261 km) long Steese Highway, a miner's trail at one time where today you can still see the signs of old mining camps as well as new ones. The road is paved for the first 44 miles (71 km) and then consists of a good gravel base until the final 30 miles (48 km), where it narrows and becomes considerably rougher. The excellent scenery along the highway and the good accommodation at Arctic Circle Hot Springs make this side trip well worth the time and money.

The Steese Highway starts in Fairbanks, *Mile 0*, at the junction of Airport Way and Richardson Highway. From there, it passes the beginning of Chena Hot Springs Rd at *Mile 4.6* (7.4 km) and then Elliott Highway at *Mile 11* (17.7 km) near Fox, a service centre. The golden past of Steese Highway can first be seen at *Mile 9.5* (15.3 km), where it passes the Goldstream Rd exit to **Gold Dredge No 8**, a five deck, 250 foot (76 metre) dredge built in 1928 that was named a national historical site in 1984. The dredge operated until 1959 and before it was closed had displaced 1065 tons (965,955 kg) of pay dirt from Pedro, Engineer and Goldstream creeks. The dredge is privately owned; it is $5 for a tour and to pan for gold afterwards.

At *Mile 16.6* (26.7 km), on the east side of

the highway, is the **Felix Pedro Monument**, whose discovery of gold nearby resulted in the boom town that was to become Fairbanks. Amateur gold panners are often in the nearby stream 'looking for colour' or you can go another 10 miles (16 km) to see a much more serious attempt at obtaining the metal. At *Mile 27.9* (45 km) you take a sharp turn up a hill to reach the old gold camp at **Chatanika**. The support centre was built in 1925 for the gold dredging that went on from 1927 to 1957 and removed an estimated $70 million in gold at yesterday's prices.

Today, the *Old FE Co Gold Camp* (tel 389-2414) is a national historical site and lodge with single rooms for $27.50. The camp also has a great sourdough breakfast served from 9 am to 2 pm Saturday and Sunday. For $10.50 you get an all-you-can-eat buffet with sourdough pancakes (of course), sourdough biscuits, eggs, French toast, potatoes, sweet rolls – the list goes on.

The first public campground along the Steese Highway is the *Upper Chatanika River State Campground* (25 sites, $5 fee) on the river at *Mile 39* (63 km). Water and firewood are usually available, but have your bug dope handy – this is mosquito country. Those with a canoe can launch their boat here. The next campground is the *Cripple Creek BLM Campground* (21 sites, $5 fee) at *Mile 60* (96.6 km), the site of the uppermost access point to the Chatanika River Canoe Trail (see the Fairbanks Paddling section in this chapter). The campground has tables, water and a nature trail nearby.

Access points for the Pinnell Mountain Trail (see the Trekking section in the Wilderness chapter) lie at *Mile 85.6* (138 km) and *Mile 107* (172 km) of Steese Highway.

The **Birch Creek Canoe Route** begins at *Mile 94* (150.4 km) of Steese Highway, where a short road leads down to a canoe launch on the creek. The wilderness trip is a 140 mile (224 km) paddle to the exit point at *Mile 147* (236.6 km) of the highway. The overall rating of the river is Class II, but there are some Class III and Class IV parts that require lining your canoe. More details on the trip can be obtained from the Fairbanks

BLM office (tel 474-2200). Ask for their brochure entitled *Alaska's River Trails – Northern Region*.

Eagle Summit, elevation 3624 feet (1105 metres), is at *Mile 108* (173.8 km), where a 0.8 mile (1.3 km) trail leads to the top. Eagle Summit is the highest point along the Steese Highway and near 21 June (summer solstice) the midnight sun can be observed skimming the horizon. The summit is also near a caribou migration route. The last campground before Central is the *Bedrock Creek BLM Campground* (eight sites, free) just beyond *Mile 119* (190.4 km).

At *Mile 127.5* (205 km), the highway reaches **Central** (pop 800 in the summer) where there is gasoline, groceries, a post office, cabins for rent and the **Circle District Museum** (tel 520-1893). The log cabin museum reflects the area's mining history and the active placer gold mining that continues today with displays indoors and outside. The admission charge is $1 and it is open daily from noon to 5 pm during the summer. Nearby is the *Central Motor Inn* (tel 520-5228) which has it all; rooms, campsites, showers, bar, liquor store, you name it.

Arctic Circle Hot Springs

Just beyond Central, the Circle Hot Springs Rd heads south and in 6 miles (9.6 km) passes the *Ketchem Creek BLM Campground* (seven sites, free), where the campsites are on both sides of the river with a footbridge connecting them. Two miles (3.2 km) beyond it is the *Arctic Circle Hot Springs Resort* (tel 520-5113), first used by miners in 1905 and today a popular spot with Fairbanks residents.

The year-round resort maintains an Olympic-sized pool in which 139°F (59°C) mineral water is pumped through at a rate of 386 gallons (1451 litres) a minute. There is also a restaurant, ice-cream parlour, hotel and the Miner's Saloon. Rustic cabins with no running water are $55 per couple, deluxe cabins with kitchen, running water and even hot tubs are $85 per couple. Or, book a bunk in their hostel upstairs in the attic for only

Top: Brooks Range (USFS)
Bottom: Old cabin on the Pribilof Islands (ED)

Top: Delta region of Southwest Alaska (USFS)
Bottom: Riverboats on the Chena River in Fairbanks (ADT)

$15 per night. It's $5 just to stop at the resort and soak.

Circle

Beyond Central, the Steese Highway passes the exit point of the Birch Creek Canoe Route at *Mile 147* (237 km) and ends at Circle (pop 90) at *Mile 162* (260.7 km).

Circle is an interesting little wilderness town that lies on the banks of the Yukon River and was the northernmost point you could drive to before the Dalton Highway was opened up. A large sign in the centre of town still proclaims this fact. The town is 50 miles (80 km) south of the Arctic Circle, but miners who established it in 1896 thought they were near the imaginary line and gave Circle its present name.

After gold was discovered in Birch Creek, Circle was a bustling log cabin city of 1200 with two theatres, a music hall, eight dance halls and 28 saloons. The Klondike reduced the town to the wilderness hamlet it remains today. You can get a feeling for the town's history by walking to **Pioneer Cemetery** which has headstones dating back to the 1800s. To find it, head upriver along the gravel road. Beyond a barricade is a trail that leads into dense underbrush and the graves are off to the left.

A city-operated campground at the end of Steese Highway consists of tables, outhouses and a grassy area along the banks of the Yukon River where you can pitch your tent. Nearby is the **Yukon Trading Post**, which includes a general store with Arctic Alaska prices, cafe, bar and motel. The bar is an especially important spot because this is the only place you can go at night (other than your car) to escape the wave of mosquitoes.

Getting There & Away

Needless to say, hitchhiking is more difficult on Steese Highway than on Chena Hot Springs Rd but not impossible. Actually in today's world, hitchhiking is probably possible anywhere. Still, you have to consider your time schedule and patience level before attempting this road.

Apart from renting a vehicle, you can

reach the resort through Spell of the Yukon Tours (tel 455-6128) if they're still running their van when you finally make it to Alaska. Sam Cox runs the company and has a basic 2 day/1 night package that includes a trip up to Circle, a night at the lodge, gold panning etc. The cost is $243 but you can probably work a deal out with him just for transport. You could also obtain a seat on 40 Mile Air's (tel 474-0518) morning mail flight. The service runs to Circle from Monday to Friday and the return fare is $120 per person.

ELLIOTT HIGHWAY

From the crossroad with the Steese Highway at Fox north of Fairbanks, the Elliott Highway extends 152 miles (244.6 km) north and then west to Manley Hot Springs, a small settlement near the Tanana River. The first 28 miles (45 km) of the highway are paved and the rest is gravel; sections past the junction with Dalton Highway are often narrow and steep. At *Mile 28* (24 km) of Elliott Highway is the trailhead, parking lot and information box for the White Mountain Trail to the Borealis-Le Fevre Cabin (see the Trekking section in the Wilderness chapter), a hike of 19 miles (30.6 km) one way.

An old Bureau of Land Management (BLM) campground, no longer maintained, is passed at *Mile 57* (91.7 km) of Elliott Highway where a bridge crosses the Tolovana River. There is still a turn-off here and the fishing is good for grayling and northern pike, but the mosquitoes are of legendary proportions. Nearby is the start of the **Colorado Creek Trail** to Windy Gap BLM Cabin. Check with the BLM office (tel 474-2200) in Fairbanks about use of the cabin during the summer.

At *Mile 71* (114 km) is the service centre of **Livengood**, where you will find a small general store. At this point Elliott Highway swings to a more westerly direction and in 2 miles (3.2 km) passes the junction the Dalton Highway (see the Dalton Highway section in the Bush chapter). From here, it is another 78 miles (125 km) south-west to Manly Hot Springs.

Manley Hot Springs

The town, which has a summer population of 150 or so, is on the west side of Hot Springs Slough and provides a public campground ($2 per night fee) near the bridge that crosses the slough. The town was first homesteaded in 1902 by J F Karshner just as the US Army Signal Corps arrived to put in a telegraph station. Frank Manley arrived a few years later and built a four-storey hotel at the trading centre which was booming with miners from the nearby Eureka and Tofly mining areas. Most of the miners have gone now but Manley left his name on the village and today it's a quiet but friendly spot known for its lush gardens, a rare sight this far north.

Just before entering the village you pass the *Manley Hot Springs Resort* (tel 672-3611) up on a hill, where most of the serious bathing is done. The relatively new resort provides rooms, a restaurant, a bar and, of course, a mineral hot springs pool. They also have showers, a laundromat and run tours up the Tanana River to see a fish camp or to go gold panning.

Within town is the *Manley Roadhouse* (tel 672-3161) offering single rooms for $30, doubles for $40 and cabins for $65. This classic Alaskan roadhouse was built in 1906 and today features antiques in its restaurant, bar and lounge. You can also wander around town and purchase vegetables from some of the residents. The produce here is unbelievable.

Moose

The Bush

The Bush, the wide rim of wilderness that encircles Anchorage, Fairbanks and all the roads between the two, constitutes a vast majority of the state's area, yet only a trickle of tourists venture into the region for a first-hand look at rural Alaska.

Cost, more than the great mountains or the mighty rivers, is the barrier that isolates the Bush. For budget-minded travellers who reach the 'Great White North' with their backpacks after hitchhiking, what lies out in the Bush is usually beyond the reach of their wallets. Apart from a few exceptions, flying is the only way to reach a specific area. Once out there, facilities can be sparse and very expensive.

Those who do endure the high expense and extra travel are blessed with a land and people that have changed little over time. The most pristine wilderness lies in the many newly created national parks and preserves found away from the road system – parks where there are no visitor centres, campgrounds or shuttle buses running trips into the backcountry. Only nature in all its grandeur is encountered. Traditional villages, where subsistence is still the means of survival, and hearty homesteaders, as independent and ingenious as they come, lie hidden throughout rural Alaska.

There are three general areas in Bush Alaska. Southwest Alaska consists of the Alaska Peninsula, the Aleutian Islands and the rich salmon grounds of Bristol Bay. The Alaska Peninsula extends 550 miles (880 km) from the western shore of Cook Inlet to its tip at False Pass. From there the Aleutian Islands, a chain of over 200 islands, curve another 1100 miles (1800 km) west into the Pacific Ocean.

Southwest Alaska is characterised by active and dormant volcanoes, a treeless terrain and the worst weather in the state. Alaska's outlying arm is where the arctic waters of the Bering Sea meet the warm Japanese Current, causing considerable

cloudiness, rain and fog. Violent storms sweeping across the Pacific Ocean contribute to high winds in the area. The major attractions of the region are Katmai National Park & Preserve at the beginning of the Alaska Peninsula, Lake Clark National Park & Preserve across Cook Inlet from Homer, and McNeil River State Game Sanctuary.

Western Alaska is a flat, treeless plain that borders the Bering Sea north of the Alaska Peninsula to beyond Kotzebue and the Arctic Circle. This flatland is broken up by millions of lakes and slow-moving rivers such as the Yukon, while the weather in the summer is cool and cloudy with considerable fog and drizzle. The most visited parts of this region are the towns of Nome and Kotzebue, and the Pribilof Islands, north of the Aleutian Islands in the Bering Sea and the location of seal-breeding grounds and bird rookeries.

The third area in the Bush is Arctic Alaska, also known as the North Slope, which lies north of the Arctic Circle. Here the Brooks Range slopes gradually to the north and is eventually replaced by tundra plains that end at the Arctic Ocean. The harsh climate and short summers produce 400 species of plants in the treeless tundra that are often dwarfed versions of those further south. Wildlife in the form of polar bears, reindeer, caribou, wolves and brown bears have adapted amazingly well to the rough conditions.

Arctic Alaska is characterised by nightless summers and dayless winters. In Barrow, Alaska's northernmost village, the midnight sun never sets from May to August. Surprisingly, the Arctic Alaska winters are often milder than those in the Interior. The summers, however, are cool at best and temperatures are rarely warmer than 45°F (8°C). Barrow attracts a small number of tourists each summer, and backpackers have discovered that the Gates of the Arctic National Park & Preserve is an expensive but intriguing place for a wilderness adventure.

Although many places are geared for tourists, with formal accommodation available most of the time, it is best to be completely self-sufficient whether you are venturing into a new wilderness preserve or into a traditional village set in its ways.

Don't just pick out a village and fly to it. It is wise to either have a contact there (someone you know, a guide company or a wilderness lodge) or to travel with somebody who does. Although the indigenous people, especially the Eskimos, are very hospitable people, there can be much tension and suspicion of strangers in small, isolated rural communities.

Southwest Alaska

There are two ways to see a small part of the Bush without flying. One of them is to drive Dalton Highway (also known as the North Slope Haul Rd). The other is to hop onto the State Marine Ferry when it makes its special run five times each summer along the Alaska Peninsula to the eastern end of the Aleutian Islands. Around 29 May, 19 June, 10 July, 21 August and 11 September (dates vary slightly from year to year), the MV *Tustumena* continues west to Sand Point, King Cove, Cold Bay and Dutch Harbor on Unalaska Island before backtracking to Kodiak.

The ferry trip is a 6 day cruise; the MV *Tustumena*, one of the oldest vessels in the state-operated fleet, leaves Kodiak on Tuesday, returns early Sunday morning and continues onto Seward that day. The boat docks at the villages only long enough to

load and unload (1 to 2 hours), but it is sufficient time to get off for a quick look around. On board are dormitory rooms, a cafeteria and a bar.

The round-trip fare for walk-on passengers to Dutch Harbor from Kodiak is $352; from Seward it is $448. The cruise is interesting and by far the cheapest way to see this part of Alaska, but those with weak stomachs should be warned that the boat ride often gets rough, especially during the September run when it is frequently hit by the stormy autumn weather. For those who want to spend more time at a village, Reeve Aleutian Airways (tel 243-4700 in Anchorage) and Peninsula Airways (tel 243-2323 in Anchorage) provide services to the Aleutian Islands as well as the Pribilof Islands and the Alaska Peninsula.

KING COVE
This town of 700 residents is a commercial fishing base at the western end of the Alaska Peninsula near the entrance of Cold Bay. Surrounded by mountains, King Cove supports a hotel, a restaurant and a busy harbour during the summer but no campgrounds. Reeve Aleutian Airways charges $332 for a one-way ticket to King Cove from Anchorage.

COLD BAY
On the west shore of Cold Bay is the town of the same name. The 160 residents are mostly government workers as the town is a major refuelling stop for many flights crossing the Pacific to or from the Orient. Russian explorers also used the bay and most likely spent the winters here on their first trips along the coast. Before they departed, Count Feodor Lutke named Izembek Lagoon in 1827 after a doctor aboard one of his ships.

A huge airstrip was built in the area during WW II; today it's the third longest in the state and the reason why the town serves as the transport centre for the entire Aleutian chain. You can still see Quonset huts and other remains from the WW II military build-up.

The town also serves as the gateway to the **Izembek National Wildlife Refuge**, which was established in 1960 to protect some 142 species of bird, primarily the black brant. Almost the entire North American population of brant, some 150,000 of them, arrive in spring and autumn to feed on large eelgrass beds during their annual migration.

A 10 mile (16 km) road runs from Cold Bay to the Izembek Lagoon; otherwise, travel in the refuge is by foot or plane. Contact the Wildlife Refuge office in Cold Bay (Pouch 2, Cold Bay, Alaska 99571) for more information. Within town, accommodation, meals and groceries are available. Reeve Aleutian Airways services the community and charges $322 for a one-way ticket from Anchorage.

UNALASKA & DUTCH HARBOR

Unalaska on Unalaska Island and its sister town Dutch Harbor on Amaknak Island, both in the Aleutian chain, lie deep in Unalaska Bay and are connected to each other by a 500 foot (152 metre) bridge. During the summer, the population of the two towns can easily exceed 2000 due to the influx of cannery workers who process seafood, most notably crab. In 1978, the towns earned more from fishing than any other USA port.

Unalaska was the first headquarters for the Russian-American Co and a cornerstone in the lucrative sea-otter fur trade in the 1700s. It was also an important harbour for miners sailing to the golden beaches of Nome. In 1939, the US built navy and army installations here; at one time 60,000 servicemen were stationed there.

In June 1942, the Japanese opened their Aleutian Islands campaign by bombing Dutch Harbor, and then took Attu and Kiska islands in the only foreign invasion of American soil during WW II. The campaign to retake the islands was a bloody one and included a 19 day battle on Attu in which American forces recaptured the plot of barren land but only after suffering 2,300 casualties and 549 deaths; the Japanese lost even more lives.

A few military relics remain around Dutch Harbor and Unalaska but in recent years the communities have begun an effort to clean them up. Attractions here now consist of the Russian Orthodox Church that was built at Unalaska in 1825 and the Sitka Spruce Plantation, six trees that the Russians planted in 1805 in Dutch Harbor that have somehow survived when all other foliage can't. Because of the treeless environment, hiking is easy on Unalaska Island and you don't have to worry about bears – there are none.

Facilities in the two towns include two lodges, restaurants, bars and grocery stores. Peninsula Airways services the two towns and charges $400 for a one-way ticket to Anchorage.

WOOD-TIKCHIK STATE PARK

At 1.5 million acres (600,000 hectares), Wood-Tikchik is the largest state park in the country. It's located 30 miles (49 km) north of Dillingham, the service and transport centre for Bristol Bay. The park preserves two large systems of interconnecting lakes that are the important spawning grounds for Bristol Bay's salmon who enter the area through the Wood River.

With the exception of five fishing lodges which only offer package stays at $3000 a week, the park is totally undeveloped. There are no campgrounds, trails, ranger stations or shelters. In short, it is an ideal place for a wilderness canoe or kayak trip. Traditional trips include running the Tikchik or Nuyakuk rivers, floating Lake Kulik into Lake Beverly or being dropped onto Nishlik or Upnuk lakes where mountains, pinnacle peaks and hanging valleys surround the lakes for the park's most impressive scenery.

The paddling season is from mid-June when the lakes are finally free of ice and snow until early October when they begin to freeze up again. Be prepared for cool and rainy weather and pack along plenty of mosquito repellent. On the open lakes you have to be cautious as sudden winds can create white-cap conditions, and white water may exist on many of the streams connecting the lakes.

Highlights of such an adventure, besides the wilderness, are the possibilities of spotting brown and black bears, beavers, moose, foxes and maybe even wolves. The fishing for arctic char, rainbow trout, Dolly Varden, grayling and red salmon is excellent in late summer.

Getting There & Away

To reach Dillingham from Anchorage, book an air ticket in advance through MarkAir (tel 243-1414); the flight costs around $350. A 24 mile (39 km) road extends from Dillingham to the village of Aleknagik on the south end of the Wood River Lakes system. But most paddlers fly in and choose the more remote Tikchik Lakes system to the north. It's not really possible to float the Wood River all the way to Dillingham due to Nushagak Bay tides, which create tidal flats in the lower portions eliminating all campsite possibilities.

Contact Yute Air (tel 842-5333) in Dillingham about chartering a float plane but expect to pay around $200 an hour for the flight in. Also ask if they need a second trip to haul your canoe in. Canoes can be rented from Wilderness Canoe Adventures (tel 842-2328 in the winter), a guide company which splits its time between Dillingham and Fairbanks in the summer. Call them before you depart for Alaska.

If you are even remotely considering paddling this area, contact the park ranger and request current information on air charters and boat rental in Dillingham. Contact the ranger at: Wood-Tikchik State Park, General Delivery, Dillingham, Alaska 99576; or call (907) 842-2375.

KATMAI NATIONAL PARK

In June 1912, Novarupta Volcano erupted violently and along with the preceding earthquakes rocked the area now known as Katmai National Park & Preserve. The wilderness was turned into a dynamic landscape of smoking valleys, ash-covered mountains and small holes and cracks (fumaroles) fuming with steam and gas. In only one other eruption in historic times, on the Greek island of Santorini in 1500 BC, has more ash and pumice been displaced.

If the eruption had happened in New York City, people living in Chicago would have heard the explosion; it was 10 times greater than the 1980 eruption of Mt St Helens in the US state of Washington. For 2 days, people in Kodiak could not see a lantern held at arm's length. An amazing aspect of this eruption, perhaps the most dramatic natural event in the 20th century, was that no-one was killed.

The National Geographic Society sent Robert Grigg to explore the area in 1916, and standing at Katmai Pass the explorer saw for the first time the valley floor with its thousands of steam vents. He named it the Valley of 10,000 Smokes. Robert Grigg's adventures revealed the spectacular results of the eruptions to the rest of the world and 2 years later the area was turned into a national monument. In 1980, the area was enlarged to 3.9 million acres (1.6 million hectares) and redesignated a national park and preserve.

Although the fumaroles no longer smoke and hiss, the park is still a diverse and scenic wilderness, unlike any in Alaska. It changes from glaciated volcanoes and ash-covered valleys to island-studded lakes and a coastline of bays, fjords and beaches. Wildlife is abundant with more than 30 species of mammals, including large populations of brown bears, some of which weigh over 1000 lb (450 kg). Katmai is also a prime habitat for moose, sea lions, arctic fox and wolves. The many streams and lakes in the park are known around the state to provide some of the best rainbow trout and salmon fishing.

The weather in the park is best from mid-June to the end of July. Unfortunately, this is also when mosquitoes, always heavy in this part of the state, are at their peak. The best time for hiking and backpacking trips is from mid-August to early September, when the autumn colours are brilliant, the berries ripe and juicy, and the insects scarce. However, be prepared for frequent storms. In fact be ready for rain and foul weather any time in Katmai and always pack warm clothing. The summer high temperatures are usually in the low 60s°F (around 15°C).

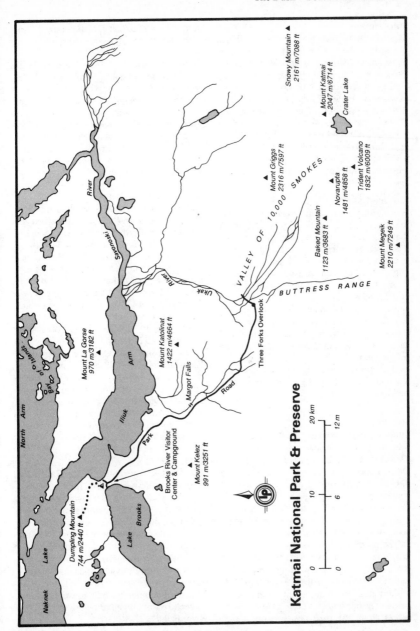

Snowy Mountain
2161 m/7088 ft ▲

▲ Mount Katmai
2047 m/6714 ft

Crater Lake

Mount Griggs ▲
2316 m/7597 ft

VALLEY OF 10,000 SMOKES

▲ Novarupta
1481 m/4858 ft

Trident Volcano
1832 m/6009 ft ▲

Baked Mountain ▲
1123 m/3683 ft

Mount Megeik
2210 m/7249 ft ▲

BUTTRESS RANGE

River

Savonoski

Three Forks Overlook

Ukak River

Mount La Gorse
970 m/3182 ft ▲

Iliuk Arm

North Arm

Bay of Islands

Mount Katolinat
1422 m/4664 ft ▲

Margot Falls

Park

Road

Naknek Lake

Brooks River Visitor
Center & Campground

Mount Kelez
991 m/3251 ft ▲

Dumpling Mountain
744 m/2440 ft ▲

Brooks Lake

Katmai National Park & Preserve

0	10	20 km
0	6	12 m

Information

Katmai is not a place to see at the last minute. Because of the cost involved in reaching the park, most visitors plan to spend at least 4 days or more to justify the expenses.

To contact the park beforehand write to: Katmai National Park, PO Box 7, King Salmon, Alaska 99613; or call on (907) 246-3305. In the USA, use the toll-free numbers to MarkAir (tel (800) 426-6784) and Katmailand (tel (800) 544-0551) for advance reservations. Katmailand is the concessionaire that handles the lodge and canoe rentals.

Brooks Camp

This summer headquarters for Katmai National Park is on the shores of Naknek Lake, 6 miles (9.6 km) from King Salmon. Facilities here include *Brooks Lodge*, where a cabin for two costs $120 per person per night, a free campground and a restaurant.

A store sells limited supplies of freeze-dried food and camp-stove fuel; it also rents tents, stoves and canoes. The canoes are $30 per day or $5 per hour, and there is some excellent paddling in the area (see the Bay of Islands Circuit in the Paddling section of the Wilderness chapter). Naturalist-led walks and evening campfire programmes are scheduled throughout the summer at the park headquarters.

Hiking

Hiking and backpacking are the best way to see the park's unusual backcountry. Like Denali National Park, Katmai has few formal trails; backpackers follow river bars, lake shores, gravel ridges and other natural routes. Many hiking trips begin with a ride on the park bus along the dirt road to the Valley of 10,000 Smokeş (see the Trekking section in the Wilderness chapter).

The only road in Katmai is 23 miles (37 km) long and ends at Overlook Cabin, where there is a sweeping view of the area. On its daily run, each bus carries a ranger who leads a short hike from the cabin to the valley below. The bus will also drop off and pick up hikers along the road but it is not a free shuttle system like at Denali National Park; the return fare is $50.

Dumpling Mountain Trail The only developed trail from Brooks Camp is a half-day trek to the top of Dumpling Mountain, elevation 2520 feet (769 metres). The trail leaves the ranger station and heads north past the campground, climbing 1.5 miles (2.4 km) to a scenic overlook. It then continues another 2 miles (3.2 km) to the mountain's summit, where there are superb views of the surrounding lakes.

Getting There & Away

Although the park is closer to Kodiak or Homer, to get from Anchorage to Katmai you first have to fly to King Salmon. A return ticket with MarkAir (tel 243-1414 in Anchorage) is $350. The airline also offers a 2 day/1 night tour that includes a fishing trip, a night in King Salmon and a day trip in the park for $418. Also check with Peninsula Airways (tel 243-2323 in Anchorage) which recently began offering a service from Anchorage to Brooks Camp for a very reasonable $320 return.

Other tour packages are offered by Katmailand Inc (tel 243-5448 in Anchorage) which has a 2 night trip that includes air fare, lodging and the bus fare to the Valley of 10,000 Smokes for $663 per person based on double occupancy. If there are more of you in the room, the price drops. A 3 night package is $746 per person.

McNEIL RIVER

The McNeil River State Game Sanctuary, across from Homer on Cook Inlet, is famous for its high numbers of brown bears from July to August. The majority of the bears gather a mile (1.6 km) upstream from the mouth of the river where salmon falls slow down the salmon and provide an easy meal. This spot is world renown among wildlife photographers and every great bear-catches-salmon shot you've ever seen was most likely taken from here. At times up to 20 brown bears can be seen feeding together below the McNeil River Falls.

The Alaska Department of Fish & Game has set up a viewing area and allows 10 visitors per day to watch the bears feed. For most visitors, viewing and photographing giant brown bears this close is an expensive side trip but a once-in-a-lifetime experience.

Permits

Visits to the game sanctuary are on a permit basis only and you're odds of drawing one from the lottery are one in 10. Write to the Alaska Department of Fish & Game, PO Box 37, King Salmon, Alaska 99613 for an application; or call (907) 246-3340. Return it with $5 by 1 April for a 15 May lottery drawing. Permits are drawn for only 10 people a day from 1 July to 25 August. If you're name is drawn, by all means take advantage of this rare opportunity in wildlife photography.

Getting There & Away

Kachemak Air Service (tel 235-8924) is based in Homer and offers a return fare of $275 to McNeil River. They make the trip whether the plane is filled to capacity (12 seats) or carries only one passenger. It lands in a tidal area during high tides. Even if you don't have a permit, check with them as they stay in constant touch with rangers at the state game area. Occasionally, cancellations or no-shows will create last-minute openings in the sanctuary's permit system.

LAKE CLARK

Apart from backpacking enthusiasts and river runners in Southcentral Alaska, few people knew about Lake Clark National Park & Preserve, 100 miles (160 km) south-west of Anchorage, until recently. Yet it offers some of the most spectacular scenery of any of the newly created parks in the state. It is within this 3.6 million acre (1.5 million hectare) preserve that the Alaska and Aleutian ranges meet. Among the many towering peaks are Mt Iliamna and Mt Redoubt, two active volcanoes clearly seen from Anchorage and the western shore of the Kenai Peninsula.

Much of the park's obscurity changed in January 1990 when Mt Redoubt erupted.

After 25 dormant years, the volcano roared back to life sending ash into the air and creating a cloud that could be seen along the western shore of the Kenai Peninsula. The spreading ash closed the Anchorage International Airport and oil terminals in the area, while 10,000 face masks were distributed to the residents of central Kenai Peninsula worried about inhaling the fine powder.

If you are contemplating a wilderness trip into the area, check with the park headquarters (tel 271-3751) in Anchorage before departing. Since most recreational activities take place in the western half of the park, chances are the eruption will have little effect on your travel plans.

Along with its now famous volcanoes, the park also features numerous glaciers, spectacular turquoise lakes (including Lake Clark, the park's centrepiece) and three designated wild rivers that have long been havens for river runners.

Wildlife includes brown and black bears, moose, red foxes, wolves and Dall sheep on the alpine slopes. Caribou roam the western foothills, while the park's watershed is one of the most important producers of red salmon in the world, contributing 33% of the US catch. Weather in the western section of the preserve, where most of the rafting and backpacking takes place, is generally cool and cloudy with light winds through much of the summer. Temperatures range from 50°F to 65°F (10°C to 18°C) June to August, with an occasional heat wave of 80°F (27°C).

Hiking

Lake Clark is another trail-less park for the experienced backpacker only. Most extended treks take place in the western foothills north of Lake Clark, where the open and relatively dry tundra provides ideal conditions for hiking. Less experienced backpackers are content to be dropped off at the shores of the many lakes in the area, camp and undertake day hikes.

There is a summer ranger station at Port Alsworth, but it is best to contact the park headquarters (tel 271-3751) in Anchorage regarding desirable places to hike and camp.

You can also write to them before departing for Alaska at: Lake Clark National Park, 222 West 7th Ave, Suite 61, Anchorage, Alaska 99513-7539.

Rafting
Float trips down any of the three designated wild rivers (the Chilikadrotna, Mulchatna and Tlikakila) are spectacular and exciting since the waterways are rated from Class III to IV. Alaska Treks & Voyages (tel 224-3960 in Seward) offer a 9 day trip on the Tlikakila River.

Getting There & Away
Access into the Lake Clark region is by small chartered plane, making the area tough to visit on a limited budget. The cheapest way to reach the park is to book a week in advance through Alaska Airlines (tel 243-3300 in Anchorage); a return ticket between Anchorage and Iliamna, a small village 30 miles (48 km) south of the park is $148. ERA Aviation, a contract carrier of Alaska Airlines, makes the flight twice a day. From Iliamna, you have to charter a plane to your destination within the park through air-taxi operators such as Iliamna Air Taxi (tel 571-1248).

Western Alaska

PRIBILOF ISLANDS
The Pribilof Islands are in the Bering Sea, 300 miles (480 km) west of Alaska's mainland and 900 miles (1400 km) from Anchorage. They are desolate, wind-swept places where the abundance of wildlife has made them tourist attractions despite the inhospitable weather. The four islands have two communities: St Paul (pop 600) and St George (pop 200) consisting mostly of Aleut Indians and government workers.

Although the Pribilof Islands are the home of the largest Aleut villages in the world, seals are the reason for the tourist trade. Every summer the tiny archipelago of rocky shores and steep cliffs becomes a mad scene when a million fur seals swim ashore to breed and raise their young. The seals spend most of the year at sea between the US state of California and Japan, but each summer they migrate to the Pribilofs, becoming the largest group of mammals anywhere in the world.

Many visitors also venture to the islands to view the extensive bird rookeries. About 2.5 million birds, made up of 200 species, nest at the Pribilofs, making it one of the largest sea-bird colonies in North America. The cliffs are easy to reach and photograph, and blinds have been erected on the beach to observe seals.

Because of strict regulations and limited facilities, most travellers choose package tours in order to visit the Pribilof Islands. Gray Line (tel 277-5581 in Anchorage) offerS a 3 day tour of St Paul that departs Anchorage on Tuesdays and Thursdays. The tour, which includes accommodation, meals, air fares and transport to the beaches and rookeries, costs $955 per person. Reeve Aleutian Airways (tel 243-4700) also runs tours to St Paul and offers longer stays including 4 days for $1090, 6 days for $1396 and even an 8 day trip for $1600.

If you do have an extra $1000 to spend, a more unique experience, while still seeing the immense wildlife, is to travel independently to St George, a smaller and much less visited island. You can stay at the *St George Hotel*, a recently designated national historical landmark, where rooms are $80 a night and you can cook your own meals in the kitchen downstairs.

Since the island isn't that big, only 5 miles (8 km) wide, hiking to within view of the wildlife is possible. Call St George Pribilof Tours (tel 563-3100) in Anchorage to reserve a room at the hotel. Then contact Peninsula Airways (tel 243-2323) to book a flight to St George; the return fare is $840.

NOME
In 1898, gold was found in Anvil Creek, giving rise to a few tents the miners initially called Anvil City. The following summer, gold was found on the beaches nearby, and

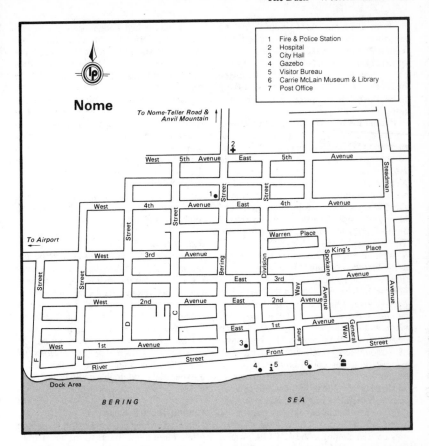

Nome

To Nome-Teller Road &
Anvil Mountain

To Airport

1 Fire & Police Station
2 Hospital
3 City Hall
4 Gazebo
5 Visitor Bureau
6 Carrie McLain Museum & Library
7 Post Office

West 5th Avenue East 5th Avenue

West 4th Avenue East 4th Avenue

Warren Place

King's Place

West 3rd Avenue

Spokane Avenue

East 3rd Avenue

West 2nd Avenue East 2nd Avenue

1st Avenue

West 1st Avenue

River Street

Dock Area

BERING   SEA

when the news finally made its way to Seattle in the summer of 1900 it set off yet another stampede of hopeful miners to Alaska. By the end of that year, there were 20,000 people in the town that was now called Nome, a place that would forever be associated around the world with gold and quick fortunes.

Nome has had its fair share of natural disasters, like much of Alaska, as fires all but destroyed the town in 1905 and 1934 and a Bering Sea storm overpowered the sea walls in 1974. However, the city survived and today it has a population of 3800 and has retained some of its frontier facade along historical Front St.

Nome serves as the transport centre for much of Western Alaska and during the summer, ocean-going barges unloading offshore are a common sight. A surge in gold prices in recent years has also given new life to the mining industry, and the lure of gold still draws people to Nome. However, it's summer tourists rather than miners which contribute to Nome's economy these days.

Things to See & Do

Nome's sights are located along Front St and

most travellers have little desire to venture any further into town. Begin at the **Nome Visitor Bureau** (tel 443-5535) which is part of the Perkins Plaza, Nome's small convention centre, on Front St in the centre of the business district. The bureau runs walking tours which describe the city's historical features and buildings.

Behind the bureau is a wooden platform on the rock sea wall that provides views of the Bering Sea and Sledge Island. To the east of the bureau on Front St is the **Carrie McLain Museum** on the 1st floor of the Kegoayah Kozga Public Library. The museum features exhibits on the Bering Land Bridge, Eskimo culture and gold-rush history; it is open Tuesday to Friday from 9 am to 5 pm and Saturday from 1 to 5 pm. There is no admission charge.

West on Front St from the visitor bureau is the **Nome City Hall**, and in a lot next to this historical building is the **Iditarod finish line arch**. The huge wooden structure is raised above Front St every March in anticipation of the mushers and their dog-sled teams ending the 1049 mile (1710 km) race here. Actually, the race is just the high point of a month-long celebration that includes such activities as golf tournaments on the frozen Bering Sea and softball games in which players wear snowshoes. All of it, of course, is merely a cure for cabin fever.

Nome's **public beach** is nearby, and in the height of the summer a few local children may be seen playing in the 45°F (7°C) water. On Memorial Day (in May), 20 to 30 residents participate in the annual Polar Bear Swim by plunging into the ice-choked waters. A warmer swim can be obtained in the public pool (tel 443-5717) at the Nome Public School. The admission charge is $2 per session.

At night, stop in at the *Board of Trade Saloon*, the oldest bar on the Bering Sea, on Front St. It's a good place to meet the locals.

Gold Dredges There are 44 gold dredges in the area surrounding the city, some of which are still being used today while many others lie deteriorating. The closest ones to Nome

are the reactivated dredges near the northern end of the Nome Airport, 2 miles (3.2 km) north of town. You can't walk through the dredges but you can view them and photograph the mining machinery from 0.5 mile (0.8 km).

Those fascinated by these relics of the gold-rush era might consider renting a car to explore the roads that extend into the Seward Peninsula from Nome. It is believed that there are close to 100 dredges scattered throughout the peninsula, many visible from the road. Stop at the Board of Trade Saloon (tel 443-2611) to rent a vehicle, and ask at the visitor bureau about the location of dredges and old steam engines that were used to obtain gold ore.

Places to Stay
There used to be a youth hostel in Nome that made this side trip affordable for backpackers. Check with the visitor bureau to see if one has been reopened but chances are pretty slim that another hostel will ever appear in Nome. The visitor bureau also has information about camping on the public beach and a list of B&Bs. Expect to pay around $55 for singles in a B&B. The *Polaris Hotel* (tel 443-2000) has singles with shared bath at $40 per night and doubles with private bath at $80.

Getting There & Away
Nome is serviced by Alaska Airlines, which offers three daily flights to the town from Anchorage. A return ticket, booked 2 weeks in advance, costs $317. Gray Line (tel 277-5581 in Anchorage) offers a package tour that spends a day in Kotzebue and another in Nome for $415. The price is based on shared accommodation and includes air fare, lodging and meals.

KOTZEBUE
Situated 26 miles (42 km) above the Arctic Circle, Kotzebue has one of the largest communities of indigenous people in the Bush; over 80% of its 3600 residents are Eskimos. Kotzebue is on the north-west shore of the Baldwin Peninsula in Kotzebue Sound, near

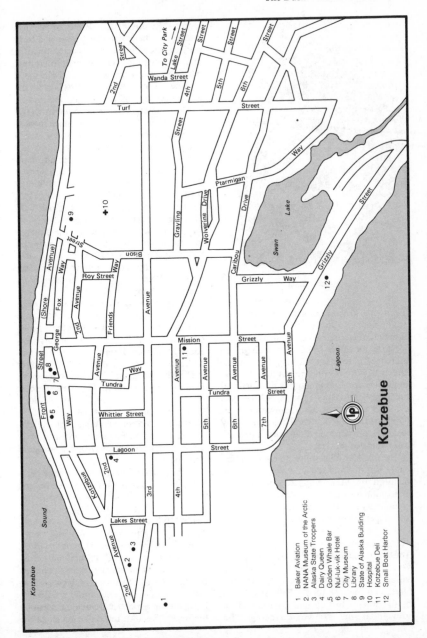

Kotzebue

Kotzebue Sound

1 Baker Aviation
2 NANA Museum of the Arctic
3 Alaska State Troopers
4 Dairy Queen
5 Golden Whale Bar
6 Nul-luk-vik Hotel
7 City Museum
8 Library
9 State of Alaska Building
10 Hospital
11 Kotzebue Deli
12 Small Boat Harbor

Eskimo Child

the mouths of the Kobuk and Noatak rivers. Traditionally, it serves as the transport and commerce centre for Northwest Alaska.

More recently, it has experienced an increase in tourism mostly through the efforts of NANA, a native corporation, and as the departure point into the new national preserves and parks nearby. NANA also manages a reindeer herd, numbering over 6000 head, on the Baldwin Peninsula. Many residents still depend on subsistence hunting and fishing to survive.

The majority of travellers to Kotzebue are either part of a tour group or are just passing through on their way to a wilderness expedition in the surrounding parks. The community is extremely difficult to visit for an independent traveller on a limited budget.

Things to See & Do
The town is named after Polish explorer Otto von Kotzebue, who stumbled onto the village in 1816 while searching for the Northwest Passage for the Russians. Much of the town's history and culture can be viewed at one of two museums. The

Ootukahkuktuvik City Museum features artefacts of the indigenous people and early settlers, including a rain parka made of walrus intestine. Independent travellers wanting to view the museum on Kotzebue Way near Tundra Way must first contact the Kotzebue City Hall (tel 442-3401).

Most tour groups visit the **Museum of the Arctic**, where 2nd and 3rd avenues meet at the western end of town. The centre is owned and operated by NANA, which offers a 2 hour programme of indigenous culture, demonstrations in Eskimo handicrafts, a visit to the adjoining jade factory and a traditional blanket toss. Independent travellers can join the museum tour, if they want to part with $20, by contacting the NANA office (tel 442-3301). Or you can just visit the museum to view the wildlife exhibits and displays on the unique natural history of Northwest Alaska; it is open daily during the summer from 8.30 am to 5.30 pm and there is no admission charge.

Perhaps the most interesting thing to do in Kotzebue is just stroll down **Front St** (also known as Shore Ave), a narrow gravel road only a few yards from the water at the northern edge of town. Here you can see salmon drying out on racks, fishing boats crowding the beach to be repaired and locals preparing for the long winter ahead. This is also the best place to watch the midnight sun roll along the horizon, painting the sea reddish gold in a beautiful scene of colour and light reflecting off the water. Beginning in early June, the sun does not set for almost 6 weeks in Kotzebue.

In the centre of town there is a large **cemetery** where spirit houses have been erected over many of the graves.

Places to Stay & Eat
There is no youth hostel or public campgrounds in Kotzebue. The only hotel, *Nul-luk-vik* (tel 442-3331), has rates from $100 per night for singles. It is a common practice among backpackers, however, to hike south of town (a quarter of a mile (0.4 km) past the airport) and pitch their tent on the beach. Keep in mind that much of the

beach around Kotzebue is difficult to camp on because it is narrow and slanted or is privately owned.

As out of place as it may seem, there is a *Dairy Queen* in town, undoubtedly the northernmost of the chain, on the corner of 2nd Ave and Lagoon St. Along with hamburgers and ice cream, it serves steaks and seafood. A cheaper place is the *Hamburger Hut* on Front St, where you can get a hamburger for around $8. There is also a *Pizza House* in town.

Paddling

Kotzebue provides access to some of the finest river running in Arctic Alaska. Popular trips include the Noatak River, the Kobuk River, the Salmon River (which flows into the Kobuk), and the Selawik River (which originates in the Kobuk lowlands and flows west into Selawik Lake).

Trips along the Kobuk National Wild River consist of floats from Walker Lake 140 miles (224 km) downstream to the villages of Kobuk or Ambler, where there are scheduled flights to both Kotzebue and Bettles, another departure point for this river. Bering Air Service (tel 443-5464) charges $70 for a one way flight from Kobuk to Kotzebue and $65 from Ambler. Most of the river is rated Class I, but some lining of boats may be required just below Walker Lake and for 1 mile (1.6 km) through Lower Kobuk Canyon. Paddlers usually plan on 6 to 8 days for the float.

The Noatak National Wild River is a 16 day float of 350 miles (560 km) from Lake Matcharak to the village of Noatak, where Bering Air has scheduled flights to Kotzebue for $40 per person one way. However, the numerous access lakes on the river allow it to be broken down into shorter paddles. The entire river is rated from Class I to II.

For more information contact the National Park office (tel 442-3890) in the Museum of the Arctic at Kotzebue, which is open Monday to Friday from 8.30 am to 5.30 pm in the summer, or write to the National Park Service (NPS) before you depart for Alaska at PO Box 287, Kotzebue, Alaska 99752.

Canoes can be rented in Kotzebue (check with the NPS for names of people renting them) or in Ambler from Ambler Air Service (tel 445-2121), which can also supply transport up the Kobuk River. It is possible to book a return, supersaver flight from Anchorage to Ambler for $432, and from there rent boats from Ambler Air Service. See the list of guide companies at the end of the Wilderness chapter.

Getting There & Away

Alaska Airlines offers a round-trip ticket to Kotzebue, if booked 2 weeks in advance, for $317 from Anchorage. You can also purchase a round-trip ticket from Anchorage with stopovers in both Nome and Kotzebue for $395. Gray Line offers a daily single-day tour of Kotzebue from Anchorage for $315 per person.

Arctic Alaska

DALTON HIGHWAY

Although officially called the Dalton Highway, this road is best known in Alaska simply as the 'Haul Rd'. This stretch of gravel winds 416 miles (666 km) north from Elliott Highway to Deadhorse at Prudhoe Bay, the community that houses the workers of what is believed to be the largest oil reserve in the USA. Prudhoe Bay is the start of the Trans-Alaska Pipeline that carries oil 800 miles (1300 km) to the ice-free port of Valdez on Prince William Sound.

After the road was completed in 1978, all but the first 56 miles (90 km) of the highway to the Yukon River was kept closed to the public. In 1981, after a bitter battle in the state legislature, the public was allowed to drive 210 miles (337 km) along the road to Disaster Creek. This section of the highway takes you into the Brooks Range and near the borders of Kanuti and Yukon Flats national wildlife refuges and the Gates of the Arctic National Park & Preserve north of them.

Mile 0 of Dalton Highway is at the junction with Elliott Highway, 73 miles (116.8

km) north of Fairbanks. The beginning is marked by an information centre that covers the route north. At *Mile 25* (40 km), there is a lookout with good views of the pipeline crossing Hess Creek. It is possible to camp around the creek, the colour of which draws an occasional amateur gold panner.

The highway begins to descend to the Yukon River at *Mile 47* (75 km), and shortly you will be able to view miles of pipeline. At *Mile 51* (82 km) of Dalton Highway, a rough road leads east 5.4 miles (8.7 km) to the Yukon River. There is a boat launch maintained by the Bureau of Land Management on the north side of the river.

The **Yukon River Bridge** is at *Mile 56* (90 km). The wooden-decked bridge was completed in 1975 and is 2290 feet (698 metres) long. On the north side of the bridge is one of two spots to purchase supplies and gasoline, and east of the highway is a rough camping area with litter barrels. Just beyond *Mile 91* (145.6 km) is a lookout with a scenic view of the road and the pipeline to the north.

At *Mile 96* (153.6 km), the highway ascends above the tree line into an alpine area where there is good hiking and berry picking. The road stays in this alpine section for the next 5 miles (8 km) before the terrain turns rugged and you pass many impressive rock outcrops and views of the surrounding mountains.

The **Arctic Circle**, near *Mile 115* (184 km) of Dalton Highway, is marked by a sign at a turn-off with parking and litter barrels. A rough road departs from the turn-off to some primitive campsites 0.5 miles (0.8 km) away. From here, for the next 64 miles (102 km), the road passes six streams and the small Grayling Lake, all of which offer superb grayling fishing.

Coldfoot (tel 678-9301), a lodge and restaurant that also sells gasoline and groceries, is at *Mile 175* (280 km), while another 5 miles (8 km) north is the spur to the *Marion Creek Campground*. The road is now near the boundaries of **Gates of the Arctic National Park** and the scenery is at its best. Wildlife is plentiful, especially Dall sheep high on the mountain slopes.

After passing *Mile 186* (297.6 km) there is a lookout where you can view the historical mining community of **Wiseman**, west of the road across the Koyukuk River. Buildings from the town's heyday in 1910 still stand, but all are private property – only a handful of people remain in Wiseman.

More spectacular mountain scenery begins around *Mile 193* (309 km) of Dalton Highway, with the first views of Sukakpak Mountain to the north and Wiehl Mountain to the east, both 4000 feet (1200 metres) in elevation. Poss Mountain, elevation 6189 feet (1885 metres), comes into view to the east in another 2.5 miles (4 km), and the Koyukuk River, a heavily braided stream, is seen near *Mile 201* (321.6 km).

Just before *Mile 204* (326.4 km) is a lookout with a 0.5 mile (0.8 km) trail leading to Sukakpak Mountain. The mounds between the road and the mountain were formed by ice pushing up the soil and vegetation.

Another lookout is passed after *Mile 206* (329.6 km), where there are good views of Snowden Mountain, elevation 5775 feet (1761 metres), 10 miles (16 km) to the northwest. Six miles (9.6 km) north of the lookout is Disaster Creek and the turnaround point for all those without a special permit to continue north onto Prudhoe Bay.

Getting There & Away

Cheap used-car rentals are available in Fairbanks (see the Fairbanks Getting Around section in the Fairbanks chapter), though you'd better ask first if they allow their vehicles on Dalton Highway. If you're driving, remember that the road is used heavily by tractor-trailer rigs driving at high speeds. Never stop in the middle of the road to observe wildlife or scenery, as the trucks have limited braking ability.

Gasoline, tyre-repair services and limited food supplies are available where the road crosses the Yukon River, 141 miles (225.6 km) north of Fairbanks, and at Coldfoot Lodge, 37 miles (59 km) south of the turnaround point. At both places gasoline costs close to $2.50 per gallon (66 cents per litre).

For more information on the road, or to obtain permits if you think you qualify, contact the Department of Transportation (tel 451-2209), 2301 Peger Rd, Fairbanks, Alaska 99701.

GATES OF THE ARCTIC

The Gates of the Arctic National Park & Preserve, one of the finest wilderness areas in the world, straddles the Arctic Divide in the Brooks Range, 200 miles (320 km) northwest of Fairbanks.

The entire park, 8.4 million acres (3.4 million hectares), extends 200 miles (320 km) east to west and lies totally above the Arctic Circle. The park extends from the southern foothills of the Brooks Range, across the range's ragged peaks and down onto the north slope. Most of the park is vegetated with shrubs and tundra, and is a habitat for grizzly bears, wolves, Dall sheep, moose, caribou and wolverines. Fishing is considered superb for grayling and arctic char in the clear streams and for lake trout in the larger, deeper lakes.

Within this preserve, you have dozens of rivers to run, miles of valleys and tundra slopes to hike and, of course, the Gates themselves. Mt Boreal and Frigid Crags are the gates that flank the North Fork of the Koyukuk River; it was through these landmark mountains that Robert Marshall found an unobstructed path northward to the arctic coast of Alaska. That was in 1929 and Marshall's naming of the two mountains has remained ever since.

Hiking

The park is a vast wilderness containing no National Park Service facilities, campgrounds or trails. Many backpackers follow the long, open valleys for extended treks or work their way to higher elevations where open tundra and sparse shrubs provide excellent hiking terrain.

Most backpackers enter the park by way of charter air-taxi out of Bettles, which can land on lakes, rivers or river bars. Extended treks across the park require outdoor experience and good map and compass skills. One of the more popular treks is the 4 to 5 day hike from Summit Lake through the Gates to Redstar Lake. Less experienced backpackers often choose to be dropped off and picked up at one lake and from there explore the surrounding region on day hikes. Lakes ideal for this include Summit Lake, the Karupa Lakes region, Redstar Lake, Hunt Fork Lake or Chimney Lake.

The lone exception to chartering a plane is the trek beginning from the Dalton Highway at either Coldfoot or Wiseman, where you can enter the park from its eastern border.

Paddling

Floatable rivers in the park include the John, the North Fork of the Koyukuk, the Tinayguk, the Alatna and the Middle Fork of the Koyukuk River from Wiseman to Bettles. The headwaters for the Noatak and Kobuk rivers are in the park (see the Kotzebue Paddling section in this chapter).

The waterways range from Class I to III in difficulty. Of the various rivers, the North Fork of the Koyukuk River is one of the most popular because the float begins in the shadow of the Gates and continues downstream 100 miles (160 km) to Bettles through Class I & II waters. Canoes and rafts can be rented in Bettles and then floated downstream back to the village.

Guide Companies

A number of guide companies run trips through the Gates of the Arctic National Park, including Sourdough Outfitters (tel 692-5252 in Bettles) who charge $1500 for an 8 day canoeing expedition on the North Fork of the Koyukuk River. Also check with Arctic Treks (tel 455-6502) if you are passing through Fairbanks or Brooks Range Expeditions (tel 692-5333) in Bettles. Both guide companies have been around for years and offer a variety of trips in the park or elsewhere in the Brooks Range.

Canoes and rafts can be rented from Sourdough Outfitters who offer unguided expeditions with arranged drop-off and pickup air services for independent backpackers.

Midnight Sun

The 2 week adventure that combines hiking from Summit Lake to Redstar Lake and then floating down the North Fork of the Koyukuk River to Bettles costs $450 per person. The company has a wide range of other unguided trips as well.

Getting There & Away

Access to the park's backcountry is usually accomplished in two steps, with the first being a scheduled flight from Fairbanks to Bettles. Check out Frontier Flying Service (tel 474-0014) or Larry's Flying Service (tel 474-9169) in Fairbanks who make regular flights to Bettles for $85 one way.

The second step is to charter an air-taxi in Bettles to your destination within the park. A Cessna 185 on floats holds three passengers and costs around $225 per hour; most areas in the park can be reached in under 2 hours of flying time from Bettles. If your destination is an hour away and there are two people in your party, the price for a drop-off and

pick-up is $4Mile 5.350 per person. Check with Brooks Range Aviation (tel 692-5444) for air charters out of Bettles.

The alternative to expensive air chartering is to begin your trip from the Dalton Highway. Travellers with time but little money can hitchhike the highway. A trickle of cars and a couple of hundred trucks use the road daily. While trucks will not stop to pick you up on the roadside, it is often possible to pick up a ride with one at the Hilltop Cafe, a truck-stop and gasoline station at *Mile 5.3* (8.5 km) of Elliott Highway.

BETTLES

This small village of 100 residents serves as the major departure point to the Gates of the Arctic National Park. Within town there is the *Bettles Lodge* (tel 692-5111), where rooms are $50 for a single and $80 for a double, a trading post for such supplies as freeze-dried food and topographic maps, and a National Park Service office (tel 692-5494).

BARROW

Barrow (pop 3000) is the largest Inupiat Eskimo community in Alaska and one of the largest in North America. Although the residents enjoy such modern-day conveniences as a local bus system and gas heating in their homes from the nearby oil fields, they remain very traditional in their outlook on life and seasonal events; this is symbolised by the spring whale hunts.

The town, the northernmost community in the USA, is the place where American humorist Will Rogers died in 1935 when the plane carrying him and Wiley Post stalled and crashed into a river, 15 miles (24 km) south of Barrow, during their Fairbanks to Siberia trip. Barrow is 330 miles (530 km) north of the Arctic Circle and less than 1200 miles (1920 km) from the North Pole.

Barrow became front page news around the world in the autumn of 1988 after several residents discovered that three grey whales had become entrapped by ice during their migration south to warmer waters off the coast of Mexico. The Eskimos, wielding chain saws, spent long hours cutting holes in the ice that allowed the mammals to breathe.

When the news media caught wind of the story, Barrow was flooded by reporters and television crews. The Top of the World Hotel was booked solid, there was a 30 minute wait to be seated at Pepe's North of the Border Mexican Restaurant and somebody was selling souvenir T-shirts (your choice of commemorative logos) on the streets of Barrow.

The unusual ordeal lasted almost 2 weeks and more than a $1 million was spent keeping the whales alive before a Soviet icebreaker finally cleared a path through the ice to open water. Two whales swam to freedom, one died and Barrow returned to its normal lifestyle after the media left. 'It was a good experience,' said an employee of a local restaurant, 'but we're glad to see it over with.'

Most people visit the town to say they've been at the top of the world or to view the midnight sun, which never sets from 10 May to 2 August. Otherwise, there is little reason to make the expensive side trip to Barrow. The return air fare from Fairbanks is $544 on MarkAir, rooms in the town's three hotels begin at over $80 per night for a single room, and occasionally there can be a feeling of tension between the indigenous people and independent travellers.

Getting There & Away

For those set on seeing Barrow, by far the best and most economical way is to book a package tour. Gray Line (tel 456-5816) in Fairbanks offers a 12 hour trip to the community for $355. Alaska Sightseeing (tel 452-8518) also has a 1 day tour from Fairbanks ($332) and an overnight trip, which is probably the best deal as it offers some time to wander around the town on your own. Based on double occupancy, the 2 day tour is $420 per person.

Human

Index

MAPS

TEXT

342 Index

Guides to the Americas

South America on a shoestring
Providing concise information for budget travellers, this guide covers Central and South America from the USA-Mexico border to Tierra del Fuego. By the author the *New York Times* nominated "the patron saint of travelers in the third world".

Argentina - a travel survival kit
This guide gives independent travellers all the essential information on Argentina — a land of intriguing cultures, 'wild west' overtones and spectacular scenery.

Baja California - a travel survival kit
For centuries, Mexico's Baja peninsula — with its beautiful coastline, raucous border towns, and crumbling Spanish missions — has been a land of escapes and escapades. This book describes how and where to escape in Baja.

Bolivia - a travel survival kit
From lonely villages in the Andes to the ancient ruined city of La Paz, Bolivia is a magnificent blend of everything that inspires travellers. Discover safe and intriguing travel options in this comprehensive guide.

Brazil - a travel survival kit
From the mad passion of Carnival to the Amazon — home of the richest and most diverse ecosystem on earth — Brazil is a country of mythical proportions. This guide has all the travel information on this fascinating country.

Canada - a travel survival kit
This comprehensive guidebook has all the facts on the USA's huge neighbour — the Rocky Mountains, Niagara Falls, ultra-modern Toronto, remote villages in Nova Scotia, and much more.

Chile & Easter Island - a travel survival kit
Travel in Chile is easy and safe, with possibilities as varied as the countryside. This guide also gives detailed coverage of Chile's Pacific outpost, mysterious Easter Island.

Colombia - a travel survival kit
Colombia is a land of myths — from the ancient legends of El Dorado to the modern tales of Gabriel Garcia Marquez. The reality is beauty and violence, wealth and poverty, tradition and change. This guide shows how to travel independently and safely in this exotic country.

Ecuador & the Galapagos Islands - a travel survival kit
Ecuador offers a wide variety of travel experiences, from the high cordilleras to the Amazon plains — and 600 miles west, the fascinating Galapagos Islands. Everything you need to know about travelling around this enchanting country.

Hawaii - a travel survival kit
Share in the delights of this island paradise — and avoid its high prices — both on and off the beaten track. Full details on Hawaii's best-known attractions, plus plenty of uncrowded sights and activities.

Mexico - a travel survival kit
A unique blend of Indian and Spanish culture, fascinating history, and hospitable people, make Mexico a travellers' paradise.

Peru - a travel survival kit
The lost city of Machu Picchu, the Andean altiplano and the magnificent Amazon rainforests are just some of Peru's many attractions. All the travel facts you'll need can be found in this comprehensive guide.

Also available:
Brazilian phrasebook and *Quechua* phrasebook.

Lonely Planet Guidebooks

Lonely Planet guidebooks cover every accessible part of Asia as well as Australia, the Pacific, Central and South America, Africa, Eastern Europe, the Middle East and parts of North America. There are four main series: *travel survival kits*, covering a single country for a range of budgets; *shoestring* guides with compact information for low-budget travel in a major region; *walking* guides ; and *phrasebooks*.

Australia & the Pacific
Australia
Bushwalking in Australia
Fiji
Islands of Australia's Great Barrier Reef
Micronesia
New Zealand
Papua New Guinea
Papua New Guinea phrasebook
Rarotonga & the Cook Islands
Samoa
Solomon Islands
Tahiti & French Polynesia
Tonga
Tramping in New Zealand

South-East Asia
Burma
Burmese phrasebook
Indonesia
Indonesia phrasebook
Malaysia, Singapore & Brunei
Philippines
Pilipino phrasebook
South-East Asia on a shoestring
Thailand
Thai phrasebook

North-East Asia
China
Chinese phrasebook
Hong Kong, Macau & Canton
Japan
Japanese phrasebook
Korea
Korean phrasebook
North-East Asia on a shoestring
Taiwan
Tibet
Tibet phrasebook

West Asia
Trekking in Turkey
Turkey
Turkish phrasebook
West Asia on a shoestring

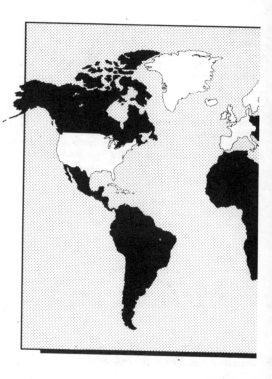

Indian Ocean
Madagascar & Comoros
Maldives & Islands of the East Indian Ocean
Mauritius, Réunion & Seychelles